The Blue Guides

Albania
Australia

Austria Austria
Vienna

Bali, Java and Lombok
Belgium and Luxembourg
Bulgaria

Czech & Slovak Czech & Slovak Republics
Republics Prague

China
Cyprus
Denmark
Egypt

France France
Paris and Versailles
Burgundy
Loire Valley
Midi-Pyrénées
Normandy
Provence
South West France
Corsica

Germany Berlin and eastern Germany

Greece Greece
Athens and environs
Crete
Rhodes and the
Dodecanese

Hungary Hungary
Budapest

Southern India
Ireland

Italy Northern Italy
Southern Italy
Florence
Rome

Venice
Tuscany
Umbria
Sicily

Jordan
Malaysia and Singapore
Malta and Gozo
Mexico
Morocco

Netherlands Netherlands
Amsterdam

Poland
Portugal

Spain Spain
Barcelona
Madrid

Sweden
Switzerland
Thailand
Tunisia

Turkey Turkey
Istanbul

UK England
Scotland
Wales
Channel Islands
London
Oxford and Cambridge
Country Houses of
England

USA New York
Museums and Galleries of
New York
Boston and Cambridge

We have done our very best to ensure that this guide is up-to-date and error free. However, things do change between editions. We should be delighted to hear from any of our readers who have comments, suggestions and corrections for the next edition of the Blue Guide. Writers of the most helpful letters will be awarded a free Blue Guide of their choice.

Tuscany

Alta Macadam

GOVANNI·DAN
TONIO·DIG OV
ANNI·PERVZZI
VIC ———— MDVII

BLUE GUIDE

A&C Black • London
WW Norton • New York

3rd edition © Alta Macadam, October 1999
Published by A & C Black (Publishers) Limited
35 Bedford Row, London WC1R 4JH

Maps and plans ©A &C Black. Maps drawn by Robert Smith; ground plans by Eugène Fleury

Illustrations © Colin Ross

ISBN 0–7136–4972–0

Published in the United States of America by
WW Norton and Company, Inc
500 Fifth Avenue, New York, NY 10110

Published simultaneously in Canada by
Penguin Books Canada Limited
10 Alcorn Avenue, Toronto,
Ontario M4V 3B2

ISBN 0–393–31949–0 USA

The author and the publishers have done their best to ensure the accuracy of all the information in *Blue Guide Tuscany*; however, they can accept no responsibility for any loss, injury or inconvenience sustained by any traveller as a result of information or advice contained in the guide.

Cover photograph of San Gimignano by Joe Cornish.
Title page illustration: coat of arms on the Palazzo Podestà, San Giovanni Valdarno.

Alta Macadam has been a writer of Blue Guides since 1970. She lives in Florence with her family (the painter Francesco Colacicchi, and their children Giovanni and Lelia). Combined with work on writing the guides she has also been associated in Florence with the Bargello Museum, the Alinari photo archive, and Harvard University at the Villa I Tatti in Florence. As author of the Blue Guides to Northern Italy, Rome, Venice, Sicily, Florence, Tuscany, and Umbria she travels extensively in Italy every year in order to revise new editions of the books.

Acknowledgements
As for the previous editions of this guide I am indebted in the first instance to **Françoise Pouncey Chiarini** who greatly assisted me in preparing the revised text of the Chianti area, the Maremma, and southern Tuscany. We received help from the Soprintendenze per i Beni Artistici e Storici of Siena (particular thanks to Bruno Santi) and of Florence (particular thanks to Rosanna Caterina Proto Pisani).

I am also very grateful to Mark and Heather Roberts, Katerine Gaja, Benedetta Origo, Lord Lambton, Mrs. Claire Ward, William E. Larson, Marta Specht, and Mark and Jocelyn Tress

Printed and bound in Great Britain by Butler and Tanner, Frome and London.

Contents

Introduction 7
How to use the Guide 9

Highlights 11

Background information
An historical introduction, by John Law 13
Place names in Italian towns and cities 21

Practical information
Planning your visit 23
Disabled travellers 24
Getting to Tuscany 24
Where to stay 27
Travelling around Tuscany 30
Food and drink 34
Eating out 36
Money and banks 37
Medical services 38
Crime and personal security 38
Local tourist offices 38
Telephone and postal services 39

Opening hours 40
Public holidays 40
Public toilets 40
Golf courses in Tuscany 40
Museums and monuments 40
Churches 41
The British Institute of Florence 41
Annual festivals and local fairs 41
Tuscan gardens 42
The Tuscan coast 43
Walking in Tuscany 44
Protected areas of natural beauty 44

Tuscany ~ the guide
1 • Florence 45
2 • Environs of Florence 95
3 • The Mugello and Val di Sieve 113
4 • The Chianti 124
5 • San Casciano in Val di Pesa and Tavarnelle 132
6 • Castelfiorentino and Certaldo 140
7 • Empoli, Vinci and west of Florence 147
8 • Prato and its province 156
9 • Pistoia 172
10 • The province of Pistoia 182
11 • Lucca 193
12 • The Garfagnana 210
13 • Versilia 217
14 • The province of Massa Carrara 223
15 • Pisa 232
16 • The province of Pisa 256

17 • Volterra and environs 266
18 • Livorno 279
19 • The coast south of Livorno and Populonia 288
20 • Grosseto and its northern province 294
21 • Massa Marittima 307
22 • The Parco Naturale della Maremma 313
23 • Orbetello and Monte Argentario 315
24 • Pitigliano and Saturnia 321
25 • Monte Amiata 328
26 • Siena 335
27 • Environs of Siena 380
28 • San Gimignano 386
29 • Colle Val d'Elsa and environs 394
30 • San Galgano and environs 403
31 • Montalcino and Sant'Antimo 405

32 · Asciano and Monteoliveto Maggiore 411
33 · Pienza and the Val d'Orcia 418
34 · Montepulciano and environs 428
35 · Chiusi and Chianciano Terme 439
36 · Arezzo 447

37 · Cortona 463
38 · The Valdichiana 473
39 · The Valdarno and Pratomagno 478
40 · The Casentino 488
41 · Sansepolcro, Anghiari and Monterchi 500
42 · The islands of Elba and Capraia 509

Glossary 515
Index to artists 519
Index 533

Maps and plans

Map of Tuscany *inside front and back covers*
Island of Elba 509

Provincial maps

Arezzo 462
Florence 98–9
Grosseto 300–1
Lucca 211
Massa Carrara 228

Pisa 258
Pistoia 185
Prato 167
Siena 382–3

Town plans

Arezzo 449
Cortona 466
Florence, centre 50
Florence, general 58–9
Livorno 283
Lucca 197
Montepulciano 430
Pienza 421
Pisa, Piazza del Duomo 235
Pisa, general 246–7
Pistoia 175
Prato 161

San Gimignano 388
Siena (I) centre 346–7
Siena (II) general 368–9
Volterra 268

Ground plans

Florence: Uffizi Gallery 65
Florence: Palazzo Pitti 69
Pisa: Duomo 237
Siena: Duomo 349
Siena: Palazzo Pubblico 343
Siena: Pinacoteca Nazionale 359

Introduction

Tuscany (in Italian Toscana) is the most famous of the twenty regions of Italy. It has an area of 22,991 square kilometres, and a population of about 3,473,000. It lies between the Apennines and the Tyrrhenian sea, bordered on the north by Emilia and Liguria, on the east by the Marche and Umbria, and on the south by Lazio. It includes the famous towns of Florence, Siena, and Pisa, as well as numerous beautiful and interesting small towns including Lucca, Cortona, Volterra, Massa Marittima, Pienza, Montepulciano, San Gimignano, and Montalcino.

It is well known for its splendid landscape, particularly that of the Chianti region between Florence and Siena with its charming low hills covered with olive groves, vineyards, woods, and isolated cypress trees, and dotted with beautiful old farmhouses. The region also includes the Apuan Alps, white with snow and marble, which form a dramatic background to the coastal plain of Versilia. The high Monte Amiata is almost always prominent in the southern Tuscan landscape. Other areas of particular natural beauty, and with their own special characteristics, include the Casentino with its country churches and castles (below the forest of Camaldoli), the Mugello, the hilly wooded area north of Florence with numerous villas and churches, and the remote areas around Pitigliano, near the southern border of Tuscany.

Although the sea coast of Versilia, which first became popular for its bathing resorts in the 18C, has lost much of its charm, beautiful stretches of coastline can still be found in the Maremma (notably the Monti dell'Uccellina) and on Monte Argentario. The island of Elba retains some unspoilt parts, and Capraia, another lovely island in the Tuscan archipelago, can now be visited.

Tuscany derives its name from the inhabitants of ancient Etruria—the Etruscans—known in Latin as *Etrusci* or *Tusci*, who probably landed at Tarquinia (now in Lazio) in the 8C BC. In *Etruria Propria* they formed themselves into a Confederation of twelve principal cities, of which Chiusi (Clevsins) was the most important in present-day Tuscany. Other member cities included Cortona, Vetulonia, Volterra (Velathri), Arezzo (Arretium), Populonia, Roselle (Rusellae), and Fiesole (Faesulae). The other four cities are Tarquinia (Tarxuna)—the most important; Veii (Veio)—the largest; Cerveteri (Caere)—all three in present-day Lazio; and Perugia (Perusia) in present-day Umbria. There were also important Etruscan settlements in the Maremma, and around Pitigliano, and Saturnia. Numerous Etruscan remains, including tombs and walls, can still be seen in these places, and important finds from excavations are exhibited in museums all over the region.

In the Middle Ages Lucca was a powerful independent town, and Pisa, at the head of its Maritime Republic, was one of the most important cities in Europe in the 12C. Siena reached the height of its power in the 12C–13C, and is still one of the most beautiful medieval towns in Italy. Numerous small hill towns survive in Tuscany as testimony to the rise of independent communes in the Middle Ages, the most famous of which is San Gimignano.

Many beautiful country churches can be seen all over the region, as well as the splendid 12C Romanesque abbey of Sant'Antimo and the 13C Gothic ruins of San Galgano. Important Tuscan monasteries and charter houses include

Monte Oliveto Maggiore, La Verna, Camaldoli, Vallombrosa, the Certosa del Galluzzo (outside Florence) and the Certosa di Pisa (near Calci).

Siena, Lucca, and Pisa (as well as Florence) have some of the most beautiful Gothic and Romanesque buildings to be seen in Italy. The early 14C Sienese school of painting produced masters such as Duccio, Simone Martini and Pietro and Ambrogio Lorenzetti. In the 13C and early 14C the great sculptors Nicola Pisano and his son Giovanni were active in Pisa.

Florence is world famous for its Renaissance buildings, but other Renaissance monuments in Tuscany include the piazza in Pienza, Santa Maria del Calcinaio in Cortona, and Santa Maria delle Carceri in Prato. Delightful enamelled terracotta works by the Florentine Della Robbia family are to be found all over the region (in Florence, Pistoia, Lucca, Impruneta, La Verna, the Valdarno, and the Casentino). The great Florentine school of painting had a wide influence over local masters whose works are preserved in country churches and small towns. Luca Signorelli left some masterpieces in his native city of Cortona, and in Arezzo and Borgo San Sepolcro some of the best works of Piero della Francesca can be seen.

Apart from the fundamental importance to western civilisation of the Florentine Renaissance, Tuscany also produced some of the greatest artists and writers of all time: Giotto, Masaccio, Brunelleschi, Donatello, Leonardo da Vinci, Michelangelo; Dante, Boccaccio, Poliziano, and Petrarca.

Towns interesting for their 19C architecture include Viareggio and Livorno, and the spa of Montecatini has elaborate buildings dating from the beginning of this century.

Numerous travellers (including poets and writers) have come to Tuscany over the centuries, and Florence, Livorno, Pisa and Bagni di Lucca have particular Anglo-American associations. Florence was an important part of the Grand Tour itinerary for British travellers in the 18C, many of whom came by boat to Livorno. The consul Sir Horace Mann and his friend Horace Walpole presided over the English community in Florence in the latter part of the century. The English colony in Pisa in the early 19C included Byron and Shelley (who drowned off Viareggio in 1822). The Brownings lived in Florence from 1847 until Elizabeth's death in 1861 and Henry James also lived there towards the end of the century. Tuscany was the setting for two of E.M. Forster's novels published at the beginning of the 20C, when Aldous Huxley and D.H. Lawrence spent much of their time writing in Tuscany.

The inhabitants of some of the larger towns in Tuscany retain notable individual characteristics, and often rivalry is strong between them. Pisa has traditionally been the enemy of Florence, and Lucca proudly independent of the two. Carrara has been an active centre of the Anarchist movement throughout this century.

Tuscany has more museums than any other region in Italy, and an increasing number of interesting small local museums are being opened, including those at San Casciano Val di Pesa, Empoli, Tavarnelle, Montelupo Fiorentino, Montalcino and Cetona, to name but a few. Tuscany is known for its gardens and it is now becoming easier to visit those in private hands. In summer there are numerous music and theatre festivals in small villages throughout the region.

How to use the Guide

The guide is divided into **chapters** which describe the main towns, with their environs, and the various provinces of Tuscany. In addition, certain areas of the region known for their distinctive landscape are also included. The chapters dedicated to the major towns are organised into a number of walking itineraries, with separate descriptions for the major monuments and museums. At the end of such chapters, places of particular interest which can be reached in less than a day are described. An exhaustive section at the beginning of the book lists all the **practical information** a traveller is likely to need in preparation for and during a visit to Tuscany. This information is integrated with specific details at the beginning of each route and at the beginning of the description of each town. Information has been given both for those who visit the area by car and those who travel by public transport.

A small selection of **hotels** has been given at the beginning of each chapter, with their official star rating, in order to give an indication of price. In making the choice for inclusion, generally speaking the smaller hotels have been favoured, those in the centre of towns, or in particularly beautiful positions in the countryside. For further information, see under 'Where to Stay' in the Practical Information section.

On the double page town plans of Siena and Pisa hotels have been marked with a number which corresponds to the key in the text (i.e. Pl.II; 3;4, or Pl.I; 3;5) given with the list of hotels at the beginning of the description of the town. Since there are two plans for Siena (called Siena I and Siena II) the first number in the key refers to the Plan (I or II), the second number to the square, and the third number to the number which marks the position of the hotel. For Pisa hotels the first number refers to the square on the Pisa plan and the second number to the number which marks the position of the hotel. On some of the single page plans hotels have been marked with a number (which corresponds to the key in the text; i.e. Pl.5).

Restaurants have also been listed at the beginning of each chapter, and these have been divided into three categories which reflect price ranges in 1999:

£££ Luxury-class restaurants where the prices are likely to be over Lire 60,000 a head (and sometimes well over Lire 100,000 a head). These are the most famous restaurants in Tuscany and they usually offer international cusine.

££ First-class restaurants where the prices range from Lire 50,000 and above. These are generally comfortable, with good service, but are not cheap.

£ Simple trattorie and pizzerie where you can eat for around Lire 25,000–40,000 a head, or even less. Although simple, and by no means smart, the food in this category, which often includes local specialities, is usually the best value.

For further information, see under 'Restaurants' on p 36.

The **most important monuments and works of art** in Tuscany have been highlighted in bold capital letters or bold type throughout the text, and **asterisks** are used to indicate works of art which are particularly beautiful or interesting. The 'Highlights' section on page 11 singles out the major monuments which should not be missed.

Bold type has also been used in **churches** to differentiate the various parts of the building (ie. the façade, south side, east end, important chapels, etc.). All churches are taken as being orientated, with the entrance at the west end and the altar at the east end, and the south aisle on the right and the north aisle on the left.

In Florence, Pisa, and Siena all the main monuments have been keyed (ie. Pl.2) against the double page **town plans** which are gridded with numbered squares. On the **ground plans** of museums and churches figures or letters correspond with the description in the text.

The **local tourist boards** (Azienda di Promozione Turistica, shortened to APT) are usually extremely helpful and are the only way of securing up-to-date information on the spot about opening times and accommodation. They have all been listed with their telephone numbers on page 39, and the information offices are listed at the beginning of each chapter and in each town. On the town maps they are marked with **i**, the symbol which is used on local signposts throughout Italy.

Opening times of museums and monuments have been given throughout (ie. 09.00–14.00; fest. 09.00–13.00), with the abbreviation 'fest.' showing times for Sundays and holidays. The times vary and often change without warning, and it is best to consult the local APT on arrival about up-to-date times. For further information, see p 40. Almost all churches close at midday and do not reopen again until 15.00, 16.00, or even 17.00 hours.

Although detailed town plans are provided, every traveller to Tuscany whether driving or using public transport, will also need a large scale **map** of the region: the best are those produced by the TCI (details on p 34).

Abbreviations used in the guide

ACI	Automobile Club Italiano
APT	Azienda di Promozione Turistica (official local tourist office)
b.	born
C	century
c	circa (about)
CAI	Club Alpino Italiano
d.	died
ENIT	Ente Nazionale per il Turismo
FAI	Fondo per l'Ambiente Italiano (founded in 1975 on the model of the British National Trust)
fest.	*festa*, or festival (ie. holiday, including Sunday)
fl.	floruit (flourished)
FS	Ferrovie dello Stato (Italian State Railways)
IAT	Information office of APT
Pl.	plan
St	Saint
TCI	Touring Club Italiano

Highlights

Famous towns
The most famous towns of Tuscany—Florence, Siena, Pisa, Lucca, Arezzo, and San Gimignano—have many of the most important buildings, works of art, and museums in the region. The Campo of Siena and the Piazza del Duomo of Pisa are unforgettable sights.

Lesser known small towns and villages
The region also has numerous less well known small towns which are extremely interesting and pleasant places to visit (and much less crowded in spring and summer than the more famous towns). These include Cortona, Pienza, Volterra, Massa Marittima, Montalcino, San Quirico d'Orcia, Pitigliano, Sansepolcro and Colle Val d'Elsa. Near Florence the towns of Prato and Pistoia, often overlooked, have much of interest.

Small **well preserved villages** in lovely countryside include (in the order they appear in the book): Uzzano, Barga, Bolgheri, Tirli, Caldana, Montepescali, Capalbio, Montefioralle, San Gusmé, Monteriggioni, Certaldo Alto, Torri, Bagno Vignoni, Castiglione d'Orcia, Cetona, Magliano in Toscana, Pereta, Sovana, Sorano, Poppi, Cennina, Anghiari, Civitella in Val di Chiana, and Lucignano.

Small museums
Besides the large museums in the famous towns, there are often excellent small museums in lesser known places such as Cortona and Volterra. Other particularly fine museums include the Museo della Collegiata di Sant'Andrea at Empoli, the museum at San Casciano in Val di Pesa, the Pinacoteca Comunale at Castiglion Fiorentino, the Museo della Cattedrale di San Zeno in Pistoia, the Museo Civico and Diocesano at Montalcino, and the Museo della Cattedrale in Pienza.

Masterpieces by famous artists
Numerous masterpieces by great artists are to be found all over the region, including the best works of Duccio, Simone Martini, Pietro and Ambrogio Lorenzetti, Fra Angelico, Filippo Lippi, Piero della Francesca, Luca Signorelli, and the sculptors Nicola and Giovanni Pisano, Donatello, and the Della Robbia family. These can easily be found by reference to the index of artists at the back of the book.

Landscape
Some of the most beautiful landscape in Tuscany can be found in the Chianti region, the Casentino, the forest of Camaldoli, the Mugello, the Garfagnana (the Parco Naturale delle Alpi Apuane and the Parco dell'Orecchiella), Monte Amiata, the Maremma (particularly in the Parco dell'Uccellina, and near Capalbio and Pitigliano, at the nature reserve of Bolgheri, the Lago di Burano, and Cala Martina and Cala Violina on the coast near Follonica). Fine countryside can also be found in parts of Monte Argentario (and the Tombolo di Feniglia), Elba, and Capraia. For details on the **gardens** and the **coast** of Tuscany, see pages 42–43.

Archaeological sites and collections

Etruscan sites and tombs in interesting towns or lovely countryside include those at Chiusi, Cortona, Vetulonia, Volterra, Arezzo, Populonia, Roselle, Fiesole, Pitigliano, Saturnia, and Artimino. **Roman** monuments are to be found at Lucca, Arezzo, Fiesole, Volterra, Cosa and Roselle. **Archaeological collections** with prehistoric, Etruscan and Roman material are kept in museums in the following towns or localities: Florence, Fiesole, Artimino, Pistoia, Pontremoli, Pisa, Siena, Volterra, Grosseto, Arezzo, Cetona, Cortona, and Chiusi.

Romanesque churches

The following are some of the most important Romanesque churches in Tuscany (apart from those in Florence, Pisa, Siena, and Lucca): Sant'Antimo, San Galgano, San Godenzo, the Duomo of Prato, the Duomo of Barga, San Piero a Grado, Abbadia Isola, the Pieve di Santa Maria a Chianni, the Collegiata of San Gimignano, the Pieve di Cellole, Mensano, the Pieve di San Lazzaro a Lucardo, the Duomo of Massa Marittima, the Collegiata of Sant'Agata at Asciano, the Collegiata of San Quirico d'Orcia, the Pieve di Romena, Gropina, the Pieve di Santa Maria in Arezzo, and San Pietro a Cedda.

Monasteries and charterhouses

Monasteries and charterhouses in Tuscany in beautiful natural settings, interesting also for their works of art, include: Monte Oliveto Maggiore, La Verna, Camaldoli, Vallombrosa, the Certosa del Galluzzo, the Certosa di Pisa, Montesenario, Sant'Anna in Camprena, Abbadia San Salvatore, Rosano, Badia a Passignano, and Lecceto.

Renaissance architecture

Masterpieces of Renaissance architecture (apart from those in Florence) include Santa Maria delle Carceri in Prato, the Tempio di San Biagio at Montepulciano, Santa Maria del Calcinaio at Cortona, and the Renaissance town of Pienza.

An Historical Introduction

By John Law

Tuscany has long fascinated foreign visitors. For this its cultural history provides a principal explanation. The region's contribution to the visual arts and architecture has been astounding in quantity and quality, in terms of technical mastery and innovation. The importance and influence of this contribution can also be gauged from the fact that Tuscany largely created the Renaissance as both a historical phenomenon and as an idea. A revealing figure here is the painter, architect and art historian Giorgio Vasari (1511–74). He came from Arezzo and his compendious and influential *Lives of the Artists*, first published in 1550, propagated the concept of the Renaissance, a period of rebirth.

Vasari shared in the belief that civilisation had reached a high point with the Roman Empire, only to decline with the barbarian invaders and the iconoclasm of early Christianity. Its eventual revival, or rebirth, Vasari located largely in Tuscany and attributed to a succession of gifted painters, sculptors and architects, most of whom were Tuscan. For Vasari, the process began with remarkable pioneers, Cimabue (c 1240–1302?) and Giotto (c 1267–1337). It reached further heights with artists like the painter Masaccio (1401–28), the sculptor Donatello (c 1386–1466) and the architect Filippo Brunelleschi (1377–1446). It attained its peak with Vasari's friend and hero, Michelangelo Buonarotti (1475–1564). And not only were most of the leading participants Tuscan; Vasari also assigned a key role in the recognition and support of talent to the Medici. Cosimo I, duke of Florence from 1537 and Grand-duke of Tuscany from 1569, was among Vasari's own patrons.

Vasari's work has had considerable bearing on the interpretation of European cultural history, and while the main focus of his attention was the fine arts and architecture, the concept of Renaissance was applied to other areas. For the poet and Latinist Francesco Petrarch (1304–74) and his humanist followers—of whom many of the leading lights were again Tuscan—literature, moral philosophy and the study of history also underwent a Renaissance, distancing the modern era in cultural terms from the Middle Ages. Moreover, the recovery of the values of ancient Rome and Greece was believed by those involved to be of more than academic or antiquarian interest. The Renaissance, and the study of the humanities, were thought to have a wider relevance for society as a whole.

But the cultural contribution of Tuscany goes beyond even the important and influential channels opened up by humanism and the Renaissance. Petrarch was a fine poet in the vernacular, and here again the Tuscan contribution was remarkable. The poets Dante Alighieri (1265–1321) and Petrarch, and the story-teller Giovanni Boccaccio (1313–75) not only raised Italian to a literary language of the highest level; they also had a profound effect on the literature of the rest of Europe. The prestige of Latin and Greek as the languages of scholarship somewhat eclipsed Italian in the 15C, but it continued as the expressive vehicle for a remarkable number of chroniclers, diarists and letter writers from the Tuscan political and mercantile elite. In the 16C the vernacular re-emerged as the language of another generation of influential writers of whom the Florentine historians and political thinkers Niccolò Machiavelli (1469–1527) and Francesco Guicciardini (1483–1540) are the most famous.

Of course, it would be misleading to suggest that the entire course of Tuscan history can match the achievements of the period c 1300 to c 1550. However the legacy of the Renaissance continued to inspire later generations of craftsmen, artists, architects, men of letters, and their patrons. It also encouraged salons, libraries, art collections and learned societies. The Accademia della Crusca of Florence is a good example; it was established in 1582 to champion the purity of the Italian language. The Accademia Etrusca was founded in Cortona in 1727 to study the pre-Roman civilisation of the region. In its turn, this tradition inspired generations of foreign artists, connoisseurs and scholars to visit Tuscany; in the 18C Florence became a principal stopping point for travellers on the Grand Tour, as Tobias Smollett vividly recalls in his *Travels through France and Italy* (1766). In the 19C and 20C the history and civilisation of Tuscany have been intensely studied. Moreover, research, curiosity and taste have not been satisfied with the major cities, the principal artists or the Renaissance period alone.

There are other reasons for foreign interest in Tuscany. Although generally a satellite of Habsburg power from 1530 to 1859, the region never sank to provincial status, like the provinces of the Papal States. This was largely due to the fact that the Medici ruled from Florence, as dukes and then Grand-dukes; in 1737 they were succeeded by the House of Lorraine which lasted—with interruptions during the Revolutionary and Napoleonic periods—down to 1859. The survival of an active court preserved a source of patronage and attracted foreign visitors, diplomats, adventurers and political exiles; Prince Charles Edward Stuart resided in Florence from 1775 to 1788. And there were other autonomous states within the boundaries of Tuscany. The city of Lucca preserved its republican constitution from the end of the Middle Ages to 1805, when it became a principality ruled by various dynasties down to 1859. Minor principalities, which also changed hands, were centred at Massa and Piombino. More famously, Napoleon was ruler of Elba from May 1814 to February 1815.

To captains of industry, however, Elba was better known for its iron ore. Deposits on the island and the mainland had been worked from pre-Roman times; the name 'Elba' was often given to foundries in 19C Britain. This introduces the point that Tuscany remained of economic importance in the modern era, if its cities had lost the commercial, financial and industrial pre-eminence they had acquired in Europe between the 12C and 14C—a phenomenon to be discussed below. Marble and alabaster were quarried in its hills. Abroad, the reputation of its olive oil preceded that of its wine. Luxury items were manufactured for export, ceramics and silk for example. From the 18C there was a growing international market for its works of art. Some of the grand-dukes actively encouraged the Tuscan economy, for example by draining the Maremma region to improve health and agricultural production, or by developing Livorno as an international port where Jewish and Protestant communities could trade and worship unmolested. The second commercial railway in Italy was built by Robert Stevenson between Livorno and Pisa (1841–44).

For a variety of reasons, therefore, Tuscany did not have to await the invention of Chiantishire or the introduction of the summer school or the art trail to become familiar to foreign—often Anglo-Saxon—visitors and residents. Furthermore, the rich travel literature and, more poignantly, the English cemetery in Florence suggest that a simple categorisation of such travellers is impossible. Some came to study art (John Ruskin, 1819–1900), others to develop the art market (Bernard Berenson, 1865–1959). The paradise of exiles attracted bohemian rebels (Shelley and Byron in Pisa, 1821–22); others aimed for a more aristocratic life-style (the Sitwells at Montegufoni, 1909–74). If the relatively liberal policies of the Tuscan grand-dukes encouraged the arrival of merchants and engineers, they also gave hope to Protestant preachers and teachers who planted churches and schools in the principal resorts and cities of the region in the 19C. Health could be a motive. Ancient spas like Bagni di Lucca were revitalised. Viareggio was an early centre for sea bathing. While some visitors were consumed by the dangers, frustrations, opportunities and responsibilities of living abroad, others found them a source of inspiration. E.M. Forster's *Where Angels Fear to Tread* (1905) and *Room with a View* (1908) were set in Tuscany. In the 19C, the politics of the Risorgimento were a source of inspiration and excitement, encouraged when Florence became capital of Italy (1865–71). A later generation was introduced to Tuscany by the war against Fascism and German occupation, and the heavy battles on the Gothic Line (1943–45). The period is captured in the writings of Iris Origo (*War in Val d'Orcia*), Eric Newby (*Love and War in the Apennines*) and Stuart Hood (*Carlino*).

Tuscany (*Toscana*) is derived from the Roman and early medieval name *Tuscia* which in turn comes from Etruria, the land of the Etruscans (*Tusci, Etrusci*). Etruscan power and civilisation were at their height from the 8C to the 4C BC. Quite apart from being seafarers with trading connections across the Mediterranean, the Etruscans settled and influenced other peoples in the Italian peninsula well beyond the frontiers of the modern region. They settled north of the Apennines and deep into what is now Umbria. They also spread southwards, through Lazio to Rome and beyond; the Tarquin rulers of Rome for around 100 years from 616 BC were an Etruscan dynasty. Lars Porsena who beseiged Rome in 508 BC was an Etruscan chieftain from Chiusi.

But the Etruscans did not create a centralised state; their civilisation was a city-based federation whose unity lay more in language, customs and religion than in political power. Eventually this proved a weakness and exposed the Etruscans to Roman conquest in the 4C BC. But although there were battles and rebellions, and Roman colonies were established (e.g. Florence, Lucca, Pisa), the Etruscans were not displaced. Their religion was respected. Some of the southern cities (Arezzo, Cortona) had welcomed Rome as an ally and Etruscan communities were accorded rights of self-government. The region did not desert Rome for Hannibal during the darkest days of the Second Punic War (217 BC), and in 90 BC its inhabitants were granted Roman citizenship. In the 3C and 2C BC, links with the capital had been strengthened with improvements and extensions to the road system, but the surviving identity of the Etruscans resulted in Tuscany being recognised as the seventh region of Italy under the emperor Augustus. Diocletian united it with Umbria in the late 3C AD, with Florence as the capital.

Whatever its frontiers, Roman regional administration was overwhelmed by the barbarian invasions, though between 535 and 553 Byzantine armies had success in regaining imperial territory from the Ostrogoths. But these gains were swept aside in the late 6C by the Lombards who occupied all Tuscany and created a duchy with its capital at Lucca (568–774).

The next fundamental change in the balance of power was created by the entry of the Franks to Italy under Pepin III (751–68) and Charlemagne (768–814) as papal champions, eventually conquering the Lombard duchy of Tuscany in 774. In 800, Pope Leo III (795–816) tried to secure his ally by crowning Charlemagne as emperor in Rome. Tuscany became part of this new western empire, and a Frankish march, or frontier province, was established with its capital at Lucca. However, as in other parts of western Christendom in the age of feudalism, effective authority was wielded from the centre only fitfully and real power was exercised by lay and ecclesiastical landlords, great monastic houses and, increasingly, by the cities.

The rise of the cities to a position of prominence in late medieval and Renaissance Tuscany was a phenomenon of such importance that it demands some explanation. Of course, none of the major centres were purely medieval foundations; all proudly claimed a Roman past, but some went back to Etruscan times and even earlier (Volterra, Chiusi, Fiesole). Whatever their precise origins, towns and cities were founded for a variety of reasons: for security, on defensive sites (Volterra); on river crossings (Florence); near good anchorages (Pisa). In Tuscany, the continuity of urban life was never broken despite the instability following the fall of the Roman Empire and the Saracen raids that intensified with the break-up of Charlemagne's empire in the 9C. A fundamental reason for urban growth—and indeed survival—was the wealth of the countryside in terms of agricultural production and raw materials. The insanitary conditions of urban life, the readiness with which their inhabitants were afflicted by famine and disease, meant that such communities depended on a steady flow of immigrants from their hinterlands. But this did not depopulate the countryside, where the majority of the population continued to live until relatively modern times. The intensity, age and variety of rural settlement—from monastic houses to villas, from medium-size towns to isolated households—points to the wealth of much of the region.

But the principal cities of Tuscany developed in economic terms far beyond the role of local market towns and centres of industry. A lead in this process was taken by Pisa which turned defensive warfare against Saracen raiders into expansion overseas, settling colonies on Corsica, Sardinia and the Balearic Islands in the 10C and 11C, participating in the crusading movement in the eastern Mediterranean and becoming a commercial and naval power of international importance.

The population of Pisa rose from around 12,000 in the mid-12C to around 20,000 in the early 13C and to around 40,000 in the late 13C, small by modern standards but large in the context of medieval Europe. The other cities of Tuscany also expanded rapidly over the same period; the economic revolution in which Pisa took part caused, and was sustained by, the development of its neighbours, Florence, Lucca, Siena. The first two became industrial giants for the production of textiles (woollen cloth and silk). All three became centres of finance, and Tuscan bankers and money-changers operated on an international scale by the 12C and 13C. For example, on the security of royal customs receipts, the Riccardi bankers of Lucca lent vast sums to Edward I of England, financing, among much else, the construction of castles in Wales. Again, the remarkably rich commercial and personal archive left by Francesco Datini (1335–1410), the merchant of Prato so vividly evoked by Iris Origo, shows business acumen at work on a local and international scale.

However, the economic upswing demonstrated most dramatically by the leading Tuscan cities was not sustained. Natural disasters intervened gradually or suddenly. The port of Pisa began to silt up and the population became increasingly exposed to malaria from the 14C. The economies of all the Tuscan cities were disrupted by the Black Death of 1348–49; its arrival in Florence was graphically described by Boccaccio in his *Decameron*. Though precise statistics are lacking, it seems likely that the plague, which became endemic, was a major factor in reducing the populations of Tuscany by at least one third.

Other checks on the economy were man-made. As in the 20C so in the 13C and 14C, heavy advances to demanding foreign clients could place the lenders in the hands of their debtors, as relations between Florentine banking houses and Edward III of England demonstrate. The Tuscan cities also faced competition, first on an Italian and later on an international scale. The rivalry of Genoa, Venice and Florence seriously weakened the naval and commercial power of Pisa; the last rival subjected Pisa to its rule in 1406. Furthermore, the commercial revolution so linked to Tuscan enterprise encouraged the development of other centres of industry, commerce and finance in Europe (e.g. Barcelona, Flanders, the Rhineland). The Medici bank, the leading Florentine finance house of the 15C, counting the papacy among its clients, did not have the resources of its 14C predecessors, and political considerations and mismanagement at the centre and branch level gradually reduced the scope of its operations. Finally, the growth of the Atlantic powers and the Ottoman Empire from the late 15C further reduced the relative importance of Tuscany in the economies of Europe and the Mediterranean. It was only in the 19C that Florence—the largest city in the region—saw its population pass the 100,000 mark, the level that it had reached c 1300.

The economic development of Tuscany earlier in the Middle Ages, its agricultural wealth and its relative accessibility by land and sea were principal reasons for the growing autonomy of its towns and cities, and their emergence in the 11C and 12C as self-governing communes. There were other factors. The authority of the emperor's representatives in the region, the marquisses of Tuscany, was only spasmodically effective and came to an end with the death of Matilda in 1115. The emperors themselves, though certainly capable of effective military and political intervention down to the 13C and even beyond, were generally distant overlords with many other preoccupations. Their struggles with the papacy, particularly intense in the late 11C and 12C, for control of the personnel and wealth of the Church proved very debilitating.

The communes that benefited from this conflict and the collapse of central authority could be represented, particularly by historians in the 19C, in a heroic and sometimes patriotic light. They could be seen in terms of a people fighting for freedom from alien rule, and also as devoted allies of the papacy and the cause of the Church. The communes could also be portrayed as breaking the repressive, reactionary, medieval power of the feudal aristocracy with weapons and policies derived from more modern economies and social attitudes.

However, historians have now become more cautious, even sceptical, when discussing the phenomenon. It was not until 1859 that Tuscany ceased to be a

satellite of the Holy Roman Empire. In the medieval period some communes—
Siena, Lucca, Pisa—could have pro-imperial, or Ghibelline, regimes that
continued to look to the emperors for protection and privileges. The confronta-
tion once seen between feudal aristocrats and bourgeois entrepreneurs is now
regarded as overdrawn. Great landowners of ancient pedigree could also have
interests in banking and commerce, like the Piccolomini of Siena. Upwardly
mobile bourgeois families enthusiastically adopted an aristocratic life-style and
acquired titles, coats of arms, country estates and well-connected marriages. If
the communes of Tuscany did try to control with force and legislation the political and military influence of noble clans, they could not end it as the castles of
the Tuscan countryside show. Moreover, they often turned to such families for
support, for example when in need of leaders and resources in time of war.

Furthermore, the communes were far from being democracies. The participa-
tion of such bodies as the *popolo* and guilds in the 13C and 14C may have
widened government, but it did not end the ascendancy of a *de facto* oligarchy of
the wealthier and longer-established families. In 14C Florence, for example, the
Arti Maggiori, or greater guilds of bankers, merchants, lawyers maintained a
predominance over the *Arti Minori* representing the much more numerous artisans and retailers. In none of the communes was the bulk of the rural or urban
population ever admitted to government. In conditions of economic hardship
this could result in violence; in July 1378 the unenfranchised day labourers of
Florence, the Ciompi, tried and failed to win for themselves a place in government.

But violence was not confined to resentful workers and peasants. Within
communal government there was little sense of loyal opposition; a regime's
enemies faced legal and fiscal penalties, fines, exile, imprisonment or death.
Beyond the borders of a city state, exiles could gather in vengeful contrary
commonwealths, though others could choose a more solitary path. Most
famously, faction in Florence condemned Dante Alighieri to exile in 1302; the
poet gradually distanced himself from other exiled Florentines and their allies,
though his bitterness never left him.

Dante's career also points to other sources of instability in the political and
social life of the communes of Tuscany. His family shared, and continued, his
exile; a strong sense of kin, often intensified by local loyalties founded on the
parish or quarter of a city, meant that patron-client relationships, a reliance on
the clan, could undermine public authority. Secondly, internal faction could
have a wider, even international, dimension as Guelfs (nominally pro-papal)
fought Ghibellines (nominally pro-imperial) for control of the cities of Tuscany
in the 13C and 14C.

Lastly, if communes were jealous of their own authority they were less
prepared to recognise the liberties of others. For reasons of military and
economic security, the towns and cities of Tuscany all sought to extend the area
of their jurisdiction, or *contado*. The larger communes also sought to bring their
rivals under their dominion. This was markedly the case with Florence whose
self-centred belief in liberty encouraged rather than inhibited its expansion in
Tuscany: Prato, 1350; Pistoia, 1351; Volterra, 1361; Arezzo, 1384; Pisa, 1406;
Cortona, 1411; Livorno, 1421.

But it can be as anachronistic to belittle as to exaggerate the achievements of
the communes. In a Europe largely dominated by monarchical forms of govern-

ment and a hierarchic view of society, they did represent an alternative: a concept of popular sovereignty; republican constitutions; more open, answerable, forms of government; greater social mobility. Such an alternative view found expression in books of statutes and the resolutions and debates of governing councils. It shaped political thought, attitudes to history and forms of propaganda. It informed the astounding range of often vivid and detailed chronicles and diaries produced in the cities of late medieval Tuscany. Even more tangibly, it was expressed in the construction of public buildings, the *palazzi*, where councils and courts met and archives and treasuries were stored. The communes also tried to improve the quality of life: establishing markets, building bridges, paving streets and squares, regulating private building, installing fountains, passing legislation on hygiene. They tried to encourage public education, the more enlightened communes supporting universities (Pisa from the 12C, Siena from the 13C). They tried to further security: fortifying the city with walls and gates; curbing powerful families who sought to build towers and castles for themselves in town and country; regulating the carrying of weapons; placing garrisons in strategic fortresses.

The sense of community could also be expressed in religious terms with the communes supporting the Church, charitable institutions and the cults associated with saints and relics. The main focus of attention was generally the cathedral, but the commune could also support hospitals and the churches associated with religious orders and local cults. The case of Siena can be taken to illustrate these general points: from ambitious plans to enlarge and embellish the cathedral, to support for the central hospital of Santa Maria della Scala; from the construction of the seat of government, the *Palazzo Pubblico*, to its decoration with frescoes expressing civic pride, piety and political beliefs; from the paving of the central *Piazza del Campo*, to the engineering feat of installing in it a public fountain, the *Fonte Gaia*.

It is in the *Campo* that the famous horse race, the *palio* between rival *contrade*, or districts, of the city is still run. This serves to introduce a further point. Loyalty to parish, family or guild was not necessarily incompatible with the common good of the wider community. Competition could be expressed in a civic context as the patronage of the guilds of Florence for the shrine of Or San Michele in the early 15C clearly demonstrates. The foundation (1495) of the beautiful Piccolomini library in the cathedral of Siena by cardinal Francesco Piccolomini (later Pius III, 1503) was in part intended to celebrate the family name and the achievements of his uncle Aeneas Sylvius (Pius II, 1458–64). It was also intended to enrich the church and contribute to learning.

As a form of government, republicanism failed to survive the Renaissance other than in Lucca. The political instability of the region had earlier seen communes come under the rule (*signoria*) of a native or foreign lord (*signore*). In some instances, such lordship could be largely nominal, like that of the Angevin kings of Naples over Florence in the early 14C. However, some *signori* were sustained by real economic and military power and the support of a faction or party of the population. This was the case with the military leader Castruccio Castracane (1281–1328) who, from a base in Lucca over which he was made duke (1327), extended his rule over a number of Tuscan cities.

But the strength of republicanism in the region and the jealousy of other families prevented signorial regimes from being more than interludes, though principalities did take root at Massa and Piombino. With the Renaissance the situation changed. In the course of the 15C, and particularly after 1434, the Medici established an ascendancy in Florence. This was not based on force, nor was the family's influence formalised in terms of office or title; they remained private citizens. Medici power was based on wealth, family alliances and patronage in the broadest sense. It depended crucially on the political and diplomatic skills of the Medici themselves, and more particularly the heads of the leading household: Cosimo (1389–68), Piero (1418–69), Lorenzo the Magnificent (1449–92). When these qualities were lacking, as happened after the death of Lorenzo, republicanism quickly re-established itself.

However informal their hold on power in the 15C, abroad the Medici had established themselves as Italian princes, and two members of the dynasty became pope: Leo X (1513–21) and Clement VII (1523–34). Papal support helped sustain the family in its periods of exile and also contributed—along with the armies of the emperor Charles V—to its eventual return in 1530, first as lords of the city and then as dukes (1532). Not only was the Medici hold on power formalised and given some legitimacy; they also inherited the ascendancy Florence had achieved over Tuscany. Thanks again to Habsburg arms, the Medici state was enlarged by the Treaty of Cateau-Cambrésis (1559) with the addition of Siena and the commune of Montalcino, both of which had put up a heroic defence of Tuscan republicanism against superior forces. In 1569 Cosimo I was created Grand-duke of Tuscany.

But if the rule of the Medici, their transformation from private citizens to princes and the construction of fortresses and citadels in Florence and elsewhere brought about the end of republican government in most of Tuscany, the legacy of the republican past was not destroyed. The civic sense and cultural vitality generated in the Middle Ages survived in Florence and the other cities of Tuscany, informing and moderating the relatively enlightened and liberal Grand-dukes down to Tuscany's unification with the kingdom of Italy in 1860.

Further reading

C. Ady, *Lorenzo dei Medici and Renaissance Italy* (London, 1955)

G. Artom Treves, *The Golden Ring. The Anglo-Florentines* (London, 1956)

K. Beevor, *A Tuscan Childhood* (London, 1995)

J. Bentley, *Italy: the Hill Towns* (London, 1990)

G. Brucker, *Renaissance Florence* (New York, 1969)

J.R. Hale, *Florence and the Medici* (London 1977)

J.R. Hale (ed.), *A Concise Encyclopedia of the Italian Renaissance* (London, 1981)

O. Hamilton, *The Divine Country* (London, 1982)

D. Hay (ed.), *The Longman History of Italy* (London, 1980–)

H. Hearder and D.P. Waley (eds), *A Short History of Italy* (Cambridge, 1962)

H. Hearder, *Italy: a Short History* (Cambridge, 1990)

C. Hibbert, *The Grand Tour* (London, 1969)

C. Hibbert, *The Rise and Fall of the House of Medici* (London, 1974)

J. Hook, *Siena* (London, 1979)

J. Keates, *Tuscany* (London, 1988)

M. Levey, *Florence. A Portrait* (London, 1996)

F. Mayes, *Under the Tuscan Sun* (New York, 1997)

I. Origo, *The Merchant of Prato* (London, 1957, 1963)

J. Pemble, *The Mediterranean Passion* (Oxford, 1988)
M. Phillips, *The Memoir of Marco Parenti. A Life in Medici Florence* (London, 1990)
D.P. Waley, *The Italian City Republics* (London, 1978)
D.P. Waley, *Siena and the Sienese* (Cambridge, 1991)

Place names in Italian towns and cities

Many of the place names in Italian towns and cities have ancient origins; the names assigned to public buildings, market places, towers, bridges, gates and fountains frequently date to the Middle Ages. But the practice of formally naming all streets and squares began in the 19C. Frequently local—even parochial—patriotism determines the choice as the community celebrates its own history and its own political, literary, religious and scientific figures, as well as famous foreign visitors.

But the choice of place names can reflect wider issues, and events and figures from Italian national history are prominently represented. Thus a united republican Italy can be celebrated in terms of concepts (e.g. Via della Repubblica, della Libertà, della Vittoria), events (e.g. Via del Plebiscito recalling the vote that preceded a region uniting with the Kingdom of Italy in the 19C), or by drawing on the gazetteer of Italian rivers, mountains, seas and cities.

Broadly speaking the national figures and events chosen tend to be representative of four phases in recent Italian history. Probably the most emotive and frequently commemorated is the Risorgimento (the Resurgence), the movement that led to the unification and independence of Italy in the 19C; among the battles commemorated are: Custoza, Lissa, Solferino, Magenta, Montebello, Mentana. For some historians, Italy's entry to the First World War represents the final phase in the pursuit of national unity; the battles and campaigns between Italy, and her allies, and the Central Powers are also frequently recorded in place names: the Isonzo; Monte Pasubio; Caporetto; Monte Grappa, the Piave; Vittorio Veneto. Opposition to Fascism and the ending of the Second World War are also commemorated in this way, as are the statesmen and events associated with the country's reconstruction, economic development and membership of the EU. Casualties in Italy's successful struggle against political terrorism (Aldo Moro, murdered by the Red Brigades in 1978) and the less successful war with organised crime (Alberto della Chiesa, killed by the Mafia in 1982) are also being so honoured.

Largely censored and deleted from the record are the events and personalities closely linked to Fascism, Italy's empire and the reigns of the last two members of the House of Savoy, Vittorio Emanuele III (1900–46) and Umberto II (1946). However, the keen-eyed observer might be able to identify traces of Fascist insignia and the Fascist system of dating (1922, when Mussolini was invited to lead the government, is year 1) on public buildings and monuments, and some street names still recall territories once ruled from Rome (e.g. Istria, Dalmazia, Albania, Libia).

Below are listed a selection of the more prominent figures and events from recent Italian history the traveller is likely to encounter time and again.

Prominent people

ALFIERI Vittorio (1749–1803), poet and dramatist.

BATTISTI Cesare, Italian patriot executed by the Habsburg regime in Trent, 12 July 1916.

CARDUCCI Giosuè (1835–1907), patriotic poet and literary critic.

CAVOUR Camille (1810–61), statesman and cautious architect of Italian unification.

CRISPI Francesco (1818–1901), statesman.

FOSCOLO Ugo (1778–1827), poet and patriot.

GARIBALDI Giuseppe (1807–82), inspirational political and military leader in the Risorgimento.

GRAMSCI Antonio (1891–1937), political thinker, Marxist, opponent of Fascism.

MANIN Daniele (1804–57), Venetian patriot and statesman, defender of that city against Habsburg forces, 1848–49.

MARCONI Guglielmo (1874–37), electrical engineer and radio pioneer.

MARGHERITA of Savoy (1851–1926), wife of King Umberto I, noted for her piety, good works and cultural patronage.

MARTIRI DELLA RESISTENZA (or DELLA LIBERTÀ), opponents of Fascism and German occupation, 1943–45.

MATTEOTTI Giacomo (1885–1924), socialist politician, assassinated by Fascists.

MAZZINI Giuseppe (1805–82), leading republican figure of the Risorgimento.

OBERDAN Guglielmo (1858–82), Italian patriot, executed by the Habsburg regime in Trieste.

RICASOLI Bettino (1809–80), Florentine statesman, instrumental in securing Tuscany's adherence to the Kingdom of Italy in 1860.

SAFFI Aurelio (1819–1890), man of letters and hero of the Risorgimento.

UMBERTO I of Savoy, King of Italy, 1878–1900.

VERDI Giuseppe (1813–1901), prolific opera composer whose output was often associated with cause of a united Italy. His surname could be read as the initials of Vittorio Emanuele Re d'Italia.

VITTORIO EMANUELE II of Savoy, King of Sardinia-Piedmont from 1849, King of Italy 1861–78.

Historic events

XI FEBBRAIO: 11 February 1929, formal reconciliation between the papacy and the kingdom of Italy.

XXIX MARZO: 29 March 1943, armistice between Italy and the Allies.

XXVII APRILE: 27 April 1945, Benito Mussolini captured by partisans in northern Italy. The Fascist leader was quickly tried and executed on 28 April.

XI MAGGIO: 11 May 1860, Garibaldi landed with 1000 men at Marsala (Sicily) and launched the military campaign that led to the Unification of Italy.

XXIV MAGGIO: 24 May 1915, Italy enters the First World War.

II GIUGNO: 2 June 1946, referendum designed to favour a republican constitution.

XX GIUGNO: 20 June 1859, papal forces and their supporters violently suppressed a pro-Unification rising in Perugia.

XIV SETTEMBRE: 14 September 1860, the forces of the Kingdom of Italy entered Perugia.

XX SETTEMBRE: 20 September 1870, Italian forces enter Rome, overthrowing papal rule.

IV NOVEMBRE: 4 November 1918, proclamation of the armistice between Italy and Austria.

Practical information

Planning your visit

When to go

The best time to visit Tuscany is in Spring or Autumn. In these seasons the countryside is at its best, covered with wild flowers in the Spring and bright with orange and yellow leaves in the Autumn. However, Spring can be unexpectedly wet until well after Easter, and Easter itself should be avoided if possible as it is the most crowded time of year throughout Italy. Autumn is often dryer and can be quite warm throughout October and even in early November. At the height of summer Tuscany can be extremely hot, and at these times it is best to go to the mountains, or to the hill towns (those above 500 metres). The coast of Versilia, and the seaside resorts in the Maremma, and the island of Elba can be extremely crowded with Italian holiday makers in July and August. As all over Italy, Tuscany is crowded with Italian school parties from March until early May. The special charm of a visit to Tuscany in winter is that even the most famous sights can be totally deserted.

Passports

These are necessary for all British and American travellers entering Italy. You are obliged to carry some means of identity with you at all times. A lost or stolen passport can be replaced by the relevant embassy in Rome: information from the British and American consulates in Florence (see 'Crime and Personal Security', p 38).

Italian Tourist Boards

General information can be obtained abroad from the Italian State Tourist Office (ENIT; Ente Nazionale Italiano per il Turismo; e-mail: www.italiantourism.com), who provide detailed information about Italy.

Canada: 1 Place Ville Marie, Suite 1914, **Montreal**, Que. H3B 2C3 (☎ 001 514-8867668, fax 514-3921429; e-mail: initaly@ican.net); **Netherlands**: Stadhoudeskade 2, 1054 ES **Amsterdam**, ☎ 003 120-6168244, fax 120-6188515; **UK**: 1 Princes Street, **London** WIR 8AY (☎. 0171 408-1254, fax 0171 493-6695; **USA: New York**: 630 Fifth Avenue, NY 10111, Suite 1565 (☎ 001 212-2454822, fax 212-5869249; **Chicago**: 500 North Michigan Avenue, Suite 2240 Chicago 1, IL 60611 (☎ 001 312-6440996, fax 312-6443019; **Los Angeles**: 12400 Wilshire Blvd, Suite 550, CA 90025 (☎ 001 310-8201898, fax 310-8206357; e-mail: enitla@earthlink.net).

Tour operators

Among the many UK tour operators offering inclusive holidays to Tuscany are the following:
Abercrombie & Kent, ☎ 0171 730 9600 *Ace Study Tours*, ☎ 01223 835055 *Citalia*, ☎ 0181 686 5533 *City Escapades*, ☎ 0181 563 8959 *CTS Travel*, ☎ 0171

637 1648 *Italian Escapades*, ☎ 0181 748 4999 *International Chapters*, ☎ 0171 722 9560 *Magic of Italy*, ☎ 0181 748 7575 *Martin Randall Travel Ltd.*, ☎ 0181 742 3355 *Prospect Music and Art Tours*, ☎ 0181 995 2163 *Specialtours*, ☎ 0171 730 2297 *Travelscene*, ☎ 0181 427 8800. The *Alternative Travel Group Ltd*, ☎ 01865 315678 specialises in walking holidays.

In Canada, *Artfocus au point* (☎ 514 937 6391, fax 514 933 5346) specialise in art and architectural tours of Italy.

Web sites on Italy
These include *Let's roam Italy* (http://tqd.advanced.org/2838); *Italytour.com* (http://www.italytour.com/); and *Italy online* (http://www.initaly.com/).

Disabled travellers
Italy is at last catching up slowly with the rest of Europe in the provision of facilities for the disabled. All new public buildings (including museums) are now obliged by law to provide access for the disabled, and specially designed facilities. In the annual list of hotels published by the local APT offices, hotels which are able to give hospitality to the disabled are indicated. Airports and railway stations provide assistance, and certain trains are equipped to transport wheelchairs. Access is allowed to the centre of towns (normally closed to traffic) for cars with disabled people, where parking places are reserved for them. For all other information, contact local APT offices, or *Chance* (☎ 045-8060110) or *Si...viaggiare* (☎ 06-23267504).

Getting to Tuscany

By air
Pisa is the main international airport in Tuscany. From the airport a train (or bus) service runs in 1hr via Pisa to Florence. There is also an international airport at **Bologna**, across the Apennines in Emilia-Romagna ('aerobus' every 20 minutes, 15 minutes journey time to Bologna station and from there trains to Florence in just over 1 hr). The small airport near the centre of **Florence** (Amerigo Vespucci at Peretola) has flights from Europe (including London Gatwick). The nearest intercontinental airport to Tuscany is **Rome** (Fiumicino) which has direct flights from numerous cities in the USA as well as from Europe. Rome's second airport (Ciampino) now also has charter flights from London Stansted.

Direct air services **from the UK** are operated by *British Airways* (☎ 0181-759 2525) and *Alitalia* (☎ 0171-602 7111) from London daily to Pisa and Bologna airports. *Go* ☎ 0845 6054321(go-fly.co.uk) flies direct from Stansted to Bologna. There are also flights from Manchester, Dublin, and Glasgow to Pisa. *Ryanair* (☎ 0541-569569) operates from Stansted to Pisa. *Meridiana* (☎ 0171-839 3333) flies from Gatwick to Florence. Details of charter flights are available through travel agencies and listings sections in many of the national newspapers, especially the Sunday newspapers, the London *Evening Standard* and in *Time Out*. Scheduled services offer special fares which are available according to season; there are reduced youth fares. *Citalia* (☎ 0181-686 5533) has fly-drive schemes.

Air services **from the USA** to Rome are operated by *Alitalia* (☎ 800 223 5730) which flies non-stop from New York, Boston, Chicago, and Los Angeles. Flights from New York to Rome are also operated by *Continental*, ☎ 800 231 0856, *Delta*, ☎ 800 241 4141 and *TWA*, ☎ 1 800 892 4141. *United*, ☎ 800 5382 929 operate between Washington DC and Rome. *British Airways, Air France, KLM* and *Sabena* offer flights connecting through London, Paris, Amsterdam and Brussels, and these are often more economical than direct flights. A direct flight operated by *Air Europe* from New York to Pisa is to be introduced in 1999.

By rail

Florence can be reached **from the UK** by the overnight sleeper from Paris Lyon; there are now frequent trains from London Waterloo through the eurotunnel via Calais to Paris Nord (in c 3 hrs). For more information, contact *European Rail Ltd*, ☎ 0171-387 0444, fax 0171-387 0888. Italian State Railways are represented in the UK by *Citalia*, ☎ 0181-686 0677, fax 0181-686 0328.

Overnight car sleeper services run May–September once a week from Calais to Bologna (for information and booking, ☎ 0272 544350 or 051 6303589).

In the USA, information is available from CIT, ☎ 212 697 1394 (New York office), ☎ 310 338 8616 (Los Angeles office). In **Canada**, there are CIT offices in Montreal (☎ 514 8459101) and Toronto (☎ 416 927 7712).

In Italy, the main line from Milan and Bologna to Rome has stations at Prato, Florence and Arezzo (although not all trains stop at Prato and Arezzo). The coastal line from Turin and Genoa serves Massa Carrara and Versilia, Pisa, Livorno, and Grosseto.

By coach

A coach service operates in two days between London (Victoria Coach Station) and Rome (Piazza della Repubblica) via Dover, Calais, Paris, Turin, Milan, Bologna, and Florence, daily from June to September, and once or twice a week for the rest of the year. Student discounts available. Information in London from *Eurolines*, ☎ 01582 456654. In Florence, contact the *SITA* office, ☎ 055 214721.

By car

The easiest approaches by road are the motorways through the Mont Blanc (closed for repairs in 1999), St Bernard, or Monte Cenis tunnels, over the Brenner pass, or along the south coast of France. The A1 motorway from Milan and Bologna to Rome runs through Tuscany from Prato to Florence, the Valdarno, Arezzo, Valdichiana, and Chiusi. The coastal motorway from the south of France and Genoa enters Tuscany at Massa Carrara and continues south through Versilia to Lucca and Pisa. The Via Aurelia (now double carriageway all the way to Civitavecchia near Rome) continues south along the coast of Tuscany via Grosseto.

British drivers taking their own cars by any of the routes across France, Belgium, Luxembourg, Switzerland, Germany, and Austria need the vehicle registration book, a valid national driving licence (accompanied by a translation, issued free of charge by the Italian State Tourist Office), insurance cover, and a nationality plate attached to the car. If you are not the owner of the vehicle, you must have the owner's written permission for its use abroad.

A Swiss Motorway Pass is needed for Switzerland, and can be obtained from the RAC, the AA or at the Swiss border. The continental rule of the road is to drive on the right and overtake on the left. The provisions of the respective highway codes in the countries of transit, though similar, have important variations, especially with regard to priority, speed limits, and pedestrian crossings. Membership of the AA (☎ 01256 20123), or the RAC (membership enquiries and insurance, ☎ 01345 3331133; route information ☎ 01345 333222) entitles you to many of the facilities of affiliated societies on the Continent. They are represented at most of the sea and air ports. Additional route information from www.autostop.it/

Motorway routes to Italy from Europe

The main routes from France, Switzerland, and Austria are summarised below:

From France, by-passing Geneva. The direct motorway route from France, enters Italy through the **Mont Blanc Tunnel** (closed for repairs at present). The road from Courmayeur to Aosta has not yet been improved. At Aosta the A5 motorway begins: it follows the Val d'Aosta. Just beyond Ivrea is the junction with the A4/5 motorway: the A5 continues south to Turin, while the A4/5 diverges east. At Santhia the A4 motorway from Turin is joined for Milan via Novara, or the A26/4 can be followed south via Alessandria, reaching the coast at Voltri, just outside Genoa.

For Tuscany there is a choice between the *Autostrada del Sole* (A1) from Milan or the Florence–Pisa motorway from Genoa. Alternatively the AI can be taken to near Parma where the AI5 diverges for the coast at La Spezia. The two latter routes avoid the Apennine pass between Bologna and Florence which carries very heavy traffic and can be subject to delays. This stretch of motorway can also be avoided when approaching from the north by continuing along the A14 beyond Bologna for Cesena, and from there taking the E45 superstrada through Romagna into eastern Tuscany (Sansepolcro and Arezzo).

To Turin from France. The most direct approach is through the **Monte Cenis Tunnel** from Modane in France to Bardonecchia. A road continues to Oulx where a motorway continues via Susa to Turin. From Turin a motorway (A6) descends direct to the coast at Savona, or the motorway (A21, A26) via Asti and Alessandria leads to Genoa; either one joins directly the coastal motorway for Pisa and Florence. Alternatively, the A4 motorway leads from Turin east to Milan for the *Autostrada del Sole*.

The coastal route from the South of France. This follows the A10 motorway through the foothills with frequent long tunnels to enter Italy just before Ventimiglia. The motorway continues past Alassio, Albenga, and Savona (where the motorway from Turin comes in), to Voltri (where the A26 motorway from Alessandria comes in) and Genoa (with the junction of the the A7 motorway from Milan). The coastal motorway continues beyond Rapallo and La Spezia into Tuscany past the resorts of Versilia, and at Viareggio divides. The left branch (A11) continues via Lucca to Florence (and the *Autostrada del Sole*), while the coastal branch (A12) continues to Pisa and Livorno and links up with the Aurelia superstrada which runs south along the Tuscan coast via Grosseto.

From Switzerland (Lausanne). The approach to Italy is usually through the **Great St Bernard Tunnel** (or by the pass in summer) which only becomes motorway at Aosta (see above).

Another motorway route from Switzerland is via the **St Gotthard Tunnel** (opened in 1980) and Lugano. The motorway (A9) enters Italy at Como and continues to Milan where the *Autostrada del Sole* (A1) begins for central Italy.

From Germany and Austria (Innsbruck). The direct approach to Italy is by the motorway over the **Brenner Pass**. The motorway (A22) continues down the Isarco valley to Bolzano and the Adige valley via Trento to Verona. Here motorways diverge west for Brescia and Milan, or east for Vicenza and Venice, or continue south via Mantua to join the A1 motorway just west of Modena for Florence and central Italy.

Where to stay

Hotels

Hotels in Italy are classified by stars as in the rest of Europe. There are five official categories of hotel from the most expensive luxury 5-star hotels to the cheapest and simplest 1-star hotels. However, these categories are bound to disappoint many travellers: the categories are now defined by the services offered (i.e. television in each room, private telephone, 'frigo-bar', etc) and often do not reflect quality. 5-star and 4-star hotels in some localities are not always on a par with hotels with the same designation in the other places in Europe.

A small selection of hotels in Tuscany has been given at the beginning of each chapter of the guide. They have been listed with their official star rating (and keyed with numbers on the town plans) in order to give an indication of price. In making the selection for inclusion, smaller hotels have been favoured, and those in the centre of towns, or in particularly beautiful positions in the countryside.

Each local tourist board (APT, see above) issues a free list of hotels giving category, price, and facilities. Local tourist offices help you to find accommodation on the spot; it is however advisable to book well in advance, especially at Easter and in summer. To confirm the booking a deposit is usually required (this can normally be made by using a credit card): you have the right to claim the deposit back if you cancel the booking at least 72 hours in advance.

Hotels equipped to offer hospitality to the disabled are indicated in the APT hotel lists. There are now numerous agencies and hotel representatives in Britain and America who specialise in making hotel reservations (normally for 5-star and 4-star hotels only). **Accommodation services** from the UK are offered by *Accommodation Line Ltd* (☎ 0171-409 1343, fax 0171-409-2606); *The Italian Connection* (☎ 0171-486 6890, fax 0171-486-6891); and *Hotel Connect* (☎ 0181 381 2233, fax 0181 381 1155); *Room Service* (☎ 0171-636 6888).

Up-to-date information about hotels and restaurants can be found in numerous annual **specialised guides** to Italy. These include *Alberghi d'Italia*, a selection of 3-star hotels published by Gambero Rosso, *Alberghi e Ristoranti d'Italia* published by the Touring Club Italiano, and the red guide *Italia: Hotel-Ristoranti*, published by Michelin.

Every hotel has to declare its **prices** annually (and these are published in the local provincial APT hotel lists, and cannot be exceeded). The total charge for the room (excluding breakfast) should be exhibited on the back of the door of the hotel room, and in the foyer there should be a list of all the rooms in the hotel with their prices. Prices usually change according to the season, and can be considerably less in off peak periods. Hotels in the more famous towns of Tuscany such as Florence and Siena are bound to be a lot more expensive than hotels of the same category in the less well known localities.

In all hotels the service charges are included in the rates. You should beware of **extra charges** added to the bill. The drinks from the 'frigo-bar' in your room are extremely expensive (it is always best to buy drinks outside the hotel). Telephone calls are also more expensive if made from your room; there is usually a pay telephone (see p 39) in the lobby which is the most economical way of telephoning (and more convenient than using the public telephones in the streets). Hotels are now obliged by law (for tax purposes) to issue an official receipt to customers: you should not leave the premises without this document.

Breakfast (which can be disappointing and costly) is by law an optional extra charge, although a lot of hotels try to include it in the price of the room. When booking a room, always specify if you want breakfast or not. If you are staying in a 2-star or 3-star hotel in a town, it is usually well worthwhile going round the corner to the nearest pasticceria or bar for breakfast. However in the more expensive hotels there are now some good buffet breakfasts provided. But even here the standard of the 'canteen' coffee can be poor: you can always ask for an 'espresso' or 'cappuccino' instead. There is a large supplement if you order breakfast in your room.

Agriturismo and self-catering

This has recently been developed throughout Italy, and provides accommodation in farmhouses (*aziende agrituristiche)* in the countryside, although many of them are no longer on working farms. There are now some 1450 farmhouses in Tuscany which provide accommodation. Terms vary greatly from bed-and-breakfast, to self-contained flats. These are highly recommended for travellers with their own transport, and for families, as an excellent (and usually cheap) way of visiting Tuscany. Some farms require a stay of a minimum number of days. Cultural or recreational activities are sometimes also provided, such as horse-back riding. A 'star' system, similar to that used to classify hotels is being introduced in the Tuscan region, using ears of corn (from one to five depending on the facilities available).

Agriturist accommodation is now usually listed in the local APT hotel brochures; otherwise a list of them is supplied by the local APT offices. More information about such holidays from *Agriturist Toscana*, 3 Piazza San Firenze, Florence (☎ & fax 055-287838), who publish an annual guide. Other associations which provide information are: *Turismo Verde Toscana*, 5 Via Verdi, Florence (☎ 055-2344925), and *Terranostra*, 2 Via dei Magazzini, Florence (☎ 055-280539; web: www.terranostra.it/servizi.htm). Terranostra publish an annual list of Agriturism accommodation called *Vacanze e Natura*. The Regione Toscana have also published a brochure entitled *Agriturismo in Toscana*, available from their office of the Dipartimento dello Sviluppo Economico, 26 Via di Novoli, 50127 Firenze (☎ 167-403192; web: www.agriturismo.regione.toscana.it).

Accommodation in historic buildings

A new type of hotel has been introduced into Italy, called a **residence** or *residenza d'epoca*. They are normally in a building, or group of houses, of historic interest, often a castle or monastery. They may have only a few rooms, and sometimes offer self-catering accommodation. They are listed separately in the APT hotel lists, with their prices.

Rented accommodation

Renting accommodation for short periods in Italy has recently become easier and better organised. Villas, farmhouses, etc., can be rented for holidays through specialised agencies. Information from ENIT offices abroad, and APT offices in Italy. Specialised **agencies in the USA** include: *The Parker Company, Ltd.*, 319 The Lynnway, Lynn, MA 01901-1810 (☎ 1-800-280-2811).

Camping

Camping is now well organised throughout Italy. In Tuscany, campsites are listed in the local APT hotel lists, giving details of all services provided, size of the site, etc. In some sites caravans and campers are allowed. The sites are divided into official categories by stars, from the most expensive 4-star sites, to the simplest and cheapest 1-star sites. Their classification and rates charged must be displayed at the campsite office. Some sites have been indicated in the text, with their star ratings. It is advisable to book in advance.

Full details of the sites in Italy are published annually by the Touring Club Italiano (TCI) in *Campeggi e Villaggi Turistici in Italia*. The Federazione Italiana del Campeggio have an information office and booking service at No. 11 Via Vittorio Emanuele, Calenzano, 50041 Florence (☎ 055-882391, fax 055-8825918). There are also two websites for further information: *Easycamping* is at www.icaro.it/ and *Faita* is at www.camping.it/italy/

Hostels

Religious organisations sometimes run hostels or provide accommodation. Information from local APT offices.

Youth Hostels

The Italian Youth Hostels Association (*Associazione Italiana Alberghi per la Gioventù*), 44 Via Cavour, 00184 Rome (☎ 06-4871152, fax 06-4880492) publish a free guide to the 61 hostels all over the country. A membership card of the AIG or the International Youth Hostel Federation (web: www.iyhf.org/) is required for access to Italian Youth Hostels. Details from the Youth Hostels Association, Trevelyan House, 8 St Stephen's Hill, St Albans, Herts AL1 2DY, and the American Youth Hostel Inc, National Offices, PO Box 37613, Washington DC 20013-7613. The regional office in Tuscany is at the *Ostello Villa Camerata*, 2 Viale Augusto Righi, Florence (☎ 055-601451, fax 055-610300).

In Tuscany there are at present youth hostels open at: **Florence** (see above); **Marina di Massa**: *Apuano*, 89 Viale delle Pinete, Partaccia; **Abetone**: *Renzo Bizzarri*; **Lucca**: *Il Serchio*, Via del Brennero, Salicchi; **Tavarnelle Val di Pesa**: *Ostello del Chianti*, Via Cassia; and **Cortona**: *San Marco*, 57 Via Maffei.

Travelling around Tuscany

By rail

The Italian State Railways (FS—*Ferrovie dello Stato*) run various categories of trains:

'ES' (*Eurostar*). International express trains running between the main Italian and European cities. They have a special supplement, approximately 30 per cent of the normal single fare, and no standing passengers are permitted, although booking is no longer obligatory except on Friday & Sunday. First and second-class carriages.

'EC' and **'IC'** (***Eurocity*** and ***Intercity***). International and national express trains, with a supplement (but cheaper than the Eurostar supplement).

Espressi. Long-distance trains (both classes) not as fast as the Intercity trains.

Diretti. Although not stopping at every station, a good deal slower than Espressi.

Interregionali. Local trains stopping at most stations.

Regionali. Local trains stopping at all stations, mostly with second-class carriages only.

Buying tickets and booking a seat. Tickets (valid for two months after the day sold) must be bought before the journey, otherwise a fairly large penalty has to be paid to the ticket-collector on the train. **In order to validate your ticket it has to be stamped at an automatic machine in the railway station before starting the journey** (there is always a machine at the beginning of each platform and sometimes half way up it). If, for some reason, you fail to do this, try to find the ticket conductor on the train before he finds you. Once the ticket has been stamped it is valid for 6 hours for distances up to 200 km, and for 24 hours for distances over 200km.

The most convenient way of buying rail tickets (and making seat reservations) is from a travel agent (but this is only possible through those who are agents for the Italian State Railways), as there are often long queues at the station ticket offices. Some trains charge a special supplement (see above), and on some, seats must be booked in advance; when buying tickets you therefore have to specifiy which category of train you intend to take as well as the destination. Trains in Italy are usually crowded especially on holidays and in summer; and it is now always advisable to book your seat for long-distance journeys when buying a ticket for a Eurocity or Intercity train. There is a booking fee of Lire 5000 and the service is available from 2 months to 3 hours before departure. In the main stations the better known credit cards are now generally accepted. Use the special ticket window when buying a ticket with a credit card.

Fares and reductions. In Italy fares are still much lower than in Britain. Children under the age of 4 travel free, and between the ages of 4 and 12 travel half price. There are also some reductions for families. For travellers over the age of 60 (with Senior citizen Railcards; show your card when buying your ticket), the **Carta Res** (valid one year) offers a 30 per cent reduction on *international* rail fares. The **Inter-rail card** (valid 1 month) which can be purchased in Britain by young people up to the age of 26, is valid in Italy (and allows a reduction of 50 per cent on normal fares). The **Carta d'Argento** and the **Carta Verde** (which both cost Lire 40,000 and are valid one year) allow a reduction on rail fares for those over 60, and between the ages of 12 and 26.

A **Chilometrico** ticket is valid for 3000 km (and can be used by up to five people at the same time) for a maximum of 20 journeys. A **Eurodomino** ticket is valid for one month's travel in a number of European countries (for 3,5, or 10 days). There is no age limit for either of these tickets.

You can claim reimbursement (on payment of a small penalty) for unused tickets and sleepers not later than 24 hours before the departure of the train. **Bicycles** are allowed on most trains (except Eurostar trains): a day ticket costs Lire 5000 on slow trains, and Lire 10,000 on Intercity, Eurocity, and Espressi. A **Carta Blu** is available for the disabled, and certain trains have special facilites for them (information from the main railway stations in Italy).

Timetables. The timetable for the train services changes on about 26 September and 31 May every year. Excellent timetables are published twice a year by the Italian State Railways (*In Treno*; one volume for the whole of Italy) and by Pozzorario in several volumes (*Sud e Centro Italia* or *Nord e Centro Italia* cover Tuscany). These can be purchased at news-stands and railway stations.

Left luggage offices are usually open 24 hours at the main stations; at smaller stations they often close at night, and for a few hours in the middle of the day.

Porters are entitled to a fixed amount (shown on notice boards at all stations) for each piece of baggage, but trolleys are now usually available in the larger stations.

Restaurant cars (sometimes self-service) are attached to most international and internal long-distance trains. Also, on most fast trains, snacks, hot coffeee and drinks are sold thoughout the journey from a trolley wheeled down the train. At every large station snacks are on sale from trolleys on the platform and you can buy them from the train window.

Sleeping cars, with couchettes, or first and second class cabins, are carried on certain long-distance trains, as well as 'Sleeperette' compartments with reclining seats (first-class only).

Train services in Tuscany are generally good. All the towns which can be easily reached by train are indicated in the text below. The main line **from Milan to Rome** has stations at Prato, Florence, Arezzo, and Chiusi, as well as numerous smaller towns (slow trains only). The main line down the coast **from Genoa to Rome** has stations at Massa, Viareggio, Pisa, Livorno, and Grosseto, as well as the smaller towns (slow trains only). There is a line from Florence via Empoli to Pisa, and via Empoli to Siena, and a secondary line from Florence to Prato, Pistoia and Lucca.

There has been interest in recent years in preserving some of the historic and most scenic railway lines in Tuscany, including the line from Asciano to Monte Antico, which is sometimes open for special excursions in May and October (for information ☎ 055-2356194 or 0577-207413).

By bus

Local country buses abound between the main towns in Italy, and offer an excellent alternative to the railways. It is difficult to obtain accurate information about these local bus services outside Italy. Details have been given in the text.

The main bus companies operating in Tuscany are: *SITA*, 15 Via Santa Caterina da Siena, Florence (☎ 055-483651), and Sansepolcro (☎ 0575-742999); *Lazzi*, 4 Piazza Stazione, Florence (☎ 166-845010 or 055-351061); *CAP*, 9 Largo Alinari, Florence (☎ 055-214637); *LFI*, 37 Via Guido Monaco, Arezzo (☎ 0575-39881); *TRA-IN*, 33 Via Trento, Poggibonsi (☎ 0577-937207).

Town buses. Now that most towns have been partially closed to private traffic, town bus services (the details of which have been given in the text) are usually fast and efficient. You buy a ticket before boarding (at tobacconists, bars, newspaper kiosks, information offices, etc.) and stamp it on board at automatic machines.

Taxis

Taxis (yellow or white in colour) are provided with taximeters; make sure these are operational before hiring. They are hired from ranks or by telephone; there are no cruising taxis. A tip of about 1000 lire is expected. A supplement for night service, and for luggage is charged. There is a heavy surplus charge when the destination is outside the town limits (ask roughly how much the fare is likely to be). Women travelling alone in the evening are sometimes entitled to a reduced rate.

By car

Tuscany has an excellent network of roads, and drivers are strongly advised to avoid motorways and *superstrade* and use the secondary roads which are usually well engineered and provide fine views of the countryside. Buildings of historic interest are often indicated by yellow or brown signposts. White road signs sometimes indicate entry into a municipal area which is (confusingly) often a long way from the town of the same name. In the larger towns the traffic tends to be chaotic, the roads congested, and parking difficult. You are strongly recommended to park outside the centre and explore towns on foot. Hotels and restaurants are almost always signed clearly (yellow signs). Information offices are marked with a yellow 'i' symbol throughout Italy.

Temporary membership of the *Automobile Club d'Italia* ('*ACI*') can be taken out on the frontier or in Italy. They provide a **breakdown service** ('Soccorso ACI', ☎ 116).

Motorways (*autostrade*). Italy probably has the finest motorways in Europe, although in the last few decades too many have been constructed to the detriment of the countryside. Tolls are charged according to the rating of the vehicle and the distance covered. There are service areas on all autostrade (open 24 hours), and, generally speaking, the FINI cafés and restaurants are usually the best. Most autostrade have SOS points every two kilometres. Contrary to French roads, motorways in Italy are indicated by green signs (and normal roads by blue signs). At the entrance to motorways, the two directions are indicated by the name of the most important town (and not by the nearest town) which can be momentarily confusing. The *Autostrada del Sole* (AI) which runs through Tuscany is less wide than some of the more recent motorways and carries very heavy traffic (including numerous lorries), especially between Bologna and Florence. Driving on this road is easier on Sundays when lorries are banned.

Superstrade are dual carriageway fast roads which do not charge tolls. They do not usually have service stations, 'SOS' points, or emergency lanes. They are also usually indicated by green signs. In Tuscany the superstrada between Florence and Siena is particularly busy at 8.00, 18.00 and on Sunday late afternoon and evening, and it is a poorly engineered road, and rather narrow.

Petrol stations are open 24 hours on motorways, but otherwise their opening times are: 07.00–12.00, 15.00–20.00; winter 07.30–12.30, 14.30–19.00. There are now quite a number of self-service petrol stations open 24hrs operated by bank notes (Lire 10,000, 50,000) or credit cards. Unleaded petrol is now available all over Italy. Petrol in Italy costs more than in England, and a lot more than in America.

Car parking. Almost every town in Tuscany (as in the rest of Italy) has taken the wise step of closing its historic centre to traffic (except for residents). This makes them much more pleasant to visit on foot. Access is allowed to hotels and for the disabled. On approaching a town, the white signs for '*centro*' (with a bull's eye) should be followed towards the historic centre. Car-parks are also sometimes indicated by blue 'P' signs; where parking is a particular problem, the best places to park near the centre have been mentioned in the main text. Some car parks are free, while others charge an hourly tariff. In some towns mini-bus services connect car parks with the centre. With a bit of effort it is almost always possible to find a place to leave your car free of charge, away from the town centre. It is forbidden to park in front of a gate or doorway marked with a *passo carrabile* (blue and red) sign. Always lock your car when parked, and never leave anything of value inside it.

Car hire is available in the main towns and at Pisa and Florence airports. Arrangements for the hire of cars in Italy can also be made through Citalia, Alitalia or British Airways (at specially advantageous rates in conjunction with their flights).

Rules of the road. Italian law requires that you carry a valid driving licence when travelling. It is obligatory to keep a red triangle in the car in case of accident or breakdown. This serves as a warning to other traffic when placed on the road at a distance of 50 metres from the stationary car. It is now compulsory to wear seat-belts in the front seat of cars in Italy. Driving in Italy is generally faster (and often more aggressive) than driving in Britain or America. Road signs are now more or less standardised to the international codes, but certain habits differ radically from those in Britain or America. Unless otherwise indicated, cars entering a road from the right are given precedence (also at roundabouts). If a driver flashes his headlights, it means he is proceeding and *not* giving you precedence. In towns, Italian drivers are very lax about changing lanes without much warning. Some crossroads in small towns have unexpected 'stop' signs. Italian drivers tend to ignore pedestrian crossings. In towns, beware of motorbikes, mopeds and Vespas, the drivers of which seem to consider that they always have the right of way.

The police (see p 38) sometimes set up road blocks on country roads to check cars and their drivers: it is important to stop at once if you are waved down by a policeman at the side of a road and you must immediately show them your driving licence and the car documents.

Maps

Although detailed town plans have been included in this book, it has not been possible, because of the format, to provide an atlas of Tuscany adequate for those travelling by car. The maps at the end of the book are only intended to be used when planning an itinerary. The Italian Touring Club publishes several sets of excellent maps: these are constantly updated and are indispensable to anyone travelling by car in Italy. They include the *Grande Carta Stradale d'Italia* on a scale of 1:200,000. This is divided into 15 sheets covering the regions of Italy: Tuscany is covered on the sheet (No. D39) entitled *Toscana*. These are also published in a handier form as an atlas (with a comprehensive index) called the *Atlante Stradale d'Italia* in three volumes (the one entitled '*Centro*' covers Tuscany). These maps can be purchased from the Italian Touring Club offices and at many booksellers; in London they are obtainable from Stanfords, 12–14 Long Acre, WC2E 9LP (☎ 0171-836 1321).

The *Istituto Geografico Militare* of Italy has for long been famous for its map production (much of it done by aerial photography). Their headquarters are in Florence (10 Via Cesare Battisti). Their maps are now available at numerous bookshops in the main Italian towns. They publish a map of Italy on a scale of 1:100,000 in 277 sheets, and a field survey partly 1:50,000, partly 1:25,000, which are invaluable for the detailed exploration of the country, especially its more mountainous regions; the coverage is however, still far from complete at the larger scales, and some of the maps are out-of-date.

Food and drink

Tuscan Food is traditionally excellent, but now good genuine cuisine is becoming less and less easy to find.

First courses

A classic first course is *minestrone*, a thick vegetable soup. In winter this is made in a richer version, called *ribollita* or *zuppa di pane*, with white beans, black cabbage, and bread. Another vegetable soup, often found in the Maremma (and the Casentino), is *acquacotta*, made with onions, basil, celery, and greens (first lightly fried) with the addition of tomatoes, toasted bread, pecorino cheese, and eggs. A summer salad (*panzanella*) has dry bread, tomatoes, fresh onions, cucumber, basil, and capers (sometimes with the addition of finely chopped green *radicchio*). *Pappa al pomodoro* is also made in summer, a thick tomato soup with bread, seasoned with basil, etc. *Crostini* are a typical hors-d'oeuvre: fresh chicken-liver paste and other 'homemade' paté of mushrooms, aubergine, etc. spread on bread and often served with cold cuts of ham and salami (*affettati*). *Prosciutto e melone* (raw Parma ham with melon) is particularly good as a first course in summer. *Bresaola* is cured beef often served with *rughetta* (rocket).

In the autumn (usually in October) *fettunta* or *bruschetta* is served: toasted bread with garlic and oil straight from the olive press; if it is topped with hot black cabbage it is called *cavolo con le fette*. Regional first course dishes include *tortelli di patate* (or *topini*), made with potatoes (found especially in the Casentino and Mugello), *pici* or *pinci*, handmade spaghetti (found in Siena), *tortelli marem-*

mani, fresh pasta filled with ricotta and spinach, *pappardelle alla lepre*, short pasta with a rich hare sauce. Black and white truffles (*tartufi*) are an expensive delicacy, often served with pasta in southern Tuscany.

Second courses

Second course meat dishes are often stewed slowly in a tomato sauce, called *in umido*. The famous *bistecca alla fiorentina*, a T-bone steak cooked over charcoal can still be found in some restaurants which offer it as their speciality. In the Maremma, wild boar (*cinghiale*) is often served, sometimes with polenta. *Scottiglia* is a traditional dish of various meats (chicken, lamb, etc.) chopped up and cooked in oil, sage, hot pepper, and tomato, served on toast. *Rosticciana* is grilled spare ribs. Traditional Florentine dishes include *fagioli all'uccelletto*, haricot beans in a tomato sauce, and *trippa alla fiorentina*, tripe in a tomato sauce with parmesan cheese. Fresh mushrooms, especially *porcini*, are served all over Tuscany in the autumn. Another good seasonal dish, often served in early spring, is *tortino di carciofi*, baked artichoke pie.

Fish dishes, for which Livorno is particularly famous, include *baccalà alla Livornese*, salt cod cooked in tomatoes, black olives, and pepper, and *cacciucco alla Livornese*, a stew of fish in a hot sauce. In Versilia *seppie in zimino* are often served, cuttlefish cooked with spinach.

Sweets

Tuscany is not famous for its sweets, although two excellent puddings produced in the autumn are *castagnaccio*, a chestnut cake with pine nuts and sultanas, and *schiacciata all'uva*, a bready dough baked in the oven, filled and topped with black grapes and sugar and seasoned with fennel. *Torta della Nonna* is a custard tart with pine nuts. *Frittelle di San Giuseppe* are fritters made with rice, eggs, milk, and lemon rind; *cenci* are simpler fritters. In Livorno *torta* is sold, a delicious thin pizza-like bread cooked with chick-peas. This is also found in Volterra, where it is called *cecina*. *Biscotti di Prato* (or *cantuccini*) are hard biscuits with almonds which are dipped in *vin santo* or *morellino* (a sweet red wine).

Tuscan wines

The best known Italian wine, *Chianti*, is produced in Tuscany. The name is protected by law and only those wines from a relatively small district which lies between Florence and Siena are entitled to the name Chianti Classico (for a fuller description, see page 130). Chianti Classico Gallo Nero (distinguished by a black cock on the bottle) is usually considered the best, but Chianti Putto and Chianti Grappolo are also very good. Other Chianti wines from different parts of Tuscany are: Chianti Montalbano, Chianti Rufina, Chianti Colli Fiorentini, Chianti Colli Senesi, Chianti Colli Aretini, and Chianti Colline Pisane.

In Tuscany the red table wine is usually of better quality than the white. Excellent red wines (not cheap) are *Brunello di Montalcino* and *Vino Nobile di Montepulciano*. Good red wine is also produced at Carmignano near Florence, and around Lucca. The most famous white wine of Tuscany is the *Vernaccia di San Gimignano*, but other good white wines are produced around Pitigliano, Montecarlo, and in the Val d'Arbia. White and rosé wines are also found in the region of Bolgheri. Elba used to produce excellent wines (now hard to find), including *Aleatico*, a dessert wine. *Vin Santo* is another dessert wine (see p 130).

More and more farms which produce wine are opening their cellars to the public, and allowing **wine tasting**. Some of the best known are mentioned below. Further information about those in the Chianti region is available from Consorzio Vino Chianti, 4 Lungarno Corsini, Florence (☎ 055-210168), Consorzio Chianti Classico, 155 Via Scopeti, Sant'Andrea in Percussina (☎ 055-8228245), and L'Associazione Nazionale Città del Vino, 34 Via Massetana Romana, Siena (☎ 0577-271556, fax 0577-271595, with an office at Suvereto, ☎ 0565-829923). There is a **wine museum** open in summer at Rufina, and *enoteche* open in the fortresses of Siena and Montalcino.

Eating out

Restaurants in Italy are called *ristoranti* or *trattorie*; there is now usually no difference between the two, although a *trattoria* used to be less smart (and usually cheaper) than a *ristorante*. Italian food is usually good and not too expensive. The least pretentious restaurant almost invariably provides the best value. Almost every locality has a simple (often family run) restaurant which caters for the local residents; the decor is usually very simple and the food excellent value. This type of restaurant does not always offer a menu and the choice is usually limited to three or four first courses, and three or four second courses, with only fruit as a sweet. The more sophisticated restaurants are more attractive and comfortable and often larger and you can sometimes eat at tables outside. They display a menu outside, and are also usually considerably more expensive. In all restaurants it is acceptable to order a first course only, or skip the first course and have only a second course. Note that fish is always the most expensive item on the menu in any restaurant.

Meal times. Lunch is normally around 13.00 or 13.30, while dinner is around 20.00 or 21.00. Some restaurants still have a **cover charge** (*coperto*, shown separately on the menu) which is added to the bill (although this has officially been discontinued). Prices include service, unless otherwise stated on the menu. **Tipping** is therefore not strictly necessary, but a few thousand lire can be left on the table to convey appreciation. Restaurants are now obliged by law (for tax purposes) to issue an official receipt to customers; you should not leave the premises without this document (ricevuta fiscale).

Restaurant prices

In each chapter a small selection of restaurants open in Tuscany in 1999 has been given, which is by no means exhaustive. The restaurants have been divided into three categories (£££, ££ and £) to reflect price ranges in 1999.

£££: Luxury-class restaurants where the prices are likely to be over Lire 60,000 a head (and sometimes well over Lire 100,000 a head). These are the most famous restaurants in Tuscany and they usually offer international cuisine.

££: First class restaurants where the prices are around Lire 50,000. These are generally comfortable, with good service, but are not cheap.

£: Simple trattorie and pizzerie where you can eat for around Lire 25,000–40,000 a head, or less. Although simple and by no means 'smart', the food in this category, which often includes local specialities, is usually the best value.

Restaurant guides

Some of the best annual guides to eating in Italy (but only in Italian) are published by Gambero Rosso (*Ristoranti d'Italia*) and Slow Food Arcigola (*Osterie d'Italia*, a guide to cheaper eating). Specialised annual guides to restaurants (mostly in the £££ and ££ categories as described above) include the red Michelin guide (*Italia: hotel-ristoranti); I Ristoranti di Veronelli*, and *Alberghi e Ristoranti* (Touring Club Italiano).

Pizzerie and self-service restaurants

Pizze (a popular and cheap food throughout Italy) and other excellent snacks are served in a *Pizzeria, Rosticceria* and *Tavola Calda*. Some of these have no seating accommodation and sell food to take away or eat on the spot.

For **picnics**, sandwiches (*panini*) are made up on request (with ham, salami, cheese, anchovies, tuna fish, etc.) at *Pizzicherie* and *Alimentari* (grocery shops). *Fornai* (bakeries) often sell delicious individual pizzas, bread with oil and salt (*focaccia* or *schiacciata*), and puff pastry topped or filled with cheese, spinach, tomato, salted anchovies, ham, etc; they also usually sell good sweet buns, rolls, and cakes. Some of the most pleasant places to picnic in towns have been indicated in the guide below.

Bars and cafés (*caffè or pasticcerie*)

These are comforable and pleasant places to have a good snack. A selection of these (in towns) is listed below. They are open all day, and most Italians eat the excellent refreshments they serve standing up. You pay the cashier first, and show the receipt to the barman in order to get served. In almost all bars, if you sit at a table you are charged considerably more (at least double) and are given waiter service (and you should not pay first). However, some simple bars have a few tables which can be used at no extra charge (it is always best to ask before sitting down). Black coffee (*caffè or espresso*) can be ordered diluted (*alto, lungo or americano*) or with a dash of milk (*macchiato*), with hot milk (*cappuccino or caffè-latte*) or with a liquor (*corretto*). In summer, cold coffee (*caffè freddo*) or cold coffee and milk (*caffè-latte freddo*) are served. A wide selection of soft drinks, wines, and spirits are also available. A *pasticceria* (usually also a caffè) always sells the best cakes since they are made on the premises. Ice-creams are always best in a *gelateria* where they are made on the spot: bars usually sell packaged ice-cream only.

Additional information

Money and banks

The monetary unit is the Italian lira (plural; lire). There are coins of 50, 100, 200, 500 and 1000 lire, and notes of 1000, 2000, 5000, 10,000, 50,000, 100,000, and 500.000 lire. there are currently three sizes of 50 and 100 lire coins. Travellers' cheques and Eurocheques are the safest way of carrying money while travelling, and most credit cards are now generally accepted in shops, hotels, and restaurants (and at some petrol stations). In the centre of the main towns there are cashpoints called Bancomat, and also automatic machines which change foreign bank notes.

Banks are usually open Monday–Friday 08.30–13.30, 14.30–15.30 (or 14.45–15.45). They are closed on Saturday and holidays, and **close early** (about 11.00) **on days preceding national holidays**. The commission on cashing travellers' cheques can be quite high. Money can be changed at exchange offices (cambio), in travel agencies, some post offices, and main stations. Exchange offices are usually open seven days a week at airports and some main railway stations. At some hotels, restaurants, and shops money can be exchanged (but usually at a lower rate).

Medical services
British citizens, as members of the EU, have the right to claim health services in Italy if they have the E111 form (issued by the Department of Health and Social Security). There are also a number of private holiday health insurance policies. First Aid services (**Pronto Soccorso**) are available at all hospitals, railway stations, and airports. **Chemist shops** (*farmacie*) are usually open Monday–Friday 09.00–13.00, 16.00–19.30 or 20.00. On Saturdays and Sundays (and holidays) a few are open (listed on the door of every chemist). In all towns there is also at least one chemist shop open at night (also shown on the door of every chemist). **For emergencies, dial 113**.

Crime and personal security
Help and advice is given to British and American travellers in Tuscany who are in difficulty by the British and American consulates in Florence (lost or stolen passports are now replaced by the relevant embassy in Rome). **British Consulate**, 2 Lungarno Corsini, Florence (☎ 055-284133); **US Consulate**, 38 Lungarno Vespucci, Florence (☎ 055-2398276).

Pick-pocketing is a widespread problem in towns all over Italy: it is always advisable not to carry valuables in handbags, and be particularly careful on public transport. Cash and documents, etc. can be left in hotel safes. It is a good idea to make photocopies of all important doucments in case of loss. Your are strongly advised to carry some means of identity with you at all times while in Italy, since you can be held at a police station if you are stopped and found to be without a document of identity.

There are three categories of **policemen** in Italy: *Vigili Urbani*, the municipal police (who wear blue uniform in winter and white during the summer and hats similar to London policemen); *carabinieri*, the military police who have local offices in every town and small village (and who wear black uniform with a red stripe down the side of their trousers); and the *Polizia di Stato*, State police (who wear dark blue jackets and light blue trousers).

Crime should be reported at once. A detailed statement has to be given in order to get an official document confirming loss or damage (essential for insurance claims). Interpreters are usually provided. For **all emergencies, dial 113**.

Local tourist offices
Tuscany is divided into sectors, each with a local tourist information office, the *Azienda di Promozione Turistica (APT)* which provides invaluable help to travellers on arrival: they supply a free list of accommodation (revised annually), including hotels, agriturist accommodation, youth hostels, and camping sites; up-to-date information on museum opening times and annual events; and infor-

mation about local transport. They also usually distribute, free of charge, illustrated pamphlets about each town, sometimes with a good plan, etc.

The headquarters are normally open Monday–Saturday 08.00–14.00, but in the towns of particular interest there is sometimes a separate APT information office (IAT), which is also often open in the afternoon.

APT offices in Tuscany:
APT Versilia, 22 Piazza Mazzini, Viareggio (☎ 0584-48881).
APT Arcipelago Toscano, 26 Calata Italia, Portoferraio, Elba (☎ 0565-914671).
APT Montecatini Terme-Valdinievole, 66 Viale Verdi, Montecatini Terme (☎ 0572-772244).
APT Chianciano Terme-Valdichiana, 7 Via Sabatini, Chianciano Terme (☎ 0578-63538).
APT Firenze, 16 Via Manzoni, Florence (☎ 055-23320).
APT Grosseto, 206 Via Monterosa, Grosseto (☎ 0564-454510).
APT Livorno, 6 Piazza Cavour, Livorno (☎ 0586-898111).
APT Massa Carrara, 24 Lungomare Vespucci, Marina di Massa (☎ 0585-240046).
APT Pisa, 26 Via Benedetto Croce, Pisa (☎ 050-40096).
APT Siena, 43 Via di Città, Siena (☎ 0577-42209).
APT Arezzo, 116 Piazza Risorgimento, Arezzo (☎ 0575-23952).
APT Abetone-Pistoia-Montagna Pistoiese, 28 Via Marconi, San Marcello Pistoiese (☎ 0573-630145).
APT Lucca, 2 Piazza Guidiccioni, Lucca (☎ 0583-491205).
APT Prato, 51 Via Muzzi, Prato (☎ 0574-35141).
APT Amiata, 25 Via Adua, Abbadia San Salvatore (☎ 0577-775811).

Telephones and postal services
There are numerous public telephones all over Italy in kiosks, bars, restaurants etc. These are operated by coins or telephone cards which can be purchased from tobacconists ('*tabacchi*', displaying a blue 'T' sign), bars, news-stands, and post offices. Telephone numbers in Italy can have from four to eight numbers. All numbers have an area code, which (since 1998) has to be used always (even for local calls). Placing a local call costs Lire 200. Directory assistance (in Italian) is available by dialling 12. Numbers that begin with 167, called *numeri verdi*, are tollfree, but require a deposit of at least 200 lire. Most cities in the world can now by dialled direct from Italy (and international telephone cards are available).

> To make an international call to Italy, dial 39 and then the full area code (ie. 055 for Florence) followed by the number.
> To make an international call from Italy dial 0044 then the area code and number.

Stamps are sold at *tabacchi* (displaying a blue 'T' sign) as well as post offices. Post offices are open Mon–Sat 08.10–13.25, and central offices in main towns are now often open 7 days a week 08.10–19.25.

Opening hours

Government offices usually work from 08.00–13.30 or 14.00 six days a week. Shops (clothes, hardware, hairdressers, etc.) are generally open from 09.00–13.00, 16.00–19.30, including Saturday, and for most of the year are closed on Monday morning. Food shops usually open from 08.00–13.00, 17.00–19.30 or 20.00, and for most of the year are closed on Wednesday afternoon. From mid-June to mid-September all shops are closed instead on Saturday afternoon.

Public holidays

The Italian national holidays when offices, shops and schools are closed are as follows: 1 January, 25 April (Liberation Day), Easter Monday, 1 May (Labour Day), 15 August (Assumption), 1 November (All Saints' Day), 8 December (Immaculate Conception), Christmas Day and 26 December (St Stephen). Each town keeps its patron Saint's day as a holiday.

Golf courses in Tuscany

18-hole courses include: *Ugolino*, 3 Via Chiantigiana, 50015 Grassina (Firenze), ☎ 055-2301009; *Punta Ala*, 1 Via del Golf, 58040 Punta Ala (Grosseto), ☎ 0564 922121); *Le Pavoniere*, Via della Fattoria 6, Località Tavola, 50047 Prato; *Versilia*, 40 Via della Sipe, 55045 Pietrasanta (Lucca), ☎ 0584-881574; *Montecatini*, Via dei Brogi, Località Pievaccia, 51015 Monsummano Terme (Pistoia, ☎ 0572-62218).

Public toilets

There is a notable shortage of public toilets in Italy. All bars (*caffès*) should have toilets available to the public (generally speaking the larger the bar, the better the facilities). Nearly all museums now have toilets. There are also toilets in railway stations and and bus stations.

 # Museums and monuments

The **opening times** of museums and monuments are given but they sometimes vary and often change without warning; when possible it is always advisable to consult the local tourist office (APT) on arrival about the up-to-date times. The opening times of state-owned museums and monuments are in the process of change: many museums and archaeological sites in Tuscany are now open seven days a week (although if they have a closing day it is still usually Monday). However, there is no standard timetable and you should take great care to allow enough time for variations in the hours shown when planning a visit to a museum or monument. Some museums in the larger cities now usually stay open on the main public holidays. In Florence, the Uffizi, Pitti and Galleria dell'Accademia are open in the evenings in summer (when they are usually less crowded).

Admission charges vary, but are usually between Lire 4000 and Lire 13,000. British citizens under the age of 18 and over the age of 60 are entitled to **free admission** to state-owned museums and monuments in Italy (because of reciprocal arrangements in Britain). During **Museum Week** (the *Settimana per i Beni Culturali e Ambientali*) there is free entrance for everyone to all state-owned museums and others are specially opened. Traditionally held early in December, for the last few years it has been held instead in March. In Florence, there is now a **booking service** (*Firenze Musei*, ☎ 055-294883, fax 055-264406) for visiting the state-owned museums, particularly useful for the Uffizi and Galleria dell'Accademia which can have extremely long queues.

Churches

Although they usually open very early in the morning (at 07.00 or 08.00), churches are normally closed for a considerable period during the middle of the day. Almost all churches close at 12.00 and do not reopen until 15.00, 16.00, or even 17.00 hours. Cathedrals and some of the larger churches (indicated in the text) may be open without a break during daylight hours. Smaller churches and oratories are often open only in the early morning, but it is sometimes possible to find the key by asking locally. The sacristan will also show closed chapels, crypts, etc., and sometimes expects a tip. Some churches now ask that sightseers do not enter during a service. Normally visitors who are not in a tour group may do so, provided they are silent and do not approach the altar in use. An entrance fee is becoming customary for admission to treasuries, cloisters, bell-towers, etc. **Lights** (operated by lire coins) have now been installed in many churches to illuminate frescoes and altarpieces, but a torch and binoculars are always useful. Sometimes you are not allowed to enter important churches or religious sanctuaries wearing shorts or with bare shoulders.

The British Institute of Florence

The British Institute of Florence is a non-profit making independent Institution, which was founded in 1917 by a group of Anglo-Florentines including Arthur Acton, Edward Hutton, G.M. Trevelyan, Lina Waterfield, and Gaetano Salvemini, and received a Royal Charter in 1923. Its scope is to promote British culture in Italy and Italian culture to English-speaking visitors and to maintain a library of English books in Florence.

The Institute runs a **language school and courses in art history** in Florence at No. 2 Piazza Strozzi (☎ 055-284033), and summer courses at Massa Marittima. Its excellent **lending library** (c 50,000 volumes, the largest collection of English books in Italy) is in Palazzo Lanfredini, 9 Lungarno Guicciardini (☎ 055-284032). Since 1989 it has been named after its benefactor Harold Acton, who died in Florence in 1993. It can be used for a small fee, and retains the atmosphere of a 19C general browsing library. The reading room has English newspapers and periodicals. Interesting public lectures are also held here.

 ## Annual festivals and local fairs

There are a number of traditional festivals in Tuscan towns which are of the greatest interest. At these times, the towns become extremely lively, and, apart from the central race or competition, numerous celebrations take place on the side, and local markets are usually held at the same time. The most important local festivals have been described in detail in the text, but a summary is given below, in case you are able to choose a period in which to visit Tuscany when some of them are taking place. They are particularly exciting events for children. Information from local APT offices.

Spring. Carnival celebrations at Viareggio, Cerreto Guidi, Borgo San Lorenzo, and Bibbiena. **Easter**: *Scoppio del Carro* (when a carriage 'explodes' with fireworks outside the duomo) on Easter Day in Florence, Good Friday passion play at Grassina. **Ascension Day**: *Festa del Grillo* (a fair where crickets are sold) in Florence. **Other festivals** include: *Palio* (horse race) at Fucecchio; *Balestro del Girifalco* (falcon crossbow contest) at Massa Marittima; *Maggiolata* (May fair) at Castiglione d'Orcia; *Palio dei Somari* (donkey race) at Torrita di Siena.

Summer. The *Palio* (horse race) at Siena, the most splendid and exciting of all annual festivals in Italy (see Ch. 26). *Calcio in Costume* ('football' game in 16C costume) in Florence; *Palio del Cerro* (athletic contests in 16C costume) at Cerreto Guidi; *Corpus Domini* procession in Prato; *Giostra del Saracino* (a tournament) in Arezzo; *Balestro del Girifalco* (falcon crossbow contest) at Massa Marittima. Marine festivities, with procession of boats at Porto Santo Stefano, Porto Ercole, Orbetello, Isola del Giglio, and Castiglione della Pescaia. Rodeo at Alberese; *Palio* (horse race) at Piancastagnaio; *Fiera di Sant'Antonino* and *Palio Marinaro* (rowing contest) in Livorno; *Palio degli Arcieri* (archery contest) in Piombino; *Disfida fra gli arcieri di Terra e Corte* (archery contest) at Fivizzano; *Festa di San Ranieri* (regatta) and *Gioco del Ponte* (a sham fight on the Ponte di Mezzo) at Pisa; *Giostra dell'Orso* (a tournament) at Pistoia; *Bravio delle Botti* (a barrel rolling contest) at Montepulciano.

Autumn. *Festa della Rificolona* (a fair when paper lanterns are carried through the streets) in Florence; *Festa dell'uva* (wine festival) and *Fiera di San Luca* (cattle fair) in Impruneta; *Sagra dei Marroni* (chestnut festival) at Marradi; Display of the *Sacro Cingolo* (Holy Girdle) in Prato; *Palio della Balestra* (crossbow contest) in Sansepolcro; *Palio* (race) at Castel del Piano; *Astiludio* (flag throwing contest) at Volterra; *Sagra del Tordo* (gastronomic 'thrush' festival) at Montalcino.

Street markets take place once a week in country towns, and local fairs are held in Florence (*Festa dell'Annunziata*), Vicchio (*Fiera Calda*), Piancastagnaio, Sansepolcro, Monte San Savino, Carmignano, and Filetto (Villafranca Lunigiana). **Specialist fairs** include the antiques fair (*Fiera Antiquariato*) at Arezzo, the first Saturday and Sunday of the month, and the cattle market at Alberese in spring. Wine fairs are held all over Chianti in autumn.

Summer music and theatre festivals in Tuscany include: *Maggio Musicale* in Florence; *Estate Fiesolana* in Fiesole; *Festival di Pentecoste* at Badia a Passignano; *Festival del Teatro* at Sorano; Puccini opera festival at Torre del Lago; *Settimana musicale senese* at the Accademia Musicale Chigiana, Siena; Music festival at Montepulciano; Theatre festival (*Teatro Povero di Monticchiello*) at Monticchiello; chamber music festival at La Foce (*Incontri in Terra di Siena*); Music and Theatre festival at Radicondoli; Buskers' festival (*On the Road*) at Pelago. Concerts are usually held at Sant'Antimo, Cennina, and Montalcino.

 ## Tuscan gardens

Gardens are a special feature of Tuscany, and it is becoming possible to visit an increasing number of private gardens, usually by previous appointment. Those described (with their opening times) are included in the following list.

In and around Florence: Giardino di Boboli (where an entrance fee is now charged), Villa di Castello, Villa della Petraia, the botanical gardens (Giardino dei Semplici), and the Giardino dell'Orticoltura. In May and June the Giardino dell'Iris and the Giardino delle Rose are open. The Villa Medici in Fiesole and Villa della Gamberaia in Settignano charge an entrance fee. The private gardens of Villa I Tatti, Villa La Pietra, Villa Le Balze, Villa Capponi, and Villa I Collazzi can sometimes be seen by previous appointment. In the environs of Florence gardens surround the Villa di Poggio a Caiano and Villa Corsi Salviati (Sesto Fiorentino).

In the Mugello, the private garden of the Castello del Trebbio is only sometimes open by previous appointment. One of the most famous gardens in Tuscany is that of the Villa Garzoni at **Collodi**. **In Lucca** the Botanical Gardens are open regularly, and in the environs there are well-known private gardens open at the Villa Reale di Marlia, Villa Mansi, and Villa Torrigiani. A camelia festival is held in March at **Pieve di Compito**, when more villa gardens are open, and there is a flower show and market. **In the Apuan Alps**, there is an alpine garden at Pania di Corfina. The Botanical Gardens at **Pisa** are one of the most important in Tuscany, and **between Pisa and Florence** there are gardens at the Villa Medici of Cerreto Guidi, and private gardens which can sometimes be visited at Bibbiani and the Villa di Belvedere at Crespina. **Siena** has a Botanical Garden, and in the environs there are private gardens at Villa di Vicobello, Celsa, and Cetinale (open by previous appointment). The Horti Leonini at San Quirico d'Orcia are open as public gardens, and at **Pienza** the hanging garden of Palazzo Piccolomini may be visited. Also in the **Val d'Orcia** the beautiful garden of La Foce is now open to the public one day a week.

Lesser known gardens include Villa La Fratta (near Torrita di Siena), La Peschiera at Santa Fiora, the Villa Rinuccini di Torre a Cona near San Donato in Collina and Villa Chigi on the outskirts of Castelnuovo Berardenga. Penelope Hobhouse has published a guide to the *Gardens of Italy* (1998).

The Tuscan coast

Much of the coast of Tuscany has been intensely developed for tourism and the beaches can be overcrowded particularly in Versilia, where Viareggio is the most popular seaside resort on the west coast of Italy. Forte dei Marmi and I Ronchi nearby are elegant resorts with beaches crowded with Florentines and Milanese in July and August. Here there is limited free access to the beaches since at the *stabilimenti* or *bagni attrezzati* you are charged for the hire of cabins and deck chairs and there is usually a refreshment kiosk. There is free access only to the *spiaggie liberi* which are often crowded and less easily accessible. However everyone is allowed to within five metres of the edge of the sea at all beaches.

The Parco Naturale Migliarino-San Rossore-Massaciuccoli between Viareggio and Livorno is a protected area of coastline (limited access). The mouth of the Serchio at Marina di Vecchiano is well preserved. There are beaches south of Livorno at Il Romito and Quercianella, at the resort of Castiglioncello, and between Cecina and Piombino (particularly attractive at Baratti and around Populonia). Cala Martina and Cala Violina are beautiful bays near Portiglione south of Follonica. The wooded headland of Punta Ala has some exclusive resorts, and the sand is particularly golden at Castiglione della Pescaia. The best preserved stretch of coastline in Tuscany (and one of the best in Italy) is near

Grosseto at the foot of the Monti dell'Uccellina (protected as the Parco Naturale della Maremma), accessible from Marina di Alberese.

Further south, the promontory of Monte Argentario has fine stretches of coast and elegant resorts (with good free beaches on the Tombolo di Feniglia). The beach near Talamone is also attractive and south of Ansedonia there is a very extensive sandy beach. The islands which form the Tuscan archipelago are now mostly protected as a national park: Elba is the most famous, with an attractive coastline crowded with holidaymakers particularly from Florence in summer (and from Germany in September), Capraia has a rocky shore (frequented by skin-divers), and Giglio also has pleasant beaches.

Walking

Hiking and walking has become more popular throughout Italy in recent years and more information is now available locally. Details have been given in the relevant chapters. Specialist guides to walking in Tuscany are now published with detailed maps (including *Walking and Eating in Tuscany and Umbria*, by James Lasdun and Pia Davis, 1997). The areas of Tuscany particularly suitable for walking are the **Garfagnana**, the **Mugello**, the **Casentino** (Monte Falterona, and the Foreste Casentinesi), and **Monte Amiata**.

The Tuscan Region and the WWF publish a guide to walking in Tuscany called *Cammina Toscana* (Arcadia). Another guide, in 2 volumes, is *A Piedi in Toscana* (ed. Iter; only available in Italian). Walking tours of Tuscany are organised by Alternative Travel Group Ltd, 69–71 Banbury Road, Oxford (☎ 01865 310399).

Protected areas of particular natural beauty

In Tuscany these include two national parks: the *Parco Nazionale di Monte Falterona, Campigna e Foreste Casentinesi*, created in 1991 and the *Parco Nazionale dell'Arcipelago Toscano*, created in 1996. There are also three regional parks (the *Parco Naturale delle Alpi Apuane* incorporating the *Parco dell'Orecchiella* reserve, the *Parco Naturale di Migliarino-San Rossore-Massaciuccoli*, and the *Parco Naturale della Maremma*). **World Wide Fund for Nature (WWF) oases** (for information, ☎ 055-477876) include Bolgheri (in the Maremma marshes near the coast), Lago di Burano, Orbetello and the Orti di Bottagone, the wooded area of Bosco di Rocconi (province of Grosseto), and further north (province of Lucca), the Oasi del Bottaccio. *Legambiente* (a society for the protection of the environment) opened its first reserve in 1998 at Bosco Tanali in the Padule di Bientina (province of Pisa). For information, ☎ 055-6585501.

A guide to the protected areas in Tuscany *Parchi, Riserve e aree protette della Toscana* was published by the WWF in 1998. Local offices of the Club Alpino Italiano (CAI), the Comunità Montana, the WWF, and the APT all provide information.

THE GUIDE

1 · Florence

Florence, in Italian *Firenze*, is one of the most famous cities in Italy. As the birthplace of the Renaissance it preserves some of the greatest works of art and most beautiful buildings in the world. From the fifteenth century onwards it became a centre of learning in the arts and sciences unparalleled since classical times. It is now a small city (380,000 inhabitants), the regional capital of Tuscany, with nearly all its beautiful buildings concentrated within a relatively small area beside the museums of the Uffizi, Pitti, and Bargello which contain the masterpieces of Florentine art. The delightful low hills which surround the city have been preserved from new buildings. The best time to visit Florence is in the winter: it can be unpleasantly crowded with tourists in the spring and unbearably hot in July and August. The river Arno, a special feature of the city, has caused disastrous floods throughout its history (last in 1966). For a fuller description of the city, see *Blue Guide Florence*.

View of Florence with the Duomo

■ Practical information

Information offices. APT, 1 (red) Via Cavour (Pl. 7; ☎ 055-290832). Comune of Florence, 29 (red) Borgo Santa Croce (Pl. 11; ☎ 055-2340444) and Piazza Stazione (beneath the bus shelter on the right side of the station), ☎ 055-212245. **Hotel booking office** (ITA) at the railway station (☎ 055-282893) on the motorway approaches to Florence (Chianti Est and Peretola Sud), and at Pisa airport.

Airports. The nearest large international airport is at **Pisa** (85km west; see Ch. 15). Direct train service in 1 hour to Florence Santa Maria Novella station (which has an Air Terminal). The train service is integrated with a *SITA* bus services (which also take one hour). The small **Florence** airport (*Amerigo Vespucci*) at Peretola, a few kilometres north of Florence, has some flights from Europe (including London Gatwick). ATAF bus no. 62 to the railway station in 20 mins, and *SITA* bus service c every hour in 15 min. **Bologna** airport also has international flights (airport bus every 20 mins in 15 mins to Bologna station, and from there trains to Florence in 60–75mins).

Railway stations. Santa Maria Novella (Pl. 6) for nearly all services. A few fast trains only stop at Campo di Marte station (beyond Pl. 8), and Rifredi station (north of Pl.2).

Buses. Although the centre of the town is very small and best visited on foot, there are four small **electric bus services** in the centre of the city which provide excellent views: line **A** & **D** both start from the railway station. Line **A** traverses the city north of the Arno and line **D** the city south of the Arno. Line **B** follows the Lungarno north of the Arno and also traverses part of the historic centre. Line **C** connects Piazza San Marco to Piazza Santa Croce. Tickets have to be bought before boarding (from newsagents, *tabacchi*, etc.). 30 day bus pass for Lire 25,000. **Information office**, Piazza Stazione (07.00–20.00, ☎ 055-5650222).

For services to the **environs**, see Ch. 2. There is a wide network of **country bus services** in Tuscany, operated by *Lazzi*, 4 Piazza Stazione (☎ 055-166 845010), *SITA*, 15 Via Santa Caterina da Siena (☎ 055-4782231), *COPIT* and *CAP*, 9 Largo Alinari (☎ 055-214637).

Car parking. Most of the centre of Florence (within the *Viali*, and in the Oltrarno; see the Plan) has been closed to private cars (from 08.30–18.30), except for residents and temporary access to hotels. Parking is difficult. At present the only large car parks with long-term parking (with hourly tariff) near to the centre of the city are at the Fortezza da Basso, Piazza Stazione (underground), Parterre (underground), and inside the walls near Porta Romana. Smaller car parks include Piazza Beccaria and Lungarno della Zecca Vecchia.

Hotels in Florence
Hotels are scattered all over the city, but it is essential to book well in advance at Easter, September and October, and in the summer.
★★★★★ *Helvetia e Bristol*, 2 Via de' Pescioni (☎ 055-287814; fax 055-288353).
★★★★ *J & J*, 20 Via di Mezzo (☎ 055-2345005, fax 055-240282); *Monna Lisa*, 27 Borgo Pinti (☎ 055-2479751, fax 055-2479755).
★★★ *Annalena*, 34 Via Romana (☎ 055-222402, fax 055-222403); *Loggiato dei Serviti*, 3 Piazza Santissima Annunziata (☎ 055-289592, fax 055-289595); *Porta Rossa*, 19 Via Porta Rossa (☎ 055-287551, fax 055-282179); *Beacci Tornabuoni*, 3 Via Tornabuoni (☎ 055-212645, fax 055-283594).
★★ *Villani*, 11 Via delle Oche (☎ 055-2396451, fax 055-215348); *Boboli*, 63 Via Romana (☎ 055-2298645, fax 055-2337169); *Casci*, 13 Via Cavour (☎ 055-211686,

fax 055-2396461); *La Scaletta*, 13 Via Guicciardini (☎ 055-283028, fax 055-289562); *Torre Guelfa*, 8 Borgo Santi Apostoli (☎ 055-2396338, fax 055-2398577).

★ *Bandini*, 9 Piazza Santo Spirito (☎ 055-215308, fax 055-282761); *Marie Luisa de' Medici*, 1 Via del Corso (☎ & fax 055-280048); *Scoti*, 7 Via Tornabuoni (☎ & fax 055-292128); *Azzi*, 56 Via Faenza (☎ & fax 055-213806).

Hotels outside the centre of Florence
These include the ★★★★ *Torre di Bellosguardo*, 2 Via Roti Michelozzi (☎ 055-2298145, fax 055-229008). For hotels in the environs, including Fiesole, see Ch. 2.
Youth Hostel (*Ostello per la Gioventù*) at *Villa Camerata*, 2 Viale Righi (☎ 055-601451, fax 055-610300).
Campsite ★★ *Italiani e Stranieri*, Viale Michelangelo (closed November to March).

Restaurants
£££ *Enoteca Pinchiorri*, 87 Via Ghibellina; *The Bristol* in the Hotel Helvetia e Bristol, 2 Via de' Pescioni.
££ *La Capannina di Sante*, Piazza Ravenna (specialising in fish); *Taverna del Bronzino*, Via delle Ruote.
££ *Latini*, 6 Via Palchetti; *Cocco Lezzone*, 26 Via del Parioncino; *Il Troia* 29 Via Porcellana.
£ *Acquacotta*, 51 Via dei Pilastri; *Benvenuto*, 16 Via Mosca; *Diladdarno*, 108 Via de' Serragli. *Alessi*, 24 Via di Mezzo (a club; membership by previous appointment; annual subscription) is run by a scholar of Renaissance cuisine who produces excellent traditional Tuscan dishes (not expensive).
Simple cheap trattorie: *La Casalinga*, 9 Via Michelozzi; *Mario*, 2 Via Rosina.

Cafés (bars) are open all day. Most customers choose to eat and drink standing up—you pay the cashier first, and show the receipt to the barman in order to get served. In almost all bars, if you sit at a table you are charged considerably more (at least double) and are given waiter service (you should not pay first).

Well-known cafés in the city, all of which have tables (some outside) include: *Rivoire*, Piazza Signoria; *Le Giubbe Rosse*, *Gilli*, both in Piazza della Repubblica; *Giacosa*, Via Tornabuoni; *San Firenze*, Piazza San Firenze; *Il Cafè*, 9 Piazza Pitti; *Cibreo*, 5 Via Andrea del Verrocchio; *Rose's*, Via del Parione. A café specialising in tea is *La Via del Tè*, 22 Piazza Ghiberti. In Settignano, *Caffè Desiderio*, 5 Piazza Tommaseo.

Cafés or **cake shops** well known for their cakes, pastries, and confectionery, include: *Dolci e Dolcezze*, 8 Piazza Beccaria; *Robiglio*, Via dei Servi and Via Tosinghi; *Giurovich*, Viale Don Minzoni; *Procacci*, Via Tornabuoni (famous for truffle sandwiches); *Gambrinus*, Via Brunelleschi; *Maioli*, Via Guicciardini; *Patrizio Cosi*, 11 Borgo degli Albizi; *Minni*, 16 Via Giacomini; and *Scudieri*, Via Cerretani. *The Forno Sartoni*, 34 Via dei Cerchi sells exceptionally good simple cakes (as well as pizzas, etc.), at reasonable prices. The *Pasticceria Alcedo Falli* in Fiesole (29 Via Gramsci) makes particularly good cakes and pastries.

Some of the best **ice-cream shops** in Florence: *Vivoli*, 7 Via Isola delle Stinche (near Santa Croce); *Badiani*, 20 Viale dei Mille; *Cavini*, 22 Piazza delle Cure; *Perchè no?*, 19 Via dei Tavolini; and *Veneta*, 7 Piazza Beccaria. Outside the centre of Florence: *La Fattoria di Maiano*, 3 Via Cave di Maiano, and *Villani*, 8 Piazza San Domenico (San Domenico di Fiesole).

Places to picnic
Some of the most pleasant spots in the city include: Forte di Belvedere, the Giardino dell'Orticoltura, the park of Villa il Ventaglio, the park of Villa Stibbert, and the gardens off Viale Machiavelli.

Admission to museums

There is now an advance booking service ('*Firenze Musei*') for State-owned museums in Florence, which is highly recommended, especially for the Uffizi and the Accademia where there can be very long queues. The telephone number is ☎ 055-294883 (fax 055-264406) and the line is open Mon–Fri 08.30–18.30, Sat 08.30–12.30. There is a booking fee of 2000 lire. You pay (no credit cards accepted) and collect your ticket from the museum, 15–30 minutes before the booked visit.

A carnet can be purchased which allows a 50 per cent reduction to the museums owned by the Comune (including Palazzo Vecchio and the Cappella Brancacci).

Consulates

British Consulate, 2 Lungarno Corsini (Pl. 10).
American Consulate, 38 Lungarno Vespucci (Pl. 5).

Churches

Anglican Church, St Mark's, 16 Via Maggio.
American Episcopalian, St James, 9 Via Bernardo Rucellai.

Institutes

British Institute, 2 Piazza Strozzi (Italian language courses), with an excellent library and reading room at 9B Lungarno Guicciardini (see p 41); *Institut Français*, 2 Piazza Ognissanti; *German Institute of Art History*, 44 Via Giuseppe Giusti, with the best art history library in Florence (post-graduate students); *Dutch Institute*, 5 Viale Torricelli; *Harvard University Center for Italian Renaissance Studies*, Villa I Tatti, Ponte a Mensola, Settignano (with a good library, open to post-graduate students); *Centro Linguistico Italiano Dante Alighieri*, 12 Via de'Bardi (Italian language courses).

Concerts and drama

Teatro Comunale (Pl. 5), 16 Corso Italia, symphony concerts and opera. Here is held the Maggio Musicale, an annual music festival (May–July). *La Pergola* (Pl. 7), 12 Via della Pergola (drama season, and chamber music concerts organised by the *Amici della Musica* in January–April and October–December). Concerts are often given by the *Orchestra Regionale Toscana* and the *Orchestra da Camera Fiorentina*.

Annual festivals and exhibitions

The *Scoppio del Carro*, on Easter Day, is a traditional religious festival held in and outside the Duomo. On 24 June, St John's Day (St John is the patron saint of Florence), a local holiday is celebrated with fireworks at Piazzale Michelangelo. A football game in 16C costume (Calcio in costume) is held in three heats during June. An Antiques Fair (the *Mostra Mercato Internazionale dell'Antiquariato*) is held biennially (next in 1999) in the autumn.

History. The Roman colony of Florentia was founded in 59 BC by Julius Caesar. The city was built on the Arno where the crossing is narrowest, and it flourished in the 2C and 3C AD. The commune of Florence came into being in the first decades of the 12C, and there followed a long drawn-out struggle between Guelfs and Ghibellines. By the middle of the 13C Florentine merchants, whose prosperity was largely based on the woollen cloth industry, were established in a privileged position in trade and commerce, and the florin, first minted in silver c 1235, and soon after in gold, was used as the standard gold coin in Europe. In the 14C Florence was one of the five largest cities in Europe. By this time Palazzo Vecchio had been built by Arnolfo di Cambio, and the two churches of Santa Maria Novella and Santa Croce were erected.

ı

The city's greatest moment of splendour came in the 15C when a new conception of art and learning symbolised the birth of the Renaissance, under the brilliant leadership of Cosimo de' Medici and, later, under his famous grandson Lorenzo il Magnifico. The origins of Florentine art in the 14C had been marked by the works of Cimabue and Giotto, who led the way for the Renaissance, which found its highest expression in the works of Brunelleschi, Donatello, and Masaccio. Numerous great artists worked together in Florence in the 15C creating remarkably beautiful paintings, buildings, and statuary. Among them were Lorenzo Ghiberti, Luca della Robbia, Beato Angelico, Filippo Lippi, and Paolo Uccello. In the later 15C Pollaiolo, Verrocchio, and Sandro Botticelli produced splendid works, and they were followed by the universal artist Leonardo da Vinci. The fame of Michelangelo, who was favoured by the patronage of Lorenzo il Magnifico, spread throughout Europe and he was recognised as the greatest artist of his time.

Despite opposition from Republican exiles, enlightened Medici rule continued into the 16C when they became grand-dukes of Tuscany. Andrea del Sarto, Pontormo, Giambologna, Benvenuto Cellini, and Bronzino represent the Mannerist era of art in the city.

The Medici were succeeded in 1737 by Austrian grand-dukes. From 1861 to 1875 Florence was the capital of the Italian kingdom. All the bridges except Ponte Vecchio were blown up in the Second World War, and in 1966 a disastrous flood of the Arno caused severe damage to the city and its works of art.

Piazza del Duomo

The Baptistery

The **Baptistery of San Giovanni (Pl. 7; **open** 08.15–19.00; fest. 08.30–13.30) is one of the oldest and most revered buildings in the city, called by Dante his *bel San Giovanni*. It was probably built in the 6C or 7C, and in any case not later than the 9C. It is a domed octagonal building of centralised plan derived from Byzantine models. In the 11C–12C the **exterior** was entirely encased in white and green marble from Prato in a classical geometrical design, which became a prototype for numerous other Tuscan Romanesque religious buildings. The cupola was concealed by an unusual white pyramidal roof (and the 11C lantern placed on top), probably in the 13C.

The bronze doors

The building is famous for its three sets of gilded bronze doors. The two doors by Lorenzo Ghiberti were erected after he won a competition in 1401, often taken as a convenient point to mark the beginning of the Florentine Renaissance.

The *south door** (1336) is by Andrea Pisano with reliefs illustrating the history of St John the Baptist. The bronze frame was added by Vittorio Ghiberti (1452–64). Over the doorway are statues of the Baptist, the Executioner, and Salome, by Vincenzo Danti (1571).

The *north door**, by Lorenzo Ghiberti (1403–24) contains scenes of the Life of Christ, the Evangelists, and the Doctors of the Church. The beautiful frame is also by Ghiberti, and his self-portrait appears in the fifth head on the left door.

FLORENCE
CENTRE

PIAZZA DELLA
INDIPENDENZA

VIA GUELFA

S. MARCO

V. DEGLI ARAZZIERI

PIAZZA
S. MARCO

Loggia

Galleria dell'
Accademia

Museo delle
Pietre Dure

Palazzo
Gerini

Palazzo
Niccolini

Cenacolo
di Fuligno

S. Apollonia

Biblioteca
Marucelliana

VIA NAZIONALE

VIA PANICALE

VIA GUELFA

VIA CHIARI

VIA TADDEA

VIA SAN GALLO

VIA CAVOUR

Stazione
S. M. Novella

VIA FIUME

VIA FAENZA

N

Mercato
Centrale

VIA DELL'ARIENTO

VIA NAZIONALE

VIA DI S. REPARATA

VIA GINORI

Biblioteca
Riccardiana

Pal.
Medici
Riccardi

i

PIAZZA
D. STAZIONE

S. Barnaba

VIA S. ANTONINO

PIAZZA
D'UNITA
ITALIANA

Cappelle
Medicee

V. CANTO
DE' NELLI

PIAZZA
S. LORENZO

VIA CAVOUR

S. Giovannino

VIA DE' PUCCI

Palazzo
Pucci

S. Michele
Visdomini

S. Maria
Novella

Cappellone
degli
Spagnuoli

V. DEL
MELARANCIO

V. DEL
GIGLIO

PIAZZA
MAD. D.
ALDOBRANDINI

S. Lorenzo

BORGO S. LORENZO

VIA RICASOLI

VIA DE' SERVI

VIA DELLA SCALA

PIAZZA
S. MARIA
NOVELLA

VIA DE' PANZANI

Biblioteca
Laurenziana

PIAZZA

Duomo

Museo
dell' Opera
del Duomo

Loggia
di S. Paolo

VIA PALAZZUOLO

VIA DE' BANCHI

VIA DE' CERRETANI

S. M.
Maggiore

Palazzo
Archivi

Battistero

Campanile
DEL DUOMO

Palazzo
dei Canonici

VIA DELL'ORIUOLO

S. Paolino

VIA DE' FOSSI

VIA DEL MORO

VIA DELLE BELLE DONNE

V. CORNINO

V. DE' AGLI

V. DE' PECORI

Museo
del Bigallo

Misericordia

VIA DELLE OCHE

S. M. in
Campo

Pal. Antinori

PIAZZA
ANTINORI

S. Gaetano

V. DE'
TORNABUONI

V. CORSI

V. CAMPIDOGLIO

V. DE' TOSINGHI

VIA DE' CALZAIOLI

S. SANTA
ELISABETTA

Palazzo
Nonfinito

BORGO D. ALBIZZI

Museo
Marino Marini

Palazzo
Larderel

Palazzo
Corsi

VIA STROZZI

PIAZZA
DELLA
REPUBBLICA

V. D. SPEZIALI

D. CERCHI

Casa di
Dante

Pal. Pazzi
Quaratesi

Palazzo
Rucellai

VIA DELLA VIGNA NUOVA

Loggia

V. D.
ANSELMI

PIAZZA
STROZZI

V. D.
VECCHIETTI

P.O.

V. DANTE ALIGHIERI

Badia
Fiorentina

VIA GHIBELLINA

PIAZZA
GOLDONI

VIA DI PARIONE

Palazzo
Strozzi

PIAZZA
DAVANZATI

S. Carlo

Orsanmichele V. D. CIMATORI

Palazzo
Uguccioni

Bargello
(Mus. Nazionale)

Palazzo
Corsini

Ponte
alle Carraia

LUNGARNO CORSINI

S. Trinita

PIAZZA
S. TRINITA

Palazzo
Bartolini

Palazzo
Davanzati

Mercato
Nuovo

VIA PORTA ROSSA

V. C. RUZZA

V. CONDOTTA

PIAZZA
D. FIRENZE

S. Firenze

VIA DELL'ANGUILLARA

S. Filippo Neri

Palazzo
Spini

Palazzo
Rosselli

Pal. di
Parte Guelfa

V. VACCHERECCIA

PIAZZA
DELLA
SIGNORIA

Palazzo
Gondi

V. D. GONDI

BORGO DEI GRECI

Ponte
S. Trinita

LUNGARNO GUICCIARDINI

BORGO S. APOSTOLI

SS.
Apostoli

ACCIAIOLI

VIA POR S. MARIA

S. Stefano

Loggia
d. Signoria

VIA DELLA NINNA

Palazzo
Vecchio

VIA VINEGIA

VIA DE' NERI

Palazzo
Capponi

S. Jacopo
sopr'Arno

BORGO S. JACOPO

Ponte
Vecchio

PIAZZA
ARCHIBUSIERI

Galleria
degli Uffizi

Loggia
d. Grano

S. Remigio

S. Spirito

VIA MAGGIO

English
Church

VIA TOSCANELLA

Mus. d. Scienza

ZA V. D. GIUDICI

V. D. SAPONAI

LUNGARNO GENERALE DIAZ

PIAZZA
MENTANA

Pal. Bardi

PIAZZA
S. SPIRITO

VIA DE' BARDI

VIA GUICCIARDINI

ARNO

LUNGARNO TORRIGIANI

Ponte
alle Grazie

S. Felicita

V. D. COSTA S. GIORGIO

Palazzo Pitti

The sculptures above of St John the Baptist, the Levite, and the Pharisee are by Francesco Rustici (1506–11), from a design by Leonardo da Vinci.

The **east door is the most celebrated work of Lorenzo Ghiberti, the completion of which took him most of his life (1425–52). It is said to have been called by Michelangelo the Gate of Paradise. The pictorial reliefs (see below), no longer restricted to a Gothic frame, depict each episode with great conciseness, and the workmanship of the carving is masterly. A copy of the door made from casts taken in 1948 was set up here in 1990, and the original panels will all be exhibited in the Museo dell'Opera del Duomo after their restoration. The subjects are: 1. *The Creation and the Expulsion from Paradise*; 2. *Cain and Abel*; 3. *Noah's Sacrifice and Drunkenness*; 4. *Abraham and the Angels and the Sacrifice of Isaac*; 5. *Esau and Jacob*; 6. *Joseph sold and recognised by his Brethren*; 7. *Moses receiving the Tablets of Stone*; 8. *The Fall of Jericho*; 9. *Battle with the Philistines*; 10. *Solomon and the Queen of Sheba*. The frame contains beautiful statuettes of Prophets and Sibyls, and medallions with portraits of Ghiberti himself and his contemporaries. The splendid bronze door-frame is also by Ghiberti. Above, the sculptural group of the Baptism of Christ, attributed to Andrea Sansovino and Vincenzo Danti, with an Angel added by Innocenzo Spinazzi (18C), has been removed and restored.

The harmonious **interior** is designed in two orders, of which the lower has huge granite columns from a Roman building, with gilded Corinthian capitals, and the upper, above a cornice, a gallery with divided windows. The walls are in panels of white marble divided by bands of black, in the dichromatic style of the exterior. The oldest part of the splendid mosaic ****pavement** in *opus tessellatum* (begun 1209) is near the Gothic font. Beside the 13C high altar is an elaborate paschal candlestick delicately carved by Agostino di Jacopo (1320). The ***tomb of the antipope John XXIII** (Baldassarre Coscia, who died in Florence in 1419) by Donatello and Michelozzo is one of the earliest Renaissance tombs in the city. This beautifully carved monument in no way disturbs the architectural harmony of the building.

The ***mosaics** in the vault are remarkably well preserved. The earliest (c 1225) are in the *scarsella* above the altar; they are signed by the monk Jacopo, who is also thought to have begun the main dome, the centre of which is decorated with early Christian motifs. Above the apse is the *Last Judgement* with a huge (8m) figure of Christ attributed to Coppo di Marcovaldo. The four bands of the cupola illustrate the *Story of Genesis*, the *Story of Joseph* (the design of some of the scenes is attributed to the Maestro della Maddalena), the *Story of Christ*, and the *Story of St John the Baptist* (some of the early episodes are attributed to Cimabue). Work on the mosaics was well advanced by 1271, but probably continued into the 14C.

The Duomo

The *Duomo (Pl. 7) the cathedral dedicated to the Madonna of Florence, **Santa Maria del Fiore**, fills Piazza del Duomo; a comprehensive view of the huge building is difficult in the confined space. It produces a memorable effect of massive grandeur, especially seen from its southern flank, lightened by the colour and pattern of its beautiful marble walls (white from Carrara, green from Prato, and red from the Maremma). The famous dome, one of the masterpieces of the Renaissance, rising to the height of the surrounding hills (from which it is nearly always visible), holds sway over the whole city.

Open 10.00–17.00; fest. 13.00–17.00; first Sat of the month 10.00–15.30. Excavations of Santa Reparata **open** 10.00–17.00 except fest. Ascent of the dome, entrance in south aisle: 08.30–18.20; Sat 09.30–17.00; first Sat of month 09.30–15.20; closed fest.

History of the Duomo. The early Christian church, dedicated to the Palestinian Santa Reparata, is thought to have been founded in the 6C–7C, or possibly earlier. The Bishop's seat, formerly at San Lorenzo, was probably transferred here in the late 7C. By the 13C a new and larger cathedral was deemed necessary, and in 1294 Arnolfo di Cambio was appointed as architect. In 1355 Francesco Talenti continued work on the building, probably following Arnolfo's original design of a vaulted basilica with a domed octagon flanked by three polygonal tribunes. By 1417 the octagonal drum was substantially finished. The construction of the cupola had long been recognised as a major technical problem, and after a competition Brunelleschi was appointed to the task, and had erected the dome up to the base of the lantern by 1436 when Pope Eugenius IV consecrated the cathedral.

The majestic ****Cupola**, the greatest of all Brunelleschi's works (1420–36), is a feat of engineering skill. It was the first dome to be projected without the need for a wooden supporting frame to sustain the vault during construction, and was the largest and highest of its time. The cupola has two concentric shells, the octagonal vaults of which are evident both on the exterior and the interior of the building; the upper section is built in bricks in consecutive rings in horizontal courses, bonded together in a herring-bone pattern. The lantern was begun a few months before the architect's death in 1446, and carried on by his friend Michelozzo. In the late 1460s Verrocchio placed the bronze ball and cross on the summit. Brunelleschi also designed the four decorative little exedrae with niches which he placed around the octagonal drum between the three domed tribunes. The balcony at the base of the cupola added by Baccio d'Agnolo was never completed, according to Vasari, because of Michelangelo's stringent criticism. The dome has been under constant surveillance since 1980 when alarm was raised about its stability (the main problem seems to be the weight of the dome which has caused fissures in the drum).

The building of the cathedral was begun on the south side where the decorative pattern of marble can be seen to full advantage. The Porta dei Canonici has fine sculptural decoration (1395–99). On the north side, the ***Porta della Mandorla** (1391–1405) is by Giovanni d'Ambrogio, Piero di Giovanni Tedesco, Jacopo di Piero Guidi, and Nicolò Lamberti. In the gable is an **Assumption of the Virgin* in an almond-shaped frame by Nanni di Banco (c 1418–20) which had an important influence on early Renaissance sculpture.

The **façade**, erected to a third of its projected height by 1420, was demolished in 1587–88; the present façade in the Gothic style, was designed by Emilio De Fabris and built in 1871–87.

Interior
The Gothic interior is somewhat bare and chilly after the warmth of the colour of the exterior, whose splendour it cannot match. The huge grey stone arches of the nave reach the clerestory beneath an elaborate sculptured balcony. The massive pilasters which support the stone vault have unusual composite capitals. Three dark tribunes with a Gothic coronet of chapels surround the huge dome. The beautiful marble **pavement** was designed by Baccio d'Agnolo, Francesco da Sangallo and others.

West wall. Mosaic of the *Coronation of the Virgin*, attributed to Gaddo Gaddi.

Ghiberti designed the three stained glass windows. The huge clock was decorated with four heads of prophets by Paolo Uccello in 1443. The recomposed tomb of Antonio d'Orso, Bishop of Florence (d. 1321) by Tino da Camaino includes a fine statue.

South aisle. In a tondo is a bust of *Brunelleschi* by Buggiano, his adopted son (1446). On the side altar, statue of a *Prophet* by Nanni di Banco. The bust of Giotto by Benedetto da Maiano bears an inscription by Poliziano. On the second altar, statue of Isaiah by Ciuffagni.

Steps lead down to the **excavations of Santa Reparata** (opening times, see above). Through a grille to the left at the bottom of the steps can be seen the simple tomb slab of Brunelleschi, found here in 1972. The architect of the cupola was the only Florentine granted the privilege of burial in the cathedral. The complicated remains of Santa Reparata (shown in a model), on various levels, include Roman edifices on which the early Christian church was built (a fine mosaic pavement of which survives), and remains of the pre-Romanesque and Romanesque reconstructions. Here are displayed finds from the excavations, including fresco fragments and plutei.

East end of the church (open to visitors only when services are not in progress). Above the octagon the great **dome** soars to a height of 91m. The fresco of the *Last Judgement* by Vasari and Federico Zuccari (1572–79) was restored in 1981–94. The stained glass in the roundels of the drum was designed in 1443–45 by Paolo Uccello, Andrea del Castagno, Donatello, and Ghiberti. Against the pillars stand 16C statues of Apostles by Jacopo Sansovino, Vincenzo de'Rossi, Andrea Ferrucci, Baccio Bandinelli, Benedetto da Rovezzano, Giovanni Bandini, and Vincenzo de'Rossi.

The marble **sanctuary** by Bandinelli (1555), with bas-reliefs by himself and Bandini, encloses the high altar, also by Bandinelli, with a wood *Crucifix* by Benedetto da Maiano. Each of the three apses is divided into five chapels with stained glass windows designed by Lorenzo Ghiberti. Above the entrance to the South Sacristy is a large lunette of the *Ascension* in enamelled terracotta by Luca Della Robbia.

In the central **apse** are two graceful kneeling angels, also by Luca, and a bronze reliquary ***urn** by Lorenzo Ghiberti with exquisite bas-reliefs.

Over the door into the **north sacristy** is another fine relief by Luca della Robbia of the *Resurrection. This was his earliest important work (1442) in enamelled terracotta. The doors were his only work in bronze. It was in this sacristy that Lorenzo il Magnifico took refuge on the day of the Pazzi conspiracy in 1478 in order to escape the death which befell his brother, Giuliano. The ***interior** has beautiful intarsia cupboards dating from 1436–45 by artists including Lo Scheggia and Antonio Manetti. The end wall was continued by Giuliano da Maiano in 1463 (possibly on a cartoon by Antonio del Pollaiolo). The carved frieze of putti is by various artists probably including Benedetto da Maiano. On the entrance wall is a fine marble lavabo by Buggiano probably based on a design by Brunelleschi.

In the pavement of the left apse is Toscanelli's huge gnomon (1475) for solar observations.

Ascending the dome. The ascent is highly recommended (for opening times see p 51). The climb (463 steps) is not specially arduous, and it follows a labyrinth of corridors, steps, and spiral staircases (used by the builders of the cupola) as far as the lantern at the top of the dome. During the ascent the structure of the dome can be examined, and the views of the inside of the cathedral from the balcony around the drum (45.5m in diameter), and of the city from the small windows and from the lantern, are remarkable. On the way down, there is a room with instruments used during the construction of the dome.

North aisle. The painting of Dante holding a copy of his *Divina Commedia* with an interesting view of Florence (1465) is by Domenico Michelino. On the side altar, Bernardo Ciuffagni, *King David*. The two splendid frescoed *equestrian memorials to the famous *condottieri*, the Englishman Sir John Hawkwood (Giovanni Acuto) who commanded the Florentine army from 1377 until his death in 1394, and Nicolò da Tolentino (d. 1434), are by Paolo Uccello and Andrea del Castagno. The bust of the organist Antonio Squarcialupi is by Benedetto da Maiano. On the last altar, Donatello (attributed), the prophet *Joshua* (traditionally thought to be a portrait of the humanist friend of Cosimo il Vecchio, Poggio Bracciolini), originally on the façade of the Duomo.

The Campanile

The *Campanile (Pl. 7; **open** 09.00–sunset daily; also 20.20–23.20 on Fridays July–Sept), nearly 85m high, was begun by Giotto in 1334 when, as the most distinguished Florentine artist, he was appointed city architect. It was continued by Andrea Pisano (1343), and completed by Francesco Talenti in 1348–59. It is built the same coloured marbles as the Duomo, in similar patterns, in a remarkably well-proportioned design. The original bas-reliefs and statues of Prophets and Sibyls in the niches have been removed to the Museo dell'Opera and have been replaced by copies.

The ascent of the bell-tower via 414 steps is interesting for its succession of views of the Duomo, the Baptistery, and the rest of the city. Although lower than the cupola, the climb is steeper.

Between the Baptistery and the Campanile is the little Gothic ***Loggia del Bigallo** built in 1351–58 probably by Alberto Arnoldi, who carved the reliefs. Beneath the loggia lost and abandoned children were shown for three days before being consigned to foster-mothers.

The **Museo del Bigallo** (open daily 08.15–13.30) is the smallest museum in the city, but one of the most charming. It preserves most of the works of art commissioned over the centuries by the Misericordia and the Bigallo from Florentine artists, including a portable triptych by Bernardo Daddi.

Across Via dei Calzaiuoli is the **Misericordia**, a charitable institution which helps those in need, and runs an ambulance service. The lay confraternity, founded in 1244, continues its work through some 2000 volunteers who, in their black capes and hoods, are a characteristic sight of Florence. The Oratory contains an altarpiece by Andrea Della Robbia and a statue of St Sebastian by Benedetto da Maiano. Other works of art can sometimes be seen on request.

Museo dell'Opera del Duomo

At No. 9 Piazza del Duomo is the *Museo dell'Opera del Duomo (Pl. 7; closed for restoration in 1999, but normally **open** 09.00–17.50; summer 09.00–18.50; fest. 09.00–13.20), in a building which has been the seat of the Opera del Duomo (responsible for the maintenance of the cathedral) since the beginning of the 15C. One of the most pleasant museums in the city, it contains material from the Duomo, the Baptistery, and the Campanile, including important sculpture.

Ground floor. When the museum reopens the following arrangement will probably be altered as the premises are to be expanded. In the entrance hall, a marble bust of Brunelleschi attributed to Giovanni Bandini, and fine marble panels from the choir of the Duomo by Baccio Bandinelli and Giovanni Bandini. In the rooms to the left are wooden models of the cupola (probably made by a contemporary of Brunelleschi), and the lantern (thought to date from 1436 and to be by the architect himself), the apparatus which may have been used in the construction of the cupola, together with the original brick moulds, and Brunelleschi's death mask.

In the large hall beyond are displayed numerous *sculptures from the old façade by Arnolfo di Cambio**, and four seated statues of the Evangelists added to the lower part of the façade by Nanni di Banco (St Luke), Donatello (*St John the Evangelist), Bernardo Ciuffagni (St Matthew), and Niccolò di Piero Lamberti (St Mark). The drawing of the old façade (never completed) of the Duomo designed by Arnolfo di Cambio was made shortly before its demolition in 1587 by Bernardino Poccetti. The room beyond contains illuminated antiphonals, wooden models (1588) for a façade for the Duomo, and reliquaries.

On the stair landing is the famous *Pietà* by **Michelangelo**. A late work, it was intended for the sculptor's own tomb. According to Vasari, the head of Nicodemus is a self-portrait. Unsatisfied with his work, Michelangelo destroyed the arm and left leg of Christ, and his pupil Tiberio Calcagni restored the arm and finished the figure of Mary Magdalen.

First floor. **Room I** is dominated by the two famous *cantorie** made in the 1430s by **Luca della Robbia** and **Donatello** for the Duomo. The original sculptured panels by Luca are displayed beneath the reconstructed Cantoria. The children (some of them drawn from classical models), shown dancing, singing, or playing musical instruments, are exquisitely carved within a beautiful architectural framework. Donatello's Cantoria provides a striking contrast, with a frieze of running putti against a background of coloured inlay. Beneath it is displayed his expressive statue in wood of *St Mary Magdalen*, thought to be a late work. Around the walls are the sixteen statues from the niches on the Campanile by Donatello (two *Prophets*, *Abraham* and *Isaac*, *Geremiah*, *Habbakuk*), Nanni di Bartolo, and Andrea Pisano.

Next door are the original *bas-reliefs from the Campanile**. The lower row are charming works by Andrea Pisano (some perhaps designed by Giotto) illustrating the *Creation of Man*, and the *Arts and Industries*. The last five reliefs (on the right wall) were made in the following century by Luca della Robbia. The upper row of smaller reliefs, by pupils of Pisano, illustrate the seven *Planets*, the *Virtues*, and the *Liberal Arts*. The *Seven Sacraments* are by Alberto Arnoldi. The lunette of the *Madonna and Child* is by Andrea Pisano.

Room II. *Four gilded bronze panels by Lorenzo Ghiberti**, removed from the east door of the Baptistery (described on p 50), have been displayed here since their restoration. The magnificent *altar of silver-gilt** from the Baptistery, is a Gothic work by Florentine goldsmiths finished in the 15C. The statuette of the *Baptist* is by Michelozzo; the reliefs (at the sides) of the Beheading of the Saint, and of his birth are by Verrocchio and Antonio del Pollaiolo. The silver *Cross** is the work of Betto di Francesco, Antonio del Pollaiolo, and others. Also displayed here are needlework *panels** from a liturgical tapestry worked by the craftsmen of the *Arte di Calimala* and designed by Antonio del Pollaiolo and sculptures by Andrea Pisano and Tino da Camaino.

Beside the Baptistery is the **Pillar of St Zenobius**, erected in the 14C to commemorate an elm which came into leaf here when the body of the bishop saint (d. c 430) was translated from San Lorenzo to Santa Reparata in the 9C.

Via de' Calzaioli (Pl. 7), on the line of a Roman road, was the main thoroughfare of the medieval city, linking the Duomo to Palazzo Vecchio and passing the guildhall of Orsanmichele. On the right is **Piazza della Repubblica** (Pl. 7), on the site of the Roman forum, and still in the centre of the city. It was laid out at the end of the 19C after the demolition of many medieval buildings. Much criticised at the time, it remains a disappointing intrusion into the historical centre of the city. It has several large cafés with tables outside.

Orsanmichele

The tall rectangular church of *Orsanmichele** (Pl. 7,11) was built as a market by Francesco Talenti, Neri di Fioravante, and Benci di Cione in 1337. The arcades were enclosed by huge Gothic windows by Simone Talenti in 1380. The upper storey was intended to be used as a granary. The decoration of the exterior was undertaken by the Guilds (or *Arti*) who commissioned statues of their patron saints for the canopied niches. They competed with each other to command work from the best artists of the age, and the statues are an impressive testimony to the skill of Florentine sculptors over a period of some two hundred years. Since 1984 restoration of the statues and niches has been underway: the restored statues are now exhibited inside the building (and most of them have been replaced on the outside by copies).

The **statues**, beginning at Via de'Calzaioli (corner of Via de'Lamberti) and going round to the right are: *St John the Baptist* (1414–16), by Lorenzo Ghiberti, the first life-size statue of the Renaissance to be cast in bronze (to be replaced by a copy); *Incredulity of St Thomas** (1466–83), by **Verrocchio** (copy), in a tabernacle by Donatello (the *stemma* above is by Luca della Robbia); *St Luke*, by Giambologna (1601; awaiting restoration), in a tabernacle by Niccolò Lamberti; *St Peter* (1408–13; a copy) attributed to Bernardo Ciuffagni; tabernacle and *St Philip* (c 1415; a copy) by Nanni di Banco; tabernacle, relief, and statues of *four soldier saints** (the *Quattro Santi Coronati*), modelled on Roman works, by **Nanni di Banco** (c 1415; removed for restoration), and *stemma* above by Luca della Robbia; *St George* by Donatello (the original statue and relief are in the Bargello); tabernacle and *St Matthew** (1419–22) by **Ghiberti** (removed for restoration); *St Stephen** by **Ghiberti** (1428) (removed for restoration); *St Eligius* (a copy) and bas-relief by Nanni di Banco; *St Mark** (a copy) by **Donatello**; *St James the Greater* and bas-relief attributed to Niccolò Lamberti;

Gothic tabernacle attributed to Simone Talenti, with a *Madonna and Child* attributed to **Giovanni Tedesco** (to be replaced by a copy), and *stemma* by Luca della Robbia; *St John the Evangelist* by Baccio da Montelupo (1515).

The **interior** of the dark rectangular hall now serves as a church (closed 12.00–16.00), and contains interesting frescoes (14C–16C), and fine Gothic stained glass windows. The Gothic *tabernacle** by **Andrea Orcagna** (1349–59) is a masterpiece of all the decorative arts. A beautiful frame of carved angels encloses a painting on the altar of the *Madonna* by **Bernardo Daddi**. On the other altar is a statue of the *Madonna and Child with St Anne*, by Francesco da Sangallo (1522).

Museo di Orsanmichele. The museum is arranged on the upper floors (opened daily on request at Orsanmichele at 09.00, 10.00. and 11.00 except the first and last Monday of the month). The **restored statues** from the exterior niches are beautifully exhibited here. From the second Gothic hall on the floor above there are **fine views** of Florence.

An overhead passageway connects Orsanmichele to **Palazzo dell'Arte della Lana**, built in 1308 by the Guild of Wool Merchants but arbitrarily restored in 1905. At the base of the tower is the little 14C oratory of Santa Maria della Tromba, with a painting of the *Madonna* by Jacopo del Casentino. **Palazzo dell'Arte dei Beccai**, also facing Orsanmichele, the headquarters of the Butchers' Guild until 1534, is now the seat of the Accademia delle Arti del Disegno (the Academy of the three trade guilds of painters, architects, and sculptors, predecessor of the Academy of Fine Arts) founded in 1563 by Vasari and his contemporaries.

On Via Porta Rossa is the 16C loggia of the **Mercato Nuovo** (Pl. 11), the Florentine straw-market (with stalls also selling leather goods, cheap lace, and souvenirs). It is known to Florentines as *Il Porcellino* from the popular statue here of a bronze boar (a copy by Tacca from an antique statue in the Uffizi to be removed and restored).

Via Porta Rossa continues to **Palazzo Davanzati** (Pl. 11; closed for restoration for several years), the Museo della Casa Fiorentina Antica, and the best surviving example of a medieval nobleman's house in Florence (despite numerous restorations). It is particularly interesting as an illustration of Florentine life in the Middle Ages. The typical 14C **façade** consists of three storeys above large arches on the ground floor. The **interior**, of great interest for its architecture and contemporary wall paintings (rare survivals of a decorative form typical of 14C houses) has been beautifully arranged with the furnishings of a Florentine house of 15C–17C (including tapestries, lacework, ceramics, sculpture, paintings, decorative arts and domestic objects). The 16C–17C furniture is a special feature of the house.

Via Pellicceria leads to **Palazzo di Parte Guelfa**, built as the official residence of the Captains of the Guelf party in the 13C. The palace was enlarged by Brunelleschi who added a hall. Nearby is **Palazzo dell'Arte della Seta**, with a beautiful stemma in the style of Donatello (the palace belonged to the guild of silk-workers).

Via delle Terme, and the parallel Borgo Santi Apostoli to the south, are both pretty medieval streets with numerous towers and old palaces.

FLORENCE

0   400 yards
0   400 metres

N

Fortezza da Basso

Palazzo dei Congressi

PIAZZA DELLA INDIPENDEN

Cenacolo di Fuligno

Ex Stazione Leopoldo

Porta al Prato

Pal. Corsini

Palazzo Ginori-Venturi

Stazione S.M. Novella

LAZZI Bus Station

Merca

La Cascine

PIAZZALE VITTORIO VENETO

American Church

Orti Oricellari

SITA Bus Station

PIAZZA D. STAZIONE

S. Maria Novella

S. Lorenz

VIALE LINCOLN

Teatro Comunale

S. Maria Novella

Ponte d. Vittoria

PIAZZA T. GADDI

V. BRONZINO

PIAZZA S. MARIA NOVELLA

Ognissanti

P.O.

Torreone

Ponte Amerigo Vespucci

PIAZZA OGNISSANTI

FIUME ARNO

PIAZZA GOLDONI

Porta S. Frediano

Ponte alla Carraia

S. Frediano in Cestello

Presb. Church

Ponte S. Trinita

PIAZZA CESTELLO

BORGO S. FREDIANO

PIAZZA DEL CARMINE

S. Spirito

Ponte Vecchi

S.M. del Carmine

PIAZZA T. TASSO

English Church

PIAZZA S. SPIRITO

Casa Guidi

PIAZZA PITTI

S. Giorgio

Palazzo Pitti

Giardino Torrigiani

S. Felice

BELLOSGUARDO

S. Francesco di Paola

Museo di Storia Naturale

Forte di Belvedere

Villa dell' Ombrellino

Giardino di Boboli

Porta Romana

Istituto d'Arte

La Colombaia

VIALE MACHIAVELLI

Santi Apostoli (Pl. 11), one of the oldest churches in the city, has a Romanesque stone façade. The basilican **interior** (open 15.30–18.30) has fine green marble columns and capitals. It contains a *sinopia of a fresco of the Madonna by Paolo Schiavo formerly on the façade; the Tomb of Prior Oddo Altoviti by Benedetto da Rovezzano; and a *tabernacle by Andrea della Robbia.

Across Via Por Santa Maria (rebuilt after 1944) is the church of **Santo Stefano al Ponte** (Pl. 11; closed for restoration since 1993), another very old church. The interior was altered by Ferdinando Tacca in 1649. The altar-steps are by Buontalenti, and the altarpieces by Santi di Tito, Matteo Rosselli, and others. In the canonry, to the right of the church the **Museo Diocesano di Santo Stefano al Ponte** (temporarily closed) displays works of art from churches in the diocese, including interesting 14C–15C Tuscan works.

Piazza della Signoria

*Piazza della Signoria (Pl. 11), dominated by Palazzo Vecchio, the town hall, has been the political centre of the city since the Middle Ages. Here, from the 13C onwards, the *popolo sovrano* met in *parlamento* to resolve crises of government. In the life of the city today, the piazza is still the focus of political manifestations. It is now a pedestrian precinct and usually crowded with tourists as well as Florentines. By 1385, when it was paved, the piazza had nearly reached its present dimensions. The 18C pavement was virtually destroyed when it was renewed in 1991.

Loggia della Signoria

The huge *Loggia della Signoria (Pl. 11), also known as *Loggia dei Lanzi* and *Loggia dell' Orcagna*, with its three beautiful lofty arches, was built in 1376–82 by Benci di Cione and Simone Talenti (probably on a design by Orcagna). It was intended to be used by government officials during public ceremonies and as an ornament to the square.

Since the end of the 18C the loggia has been used as an open-air museum of sculpture. The magnificent bronze ***Perseus*** was commissioned from Cellini by Cosimo I in 1545 (removed and being restored in a ground-floor room of the Uffizi; adm. by appointment). Perseus is shown trampling Medusa and exhibiting her severed head. The original bas-relief and statuettes from the pedestal are now in the Bargello. The *Rape of a Sabine* (1583), a three-figure group, is Giambologna's last work, and one of the most successful Mannerist sculptures. Also here are two lions, one a Greek work, the other a 16C copy; *Hercules and the Centaur*, by Giambologna; the *Rape of Polyxena*, by Pio Fedi; and Roman statues.

Michelangelo's famous **David** was commissioned by the city of Florence in 1501 and set up in front of Palazzo Vecchio in 1504 as a political symbol, representing the victory of Republicanism over tyranny. It was removed to the Accademia in 1873 and replaced here by a copy. The colossal statue of *Hercules and Cacus*, an unhappy imitation of the David, was sculpted in 1534 by Bandinelli. Donatello's statue of *Judith and Holofernes* has been replaced by a copy (original inside Palazzo Vecchio, see below).

The **Neptune Fountain**, by Ammannati, is dominated by a colossal flaccid figure of Neptune, known to Florentines as '*il Biancone*' (the 'white giant'). The more successful elegant bronze groups on the basin were carved by Giambologna,

Andrea Calamech, and others. The porphyry disk in the pavement in front of fountain marks the spot where Savonarola, the Dominican prior of San Marco, was burnt at the stake as a heretic after his excommunication in 1498. The fine bronze equestrian monument to Cosimo is by Giambologna.

At the end of the piazza, towards Piazza San Firenze, is the **Tribunale di Mercanzia** (or Merchants' Court), founded in 1308 and established in this building in 1359. Palazzo Uguccioni (No. 7) has an unusual but handsome façade attributed to Mariotto di Zanobi Folfi (1550), with a bust of Francesco I by Giovanni Bandini. Above a bank at No. 5 is displayed the **Collezione Della Ragione** (**open** 09.00–14.00 except Tuesday; fest. 08.00–13.00), a representative collection of 20C Italian art left to the city in 1970 by Alberto della Ragione.

Palazzo Vecchio

*Palazzo Vecchio, also known as *Palazzo della Signoria* (Pl. 11; **open** 09.00–19.00; fest. 08.00–13.00. There is a café and restaurant), the medieval Palazzo del Popolo, is still the town hall of Florence.

On a design traditionally attributed to Arnolfo di Cambio (1298–1302), it is an imposing fortress-palace built in pietra forte on a trapezoidal plan and became the prototype of many other town halls in Tuscany. The façade has remained virtually unchanged: it has graceful two-light windows and a battlemented gallery. It was the tallest edifice in the city until the 15C; the tower (1310), asymmetrically placed, is 95m high. Many of the rooms on the upper floors are open to the public, or used for exhibitions.

> The palace stands on part of the site of the Roman theatre of Florence built in the 1C AD. The *priori* (priors) lived here during their two months' tenure of office in the government of the medieval city. In 1433 Cosimo il Vecchio was imprisoned in part of the tower known as the Alberghetto, before being exiled. In 1540 Cosimo I moved here from the private Medici palace in Via Larga. It became known as Palazzo Vecchio after 1549 when the Medici grand-dukes moved out and took up residence in Palazzo Pitti. From 1865 to 1871 it housed the Chamber of Deputies and the Foreign Ministry when Florence was capital of the Kingdom of Italy.

Above the entrance is a frieze (1528) dedicated to *Cristo Re*. The **courtyard** was reconstructed by Michelozzo (1453), and the elaborate decoration added in 1565 by Vasari on the occasion of the marriage between Francesco, son of Cosimo I, and Joanna of Austria. The fountain bears a copy of Verrocchio's putto, now inside the palace. The statue of *Samson killing the Philistine* is by Pierino da Vinci. In the 14C **Sala d'Arme** exhibitions are held. The rest of the ground floor is taken up with busy local government offices (and the ticket office).

First floor

A monumental **double grand staircase** by Vasari ascends to the immense *Salone dei Cinquecento**, built by Cronaca in 1495 for the meetings of the Consiglio Maggiore of the Republic. Leonardo da Vinci and Michelangelo were commissioned to paint huge murals of the Florentine victories at the battles of Anghiari (over Milan) and Cascina (over Pisa) on the two long walls. Only the cartoons and a fragment by Leonardo were ever completed; these were copied and studied by contemporary painters before they were lost. The room was transformed by Vasari in 1563–65 when the present decoration was carried out in honour of Cosimo I, and the Florentine victories over Siena and Pisa, by Giovanni Stradano, Jacopo Zucchi, and Giovanni Battista Naldini. **Michelangelo's** *Victory*, a strongly knit two-figure group, was intended for a niche in the tomb of Julius II in Rome. Giambologna's *Virtue overcoming Vice* was commissioned as a pendant (the original plaster model is displayed here). The statues of the *Labours of Hercules* are Vincenzo de'Rossi's best works.

An inconspicuous door (opened on request) gives access to the charming *Studiolo of Francesco I*. This tiny study is a masterpiece of Florentine Mannerist art created by Vasari and his school. It is entirely decorated with paintings and bronze statuettes celebrating Francesco's interest in the natural sciences and alchemy, by Il Poppi, Bronzino, Vincenzo Danti, Vasari, Santi di Tito, Giovanni Battista Naldini, Giovanni Battista Stradano, Alessandro Allori, Giovanni Bandini, Maso di San Friano, Giambologna, Vincenzo de'Rossi, Giovanni Maria Butteri, Alessandro Fei, Bartolomeo Ammannati, and Jacopo Zucchi.

The Town Council still meets in the **Sala dei Dugento**, reconstructed in 1472–77 by Benedetto and Giuliano da Maiano, who also executed the magnificent wood ceiling (with the help of Domenico, Marco and Giuliano del Tasso). The *tapestries* made in Florence by Bronzino, Pontormo, Salviati, and Allori have been removed since 1983 for restoration.

The **Quartiere di Leone X** was decorated for Cosimo I by Vasari, Marco da Faenza, Giovanni Stradano, and others with paintings illustrating the political history of the Medici family. Only the Sala di Leone X is at present open.

Second floor
Stairs lead up to the **Quartiere degli Elementi**, also decorated by Vasari and assistants. In a little room here is displayed the original of Verrocchio's *Putto with a dolphin*, removed from the courtyard. In some of the rooms are fine cabinets in pietre dure. The **Terrazza di Saturno** has a good view of Florence.

A balcony leads across the end of the Sala dei Cinquecento. The apartments of Cosimo I's wife are known as the **Quartiere di Eleonora di Toledo**. The *chapel* was entirely decorated by Bronzino. In the **Sala di Ester** is a painting of 1557 which shows the lost fragment of the *Battle of Anghiari* by Leonardo, probably the best copy that has survived. Beyond the **Cappella della Signoria** decorated by Ridolfo del Ghirlandaio is the **Sala d'Udienza** with a superb *ceiling* by Giuliano da Maiano and assistants. The *doorway* crowned by a statue of Justice is by Benedetto and Giuliano da Maiano. The mural paintings (1545–48) are by Salviati. The **Sala dei Gigli** (decorated with Florentine lilies) has another magnificent *ceiling*, and frescoes by Domenico Ghirlandaio. Here is displayed Donatello's bronze statue of *Judith and Holofernes*, removed from Piazza della Signoria and recently restored. It is one of his last and most sophisticated works. The **Cancelleria** (chancellor's office) was Niccolò Machiavelli's office when he was government secretary. The **Guardaroba** (wardrobe or cloakroom) contains 57 maps illustrating the entire known world by Fra Egnazio Danti and Stefano Bonsignori (1563–81).

The **Collezione Loeser** (which includes a *portrait of Laura Battiferri*, wife of Bartolomeo Ammannati, by Bronzino) is kept in the Quartiere del Mezzanino. The **tower**, from which there is a fine view, was reopened to the public in 1998.

Galleria degli Uffizi

The massive *Palazzo degli Uffizi (Pl. 11) extends from Piazza della Signoria to the Arno. The unusual U-shaped building with a short façade on the river front was begun in 1560 by Vasari, and completed according to his design by Alfonso Parigi the Elder and Bernardo Buontalenti. It was commissioned by Cosimo I to serve as government offices (*uffici*, hence uffizi). Resting on unstable sandy ground, it is a feat of engineering skill. The use of iron to reinforce the building permitted extraordinary technical solutions during its construction, and allowed for the remarkably large number of apertures.

■ Gallery **open** winter 08.30–18.50; fest. 08.30–13.50; summer 08.30–21.00; fest. 08.30–20.00; closed Monday. To book in advance, ☎ 055-294883, see p. 48. **Corridoio Vasariano** and **Collezione Contini-Bonacossi**, visits by appointment only ☎ 055-294883. There is a **café** with a terrace on the third floor.

The ****Galleria degli Uffizi** is the most important collection of paintings in Italy and one of the great art collections of the world. The origins of the collection go back to Cosimo I, and numerous members of the Medici dynasty continued to add works of art in the following centuries. The last of the Medici, Anna Maria Lodovica, bequeathed her inheritance on the people of Florence in 1737. All the works are well labelled and the collection is arranged chronologically by school. The following description includes only some of the most important paintings and sculptures. More rooms are to be opened on the first floor and the collection rehung, and a new exit constructed on Piazza Castellani. Rooms 35–40 and 42–45 are still closed following severe damage to the west corridor in 1993 from a car bomb (placed by the Mafia).

A series of large rooms on the **ground floor** were restored and opened in 1998 which house ticket offices (separate one for pre-booked visits), bookshops, information centres, and cloakrooms. Beyond the staircase, in a hallway, is a detached fresco of the *Annunciation* by Botticelli. A room nearby incorporates the remains of the church of **San Pier Scheraggio** (founded c 1068) a series of *frescoes of illustrious Florentines by **Andrea del Castagno** are displayed.

There is a lift for the picture galleries on the third floor (although it is now officially reserved for the use of the disabled and the gallery staff). The **staircase**, lined with antique busts and statues, leads up past the **Prints and Drawings Room**, with one of the finest collections in the world, particularly rich in Renaissance and Mannerist works (shown in *Exhibitions).

Third floor

The **vestibule** (A) contains good antique sculpture. The long U-shaped gallery provides a fine setting for the superb collection of antique sculptures (mostly Hellenistic works). **Room 2** contains three famous paintings of the *Maestà* by **Cimabue, Duccio di Boninsegna** (both c 1285), and **Giotto** (painted some 25 years later). **Room 3** displays works of the 14C Sienese school including, the Lorenzetti brothers, and an *Annunciation*, one of Simone Martini's most famous works. **Room 4**. Florentine school of the 14C (Bernardo Daddi, Nardo di Cione, Giovanni da Milano, and others). **Rooms 5 & 6**. Works by Lorenzo Monaco and Gentile da Fabriano, including two charming *Adoration of the Magi*.

Room 7 (Florentine school of the early 15C). Domenico Veneziano, *Madonna enthroned with saints*; **Piero della Francesca**, *portraits of *Federico di Monte-feltro* and Battista Sforza; **Paolo Uccello**, *Battle of San Romano*. **Room 8** contains some lovely *works by **Filippo Lippi** (including the *Coronation of the Virgin*, *Madonna and Child with two angels*). **Room 9**. Paintings by Piero and Antonio del Pollaiolo (*Six Virtues, and Saints Vincent, James, and Eustace*, from San Miniato) and Botticelli (*Story of Holofernes*).

Rooms 10–14. This area has been converted into one huge room to display the masterpieces of **Botticelli**, including the famous *Primavera* and *Birth of Venus*. The *Primavera* is an allegory of Spring, richly painted on poplar wood; the *Birth of Venus*, classical in inspiration, and is painted with a remarkable light-ness of touch. Other works by Botticelli here include: *Adoration of the Magi*, *Calumny of Apelles*, *Pallas and the Centaur*, and *Madonna of the Magnificat*. Also here, Hugo van der Goes, *Triptych* commissioned by the Portinari family.

Room 15. Here are displayed the early Florentine works of **Leonardo da Vinci** (*Annunciation*, and the *Adoration of the Magi*, an unfinished composi-tion), together with paintings by his master **Verrocchio** (*Baptism of Christ*). Also works by Perugino, Luca Signorelli, Piero di Cosimo, and Lorenzo di Credi.

Room 18. The beautiful octagonal *Tribuna** was designed by Buontalenti, and contains the most important *sculptures** owned by the Medici (the famous *Medici Venus*, a copy of the Praxitelean *Aphrodite of Cnidos*; the *Arrotino*; the *Dancing Faun*; and *Apollino*). Around the walls are a remarkable series of distin-guished court *portraits**, many of them the family of Cosimo I commis-sioned from **Bronzino**.

Room 19. **Luca Signorelli**, *tondi of the *Madonna and Child* and *Holy Family*. **Room 20** is devoted to **Dürer** (*Adoration of the Magi*) and the German School, including Cranach (*Adam and Eve*). **Room 21** (Venetian School): works by **Giovanni Bellini**, (*Sacred Allegory*), **Giorgione**, and Cima da Conegliano. **Room 22** contains German and Flemish works: *portraits by **Holbein**, and Joos van Cleve the Elder; and works by Albrecht Altdorfer, Gerard David (*Adoration of the Magi*) and others. **Room 23**: *triptych* by **Mantegna**; and works by Bernardo Luini and **Correggio**.

The short **south corridor** (good view of the Arno) displays some more fine sculpture.

Room 25 contains the famous *Tondo Doni** of the *Holy Family*, the only finished oil painting by **Michelangelo**, and works by Mariotto Albertinelli. In **Room 26** are some famous works by **Raphael**: *Madonna del Cardellino*, *Leo X* with Cardinals Giulio de'Medici and Luigi de'Rossi, and a self-portrait; works by **Andrea del Sarto**. Fine portraits by Pontormo are displayed in **Room 27**, together with works by Bronzino, and Rosso Fiorentino.

Room 28 is devoted to **Titian**, including some of his masterpieces (*Flora* and *Venus of Urbino*) and some very fine portraits. Also displayed here is the *Death of Adonis* by Sebastiano del Piombo.

Rooms 29–30 are devoted to Dosso Dossi and Parmigianino and the 16C **Emilian school**.

Room 31 displays works by Paolo Veronese (*Annunciation*, *Holy Family with St Barbara*) and the **Veneto school** is also represented in **Room 32** (by Tintoretto, the Bassano, and Paris Bordone).

UFFIZI GALLERY

South Corridor

24
23
22
21
20
19
18
17
15
16
10 - 14
9
8
7
6 2
5
4 3
A
1

East Corridor

25 26 27 28 30
29
B
33 32 31
34
35
C
41
42

West Corridor

43 44
45
WC
Bar

0 metres 30

Room 33 has works by the **French school**, including François Clouet (equestrian portrait of Francis I). **Room 34** has more works by the **Venetian school**, including Lorenzo Lotto and Giovanni Battista Moroni (**Count Pietro Secco Suardi*).

Room 35 is at present used to display the masterpieces of the gallery in the last rooms (41–45) which are still closed for repair.

Room 41. Rubens, huge canvases illustrating the history of *Henri IV*, *Philip IV of Spain*, *Isabella Brandt; *Van Dyck*, portraits, including an equestrian portrait of the *Emperor Charles V*; Sustermans, Galileo Galilei.

The **Niobe Room (Room 42)**, restored in 1998, contains Roman statues of Niobe and her children and the neo-Attic Medici vase.

Room 43. Works by **Caravaggio** (**Sacrifice of Isaac*), Annibale Carracci (*Bacchic scene*), and Claude **Lorrain** (seascapes).

Room 44 has three *portraits by **Rembrandt** (two of them self-portraits), and Dutch and Flemish works (Jan Steen, Jacob Ruysdael and others).

Room 45 contains 18C works by Piazzetta, Giovanni Battista Tiepolo, Francesco Guardi, Canaletto, Alessandro Longhi; and portraits by Etiene Liotard, Francesco Xavier Fabre, and Goya. On the landing by the **stairs** down to the exit is a sculptured boar (copy of a Hellenistic original).

Corridoio Vasariano

The Corridoio Vasariano (**B**) is a covered passageway built by Vasari in 1565 to connect Palazzo Vecchio, via the Uffizi and Ponte Vecchio, with Palazzo Pitti. It has been restored after severe damage in 1993, for opening times see p. 63. It offers unique views of the city, and is hung with notable paintings including 17C works, and a celebrated ***collection of self-portraits** (begun by Cardinal Leopoldo), by **Vasari**, Bronzino, Salvator Rosa, Rubens, Rembrandt, Van Dyck, Velazquez, Hogarth, Reynolds, David, Delacroix, Corot, Ingres, and many others.

The **Collezione Contini-Bonacossi** was arranged in a wing of the Uffizi in 1998 (entrance on Via Lambertesca; for opening times see p.63). It contains Italian paintings (many by artists not represented elsewhere in the Uffizi), Spanish works, and 15C–17C majolica and furniture, ceded to the Italian state in 1974. Among the most important works are Madonnas by Duccio, Sassetta, and Andrea del Castagno.

Ponte Vecchio

The fame of **Ponte Vecchio** (Pl. 11; **open** to pedestrians only), lined with quaint medieval-looking houses, saved it from damage in 1944. It was the only bridge over the Arno until 1218. The present bridge of three arches was reconstructed after a flood in 1345 probably by Taddeo Gaddi (also attributed to Neri di Fioravante). The **jewellers' shops** have pretty fronts with wooden shutters and awnings; they overhang the river supported on brackets. The excellent jewellers here continue the traditional skill of Florentine goldsmiths whose work first became famous in the 15C. Above the shops on the left side the round windows of the Corridoio Vasariano can be seen. From the opening in the centre there is a view of Ponte Santa Trìnita.

Santa Felìcita

The Oltrarno. Via Guicciardini continues towards Piazza Pitti; on the left opens Piazza Santa Felicita with a granite column of 1381 marking the site of the first Christian cemetery in Florence. Here is **Santa Felìcita** (Pl. 11), probably the oldest church in Florence after San Lorenzo. The early-Christian church, dedicated to the Roman martyr, St Felicity, was last rebuilt in 1736 by Ferdinando Ruggeri in a 15C style.

The fine **interior** is notable chiefly for the superb *works (1525–27) by Pontormo in the **Cappella Capponi** (an altarpiece of the *Deposition*, and frescoes of the *Annunciation*, and the *Evangelists*). The church also contains altarpieces by Antonio Ciseri and Simone Pignone. The high altarpiece is attributed to Francesco Brina. In the **Sacristy** are works by Taddeo Gaddi, Niccolò di Pietro Gerini and Luca della Robbia.

The Pitti Palace and the Boboli Gardens

The Pitti Palace

*Palazzo Pitti (Pl. 10) was built by the merchant Luca Pitti, an effective demonstration of his wealth and power to his rivals, the Medici. The majestic golden-coloured palace is built in huge rough-hewn blocks of stone of different sizes. Its design is attributed to Brunelleschi although it was begun c 1457, after his death. Luca Fanelli is known to have been engaged on the building, but it is generally considered that another architect, whose name is unknown, was also involved. The palace remained incomplete on the death of Luca Pitti in 1472; by then it consisted of the central seven bays with three doorways. Bartolomeo Ammannati, and then Giulio and Alfonso Parigi the Younger completed the building, and the two rondò were added in the 18C and 19C.

In 1549 the palace was bought by Eleonora di Toledo, wife of Cosimo I. It became the official seat of the Medici dynasty of grand-dukes after Cosimo I moved here from Palazzo Vecchio. The various ruling families of Florence continued to occupy the palace, or part of it, until 1919 when Vittorio Emanuele III presented it to the State.

The splendid ***courtyard** by Ammannati serves as a garden façade to the palace. It is a masterpiece of Florentine Mannerist architecture, with bold rustication in three orders. Under the portico to the right is the entrance to the celebrated ****Galleria di Palazzo Pitti** or **Galleria Palatina**, formed in the 17C by the Medici grand-dukes, and installed here in the 18C. The splendid ceilings in the reception rooms on the *piano nobile* were decorated in the 17C by Pietro da Cortona for the Medici grand-dukes. They contain the masterpieces of the collection, including numerous famous works by Raphael and Titian. The arrangement of the pictures (most of them richly framed) still preserves to some extent the character of a private royal collection of the 17C–18C, the aesthetic arrangement of the rooms being considered rather than the chronological placing of the paintings. This produces a remarkable effect of magnificence even though in some cases the pictures (all of which are well labelled) are difficult to see on the crowded walls.

■ **Admission**. Tickets for all the museums in the palace are sold off the right side of the courtyard, left of the main staircase leading up to the Galleria Palatina and Museo d'Arte Moderna (**booking service**, ☎ 055-294883; see p.48). A cumulative ticket, valid for 3 consecutive days, can also be bought (cheaper after 16.00). The rooms are not numbered: the numbers given in the description below refer to the floor plan of Palazzo Pitti on p 69.

Galleria Palatina (ticket valid also for the **Appartamenti Reali**, but in winter these can only be visited by previous appointment, ☎ 055-294883) 08.30–18.50; fest. 08.30–13.00; summer 08.30–21.00; fest. 08.30–20.00; closed Monday.

Galleria d'Arte Moderna (second floor) and **Museo degli Argenti** (entered from the left side of the courtyard) daily 08.30–13.50; closed the second and fourth Sun of every month and the first, third and fifth Monday of every month. The Galleria del Costume is closed for restoration.

Galleria Palatina

The **grand staircase** by Ammannati ascends to the entrance to the Galleria Palatina. From the three reception rooms (straight ahead—1, 2, and 21), there is a view of the courtyard and Boboli gardens. Beyond these are the 'minor' rooms of the gallery (rooms 22–23 and 10–19). The six reception rooms (4–9) overlooking Piazza Pitti which contain the famous masterpieces of the collection, are visited at the end.

From the **Sala del Castagnoli** (**21**), containing a magnificent 19C circular table in *pietre dure*, is the entrance to the so-called **Volterrano wing** (sometimes closed). Here the **Sala delle Allegorie** (**22**) contains works by Volterrano and Giovanni da San Giovanni. The rooms beyond (23–31) contain works by Cigoli, Carlo Dolci, Empoli, Lorenzo Lippi, Cristoforo Allori, Jacopo Ligozzi, Jacopo Vignali, Giovanna Garzoni, Francesco Furini, Giovanni Bilivert, Francesco Curradi, and Salvator Rosa.

From the Sala del Castagnoli (see above) is the entrance to a series of rooms decorated in the neo-classical style which contain the smaller works in the collection. The **Sala di Musica** (**20**) was built in 1811–21. The **Galleria del Poccetti** (19) displays portraits by Rubens, Pontormo, Peter Lely, and Niccolò Cassana.

The **Sala di Prometeo** (**14**) contains: Baldassarre Peruzzi, *Dance of Apollo with the Muses*; Filippo Lippi, **Tondo of the Madonna and Child*, one of his best works; Guido Reni, *Young Bacchus*; Botticelli (attributed), *Portrait of a lady in profile*; and works by Pontormo, Francesco Botticini, Luca Signorelli, and Marco Palmezzano. Rooms 15–18 are not always open. A **corridor** (**15**) with small Flemish paintings leads to the **Sala della Giustizia** (**16**) with fine portraits by Titian (**Portrait of a man*, once thought to be Vincenzo Mosti) and Tintoretto. The **Sala di Flora** (**17**) contains the *Story of Joseph* by Andrea del Sarto; and the **Sala dei Putti** (**18**) the *Three Graces* by Rubens.

The **Sala di Ulisse** (**13**) reached from the Sala di Prometeo (**14**) contains fine portraits by Moroni and Tintoretto. Also, Filippino Lippi, **Death of Lucrezia*; and Raphael, **Madonna dell'Impannata*. Beyond the delightful **Empire Bathroom** (**12**) the **Sala dell'Educazione di Giove** (**11**) contains: *Judith with the head of Holofernes* by Cristofano Allori, and the *Sleeping Cupid*, a late work by Caravaggio; also typical pious works by Carlo Dolci. The ***Sala della Stufa** (**10**) is beautifully frescoed by Pietro da Cortona showing the *Four Ages of the World*, his first work in the palace (1637).

PALAZZO PITTI

Fontana del Carciofo

Cortile dell' Ammannati

XV
XIV
XIII
XII
XI
X
IV
III
II
I

XVII
XVI
XVIII
XIX
XX
XXI
Sala Bianca

VIII
IX
VII
VI
V

Grand Staircase

1
2
3
21
4
5
6
7
8
9

30 29 28
32
33 31
26
23 22
24 20
27
19
17 16
Cortile della Fama
18
15
14
13
12
11
10

First Floor

Galleria Palatina and
the State Apartments

To the left is the entrance to the six rooms on the *piano nobile* overlooking Piazza Pitti which house the masterpieces of the collection. The **Sala dell'Iliade** (**9**) contains portraits by Sustermans, Francesco Pourbus the Younger, Ridolfo del Ghirlandaio, and Joos van Cleve; Andrea del Sarto, two large paintings of the **Assumption*; **Titian**, **Philip II of Spain*, **Diego de Mendoza*; **Raphael**, **Portrait of a woman expecting a child*.

The next five reception rooms (8–4) have beautiful Baroque **ceilings decorated in the 17C by Pietro da Cortona for Ferdinando II. **Sala di Saturno** (**8**): **Raphael**, **Madonna della Seggiola*, a beautifully composed tondo, among the artist's most mature and most popular paintings; **Maddalena Doni, and her husband*; *Vision of Ezekiel*; *Madonna del Baldacchino*; *Cardinal Tommaso Inghirami*; **Madonna del Granduca*, an early work showing the influence of Leonardo; Perugino, **Deposition*; and works by Ridolfo del Ghirlandaio, Annibale Carracci and others.

The **Sala di Giove** (**7**). Venetian School, **Three Ages of Man* (attributed to Giorgione); Raphael, **Portrait of a lady (La Velata)*, one of his most beautiful paintings; works by Andrea del Sarto (including **Young St John the Baptist*) and Fra Bartolomeo (**Deposition*).

Sala di Marte (**6**). Portraits by Tintoretto (*Luigi Cornaro*), Van Dyck (*Cardinal Bentivoglio*), Paolo Veronese, and Titian (**Cardinal Ippolito de'Medici*); **Rubens**, **Consequences of War*, a huge allegorical painting, and **The Four Philosophers* (represented by Rubens, his brother Filippo, Justus Lipsius, and Jan van Wouwer).

Sala di Apollo (**5**). Portraits by Van Dyck, Rubens, and Sustermans; Guido Reni, Cleopatra; Andrea del Sarto, **Holy Family*, and **Deposition*; Rosso Fiorentino, *Madonna enthroned*; **Titian**, **Portrait of a gentleman*, once thought to be the Duke of Norfolk, and **Mary Magdalen*.

The **Sala di Venere** (**4**) has the earliest ceiling (1641–42), executed by Pietro da Cortona for Ferdinando II. The paintings here include: **Titian**, **Concert* (a famous work, also attributed to Giorgione); **Pietro Aretino*, a splendid portrait; and **Portrait of a lady (La Bella)*; Rubens, *Ulysses in the Phaecian Isle*, and **Return from the hayfields*; seascapes by Salvator Rosa. The **Venus Italica* was sculpted by Canova, and presented by Napoleon in exchange for the Medici *Venus* which he had carried off to Paris.

Appartamenti Reali. The other half of the *piano nobile* along the façade of the palace is occupied by the **Appartamenti Reali* (3, 1–XXI). These lavishly decorated rooms were used as state apartments from the 17C onwards by the Medici and Lorraine grand-dukes and later by the royal house of Savoy. They were beautifully restored in 1993 to their appearance in 1880–1911. The contents, which reflect the eclectic Victorian taste of the Savoy rulers, as well as the neo-Baroque period of the 19C Lorraine grand-dukes, include splendid silk curtains, drapes, wall hangings and furnishings made in Florence and France; sumptuous gilded chandeliers, neo-classical mirrors and frames; early 19C carpets from Tournai, huge oriental vases; furniture decorated with pietre dure; and portraits of the Medici by Sustermans.

Second floor. Above the Galleria Palatina is the **Galleria d'Arte Moderna** (adm. see p. 68). The collection is particularly representative of Tuscan art of the 19C, notably the *Macchiaioli* school (including Giovanni Fattori, Silvestro Lega, Telemaco Signorini). Many of the rooms on this floor were decorated in the 19C by the last Lorraine Grand-dukes Ferdinando III and Leopoldo II. In every room there is a detailed catalogue of the works displayed which cover the period from the mid-18C up to the end of the First World War. They are arranged chronologically and by schools. The collection of 20C works is particularly representative of the years between the two world wars.

In the Palazzina della Meridiana, the southern wing of the palace, which was begun in 1776 by Gaspare Maria Paoletti, is the **Galleria del Costume** (admission with the same ticket as the Galleria d'Arte Moderna, but also closed for restoration) which illustrates the history of costume from the 18C to the early 20C.

Museo degli Argenti

The *Museo degli Argenti (for admission, see above), arranged in the summer apartments of the grand-dukes, is entered from the left side of the courtyard. Although always known as the 'silver' museum it contains a great miscellany of decorative arts. The main room contains exuberant and colourful frescoes by Giovanni da San Giovanni. In the **Sala Buia** is displayed the magnificent *collection of vases in *pietre dure* which belonged to Lorenzo il Magnifico, most of which date from the late Imperial Roman era. The reception rooms are decorated with trompe l'oeil frescoes by Angelo Michele Colonna and Agostino Mitelli.

The rooms towards the gardens were the living quarters of the grand-dukes. Here, and on the mezzanine floor, are displayed their eclectic collection of personal keepsakes, gifts presented by other ruling families, objets d'art made specially for them, and the *jewellery collection of the electress Anna Maria Lodovica de' Medici.

Boboli Gardens

On the hillside behind Palazzo Pitti lie the magnificent *Boboli Gardens (Pl.10, 14), laid out for Cosimo I by Tribolo and extended in the early 17C.

■ **Open** 09.00–sunset; except first and last Mon of the month. The main entrance is in the courtyard of Palazzo Pitti (ticket office also in the courtyard); there are three other entrances (and exits) at the Annalena Gate in Via Romana, the Porta Romana gate, and, at the top of the gardens, at Forte di Belvedere.

The biggest park in the centre of Florence, it is laid out on two main axes. The lower gardens, with 17C arboured walks on either side of a splendid long cypress avenue (the *Viottolone*) and the *Isolotto* with its fruit trees in pots, are the most attractive. The vegetation is predominantly evergreen with tall double hedges and ilex woods. About 170 statues decorate the walks, many of them restored Roman works and others dating from the 16C and 17C (some are removed for restoration or replaced by copies). The **amphitheatre** was designed by Ammannati in imitation of a Roman circus.

At the top of the garden in the secluded Giardino del Cavaliere (charming views) is the **Museo della Porcellana** (open 09.00–13.50, exc Mon & 2nd and 4th Sun of month) displaying 18C–19C porcelain. Near here, there is a gate into the Forte di Belvedere (see p. 93). Near Piazza Pitti exit is the 16C *Grotta Grande** (closed for restoration).

Around Piazza San Marco

The Galleria dell'Accademia

The entrance to the *Galleria dell'Accademia (Pl. 3,7) is at No. 58 Via Ricasoli. It is visited above all for its famous works by Michelangelo, but it also contains an important collection of Florentine paintings. The collection was formed in 1784 with a group of paintings given, for study purposes, to the Academy by Pietro Leopoldo I. Since 1873 some important sculptures by Michelangelo have been housed here, including the *David*.

Open 08.30–18.50; summer 08.30–21.00); closed Mon; booking service, ☎ 055-294883, see p. 48.

The galleria contains **sculptures** by **Michelangelo**. The four *Slaves* or *Prisoners* (c 1521–23) were begun for the tomb of Julius II in Rome which was never finished. The *St Matthew* (1504–08), one of the twelve apostles commissioned from the sculptor by the Opera del Duomo, was the only one he ever began. These are all magnificent examples of Michelangelo's unfinished works, some of them barely blocked out, the famous *non-finito*, still much discussed by scholars. The *Pietà* from Santa Rosalia in Palestrina is an undocumented work, and is not now usually considered to be by Michelangelo's own hand.

The **Tribune** was specially built in 1882 to exhibit the *David* by **Michelangelo** (1501–04) when it was removed from Piazza della Signoria. It is perhaps the most famous single work of art of western civilisation, and has become all too familiar through endless reproductions, although it is not the work by which Michelangelo is best judged. It was commissioned by the city of Florence to stand outside Palazzo Vecchio where its huge scale fits its setting. The figure of David, uncharacteristic of Michelangelo's works, stands in a classical pose suited to the shallow block of marble, 4.10m high. The hero, a young colossus, is shown in the moment before his victory over Goliath. A celebration of the nude, the statue established Michelangelo as the foremost sculptor of his time at the age of 29.

The Pinacoteca

Off the Galleria (see above) is the entrance to four rooms of the Pinacoteca with 15C and 16C Florentine paintings including: Lo Scheggia, *frontal of a *cassone* or marriage-chest of the Adimari family showing a wedding scene in front of the Baptistery; works by Mariotto di Cristofano, Botticelli (two *Madonnas*), Alesso Baldovinetti (*Trinity and Saints*), Lorenzo di Credi (*Adoration of the Child*), Raffaellino del Garbo, Cosimo Rosselli, and others. The last room contains works by Francesco Granacci, Mariotto Albertinelli, Filippino Lippi and Perugino (*Descent from the Cross*).

At the end of the hall to the left of the *David* is a huge room which displays 19C works by Academicians, including plaster models by Lorenzo Bartolini. Off the hall are three more rooms containing early Tuscan works of the 13C–14C. The **first floor**, with a *Pietà* by Giovanni da Milano, also has Florentine paintings of the 14C and 15C, including works by Lorenzo Monaco.

The very fine **Museum of Musical Instruments** (with stringed instruments by Stradivari, Guarneri, Arnati, and Ruggeri, and a harpsichord by Cristofori), which belongs to the Conservatorio Cherubini is to be arranged in another part of the building.

At No. 78 Via Alfani is the **Museo dell' Opificio delle Pietre Dure** (oper Tues, and Wed 09.00–14.00; Thurs, Fri, & Sat 09.00–19.00; closed fest. exc the 3rd Sun of the month), which documents the history of the Opificio founded in 1588 by the Grand-duke Ferdinando I.

The refined craft of working hard or semi-precious stones (*pietre dure*) was perfected here. Beautiful mosaics were made to decorate cabinets and table-tops, some of which are exhibited here. This is also the seat of a State restoration and conservation laboratory, and restoration school.

Nearby is the **Rotonda di Santa Maria degli Angeli** (now used by the university; no adm.), one of the first centralised buildings of the Renaissance begun by Brunelleschi in 1434 and left unfinished.

Via dei Servi is lined with a number of handsome 16C palaces, including Palazzo dei Pucci attributed to Ammannati. The church of **San Michele Visdomini** (or San Michelino) contains a *Holy Family* by Pontormo. The street tabernacle here encloses a fresco by Cosimo Rosselli. Via dei Servi leads to Piazza Santissima Annunziata.

Piazza Santissima Annunziata

*Piazza Santissima Annunziata (Pl. 7), designed by Brunelleschi, is surrounded on three sides by porticoes. It is the most beautiful square in Florence. The equestrian statue of the Grand-duke Ferdinando I is by Giambologna, and the two fountains by Tacca.

The ***Spedale degli Innocenti**, opened in 1445 as a foundling hospital, the first institution of its kind in Europe, is still operating as an orphanage and as an institute dedicated to the education and care of children. Brunelleschi began work on the building in 1419, and the ***Colonnade** of nine arches is one of the first masterpieces of the Renaissance. It takes inspiration from classical antiquity as well as from local Romanesque buildings. In the spandrels are delightful ***medallions**, perhaps the best known work of Andrea della Robbia (1487), each with a baby in swaddling-clothes against a blue background.

The Convent may be visited to see the Museo dello Spedale degli Innocenti (**open** 08.30–14.00 except Wed). Among Brunelleschi's works are the Chiostro degli Uomini (with a lunette by Andrea Della Robbia), and the oblong ***Chiostro delle Donne**, with 24 slender Ionic columns beneath a low loggia. Stairs lead up to the Loggia, with detached frescoes. In the Long Gallery are Florentine paintings, including the splendid *Adoration of the Magi* by Domenico Ghirlandaio. The *Madonna and Child* is one of the most beautiful works by Luca della Robbia.

The church of Santissima Annunziata

The church of the *Santissima Annunziata (Pl. 7), was founded by the seven original Florentine members of the Servite Order in 1250 and rebuilt, along with the cloister, by Michelozzo and others in 1444–81. The series of frescoes on the walls of the **Chiostrino dei Voti** is particularly interesting since most of them were painted in the second decade of the 16C by the leading painters of the time: (right to left): Rosso Fiorentino, *Assumption*; Pontormo, *Visitation*; Franciabigio, *Marriage of the Virgin*; Andrea del Sarto, *Birth of the Virgin, Coming of the Magi*. The frescoes by Alesso Baldovinetti (*Nativity*) and Cosimo Rosselli

(*Vocation and Investiture of San Filippo Benizzi*) are earlier works. The last five frescoes (damaged) are works by Andrea del Sarto.

Interior. The heavily decorated and dark interior has a highly venerated shrine of the Madonna. The huge *tabernacle was designed by **Michelozzo** and executed by Pagno di Lapo Portigiani. On the **south side**, monument to Orlando de'Medici, by Bernardo Rossellino, and a *Pietà* by Bandinelli who is buried here. The fine organ is by Domenico di Lorenzo di Lucca (1521).

The unusual circular **tribune** was begun by **Michelozzo** and completed in 1477 by Leon Battista Alberti. In the cupola is a fresco by Volterrano. The high altar dates from the 17C. Near the *tomb of Bishop Angelo Marzi Medici, signed by Francesco da Sangallo (1546), is the **burial place of Andrea del Sarto**. In the semicircular chapels which radiate from the **sanctuary** are paintings by Alessandro and Cristofano Allori, Bronzino (*Resurrection*), and a statue of *St Roch* by the famous German sculptor (born around 1450) Veit Stoss. The east chapel is the **burial place of Giambologna**; it contains reliefs and a *Crucifix* by him, and statues by his pupils including Francavilla. The *Madonna* is attributed to Bernardo Daddi.

The **sacristy**, with a fine vault, was built by Pagno di Lapo from Michelozzo's design. On the **north side**, statue of the *Baptist* by Michelozzo; an *Assumption* by Perugino; and a *Crucifixion* by Giovanni Stradano. The *Last Judgement* by Alessandro Allori is derived from Michelangelo's fresco in the Sistine Chapel. The last two chapels contain a *Holy Trinity with St Jerome, and *St Julian and the Saviour, two frescoes by Andrea del Castagno.

The cloisters. The cloisters are known as the **Chiostro dei Morti** because they have memorial stones to the dead. Over a side door into the church, is the *Madonna del Sacco, one of the best works by **Andrea del Sarto**. The other lunettes contain 17C frescoes by Andrea Mascagni, Bernardino Poccetti, Matteo Rosselli, and Ventura Salimbeni. The **Cappella di San Luca** has belonged to the Accademia delle Arti del Disegno since 1565. It contains works by Vasari, Pontormo, Alessandro Allori, Luca Giordano, and Montorsoli.

Just out of the square, at No. 4 Via Gino Capponi, is the **Cloister of the ex-Compagnia della Santissima Annunziata (or di San Pierino)**. There is a lunette by Santi Buglioni over the portal, and a delightful little cloister with frescoes (c 1585–90) by Bernardino Poccetti and others.

East of the square, at No. 38 Via della Colonna, is the *Museo Archeologico** (Pl. 7; **open** 09.00–14.00; fest. 09.00–13.00 exc Mon), with one of the most important collections of Etruscan antiquities in existence (it has been undergoing rearrangement for years, and parts of the museum are often closed).

On the **ground floor** is displayed the famous *Chimera, an Etruscan ex-voto (late 5C or early 4C BC) and a silver *amphora (380–390 AD). On the **first floor** is the **Egyptian Museum**, with statues, bas-reliefs, sarcophagi, etc., and a Hittite Chariot in wood and bone from a Theban tomb of the 14C BC. The Etruscan, Greek, and Roman sections of the museum contain bronze statues including the *Idolino (probably a Roman copy of a Greek original), a *horse's head (2C–1C BC), Minerva (restored), the *Arringatore (late Republican). Also Etruscan urns, and a collection of precious *gems. On the ground floor of a new pavilion is the first section of the Etruscan Topographical Museum with finds from Etruria including the Mater Matuta, a canopic vase of c 440 BC and the tomb of Larthia Seianti (150 BC). On the second floor are eleven rooms of *Attic vases including the famous *François Vase, made in Athens c 570 BC.

Piazza San Marco

Piazza San Marco (Pl. 3) is one of the liveliest squares in the city. Here, beneath the Loggia dell'Ospedale di San Matteo, is the seat of the Accademia di Belle Arti, an art school opened in 1784. Across Via Cesare Battisti are the administrative offices of the University of Florence, and on Via La Pira is the **Giardino dei Semplici** (open Mon, Wed and Fri 09.00–12.00; Mon & Fri also 14.30–17.00), a botanical garden laid out in 1545–46 by Tribolo for Cosimo I.

Museo di San Marco

The north side of the square is occupied by the Dominican church and convent of San Marco. The convent contains the *Museo di San Marco (Pl. 3; **open** 08.30–13.50; closed 1st, 3rd, & 5th Sun and the 2nd and 4th Mon of the month), famous for its works by the **Blessed Fra' Angelico** who was a friar here.

Cosimo il Vecchio founded a public library here, the first of its kind in Europe. Antonino Pierozzo (1389–1459) and Girolamo Savonarola (1452–98; see p. 61) were famous priors of the convent.

The beautiful **Cloister of St Antonino** was built by Michelozzo. The lunettes with scenes from the life of St Antonino are by Bernardino Poccetti. In the corners are frescoes by Fra Angelico. The **Pilgrims' Hospice**, also by Michelozzo, contains a superb *collection of paintings by Fra Angelico, many of them from Florentine churches (all well labelled), including the *Tabernacle of the Linaioli, with a marble frame designed by Ghiberti. The **Great Refectory** and adjoining rooms display 16C and 17C works (Fra Bartolomeo, Giovanni Antonio Sogliani, etc.). The **Chapter House** contains a large *Crucifixion and Saints by Fra Angelico and assistants, and the Small Refectory a charming Last Supper by Domenico Ghirlandaio and his workshop.

First floor. The *dormitory* consists of 44 small monastic cells beneath a huge wooden roof, each with their own vault and adorned with a fresco by Fra Angelico or an assistant. The *Annunciation, at the head of the stairs, is justly one of the most famous works of the master. Among the most beautiful frescoes are those in Cells 1, 3, 6, and 9, and the Madonna enthroned in the corridor. **Savonarola's cell** contains two portraits by Fra Bartolomeo. The *library*, a light and delicate hall, is one of the most pleasing of all Michelozzo's works; it contains illuminated choirbooks and psalters.

The **church of San Marco** (Pl. 3) contains a *Madonna and saints by Fra Bartolomeo; an 8C mosaic of the *Madonna in prayer; and the tomb slabs of the famous humanist scholar and Platonic philosopher Pico della Mirandola (1463–94) and his friend the poet Poliziano (Angelo Ambrogini, 1454–94).

Just out of Piazza San Marco, in Via Cavour (Pl. 7,3) is the **Casino Mediceo**, built by Buontalenti and now occupied by the law courts. This was the site of the Medici Garden where Cosimo il Vecchio and Lorenzo il Magnifico collected antique sculpture, and where the sculptor Bertoldo is said to have held a school of art in the mid 15C. At No. 69 is the **Chiostro dello Scalzo** (Pl. 3; **open** Mon

& Thur 09.00–13.00), with fine *frescoes in monochrome by Andrea del Sarto and Franciabigio.

A short way west of Piazza San Marco is the former convent of **Sant' Apollonia** (Pl. 3; open 08.30–13.50 exc 1st, 3rd, & 5th Sun of month, and 2nd & 4th Mon) which contains a *Last Supper, the masterpiece of **Andrea del Castagno**, and other works by him.

Around Piazza San Lorenzo

Palazzo Medici-Riccardi

Via Cavour leads south from Piazza San Marco to *Palazzo Medici-Riccardi (Pl. 7), now the seat of the Prefect. This town mansion was built for Cosimo il Vecchio by Michelozzo after 1444, and was the residence of the Medici until 1540 when Cosimo I moved into Palazzo Vecchio. Its rusticated façade served as a model for other famous Florentine palaces. The **courtyard** is decorated with medallions ascribed to Bertoldo.

A staircase leads up to the dark little *chapel (open 09.00–13.00, 15.00–18.00; closed Wed) the only unaltered part of Michelozzo's work, with a beautiful ceiling and marble inlaid floor. The walls are entirely covered with decorative *frescoes, the masterpiece of Benozzo Gozzoli of the *Procession of the Magi to Bethlehem*, which includes portraits of the Medici (shown with their emblem of the three ostrich feathers). The decorative cavalcade is shown in a charming landscape with hunting scenes. The **gallery** (lift) has a vault fresco by Luca Giordano (1683), and a *Madonna and Child* by Filippo Lippi.

The back of Palazzo Medici-Riccardi stands on Via de' Ginori, with a number of fine palaces and the **Biblioteca Riccardiana** (1718). Here is Piazza San Lorenzo (Pl. 7), filled with a busy **street market** (with cheap leather-goods and clothing).

San Lorenzo

The church of *San Lorenzo (Pl. 7) was intimately connected with the Medici after they commissioned Brunelleschi to rebuild it in 1425–46. It is the burial place of all the principal members of the family from Cosimo il Vecchio to Cosimo III. Thought to be the earliest church in Florence, a basilica on this site was consecrated by St Ambrose of Milan in 393. The grandiose façade designed by Michelangelo was never built; the exterior remains in rough-hewn brick.

■ Admission. The **Biblioteca Laurenziana** is open 09.00–13.00 except Sun; although it is closed at present for restoration.

The **church** is open 08.00–12.00, 15.30–18.30.

The **Old Sacristy** is open Mon, Wed, Fri & Sat 10.00–11.45; Tues & Thurs 16.00–17.45.

The **Medici Chapels** are open 08.30–16.50 except the 2nd & 4th Sun of the month, and the 1st, 3rd, and 5th Mon of the month. The drawings attributed to Michelangelo in a room beneath the Medici Chapels can only be seen by appointment at the ticket office 09.30–12.00.

The grey cruciform **interior**, built with pietra serena, with pulvins above the Corinthian columns in pietra forte, is one of the earliest and most harmonious architectural works of the Renaissance. It was completed on Brunelleschi's design by Antonio Manetti (1447–60) and Pagno di Lapo Portigiani (1463).

In the **south aisle**, *Marriage of the Virgin* by Rosso Fiorentino, and *tabernacle* by Desiderio da Settignano. The two bronze *pulpits in the nave are the last works of Donatello, finished by his pupils Bertoldo and Bartolomeo Bellano. Beneath the dome a simple inscription, with the Medici arms, marks the grave of Cosimo il Vecchio *Pater Patriae*.

Off the north transept is the *Old Sacristy** (1420–29; restored in 1998) by Brunelleschi, one of the earliest and purest monuments of the Renaissance, with a charming vault. The decorative details are by Donatello (the *tondi in the pendentives and lunettes, the reliefs above the doors, and the doors themselves). In the centre is the **sarcophagus of Giovanni di Bicci de'Medici** and Piccarda Bueri, by Buggiano. Set into the wall is the magnificent porphyry and bronze sarcophagus of Giovanni and **Piero de'Medici** by Verrocchio. In a chapel in the north transept is an *Annunciation* by Filippo Lippi, and a 19C monument marking the **burial place of Donatello**.

From the 15C cloister a staircase ascends to the *Biblioteca Laurenziana** (Pl. 7); begun by Michelangelo c 1524 to house the collection of MSS made by Cosimo il Vecchio and Lorenzo il Magnifico.

The heavily decorated **vestibule**, filled with an elaborate staircase was constructed by Vasari and Ammannati on Michelangelo's design. The peaceful **reading room** provides an unexpected contrast. The collection is famous above all for its Greek and Latin MSS. *Exhibitions are held every year.

The Medici Chapels

The entrance to the **Cappelle Medicee** (or Medici Chapels; Pl. 7) is from outside San Lorenzo, in Piazza Madonna degli Aldobrandini.

From the crypt a staircase leads up to the *Cappella dei Principi**, the opulent, if gloomy, mausoleum of the Medici grand-dukes begun by Matteo Nigetti (1604). Its minor details were completed only in the 20th century. It is a tour de force of craftsmanship in pietre dure. A passage to the left leads to the so-called *Sagrestia Nuova** (or New Sacristy), begun by Michelangelo and left unfinished when he departed from Florence in 1534. It is built in dark pietra serena and white marble in a severe and idiosyncratic style. Here are the famous ****Medici Tombs** of Lorenzo, Duke of Urbino, and Giuliano, Duke of Nemours with statues of the dukes, and allegorical figures of *Dawn* and *Dusk*, *Night* and *Day*, all superb works **by Michelangelo**. On the entrance wall is the *Madonna and Child*, also by Michelangelo, intended for the monument to Lorenzo il Magnifico and his brother Giuliano.

On the walls behind the altar, architectural graffiti have been uncovered, attributed to Michelangelo and his pupils including Tribolo. Nearby is a little room (adm. by appointment at the ticket office, 09.30–12.00) where charcoal *drawings of great interest were discovered on the walls in 1975, attributed by most scholars to Michelangelo himself.

The animated Via dell'Ariento behind San Lorenzo with numerous market stalls leads past the huge **Mercato Centrale** (in a cast-iron market building by Giuseppe Mengoni, 1874), the biggest food market in Florence, to the busy Via Nazionale. In Via Faenza, just to the left, is the so-called **Cenacolo di Fuligno**

(Pl. 2; **open** 09.00–12.00 by appointment, ☎ 055-286982) with a fresco of the *Last Supper* by Perugino. At the station end of Via Nazionale, at No. 15 Largo Alinari is the headquarters of **Fratelli Alinari**, a firm founded in 1852 and famous for its black and white photography. Alinari's photo archive and a museum here are open to the public.

Around Piazza Santa Maria Novella

Santa Maria Novella
*Santa Maria Novella (Pl. 6; closed between 11.30–15.30) is the most important Gothic church in Tuscany. The Dominicans were given the property in 1221 and building was begun in 1246 at the east end. The Dominican friars, Sisto and Ristoro are thought to have been the architects of the impressive nave, begun in 1279. The church was completed under the direction of Fra Jacopo Talenti in the mid-14C.

The lower part of the beautiful marble ***façade**, in a typical Tuscan Romanesque style, is attributed to Fra Jacopo Talenti. In 1456–70 Leon Battista Alberti was commissioned by Giovanni di Paolo Rucellai to complete the upper part of the façade. Its classical lines are in perfect harmony with the earlier work. To the right of the façade are the Gothic *avelli* or family-vaults of Florentine nobles, which extend around the old cemetery. The campanile, also attributed to Fra Jacopo Talenti, was grafted onto an ancient watch tower.

Interior
The spacious nave has remarkably bold stone vaulting, its arches given prominence by bands of dark grey pietra serena. The stained glass in the rose window at the west end is thought to have been designed by Andrea di Bonaiuto (c 1365). Over the west door is a good fresco of the *Nativity*, thought to be an early work by Botticelli.

In the **south aisle** are 16C altarpieces by Girolamo Macchietti, Giovanni Battista Naldini, Jacopo del Meglio, and Jacopo Ligozzi. In the **south transept** are Gothic tombs including that of Joseph, Patriarch of Constantinople (died in Florence in 1440), with a contemporary fresco of him.

Steps lead up to the **Cappella Rucellai** (light on left) which contains a marble *statuette of the Madonna and Child signed by Nino Pisano, and the bronze tomb slab of Francesco Leonardo Dati, by Ghiberti. The walls have traces of 14C frescoes.

Cappella dei Bardi. This chapel has damaged frescoes in the lunettes attributed to Cimabue, and an altarpiece by Vasari.

Cappella di Filippo Strozzi. Exuberant ***frescoes by Filippino Lippi** illustrate stories from the *Life of St Philip the Apostle and St John the Evangelist*. Behind the altar, ***tomb** of Filippo Strozzi, exquisitely carved by Benedetto da Maiano. In his *Decameron* Boccaccio uses this chapel as the meeting-place of a group of young people during the Plague year of 1348.

On the main altar is a bronze *Crucifix* by Giambologna.

In the **sanctuary** (light behind the altar) are delightful ***frescoes** commissioned by Giovanni Tornabuoni. They are the **masterpiece of Domenico Ghirlandaio**; he was assisted by his brother Davide, his brother-in-law, Sebastiano Mainardi, and his pupils (including perhaps the young Michelangelo). In the scenes from the *life of St John the Baptist, and of the Virgin*, many of the figures are portraits of the artist's contemporaries, and the whole cycle mirrors Florentine life of the late 15C. On the end wall are the two kneeling figures of the donors, Giovanni Tornabuoni and his wife Francesca Pitti.

North transept. The Cappella Gondi with marble decoration by Giuliano da Sangallo contains the famous wood *Crucifix* by Brunelleschi traditionally thought to have been carved to show Donatello how the Redeemer should be represented. The Cappella Gaddi has paintings by Alessandro Allori and Bronzino. At the end of the transept the *Cappella Strozzi* is a remarkably well-preserved example of a Tuscan chapel of the mid-14C. The *frescoes* of the *Last Judgement, Paradise*, and *Inferno* are the most famous work of **Nardo di Cione** (c 1357). The fine *altarpiece* is by his brother, Orcagna.

The **sacristy** has a fine cross-vault by Fra Jacopo Talenti and stained glass windows dating from 1386. The lavabo is by Giovanni della Robbia, and the *Crucifix* (removed many years ago for restoration) is an early work by **Giotto**. The paintings are by Jacopo Ligozzi, Giovanni Stradano, Pietro Dandini, and Vasari.

The altarpieces in the **north aisle** are by Alessandro Allori, Vasari, and Santi di Tito. Also here is the famous *fresco of the Trinity with the Virgin and St John the Evangelist and donors*, a remarkable work by Masaccio. The pulpit was designed by Brunelleschi.

Museo di Santa Maria Novella

To the left of the church is the entrance to the *Museo di Santa Maria Novella (**open** 09.00–14.00; fest. 08.00–13.00; closed Friday). The Romanesque *Chiostro Verde* has damaged *frescoes by Paolo Uccello (c 1446) painted in *terraverde* and illustrating stories from Genesis: (in the East walk) the *Creation of Adam*, and the *Animals*, and the *Creation and the Temptation of Eve*, and *Flood*, the *Recession of the Flood* (with Noah's ark), and the *Sacrifice and Drunkenness of Noah*. The other frescoes in the cloisters also date from the first half of the 15C.

Off the cloister opens the *Cappellone degli Spagnuoli, or *Spanish Chapel*. It received its name in the 16C when it was assigned by Duchess Eleonora di Toledo to the Spanish members of her suite. It was originally the chapter house built by Jacopo Talenti in the mid-14C with a splendid cross-vault. It is entirely covered with colourful *frescoes* by **Andrea di Bonaiuto** (Andrea da Firenze) dating from c 1365. They represent the *Mission, Works*, and *Triumph of the Dominican Order* (including the artist's vision of the completed Duomo), and the *Triumph of Catholic doctrine personified in St Thomas Aquinas*. In the Chiostrino dei Morti are frescoes dating from the mid-14C.

The large **refectory** has fine cross-vaulting. The fresco of the *Manna in the Desert* by Alessandro Allori surrounds a good fresco of the *Madonna and Child* attributed to a follower of Agnolo Gaddi. Here, and in the adjoining chapel, are displayed church silver, charming reliquary busts by the Sienese school, and vestments.

Piazza Santa Maria Novella, with its irregular shape, was created by the Dominicans at the end of the 13C. The two obelisks were set up in 1608 (resting on bronze tortoises by Giambologna) as turning posts in the course of the annual Palio dei Cocchi. Beneath the 15C Loggia di San Paolo is a beautiful *lunette showing the *Meeting of Saints Francis and Dominic* by Andrea Della Robbia. In the house on the corner of Via della Scala Henry James wrote

Roderick Hudson in 1872. The **Farmacia di Santa Maria Novella** at No. 16 Via della Scala is (**open** 09.00–13.00, 15.30–19.30 except Saturday afternoon and Monday morning) is of ancient foundation, decorated in neo-Gothic style in 1848. The charming old chemist's shop has 17C vases.

Ognissanti

The church of Ognissanti (Pl. 6), reached by Via de'Fossi and Borgo Ognissanti, was founded in 1256 by the Umiliati, a Benedictine Order skilled in manufacturing wool. The church was rebuilt in the 17C; the façade incorporates a terracotta attributed to Benedetto Buglioni.

On the south side are two frescoes by Domenico and Davide Ghirlandaio; the *Madonna della Misericordia* protects the Vespucci whose family tombstone (1471) is in the pavement. Between the third and fourth altars, on the north and south side are *St Jerome* by Domenico Ghirlandaio, and *St Augustine's vision of St Jerome*, by Botticelli, both painted c 1481. Elsewhere in the church are altarpieces by Santi di Tito, Matteo Rosselli, Maso di San Friano, and Jacopo Ligozzi. Botticelli (Filipepi) is buried in the south transept. The sacristy has late 13C wall paintings, and works by Taddeo and Agnolo Gaddi.

From the **cloister** with 17C frescoes by Jacopo Ligozzi, Giovanni da San Giovanni, and others, is the entrance (**open** Monday, Tuesday, and Saturday 09.00–12.00) to the **refectory** with a *Last Supper* by Domenico Ghirlandaio. In the piazza is Palazzo Lenzi (now the French Consulate and French Institute) built c 1470, with restored graffiti.

Ponte Santa Trìnita (described below) crosses the Arno at the beginning of **Via Tornabuoni** (Pl. 7), the most elegant street in Florence with fashionable shops. Here is *Palazzo Spini-Feroni** (1269; restored), one of the best preserved and largest private medieval palaces in the city.

Santa Trìnita

Opposite is the church of *Santa Trìnita (Pl. 11), dating in its present Gothic form from the end of the 14C. The façade was added by Buontalenti in 1593.

On the west wall, the interior façade of the Romanesque building survives. **South aisle**. **Third chapel**, altarpiece by Neri di Bicci, and detached fresco and sinopia by Spinello Aretino; the **fourth chapel** is entirely frescoed by **Lorenzo Monaco**, who also painted the beautiful *altarpiece of the *Annunciation*; **fifth chapel**, part of a monument to St John Gualberto by Benedetto da Rovezzano. Outside the **choir chapels** are remains of frescoes by Giovanni del Ponte.

The *Sassetti Chapel** contains frescoes of the *Life of St Francis* by Domenico Ghirlandaio. They include views of Florence and portraits of the Medici and personages of the Renaissance city. The *altarpiece of the *Adoration of the Shepherds*, also by Ghirlandaio, is flanked by the donors, Francesco Sassetti and his wife Nera Corsi. Their tombs are attributed to Giuliano da Sangallo. In the sanctuary is a triptych by Mariotto di Nardo and remains of vault frescoes by Alesso Baldovinetti. In the second chapel left of the altar is the *tomb of Benozzo Federighi by Luca Della Robbia (1454–57).

North aisle, **Fifth chapel**, *Mary Magdalen*, a wooden statue by Desiderio da Settignano (finished by Benedetto da Maiano); fourth chapel, frescoes by Neri di Bicci and Bicci di Lorenzo; second chapel, paintings by Ridolfo del Ghirlandaio.

In Piazza Santa Trìnita, with the **Column of Justice**, a granite monolith from the Baths of Caracalla in Rome, are **Palazzo Buondelmonti**, with a façade attributed to Baccio d'Agnolo, and, perhaps, his best work, **Palazzo Bartolini Salimbeni**. Beyond several more handsome palaces rises the huge *Palazzo Strozzi** (Pl. 7; used for exhibitions), the last and grandest of the magnificent Renaissance palaces in Florence, built for Filippo Strozzi by Benedetto da Maiano in 1489 (and finished by Cronaca).

Via della Vigna Nuova leads past the home (1614) of Sir Robert Dudley, and the house where George Eliot stayed while gathering material for *Romola*, to *Palazzo Rucellai** (Pl. 6). This was designed for Giovanni Rucellai by Leon Battista Alberti and executed by Bernardo Rossellino (c 1446–51).

Behind the palace, the former church of **San Pancrazio**, has been converted into the **Museo Marino Marini** (open 10.00–17.00; fest. 10.00–13.00; closed Tues) displaying sculptures by Marino Marini (1901–80), who bequeathed them to the city. The fine classical porch is by Alberti. Important exhibitions are held in the crypt.

At No. 18 Via della Spada is the entrance to the remarkable **Cappella di San Sepolcro** (usually **open** only on Sat at 17.30 except July–Sept) built in 1467 also by Alberti for Giovanni Rucellai. It contains a *model in inlaid marble of the Sanctuary of the Holy Sepulchre.

At No. 19 Via Tornabuoni **Palazzo Larderel**, attributed to Giovanni Antonio Dosio, is a model of High Renaissance architecture. Opposite is the huge church of **San Gaetano**, the most important 17C church in the city (**open** 09.00–12.00; 15.30–18.00). The **façade** is by Pier Francesco Silvani, and the **interior** was built in *pietra serena* in 1604–49 by Matteo Nigetti and Gherardo Silvani. Nearly all the frescoes and altarpieces were painted in the 1630s and 1640s by Jacopo Vignali, Matteo Rosselli, Giovanni Bilivert, Lorenzo Lippi, and others.

*Palazzo Antinori** (Pl. 7), attributed to Giuliano da Maiano (1461–69), is one of the most beautiful smaller Renaissance palaces in Florence. Nearby, on Via de'Cerretani is the Gothic Cistercian church of **Santa Maria Maggiore** (**open** 07.00–12.00, 15.30–17.30. It contains frescoes by Mariotto di Nardo, a Byzantine relief in painted wood of the *Madonna enthroned* attributed to Coppo di Marcovaldo (removed for restoration), and an effigy of Bruno Beccuti attributed to Tino da Camaino.

Palazzo del Bargello

*Palazzo del Bargello (Pl. 11), a massive battlemented medieval fortified building in pietra forte, was erected in 1250 as the Palazzo del Popolo. Building was continued in the 14C and it was well restored in the 19C. At first the seat of the *Capitano del Popolo*, it became the residence of the Podestà, the governing magistrate of the city, at the end of the 13C. From the 16C, as the police headquarters, it became known as the *Bargello*.

Museo Nazionale del Bargello

The palace now contains the **Museo Nazionale del Bargello, famous for its superb collection of Florentine Renaissance sculpture, including numerous works by **Donatello** and the **della Robbia family**. 16C Florentine sculpture is well represented by **Michelangelo**, **Cellini**, and **Giambologna**, among others, and an exquisite collection of small Mannerist bronzes. There is also a notable collection of decorative arts (**open** 08.30–13.50; closed the 1st, 3rd, & 5th Sun of the month, and the 2nd & 4th Mon of the month).

The fine **hall** (right) contains 16C sculptures by Michelangelo and his Florentine contemporaries. Works by Michelangelo include: *Bacchus drunk* (an early work; c 1497); *tondo of the Madonna and Child with the infant St John* made for Bartolomeo Pitti; *bust of *Brutus* (c 1539–40); and *Apollo* (or *David*). Other sculptors well represented here include Jacopo Sansovino (Bacchus), Bartolomeo Ammannati, Bandinelli (bust of *Cosimo I, Adam and Eve*), De'Rossi (*Dying Adonis*), Cellini (*Narcissus, Apollo* and *Hyacinthus,* *bronzes from the pedestal of his statue of *Perseus*, bust of Cosimo I), and Giambologna (*Mercury*).

The Gothic **courtyard** displays more 16C sculptures. A room off the courtyard displays 14C sculpture (Arnolfo di Cambio, Tino da Camaino).

First floor

The **Loggia** contains more works by Giambologna. The **Salone del Consiglio Generale**, a fine vaulted hall, displays superb sculptures by **Donatello** and his contemporaries. Works by Donatello include: *St George* from Orsanmichele (in a reconstructed tabernacle), two statues of *David*, one in bronze and one in marble, *Atys-Amorino*, a bronze putto, the Marzocco (heraldic lion), a bust of a youth with a medallion at his neck, and *bust of Niccolò da Uzzano (the last two both attributed to Donatello). Also here: Desiderio da Settignano, *busts of a young woman and a boy; fine works by Giovanni di Bertoldo; Michelozzo, *reliefs of the Madonna; Luca della Robbia, *Madonnas* in enamelled terracotta, and two marble reliefs of St Peter; the two trial *reliefs of the *Sacrifice of Isaac* by Ghiberti and Brunelleschi made for the competition for the second bronze doors of the Baptistery; and a *reliquary urn by Ghiberti.

The other rooms on this floor contain a beautifully displayed *collection of **decorative arts** (seals, glass, enamels, ecclesiastical ornaments, jewellery, goldsmiths' work, *ivories, and majolica). The Cappella del Podestà contains restored frescoes attributed to the school of Giotto.

Second floor

Room 13 contains a number of colourful enamelled terracottas by Giovanni della Robbia and cases of medals and plaquettes. **Room 14** displays beautiful *works by Andrea della Robbia. **Room 15**: sculptures by **Verrocchio** and a number of fine Renaissance portrait busts. Works by Verrocchio include his bronze *David*, and a *bust of a *lady holding flowers*. Also here are works by: Antonio del Pollaiolo (*bust of a young cavalier, and *portrait-bust of a man); Mino da Fiesole (marble *portrait busts, and two *Madonnas*); Benedetto da Maiano (*Pietro Mellini*); Antonio Rossellino; and Francesco Laurana (*bust of *Battista Sforza*).

The **Medagliere Mediceo** (**Rooms 18** and **19**) contains the collection of Italian medals begun by Lorenzo il Magnifico, including works by Pisanello, and busts by Bernini and Algardi.

The **Salone del Camino** (**Room 16**) contains a superb display of small *Renaissance bronzes**, by Antonio Pollaiolo (*Hercules and Antaeus*), Cellini, Giambologna, Tacca, Tribolo, Bandinelli, Il Riccio, Danese Cattaneo, etc. The fine *chimneypiece is by Benedetto da Rovezzano. The anatomical figure made in wax by Lodovico Cigoli was cast by Giovanni Battista Foggini. Also on this floor (not always open) is a magnificent collection of *arms and armour.

In Piazza San Firenze is *Palazzo Gondi by Giuliano da Sangallo (c 1489), and San Firenze, a large building now occupied by the law courts, by Francesco Zanobi del Rosso (1772). Next door is the church of San Filippo Neri (1633) with an interior of 1712.

The Badia Fiorentina

Opposite the Bargello, in Via del Proconsolo, is the Badia Fiorentina (Pl. 11), the church of a Benedictine abbey founded in 978 by Willa, the widow of Uberto, Margrave of Tuscany. The graceful, slender campanile (undergoing a lengthy restoration) is Romanesque (1307) below and Gothic (after 1330) above.

The 17C interior (at present only open for services) contains a painting of the *Madonna appearing to St Bernard by Filippino Lippi; a sculpted altarpiece, the tomb of Bernardo Giugni, and (north transept), *monument to Ugo, Margrave of Tuscany, all by Mino da Fiesole; and frescoes attributed to Nardo di Cione.

The Chiostro degli Aranci (at present closed), by Bernardo Rossellino, has an interesting fresco cycle with scenes from the life of St Benedict by an artist known as the Maestro del Chiostro degli Aranci (c 1430).

Via Dante Alighieri leads left from Via del Proconsolo to Piazza San Martino with the splendid 13C Torre della Castagna, and the little chapel of San Martino del Vescovo decorated with charming frescoes by the workshop of Ghirlandaio (Francesco d'Antonio del Chierico?) illustrating the life of St Martin and works of charity. The area is traditionally associated with the great Florentine poet Dante Alighieri, who was probably born on the street that now bears his name. The so-called Casa di Dante is in a group of houses restored in the 13C style in 1911. In the little church of Santa Margherita de'Cerchi Dante is supposed to have married Gemma Donati (it contains an altarpiece by Neri di Bicci).

At No. 10 Via del Proconsolo is the handsome Palazzo Pazzi-Quaratesi attributed to Giuliano da Maiano. Here begins *Borgo degli Albizi, one of the most handsome streets in the city, lined with numerous fine palaces, including two (Nos 28 and 26) by Bartolomeo Ammannati. Across the borgo is Palazzo Nonfinito, begun in 1593 by Buontalenti. It now houses the Museo Nazionale di Antropologia ed Etnologia (open Thursday, Friday, Saturday, and the third Sunday of the month, 09.00–13.00), founded in 1869 by Paolo Mantegazza, and probably the most important museum of its kind in Italy. The most interesting material comes from Africa, North Pakistan, South America, Mexico, Asia. The exhibits from the Pacific Ocean were probably acquired by Captain Cook on his last voyage.

At No. 24 Via dell'Oriuolo is the Museo di Firenze com'era (Pl. 7; open 09.00–13.00; fest. 08.00–13.00; closed Thurs), a topographical historical museum of the city. The maps, paintings, and prints displayed in several rooms of the old Convento delle Oblate illustrate the life of the city since the 15C. Nearby is the hospital of Santa Maria Nuova founded in 1286 by Folco Portinari with a portico by Buontalenti, and the church of Sant'Egidio, both with a number of interesting works of art.

Piazza Santa Croce (Pl. 11), an attractive and spacious square, is the centre of a distinctive district of the city. Some houses in the piazza have projecting upper storeys resting on *sporti*. Palazzo dell'Antella, built by Giulio Parigi, has a worn polychrome façade painted in 1619. Palazzo Cocchi (Serristori) at the end of the square has recently been attributed to Giuliano da Sangallo.

Around Piazza Santa Croce

Santa Croce
*Santa Croce (Pl. 11,12), the Franciscan church of Florence, was rebuilt c 1294 possibly by Arnolfo di Cambio. The neo-Gothic **façade** dates from 1853.

The huge, wide **interior** (open 08.00–12.30, 15.00–18.30; summer 08.00–18.30; fest. 15.00–18.00) has an open timber roof. The Gothic church was rearranged by Vasari in 1560. For five hundred years it has been the custom to bury or erect monuments to notable citizens of Florence in this church; it is the burial place of Ghiberti, Michelangelo, Machiavelli, and Galileo.

South aisle. First pillar, *Madonna del Latte* a relief by Antonio Rossellino. The **tomb of Michelangelo** was designed by **Vasari**. The neo-classical cenotaph to **Dante** (buried in Ravenna) is by Stefano Ricci. The *pulpit is by Benedetto da Maiano. There follow monuments to Vittorio Alfieri (by Antonio Canova), and to **Niccolò Machiavelli** (by Innocenzo Spinazzi, 1787). The altarpieces in this aisle are by Vasari, Jacopo Coppi di Meglio, Alessandro del Barbiere (*Flagellation of Christ*), and Andrea del Minga (*Agony in the Garden*). By the side door is the *Cavalcanti tabernacle** with a beautiful high relief of the *Annunciation* by **Donatello**. The *tomb of Leonardo Bruni** by **Bernardo Rossellino** (c 1446–47) is one of the most harmonious and influential sepulchral monuments of the Renaissance.

South transept. The **Castellani Chapel** contains decorative *frescoes by Agnolo Gaddi and assistants. The **Baroncelli Chapel** has *frescoes by Taddeo Gaddi (father of Agnolo), a pupil of Giotto. The restored altarpiece of the *Coronation of the Virgin* is by Giotto and his workshop. Also here is a 15C fresco of the *Madonna* by Sebastiano Mainardi, and a 16C statue of the *Madonna and Child* by Vincenzo Danti.

The *Sacristy** has frescoes by Taddeo Gaddi, Spinello Aretino (attributed), and Nicolò di Pietro Gerini, and, in the **Rinuccini Chapel**, *frescoes by Giovanni da Milano, one of the most gifted followers of Giotto. The **Medici Chapel** by Michelozzo contains an *altarpiece by Andrea della Robbia.

Bardi and Peruzzi Chapels. The small rectangular vaulted **chapels at the east end** are famous for their **frescoes by Giotto** and his school. The two chapels right of the sanctuary were decorated by Giotto; the frescoes are damaged and in poor condition. The *Peruzzi Chapel** contains scenes from the life of *St John the Evangelist* and of *St John the Baptist* painted in his maturity (the altarpiece is by Taddeo Gaddi); the frescoes illustrating the story of *St Francis* in the *Bardi Chapel** were designed by Giotto, but some of them may have been executed by his pupils. The painting of *St Francis* on the altar dates from the 13C.

The **sanctuary** is frescoed with the *Legend of the Cross* by Agnolo Gaddi (c 1380), who also designed the fine stained glass lancet windows. The polyptych is by Nicolò Gerini and Giovanni del Biondo, and the *Crucifix* above by the Master of Figline. In the last two east chapels are frescoes of the *Lives of St Lawrence and St Stephen* by Bernardo Daddi, and colourful and well-preserved frescoes of the *Life of St Sylvester* by Maso di Banco, perhaps the most original follower of Giotto, who also probably painted the *Last Judgement* in the Gothic tomb here.

North transept. The **Niccolini Chapel** designed by Giovanni Antonio Dosio, has frescoes by Volterrano, statues by Francavilla, and paintings by Alessandro Allori. The second **Bardi Chapel** contains a wooden *Crucifix* by Donatello. The story told by Vasari of Brunelleschi's complaint that it was a mere peasant on the cross is now thought to be apocryphal. In the **Salviati Chapel** is the *tomb of Princess Sofia Czartoryska (d. 1837) with a Romantic effigy by Lorenzo Bartolini.

North aisle. By the side door, *monument to Carlo Marsuppini** (d. 1453) by Desiderio da Settignano. The classical sarcophagus may be the work of Verrocchio. In the pavement between the fifth and fourth altars is the handsome tomb-slab with niello decoration of Lorenzo Ghiberti, and his son Vittorio. The **monument to Galileo Galilei** (1564–1642) was set up by Giovanni Battista Foggini in 1737 when the great scientist was allowed Christian burial inside the church. In the nave is the tomb-slab of his ancestor and namesake, a well-known physician in 15C Florence. The altarpieces in this aisle are by Giovanni Stradano, Santi di Tito (*Supper at Emmaus* and *Resurrection*), and Giovanni Battista Naldini.

Museo dell'Opera di Santa Croce
On the right of the church is the entrance to the conventual buildings and the Museo dell'Opera di Santa Croce (Pl. 12; open 10.00–12.30, 14.30–18.30; winter, 10.00–12.30, 15.00–17.00; closed Wednesday).

In the first cloister (14C) is the charming *Cappella dei Pazzi**, one of the most famous works of Brunelleschi (1442–46). The **portico** may have been designed by Giuliano da Maiano; the shallow cupola bears delightful enamelled terracotta decoration by Luca della Robbia, who also made the medallion with *St Andrew over the door. The beautiful calm **interior** is one of the masterpieces of the early Renaissance. The twelve *roundels of the seated Apostles are by Luca della Robbia; the polychrome roundels of the Evangelists may have been designed by Donatello. The **second cloister** is another beautiful work by Brunelleschi.

Off the first cloister is the entrance to the Museo dell'Opera di Santa Croce. In the fine Gothic **refectory** is displayed Cimabue's great *Crucifix* which has been restored after it was almost completely destroyed in the flood of 1966. The huge *fresco** of the *Last Supper* on the end wall and below the *Tree of the Cross* is by **Taddeo Gaddi**. Also here are fragments of a large fresco by Orcagna of the *Triumph of Death and Inferno* detached from the nave of the church, and several other fine 14C–15C frescoes (including one with a view of the Baptistery and Duomo). In a reconstructed tabernacle is Donatello's colossal gilded bronze *St Louis of Toulouse*, from Orsanmichele. The other rooms contain more frescoes (14C–17C), della Robbian terracottas, interesting large sketches detached from walls of the Cappella dei Pazzi, and sculptures by Tino da Camaino. Beneath the colonnade, just before the exit from the cloister, is a memorial to Florence Nightingale, named after the city where she was born.

To the right of Santa Croce is the huge **Biblioteca Nazionale** (severely damaged in 1966). At the other end of Piazza Santa Croce **Via dei Benci**, with its old rusticated houses, runs towards the Arno. The polygonal 13C Torre degli Alberti has a 15C loggia below. Nearby (No. 20) is **Palazzo Mellini Fossi** with a frescoed façade (beautifully restored in 1996) dating from 1575. Palazzo Bardi alle Grazie (No. 5) is an early Renaissance palace attributed to Brunelleschi; No. 1, Palazzo Malenchini was reconstructed on the site of a 14C palace of the Alberti where the great architect Leon Battista died in 1472.

Off the interesting old Via dei Neri a road (right) leads to the **church of San Remigio**, founded in the 11C. The fine Gothic interior (often closed) contains a *Madonna and Child* by a follower of Cimabue known as the Master of San Remigio. Nearby is the interesting medieval Piazza Peruzzi, and Via dei Bentaccordi which takes its shape from the curve of the Roman amphitheatre (2C–3C AD) once on this site. The church of **San Simone,** founded in 1192–93, has a fine interior by Gherardo Silvani (1630), and an altarpiece of *St Peter enthroned* (1307); opposite is Palazzo da Cintoia, one of the best preserved medieval palaces in the city.

Casa Buonarroti

From the north side of Santa Croce Via delle Pinzochere leads to Via Ghibellina, where, at No. 70 is the *Casa Buonarroti (Pl. 12; **open** 09.30–13.30 exc Tues); a charming museum, usually uncrowded, and extremely well maintained. Three houses on this site were purchased in 1508 by Michelangelo who left the property to his only descendant, his nephew Leonardo.

The **ground floor** is used for interesting exhibitions. Also displayed here are: a statue of *Venus* attributed to Vincenzo Danti, and part of the eclectic collection of antiquities and Renaissance works made by Michelangelo's descendants, including a copy from Titian of a *love scene and Etruscan stelae.

First floor. Two early works by Michelangelo: ***Madonna of the Steps**, a marble bas-relief, carved at the age of 15 or 16, and a **battle relief**, modelled on a Roman sarcophagus. The wooden model for the façade of San Lorenzo was designed by Michelangelo (but never carried out). The *torso, a model in clay and wood for a river god, is also by Michelangelo. A selection of his **drawings** owned by the museum are shown in rotation.

The four rooms decorated in 1613 by Michelangelo Buonarroti the Younger in celebration of his great-uncle and his family, contain paintings by Cristofano Allori, Giovanni Biliverti, Empoli, Giovanni da San Giovanni, Matteo Rosselli, Jacopo Vignali, and others. Also here: *portrait of Michelangelo* attributed to Giuliano Bugiardini, a predella by Giovanni di Francesco, Roman and Etruscan sculpture and small bronzes, and bozzetti by Michelangelo (the allegorical model in terracotta in case 408), and his followers including Tribolo. The ***Crucifix** in painted poplar wood was found in Santo Spirito in 1963 and is now generally attributed to Michelangelo (it is to be returned to the church).

The church of **Sant'Ambrogio** (Pl. 8), to the north, was rebuilt in the late 13C. It contains a number of interesting frescoes including a *Madonna enthroned with saints*, attributed to the school of Orcagna. In the chapel on the left of the high altar is an exquisite ***tabernacle** by **Mino da Fiesole** (who is buried here), and a large *fresco by Cosimo Rosselli of a procession with a miraculous chalice (preserved here) in front of the church. On the north side, *Angels and Saints* by Alesso Baldovinetti surrounding a *Nativity* by his pupil Graffione. Cronaca (d. 1508) and Verrocchio (d. 1488) are both buried here.

Nearby is the produce **market of Sant'Ambrogio** and the *Mercatino*, a flea market in Piazza dei Ciompi, with Vasari's graceful Loggia del Pesce (removed from the Mercato Vecchio). Lorenzo Ghiberti lived in Piazza dei Ciompi, and Cimabue lived in Borgo Allegri which was given this name, according to Vasari, after his painting of the *Maestà* (now in the Uffizi) left his studio in a joyous procession down the street.

To the north, beyond the huge **Synagogue** (1874–82) with a green dome (and a small museum), is the ex-convent of **Santa Maria Maddalena dei Pazzi** (Pl. 8), on Borgo Pinti (No. 56). The *cloister is by Giuliano da Sangallo. The church has a fine Baroque sanctuary (1675, by Ciro Ferri) and altarpieces by Carlo Portelli, Matteo Rosselli, Domenico Puligo, and Santi di Tito. In the **Chapter House** (open 09.00–12.00, 17.00–19.00; or ring at No. 58) is a beautiful and very well preserved *fresco of the *Crucifixion and Saints* by **Perugino**, one of his masterpieces.

Along the Arno

Ponte alla Carraia (Pl. 10), first constructed in 1218–20, was the second bridge to be built over the Arno. It was rebuilt and repaired several times, and reconstructed after it was blown up in 1944. At the north end, Lungarno Vespucci, opened in the 19C, leads away from the centre of the city towards the park of the Cascine past two modern bridges.

The **Cascine** (Pl. 1,5) is a huge public park (not as well maintained as it might be, and not safe at night) which skirts the Arno for 3.5km. It was used as a ducal chase by the Medici grand-dukes in the 17C, and festivals were held here. It was first opened regularly to the public c 1811. In these gardens the *Ode to the West Wind* was conceived and chiefly written by Shelley in 1819. At the far end is a monument to the Maharajah of Kolhapur who died in Florence in 1870. From here the view is dominated by a suspension bridge (1978) over the Arno.

Lungarno Corsini leads past the huge **Palazzo Corsini** (Pl.1, 5) built between 1656 and c 1737 in a grandiose Roman Baroque style. It contains the most important private art collection in Florence (adm. by appointment only at 11 Via Parione). In rooms frescoed by Alessandro Gherardini and Antonio Domenico Gabbiani it is particularly interesting for its **paintings of the 17C Florentine school**. It also contains a *Madonna* by Pontormo, a *Crucifix* by Giovanni Bellini, a cartoon attributed to Raphael of his portrait of Julius II, and works attributed to Signorelli and Filippino Lippi. The palace is also now used for important exhibitions.

Farther on is **Palazzo Masetti** (now the British Consulate) where the Countess of Albany, widow of Prince Charles Edward Stuart, lived from 1793 to her death.

*Ponte Santa Trìnita** (Pl. 10) was first built in 1252. The present bridge is an exact replica of the bridge begun by Ammannati in 1567 and destroyed in 1944. The high flat arches (catenaries) which span the river recreate the unique curve of a chain suspended from two terminal points. They are perfectly proportioned and the bridge provides a magnificent view of the city. The statue of *Spring* on the parapet is the best work of Pietro Francavilla (1593).

Lungarno Acciaioli continues to **Ponte Vecchio** (described above). The modern buildings on both banks of the river near the bridge replaced the medieval houses which were blown up in 1944 by the Germans in order to render Ponte Vecchio impassable.

Museo di Storia della Scienza

Beyond the Uffizi lies Piazza dei Giudici with the medieval Palazzo Castellani which now contains the *Museo di Storia della Scienza (Pl. 11; **open** 09.30–13.00; Mon, Wed & Fri also 14.00–17.00; closed fest.), a beautifully displayed and well maintained collection of scientific instruments. A large part of the collection was owned by the Medici grand-dukes. Excellent hand-lists are lent to visitors.

First floor. **Room I**: astrolabes, quadrants, solar clocks, and mathematical instruments. **Room II**: German instruments, and navigational instruments, including some invented by Sir Robert Dudley. **Room III**: scientific instruments made for the Medici grand-dukes. **Room IV**: precious collection of instruments which belonged to **Galileo**, including his compass, the lens he used in discovering the four largest moons of Jupiter (cracked by him before he presented it to Ferdinando II), and the Giovilabio; models of his inventions. **Room V**: astronomy, including Galileo's two wooden telescopes. **Room VI**: lenses and prisms. **Room VII**: globes, including the armillary sphere made by Antonio Santucci in 1588. **Room VIII**: microscopes. **Room IX**: material relating to the Accademia del Cimento, an experimental academy founded by Cardinal Leopoldo in 1657 (including elaborate glass). **Room X**: barometers, thermometers and rain gauges. **Room XI**: astronomy in the 18C and 19C (large telescopes). *Second floor*. **Room XII**: mechanical clocks. **Room XIII**: mathematical instruments (18C–19C). **Room XIV**: magnetic and electrostatic machines. **Room XV**: pneumatic apparatus. **Rooms XVI–XVII**: demonstration models made in 1775 illustrating mechanical principals. **Room XVIII**: surgical instruments and anatomical models. **Room XIX**: history of pharmaceutical research. **Room XX**: instruments concerning fluids and gases. **Room XXI**: weights and measures.

Upstream is **Ponte alle Grazie** (Pl. 11), first built in 1237 and replaced after 1944 by a modern bridge. Via dei Benci leads northwards away from the bridge.

Museo Horne

Here, at No. 6 Palazzo Corsi, attributed to Cronaca, is the **Museo Horne** (Pl. 11; **open** 09.00–13.00, except fest.). The interesting collection of 14C–16C paintings, sculptures, and decorative arts (notable furniture and majolica) was presented to the nation, along with his house, by the English art historian Herbert Percy Horne (1864–1916). A handlist is lent to visitors.

First floor. Paintings by Masaccio (attributed), Pietro Lorenzetti, Bernardo Daddi, Benozzo Gozzoli, **Giotto** (*St Stephen*), Filippino Lippi, Beccafumi (*tondo of the Holy Family*), and Renaissance sculptures. *Second floor*. 15C furniture, and paintings by the Master of the Horne Triptych, Neri di Bicci, and Simone Martini (attributed).

Museo Bardini

Across the river, at the other end of the bridge is Piazza dei Mozzi, with the large Palazzo Bardini (No. 1), built by the famous antiquarian and collector Stefano Bardini in 1883. It houses his huge art collection, bequeathed to the city in 1923 as the Museo Bardini (Pl. 11; temporarily closed).

His eclectic collection includes architectural fragments, sculpture, paintings, the decorative arts, furniture, ceramics, carpets, arms and armour, and musical instruments, etc. Many of the rooms were built specially to contain the fine doorways, staircases, and ceilings from demolished buildings. The rooms are crowded with a miscellany of works.

Ground floor. Medieval and Renaissance architectural fragments; classical sculpture; medieval sculpture (statue of *Charity* attributed to Tino da Camaino); altarpiece attributed to Andrea della Robbia.

First floor. Armour; sculpture (reliefs attributed to Donatello); paintings (*St Michael* by Antonio Pollaiolo); and musical instruments.

The Palazzi dei Mozzi, on Via de'Bardi, built in the 13C–14C are among the most splendid private houses of medieval Florence. The severe façades in pietra forte have arches on the ground floor. The building, together with a huge collection of decorative arts, was left to the State in 1965 by Ugo, son of Stefano Bardini, and there are long-term plans to open it to the public, along with the huge garden which climbs the hillside behind.

*Via di San Niccolò, a narrow medieval street, leads left to the church of **San Niccolò Sopr'Arno** (Pl. 11), with several interesting 15C frescoes, including the *Madonna della Cintola* (in the sacristy), attributed to Alesso Baldovinetti, and *St Ansano*, attributed to Francesco d'Antonio. The road continues past the pretty 14C Porta San Miniato (right) to the massive Porta San Niccolò with a high medieval tower (c 1340).

The winding *Via de'Bardi leads right from Piazza dei Mozzi past a series of fine old town houses back to Ponte Vecchio.

The Oltrarno

In the characteristic district on the south bank of the Arno known as the *Oltrarno*, the two most important churches are Santo Spirito and Santa Maria del Carmine, and around them focuses the life of this part of the city.

Santo Spirito

The church of *Santo Spirito (Pl. 10; **open** 10.00–12.00, 16.00–18.00 exc Wed pm) was rebuilt by Brunelleschi in 1444. Building was continued after his death by Antonio Manetti and others. The slender campanile is by Baccio d'Agnolo (1503), and the modest façade dates from the 18C.

The *interior*, designed by Brunelleschi, was executed mostly after his death and modified in the late 15C. It is remarkable for its harmonious proportions, its solemn colour, and the perspective of the colonnades and vaulted aisles. The plan is a Latin cross with a dome over the crossing. The columns, with fine Corinthian capitals, are carried round the transepts and east end forming an unbroken arcade with 38 chapels in semi-circular niches.

The Baroque **high altar** by Giovanni Caccini disturbs the harmony of the architecture. The interior façade was designed by Salvi d'Andrea (1483–87), and the stained glass oculus is from a cartoon by Perugino.

South aisle chapels. 2nd chapel, *Pietà*, a free copy of Michelangelo's famous sculpture in St Peter's by Nanni di Baccio Bigio; **4th chapel**, Giovanni Stradano, *Christ expelling the money-changers from the temple*; **6th chapel**, Passignano, *Martyrdom of St Stephen*.

South transept chapels. 10th chapel, *Madonna del Soccorso*, a painting of the early 15C; **12th chapel**, Filippino Lippi, **Madonna and Child, with the young St John, saints, and donors*, one of his finest works; **13th chapel**, Felice Ficherelli, copy of Perugino's *Vision of St Bernard*, now in Munich; **14th chapel**, Giovanni Camillo Sagrestani, *Marriage of the Virgin* (1713), his best work.

Chapels at the east end. 15th chapel, *Madonna and Saints*, a good painting in the style of Lorenzo di Credi; **16th chapel**, Maso di Banco, polyptych; **17th chapel**, Aurelio Lomi, *Epiphany*; **18th & 19th chapels**, Alessandro Allori, *martyred saints*, **Christ and the adulteress*; **21st & 22nd chapels**, 15C Florentine paintings.

North transept chapels, 23rd chapel, Agnolo and Donnino di Domenico Mazziere, *Madonna enthroned between Saints*; **24th chapel**, **St Monica and Augustinian nuns in black habits*, traditionally attributed to Botticini, but possibly by Verrocchio; **25th chapel**, Cosimo Rosselli, *Madonna enthroned between Saints*; **26th chapel**, sculpted **altarpiece by Andrea Sansovino; **27th chapel**, **Trinity with Saints*, a good painting of the late 15C, by the Mazziere brothers; **28th chapel**, Raffaellino dei Carli, **Madonna enthroned with Saints*.

A door beneath the organ in the north aisle leads into a grandiose ****vestibule** built by Cronaca in 1491. The ****sacristy**, taking its inspiration from Brunelleschi, was designed by Giuliano da Sangallo.

To the left of the church, at No. 29, is the entrance to the **Cenacolo di Santo Spirito** (open 09.00–14.00; fest 08.00–13.00; closed Mon) in the refectory of the 14C convent; the only part of it of this date to survive. Above a fresco of the *Last Supper* (almost totally ruined) is a huge **Crucifixion*, both of them painted c 1360–65 and attributed to Andrea Orcagna and his bottega. Also displayed here is the **Fondazione Salvatore Romano**, an interesting collection of sculpture, notable for its Romanesque works. There are two statuettes by Tino da Camaino, and sculptures attributed to Jacopo della Quercia, Donatello, and Ammannati.

Piazza Santo Spirito is one of the most attractive little squares in the city, the scene of a small daily market. ****Palazzo Guadagni** (No. 10) was probably built by Cronaca c 1505. Via Sant'Agostino leads to Via de' Serragli, a long straight road with handsome 17C–18C palaces. Via Santa Monica continues past a tabernacle by Lorenzo di Bicci into **Piazza del Carmine**.

Santa Maria del Carmine

Here is the rough stone façade of the church of Santa Maria del Carmine (Pl. 10), famous for its frescoes by Masaccio in the Cappella Brancacci, which escaped destruction in a fire in 1771 that ruined the rest of the first church.

Open 09.00–12.00, 16.30–18.00. Brancacci Chapel **open** 10.00– 17.00 (fest. 13.00–17.00) except Tues.

The huge, broad **interior** was rebuilt in an undistinguished late Baroque style. At the end of the north transept is the sumptuous ****Chapel of Sant'Andrea Corsini** by Pier Francesco Silvani, one of the best Baroque works in

Florence. The ceiling is by Luca Giordano, and the marble and silver reliefs by Giovanni Battista Foggini. The Gothic **sacristy** has frescoes from the life of St Cecilia by the school of Bicci di Lorenzo.

The Brancacci Chapel

The ****Brancacci Chapel**, in the south transept, is now entered at No. 14 in the piazza through the early 17C cloisters. The **frescoes** illustrating the life of St Peter were commissioned by Felice Brancacci c 1424 from **Masolino** and **Masaccio**. Seriously damaged in the 18C and 19C, they were restored in 1983–89, and many of the details formerly obscured by surface mould can now be seen. The design of the whole fresco cycle may be due to Masolino, but his pupil Masaccio seems to have continued work on them alone in 1428. Later that year Masaccio himself broke off work abruptly on the frescoes and left for Rome where, by the end of the year, he had died at the early age of 27. The frescoes were at once recognised as a masterpiece and profoundly influenced Florentine art of the Renaissance. All the major artists of the 15C came here to study the frescoes which combine a perfect application of the new rules of perspective with a remarkable use of chiaroscuro. The cycle was completed only some 50 years later by Filippino Lippi (c 1480–85) who carefully integrated his style with that of Masaccio, possibly following an earlier design.

The **frescoes** are arranged in two registers. **Upper row** (right to left): Masolino, *Temptation of Adam and Eve*; Masolino, *St Peter, accompanied by St John, brings Tabitha to life and heals a lame man* (the figures on the extreme left may be by Masaccio); Masaccio, **St Peter baptising*; Masolino, *St Peter preaching*; Masaccio, **The Tribute money*, perhaps the painter's masterpiece; Masaccio, **Expulsion from Paradise*, one of his most moving works.

Lower row (right to left): Filippino Lippi, **Release of St Peter from prison*; Filippino Lippi, *Saints Peter and Paul before the proconsul*, and *Crucifixion of St Peter*; Masaccio, *Saints Peter and John distributing alms*; Masaccio, **St Peter, followed by St John, healing the sick with his shadow*; Masaccio, **St Peter enthroned with portraits of friars*, his last work, and *St Peter bringing to life the Emperor's nephew*, finished by Filippino; Filippino Lippi, *St Peter in prison visited by St Paul*. The altarpiece of the *Madonna del Popolo* is a Tuscan Byzantine work of the mid-13C attributed to Coppo di Marcovaldo.

Borgo San Frediano (Pl. 10,9), at the north end of the piazza, gives its name to a characteristic district with numerous artisans' houses and workshops. The large church of **San Frediano in Cestello** with its main entrance on the Arno was rebuilt with a fine dome in the 17C by Antonio Maria Ferri. It contains late 17C and early 18C paintings and frescoes by Francesco Curradi, Jacopo del Sellaio, Giovanni Camillo Sagrestani, Alessandro Gherardini, Antonio Domenico Gabbiani, and others.

The fortified **Porta San Frediano** (Pl. 5,9) is the best preserved part of the last circle of city walls built by the commune in 1284–1333. The gate, built in 1324, perhaps by Andrea Pisano, has a high tower and huge wooden doors.

Via di Santo Spirito (Pl. 10) runs parallel to the Arno in the other direction, past the 17C Palazzo Rinuccini, Palazzo Manetti with a 15C façade (the home of Sir Horace Mann in 1740–86 while he was serving as English envoy to the Tuscan court), and Palazzo Frescobaldi. On Lungarno Guicciardini (Pl. 10) is

Palazzo Lanfredini by Baccio d'Agnolo with bright (restored) graffiti decoration. On the first floor is the library of the **British Institute** (see p. 41). A non-profit making independent Institution, it was founded in 1917, and received a royal Charter in 1923. Its scope is to promote British culture in Italy and Italian culture to English-speaking visitors. The excellent lending library (c. 50,000 volumes) has the largest collection of English books in Italy. The institute also runs a well-known language school at No. 2 Piazza Strozzi.

From the foot of Ponte Santa Trìnita the handsome **Via Maggio** (Pl. 10) leads away from the Arno. Its name (from *Maggiore*) is a reminder of its origin as the principal and widest street of the Oltrarno. Palazzo Ricasoli (No. 7) was built at the end of the 15C. Palazzo Machiavelli (No. 16–18) was bought in 1877–1905 by **St Mark's Anglican Church**. The church, in part of the ground floor, was designed in 1877–79 for Anglo-Catholic zealots led by the Rev. Charles Tooth, and its pre-Raphaelite decoration survives virtually intact. It can usually be visited on request (10.00–12.00) at the vicar's residence on the floor above, and services are held every Sun at 10.30 am. Palazzo di Bianca Cappello (No. 26), with good graffiti decoration attributed to Bernardino Poccetti, was built by the Grand-duke Francesco I for Bianca Cappello. Palazzo Ridolfi (No. 13) dates from the late 16C, and Palazzo Commenda di Firenze (No. 42), first built in the late 14C, was reconstructed in the 16C.

Via Maggio ends in **Piazza San Felice** (Pl. 10). No. 8 is the 15C **Casa Guidi** (open Apr–Nov, Mon, Wed, & Fri 15.00–18.00; ring the bell), where **Robert and Elizabeth Barrett Browning** rented a flat on the first floor and lived after their secret marriage in 1846 until Elizabeth's death in 1861. Since 1993 it has been owned by Eton College and is leased to the Landmark Trust. It has been restored as far as possible to its simple appearance in the Brownings' day: during their stay here both poets wrote some of their most important works, including Elizabeth's *Casa Guidi Windows,* and Robert's *The Ring and the Book.*

San Felice is a Gothic church with a Renaissance façade by Michelozzo. It contains a large **Crucifix* attributed to Giotto or his workshop, a *Triptych* by Neri di Bicci, and a *Triptych* by a follower of Botticelli.

Via Romana continues southwest to Porta Romana (Pl. 13), a well-preserved gate built in 1327 on a design by Andrea Orcagna. No. 17, Palazzo Torrigiani, was built in 1775 as a natural history museum, known as **La Specola**. Here in 1814 Sir Humphry Davy and Michael Faraday used Galileo's great burning glass to explode the diamond. It now contains a **Zoological Museum** (open 09.00–13.00 except Wed) with a remarkable collection of anatomical models in wax, many of them by Clemente Susini (1775–1814).

In **Piazza Pitti**, dominated by the huge Palazzo Pitti (see p. 67), the pretty row of houses facing the palace includes the home of Paolo dal Pozzo Toscanelli (1397–1482), the famous scientist and geographer. While staying at No. 21 in 1868 Dostoyevsky wrote *The Idiot.*

Via Guicciardini continues to Ponte Vecchio; on the left is the ancient Borgo San Jacopo with the Torre Marsili di Borgo, a fine towerhouse, and the church of **San Jacopo sopr'Arno** with an 11C portico transported here in the 16C from a demolished church.

To San Miniato

San Miniato can be reached directly from the station or Piazza Duomo by Bus 12 or 13, or on foot by the steps from Porta San Niccolò (Pl. 12). However, if you have time, the following route on foot is highly recommended (and Bus 12 or 13 can be taken back from San Miniato).

Near Ponte Vecchio the narrow Costa San Giorgio (Pl. 11) winds up the hill towards Forte di Belvedere past the pretty Costa Scarpuccia (left). The church of **San Giorgio sulla Costa** has a good Baroque interior by Giovanni Battista Foggini, altarpieces by Tommaso Redi, Jacopo Vignali, and Passignano. Beyond the house (No. 19) purchased by Galileo for his son Vincenzio, the road reaches **Porta San Giorgio** with a fresco by Bicci di Lorenzo. Built in 1260 this is the oldest gate in the city to have survived. Here is the entrance to *Forte di Belvedere** (Pl. 11, 15), a huge fortress designed by Buontalenti for Ferdinando I in 1590. From the ramparts (**open** 09.00–20.00 except when exhibitions are being mounted or dismantled) there is a splendid *view** in every direction. There is a gate (and ticket office) for the Boboli Gardens (see p. 71).

*Via di San Leonardo** (Pl. 15), one of the most beautiful country roads on the outskirts of the city, leads to the church of **San Leonardo in Arcetri** which contains an early 13C *pulpit, and several 15C paintings.

*Via di Belvedere (Pl. 15), a picturesque country lane, follows the straight line of the city walls (first built in 1258) from Forte di Belvedere to Porta San Miniato. From here Via del Monte alle Croci or Via di San Salvatore al Monte return uphill.

San Miniato al Monte

Across the busy Viale Galileo, a monumental flight of steps leads up past a cemetery (1839) to *San Miniato al Monte (Pl. 16; closed in winter 12.00–14.00; in summer 13.00–15.00).

The finest of all Tuscan Romanesque basilicas, with its famous **façade**, it is one of the most beautiful churches in Italy. Its position on a green hill above the city is incomparable. Deacon Minias is thought to have been martyred c 250 during the persecutions of Emperor Decius and buried on this hillside. The church was built in 1013 by Bishop Hildebrand on the site of Decius' tomb.

The *façade**, begun c 1090, is built of white and dark greenish marble in a beautiful geometrical design reminiscent of the Baptistery. The mosaic (restored) of *Christ between the Virgin and St Minias* dates from the 13C. The tympanum is crowned by an eagle, emblem of the Arte di Calimala (the cloth-importers guild) who looked after the fabric of the building.

The fine *interior** built in 1018–63, with a raised choir above a large hall crypt, is practically in its original state. In the centre of the pavement are seven superb marble intarsia *panels (1207) with signs of the zodiac and animal motifs. At the end of the nave is the *Cappella del Crocifisso**, an exquisite tabernacle by Michelozzo (1448). The painted panels are by Agnolo Gaddi, and the enamelled terracotta roof and ceiling by Luca della Robbia.

In the aisles are a number of 13C–15C frescoes. On the north wall is the *Chapel of the Cardinal of Portugal**, begun by Antonio Manetti in 1460. The exquisitely carved *tomb of the Cardinal is by Antonio Rossellino and the ceiling, with five *medallions, by Luca della Robbia. The altarpiece of *Three Saints* by Antonio and Piero del Pollaiolo is a copy of the original in the Uffizi. The

Annunciation is by Alesso Baldovinetti. Before the **choir** is a beautiful marble *transenna** dating from 1207, and *pulpit**. The low columns in the choir have huge antique capitals. The large apse mosaic, representing *Christ between the Virgin and St Minias* (1297), was first restored in 1491 by Alesso Baldovinetti.

The **sacristy** (south side) is entirely frescoed with scenes from the *Life of St Benedict*, one of the best works of **Spinello Aretino** (restored in 1840). The 11C Crypt has slender columns with antique capitals. The original 11C altar contains the relics of St Minias. The frescoes are by Taddeo Gaddi.

The massive stone **campanile** was begun after 1523, but never finished. During the siege of Florence (1530) Michelangelo mounted two cannon here, and protected the bell-tower from hostile artillery by a screen of mattresses. The battlemented **Bishop's Palace** dates from 1295 (restored). There is a splendid **view** from the terrace in front of the church.

In a grove of cypresses on the side of the hill is the church of **San Salvatore Al Monte**, a building of gracious simplicity by Cronaca, called by Michelangelo his *bella villanella* (his pretty country maid). Steps lead down to **Piazzale Michelangelo** (Pl. 16), a celebrated viewpoint much visited by tourists. From the balustrade on the huge terrace is a remarkable panorama of the city. **Viale dei Colli** (bus 13), a fine roadway 6km long, was laid out by Giuseppe Poggi in 1865–70. It is one of the most panoramic drives near Florence.

The Viali

The wide avenues (or *viali*) form a ring-road busy with traffic around the centre of the city, north of the Arno. They were laid out in 1865–69 by Giuseppe Poggi after he had demolished the last circle of walls built in 1284–1333; he left some of the medieval gates as isolated monuments.

Viale Filippo Strozzi skirts the huge **Fortezza da Basso** (Pl. 2). This massive fortress, on a grand scale (with its exterior wall still intact), was built for Alessandro de'Medici in 1534 by Antonio da Sangallo. It became a symbol of Medici tyranny, and Alessandro was assassinated here by his cousin Lorenzino in 1537. It is now used partly as a restoration laboratory for paintings, by the Opificio delle Pietre Dure—one of the two official schools of restoration in Italy—and partly as an international exhibition centre. Public gardens have been laid out on the glacis.

From the Fortezza a bus (No. 4 from Piazza Unità d'Italia near the station) runs northeast to the *Museo Stibbert** (open 10.00–13.00, Fri, Sat & Sun, 10.00–18.00; winter 10.00–14.00, Sat 10.00–18.00; closed Thurs). It was created by Frederick Stibbert (1838–1906), born in Florence (his mother was Italian). His eclectic collection, with an extraordinary variety of objects, is crammed into 57 period rooms designed by him, producing a remarkably bizarre atmosphere. Stibbert was particularly interested in armour and costume, and the museum is famous for its armour (including a remarkable collection of Asiatic armour). The park, also created by Stibbert, is open daily (09.00–dusk except Thur morning and Sun afternoon).

Across Viale Strozzi is **Palazzo dei Congressi** (1964), an international conference centre. At No. 14 is the **Istituto Geografico Militare**, the most important cartographical institute in Italy. Viale Lavagnini continues towards Piazza della Libertà. In Via Leone X (left) is the delightful **Russian Church**

(Pl. 3) built in 1904 by Russian architects. It is owned by the Russian Orthodox community of Florence and is open for services on the third Sunday of the month. In the arcaded **Piazza della Libertà** is the medieval Porta San Gallo and a triumphal arch erected in 1739.

To the north of the square is Ponte Rosso near which is the entrance to the **Giardino dell'Orticoltura**, a horticultural garden created in 1859 (**open** daily) with an elaborate greenhouse (1880; by Giacomo Roster). Via Bolognese begins here and leads uphill out of the city (bus 25) past a number of villas including **Villa La Pietra** (No. 120), the former residence of the aesthete and historian Sir Harold Acton (1904–94) and left by him to New York University. The beautiful Italianate *garden (with topiary laid out in 1904) can sometimes be seen by written application, ☎ 055-474448. The villa contains one of the most interesting private art collections in Florence (no admission).

The Viali continue to **Piazza Donatello**, in the centre of which is the **English Cemetery** (Pl. 4; **open** 09.00–13.00, 15.00–17.00, except fest. Ring at the main gate) on a mound shaded by cypresses. Here are buried Elizabeth Barrett Browning, Isa Blagden, Arthur Hugh Clough, Walter Savage Landor, Frances Trollope, Theodore Parker of Lexington, Robert Davidsohn, the German historian of Florence and Gian Pietro Vieusseux the Swiss bibliophile.

San Salvi

From the next square, **Piazza Beccaria** (Pl. 8,12), the ex-convent of San Salvi is reached (bus 6 from the Duomo and Piazza San Marco). In the refectory (entrance at No. 16 Via San Salvi; **open** 08.30–13.50 exc the 1st, 3rd, and 5th Sun of the month and the 2nd and 4th Monday of the month) is the celebrated *Cenacolo di San Salvi** by **Andrea del Sarto** (c 1520–25), a masterpiece of Florentine fresco, remarkable for its colouring, and one of the most famous frescoes depicting the *Last Supper* in Italy. 16C altarpieces and other works by Andrea del Sarto are displayed in the conventual buildings.

Nearby is the sports ground of Campo di Marte with the **Stadio Comunale**, a remarkable building (1932) by Pier Luigi Nervi (enlarged in 1990).

2 · Environs of Florence

San Domenico and Fiesole

The small town of Fiesole is the most famous place in the immediate environs of Florence and is a particularly pleasant place to stay (especially in summer when it is cooler than Florence) since most of the hotels are in good positions with gardens. It is interesting for its Etruscan walls, Roman theatre, archaeological museum, collection of Attic vases, and the little Museo Bandini. The country lanes near the town are particularly beautiful.

■ Practical information

Information office. IAT, 37 Piazza Mino, Fiesole (☎ 055-598720; fax 055-598822). *APT* Firenze (☎ 055-290832).

Bus from Florence. No. 7 about every 20 mins (from the station and Piazza San Marco) via San Domenico.

Car parking in Fiesole can be difficult. There are only two free car parks, in Piazza

Mercato and below the Teatro Romano; the central car park in Piazza Mino has an hourly tariff.

Hotels
★★★★ *Villa San Michele*, 4 Via Doccia, with restaurant and swimming pool (☎ 055-59451, fax 055-598734); *Villa Aurora*, 39 Piazza Mino, with restaurant (☎ 055-59100; fax 055-59587).

★★★ *Villa Bonelli*, 1 Via Poeti, with restaurant (☎ 055-59513; fax 055-598942); *Bencistà*, 4 Via Benedetto da Maiano (☎ & fax 055-59163).

Rooms to let at the *Villa San Girolamo*, Via Vecchia Fiesolana.

Campsite. ★★★ *Panoramico*, 1 Via Peramonda.

Restaurants
Maiano. ££ *Le Cave di Maiano* (☎ 055-59133); *La Graziella* (☎ 055-599963).
San Domenico. £ *Pizzeria San Domenico.*

Lovely places to **picnic** include the park below San Francesco; near the Roman theatre; near Maiano; and off the *Strada dei Bosconi* (en route to Vincigliata).

San Domenico di Fiesole
From Viale Alessandro Volta (where the park of **Villa il Ventaglio** is open daily) in Florence, Via di San Domenico ascends the hillside offering a beautiful view of Fiesole and its villas to **San Domenico di Fiesole**, a little hamlet with several handsome private villas.

The 15C church of **San Domenico** has a 17C portico and campanile (by Matteo Nigetti). Inside the church, first north chapel, **Fra Angelico**, *Madonna with Angels and Saints* (c 1430). The architectural background was added by Lorenzo di Credi in 1501, when the frame was redesigned (the saints are by a follower of Lorenzo Monaco). The other altarpieces are by the school of Botticelli (*Crucifixion*), Lorenzo di Credi (*Baptism of Christ*), Giovanni Antonio Sogliani (*Epiphany*), and Jacopo da Empoli (*Annunciation*).

In the Convent of San Domenico, St Antoninus and Fra Angelico were both friars. In the little **Chapter House** (ring at No. 4) is a *Crucifixion* and *Madonna and Child* by Fra Angelico.

The narrow Via della Badia descends (left; beware of traffic) from San Domenico to the *Badia Fiesolana*, the cathedral of Fiesole until 1028. Standing in a beautiful location, it was rebuilt in the 15C under the direction of Cosimo il Vecchio. The **European University Institute** was established in the conventual buildings in 1976. The rough stone front incorporates the charming *façade* of the smaller Romanesque church with inlaid marble decoration. The simple cruciform *interior* (open for services, or sometimes by request at the European University) is attributed to a close follower of Brunelleschi.

From San Domenico the ascent to Fiesole may be made either by the main road or by the shorter and prettier old road (Via Vecchia Fiesolana, very narrow and steep); both are lined with fine villas and beautiful trees and provide splendid views of Florence.

Fiesole
Fiesole (295m) is a little town (14,000 inhab.) set in a magnificent position on a thickly wooded hill overlooking the valleys of the Arno and the Mugnone. It has always been a fashionable residential district with fine villas, gardens and

stately cypress groves. An Etruscan city, its foundation preceded that of Florence by many centuries, and, with its own local government, it is still proudly independent of the larger city. It is crowded with Florentines and visitors in summer when its position makes it one of the coolest places in the neighbourhood of the city.

History. Excavations have proved that the hill was inhabited before the Bronze Age. The site of Faesulae, on a hilltop above a river valley, was typical of Etruscan settlements. Probably founded in the 6C or 5C BC from Arezzo, it became one of the chief cities of the Etruscan confederacy. It was the most important town in Etruria after its occupation by the Romans. The ascendancy of Florence over the older city was only finally assured as a result of a decisive battle in 1125.

The bus from Florence (No. 7; see above) terminates in Piazza Mino da Fiesole, the main square, with the *IAT* information office. The **cathedral**, founded in 1028, was over-restored in the 19C. The tall battlemented bell-tower dates from 1213. The bare stone **interior** has a raised choir above a hall crypt. The massive columns have fine capitals (some of them Roman). Above the west door is a statue of St Romulus in a garlanded niche by Giovanni della Robbia. In the Cappella Salutati (right of the choir) are frescoes by Cosimo Rosselli, and the *tomb of Bishop Salutati with a fine portrait bust, and an *altar-frontal, both superb works by Mino da Fiesole. Over the high altar is a large *altarpiece by Bicci di Lorenzo. The crypt has interesting primitive capitals.

At the upper end of the piazza is the old **Palazzo Pretorio** next to the church of **Santa Maria Primerana**, with a quaint porch. The equestrian monument (1906) in the square celebrates the meeting between Vittorio Emanuele II and Garibaldi at Teano. At the opposite side of the piazza, between the 17C Seminary and Bishop's Palace, Via San Francesco, a very steep paved lane, climbs up the hill past a terrace offering a fine ***view** of Florence. The ancient church of **Sant'Alessandro** contains cipollino marble *columns with Ionic capitals and bases from a Roman building. At the top of the hill (345m), on the site of the Etruscan and later Roman acropolis are the convent buildings of **San Francesco**. The church contains altarpieces by Neri di Bicci, Piero di Cosimo, and Raffaellino del Garbo. A small missionary **museum** contains Eastern objets d'art. The wooded hillside is a public park.

Roman theatre and museum

From Piazza Mino the street behind the apse of the cathedral leads to the entrance to the *Roman theatre and museum (**open** 09.00–dusk exc 1st Tues of the month; ticket also valid for the Museo Bandini).

From the terrace there is a good comprehensive view of the excavations, which were begun in the 19C, in a plantation of olive trees. The **Roman theatre** (1C BC) held 3000 spectators (the seats on the right side are intact; the others have been restored). To the right are the **Roman baths**, reconstructed in 1892, probably built in the 1C AD and enlarged by Hadrian. A small terrace provides a fine view of a long stretch of **Etruscan walls** which enclosed the city. Northwest of the theatre is a **Roman temple** (1C BC), and, on a lower level, remains of an Etruscan Temple (3C BC).

The **museum**, built in 1912, contains a topographical collection (well

PROVINCIA DI
FIRENZE

labelled) from Fiesole and its territory (she-wolf in bronze, Bronze Age material, Etruscan stelai, urns, architectural fragments from the theatre and temples, and the Stele Fiesolana (5C BC). Also displayed here is the splendid *Costantini Collection of Greek vases.

In Via Dupré is the small **Museo Bandini**, a collection of 13C–15C Florentine paintings by Bernardo Daddi, Neri di Bicci, Taddeo Gaddi, Lorenzo Monaco, and Bicci di Lorenzo, etc. in a pretty little palace built for the collection in 1913.

EMILIA
ROMAGNA

Palazzuolo
sul Senio

Marradi

477

MUGELLO

Vicchio   67

S. Godenzo

Dicomano

SIEVE

Rufina

ontassieve   70

Pelago   AREZZO

Saltino

Sammezzano   Vallombrosa

Reggello

Cascia

Figline Valdarno

The hills around Fiesole

There are many beautiful old roads in the vicinity of Fiesole. Even though most of them are very narrow, they are still used by cars, and if you are on foot you should take great care of the traffic.

From Piazza Mino, Via Santa Maria and Via Belvedere climb up the hill (with superb views) to the wall along the east limit of the Etruscan city. Below are the beautiful woods of Montececeri crossed by footpaths.

***Via Vecchia Fiesolana** descends steeply from the Piazza Mino and passes the **Villa Medici** built by Michelozzo for Cosimo il Vecchio. The beautiful garden (at its best after Easter) is one of the earliest of the Renaissance, and has a superb view of Florence. The entrance is on the main road at No. 2 Via Beato Angelico; it is privately owned but willingly shown, usually on weekdays 09.00–15.00, and on Sat 09.00–12.00. Opposite (No. 26) is **Villa Le Balze**, owned by Georgetown University since 1979, with a beautiful garden designed by Cecil Pinsent (which can sometimes by seen on request). A by-road leads to **Fontelucente** where there is a church built over a spring. It contains a triptych by Mariotto di Nardo. In Via Dupré is **Ville Le Coste** (No. 18) where the painter Primo Conti (1900–88) lived, and which contains a collection of his works (**open** 10.00–13.00 except Monday and fest.)

The pretty **Via Benedetto da Maiano** diverges from the main Florence road below Fiesole for the hamlet of **Maiano**. The church contains a painting by Giovanni Battista Naldini. Nearby are disused quarries of pietra serena.

Via del Salviatino returns down to Florence past the gate of the **Villa di Maiano** restored in 1863 as the residence of John Temple Leader, who acquired many farms and villas between Fiesole and Settignano, and planted the woods in this district. Via Benedetto da Maiano continues to Ponte a Mensola (see below).

From Piazza Mino in Fiesole (see above) the main street continues uphill and, beyond Borgunto, the **Strada dei Bosconi** leads out of the town with increasingly beautiful views over the wide Mugnone valley to the north. It continues to L'Olmo where it joins Via Faentina which leads north for the Mugello valley (see Ch. 3), while, soon after leaving Fiesole, a by-road diverges right for Montebeni and Settignano. It runs along a ridge round the north shoulder of Monte Ceceri through magnificent woods, planted by John Temple Leader in the 19C. Just beyond **Villa di Bosco di Fontelucente**, with an interesting garden redesigned after the Second World War by Paolo Peyron (sometimes shown on request), there is a superb view of Florence. The road climbs to a fork; the road on the right continues past **Castel di Poggio** (usually open at weekends, 15.00–19.00, in May–July, Sept & Oct). It was rebuilt in the late 15C and a wing added in 1820 (and restored in the neo-Gothic style in 1922). There are splendid views. The road descends, lined with magnificent cypresses, past the **Castello di Vincigliata**, the ruins of which were rebuilt in neo-Gothic style in 1855 by John Temple Leader. Privately owned, and being restored, it is now sometimes open to the public (☎ 055-599478). The castle was used by Temple Leader as a museum. The road goes on downhill past Villa I Tatti for Settignano (see below).

Longer trips may be taken to the north of Fiesole, to the Convento della Maddalena, Pratolino, and Montesenario, all described below.

Ponte a Mensola and Settignano

■ Practical information
Bus from Florence. No. 10 (from the station and Piazza San Marco) via **Ponte a Mensola** (service about every 20 mins, journey time about 30 mins).

Rooms to let at the Benedictine convent *Villa Linda*, 5 Via Poggio Gherardo (☎ 055-603913).

Restaurants
££ *Osvaldo*, Ponte a Mensola.
£ *La Capponcina*, 17 Via San Romano, Settignano.
There are numerous places to **picnic** near Ponte a Mensola and Settignano.

Ponte a Mensola
At the foot of the hill of Settignano in the village of Ponte a Mensola, Via Poggio Gherardo branches left from the main road past the Villa di Poggio Gherardo, traditionally thought to be the setting for the earliest episodes in Boccaccio's *Decameron*. In 1888 it was purchased by Janet and Henry Ross. (Janet wrote some excellent books on Tuscany and created a lovely garden here.)

Nearby is **San Martino a Mensola**, a Benedictine church of the 9C, founded by St Andrew, thought to have been a Scotsman and archdeacon to the bishop of Fiesole, Donato, who was probably from Ireland. In the graceful 15C **interior** is a **Triptych of the Madonna enthroned with two female Saints* by Taddeo Gaddi, and, on the high altar, a triptych with the donor Amerigo Zati by a follower of Orcagna (1391), known as the Master of San Martino a Mensola. In the north aisle is an **Annunciation* by a follower of Fra Angelico, and a **Madonna and four saints* by Neri di Bicci. A tiny museum contains a wooden **casket, decorated with paintings by the school of Agnolo Gaddi, which formerly contained the body of St Andrew and a reliquary bust of the saint (late 14C).

Nearby is **Villa I Tatti** (entrance on Via Vincigliata), the former home of Bernard Berenson (1865–1959), the art historian and collector, and left by him to Harvard University as The Center of Italian Renaissance Studies. It contains his library (open to post-doctorate scholars), his *collection of Italian paintings, and a beautifully kept Italianate garden, laid out by Cecil Pinsent in 1911–15. The house and garden are shown to scholars with a letter of presentation, only by appointment.

The pretty by-road continues up the hill through woods past the castles of Vincigliata and Poggio to Fiesole (see above). In Via Vincigliata at the bottom of the hill are two plaques recording the writers and artists who lived and worked in the neighbourhood. The **Villa Boccaccio** (Via di Corbignano) was owned by the father of Giovanni Boccaccio who probably spent his youth here.

Settignano

From Ponte a Mensola the road continues up to Settignano winding across the old road; both have fine views of the magnificent trees on the skyline of the surrounding hills. **Settignano** (178m), a peaceful village, is known for its school of sculptors, most famous of whom were Desiderio and the brothers Rossellino. In the church is a *Madonna and Child with two angels*, attributed to the workshop of Andrea della Robbia. In the lower Piazza Desiderio there is a superb view of Florence.

The numerous narrow lanes in and around Settignano, mostly with splendid views over unspoilt countryside are well worth exploring on foot.

In Via Capponcina is **Villa Michelangelo** (No. 65; no admission) where Michelangelo passed his youth. Via Rossellino diverges right from the narrow main road of Settignano to **Villa Gamberaia** (No. 72) which has a famous *garden (open weekdays 09.00–17.00; entrance fee; ring), remarkable for its topiary, azaleas, and ancient cypresses and pine trees.

Villamagna

■ Practical information

Bus from Florence. No. 33 from the station to Bagno a Ripoli (c every 20 mins in 45 mins), and from there Bus No. 48 (infrequent service, about every hour) to Villamagna (in about 45 mins).

Hotel ★★★★★ *Villa La Massa*, at Candeli, with restaurant and swimming pool (☎ 055-6510101, fax 055-6510109).

Above the Arno to the east of Florence is **Vicchio di Rimaggio** with the church of **San Lorenzo** (only open on Sunday). The portico has a good fresco of *St Lawrence with two angels* by the circle of Cosimo Rosselli over the door. Inside there are two 15C ciborium and a *Madonna and Child* attributed (from this work) to the Maestro di Vicchio di Rimaggio (c 1300).

Farther east (about 11km from Florence), above woods, is **Villamagna** with the church of **Pieve di San Donnino** (if closed, ring at the priest's house at No. 1 in the lane above the church to the right). The church was in existence by the 11C, and it preserves its Romanesque appearance.

South aisle. Stucco relief of the *Madonna and Child* surrounded by a 17C painting, and a triptych by Mariotto di Nardo, and the body of the Blessed Gherardo in a 16C urn. At the east end of the south aisle, frescoes attributed to the Maestro di Signa, and near the high altar, 16C *Crucifix*.

At the east end of the **north aisle** *Madonna and Child with two Saints by Francesco Granacci, who was born in Villamagna. On the north altar, fine 15C painting of the Madonna and Saints in its original frame, and above the 16C font, a 14C painting of Saints John the Baptist and Anthony Abbot. A road (about 2km) leads uphill ending at the church of **Incontro** which offers a splendid view (557m).

Poggio Imperiale and Pian de' Giullari

▣ Practical information

Bus from Florence. No. 11 (every 5–10 mins) from Piazza San Marco, Via Martelli, and Via Serragli for Poggio Imperiale (in about 20 mins). Also Bus No. 38 (request service only, ☎ 167-019794) from Porta Romana for Poggio Imperiale (Largo Fermi) and for Pian de' Giullari (in about 10 mins).

Restaurants
££ Omero, 11 Via Pian de' Giullari.

Outside Porta Romana (Pl. 13,14) Viale del Poggio Imperiale, a long straight cypress avenue lined with handsome villas surrounded by gardens leads up to the huge **Villa di Poggio Imperiale** (now a school; adm. readily granted by previous appointment) with a neo-classical façade by Pasquale Poccianti and Giuseppe Cacialli (1814–23). After 1565 this was the residence of the grand-dukes of Florence. Some of its rooms are decorated by Matteo Rosselli (1623), and others by Giuseppe Maria Terreni (1773).

To the left of the villa, in Largo Fermi, is the entrance to the **Observatory of Arcetri**, founded in the 19C and with a high international reputation in the scientific field.

Via San Leonardo (see p. 93) leads back towards Florence while Via Guglielmo Righini winds up past **Villa Capponi** (No. 3), with a beautiful 16C *garden (privately owned) to **Torre del Gallo**, reconstructed in medieval style by Stefano Bardini in 1904–06.

The road coninues to the pretty little village of **Pian de' Giullari** where **Villa di Gioiello** (No. 42; not open to the public, but for permission to visit, ask at the observatory) was the house where the aged Galileo lived, practically as a prisoner, from 1631 onwards. After he was condemned by the Inquisition in 1633 he avoided imprisonment through the good offices of Grand-duke Ferdinando II but was constrained to live here for the rest of his life; he died in 1642.

Monteoliveto and Bellosguardo

▣ Practical information

Buses from Florence. For **Monteoliveto** Bus No. 12 from the station to Viale Raffaello Sanzio and to Piazza Torquato Tasso for **Bellosguardo** (Pl. 9; a walk of about 20 mins). Bus No. 42 (request service only ☎ 167-019794) for **Bellosguardo** (going on to Marignolle, in about 15 mins) departs from Porta Romana.

On the south bank of the Arno, near Ponte della Vittoria (Pl. 5) is the thickly wooded hill of **Monteoliveto** with some beautiful private villas. It is reached via Viale Raffaello Sanzio and (right) Via di Monteoliveto (Pl. 9; a walk of about 15 mins). A military hospital occupies the convent of the church of **San Bartolomeo** (for adm. ring at No. 72A). It contains frescoes by Bernardino Poccetti and Sodoma (*Last Supper*; very damaged), and an altarpiece by Santi di Tito. The road ends in front of an entrance to the **Villa Strozzi** (open daily, 09.00–dusk), a wooded park.

Bellosguardo

The adjoining hill to the south is aptly called Bellosguardo (Pl. 9), which offers superb views of Florence. It can be reached by foot (in about 15 mins) from Monteoliveto by the pretty Via di Monteoliveto, but the most direct approach from the centre of Florence is from Piazza San Francesco di Paola (Pl. 9).

In the piazza is an ex-convent (No. 3; no adm.) bought by the sculptor Adolf Hildebrand in 1874, surrounded by a beautiful park, and the fantastic Villa Pagani built by Adolfo Coppedè in 1896. Via di Bellosguardo climbs uphill, with a view (right) of **Villa dello Strozzino** a beautiful Renaissance villa. On the right, beside a group of pine trees, is **Villa Brichieri-Colombi** (No. 20) owned in 1849–73 by Miss Isa Blagden who was often visited here by the Brownings. Henry James wrote *The Aspern Papers* while staying at the villa in 1887.

A road on the left leads to the **Torre di Bellosguardo** with a delightful garden. From the quiet Piazza di Bellosguardo is the entrance to the **Villa dell'Ombrellino,** where Violet Trefusis lived until her death in 1973. It was ostentatiously restored in 1988 as a trade centre. Via San Carlo leads out of the opposite side of the piazza to **Villa di Montauto** where Nathaniel Hawthorne stayed in 1859. Via Piana continues from Piazza di Bellosguardo to Via di Santa Maria a Marignolle which leads left (no entry to cars) to **Villa La Colombaia** (No. 2), now a convent school, where Florence Nightingale was born.

The Certosa del Galluzzo

■ Practical information

Buses from Florence. Nos 36 & 37 from the station (every 15 mins) to a request stop below the Certosa (in about 30 mins).

Restaurant
££ *Da Bibe*, 1 Via delle Bagnese, Ponte all'Asse.

Outside Porta Romana, Via Senese (Pl. 13) climbs uphill, and continues through the village of Galluzzo, just beyond which, on a picturesque hill to the right of the road, is the ***Certosa del Galluzzo*** (open 09.00–12.00, 15.00 or 14.30–17.00 or 18.00; closed Mon. Tours are given by a monk). The monastery was founded in 1342 by Niccolò Acciaioli.

In the **church** is the *tomb-slab of Cardinal Agnolo II Acciaioli, now attributed to Francesco da Sangallo. The **Chapter House** has another expressive tomb-slab with a fine effigy by Francesco

A Della Robbian tondo in the Great Cloister of the Certoso del Galluzzo

da Sangallo, and a fresco of the *Crucifixion* by Mariotto Albertinelli. The secluded ***Great Cloister** with tondi by the della Robbia, is surrounded by the monks' cells (one is open). On the upper floor of the **Palazzo degli Studi**, a fine Gothic hall, is a **picture gallery** with five frescoed *lunettes of the Passion cycle by Pontormo, detached from the cloister and painted while he was staying in the monastery in 1522. There are also 14C and 15C Florentine paintings.

The Medici Villas of Careggi, La Petraia and Castello

■ Practical information

Buses from Florence. No. 14C (every 10 mins) from the station or Via de' Pucci to the **Villa di Careggi** (the penultimate request stop before the terminus, in about 30 mins). Bus No. 28 from the station (every 5–10 mins), for the Medici villas of **La Petraia** and **Castello** (request stop at Il Sodo, in about 35 mins).

A bus is recommended to cross the uninteresting northern suburbs of Florence, but pretty country walks may be taken in the hills behind Careggi and La Petraia.

Restaurants
Cercina. ££ *Trianon*, and *I Ricchi;* **Serpiolle. ££** *Strettoio*, 7 Via di Serpiolle and *Dulcamare Club*, 2 Via Dante da Castiglione. **£** *Osteria della Fettunta*, Via Reginaldo Giuliani (near Villa della Petraia).

Villa Medicea di Careggi
In the northern suburbs, beside the Careggi hospital buildings is the **Villa Medicea di Careggi**. Set in a well-wooded park, it is now used as offices by the hospital (**open** 08.00–18.00; Sat 08.00–14.00; closed fest. ☎ 055-4279981). A 14C castellated farmhouse here was enlarged (and a loggia added) by Michelozzo for Cosimo il Vecchio in 1434. This was the literary and artistic centre of the Medicean court, and the meeting place of the famous **Platonic Academy** which saw the birth of the humanist movement of the Renaissance. Cosimo il Vecchio, Piero di Cosimo, and Lorenzo il Magnifico all died in the villa. In 1848 it was restored by Francis Sloane.

There are pretty country lanes in the hills behind Careggi, especially towards **Cercina** where there is a fine Romanesque church.

Villa Medicea della Petraia and Villa Medicea di Castello
Villa Medicea della Petraia (open 09.00–dusk except on the 2nd and 3rd Mon of the month) was once a castle of the Brunelleschi but the villa was rebuilt in 1575 for the Ferdinando I by Buontalenti. In 1864–70 it was a favourite residence of Vittorio Emanuele II, and in 1919 it was presented to the State by Vittorio Emanuele III. A pretty **garden** and moat (filled with carp) precede the villa, which still preserves a tower from the old castle. On the upper terrace is the base of a fountain by Tribolo and Pierino da Vinci. A magnificent **park**, with ancient cypresses, extends behind the villa to the east.

The courtyard of the **villa** has decorative *frescoes illustrating the history of the Medici family, by Volterrano and Cosimo Daddi. In a room here is displayed the bronze group of *Antaeus and Hercules* by Ammannati from the fountain in Villa di Castello. The rooms were furnished as state apartments in the 19C. On the first floor the private apartments, decorated in neo-classical style, contain the original bronze statue of *Venus* by Giambologna, removed from the fountain in the garden. The gaming room is a remarkable period piece hung with 17C paintings.

In Via della Petraia is **Villa Il Bel Riposo** where Carlo Lorenzini (Collodi) lived while writing *Pinocchio*, and the **Villa Corsini** rebuilt in 1698 by Antonio Ferri, with an interesting Baroque façade. A plaque records the death here in 1649 of Sir Robert Dudley (see p. 285). The villa and garden are sometimes open for exhibitions and concerts.

In front of the villa, Via di Castello leads shortly to **Villa Medicea di Castello** (admission to the gardens only, times as for La Petraia), now the seat of the Accademia della Crusca, founded in 1582, for the study of the Italian language. The villa was acquired by Giovanni and Lorenzo di Pierfrancesco de'Medici, Lorenzo il Magnifico's younger cousins, around 1477. Here they hung Botticelli's famous *Birth of Venus*. The typical Tuscan **garden*, described by numerous travellers in the 16C and 17C, was laid out by Tribolo for Cosimo I in 1541. The *fountain by Tribolo was crowned by a bronze group by Ammannati (now kept in Villa della Petraia). The gardens also contain a grotto, a colossus by Ammannati, and an orangery.

Lovely country walks may be taken in the lanes on the hillside above Via Giovanni da San Giovanni. A narrow rural road (Via di Castello; parallel to the main road lower down the hill) continues beyond Villa di Castello towards Sesto passing **Quinto** where there is an Etruscan tomb known as 'La Montagnola' (ring at No. 95 on Saturday or Sunday, 10.00–13.00) with a remarkable domed tholos burial chamber in the tumulus.

Sesto Fiorentino

■ Practical information

Buses from Florence. No 28 (every 5–10 mins) from the station terminates at Sesto Fiorentino (in about 45 mins).

Hotel

★★★★ *Villa Villoresi*, 2 Via Ciampi, Colonnata, with restaurant and swimming pool (☎ 055-443212, fax 055-442063).

Sesto Fiorentino is a small town (41,000 inhab.) in the northern suburbs of Florence. As you enter the town you will see **Villa Corsi Salviati** on the left with its 18C garden. Exhibitions are held here. Next to the Ginori porcelain factory, entered at No. 31 Via Pratese, is the **Museo delle Porcellane di Doccia** (open Tues, Thur, and Sat 09.30–13.00, 15.30–18.30 except in Aug) in a fine building by Piero Berardi (1965). It contains a large well-displayed *collection of porcelain made in the famous Doccia factory founded by Carlo Ginori in 1735. The firm, known as Richard-Ginori since 1896, continues to flourish. Across the road, in an inconspicuous one-storey warehouse, Ginori seconds can be purchased.

At the foot of the hills is the **Villa Ginori** at Doccia, with a huge park and cypress avenue, created by Leopoldo Carlo Ginori in 1816. Here exceptionally interesting remains of the old Ginori factory survive.

From Sesto a road leads north via Colonnata to the *Strada Panoramica dei Colli Alti* (a panoramic road across the hills) which skirts the wooded slopes of **Monte Morello** (934m), with magnificent views, as far as Via Bolognese (see below).

Pratolino and Montesenario

■ Practical information

Buses from Florence. No. 25 (every 15–30 mins) from Piazza San Marco for Pratolino (in about 45 mins); there is no public transport to Montesenario.

Trains from Florence. A secondary railway line reopened in 1999 which connects Florence to Borgo San Lorenzo has a station at Le Caldine.

Hotels
Pratolino.★★★★ *Villa Demidoff*, with pool (☎ 055-409772; fax 055-409781).
Bivigliano. ★★★ *Giotto* (☎ 055- 406608; fax 055-406730).
Olmo. on the Via Faentina: ★★★ *Dino*, with restaurant (☎ 055-548932; fax 055-548934).

Campsite
Bivigliano. ★★ *Poggio degli Uccellini*.

Restaurants
Pratolino. ££ *Villa Vecchia*.
Olmo (Torre di Buiano). £ *Casa del Prosciutto*, 58 Via Bosconi; £ *Da Mario*, 428 Via Faentina.

Villa Demidoff (Pratolino)

North of Florence, reached by the Via Bolognese (which leaves the city north of Piazza della Libertà, Pl. 3) is the huge park of **Villa Demidoff**, the entrance of which is at **Pratolino**. Some 17–18 hectares of the splendid well-kept park belong to the Province (**open** March on fest. 10.00–18.00; Apr–Sept on Thur, Fri, Sat & Sun 10.00–20.00; and in Oct on fest. 10.00–19.00; car park on the left of the main road).

A remarkable garden with numerous fountains was created here in 1569 for Francesco I de' Medici by Buontalenti, the most famous of which was Giambologna's colossal statue (about 10 metres high) of *Appennino* (1579–80), which is still one of the most extraordinary sights in Italy (the huge figure symbolising the Apennine mountains crouches on a natural rock above a pool surrounded by trees). Other areas of the gardens have been or are being restored. The Paggeria (servants' quarters) of the Medici villa was restored as the residence of the Demidoff family when they bought the estate in 1872 and transformed the park.

Farther north is the little hill resort of **Bivigliano** where the church of San Romolo (**open** at weekends) contains a della Robbian terracotta, and a 15C wooden statue of *St John the Baptist*. The 16C Villa di Bivigliano, surrounded by a large park, where concerts are sometimes held, can be visited by appointment (☎ 055-406717).

Convent of Montesenario

On a hill-top (817m) is the convent of Montesenario. On foot, there is a path starting from the approach road up through the woods past the cemetery and some grottoes; for drivers, there is a car park at the top of the hill. The *views are superb, and on a clear day you can see the whole of the Mugello valley. Seven Florentine merchants became hermits here and established the Servite Order of mendicant friars in 1233. In the piazzale are two statues of Saints (1754) by Pompilio Ticciati.

The church and convent were enlarged by Cosimo I in 1539, and then rebuilt in 1717. The clock tower dates from 1834. The **church** (open daily) has an 18C interior with elaborate stuccoes and a fresco by Antonio Domenico Gabbiani in the vault. In the sanctuary is a *Crucifix* in polychrome stucco by Ferdinando Tacca, and two paintings by Tommaso Redi. In the choir, behind, are paintings by Giuseppe Bezzuoli (*Assunta*, 1849), Giuseppe Cassioli (*St Joseph*, 1937), and Pietro Annigoni (*Seven founders of the Order*, 1985). The Oratory of San Filippo contains a 15C polychrome terracotta *Deposition* group. Off the nave is the Chapel of the Seven Founders added in 1933 in a neo-Gothic style by Giuseppe Cassioli (who also made the urn over the altar). Above the door into the Sacristy, which contains two grisaille paintings, is a 14C painting of the *Madonna and Saints*. In the refectory of the **convent** (admission on request) is a frescoed *Cenacolo* by Matteo Rosselli.

On the **Via Faentina** which follows the Mugnone valley north of Florence, just beyond the village of **Le Caldine** is the convent of the **Maddalena** on the right of the road. This was a hospice of the Dominican convent of San Marco, and until recently was run by two friars. It is at present closed to the public (for information ☎ 055–540039). Here Fra Bartolomeo lived and painted several frescoes, including the *Noli me Tangere* in the little chapel in the orchard. The convent was built c 1470–85 probably on a design by Michelozzo. The **church** contains a *Madonna in Maestà* attributed to the Master of the Horne triptych, and an *Annunciation* by Fra Bartolomeo above a presepio with terracotta figures attributed to Andrea della Robbia.

Rovezzano, Santa Brigida, Pontassieve

This district is east of Florence near the Arno. Sant' Andrea a Rovezzano can be reached by bus and Pontassieve by train. The other places described below cannot be reached by public transport.

■ Practical information

Buses from Florence. No. 14 (every 10 mins) from the station and Piazza Duomo for Sant' Andrea a Rovezzano (in about 30 mins).

Trains from Florence. Pontassieve has a railway station (slow trains only stop here, in about 10 mins from Santa Maria Novella).

Restaurants
Consuma. £ *Dal Consumi* for good snacks.
Santa Brigida. £ pizzeria.
Monteloro. ££ restaurant.

To the east (on the outskirts) of Florence, on the main road which follows the Arno, is **Rovezzano**. In Piazzetta Benedetto da Rovezzano is a tabernacle with a *Crucifixion* by Franciabigio. The church of **San Michele** (rebuilt in 1840) contains a painted *Crucifix* dated 1400, and a *Madonna enthroned* by the Maestro della Maddalena. The church of **Sant'Andrea a Rovezzano** has a fine Romanesque campanile. In the neo-classical interior with frescoes by Luigi Ademollo, is a beautiful relief of the *Madonna* (c 1450) by Luca della Robbia, and an early 13C painting of the *Madonna and Child*. A marble statuette of the

Madonna and Child by a follower of Giovanni di Balduccio is kept in the canonica. Just before **Compiobbi** is the **Florence British Military Cemetery**, with 1551 graves from the Second World War. A pretty country road diverges from the main road towards Fiesole via **Gricigliano** where the 15C–16C Villa Martelli, with a fine garden, is now a monastery (the monks sell produce and Mass is held here in Gregorian chant on Sundays at 11.00), and the hamlet of **Monteloro**.

Between Compiobbi and Pontassieve is the locality of **Le Sieci**, with the **Pieve di San Giovanni Battista a Remole** with a fine tall campanile. The church is usually open 16.00–18.30; if closed ring at the priest's house in the garden beyond the portico. In the right aisle is the font composed of various coloured marbles in 1753, behind a 15C balustrade. On the wall is a statuette of *St John the Baptist* by the bottega of Giovanni della Robbia. At the end of the aisle is a 15C ciborium in pietra serena. On the east wall, **Crucifixion, with the Madonna and St John*, attributed to the school of Botticelli. In the chapel to the left, 14C fresco fragments and a **Madonna and Child*, attributed to the Master of Remole, who acquired his name from this work.

North of Le Sieci is the castle of **Torre a Decima**, approached by a pretty road lined on one side by cypresses. It was owned by the Pazzi family from the 13C, and was restored in 1950. The wine cellars can sometimes be visited by appointment.

Higher up, in a beautiful position, is **Doccia** where the church of Sant'Andrea (entrance through the little courtyard behind) contains a tiny della Robbian tabernacle and a *Madonna and Saints* by the school of Ghirlandaio. The *Crucifix and saints* by Ignazio Hugford is in very poor condition. Outside is a medieval well, now covered with posters. A narrow road below Doccia is signposted for Santa Brigida. It winds up and down through woods and lovely rolling hills, with a view left of the castle of Torre a Decima. Beyond Fornello is La Villa with a handsome villa, where another road comes in from Molino del Piano.

Santa Brigida has a church with a square tower and an unusual plan. It contains a **Madonna and Child with two Saints* attributed to the Maestro di San Martino alla Palma, a 16C painted *Crucifix*, and a little carved tabernacle of 1483. On the intrados of the choir arch there are unusual carvings. At the west end are two 16C polychrome busts in niches. The apse has interesting frescoes. From the terrace there is a lovely view of the unspoilt countryside.

Below Santa Brigida is the **Castello del Trebbio** (not to be confused with the Castello del Trebbio outside San Piero a Sieve described in Ch. 3), right on the road. It was built by the Pazzi family in the 13C but has been restored. Visitors are invited into the courtyard. On the floor of the valley is the *pieve* of **Lubaco** with a Romanesque apse.

Pontassieve (16,500 inhab.), an important centre of the *Chianti Rufina* wine trade, stands to the east of Florence at the confluence of the Sieve and Arno Rivers. The old Medici bridge (1555; attributed to Bartolomeo Ammannati; restored) across the Sieve, can be seen upstream from the main road bridge. The town was severely damaged in the Second World War.

From Pontassieve begins the road for the Casentino—the beautiful wooded upper valley of the Arno (described in Ch. 40)—across the Consuma Pass. Off this road is **Nipozzano**, a picturesque hamlet spread out along a ridge backed by cypresses, with the 17C Villa Albizi (Frescobaldi) behind a low wall, a church, and remains of an 11C castle. There are pretty farmhouses in the vicinity and views all the way to Vallombrosa. The farm produces a well-known wine (the cellars can sometimes be visited by appointment).

Diacceto, also surrounded by vineyards, has the church of San Lorenzo (open only at weekends), rebuilt in 1872, which contains a della Robbian *Madonna and Child with Saints*. At nearby **Pelago**, a festival (called *On the Road*) of buskers and street players is held in July. Opposite a little Oratory preceded by a portico (and containing a small 15C wood *Crucifix*), a road leads into Piazza Ghiberti, named after the great sculptor Lorenzo, who was born here, probably in 1378. This delightful ancient **market square** preserves its old pump and a medley of houses. Via Roma leads out of the piazza past an old tower, and steps continue up past the handsome town hall and beneath two arches to the tiny Piazza Cavalcanti at the top of the village. In the church of San Clemente a small museum was opened in 1994. The works from churches nearby include a triptych by Niccolò di Pietro Gerini.

The main road continues to Borselli. Near Borselli, on the Pomino road, is the Romanesque church of **Tosina** which contains a beautiful triptych by Mariotto di Nardo (1389; restored in 1989). **Consuma**, a summer and ski resort is a few metres below the Pass (1023m) connecting the Pratomagno with the main Apennine chain.

Southwest of Pontassieve (see above) is the Villa of **Altomena**. A Guidi family castle and a church have been incorporated into the villa which is surrounded by extensive vineyards and olive groves. The church contains a *Madonna and Child with Saints* attributed to the circle of Domenico Ghirlandaio.

A by-road leads across the Arno from Pontassieve to the village of **Rosano**, in a peaceful position by the river. By a pretty tabernacle a narrow road leads shortly to the well-kept Benedictine convent of Santa Maria, founded in 780, and now housing some seventy nuns (ring for **admission** on the right of the courtyard at the closed order).

The **church** has a Romanesque façade and a fine 11C–12C campanile. Mass is celebrated with Gregorian chant at 7am on weekdays and at 10am on holidays. The presbytery is raised above the pretty crypt which has a 12C altar. In the right aisle is a font (1423) and to the right of the high altar, *Annunciation* by Giovanni dal Ponte (1434). On the east wall is a fine painted *Crucifix* (in very poor condition) by an unknown master of the late 12C or early 13C. In the chapel at the base of the campanile, *Annunciation* by Jacopo di Cione. A 16C wood ciborium has been removed to the convent. The nuns have a laboratory for the restoration of books. A beautiful road climbs to Villamagna (described above).

Bagno a Ripoli

■ Practical information

Bus from Florence. No. 33 from the station (every 20 mins) to Bagno a Ripoli in about 45 mins.

South of the Arno, approached across Ponte San Niccolò, is the large scattered Comune of **Bagno a Ripoli**, a pleasant residential area on low hills with fine views. On the approach, beyond the district of Sorgane, much criticised when it was built in 1962–70, is the **Pieve a Ripoli** (San Pietro), first mentioned in the 8C, with a beautiful interior.

North of the centre of Bagno a Ripoli, at Quarto, is the church of Santa Maria, restored in 1930 by Giuseppe Castellucci. It contains a triptych with a central panel by Bicci di Lorenzo, and side panels by the bottega of Bernardo Daddi, as well as a painting signed and dated 1391 by a certain Francesco.

Near the Arco di Camicia, is the church of **Santo Stefano a Paterno** rebuilt in 1934. It contains a painted *Crucifix* by a follower of Cimabue (late 13C). From **L'Apparita** there is a good view of Florence.

The church of **San Quirico a Ruballa** (1763) contains a *Madonna and Child with the young St John* by Domenico Puligo, a painted *Cross* of c 1330, and a small wooden 14C statue of the *Madonna and Child*. Close to the motorway (at Osteria Nuova) is the church of **San Giorgio a Ruballa**, restored by Nicolò Matas in 1863. It contains a *Madonna and Child with Saints* dated 1336, and a painted Cross, a late work by Taddeo Gaddi.

San Donato in Collina is in a beautiful position, with fine villas. To the northeast is the splendid 18C **Villa Rinuccini di Torre a Cona** with a medieval tower. It has a cypress avenue and Italianate garden surrounded by a fine park (not open to the public). **Palazzolo**, has a neo-Gothic church, and nearby is the Romanesque church of **San Lorenzo a Cappiano** (open Sunday morning only) with an 18C interior and a *Madonna and Child* attributed to the Maestro di Barberino.

Antella, Grassina and Impruneta

■ Practical information

Information office open Apr–Dec at Impruneta: 1 Via Mazzini (☎ 055-2313729).

Buses from Florence. No. 32 from the station (about every 10 mins) to Ponte a Ema and Antella (in about 35 mins); Bus 31 from the station (about every 10 mins) to Grassina (in about 45 mins). For Impruneta, services run by *CAP* c every hour (Largo Alinari, off Piazza della Stazione) in 40 mins.

Campsite. ★★ *Camping Internazionale,* open in summer, at Bottai near Impruneta.

Restaurant near Impruneta: *I Tre Pini* (at Pozzolatico).

Florence is left by Piazza Ferrucci at the south end of Ponte San Niccolò (Pl. 12). The road signposted to Grassina crosses a piazza in front of the **Badia a Ripoli**, a pretty 16C porticoed church flanked by its tall campanile. A Benedictine convent, founded in 790, it became a Vallombrosan monastery in the 12C. Since its suppression in 1808 it has been a parish church. The interior, enlarged in 1598, has a Latin cross plan with a crypt. It was restored to its original state in 1930 when the later painted decoration and stuccowork was destroyed.

The altarpieces include: Agostino Veracini, *St John Gualberto* (c 1744); Nicodemo Ferrucci, *Crucifixion and Saints*; Jacopo Vignali, *Madonna and Child* (1630); Giovanni Camillo Sagrestani, *Scene from the life of Countess Matilda* (1706), and Francesco Curradi, *Madonna and Child in glory*. In the sacristy are fine inlaid cupboards and a frescoed frieze attributed to Bernardino Poccetti (1585). Another fresco by Poccetti (a lunette showing the *Marriage at Cana*), signed and dated 1603–4 in the refectory of the convent has recently been restored.

Near **Ponte a Ema** is the **Oratorio di Santa Caterina dell'Antella**, restored in 1998 (for **admission**, ☎ 055-6390356, the Comune di Bagno a Ripoli). The stone façade was originally frescoed (the lunette over the doorway representing the *Madonna and Child* is by Spinello Aretino). The nave is divided into two bays with cross-vaults containing figures of the Evangelists. On the walls is a **cycle of frescoes* of the *life of St Catherine* by Spinello Aretino (c 1390). Flanking the apse are figures of *Saints Anthony* and *Catherine* attributed to Pietro Nelli (c 1360). Another cycle of frescoes (c 1360) also devoted to St Catherine and attributed to the Master of Barberino decorates the apse. The original altarpiece is by Agnolo Gaddi.

Grassina is a large village which is famous for its Good Friday Passion play. The golf-course at **Ugolino** (18 holes) was created in 1933 to satisfy the British colony in Florence (the first golf course was made in the grounds of one of the Demidoff properties in 1889). The Club House was built by Gherardo Bosio and the greens beautifully landscaped between olive trees, cypresses, and pines.

Impruneta

Impruneta (correctly, L'Impruneta; 275m), is a large village (13,600 inhab.) on a plateau, where the great cattle fair of St Luke is still celebrated (mid-October), although it has now become a general fair. The clay in the soil has been used for centuries to produce terracotta for which the locality is famous. The kilns here still sell beautiful pottery (flower pots, floor tiles, etc).

The Collegiata

In the large central piazza (where the fair is held) is the **Collegiata** (Santa Maria dell'Impruneta), with a high 13C tower, and an elegant portico by Gherardo Silvani (1634). The **interior** was restored, after severe bomb damage in 1944, to its Renaissance aspect which it acquired in the mid-15C under the Pievano Antonio degli Agli. At the west end is the 16C organ and early 18C cantoria, restored and returned here in 1992. **South side**. First altar, Cosimo Gamberucci, *Martyrdom of St Lawrence*; second altar, Passignano, *Birth of the Virgin*. In the nave chapel, where the Pievano Antonio degli Agli lies buried in a 15C tomb, there is a bronze *Crucifix* by Felice Palma.

At the **entrance to the presbytery** are two chapels (c 1452) attributed to Michelozzo, with beautiful ***decoration in enamelled terracotta by Luca and Andrea della Robbia**. They were reconstructed and restored after bomb damage. The chapel on the right was built to protect a relic of the True Cross given to the church by Pippo Spano in 1426. It contains an enamelled terracotta ceiling and an exquisite relief of the *Crucifixion with the Virgin and St John* in a tabernacle, flanked by the figures of St John the Baptist and a bishop saint. Beneath is a charming predella of adoring angels. The chapel on the left protects a miraculous painting of the *Virgin* traditionally attributed to St Luke which was ploughed up by a team of oxen in a field near Impruneta. For centuries it was taken to Florence to help the city in times of trouble. It had to be restored in the 18C by the English painter Ignazio Hugford. The beautiful ceiling is similar to the one in the other chapel. The frieze of fruit on the exterior incorporates two reliefs of the *Madonna and Child*. The figures of Saints Luke and Paul flank a tabernacle which contains the image of the *Madonna and Child* (usually covered; exposed only on religious festivals). The silver altar frontal designed by Giovanni

The della Robbia family

The art of enamelled terracotta was invented in the 1440s by Luca della Robbia. The secret of the chemical composition he used for the enamelling (a lead glaze with the addition of oxides) was handed down through three generations of his family (who had their kiln and workshop in Via Guelfa in Florence), and then lost. Tuscany is full of these colourful luminous works, usually blue and white, used in the decoration of buildings and for altarpieces and numerous half-length Madonna reliefs which became popular for private devotion.

Luca (1399/1400–82) started life as a highly skilled and sensitive marble sculptor (his earliest work and masterpiece is the Cantoria now in the Museo dell'Opera del Duomo in Florence) and was very successful in his very long life. He is generally recognized as one of the most important early Renaissance sculptors, and was clearly influenced by classical art. His best enamelled terracotta works can be seen in Florence (in the Bargello Museum, the Duomo, and Cappella Pazzi), Pistoia (the *Visitation* in the church of San Giovanni Fuorcivitas), and here at Impruneta.

His nephew **Andrea** (1435–1525) worked with him, and then went on to produce his own very beautiful works at La Verna, the Spedale degli Innocenti in Florence, and at the Osservanza outside Siena. Some of his finest works are also in the Bargello Museum in Florence. He had five children, all of whom produced enamelled terracotta works. The most skilful one was **Giovanni** (1469–1530) who made use of more colours as can be seen in his numerous works in Tuscany (including those in Florence, in the Bargello Museum, and in the cloister of the Certosa di Galluzzo in the environs). There was a revival of interest, particularly in England, in della Robbian works in the late 18C and they were imitated with some success in the 19C.

Battista Foggini replaces a 15C relief now exhibited in the treasury (see below). Five large 18C paintings have recently been returned to the church, depicting Miracles of the Virgin, including two fine works by Gian Domenico Ferretti.The large **high altarpiece** (1375) was partially recomposed after it was shattered in the Second World War. Traditionally attributed to Tommaso del Mazza, it is now thought to be the work of Pietro Nelli with the help of Niccolò di Pietro Gerini. The carved and inlaid choirs stalls date from 1522.

On the **north side** of the nave are altarpieces by Matteo Rosselli (*Martyrdom of St Sebastian*) and Empoli (*Calling of St Peter*), and a 16C cantoria. In the baptistery is a late 16C font with a 14C relief of the *Baptism of Christ*. A door beneath the portico on the right leads into two cloisters; off the second (left) is the little crypt (11C), with sculptural fragments.

The entrance to the **treasury** is on the left of the church door (open Fri, 10.00–13.00, Sat 15.00–18.30; Sun 10.00–13.00, 15.00–18.30; in summer: Thur and Fri 10.00–13.00, Sat and Sun 10.00–13.00, 16.00–19.30). Above the portico of the church are displayed a gilded silver *Cross attributed to Lorenzo Ghiberti (c 1420–25); two paxes attributed to Antonio di Salvi; a Cross of the 13C and 14C; fifteen silver votive vases of 1633; and 17C and 18C church silver. The marble schiacciato relief (c 1448) attributed to a follower of Donatello or the circle of Filarete shows the discovery of the miraculous painting of the *Madonna of Impruneta* (see above). In two other rooms are displayed eleven *illuminated choirbooks including one attributed to Lippo di Benivieni (c 1310–20), five attributed to the bottega of Pacino di Bonaguida (mid-14C), and three by Antonio di Girolamo da Ugolino (1537–39). The patchwork cushion and linen and silk veil were found in the tomb of Antonio degli Agli (d. 1477; see above) in 1944. Vestments are to be exhibited in another room.

3 · The Mugello and the Val di Sieve

The **Mugello** is the area north of Florence which extends either side of the Sieve river. The beautiful landscape consists of wooded hills rising above the cultivated valley. Numerous churches and villas are dotted around the hills. The small towns of Borgo San Lorenzo, San Piero a Sieve, and Scarperia contain interesting buildings, and Vicchio is famous as the birthplace of Giotto.

The **Alto Mugello** extends up to the Apennine passes and the border with Emilia-Romagna. Borgo San Lorenzo—the main town in the Mugello area—was severely damaged by earthquake in 1919, and the Mugello suffered further in the last World War from its proximity to the 'Gothic Line' (the German defensive line established in the autumn of 1944 which was only broken by the Allies in the spring of 1945) across the ridge of the Apennines between Versilia and Rimini.

The **Val di Sieve** is the area northeast of Florence around the wine-growing centres of Pontassieve and Rufina. The whole area has been opened up in the last ten years or so to hikers with a number of nature trails: information from the *Comunità Montana*, who publish a guide and a map.

■ Practical information

Information offices. *Comunità Montana Mugello*, 45 Via Togliatti, Borgo San Lorenzo (☎ 055-8495346), which also provides information about hiking. *Turismo e Ambiente*, 6 Via Bandini, Borgo San Lorenzo (☎ 055-8458793). *Borgoinforma*, 1 Piazza Garibaldi, Borgo San Lorenzo (☎ 055-8456230).

Getting there from Florence
By road. There are two direct roads from Florence to the **Mugello**: the Via Faentina (N302), the most attractive road, and the Via Bolognese (N65) which offers a slightly faster approach. The Faentina can also be joined at l'Olmo from a beautiful secondary road which leads along the hills beyond Fiesole (see p. 100). The **Val di Sieve** can be reached directly from Florence east along the Arno on the Arezzo road (N69) as far as Pontassieve, and then by N67 which follows the Sieve north to Rufina and Dicomano.

By bus. *SITA* and *CAP* provide a frequent service from Florence to San Piero a Sieve (in 50mins) and to Borgo San Lorenzo (in 1 hour). Other services connect Borgo San Lorenzo to San Piero a Sieve, Cafaggiolo, and Scarperia as well as Vicchio and Dicomano.

By rail. A secondary line from Florence to Faenza runs via Pontassieve, Rufina, Dicomano, and Vicchio to Borgo San Lorenzo (in 60–70 minutes). The secondary line along the Faentina (via Le Caldine and Vaglia) from Florence (Campo di Marte station) to Borgo San Lorenzo (which was put out of action in the Second World War) was reopened in 1999. It also has a station at San Piero a Sieve. At present there are four trains a day in each direction and the scenic journey from Florence to Borgo takes about 45 mins (for information ☎ 055-8459116).

Hotels
Near **Borgo San Lorenzo**. ★★★ *Villa Ebe*, 11 Via Ferracciano (☎ 055-8457507; fax 055-848567); *Tre Fiume*, 16 Via Madonna dei 3 Fiumi (near Ronta).
Marradi. ★★★ *Il Lamone*, 28 Viale Baccarini (☎ 055-8045023).
Palazzuolo sul Senio. ★★★ *Senio*, 1 Borgo dell'Ore, with restaurant (see below; ☎ 055-8046019; fax 055-8046485).
San Piero a Sieve. ★★ *La Felicina*, 14 Piazza Colonna (☎ 055-8498181; fax 055-8498157) with restaurant.
Vicchio. ★★★ *Villa Campestri* (in a beautiful villa near Sagginale at Campestri), 19 Via di Campestri (☎ 055-8490107; fax 055-8490108).
San Godenzo. ★★ *Silvano*, 69 Via Forlivese (☎ 055-8374043; fax 055-8374397).
Rufina. ★★★ *La Speranza*, 14 Via Piave (☎ 055-8397027; fax 055-8397028).

Agriturismo accommodation. This is available in most of the above localities. Accommodation booking service run by *Promo Mugello, Consorzio di Promozione Turistica*, 5/6 Piazza Martin Luther King, Borgo San Lorenzo (☎ 055-8458742).

Campsites
Palazzuolo sul Senio. ★★ *Visano*, 19 Via Faggiola (☎ 055-8046106).
San Piero a Sieve. ★★★ *Mugello Verde*, 39 Via Massorondinaio (at La Fortezza; (☎ 055-848511, fax 055-8486910).
Barberino di Mugello. ★★ *Il Sergente*, 24 Via Santa Lucia, Monte di Fò (☎ 055-8423018).
Firenzuola. ★★ *Lo Stale*, Bruscoli Postiglione (☎ 055-815297).
Vicchio. ★★ *Vecchio Ponte*, 16 Via Costoli (☎ 055-8448638) and *Valdisieve*, Via Rossoio Caldeta (☎ 055-838246).

Restaurants
Vetta Le Croci. ££ *Feriolo*, and £ *Las Vegas*.
Borgo San Lorenzo. ££ *Collefertili*, Località Arliano (☎ 055-8495201).
Marradi. ££ *Il Camino*.
Palazzuolo sul Senio. £££ *Locanda Senio*, 1 Borgo dell'Ore (☎ 055-8046019).
Val di Sieve (Pontassieve). ££ *La Casellina*, 28 Via Colognese (☎ 055-8397580) and ££ *Torre al Sasso*, 51 Via Montestrini (☎ 055-8300086).

Market at Borgo San Lorenzo on Tuesdays.

Borgo San Lorenzo
Borgo San Lorenzo (14,800 inhab.) in the centre of the Sieve valley is the main town of the Mugello. Up until the 1950s it was a thriving market town, and since the 1960s numerous small industries have set up factories on the plain, towards Scarperia.

> **History**. Of ancient foundation, Borgo San Lorenzo was once a possession of the Ubaldini, and from the 10C was owned by the Bishop of Florence. In a central position, on a crossing of the Sieve, it became a dominion of Florence after 1290. It suffered a severe earthquake in 1919. The famous Chini ceramic factories, founded by Galileo and Chino Chini, both natives of Borgo, were active here from 1906–44, producing very fine ceramic decoration and stained glass, much of it still to be found in the town.

In the pleasant old town centre is the **Palazzo del Podestà** with numerous well-preserved coats of arms on its façade (including della Robbian works). It is now the seat of the Biblioteca Comunale: on the ground floor are more coats of arms and frescoes including a 16C Florentine *Madonna and Child with Saints*.

Nearby is the large Pieve di San Lorenzo, first mentioned in 941 and rebuilt in the 12C. It was altered later and restored in 1937 after earthquake damage. The campanile is described below.

Interior. The pretty side altars were erected in 1503. **North aisle: first altar**, 17C Florentine school, *Saints Anthony Abbot and Anthony of Padua*; **second altar**, Matteo Rosselli, *Madonna and Saints Domenic and Francis*; **third altar**, Bachiacca (attributed), *Saints Benedict, Sebastian, and Domenic* (with angels in the lunette above); **fourth altar**, Jacopo Vignali, *Madonna in glory with Saints* (removed). Over the **high altar**, 14C painted *Crucifix*, and in the apse, mural painting by Galileo Chini (1906). At the end of the **South aisle**, *Madonna*, a ruined fragment attributed to Giotto. **Fourth altar**, Agnolo Gaddi (attributed), *Madonna enthroned with Angels*; **third altar**, Paolo Colli (d. 1822), *St Michael*, and a 15C polychrome terracotta bust of *St Lawrence*. Beyond a 16C fresco of the *Madonna* (removed), the second altarpiece of the *Lamentation over the Dead Christ* is by Cesare Velli (1591).

Outside the church is the **Tabernacle of St Francis**, brightly decorated in 1926 with paintings and polychrome terracotta by the Chini workshop (restored in 1989).

Corso Matteotti divides the old town roughly in half. Just before it passes beneath a gate with a clock tower (which still keeps the hours) a side street right leads to the foot of the unusual **Campanile of San Lorenzo**, built in 1263 above the apse. It is circular beneath and irregularly hexagonal above.

Corso Matteotti continues towards a less attractive part of the town past the police station (with a ceramic eagle by Chini) and some way further on ends beside the **Santuario del Santissimo Crocifisso** on the edge of town. This centrally-planned building was built by Girolamo Ticciati in 1714–43 on the site of an oratory dedicated to a *Crucifix*, believed to work miracles and venerated since c 1400. It was ruined in the earthquake of 1919 but has been reconstructed.

Interior. The fine high altarpiece of the guardian angel protecting Borgo from the earthquake of 1835 is by Giuseppe Bezzuoli. Behind it is kept the miraculous *Crucifix* attributed to the school of Giovanni Pisano, exhibited only on the first Sunday of every month. The eight paintings of the *Passion of Christ* are by Luigi Sabatelli and the right altarpiece (the *Baptism of Constantine*) is by Ignazio Hugford. The Cappella della Compagnia, off the left side of the church, has **stained glass** by the Chini workshop (1922).

On the left of the sanctuary is the deconsecrated Gothic church of **San Francesco** (privately owned; ring for adm. at the ex-convent) with an interesting Cistercian interior and recently restored Giottesque frescoes. Nearby is the large **Villa Pecori-Giraldi**, with a 16C façade and a 19C tower. Owned by the Comune it is being restored (interesting Art Nouveau details in the interior). The park is open to the public.

On the other side of the town, in Piazza Dante (with a public garden), is the headquarters of the **Misericordia** (1908) with a neo-Gothic exterior and a majolica *Pietà* by Galileo Chini over the doorway. Inside the chapel are two side altars and two kneeling angels in enamelled terracotta by Galileo Chini, who also painted the apse.

The Alto Mugello

The Via Faentina leads north from Borgo San Lorenzo to the town of Marradi, near the border with Emilia-Romagna. The district is known as the 'Alto Mugello'. An annual running race known as the *100 kilometri del passatore* is held on this road from Faenza to Florence in Spring.

A few kilometres north of Borgo San Lorenzo, right of the Via Faentina, is the church of **San Giovanni Maggiore** (open on Sunday), surrounded by farm buildings. It has a portico and an 11C octagonal campanile. Founded in the 10C, the church was rebuilt by Francesco Minerbetti in 1520–30 and transformed in the 19C. It contains an elegant 12C *ambone. The stained glass is by the Chini factory, and the nave was frescoed in 1843 by Pietro Alessi Chini.

Further north, near **Ronta**, a quiet little summer resort, is the **Madonna dei Tre Fiumi** in a fine position. Here an interesting privately-owned water mill, the **Antica Mulino Margheri** which is still in operation can be visited on request (☎ 055-8403051). The **Colle di Casaglia** (913m) is the hill dividing the Sieve and Lamone valleys.

Marradi lies in a narrow stretch of the Lamone valley, at the foot of the Apennines which divide Tuscany from Emilia-Romagna. It came under Florentine rule from 1428 onwards. Its capture by the Allies in 1944 made a breach in the German Gothic line (see p. 113). The Piazza Le Scalelle is named after a mountain pass which was the scene of a victory of the citizens of Marradi in 1358 over Corrado Lando, a count from Württenberg who was forced to lead his mercenary army south via the territory of Marradi in order to avoid Florence. Having wrought much damage to Marradi, they were ambushed by the angry citizens; Carrado's brother died and he himself was wounded and taken prisoner.

On the outskirts of the town is the Teatro degli Animosi, built in 1792 by Giulio Mannaioni (restored and reopened). Outside the town is **Badia del Borgo** (first documented in 1025), reconstructed in 1741–65. In the sacristy 15C paintings attributed to the Master of Marradi are preserved.

Palazzuolo sul Senio

A winding mountain road connects Marradi with Palazzuolo sul Senio in the Senio valley to the northwest. It was ruled by the Ubaldini family until 1362 when it came under Florentine dominion. In the picturesque 14C Palazzo dei Capitani is the **Museo della Civiltà Contadina**, a fine local ethnographical museum (open 16.00–19.00 in July and August, ☎ 055-8046008). Next to it, above a garden, is the church of Santi Carlo e Antonio with an interesting 17C interior. The parish church of Santo Stefano contains Florentine 16C–17C paintings, decorations by Dino Chini (1945), and a small museum. The medieval **Pieve di Misileo** (rebuilt in 1781), near Palazzuolo, preserves a Romanesque crypt and a 15C painting of the *Madonna and Saints* (recently restored).

Another road leads north from Borgo San Lorenzo via **Luco di Mugello** (where the hospital, in a former monastery, has a beautiful Renaissance courtyard), to **Grezzano**. Here in the **Casa d'Erci**, an old farmhouse, is a delightful private museum (open on holidays 14.30–18.30; summer 15.30–19.30, or by appointment, ☎ 055-8457197) of agricultural implements and artisans' tools, all of them still in working order, illustrating life in the Mugello up until the last War. It is organised by a group of local volunteers.

San Piero a Sieve

To the west of Borgo San Lorenzo is **San Piero a Sieve** at a crossroads connecting the Mugello plain with the Apennine passes via Scarperia and Barberino del Mugello, and where the river Sieve meets the Carza. The **Pieve di San Pietro**, at the entrance to the village on the main road from Vaglia, was founded in the 11C and altered in the 18C. The baptismal font is a fine work by the della Robbia. Above the high altar is a wood *Crucifix* attributed to Raffaello da Montelupo. It also has stained glass windows and a painting of *St Peter*. Outside is a statue of *St Peter* by Girolamo Ticciati (1768) and a war memorial. Across the main road Via della Compagnia ascends past a little 13C oratory to Palazzo Adami with terracotta decorations.

A valley in the Mugello.

A country track continues up to the large 16C **Fortezza di San Martino**, surrounded by pine woods. It was designed for the Medici by Bernardo Buontalenti to guard Florence from the north. It is one of the most interesting examples of Renaissance military architecture left in Tuscany and is to be restored and eventually opened to the public.

From Palazzo Adami, Via dei Medici descends through Piazza Gramsci past the large **Villa Schifanoia** (formerly Medici) built in terraces on the hillside with a dovecot in the tower, and (right) an ancient house with arches, past the **Municipio** with polychrome majolica decoration (1925), into the central Piazza Colonna.

Bosco ai Frati

Outside the village, just after a bridge over the Sieve, a by-road (signposted) leads left to Bosco ai Frati, a charming little convent (four friars live here) in pretty wooded country (known locally for its mushrooms). Visitors are shown around by one of the friars (closed 12.00–15.00). The convent was founded before 1000 and the Franciscans came here in 1212. In 1273 St Bonaventura was staying in the convent when Gregory X appointed him Cardinal. The story is told that the saint was washing dishes in the scullery and told the messenger to hang his cardinal's hat on a tree nearby. The convent was purchased by Cosimo il Vecchio in 1420 and he employed Michelozzo to restore the church and convent (he added the fine porch behind the church). Off the cloister a little museum contains a *Crucifix, attributed to Donatello (restored after earthquake damage). Another *Crucifix*, attributed to Desiderio da Settignano was stolen in 1969.

The Medici Villas of Trebbio and Cafaggiolo

A few kilometres west of San Piero a Sieve are the delightful Medici fortified villas of Trebbio and Cafaggiolo. They are reached off the main road (N65) to

Barberino di Mugello. The **Castello del Trebbio**, in a lovely elevated position, is surrounded by a hamlet and pretty woods (privately owned; for **adm.** ☎ 055-8458793 *Turismo e Ambiente*, Mon, Wed or Fri). The castle, surrounded by cypresses, was built by Michelozzo for Cosimo il Vecchio in 1461 as a country residence. It remained the property of the Medici until 1644. A beautiful Italianate 15C **garden** with a long 17C pergola survives. The villa was the residence of Giovanni Dalle Bande Nere and Maria Salviati, and Amerigo Vespucci may have been a guest here in 1476. The kitchen and a small living room on the ground floor are also usually shown.

The **Villa di Cafaggiolo**, a huge castle behind a garden railing can be seen from the main road (privately owned; **adm.** as for Trebbio). It is surrounded by a park with some fine trees. This was the first country villa that Michelozzo built for Cosimo il Vecchio. It was erected in 1451 on the site of a castle. In 1500, Pierfrancesco de' Medici founded a ceramic manufactory in the buildings to the left of the villa. It was famous for its products especially up to c 1520. Leo X stayed here in 1515, and it was the favourite country house of Ferdinando I and of the Lorraine grand-dukes. It was bought by the Borghese family in 1864.

The impressive exterior, with corbelling below the eaves and decorated with battlements, formerly had two towers and was once surrounded by a moat. It is more interesting than the interior, which has some 19C decorations restored in 1887 by the Chini brothers on the ground floor.

Beyond Cafaggiolo, towards Barberino, is the site of the huge artificial lake of **Bilancino** built between 1984 and 1998. The dam here controls the waters of the Sieve (and their confluence with the Arno at Pontassieve in times of flood), and will increase Florence's supply of drinking water. The process of filling the basin with some 69 million cubic metres of water will not be completed until at least 2000. There are long-term plans to use the lake, which will have an area of about 5 sq km, for boating and wind-surfing. This extremely costly and ambitious project was fraught with problems and legal proceedings are in process to discover how the funds have been used.

Galliano, off the road to the right, was founded in 1048 by the Ubaldini family at the foot of an Apennine pass (remains of its fortifications survive). The Pieve has a dome frescoed by Tito Chini (1920). Inside is a *Madonna and Child* attributed to Margaritone di Arezzo and a *Madonna and Child with Saints* attributed to the school of Ghirlandaio. In the adjoining oratory is an *Annunciatory Virgin* by Davide Ghirlandaio. In the church of Santo Stefano a Rezzano nearby is a *Madonna and Saints* attributed to Filippino Lippi.

Barberino di Mugello is well known because of its vicinity to the Florence–Bologna motorway. A hamlet grew up here in the 11C around a castle belonging to the Cattani family. Of great strategic importance on an Apennine pass, it was sacked by many armies, including that of Sir John Hawkwood (in 1364); see p. 461. It was badly damaged in the last War. Palazzo Pretorio, in Piazza Cavour, has a portico attributed to Michelozzo. The Pieve of **San Silvestro** contains a precious organ (16C–19C), and an **enamelled terracotta font** (moved from the church of Sant'Andrea a Camoggiano) by Giovanni della Robbia and the Oratory next door has good examples of carved woodwork.

The church of **Cavallina**, south of the town, contains a fine carved tabernacle attributed to Mino da Fiesole, and a 16C *Madonna and Child with Saints*.

Also just outside Barberino is the Badia di **Santa Maria a Vigesimo** with a fine façade and interior of 1740–47 (restored in 1996). Beneath the organ of 1744 is a Rococo cantoria. The paintings include a 15C *Virgin Annunciate* and a *Birth of the Virgin* by Ignazio Hugford.

The church of Sant'Andrea at **Camoggiano**, across the motorway, has a pretty façade (1470) with a little portico, and, inside, late 14C frescoes by the Florentine school. Next door is the Renaissance Palazzo Cattani with a good courtyard.

North of Barberino is the Pieve of **San Gavino Adimari** rebuilt in 1267, with an 18C interior and an interesting tomb slab carved with Christian symbols. Beyond **Panna**, where mineral water is bottled, is the **Passo della Futa** (903m) one of the main Apennine passes. The strongest German defences in the Gothic line (see p. 113) in the Second World War were here, but the position was altered when the Allies captured the Giogo Pass and Firenzuola. Just beyond (851m), a summer and winter holiday resort is the **Passo della Raticosa** (968m) with an old custom-house on the border with Emilia, see *Blue Guide Northern Italy*.

Scarperia

North of San Piero a Sieve is Scarperia (5700 inhab.) which was founded in 1306 by the Florentines to protect her territories from invading armies from across the Apennines. The town preserves its interesting rectangular plan laid out on either side of the main road which connected Florence to Bologna (now Via Roma) with the castle in the centre. In 1415 it became the seat of a vicariate of the Florentine Republic, with jurisdiction over the whole of the Mugello. The craft of making knives has been practised here probably since the 14C; it was a flourishing industry from the 15C up until the early 20C. In 1542 the village suffered from an earthquake, and after the Lorraine grand-dukes opened the new road across the Futa Pass in 1752, Scarperia lost its importance.

At the entrance to the town is the little **Oratorio della Madonna dei Terre-moti** with a charming fresco of the *Madonna and Child enthroned* (c 1448) attributed to the circle of Francesco d'Antonio (or the school of Filippo Lippi). Beyond the little public garden (with a view) is the lovely walled garden of the **Torrino**, a 15C tower restored in 1930 (**adm**. by appointment with *Turismo e Ambiente*, ☎ 055-8458793 Mon, Wed, or Fri.) It contains a private museum with an eclectic collection, including Etruscan vases medieval urns and paintings on nine floors and Art Nouveau tiled decoration by the Chini workshop.

The main road runs straight up to the centre of the town with the splendid *Palazzo dei Vicari (open Sat 15.30–19.00; fest. 10.00–13.00, 15.30–19.00, or by appointment at the Biblioteca Comunale, ☎ 055-8430671), built in 1306 perhaps on a design by Arnolfo di Cambio. It has a very tall tower and numerous coats of arms all over its façade, some in enamelled terracotta by the della Robbia family and Benedetto Buglioni. The imposing **atrium** (restored in 1889 by Gaetano Bianchi), covered with more coats of arms and late 14C frescoes (including a *Madonna and Child*), leads into the long rectangular courtyard which stretches as far as the hillside. The staircase leads up past a huge fresco of *St Christopher* (c 1412) to the **first floor**. Here is a fine fresco of the *Madonna and Child with Saints* by the school of Ridolfo del Ghirlandaio (1554). The Sala del Consiglio has more frescoes (15C–19C) with coats of arms. The Sala del Sindaco, with 14C and 15C paintings, a 16C fireplace, and polychrome terracotta relief of the *Madonna and Child*, may also be visited.

In the piazza, opposite Palazzo dei Vicari, is the parish church of **Santi Jacopo e Filippo** founded in the 14C but rebuilt, with a neo-Gothic campanile.

Interior. Left side: **first altar**, Matteo Rosselli, *Crucifixion and Saints*; **second altar**, *Annunciation*, a fine painting recently restored and attributed to Giovanni Balducci. In the chapel to the left of the main altar, small marble tabernacle, an early work by Domenico Rosselli and a small wooden *Crucifix* attributed to Jacopo Sansovino. In the apse, late 15C wooden *Crucifix*. In the chapel to the right of the main altar is a beautiful marble tondo of the *Madonna and Child* by Benedetto da Maiano (in its original wooden frame). The second altarpiece on the right side (*Birth of the Virgin*) is by Matteo Rosselli, and on the wall is a fragment of a 15C fresco. Also in the piazza, with a large window, is the **Oratorio della Madonna di Piazza** (door usually unlocked) with a Gothic tabernacle enclosing a fine painting of the *Madonna and Child* by Jacopo del Casentino (restored in 1986), within a 15C marble frame.

To the right of Palazzo dei Vicari, at No. 19 Via Solferino is the **Museo dei Ferri Taglienti**, an artisan's workshop (admission as for Palazzo dei Vicari) showing how knives were manufactured. From the public gardens (see above) a road runs down the edge of the hillside by the **Oratorio della Madonna del Vivaio** built on a design by Alessandro Galilei in 1724–41. It is a centrally-planned church surmounted by a tall drum and lantern, with an interesting neo-classical interior (closed since 1960).

The district of Scarperia

Sant'Agata, a short way west of Scarperia, has an interesting Pieve (open all day), documented since 984. The exterior is prettily decorated and the low tower has a clock. The interior is remarkable for its unusual columns on huge square bases which rise directly to the wooden roof beams. At the west end the baptismal font is enclosed by Romanesque marble intarsia panels (1175; formerly part of an ambone). On the wall is a Romanesque statuette. In the chapel to the right of the high altar, *Mystical Marriage of St Catherine*, a fine painting by Bicci di Lorenzo enclosed in a 16C wooden tabernacle. On the triumphal arch are two tabernacles with the *Madonna* and *Annunciatory Angel* attributed to the bottega of Cristofano Allori. Over the west door, Romanesque statue of St Agata. The high altarpiece attributed to Giovanni del Biondo (c 1377) or Jacopo di Cione has been removed for restoration.

Beside the 17C Palazzo Salviati, Chiasso Salviati leads out of the village into open country. Below the church is a Romanesque bridge and old water mill. A delightful little private museum, the **Teatrino degli Automi Meccanici di Faliero Lepri**, has mechanical tableaux of local peasant life (1920–50), usually open (☎ 055-8406750).

Just to the south of Scarperia is the church of **Santa Maria a Fagna**. Founded before 1018, the façade and interior were decorated in 1770. The church (for the key ring at the house on the right) contains a handsome 12C *ambone and font, an *Assumption of the Virgin*, signed and dated 1587 by Santi di Tito, a 15C Florentine *Madonna and Child* attributed to Fra Diamante or Pseudo Pier Francesco Fiorentino, and a wax early 19C sculpture of the *Dead Christ* by Clemente Susini.

Another country road from Scarperia (signposted Luco di Mugello) passes the isolated little church of **San Michele a Figliano** which contains a font and altar by the Chini factory (who also designed the war memorial outside). Nearby is the **Villa Frescobaldi a Corte** with a fine park (no adm.).

To the north of Scarperia is the neo-classical **Villa il Pelagio** (left), once a residence of the Borghese family, with a garden. Beyond the **Giogo di Scarperia** (882m), an Apennine pass, is **Firenzuola**, a 14C Florentine colony, with a gateway at either end of its arcaded main street. The town was laid out on symmetrical lines within rectangular bastions, designed by Antonio da Sangallo the Elder, but it was very badly damaged in the Second World War. The German Gothic line (see p. 113) was pierced here by the American fifth Army in September 1944 after heavy fighting.

The road then follows the Santerno river through hills with interesting rock formations and numerous quarries of *pietra serena*. To the north, on the Emilian border just outside Moraduccio is a British Military Cemetery.

South of Borgo San Lorenzo

South of Borgo San Lorenzo, in beautiful countryside off the two roads from Florence between Polcanto and Vaglia, is the **Badia di Buonsolazzo**, a Benedictine foundation with a worn 18C façade. At **Faltona**, on the Via Faentina, is the church of Santa Felicità. The church (usually locked), with a tall tower, contains a stained glass window (in the chapel of the Rosario, 1647) of St Felicity with her seven children, recently restored and attributed to the circle of Andrea del Castagno. Nearby is the well-kept, privately-owned 18C **Villa Guiducci a Serravalle** (with a painted coat of arms on the bright yellow façade).

On the south bank of the river Sieve, is **Santa Maria ad Olmi**, a conspicuous church with a bell tower, next to an elegant villa. The church dates from the 16C and contains a 15C tabernacle which encloses a 14C fresco, and paintings by Alessandro Allori and Carlo Portelli (if closed, ring at No. 4). Francesco I and Bianca Cappello stayed in the villa in 1585 when Alessandro Allori painted Bianca's portrait in fresco (detached in 1871 and now exhibited in the Tribuna of the Uffizi).

From Olmi a road leads south to through an unspoilt valley to the little village of Poggiolo-Salaiole past the **Villa de Le Viterete** (1624), the buildings of which line the edge of the road next to a little chapel (the garden façade, difficult to see, has a loggia), and the 15C **Villa La Bartolina** (recently restored) with a fine ground floor loggia of four arches.

On the left of the Sagginale road is **Lutiano Nuovo**, a little group of houses with a roadside tabernacle protecting a ceramic *Madonna and Child* by the Chini (1914). A road diverges right for the church of **San Cresci** in a lovely position above the valley. It has a splendid tall campanile with windows on four stories. Founded in the 9C, it was rebuilt in 1701–04 by Giovanni Battista Foggini (reconstructed after the earthquake in 1919).

Sagginale has a circular church built in 1969. A *Madonna and Child with two angels* by the Master of the Madonna Straus, and a silver reliquary bust of San Cresci by Giovanni Battista Foggini and Bernardo Holzmann also belong to the church. Nearby is **Barbiana** where Don Lorenzo Milani (1923–67) was parish priest. He was also a writer and educator and founded a remarkable local school here for children from poor families based on the development of liberty and socialisation. Together with his pupils he wrote *Lettera ad una professoressa* (*Letter to a teacher*), published in 1967.

Vicchio, Dicomano and the Val di Sieve

Vicchio

Vicchio, is famous as the **birthplace of Giotto** and **Fra Angelico**. Benvenuto Cellini had a house here from 1559–71 (on Corso del Popolo; plaque). A picturesque bridge crosses the Sieve. Part of the medieval walls (1324) survive. In Piazza della Vittoria is the polygonal Torre dei Cerchiai beside a neo-classical loggia. The centre of the little town is Piazza Giotto which has a bronze monument to the painter by Italo Vagnetti (1901). The **Museo Civico Beato Angelico** has an interesting collection of works of art from churches in the region, but it has been closed for many years (although there are at last plans to restore it).

A few kilometres outside Vicchio, signposted off the main road to Borgo San Lorenzo, is **Vespignano** where the house in which Giotto is thought to have been born has been restored and opened to the public. It contains photographs of his major works (ring for admission: **open** summer, Tues, Thur, Sat, and Sun, 15.00–19.00; winter, Sat and Sun, 15.00–19.00).

On the hillside above the house is the church of San Martino which contains a *Madonna and Child* by Paolo Schiavo and a tabernacle by Mino da Fiesole. A path

Giotto di Bondone

Giotto di Bondone (1266/7–1337), known to have been born in Vespignano, introduced a new style of painting which was to have a profound influence on the course of Italian art. His painting had a realism, monumentality and sense of volume which had never been achieved in medieval painting or by his master Cimabue. He was immediately recognised by his contemporaries as a great painter. He was admired in his lifetime by Petrarch and Boccaccio, and his friend Dante mentions him in his *Divina Commedia* (*Purgatorio*; Canto XI, 91–92):

> *Credette Cimabue, nella pittura,*
> *Tener lo campo, ed ora ha Giotto il grido...*

> (Cimabue thought he commanded the field in painting,
> and now Giotto has the acclaim...)

Among his famous masterpieces are the fresco cycles in the Scrovegni chapel in Padua, and in the upper church of San Francesco in Assisi, and in the Peruzzi and Bardi chapels in Santa Croce in Florence. One of his most beautiful paintings is the *Maestà* painted for the church of Ognissanti in Florence and now in the Uffizi. As capomaestro of the cathedral works in Florence he designed the campanile. He is also known to have worked for the papacy in Rome, the Anjou in Naples and the Visconti in Milan. His art was closely studied by Masaccio, Leonardo, and Michelangelo. A fragment of a painting of the Madonna attributed to him can be seen near Vicchio in the Pieve at Borgo San Lorenzo.

leads across fields to the little Cappellina della Bruna protected by cypresses, which preserves a damaged fresco attributed to Paolo Schiavo (restored in 1985).

Dicomano

Dicomano is a flourishing small market town of ancient origins, with some arcaded streets. The town hall occupies a large neo-classical building (1888). A road leads up above the town to the 12C Romanesque **Pieve di Santa Maria** with a squat campanile (if closed ring at the priest's house, No. 25 on the left). The small **interior** has low stone arcades and a wooden roof. On the south wall is a polychrome terracotta relief of the *Marriage of St Joachim and Ann* by the della Robbian school. A painting of the *Madonna of the Rosary* by Santi di Tito has been removed for restoration. At the end of the **south aisle**, *Nativity* attributed to the school of Bronzino in a splendid Mannerist frame.

On the east wall, *Assumption* by Francesco Curradi in another fine frame. Behind the altar is a tiny della Robbian polychrome tabernacle. **North aisle**. Giorgio Vasari (attributed), *Madonna and Saints*; school of Ghirlandaio, *Madonna enthroned with Saints*; and a beautiful 14C triptych of the *Madonna with Saints*.

On the north side of the town is the **Oratorio di Sant'Onofrio**, a splendid neo-classical building by Giuseppe del Rosso (1796), preceded by a portico of four columns. The church of **Sant'Antonio** (rebuilt in 1938; usually locked) contains a della Robbian relief (1504; heavily restored after damage in 1919) and a 14C *Madonna and Child with Saints*.

Important Etruscan excavations (6C BC) have taken place southeast of Dicomano at **Frascole** (sometimes open, ☎ 055 838541).

San Godenzo

A road leads northeast from Dicomano to the Passo del Muraglione on the border with Emilia-Romagna passing San Godenzo. The town is noted for its *abbey church, a massive Romanesque building founded in 1028 by Jacopo il Bavaro, Bishop of Fiesole. It stands above the main street, in Piazza Dante Alighieri. In 1308 a meeting took place in the abbey of members of the Guelf party in exile from Florence, including Dante.

The plain stone **interior** has the presbytery raised above the crypt. On the parapet is a pretty frieze of inlaid marble. The polyptych of the *Madonna and Saints* attributed to Bernardo Daddi was repainted in 1533. The apse mosaic of the *Coronation of the Virgin* is by Giuseppe Cassioli (1929). In the left aisle is an *Annunciation* attributed to Franciabigio, and a wooden *statue of *St Sebastian* by Baccio da Montelupo (1506; restored in 1988).

Nearby is **Castagno d'Andrea**, thought to have been the birthplace of the painter Andrea del Castagno (1417 or 1419–57). In the parish church (rebuilt after the the Second World War) are frescoes of the *Crucifixion* by Pietro Annigoni (1958). Here is an entrance to the **Parco Nazionale delle Foreste Casentinesi, Monte Falterona e Campigna** (see p. 492), an extensive protected wooded area of the Apennines.

The **Passo del Muraglione** (907m), an Apennine pass above the border with Emilia-Romagna, is named after the massive wall erected here in 1836 by Leopoldo II to shelter travellers from snow and icy winds. To the north, where the Troncalosso and Acquacheta rivers meet, is the charming **Acquacheta** waterfall (130m), sung by Dante (*Divina Commedia; Inferno*, XVI, 94–102).

South of Dicomano is **Londa** (where Etruscan remains have been found) on a secondary road which leads to Stia in the Casentino (see Ch. 40). Farther south, a beautiful by-road winds up through vineyards past some lovely old farmhouses to **Castiglioni**, with a 12C church (altered in 1926) from where there is a view below of the tiny little fortified borgo of Castello di Castiglioni.

Beyond **Petrognano**, with a church rebuilt in 1925 and the 18C Villa Budini Gattai, and Rimaggio, the tower of the pieve of **San Bartolomeo in Pomino** is conspicuous ahead. The church was founded in the 12C–13C (if closed, ring at no. 60). It has an attractive tall basilican interior with stone arches and a raised chancel. On the left altar, *Madonna and Saints Sebastian and Anthony Abbot*, a fine work attributed to the Master of San Miniato, and on the wall a della Robbian *Madonna and Child with two Saints*. On the right wall is a detached fresco of *St James* with its sinopia. The stained glass and mosaic lunette of the *Madonna with two angels* outside the west door date from 1933. **Rufina** has been famous as a wine-growing centre since 1760 (*Chianti Rufina* is bottled here). Above the town (but hidden by its park) is the 16C Villa di Poggio Reale, approached by a long cypress avenue. It is the seat of the **Museo della Vite e del Vino della Vald-isieve** (closed for restoration), illustrating wine production in the area.

The tall 12C tower of **Montebonello** is conspicuous on the other side of the river where a road leads to **Santa Maria in Acone**. The road crosses a stream and then narrows to climb uphill. An unsurfaced road leads past a farm and ends in front of the church (key at the house next door). The lunette over the main door, the apse and the high altar were decorated by the Chini at the beginning of this century. A painting of the *Madonna and Saints* by the school of Ghirlandaio has been removed to the Misericordia at Pontassieve.

4 · The Chianti

The beautiful hilly region between Florence and Siena is known as the **Chianti** district. Its characteristic landscape includes numerous carefully tended vineyards, orchards, and olive groves, as well as wilder wooded areas. It is perhaps at its most beautiful in autumn when the leaves of the vines and deciduous trees turn to gold and stand out amidst the silver olive trees, and dark green cypresses and pines. It is at this time that the vintage (*vendemmia*) takes place. Picturesque villages and castles often dominate the hills and offer spectacular panoramas. Some of the most typical and beautiful parts of the countryside can be explored on white unsurfaced roads. Also in this area are many old Romanesque country churches (*pieve*). Vineyards surround the typical, elegant farmhouses known as *case coloniche*. Many of them were built in the 18C during the agricultural reforms carried out by Grand-duke Pietro Leopoldo, and they are often beautifully sited with characteristic towers (formerly dovecots). Some of them have been carefully restored in the last few decades, often by foreigners. The north-western district of the Chianti region is described in Chapter 5.

The name 'Chianti' is probably of Etruscan origin. The boundary between the Province of Florence (north) and that of Siena (south) divides the Chianti district roughly in half. Most of the castles originated as part of the *Lega del Chianti* (Chianti League): they were fortified strongholds built by the Florentines in the 12C against the Sienese and owned by rich Florentine families and landowners

Towns and castles were lost and won (the Florentines were heavily defeated at Monta-perti in 1260) but in 1559 Siena, and her entire territory, was forced to capitulate to the Grand-duke of Tuscany, Cosimo I de'Medici.

■ Practical information
Information offices. APT of Florence (☎ 055-290832) for Greve, and Panzano; and *APT* of Siena (☎ 0577-280551) for Radda, Gaiole, Castellina in Chianti, and Castelnuovo Berardenga. There is a local tourist office in Greve (Via Luca Cini, ☎ 055-8545243).

Getting there
By car. The prettiest **road** from Florence is the **Via Chiantigiana** (N222) via Grassina near Impruneta (see Ch. 2) to Greve in Chianti, Panzano, and Castellina in Chianti. South of Panzano another lovely road traverses beautiful countryside in the heart of the Chianti region via Radda and Gaiole.

By bus. Frequent services run by *SITA* from Florence (*SITA* bus station, 15 Via Santa Caterina da Siena, off Piazza Stazione) to Greve in 1hr. Some services leave Florence by Porta Romana, and run via Galluzzo and the Cassia as far as Terme di Firenze, and others leave Florence by Piazza Beccaria, and run via Ponte a Ema, Grassina, Ugolino, and Strada in Chianti. From Greve the bus continues to Panzano (and, infrequently, to Lamole, Radda and Castellina). Another *SITA* service (once or twice a day) runs via Grassina, Greve, and Panzano to Radda and Gaiole (in 2hrs).

Hotels
There are a number of fine hotels in beautiful quiet positions in the country, mostly three and four star, and nearly all of them with swimming pools. There is however a scarcity of cheaper hotels and campsites.

Greve in Chianti. ★★★ *Del Chianti*, swimming pool, 86 Piazza Matteotti (☎ & fax 055-853763).
Passo dei Pecorai. ★★ *Da Omero*, 68 Via Giovanni Falcone (☎ & fax 055-850716).
Panzano. ★★★ *Villa Sangiovese*, swimming pool, 5 Piazza Bucciarelli (☎ 055-852461; fax 055-852463) and *Villa Le Barone*, swimming pool, 19 Via San Leolino (☎ 055-852621; fax 055-852277).
Radda in Chianti. ★★★★ *Relais Fattoria Vignale*, swimming pool, 8 Via Pianigiani (☎ 0577-738300; fax 0577-738592); ★★★ *Vescine* (*Il Relais del Chianti*; ☎ 0577-741144; fax 0577-740263).
Gaiole in Chianti. ★★★★ *Castello di Spaltenna*, swimming pool (☎ 0577-749483; fax 0577-749269); ★★★ *Residence San Sano* at Lecchi, 6km south, swimming pool (☎ 0577-746130; fax 0577-746156).
Castelnuovo Berardenga. ★★★★ *Relais Borgo San Felice*, swimming pool (☎ 0577-359260; fax 0577-359089); *Villa Arceno*, swimming pool, località Arceno (near San Gusmè; (☎ 0577-359292; fax 0577-359276); ★★★ *Il Fortilizio*, on the Chiantigiana at il Colombaio (☎ 0577-55229; fax 0577 56170).
Castellina in Chianti in the vicinity are a number of hotels with swimming pools: ★★★★ *Villa Casalecchi* (☎ 0577-740240; fax 0577-741111) and *Tenuta di Ricavo* (☎ 0577-740221; fax 0577-741014); ★★★ *Belvedere di San Leonino* (☎ 0577-740887; fax 0577-740924); *Colle Etrusco Salivolpi* (☎ 0577-740484; fax 0577-740998); *Il Colombaio*, 29 Strada Chiantigiana (☎ & fax 0577-740444).
In an historic palazzo in the centre of Castellina: ★★★ *Palazzo Squarcialupi*, also with swimming pool, 26 Via Ferruccio (☎ 0577-741186; fax 0577-740386).

Agriturismo accommodation

Numerous localities including Greve, Radda, Gaiole, and Castellina in Chianti offer *Agriturismo* accommodation (listed in the *APT* hotel lists. Information also from Agenzia Colline Verdi, 12 Via della Rocca, Castellina in Chianti, ☎ & fax 0577-740620).

Campsite ★★ *Luxor srl* (☎ 0577-743047) open in summer at Castellina in Chianti (with swimming pool and restaurant).

Restaurants

Restaurants also tend to be expensive in the Chianti region. Some of the cheaper ones are listed below.

Montefioralle. £ *Taverna del Guerrino.*

Strada in Chianti. ££ *Il Padellina.*

La Panca. £ *Trattoria Le Cornacchie.*

Passo dei Pecorai. £ *Casprini da Omero.*

Radda in Chianti. £ *Le Vigne,* Podere Le Vigne.

Gaiole. £ *Il Carlino d'oro,* San Regolo.

Volpaia. *Osteria la Bottega di Volpaia* (snacks).

Castelnuovo Berardenga. £ *La Bottega del 30,* and *Nonna Luisa* at Corsignano.

Castellina in Chianti. £ *La Torre* in Piazza del Comune.

Wine tasting. In many of the larger estates the **wine cellars** (*cantine*) may be visited, and wine purchased. Wine-tasting and snacks are also often provided by appointment (telephone numbers are given in the text below where this applies: booking is usually necessary at least three days in advance). Information from local tourist offices and the Consorzio del Chianti, 4 Lungarno Corsini, Florence (☎ 055-212333), and the Consorzio del Marchio Storico Chianti Classico, 155 Via Scopeti, Sant'Andrea in Percussina, San Casciano Val di Pesa (☎ 055-8228245). **Annual wine festival** in the third week of September in Greve in Chianti.

Greve in Chianti

Greve in Chianti, a pretty market town (10,000 inhabitants), is one of the centres of the wine trade. It has an attractive triangular **piazza**, with porticoes along two sides, which provides a perfect setting for the annual fair. The monument commemorates Giovanni da Verrazzano (d. 1528), the explorer of the North American coast. The church of **Santa Croce**, rebuilt in the neo-classical style, has a painting by Bicci di Lorenzo. In Piazza Matteotti is a little puppet theatre which gives regular performances for children in summer.

On a hill, just outside the town, is the little church of **San Francesco** containing a glazed terracotta *Deposition* by Santi Buglioni. The conventual buildings are to house a local museum (due to open in 1999) for works of art from churches in the neighbourhood. These will include altarpieces by Francesco Granacci, Raffaellino del Garbo, and Francesco Curradi, some interesting 14C–15C sculptures, liturgical objects, and an archaeological section.

To the west is the charming little village of **Montefioralle**, the birthplace of the Vespucci family. It is perched on a hill, partly surrounded by its old walls, and has remains of a medieval castle. The village has preserved its medieval character and there are fine views all around. In the church of Santo Stefano is a large icon of the *Madonna and Child* by a 13C Florentine painter, and paintings of the *Trinity with four Saints* and an *Annunciation with Saints John the Baptist and Stephen*, both 15C Florentine works.

On a nearby hill is **San Cresci**, a Romanesque church in a beautiful position.

The 12C façade has the unusual feature of a narthex and brick decoration round the entrance and window arches. The interior has undergone numerous alterations over the centuries and what we see is mostly 19C. Some damaged remains of early frescoes have been uncovered under whitewash. A beautiful unsurfaced road continues, through woods, to Badia di Passignano (see Ch. 5). The area around Greve is particularly rich in medieval castles, mostly privately owned, each surrounded by its estate which produces its own wine.

To the north, by-roads lead off on the right to the former castle of **Uzzano** (☎ 055-853032), now transformed into a villa with a porticoed courtyard. The drive uphill through woods and cypress trees offers some splendid views.

Nearby is the romantic-looking fortified farmhouse of **Colognole** (private) at the end of a long cypress alley. Beyond is the elegant **Villa Calcinaia**, for centuries the property of the Capponi family, with fine gardens (☎ 055-853008).

Further north are the castles of **Verrazzano** (☎ 055-853049) and **Vicchiomaggio** (☎ 055-853003), both in fine positions. On the main road is the **Passo dei Pecorai**(344m), off which is the castle of **Gabbiano** (☎ 055-821053) with four round corner towers and an impressive towered entrance. On the road to Impruneta are terracotta furnaces at **Ferrone**.

On the Via Chiantigiana, 2km beyond Chiocchio is a pretty road running parallel to the Sezzate river. The impressive castle of **Mugnana** (private), surrounded by cypress trees, faces the little medieval village of **Sezzate** across the valley. Further along is the villa and little church of **Cintoia** with its castle, or fortified village, on the hill. Just before reaching La Panca, a by-road leads to the Vallombrosan abbey of **Montescalari** (698m), incorporated into 17C farm buildings.

Off the road to San Polo in Chianti are by-roads for **Castel Ruggero** (☎ 055-642976), **Villa Tizzano** with the little church of Santo Stefano, and the Fattoria di **Vitiano** (☎ 055-855037), all with fine views. The main road continues via Strada and Grassina to Florence.

Panzano

Panzano (498m), originally a medieval castle, still preserves some of its old walls and towers. Its strategic and picturesque position is best appreciated on the approach from San Casciano. There is one main street leading to the church of **Santa Maria** which was completely renovated a century ago. It has a few paintings including a late Gothic *Madonna and Child* attributed to Bernardo di Stefano Rosselli encased in a larger picture with saints and angels. In the nearby oratory is an *Annunciation* attributed to Michele di Ridolfo del Ghirlandaio.

Approximately 1km south of Panzano is its *pieve*, **San Leolino**, beautifully situated on a hill. This fine Romanesque church (the elegant portico was added in the 16C) has a nave and two aisles terminating in three apses; a little door in the right aisle leads to the cloister. The church has several interesting works: an altarpiece of the *Madonna between Saints Peter and Paul*, and stories from their lives, attributed to Meliore di Jacopo (mid-13C), a triptych by the Maestro di Panzano (15C), a *Madonna enthroned with two angels* of the 15C Florentine school, a polyptych over the high altar by Mariotto di Nardo, and two glazed terracotta tabernacles attributed to Giovanni della Robbia. On the left wall is a reliquary bust of St Euphrosynus.This bishop saint was venerated in a nearby oratory, 1km further south off the main road, behind which is a little Romanesque chapel with a carved altar over a well, whose waters were believed to be miraculous.

All around Panzano are numerous villas and *case coloniche* in beautiful countryside. To the north is the 15C villa of **Vignamaggio**, which has a fine Italian garden (which can be visited, together with the cellars, by appointment ☎ 055-8544840). The road continues towards the hills to the picturesque village of **Lamole** and its medieval castle, above the source of the river Greve.

West of Panzano, off a pretty road to Badia a Passignano, is **Rignana** (☎ 055-852065), a little group of farm buildings and a medieval tower. Concerts are given in summer in the nearby church of Santa Maria.

> ### *Agriculture in the Chianti region*
> The agricultural landscape of Tuscany has changed since the 1950s and 1960s when the centuries old sharecropping (*mezzadria*) system of farming came to an end. Until then the peasant families of Tuscany had lived on small holdings (*poderi*) taking a proportion of the crops in return for their work for the landowner. As a result the land was intensely cultivated, often in terraces, with small vineyards, olive groves, and orchards of fruit trees and vegetables. White oxen were used to till the land. With the growth of industrialisation and the booming economy in the post-war years many tenant farmers left the rural life of the country for the towns. Although a few small *poderi* can still be seen, characterised by the variety of crops grown in a small area, with the vines often strung between olive and fruit trees, most of the cultivated land in Tuscany is now owned by large estates surrounded by extensive vineyards which have considerably altered the look of the countryside, particularly in the Chianti region. Many producers now sell their wine and other products directly from their farms (*fattorie*). The beautiful old farm houses (*case coloniche*) and their outhouses, where once the peasants lived with their familes above the stables and barns, are now being restored and bought up by wealthy Italians and foreigners or developed for agriturist accommodation.

Radda in Chianti

Radda in Chianti, another major wine centre, was the principal castle of the Chianti League in the 13C. Although something survives of its walls and fortifications, the medieval hill town has been extensively transformed. In the central piazza is the 15C **Palazzo del Podestà** which has numerous coats of arms on its façade; there is a fine view from the main hall. Opposite are steps leading to the heavily restored church of **San Niccolò**. Outside the town, near the sport fields, is the church of **Santa Maria al Prato**, originally Romanesque but rebuilt in the 17C with the addition of a portico. The adjoining convent of **San Francesco** is destined to become a museum for works of art from churches in the district.

The **Castello di Volpaia** (☎ 0577-738066) stands in a splendid panoramic position (617m).Wine has been produced here since the 11C. In the tiny fortified hamlet there is a small Renaissance church called *La Commenda*. Modern art exhibitions are held here in September.

South of Radda is the **Villa Vistarenni** (☎ 0577-749439). Its monumental

16C façade rises majestically above the surrounding vineyards. The villa origically belonged to the Strozzi family and has fine cellars excavated in the underlying rock, which can be visited.

The **Badia di Coltibuono** (628m), a former Vallombrosan abbey, is surrounded by beautiful oak and pine woods. The monastery has been transformed into a villa (with a restaurant and wine cellars). The main structure in grey stone dates from the 11C–12C and it has an impressive crenellated tower; the church can also be visited.

Gaiole in Chianti owes its importance as a market town to its position as a crossroads between the Chianti district and the upper Arno valley. The surrounding area is very beautiful. On a hill to the west is the medieval castle of **Vertine**. Just east of Gaiole is the village of **Barbischio**, picturesquely perched on a hill covered with rocks and wild vegetation. The impressive castle of **Meleto** (private), to the south, is one of the best preserved castles originally forming part of the Chianti League. It has two massive circular towers, one of which still has its original defences, dominating extensive vineyards. The interior was transformed into a villa in the 18C.

On the road between Radda and San Sano, in a beautiful setting, is one of the oldest Romanesque churches in the Chianti district, **San Giusto in Salcio**. Together with its impressive bell-tower, it has been extensively restored in recent times.

San Polo in Rosso (☎ 0577-746070) is another interesting early *pieve*. It was formerly situated on the boundary separating the territories of Florence and Siena and was therefore incorporated into a fortified castello, probably in the 13C. It is a picturesque group of buildings with an interesting bell tower and a cloister.

One of the most impressive castles in the Chianti is the **Castello di Brolio** (533m), the home of the Ricasoli family since the 12C, and well-known for its wine. Strategically placed at the south end of the Chianti hills, it was for centuries disputed between Florence and Siena. The impressive fortifications surrounding the castle date in part from the 15C–16C but were heavily restored in the 19C. The palace was rebuilt in 1860 in Sienese Gothic style (**open** daily, except Fri, 10.00–12.00, 15.00–18.00). The 14C chapel has a modern mosaic on the façade and contains a polyptych by Ugolino di Nerio (14C); in the crypt are the family tombs. Bettino Ricasoli, the eminent statesman and philanthropist, died here in 1880. The magnificent view to the south stretches from Monte Amiata to Siena and the hills beyond.

To the south is **San Gusmé**, one of the most picturesque villages in the area, surrounded by its original walls complete with two gateways. An excellent white wine (Val d'Arbia) is produced in this area.

Further south is **Castelnuovo Berardenga**, where little survives of the 15C castle, except for the clock-tower and a stretch of walls and a watch tower. The church of **Santi Giusto e Clemente** has a neo-classical façade. Inside is a *Madonna and Child* by Giovanni di Paolo, signed and dated 1426 and a *Madonna* by Andrea di Niccolò, removed from the nearby Pieve di Pacina. The **Villa Chigi** has fine gardens which may be visited on Sundays (10.00–dusk).

At **Montaperti**, west of the river Arbia, is the hill where the Florentine Guelf army was defeated by Siena and Florentine exiles on 4 September 1260 in the

The wines of Tuscany

The world-famous **Chianti red wine** is produced from a careful blend of white and black grapes perfected over many centuries: it was already exported to England in the 17C. The blend is composed of black *Sangiovese* grapes, black *Canaiolo* grapes (traditionally grown in Tuscany), and white *Trebbiano* and *Malvasia* grapes. Only wine produced from grapes grown in a limited geographical area (first officially established in 1716 and the boundaries redrawn in 1932) can bear the label of the black rooster on a yellow ground in a red circle and be called *Chianti Classico gallo nero*. This area, which is strictly controlled, includes San Casciano Val di Pesa, Greve, Castellina, Radda, Gaiole, Castelnuovo Berardenga, Barberino Val d'Elsa, Tavarnelle and Poggibonsi. The other Chianti wines, some of which rival the *classico*, include *Chianti Colli Aretini, Chianti Colli Fiorentini, Chianti Colli Senesi, Chianti Montalbano,* and *Chianti Rufina*. The bright ruby-red Chianti is drunk younger than most French wines. It has between 11.5 and 13 degrees of alcoholic content, and normally is unsuitable for long storage.

The soil and climate of this area of Tuscany is particularly adapted for the vines, which have been planted here since Etruscan times. The grape harvest (*vendemmia*) takes place for a few weeks, usually in late September or early October when the grapes are fully ripe and the weather sunny and dry. The wine-making process usually includes a double fermentation (known as the *governo*).The very best wine is produced in small orchards where the vines are strung between olive trees and the land between them cultivated. However, nowadays most of the wine is produced in extensive vineyards, intensely cultivated on the hillsides. Sulphite free wine is now unfortunately difficult to find, although often it is possible to purchase excellent locally produced wine which is not bottled but can be bought in bulk from small farms. The larger estates now often only sell bottled wine, and organise wine tasting and tours of the cellars.

Vin Santo is an amber dessert wine (17–18 degrees of alcoholic content) produced in Tuscany and Umbria, in particular in the Chianti region (and at Carmignano), similar in taste to an excellent sherry. It is made from selected white bunches of grapes which are laid out on cane mats to dry in the autumn sun after the *vendemmia*. After a few months, usually before Christmas, they are pressed two or three times and the grape-juice or must (*mosto*) is then stored in small casks (*caratelli*), preferably made out of chestnut or oak, and sealed with cement. It is then aged for a minimum of three years (but sometimes for as long as 20 years) in a room, usually indoors under the eaves (in a place subject to the varying temperature of the seasons) rather than in a wine cellar.

Vin Santo is thought to have acquired its name through its association with Holy Week (*La Settimana Santa*) when the wine was usually transferred to bottles, but others maintain that it was called 'Santo' because it was the wine which was normally used at Mass. Yet another theory is that the name comes from the Greek island of Xanthos where a similar wine was produced. Many small wine producers still make excellent Vin Santo for home consumption, but it is also produced on a commercial scale. It is often served with dry almond biscuits (*biscotti di Prato*) at the end of a meal.

battle, dramatically referred to by Dante (*La Divina Commedia; Inferno*, X, 85). A pyramid commemorates the battle. Nearby is the **Pieve di Sant'Ansano** (founded in the 7C). A footpath leads to an octagonal chapel over the spot where St Ansanus, first patron saint of Siena, was allegedly martyred in the 4C.

Castellina in Chianti and environs

Castellina in Chianti (578m) is a small well kept medieval town, with a 15C castle and town gate, which dominates the Arbia, Elsa, and Pesa valleys, with spectacular views of woods, vineyards, olive groves, and scattered *case coloniche*. It has a modern suburb which meets the demands of the expanding wine trade, and smart shops which cater for its many visitors. On the northern side the 15C defence walls are relatively well preserved, and a remarkable walkway (Via delle Volte) follows the eastern line of walls (it was vaulted at a later date and has recently been restored). The fine castle (now the town hall) has a tower and battlements. In the parish church (rebuilt after the last War) is a detached fresco of the *Madonna and Child* by Lorenzo di Bicci, and the shrine of St Fausto, invoked either in times of torrential rain or drought.

Just outside the town is the impressive Etruscan tomb of **Montecalvario** (7C BC) surrounded by pine trees. The tumulus has a diameter of 50 metres and houses four tombs connected by covered passages. Remains of the town walls and a well have been discovered in Castellina, which was situated on an important crossroads in Etruscan times. A few pieces of Etruscan pottery are exibited in the town hall.

A particularly beautiful road descends westwards to Poggibonsi (see Ch. 29) past the little 12C Romanesque church of **San Pietro a Cedda**. It has carved architraves over the front and side doors, a square bell-tower, and an apse decorated with blind arcades. The simple **interior** (open only for Mass on Sat at 17.30, and Sun at 10.30) is built entirely of stone, with a timber roof. A large transversal arch resting on the elaborately carved capitals of two half columns divides the nave. The apse has a lancet window and delicately carved decoration. There are two frescoes of saints (15C) and a reproduction of a triptych of the *Madonna and Child with Saints* of the 15C Florentine school (the original has been removed to the Museo Civico of Colle Val d'Elsa). A little beyond is a fine view of the castle of Strozzavolpe on a hill to the left (described in Ch. 29).

The Via Chiantigiana south of Castellina runs along a ridge offering a variety of extensive views, passing the little hamlet of **Fonterutoli** and crossing the village of **Quercegrossa**. Here, in the Romanesque church is a group of painted terracotta figures attributed to Francesco di Giorgio Martini representing the *Lamentation of the dead Christ*.

Farther south, in beautiful countryside and with a lovely view of Siena, is the **Certosa di Pontignano**, a monastery founded in 1343 and enlarged in the 15C and 16C. It is now attached to Siena University and used for conferences. A fine Renaissance cloister leads to a smaller cloister surrounded by a portico and an upper loggia. A third cloister has remains of frescoes by Bernardino Poccetti. The church also has frescoes by Poccetti and other artists and some fine carved choirstalls by Domenico Atticciati all dating from the 16C. Another chapel has a *Crucifixion* by Francesco Vanni and works by Giuseppe Nicola Nasini.

Olive oil

Some of the best Italian **olive oil** is produced in Tuscany, much of it in this region. The olives, which are at first green and then turn black as they ripen, are still harvested by hand so as not to damage the trees: ladders are propped up against the trees from which the olives are picked into baskets, and sheets (sometimes parachutes left over from the Second World War) spread out on the ground beneath to collect the olives as they fall. The harvest, in late autumn, usually takes many weeks or even months. The olives are then taken to an olive press, once a stone mill worked by mules, but now mechanically operated. To facilitate the pressing the olives are usually slightly heated, but purists make sure the temperature of the olives is not altered. The oil straight from the first pressing is the best and can be labelled *olio extra vergine di oliva* if its acidity is less than 1 per cent. When newly pressed it has a bright green colour and a particularly aromatic flavour. Its qualities are especially appreciated on garlic toast (*bruschetta* or *fettunta*) or as a dip for raw vegetables (*pinzimonio*).

The land is usually left to rest until February when the soil is dug and loosened around the large roots of the olive trees and then fertilised. The pruning of the trees in March is a very long and laborious process done with a hand-saw and secateurs. The branches are then sprayed with copper sulphate.

The olive oil of Tuscany is considered one of the best in Italy, with a particularly strong flavour, and this is the most northerly part of the country where olive trees thrive (in northern Italy the climate is too cold, except for a few very limited areas such as Liguria and around Lake Garda). The trees, if carefully tended, usually flourish and bear fruit for hundreds of years, although an exceptionally harsh winter in 1984 killed numerous olive trees in Tuscany (many of these have been replanted and are beginnng to bear fruit). Low hills are the ideal terrain for olives. Olive oil, which is expensive even in Italy, is recognised for its exceptional nutritional value and as one of the most healthy vegetable oils, both in its raw state and when heated for cooking or frying. It is the basis of Italian cuisine, and replaces butter in the Mediterranean diet. Local recipes provide numerous different ways of preserving or pickling the olives both when green and when black, to be eaten as hors-d'oeuvre.

5 · San Casciano in Val di Pesa and Tavarnelle

This beautiful district, offering spectacular views of the delightful countryside, is also in the Chianti area. The chapter focusses on places near the Via Cassia (N1), a Roman road from Rome to Florence, paved c 154 BC, which runs through splendid countryside and passes many places of interest. Both **San Casciano** and **Tavarnelle** now have interesting small diocesan museums, and **San Donato in Poggio** is a particularly well preserved village.

■ Practical information

Information offices. APT of Florence (☎ 055-290832). Local tourist offices in San Casciano Val di Pesa (☎ 055-8229558) and Tavarnelle (☎ 055-8077832).

Getting there

By road. The Via Cassia or the Via Chiantigiana (see Ch. 4) are by far the most pleasant routes between Florence and Siena. The **superstrada** which runs roughly parallel to the Cassia and has exits at all the main places of interest, is a poorly engineered road, with no emergency lane, and is usually very busy. It has no service stations.

By bus. Frequent bus services run by *SITA*. From Florence via Porta Romana, Galluzzo, San Casciano, San Donato in Poggio, to Tavarnelle in 1hr 20mins; also via Sant'Andrea in Percussina to San Casciano and Mercatale.

Hotels

San Casciano in Val di Pesa. ★★★ *L'Antica Posta*, 1 Piazza Zannoni (☎ 055-822313; fax 055-822278).
Tavarnelle. ★★ *Torricelle Zucchi*, a particularly well-run hotel, 32 Via Cellini at Sambuca (☎ 055-8071780; fax 055-8071102).

Agriturismo accommodation is widely available (information from the local tourist offices).

Youth Hostel. *Ostello del Chianti* (enlarged in 1998), 137 Via Roma, Tavarnelle (☎ 055-8077009).

Campsites at **Barberino Val d'Elsa**: ★★ *Semifonte*, 4 Via Ugo Foscolo (☎ & fax 055-8075454; open March–Nov); and at **Marcialla**: *Toscana Colliverdi* (☎ 0571-669334; open March–Sept).

Restaurants

San Casciano. ££ *Cantinetta del Nonno*, 18 Via IV Novembre; *Nello*, 64 Via IV Novembre; *Malia sul Ponte*, 130 Via Scopeti; and *Matteuzzi*, 8 Via Certaldese.
For restaurants in **Cerbaia**, see Ch 6.
Sant'Andrea in Percussina. ££ *Scopeti*.
Mercatale. ££ *Il Salotto del Chianti*.
Bargino. ££ *del Pesce*, excellent fish restaurant.
Tavarnelle. ££ *La Gramola*; at **La Romita**, 3km north: ££ *La Fattoria*; at **Marcialla**. 4km west: £ *Il Frantoio*.
Badia a Passignano. ££ *La Scuderia*; at Rignana, 3km south: ££ *La Cantinetta*.
San Donato in Poggio. ££ *Villa Francesca* and ££ *La Toppa*. Excellent cheap pizzeria at the Circolo open at weekends in winter; in summer it is operated by volunteers from the Unione Sportivo next to the playing field (daily in June and July). Between San Donato and Panzano at La Piazza, ££ *Osteria della Piazza*.
Lucardo. £ *C'era una volta*.
Barberino Val d'Elsa. ££ *La Bustecca* (also pizzeria); £ *Pizzeria l'Archibugio*.

Annual festivals. At Badia a Passignano a **chamber music festival** is held at Pentecost (early June); information from the *Amici della Musica*, Tavarnelle Val di Pesa (☎ 055-8076426). A three-day **country fair** (*Giardino in fiore*) is held in September at Villa Le Corti near Mercatale.

San Casciano in Val di Pesa

San Casciano in Val di Pesa is a small town (14,500 inhab.) situated on a hill which dominates the beautiful hilly landscape of the Chianti district with extensive views all around. From a signposted car park steps lead up to the town centre. Inside the walls it is a short walk to Piazza Pierozzi where an archway, beneath the clock-tower, leads to the ***Collegiata***, rebuilt in 1793 on the site of a Romanesque church. Over the baptismal font is a fresco of the *Madonna and Child with Saints John the Baptist and Stephen* by an early 15C Florentine master. Above the high altar is a painted wooden *Crucifix* by the workshop of Baccio da Montelupo, and, in the choir, *Glory of St Cassiano* by Luigi Pistocchi. On the altar to the left is a detached fresco of the *Madonna and Child* (c 1500) and on the left wall of the nave, an *Annunciation* by Fra Paolino.

The church of **Santa Maria del Gesù** (known as Il Suffraggio), in Via Roma, is now the **Museo di Arte Sacra** (open Sat 16.30–19.00; fest. 10.00–12.30, 16.00–19.00). The museum contains works from San Casciano and from many of the nearby country churches. Inside, on the high altar, *Madonna and Child* by Lippo di Benivieni, and other 15C and 16C paintings including a *Coronation of the Virgin* by Neri di Bicci (1481) in the nave. In a little room to the right is a polychrome marble statue of the *Madonna and Child* inscribed Gino Micheli (1341).

In the adjoining **oratory** are two important paintings: a *Madonna and Child* by Ambrogio Lorenzetti, one of the artist's earliest works, dated 1319, and the **San Michele altarpiece**, a rare 13C Florentine work, attributed to Coppo di Marcovaldo, both from the church of Sant' Angelo at Vico l'Abate. Other interesting gold-ground panels include *Madonnas* by the Master of the Horne Triptych, Jacopo del Casentino and Cenni di Francesco; a *Crucifix* attributed to the Master of San Lucchese, on the end wall; a triptych by the Master of San Iacopo a Mucciana and the *Martyrdom of St Lucy* by Simone Pignoni. In the centre is a marble pedestal, possibly of a baptismal font, composed of carvings representing the *Annunciation, Nativity*, and *Annunciation to the Shepherds*, attributed to the Master of Cabestany (French or Spanish, second decade of the 12C). There are a number of showcases, also on an upper floor, displaying liturgical objects, church silver, vestments, etc.

From Piazza Pierozzi Via Morrocchesi leads to the church of the **Misericordia** (Santa Maria del Prato), a 14C Gothic church rebuilt in the late16C (if closed, entrance through the adjacent Confraternity). The church has several fine works (well labelled): a painted *Crucifix with the mourning Virgin and St John* by Simone Martini (c 1325); *Madonna and Child, St Francis and St Peter* by Ugolino di Nerio; an enthroned *Madonna with Saints and Angels*, dated 1516, by a Florentine artist; other 17C paintings by Francesco Furini, Rutilio Manetti and Jacopo Vignali; marble **pulpit** with reliefs representing the *Annunciation* by Giovanni di Balduccio (1339).

Outside the old walls, next to a terrace with a fine view, is the church 15C of **San Francesco** (founded 1492). The church was renovated and the portico added in the 18C. Inside, on the left, is an altarpiece of the *Madonna and Child between Saints Francis and Mary Magdalen* by Biagio d'Antonio, and, right, a Sienese *Crucifix* (c 1360).

Environs of San Casciano

On the pretty road leading west to Cerbaia are several Romanesque churches in picturesque settings. They are generally open only for services on Sunday morning, but at other times ring at the priest's house. Most of their contents have been removed for safe keeping to the Museum in San Casciano (see above). Just outside San Casciano a narrow by-road diverges steeply left (signposted *Vivai Orlandi*) to **Santa Maria ad Argiano**, a Romanesque church largely rebuilt in the 18C. The church of **San Martino ad Argiano** has a Romanesque façade with terracotta decorations and an 18C portico. Next to it is the Oratory of the Santissima Annunziata, which has fine 17C furniture, an *Annunciation* by Cesare Dandini and a painting of *Saints Augustine, Ambrose, and Carlo Borromeo* by Fabrizio Boschi. A cypress avenue leads to the villa and church of **San Pietro a Montepaldi**, with a simple Romanesque façade and Baroque interior.

Near Talente is **San Giovanni in Sugana**, one of the oldest and most important Romanesque churches in the diocese of Florence. It was considerably restored and provided with a cupola in the 16C. It contains some glazed terracotta works by the della Robbia and Buglioni, and a *Crucifixion* by Pier Dandini. It preserves parts of its original structure and has an elegant 16C cloister with an upper loggia, carved doorways and a two-light Romanesque window. **Cerbaia,** on the Via Volterrana, is described in Ch. 6.

To the north of San Casciano, in woods, is the hamlet of **Sant'Andrea in Percussina** with the *Albergaccio* where Niccolò Machiavelli lived in exile from Florence in 1513 and wrote *Il Principe*. The hostelry (☎ 055-828471) here succeeds the one frequented by the politician and writer. The Romanesque church of Sant'Andrea has an elegant Renaissance interior with a small dome, a 17C *Presentation in the Temple* and some fragmentary frescoes (14C–15C).

Nearer Florence, at Spedaletto, a path leads to **Santa Maria a Casavecchia**, a Romanesque church beautifully situated with a view of Brunelleschi's dome in the distance. Inside is a relief of the *Assumption* in glazed terracotta by Benedetto Buglioni (c 1515). Off the Cassia, following the road to Greve just beyond Tavarnuzze is the **US Military Cemetery** with the graves of 4403 American soldiers who died in service north of Rome in 1944–45 (**open** daily 08.00–17.00). At the **Terme di Firenze** there is a public swimming pool.

On the northern outskirts of San Casciano is the Romanesque church of **Santa Cecilia a Decimo**. A church existed here in the time of Charlemagne, but the present structure, including an impressive bell-tower, dates from the 12C. The portico was added in the 16C. The **interior**, elegantly decorated with stucco-work (1728) has a nave and two aisles separated by arches. On the altar is a *Madonna and Child with Saints Lawrence and Cecilia* by Michele di Ridolfo del Ghirlandaio. The small fresco of the *Madonna and Child* is by Cenni di Francesco. Behind the church are picturesque old farm buildings.

A pretty road leads south from San Casciano to Certaldo. It passes the tiny village of **San Pancrazio**. In a little piazza at the top of the hill is the Romanesque *Pieve* (10C) beside a fortified tower (the key may be obtained from the priest's house next door). It has a 17C portico, but the nave and aisles and two small apses correspond to the original structure. The paintings include a *Crucifixion* by Santi di Tito, 1590. In a nearby room are frescoes of the *Liberal Arts* and representations of *Virgil, Dante and Petrarch* attributed to Cosimo Gheri who also painted two altarpieces for the church.

Lucardo, a hamlet with remains of a castle, is beautifully situated on a hill overlooking the Pesa and Elsa valleys. The interior of San Martino church (key from the adjacent canonica) was renewed in the Baroque period and decorated with stuccowork. There are several paintings, including a *Madonna and Child with Saints Peter, John the Baptist, Martin, and Justus* attributed to Ridolfo del Ghirlandaio. A record of the castle, of which only a tower and parts of the walls now survive, dates from the 8C.

A little further south, beyond a handsome *casa colonica* with a tower, an unsurfaced road leads to the **Pieve di San Lazzaro a Lucardo**, dating from the late 11C and a fine example of early Romanesque architecture. It is surrounded by medieval buildings and has an impressive tower (the upper part is restored) next to the remains of the former cloister. The church is built entirely of sandstone and has a basilican plan with a nave and two aisles divided into seven bays by pillars, and a raised chancel terminating in three apses. The crypt was discovered during restoration work. There are frescoes on the left wall and on two pilasters by Cenni di Francesco. The porch over the entrance was added in the 19C. The road continues through rolling countryside, with a view of San Gimignano, as it approaches Certaldo (see Ch. 6).

On the pretty road to Mercatale, east of San Casciano, is the 16C **Villa Le Corti**, attributed to Santi di Tito, belonging to the Corsini family (a three-day fair, 'Giardino in fiore' is held here in September). Just before reaching Mercatale an unsurfaced road diverges left to **Luiano**. Here, near a group of houses beside a villa, is the small Romanesque church of Sant'Andrea (11C) at the end of a footpath. It is one of the earliest churches in the Florentine diocese, and maintains its Romanesque structure and plan. The exterior, in white *alberese* stone, is well preserved. There is a fine view towards Impruneta.

Beyond Mercatale, at the crossroads known as Le Quattro Strade, the road to the right leads past an old fortified farmhouse to **Santo Stefano a Campoli**, dating from the 12C. It has a 17C portico, and the interior was remodelled in the 18C (key in the afternoons from the house next door). It contains a *Madonna and Child with Saints*, attributed to Franciabigio and a small 15C *Madonna and Child with the infant St John*. From Le Quattro Strade there is a beautiful road to Panzano (see Ch. 4).

Tavarnelle

The main road runs through the long village of Tavarnelle at the south end of which is the church of **Santa Lucia a Borghetto**. This Franciscan church, first recorded in the 13C, is one of the few examples of Gothic architecture in the district. Typically sober in form, and built from simple bricks and pebbles, it contains fresco fragments and a 14C Florentine painted *Crucifix*. Something survives of the former cloister on the right. The façade was considerably restored at the beginning of this century.

Off the main road at the north end of Tavarnelle, beyond the turning for Morocco, is the Romanesque church of **San Pietro in Bossolo** in a lovely position. The church, preceded by a portico, is wedged between a tall bell-tower and the Canonica which houses the **Museo di Arte Sacra**. The interior of the church, restored to its original aspect, is very simple and opens onto a small cloister.

The museum contains works of art and liturgical objects from churches in the district (**open** Sat 16.00–19.00; fest. 09.00–13.00, 16.00–19.00). The paintings include a *Madonna and Child* attributed to Meliore (c 1280); *Madonnas* by

Rossello di Jacopo Franchi and the Master of Marradi; several altarpieces by Neri di Biccifrom the convent of Morrocco (see below) which were commissioned in 1473–75 by Niccolò Sernigi whose portrait was also painted by the artist. There are paintings by the Master of Tavarnelle; Lorenzo di Bicci, Jacopo da Empoli, and a number of works by later Florentine artists. The liturgical objects include two **13C processional crosses**. There is a fine collection of church plate (15C–19C), vestments, ex-votos, and reliquaries.

At **Morrocco** is the Carmelite convent of Santa Maria del Carmine, founded in 1460. Since 1982 it has housed a small community of Discalced Carmelite sisters from Australia (Sunday Mass at 09.30; ☎ 055-8076067). The church is flanked by a loggia with remains of 15C frescoes. Inside is a glazed terracotta della Robbian lunette of the *Annunciation* and a portrait in a garlanded tondo of Niccolò di Giovanni Sernigi, founder of the convent, by Andrea della Robbia. The paintings have been removed to the Museum of Tavarnelle (see above). A venerated 13C icon formerly on the high altar was stolen in 1980.

Badia a Passignano

Near Sambuca a pretty by-road (signposted) leads uphill to the Badia di Passignano (341m), in a delightful setting, enclosed by cypress trees and surrounded by vineyards and olive groves. The monastery was founded in 1049 by an abbot of the Vallombrosan Order created by St Giovanni Gualberto, who died here in 1073 and was canonised in 1193. Little survives of the original monastery, except perhaps the crypt of the church of San Michele. The oldest parts, including the church façade and bell-tower, date from the later 13C but are much restored. The outer walls and cloisters were added in the mid-15C when the monastery was enlarged and later embellished with numerous frescoes. The two smaller towers and battlements we see today were added in the late 19C after the abbey was sold at auction and bought by a certain Count Dzieduszycki. The present Vallombrosan community was reinstated here in 1986 (the monastery is **open** to the public Sun afternoon, or on request, ☎ 055-8071622). A **music festival** is held in the abbey in June (see 'Festivals', p. 133).

Badia a Passignano

At the end of a cypress avenue, beyond an arched doorway, is a large court-yard, with the abbey church of San Michele Arcangelo (described below). Opposite is the entrance to the **monastery**, beside a terrace and an Italianate garden. A fine 15C stone doorway with a carved and inlaid door gives access to the **cloister**. The upper loggia, which was enclosed and provided with windows in the 18C, has frescoes of the *Life of St Benedict* by Filippo d'Antonio Filippelli (1483). The red brick dome of the church (described below), visible from the cloister, was added in 1602. The large **refectory** has a painted *cenacolo*, a life-size fresco representing the *Last Supper*, covering the end wall, by Domenico and Davide Ghirlandaio, dated 1476. The two lunettes above of *Adam and Eve driven out of Paradise* and *Cain slaying Abel* (1474) are by Bernardo di Stefano Rosselli. There are also remains of other frescoes, a carved stone pulpit and corbels and a monumental fireplace.

A small **chapel**, with a fresco of the *Annunciation* by Filippelli, has stairs leading to the church of **San Michele Arcangelo**. Originally Romanesque, it was remodelled in the late 16C. The choir-stalls were carved by a Vallombrosan monk, Michele Confetto, in 1549; the two altarpieces, separating the choir from the nave, representing the Nativity and the Three Archangels are by Michele di Ridolfo del Ghirlandaio. The impressive statue of St Michael the Archangel defeating the Dragon is a rare 13C marble sculpture which originally stood on the roof above the entrance to the church. It is the only important surviving work from the Romanesque monastery.

The spacious **sacristy**, off the south transept, dates from the 15C. It contains a stone tabernacle with painted wooden shutters made for St Giovanni Gualberto's **reliquary bust**. This superb work, composed of a silver and silver gilt head resting on a gilded base, was made in Siena in 1324–32. It is decorated with scenes from the saint's life in coloured enamel. The fine sacristy cupboards are by Domenico Atticciati (1580) and the eight small paintings are attributed to Francesco Curradi.

In 1598–1602 Domenico Cresti, a native of the village, and known as *Il Passignano* remodelled the east end of the church creating three chapels, a transept and a dome (frescoed by Giuseppe Nicola Nasini in 1706). Passignano was responsible for all the frescoes in the **central chapel** dedicated to St Michael: *God the Father in Glory* in the vault, the four *Cardinal Virtues* in the spandrels, and the *Evangelists* in painted niches. He also painted the three large altarpieces representing the *Apparition of St Michael on Mount Gargano* (right), the *Apparition of the Madonna* (centre), and *St Michael defeating Lucifer* (left). The statues of *Saints Peter and Paul* are by Andrea Ferruzzi.

The chapel on the right is dedicated to St Sebastian and St Atto, a Vallombrosan abbot. All the paintings, including the frescoes in the south transept illustrating the life of Atto, are by Benedetto Veli (1600).

The left-hand chapel is dedicated to St Giovanni Gualberto and contains his tomb which lies beneath a reclining marble figure by Giovanni Caccini (1580). The design of the chapel and the *Glory of the Saint* frescoed in the vault are by Alessandro Allori (1580), who also painted, with assistants, the scenes of the saint's life in the north transept, and the large **fresco** of the *Transportation of the Relics*, depicting numerous portraits of members of the clergy and congregation. The altarpiece of the chapel which shows Pope Celestino III proclaiming the saint's canonisation in 1193 is by Giuseppe Nicola Nasini (1709). The two other altarpieces representing the *Ordeal by Fire of St Peter Igneus* (right) and *Giovanni Gualberto forgiving his brother's murderer and praying before the Crucifix of San Miniato* (left) are by Giovanni Butteri(1600). Steps lead down to the small 10C **crypt**.

The little village church of **San Biagio**, approached by a flight of steps outside the abbey walls, dates from the 14C and has some remains of frescoes inside.

San Donato in Poggio

This is a charming fortified medieval village in a beautiful setting. A main street connects the two gates with the piazzetta in the centre, containing an elegant Renaissance palace, a well and a little gothic church. There are remains of the old walls and many of the houses still preserve their original character.

Just outside the village is the **Pieve**, a beautiful Romanesque church of the late 12C, with three apses, built out of large blocks of cream-coloured *alberese* stone. The upper part of the square crennellated tower is of darker stone. Inside, simple piers divide the aisles from the nave, which is considerably higher. A little chapel on the right contains a baptismal **font** by Giovanni della Robbia (1513) with reliefs of the *Life of St John the Baptist*, and a small collection of paintings among which is a *Coronation of the Virgin* by Giovanni del Biondo. Over the high altar is a *Crucifix* by a follower of Giotto.

On the road between San Donato and Castellina is the sanctuary of the **Madonna di Pietracupa** (open daily 11.00), a late-Renaissance church (1595) surrounded by a portico. Inside are three altarpieces by Passignano; the one on the high altar surrounds a venerated image of the *Madonna*. The beautiful road continues to Castellina in Chianti (see Ch. 4) along a ridge, with magnificent views across the Elsa valley towards San Gimignano and the hills beyond.

Just south of Tavarnelle is the little village of **Barberino Val d'Elsa**. It preserves its medieval defence walls and a gateway at either end of the main street, which is named after the poet Francesco da Barberino (1264–1348). The 14C **Ospedale dei Pellegrini** (pilgrims' hospice), just inside the walls, is now the public library. There are several elegant palaces (restored), including the **Palazzo Pretorio** with coats of arms on the façade. The church of **San Bartolomeo** was rebuilt by Giuseppe Castellucci at the beginning of this century. A *Madonna and Child* by Bicci di Lorenzo and a bronze bust of Beato Davanzato by Pietro Tacca are preserved in the Canonica.

South of Barbarino is the **Pieve di Sant'Appiano**, a 10C Romanesque church extensively rebuilt in brick in the 12C after its tower fell down, destroying much of the original building. The **interior** is finely proportioned with brick columns separating the nave from the aisles, and carved capitals. To the right of the entrance from the Romanesque cloister is a marble tomb slab carved with the effigy of Raffaello Gherarduccio dei Gherardini (1331). The chapel left of the choir has remains of frescoes and a *Madonna and Child with Saints* by a 16C Florentine artist. Against the wall on the left is the shrine of St Appiano, which was originally under the main altar. According to tradition, St Appiano was the first evangeliser of the Val d'Elsa. In the nave are three frescoes of saints by the school of Ghirlandaio.

The **cloister**, which still preserves a fine door and three windows of the original sacristy, leads to the **canonica**. It has a 15C hall with fresco decoration and the arms of the Catellini family, protectors of the pieve, and a small collection of paintings awaiting restoration. In front of the simple façade of the church are four columns which were part of the former **baptistery** (pulled down in the early 19C) which had an unusual octagonal plan with a dome and crypt. Next to the cloister an **Antiquarium** has recently been opened. It contains Etruscan and Roman objects from the surrounding district (**open** Sat and Sun, 15.00–19.00). Nearby is the picturesque medieval village of **Linari**.

A by-road leads west through beautiful countryside from Barberino Val d'Elsa to Certaldo passing the Villa of Petrognano before reaching a crossroads where there is a circular chapel surrounded by cypresses. It is known as '**La Cupola**' since it reproduces in miniature Brunelleschi's cupola of Florence Cathedral. It has recently been restored, and forms a charming landmark. It was built in 1597 by Santi di Tito to commemorate the former town of **Semifonte**. Originally enclosed in star-shaped walls, in a strategic position close to the Francigena and Volterrana roads, Semifonte was the stronghold of the powerful Conti Alberti. It became such a threat to Florence that it was razed to the ground after a siege lasting four years which ended in 1202. Nearby is the church of **Santa Maria a Bagnano**. Its precious paintings have unfortunately had to be removed for safekeeping and are now housed temporarily in the Canonica of Certaldo. Works from other churches in the neighbourhood have also been removed to Certaldo (see Ch. 6).

6 · Castelfiorentino and Certaldo

These two small towns, both in the province of Florence, although little visited, contain important works of art. Castelfiorentino has frescoes by Benozzo Gozzoli and 18C Florentine artists, and Certaldo, where Boccaccio spent the last years of his life, has more frescoes by Gozzoli. Interesting early 16C sculptures can be seen at San Vivaldo. The **Via Volterrana**, considered one of the most beautiful roads in Tuscany, which links Florence to Volterra, runs through Castelfiorentino, and passes Cerbaia, Montespertoli, Gambassi Terme and Il Castagno.

■ Practical information

Information office. APT of Florence (☎ 055-290832). *Pro-loco* in Certaldo, 16 Via Boccaccio (☎ 0571-664944).

Getting there
By rail. Services from Florence to Empoli in 20mins. From Empoli (with some through trains from Florence) to Castelfiorentino (in 15 mins) and Certaldo (in 30 mins).

By bus. Buses run by *SITA* (infrequent daily service) from Florence (via Porta Romana and Galluzzo) to Cerbaia, Montespertoli, Castelfiorentino, and Certaldo (in 1hr 40 mins). A service links Florence to Volterra along the Via Volterrana once a day (in 2hrs 40 mins).

Hotels
Castelfiorentino. ★★ *Lami*, 82 Piazza Gramsci (☎ & fax 0571-64076).
Certaldo. In Certaldo Alto: ★★ *Il Castello*, restaurant (☎ & fax 0571-668250) and *Osteria del Vicario*, rooms to let (☎ 0571-668228).

Gambassi Terme has ★ hotels.
Montaione. ★★★ *Vecchio Molino* (☎ & fax 0571-697966).

Campsite. ★★ *Toscana Colliverdi* (☎ 0571-669334), 10km west of Certaldo at Marcialla (open March–Sept).

Restaurants
Montespertoli. ££ *La Terrazza*, Viale Matteotti and at Montagnana ££ *Il Focolare*; £ *Baccaiano* at Baccaiano.
Cerbaia. £££ *Tenda Rossa*, considered by many to be one of the best restaurants in Tuscany.

Castelfiorentino

Castelfiorentino (population 17,500) is an industrial town on the river Elsa, with the old walled town above on a rocky spur. Originally a castle in a strategic position for the defence of Florence (hence its name), Castelfiorentino owed its importance to its position on the pilgrim road to Rome, the Via Francigena.

Santa Verdiana and the lower town

At the entrance to the lower town is the church of **Santa Verdiana** rebuilt in the 18C on the site of the former Romanesque church of Sant'Antonio. The elegant façade, with a portico, is by Bernardo Fallani and Giuseppe Manetti.

Interior. This is entirely decorated with frescoes by a group of 18C Florentine artists to an overall architectural design by Foggini which forms a unique and charming complex of exceptional freshness and luminosity. The nave vault, the twelve hemispherical domes of the side chapels and the paintings of the apse and altars depict the legend, miracles and apotheosis of Santa Verdiana. This local saint, after making a pilgrimage to Santiago di Compostela and another to Rome, chose to live the rest of her life as an anchoress in a walled-up cell (in the church crypt). Renowned for her holiness, Verdiana died c 1242 after living 34 years in the company of two snakes which were sent, in answer to her prayers, to try her patience.

The *Glory of St Verdiana* in the nave vault is by Alessandro Gherardini (1708), with painted architecture by Lorenzo del Moro. The cupola above the transept representing the saint received into heaven is by Matteo Bonechi (1716). The small domes were frescoed by Giovanni Camillo Sagrestani, Agostino Veracini, Ranieri del Pace, Antonio Puglieschi, and Niccolò Lapi. The altarpieces include: Jacopo da Empoli, *Assumption of the Virgin* (enlarged by Gherardini a century later with the addition of putti); Orazio Fidani, *Ecstasy of St Francis* (1644); Simone Pignoni, *Charity of St Thomas of Villanova* (1664); Giovanni Martinelli, *Three Saints*; and Giovanni Domenico Ferretti, two *Scenes from the life of St Verdiana*.

Three large paintings dating from the 1630s (*Reclusion of St Verdiana* by Giovanni Battista Ghidoni, her death by Bartolomeo Salvestrini, and her funeral by Filippo Tarchiani), removed from the apse in the 19C, have been restored and will be returned here to their original frames, thus completing the recent restoration of the entire church.

In the Canonica of Santa Verdiana a small **museum** was opened in 1999 with earlier works from the church, including paintings by Taddeo Gaddi, Taddeo di Bartolo, and Francesco Granacci. It also houses paintings and sculptures from the churches of Voltigiano, Cambiano, Ortimino, and Petrazzi, as well as illuminated manuscripts and liturgical objects.

Across the garden in front of Santa Verdiana is the apse of **San Francesco**, a 13C Franciscan church built in brick, which was badly flooded in 1966 and is now being restored. It has 14C frescoes by Giovanni del Biondo.

Upper town

Signposts (*Affreschi del Gozzoli*) indicate the way to the upper town. Here at No. 41 Via Tilli (named after Michelangelo Tilli, the 17C physician, botanist, and philosopher) the **Biblioteca Comunale** (open Tues, Thur, and Sat 16.00–19.00; fest. 10.00–12.00, 16.00–19.00) houses detached **frescoes** by **Benozzo Gozzoli**. The frescoes came from two chapels in the area. Those of the Tabernacle of the Madonna della Tosse come from Castelnuovo d'Elsa, a few kilometres north of Castelfiorentino. On the tabernacle vault is a figure of *Christ with the four Evangelists* above a trompe-l'oeil altarpiece representing the *Madonna and Child enthroned with Saints Peter, Catherine, Margaret and Paul* surrounded by angels holding up a red curtain. On the two side walls are the *Dormition of the Virgin* and her *Assumption*. The frescoes were painted by Benozzo Gozzoli and his workshop in 1484. The larger *Tabernacle of the Visitation*, dated 1490, was situated in Castelfiorentino, near the river. These frescoes, which had suffered from damp and flooding, were detached in 1965, uncovering the fine *sinopie*, or underdrawings. Although in fragmentary condition, the surviving scenes illustrating the *Life of the Virgin* are a typical example of Gozzoli's charming narrative style. The episodes, painted in a rich range of colours, are transformed into scenes of everyday life, full of picturesque details, with architectural and landscape backgrounds. Benozzo Gozzoli, a pupil of Fra Angelico with whom he worked in Orvieto and Rome, is famous for his frescoes in the Medici-Riccardi chapel in Florence (1462). He travelled extensively, working in Pisa and in the Elsa Valley, assisted towards the end of his life by his sons.

Via Tilli leads into **Piazza del Popolo**. The clock tower of the **Municipio** (on the left), has a bell which chimes every hour when the little seated soldier, called *Membrino*, strikes it with a hammer.

Steps lead up from the piazza to the Romanesque church of **San Leonardo**, whose interior was rebuilt in the 16C. It has a pretty cupola which comes into view as one climbs up the adjacent street leading to the 12C **Pieve di Sant' Ippolito** (originally San Biagio, the parish church of the medieval Castello). It stands at the top of a flight of steps in a beautiful panoramic position dominating the countryside and the towers and rooftops of the old town. The simple brick **façade** is decorated with a two-light window over the doorway and ceramic dishes. A marble inscription records the creation of the Tuscan League in 1197, the first Treaty between Volterra, Lucca, Siena, San Miniato, and Florence. The simple **interior** (extensively restored; if closed, the key is available from the old people's home next door) has fine proportions. Over the baptismal font is a frescoed lunette with a half-length figure of the *Dead Christ and two angels* (14C). Over the high altar is a *Crucifix* of the same period. On the left side of the church is a bell-cot with three bells, one of which is dated 1253. The elegant apse is visible from the garden (access from the church sacristy) which is partly enclosed by the old walls with remains of two towers.

North of Castelfiorentino, on the road to Castelnuovo d'Elsa, is the chapel of the **Madonna della Tosse**, where Benozzo Gozzoli's frescoes (see above) will eventually be reinstalled. Nearby is the **Pieve di Coiano** dedicated to Saints Peter and Paul, on a hill (182m). This ancient church, founded in the 11C, has a Pisan-type façade with a two-light window and remains of 14C frescoes.

Montespertoli

Montespertoli is a small market town between Castelfiorentino and San Casciano on the Via Volterrana, at the heart of an important wine-growing area (which produces *Chianti Putto*, *Chianti Colli Fiorentini*, *Montalbano* and *Galestro*, see p. 130). The main piazza, forming a triangle with a well at the centre, has an interesting 17C building surrounding the **Oratory of the Misericordia** with two gabled clock-towers surmounted by small bells. Also facing the piazza is the church of **Sant'Andrea** (16C, but rebuilt after the Second World War) which has an early 12C baptismal font, decorated with marble inlay. Over the high altar is a 14C *Crucifix* and there is a damaged triptych by Niccolò Gerini.

South-west of Montespertoli (on the Tresanti road) is the pieve of **San Pietro in Mercato** which derived its name from the important market, held here until the late 15C (**open** Sun 11.00). The original church was probably founded in the 10C; the present building consecrated in 1057. It has a basilican plan with three apses and a nave and two aisles separated by simple arched piers. Left of the entrance, beneath a lunette with a fresco of the *Baptism of Christ* by the school of Ghirlandaio, is a 12C font, with geometrical motifs inlaid in coloured marble.

The **Museo di Arte Sacra** in the adjacent monastery houses works removed for protection from churches in the neighbourhood, including Sant'Andrea a Botinaccio, San Biagio a Poppiano, Santa Maria a Torri, San Bartolomeo a Tresanti, and San Giusto a Montalbino. There are some interesting gold-ground panels by Cenni di Francesco and Bicci di Lorenzo; a charming early painting of the *Madonna and Child* by Filippo Lippi; another *Madonna* by Andrea di Giusto; and altarpieces by Neri di Bicci. There is a 12C baptismal font, a della Robbia relief of *St Jerome in the desert*, liturgical objects (15C–18C), a 13C Limoges plate, fine processional Crosses, manuscripts and vestments.

In beautiful countryside east of Montespertoli on the road to San Casciano is **Poppiano**, a 13C castle belonging to the Guicciardini family, famous for its wine (*Chianti Colli Fiorentini*).

The Via Volterrana proceeds towards Florence past the **Villa of Montegufoni**, originally a medieval castle of the Accaiuoli family. Its tower, built in 1386, was modelled on that of Palazzo Vecchio in Florence. The story is told that the owner of the castle had taken an oath that if St Anthony answered his prayers he would never live out of sight of the tower of Palazzo Vecchio. When his prayers were granted he decided to build a copy of the tower in order to avoid moving from his country estate. The villa was rebuilt in the 17C, together with the little church of San Lorenzo which contains a fresco of *St Lawrence* by Gian Domenico Ferretti (1764) and a painted *Crucifix* by Taddeo Gaddi. The villa was purchased in 1910 by Sir George Reresby Sitwell (author of *An essay on the making of gardens* (1909). He was father of the three writers, Edith, Osbert and Sacheverell. Sir George spent 28 years restoring the castle, making pseudo-Gothic alterations, and redesigned the garden. He stayed on during the Second World War when many paintings from the Uffizi were stored here for safety. Osbert, who described the family holidays at the villa in his autobiography, died here in 1969 (it is now a hotel-residence).

Beyond Montagnana and Cerbaia is the Romanesque church of **Sant'**
Alessandro a Giogoli (12C), beautifully situated on a hill. At a bend in the Via
Volterrana is a view of **I Collazzi** (private), one of the grandest villas on the
outskirts of Florence. It was built in the Renaissance style in the mid-16C to the
design of Santi di Tito surrounded by olive groves and cypress trees.

Certaldo

Like many other Tuscan towns, Certaldo (population 15,600) is divided between
its medieval walled town on a hill and the modern residential and industrial
suburb spread out below. Etruscan and Roman in origin, Certaldo was also situated on the Via Francigena.

Lower town

In the lower town is the main square, **Piazza Boccaccio** (car park), with a
marble statue by Augusto Passaglia (1879) which was commissioned to celebrate the fifth centenary of the death of Giovanni Boccaccio (1313–75), the
celebrated author of the *Decameron*, who died at Certaldo, and may also have
been born here. The pseudo-Romanesque church of **San Tommaso**, patron
saint of Certaldo, was founded in 1843. The adjacent **Canonica** at present
houses some of the works removed from local churches and destined for the
Diocesan Museum, which will be in the upper town. The paintings include: a
monumental 13C *Crucifix* and a polyptych by Puccio di Simone from San
Donnino; *Madonna and Child* by the Master of Bagnano; a triptych by a close
follower of Duccio; the *Madonna of the Rosary* by Bernardo Monaldi and other
paintings from Santa Maria a Bagnano. A fresco of the *Madonna* standing in a
niche is by Cenni di Francesco from San Martino a Maiano. Four predella scenes
illustrating the *Life of Beata Giulia* of Certaldo are attributed to Paolo Uccello
from the church of Santi Michele e Jacopo (see below). They depict her saving a
child by miraculously passing through a fire unscathed, and thanking the children of Certaldo with flowers for having brought her bread.

Giovanni Boccaccio

Giovanni Boccaccio (1312–75) was born in Paris, where his Florentine
father had mercantile interests. He lived most of his life in Florence and
acted as ambassador for the city after 1350. He is famous for his
Decamerone (1348–58), a brilliant secular work which established him
as the father of Italian prose, and which had a great influence on European writers (including Chaucer). His close friends included Petrarch and
Dante.

Certaldo Alto

Certaldo Alto, the upper town (signposted) is reached on foot in c 10min. Built
almost entirely of brick, the upper town has considerable charm and maintains
its medieval character, despite some damage from the Second World War. Its
walls and gateways, dating from the 13C–15C, are well preserved. All the principal buildings, as well as some attractive houses, face onto Via Boccaccio.

Half-way up on the left is the **Casa del Boccaccio** (rebuilt in 1947), with a
tower and loggia, which was bought and restored in the early 19C by Marchesa
Carlotta dei Medici Lenzoni. Boccaccio is known to have spent part of his later

years here (or in the contiguous house), enjoying a peaceful and simple life. He was buried in the nearby church. The house (**open** daily 09.00–12.00, 15.00–18.00) is now a museum and the *Centro Nazionale di Studi sul Boccaccio*, with a small library containing editions and translations of his writings. On the first floor is a fresco representing Boccaccio in his study which was commissioned from Pietro Benvenuti by the Marchesa Carlotta in 1826.

On the left of the little piazza is the **Compagnia dei Bianchi** which will house the Diocesan Museum (see above). Opposite is the church of **Santi Michele e Jacopo**. The simple brick façade dates from the 13C, the interior was restored to its original Romanesque appearance at the beginning of this century. Temporarily placed on the right of the entrance is the Tabernacolo dei Giustiziati, a small frescoed chapel representing *Christ being taken down from the Cross, Saints* and other scenes, painted by Benozzo Gozzoli and Giusto d'Andrea in 1466. In a niche is an urn containing the body of Beata Giulia, who lived thirty years walled up in a cell next to the sacristy in order to devote herself to prayer and meditation. Her death in 1367 was announced by the mysterious tolling of all the bells in Certaldo. The predella (described above) was formerly on the altar of her chapel. Nearby is a glazed terracotta relief of the *Madonna of Mercy with two kneeling Saints* and two small della Robbia tabernacles (c 1500) on either side of the altar. A door leads to the pretty 16C cloister. Beyond, in a round niche, is a bust of Giovanni Boccaccio by Giovan Francesco Rustici (1503) with an epitaph; his modern tombstone is now in the centre of the nave. To the left of the entrance is a niche with a fresco of the *Madonna and Child with Saints* of the 14C Sienese school.

Beyond the church is **Palazzo Pretorio**, originally the castle of the Conti Alberti, with its façade decorated with picturesque coats of arms in stone and glazed terracotta which record the Governors (*Vicari*) sent from Florence. The **interior** is **open** in summer 09.30–12.30, 16.30–19.30; in winter 10.00–12.00, 15.00–18.00. Around the courtyard are the rooms where justice was administered, dungeons, and a chapel with a fresco of *Doubting Thomas* attributed to Benozzo Gozzoli. Several rooms have fine doorways, fireplaces and some fresco decoration. There is also a small collection of Roman and medieval finds from local excavations. A staircase leads up to the rooms of the former governors where temporary exhibitions are held.

A terraced garden and a walkway overlooking the town walls provide a splendid view stretching from the hills of the Val d'Elsa to San Gimignano. Across the garden on the ground floor is the side entrance to the 13C church of **Santi Tommaso e Prospero** which contains a few damaged 15C frescoes and some *sinopie* by Gozzoli.

Environs of Certaldo

Gambassi Terme is a small spa to the west of Certaldo which is known for its springs of *Acqua Pillo*. It has an attractive public garden outside the **Palazzo Civico** which houses a small collection of Etruscan and Roman finds excavated in the area. The town was already known in medieval times for its glass production (still manufactured here). It was the birthplace of Domenico Livi who made some of the stained-glass windows of Florence Cathedral in the 1430s.

A short distance north of Gambassi on the road to Castelfiorentino is the **Pieve di Santa Maria a Chianni**, a Pisan-Romanesque church of the late 13C, with three orders of blind arches on the façade. The exterior is built of honey-coloured sandstone. Fine lancet windows and two tall half-columns with interesting capitals decorate the exterior of the north transept. The Latin-cross interior has a basilican plan and raised chancel with a wide transept and five apses (the central apse was altered in the 16C). The columns dividing the nave from the aisles differ in type and size and have capitals decorated with floral, geometrical, and anthropomorphic motifs. There is a copy by Santi di Tito of Andrea del Sarto's Gambassi altarpiece depicting the *Madonna and Child surrounded by six Saints* (now in the Pitti Gallery in Florence).

Montaione, on a hill, now has an unattractive modern suburb. Etruscan and Roman in origin, the medieval **Castle**, which had survived with its walls, towers and gates almost intact, suffered considerable damage in the Second World War. The old town has a simple plan of three parallel streets with a central piazza. The 13C church of **San Regolo**, was rebuilt in 1635 by Scipione Ammirato il Giovane, to a design perhaps by Bartolomeo Ammannati. The imposing bell-tower dates from 1795. In the church is a 13C *Madonna and Child* by a follower of Cimabue. The **Palazzo Pretorio** dates from the 15C and its façade is decorated with numerous coats of arms. It now houses a local **museum** (**opened** on request at the Comune, ☎ 0571 69031), which contains an interesting collection of fossils, minerals, and prehistoric stone implements.

San Vivaldo

South of Montaione a road passes the public park of Poggio all'Aglione and continues through woods to San Vivaldo in the Bosco di Camporena. This was originally a hermits' retreat and is associated with Beato Vivaldo Stricchi of San Gimignano, a Franciscan tertiary, who was found dead in a hollow tree in 1320. A chapel was built on the spot under the custody of Franciscan friars. In 1500–15 a friar named Tommaso created here a mystical itinerary or ideal pilgrimage to the Sacro Monte, or Holy Mountain, of Jerusalem, with 30 chapels containing tableaux representing the Life and Passion of Christ. Not all of these survive but 18 have been restored. The sequence comprises: the *Annunciation, Flight into Egypt, Supper in the house of Simon the Pharisee, Last Supper, Christ praying in the Garden of Gethsemane, House of Pilate, Flagellation and Mocking of Christ, Jesus Condemned, Way to Calvary, Meeting with Mary His Mother, Meeting with the Holy Women, Veronica, Crucifixion, Deposition, Noli me Tangere, Doubting Thomas, Ascension* and *Pentecost*. The terracotta figures are mostly Florentine, from the della Robbia and Buglioni workshops, although a few are attributed to the Sienese sculptors Rustici and Cozzarelli.

The chapels lead to the 15C church of **Santa Maria in Camporena** with a portico. It has a Romanesque *Crucifix* and an altarpiece of the *Madonna and Child with Saints Jerome, Francis, and Vivaldo* by Raffaellino del Garbo.

West of San Vivaldo, in a more open landscape with clay downs and some interesting rock formations, is the hill-top village of **Castelfalfi** which has a little Romanesque church dedicated to St Florian.

The Via Volterrana (*Strada Provinciale* No. 4) passes through **Il Castagno**. There is a fine view of Volterra, described in Ch. 17, in front of a range of hills. The road continues west through wild and sparsely inhabited countryside and, after crossing the river Era, proceeds uphill past woods and olive groves. Volterra is approached from the northwest with the church of Santi Giusto e Clemente forming a prominent landmark. On either side are dramatic views of the precipices and eroded slopes of Le Balze.

7 · Empoli, Vinci, and west of Florence

■ Practical information

Information offices. APT Florence (☎ 055-290832). At Vinci, Ufficio Turistico (for Vinci, Empoli, Cerreto Guidi, and Montelupo), 11 Via della Torre (☎ 0571-568012). At Empoli, *Pro Loco*, 98 Via Giuseppe del Papa (☎ 0571-76115). At Fucecchio, Pro Loco, 48 Via Roma (☎ 0571-20035).

Getting there

By car. The *superstrada* from Florence to Pisa which begins in the southern suburbs of Florence near Scandicci has exits at Montelupo Fiorentino and Empoli. The old road (N67) is not very attractive as it has been ribbon-developed and is lined with small factories.

By bus. Lazzi run services from Florence for Lastra a Signa, Montelupo, Empoli. From Empoli (*Lazzi* and *COPIT*) frequent services for Vinci (in 20mins).

By rail. On the main line from Florence to Pisa. Frequent service to Empoli (in 20–30 mins; the railway station is 10 mins' walk from the Collegiata). Slow trains on this line also stop at Montelupo. One of the earliest lines in Italy, it was in fact a project by Robert Stephenson for the Tuscan grand-dukes (1838–40; completed in 1844–48). Empoli is also a junction for the Florence–Siena secondary line.

Hotels

Empoli. ★★★ *Tazza d'oro,* 16 Via Giuseppe del Papa (☎ 0571-72129; fax 0571-70073); *Commercio,* 16 Piazzetta Ristori, (☎ 0571-77247; fax 0571-711681); *Il Sole,* 18 Piazza Don Minzoni (☎ 0571-73779; fax 0571-79871).
Vinci has three ★★★ hotels and agriturist accommodation.
Cerreto Guidi. ★★★ *Il Tegolo,* with restaurant, 16 Via Corliano (☎ 0571-559011, fax 0571-559038).
Montelupo Fiorentino. ★★★ *Baccio da Montelupo,* 3 Via Don Minzoni (☎ 0571-51215, fax 0571-51171).

Restaurants

Empoli. £££ *Bianconi,* 70 Via Tosco-Romagnola (2km outside the town on the Florence road); *Il Galeone,* 67 Via Curtatone e Montanara.
£ *Sant'Andrea,* Via Salvagnoli; *Il Petrarca,* 122 Viale Petrarca; *Sciabolino,* 14 Via Ormicello; *Da Cioffi,* 333A Via Valdorme.
Lastra a Signa. £££ *Antica Trattoria Sanesi.*

Empoli

Empoli, 32km west of Florence, is a pleasant small town spaciously laid out (after damage in the Second World War) around two long parallel shopping streets either side of the small piazza which lies in front of the Collegiata. It has long been famous for its glass factories, and is now an important commercial centre of the clothing industry.

History. In 1984 excavations revealed Roman remains in the centre of Empoli. The town grew up around the church of Sant'Andrea after 1119. Here in 1260 the Ghibelline party held their famous parliament after their victory at Montaperti; the proposal to raze Florence to the ground was defeated by Farinata degli Uberti, who is honoured for his protest by Dante (*Divina Commedia, Inferno*, X). Jacopo Chimenti, the painter, known as Empoli (1551–1640) was a native of the town.

The **glassworks** of Empoli have long been known for their production of green glass, including the characteristic wine fiasco (protected by straw) which was first produced here in large quantities at the beginning of this century. Glassworks still operating here include: *Consorzio Centrovetro*, Piazza Guido Guerra and *Consorzio Toscanavetro*, Piazza Gramsci; also at Monticiana, 6km outside the town.

From the station, the wide straight Via Roma leads to Piazza della Vittoria and the oratory of the **Madonna del Pozzo**. The design, by Andrea Bonistalli (1621) is interesting. A long nave, surrounded on the exterior by a portico, precedes a pretty octagonal domed sanctuary. At No. 16 in the piazza is the musician **Ferruccio Busoni's House**, in which there is a small museum. Busoni (1866–1924), as a pianist, was a child prodigy. He travelled widely in Europe and is known for his piano concerto and opera *Doktor Faust* (completed by a pupil in 1925).

From the right of the oratory Via Giuseppe del Papa leads to the Canto del Pretorio where on the right is **Piazza Farinata degli Uberti**, the pleasant arcaded central square. Here there is a large fountain with four amusing lions by Luigi Pampaloni (1827). There is also a local **museum of Paleonthology** (**open** Thur, Sat & Sun 17.00–20.00) with a well illustrated collection of fossils from the Pliocene period, including numerous shells, found in central Tuscany.

The **Collegiata di Sant'Andrea**, documented as early as 780, was begun in its present form in 1093. The handsome black-and-white marble **façade** recalls that of San Miniato al Monte in Florence. It was probably begun in the mid-12C, and the upper part is a successful imitation of this style carried out when the church was enlarged in the 18C by Ferdinando Ruggeri. The marble portal dates from 1546. The **interior** by Ruggeri has a ceiling painting by Vincenzo Meucci and Giuseppe del Moro which was reconstructed after severe damage in the last War. On the west wall, fresco of *Christ with instruments of the Passion* attributed to Raffaello Botticini.

South side. First chapel, venerated 14C *Crucifix*, and a painting of 1808 symbolising the recovery from the plague. **Second chapel**, interesting detached 14C Florentine fresco of the *Martyrdom of St Lucy* (with white oxen). On the high altar by Zanobi del Rosso (1785), triptych by Lorenzo di Bicci. On the **east wall**, fresco of the *Martyrdom of St Andrew* by Ferdinando Folchi (1862). To the left of the presbytery is the entrance to two oratories, the second of which is used as a sacristy. Here are the remains of a della Robbian tiled pavement around the altar. Outside the chapel at the end of the left transept is a very ruined fresco of *St Joseph* attributed to Empoli (right). The statuette of the *Madonna* on the altar (repainted) is attributed to the bottega of Buglioni.

North side. Fourth chapel, 17C painting of the *Madonna and Saints*, and (first chapel) reliquary cupboard of c 1724.

Museo della Collegiata di Sant'Andrea

In the courtyard (to the right of the façade) is the entrance to the *Museo della Collegiata di Sant'Andrea, one of the first local museums in Tuscany, founded in 1859. The museum contains fine works of art from the Collegiata and other churches in the area, as well as private donations. The museum was reopened in 1990 and the sculptures, frescoes, and paintings (many of them recently restored) are beautifully displayed and well labelled

Open 09.00–12.00, 16.00–19.00 except Mon. The ticket includes admission to the church of Santo Stefano degli Agostiniani (see below), usually only **open** 09.00–12.00.

Room 1 was formerly part of the church of San Giovanni Evangelista, transformed into a baptistery in the 15C and connected by a passageway to the Collegiata. Here is a *font dated 1447, an exquisite and unusual work recently attributed to Bernardo Rossellino. The *fresco of ***Christ in Pietà*** (detached from the window wall in 1946, and restored in 1987) is a superb work by **Masolino** (1424–25). Also here are frescoes and sinopie of *Saints* by Lo Starnina (1409).

Room 2: stoup of 1557; lectern of English workmanship donated to the Collegiata in 1520; bas-relief of the *Madonna and Child* attributed to Mino da Fiesole; small tondo of the *Madonna and Child*, an early work by Tino da Camaino; terracotta dossal of the *Madonna enthroned with Saints* attributed to Santi di Buglioni.

Room 3 contains 14C and 15C paintings. Master of 1336 (Pistoian school), *Madonna and Child with Saints*; works by Niccolò di Pietro Gerini; Lorenzo di Bicci, *Crucifixion and Virgin of the Holy Girdle*. The early 15C painting for an altar step of the *Miracle of the Almond Tree and the brotherhood of the Compagnia del Crocifisso* depicts a miracle which took place in Empoli in 1399. The brothers (shown in hooded white cloaks) were on their way to Val di Marina to invoke the end of a plague which was afflicting the inhabitants of Empoli. They leant their crucifix against a dead almond tree which miraculously came into flower, signalling the end of the plague. Also here, Ambrogio di Baldese (attributed), *Madonna del Latte*; Agnolo Gaddi (attributed), triptych; Cenni di Francesco, *Saints*; Mariotto di Nardo, *Madonna and Child*. The polychrome wood statue of *St Stephen* is signed and dated 1403 by **Francesco da Valdambrino**.

Room 4. Rossello di Jacopo Franchi, triptych; Master of Signa, *Saints*; Lorenzo Monaco, *Madonna enthroned with Saints*; Filippo Lippi, *Madonna enthroned between Angels and Saints* (a very small work); *Madonna of Humility with four Saints* (1404) by Lorenzo Monaco; Bicci di Lorenzo, *Madonna and Saints*. The polychrome wood statue of the penitent *Magdalene* (dated 1455) is attributed to Don Romualdo da Candeli and Neri di Bicci. **Room 5** displays works by Francesco Botticini and his son Raffaello. The *tabernacle of St Sebastian* (c 1475) contains exquisite paintings of two angels by Francesco Botticini and a beautiful statue of *St Sebastian* by Antonio Rossellino. Also by Francesco Botticini, *Annunciation, and angel musicians*. Works by Raffaello Botticini include *Saints Sebastian and Jerome*, and a predella.

Room 6: Jacopo da Empoli, *Incredulity of St Thomas*; 17C Florentine painter, *Assumption of the Virgin*; tabernacle of the *Holy Sacrament*, an elaborate work by Francesco and Raffaello Botticini; Jacopo del Sellaio, *Madonna and Child, Madonna and Saints*; Giovanni Antonio Sogliani, *St Blaise* (in a splendid frame); Pier Francesco Fiorentino, *Madonna enthroned with Saints*. The upper walk of the Cloister (closed in winter) displays della Robbian works in enamelled terracotta, including a tondo of the *Holy Father* by Andrea and dossals by Benedetto Buglioni and his bottega. A precious collection of ten illuminated missals (13C–16C) will be displayed in the museum in the future.

Santo Stefano degli Agostiniani

Near the museum, in Via dei Neri, is the 14C church of **Santo Stefano degli Agostiniani** (open with the same ticket as for the Museo della Collegiata, 09.00–12.00 except Monday). The church, with no façade, is important for its remains of frescoes by Masolino.

Interior. The organ at the west end, with an elaborate gallery of 1756, dates from 1558. South side. The **first chapel** was frescoed with the Legend of the True Cross in 1424 by Masolino; the scenes were destroyed in 1792 except for the intrados of the entrance arch, the window frame, and a niche with trompe l'oeil shelves. However the *sinopie have survived here. Beyond the second chapel with a 17C wood dossal, the **fourth chapel** has remains of frescoes and sinopie (restored in 1989) attributed to the bottega of Bicci di Lorenzo. Here has been placed a damaged tomb slab of an Augustinian monk dated 1432. Beyond is the entrance to an **Oratory** (1510) with carved benches by Nofri d'Ascanio and a copy of a Deposition by Cigoli (removed by Ferdinando II and now in the Galleria Palatina in Florence), carried out in 1690 by Antonio Domenico Gabbiani.

South transept. Here there are more fresco fragments by Masolino: a group thought to represent the pupils of St Ivo, and a lunette of the *Madonna and Child with two angels.

To the right of the high altar is the entrance of the **Oratory of the Santissima Annunziata**, with two beautiful *statues of the *Annunciation* by Bernardo Rossellino (c 1447). In the chapel on the left of the high altar, Passignano, *Adoration of the Shepherds* (1621).

North side. **Fourth chapel**, altarpiece of the *Assumption* by Mario Balassi (1659); the **third chapel** was decorated in 1759–63 with frescoes by Vincenzo Meucci and Giuseppe del Moro. **Second chapel**, Rutilio Manetti, *Martyrdom of St Catherine* (1627) and frescoes by Ottavio Vannini. In the **first chapel**, the *Madonna of the Rosary* by Francesco Furini encloses a painting of *St Nicholas of Tolentino* protecting Empoli from the plague by Bicci di Lorenzo (1445).

At the far end of Via Giuseppe del Papa is Via della Noce, in which are remains of the **Porta Pisana** (1487; damaged in the Second World War), the only part to survive of the once-famous walls of Empoli (demolished in the early 19C) .

Churches of interest on the outskirts of Empoli include **Santa Maria a Ripa** (works by the della Robbia, Santi Buglioni, Giovanni Antonio Sogliani), **Pianezzoli** (15C pulpit and a *Madonna and Child with Saints* signed and dated 1593 by Ludovico Cigoli) and **Monterappoli** (fresco attributed to Raffaello Botticini).

Pontorme

On the eastern outskirts of Empoli is the unattractive suburb of Pontorme, birthplace of the painter Jacopo Carucci, called Pontormo (1494–1556; plaque set up in 1956 by Emilio Cecchi on the house at No. 97 on the main road). The small church of **San Michele** (identified by its tall domed campanile; inconspicuous sign off the main road) contains *St John the Evangelist and *St Michael Archangel (c 1519) by Pontormo. In a niche with very faded frescoes of the *Baptism of*

Christ, also attributed to Pontormo, is a handsome round 15C marble font. On the fine gilded wood high altar is a ciborium and two paintings by Girolamo Macchietti of *St Michael Archangel* and *St John the Baptist*. In the chapel to the left of the high altar, **Immaculate Conception* by Lodovico Cigoli (c 1590).

A short distance from the church, on the outskirts of the village, is the church of **San Martino**, with a brick façade which incorporates a bellcote. The attractive simple interior (if closed, ring at the house on the right) contains (behind the left altar), a good 15C fresco fragment of two saints (restored in 1985). On the left of the apse arch is a statuette of the *Madonna and Child* by Michele da Firenze. Above, on either side of the apse arch are two paintings of five saints attributed to Giovanni Toscani.

Vinci

On the southwest slope of Monte Albano, 11km north of Empoli, in beautiful countryside, is the little village of Vinci, famous as the birthplace of Leonardo da Vinci (see box, p 152).

The restored 13C **castle** of the Guidi family houses the particularly interesting ****Museo Leonardiano** (open daily 09.30–18.00 or 19.00), beautifully rearranged in 1986. It contains numerous ****models** which are interpretations of the drawings of machines invented by Leonardo, exhibited beside facsimiles of his drawings (well labelled, also in English). Next door is the Biblioteca Leonardiana, a library relating to Leonardo (**open** Tues–Fri 15.00–19.00). The nearby church of Santa Croce preserves the font in which Leonardo is supposed to have been baptised. A 17C painting of *Mary Magdalene* here was restored in 1997 and attributed to Alessandro Rosi.

Above Vinci is the hamlet of **Anchiano** (also approachable on foot by an old path, c 2km long), amidst magnificent olive groves. Here is the house which is traditionally thought to be the actual birthplace of Leonardo. It was restored in 1952 as a humble memorial to him (open as for the castle). In the lower town is the church of the *Santissima Annunziata*, preceded by a porch, with an *Annunciation* (over the high altar), attributed to Fra Paolino da Pistoia.

A road, with splendid views, connects Vinci and Pistoia (see Ch. 9) crossing Monte Albano.

A short way southeast of Vinci is the Pieve di **Sant'Ansano in Greti** founded before 998, which preserves interesting sculptures and a painting by Rutilio Manetti.

Between Empoli and Vinci is **Cerreto Guidi**, a centre of wine production (*Chianti Putto*). The **Villa Medici** here has been restored (**open** 09.00–19.00; except the 2nd and 3rd Mon of the month). It is approached by a splendid double ramp built in brick to a design of Buontalenti. The villa, incorporated in a castle, was begun in 1565. The early Medici grand-dukes used the palace which now contains portraits of the family, and decorations carried out in the early 20C. The small Baroque garden was designed in the 18C by Ferdinando Ruggieri. In the church next door (open only on Sunday) is a **font by Giovanni della Robbia.

Fucecchio on the western border of the province of Florence, was founded before the 11C. Nearby a bridge carried the Via Francigena (a stretch of which can still be seen at Galleno) across the Arno (for a description of this pilgrimage route to Rome, see p. 423). The town was beseiged in 1323 by Castruccio Castracani and after 1330 came under Florentine rule.

Leonardo da Vinci

Leonardo da Vinci (1452–1519) was the illegitimate son of a notary. At 17 he went to work in Verrocchio's studio in Florence and stayed there until around 1476. His early works produced at this time are preserved in the Galleria degli Uffizi: the *Annunciation, Adoration of the Magi,* and the *Baptism of Christ.* He was in Milan c 1482–99 where he worked as sculptor for Ludovico Sforza and where he painted the *Virgin of the Rocks* (now in the Louvre) and the *Last Supper* (Cenacolo) on the refectory wall at the convent of Santa Maria delle Grazie. When he returned to Florence in 1503 he worked in the Salone dei Cinquecento in Palazzo Vecchio with Michelangelo and his unfinished mural of the *Battle of Anghiari* (now lost) was carefully studied by contemporary artists. He returned to Milan in 1506–13, and after a time in Rome, spent the last two years of his life in France. He died in 1519 at Amboise where he is buried.

Perhaps the most famous Italian of all time, he was not only known as a painter (although only about 30 works by his own hand survive), but also for his 'universal' talents illustrated in his writings and notebooks. He had extraordinary skills as an architect, military engineer, anatomist, botanist, mechanic and hydraulic engineer. The exquisite drawings by Leonardo which have survived in Italy are kept in Florence at the Gabinetto dei Disegni e Stampe in the Uffizi, at the Ambrosiana in Milan, and the Biblioteca Reale in Turin, although the most important collection of his drawings (which number around six hundred) now belong to the Royal Library at Windsor Castle. The models which have been made in this century, some of which are exhibited at Vinci (and others in the Science Museum in Milan) are interpretations of his drawings which illustrated concepts of physics and were studies of machinery and apparatus, including a submarine, an underwater diving suit, a parachute, flying machine, and a tank.

His greatest pictorial work, which was to have a profound influence on generations of artists, the *Last Supper,* survives in Milan (its restoration was completed in 1999). Also in Milan is his portrait of a Musician (in the Ambrosiana), and his mural decoration of the Sala delle Asse in the Castello Sforzesco. Two other paintings by him which are still in Italy are in the Galleria Nazionale in Parma (the head of a girl) and the Vatican picture gallery (*St Jerome*). All his other known works are in important museums outside Italy, including the portrait of Monna Lisa (*La Gioconda*), a painting begun in Florence, which is now the most famous work in the Louvre.

In the central Piazza Vittorio Veneto a long flight of steps leads up to the large church of **San Giovanni Battista**, founded in the 10C and rebuilt in the 18C. It contains on the north side (first altar) a *Madonna and Saints* (in very poor condition) by the 16C Florentine school beneath a fragment of a Baptism of Christ, and (on the last altar) a 16C marble relief of the *Madonna and Child*. On the left side of the church is a terrace with a panoramic view. Here is the church of **San Salvatore** (Misericordia) preceded by a pretty loggia. In the interior (closed order of nuns), on the third south altar, is an *Allegory of the Conception* by Giorgio Vasari (one of several versions of this painting by the artist).

In the piazza, opposite Palazzo del Podestà, another flight of steps leads up to

Palazzo Corsini (14C, enlarged in the 15C) which now houses the Biblioteca Comunale. It is being restored and will house the **Museo di Fucecchio**, with some archaeological material, and paintings by Zanobi Machiavelli (*Madonna in Adoration*), the Maestro dei Paesaggi Kress (*Trinity and Evangelists* and *Nativity with Saints*), and Berlinghiero Berlinghieri (*Saints*).

Montelupo Fiorentino

East of Empoli is Montelupo Fiorentino, an attractive village where the Pesa and Arno rivers meet. Its 14C fortifications still determine the layout of the old centre. It was fortified by the Florentines in opposition to the now demolished stronghold of Capraia, beyond the river. Baccio da Montelupo (1469–1535) and his son Raffaello (c 1505–66), both sculptors and architects, were born here.

The approach road passes the fine **Villa dell'Ambrogiana** (now used as a prison), a Medici hunting lodge. It has a square plan with four angle towers and was reconstructed after 1587, possibly to a design by Buontalenti. It once had a garden on the Arno with fountains and grottoes.

Across the river Pesa off the main street of Montelupo, roads lead up towards the castle past the restored **Palazzo Pretorio** with a neo-Gothic loggia. This is now the **Museo Archeologico e della Ceramica** (open 09.00–12.00, 14.30–19.00 exc Mon; the museum is to be expanded and rearranged). In the 15C and early 16C Montelupo was one of the most important centres of ceramic production in the Mediterranean. The modern display is accompanied by detailed explanations.

Ground floor. The archaeological collection is displayed here. **Room 1** contains Paleolithic finds, and **Room 2** Bronze Age weapons. Imported vases from Greece and Southern Italy, and Etruscan and Roman material are displayed in **Room 3**. Remains of 15C frescoes, and medieval finds are in **Room 4**.

Upper floor. **Rooms 5** and **6** contain a didactic display of ceramic manufacture. **Rooms 7–10** contain examples of majolica produced in Montelupo, arranged chronologically. The earliest potteries dating from the late 13C produced green and brown ware mostly with geometric designs. By the late 14C cobalt blue was also widely used. The production in the 15C reflected the influence of Hispano-Moresque ware. There was a notable

An example of majolica from Montelupo Fiorentino

decline in the industry in the late 16C and 17C when the so-called 'arlecchino' style was introduced on a yellow ochre ground. The museum also has examples of ceramics produced in the rest of Italy and a room is dedicated to Paolo Azzati who donated his large private collection of ceramics to the museum.

In Via Bartolomeo Sinibaldi, just below the museum, is the church of **San Giovanni Evangelista** with a *Madonna enthroned with Saints Sebastian, Lorenzo, John the Baptist, and Roch* by Botticelli and his workshop. At the top of the castle hill is the church of **San Lorenzo** (the custodian lives nearby) with fresco fragments signed and dated 1284 by Corso di Buono. The tall, square campanile was probably once one of the castle towers.

To the south of Montelupo, is the Pieve di **Sant'Ippolito** of the 11C, with a marble ciborium by a 15C Florentine sculptor.

Across the Arno is **Capraia** (see above). Excavations in progress at Montereggi alla Castellina have revealed Etruscan and Roman remains. **Limite**, to the west, is well known for its boat builders. To the east of Montereggi, on the hill of **Bibbiani** is a villa with **gardens** laid out in the mid-19C by Cosimo Ridolfi, often visited by Giacomo Puccini (**open** Apr–July, and mid-Sept–Oct on Fri and Sun 09.00 and 11.00; information from the Comune di Capraia e Limite).

Lastra a Signa

East of Montelupo is Lastra a Signa, a large village near the confluence of the Vingone and the Arno, once famous for the production of straw hats. The medieval centre (right of the main road) is remarkable for its walls built in 1380, with three gates, which were strengthened by Brunelleschi c 1424. Here is the **Loggia di Sant'Antonio** (it has been undergoing restoration for many years, now almost completed), formerly a hospital erected at the expense of the Arte della Seta (silk-weavers' guild) in 1411. The portico of six arches (the seventh is walled up) has traditionally been attributed as an early work to Brunelleschi. Nearby is the **ex-Palazzo Pretorio**, a little building (in need of restoration), with the escutcheons of many podestà. Just out of the main square is the church of **Santa Maria alla Lastra** (for admission ask at the Misericordia), rebuilt in 1904, with a *Madonna and Child* by the school of Cimabue.

Just outside the town, off the main road to Montelupo (signposted), is the church of **San Martino a Gangalandi**, at the end of an attractive row of houses. Founded in the 12C or earlier, it has a restored campanile and a 15C loggia at the side. The baptistery at the west end is decorated on the exterior and in the vault with frescoes by Bicci di Lorenzo and his school (1432; restored in 1982). The font was sculpted by a follower of Ghiberti. Here is hung a painting of *St John the Baptist* attributed to Bernardo Daddi (1346; in very poor conditon). Over the first south altar is an unusual painting of *Saints Margaret, Catherine of Alexandria, Catherine of Siena, Mary Magdalene and Apollonia*, attributed to Piero Salvestrini da Castello, a pupil of Poccetti. Over the third south altar, *Immaculate Conception* by Matteo Rosselli (1615). The fine semicircular apse was decorated in *pietra serena* by Leon Battista Alberti, who was rector here from 1432–72. The high altar bears the date 1366. On the north wall is a large detached fresco of *St Christopher*, and fragments of 14C frescoes over the second altar.

A small **museum** has recently been opened (**open** by request, preferably by appointment) above a little room with fine capitals, now used as the sacristy, off the left side of the church. It contains 18C church silver and paintings including a *Madonna of Humility* by Lorenzo Monaco (from San Romolo a Settimo), a trip-tych with the *Assumption and four Saints* by Bicci di Lorenzo and a *Madonna and Child* attributed to Jacopo del Sellaio.

In the hills to the southwest is **Malmantile** castle (1424), an outpost of Castracani, the military adventurer who died in 1328, against the Florentines, celebrated in a poem by Lorenzo Lippi, *Il Malmantile racquistato*, published 11 years after his death in 1676.

Opposite Lastra a Signa, on the other side of the Arno, is **Signa**, with an old district on the hill where the church has 13C frescoes and a painting attributed to Lorenzo Monaco. In the church of San Giovanni Battista, in the lower town, the body of Beata Giovanna da Signa is preserved. Frescoes of 1441 and 1462 illustrate stories from her life.

Further north (8km) is **Campi Bisenzio**, now a large industrial suburb of Florence, but of ancient origin. It was granted privileges in 780 by Charlemagne. Situated in low-lying ground, it has often been subject to flooding from the river Bisenzio. In Piazza Matteotti are **Palazzo del Podestà**, with coats of arms on its façade, and the **Pieve di Santo Stefano**, founded in 936. It was restored in neo-classical style in 1835 and given its façade in 1938. It contains two fine stoups, a fresco of the *Annunciation* by Paolo Schiavo, a painting of *St Anthony Abbot and the angel* by Francesco Curradi (c 1650), and an altarpiece of the *Madonna and Child with Saints* attributed to Sebastiano Mainardi. In the adjoining **Teatro della Pieve** (formerly an oratory) is a fresco fragment of the *Annunciation* and *Holy Trinity* attributed to Raffaellino del Garbo. The **Teatro Dante** was built by Falcini in 1871. Across the Bisenzio is the **Rocca Strozzi** rebuilt in 1377 and the church of **Santa Maria** which contains a chapel frescoed by Mariotto di Cristofano in 1420, and a 15C *Crucifix*.

On the Florence road is the suburb of **Brozzi**, where the church of Sant'Andrea has frescoes by Domenico Ghirlandaio and pupils. Nearby is **Peretola** which was the home of the Vespucci family before they moved to Florence. The church of Santa Maria contains a *tabernacle by Luca della Robbia (1441). The small airport for Florence, at Peretola (see Ch. 1) is beside the motorway which runs from Florence to the coast. At the Firenze-Nord exit is the church of San Giovanni Battista, built in 1960–64 by Giovanni Michelucci.

Badia di San Salvatore a Settimo

East of Lastra a Signa, on the south bank of the Arno, is the Badia di San Salvatore a Settimo, a 10C abbey, rebuilt for Cistercians in 1236–37, walled and fortified in 1371, and restored after 1944. The **church** has a rebuilt campanile and a Romanesque **façade** with a round 15C window (only open for services; at other times ring the (inconspicuous) bell by the gate to the left of the façade).

Over the second altar on the south side, Lodovico Buti, *Martyrdom of St Lawrence* (1574). Behind the high altar in *pietre dure* is the choir with a della Robbian enamelled terracotta frieze of cherubim and the Agnus Dei, and two frescoed tondi of the *Annunciation* by the school of Ghirlandaio. On the left of the high altar is a little marble *tabernacle*, beautifully carved and attributed to Giuliano da Sangallo. The chapel on the left of the high altar has good *frescoes* (in poor condition) by Giovanni di San Giovanni (1629). They depict scenes from the lives of Saints Stephen, Benedict, Bernard and Laurence, with God the Father in the dome and the Evangelists in the spandrels. The wall-tomb of the Countesses Gardia and Cilla (d. 1096)—a rare example of a pre-Romanesque tomb—on the north side dates from 1096. In the sacristy two paintings which were once in the church are displayed: the *Adoration of the Magi* and an unusual scene of *Christ at the sepulchre*, both attributed to Ghirlandaio or his school.

The remains of the **monastery** (carefully restored and now privately owned, but sometimes courteously shown; ring at the cloister) include much of the old fortifications, and the chapterhouse and the remarkable vaulted lay brothers' hall.

Near the Badia is the church of **Santi Giuliano e Settimo**, an 8C building, altered in subsequent centuries.

South of the main road between Lastra a Signa and Florence is **San Martino alla Palma** (open only for services; at other times ring at the green door under the portico) in a magnificent position among low, rolling hills (easily visible from the main road). It was founded in the 10C, and contains a charming *Madonna* by a follower of Bernardo Daddi known, from this painting, as the Master of San Martino alla Palma (1325–30).

On the other side of the motorway, which skirts the west side of Florence, is the huge suburb of **Scandicci** where much new building has taken place since the Second World War. To the south, beyond Vingone, is **San Paolo a Mosciano**. D.H. Lawrence stayed in the Villa Mirenda (next to the little cemetery and church) in 1926–27 while completing *Lady Chatterley's Lover* (first published in Florence in 1928).

8 · Prato and its province

Prato (163,000 inhab.) is a rapidly expanding industrial town, known as the Manchester of Tuscany, and long famous for its wool factories; it is one of the most important centres of the textile industry in Europe. In 1992 it became the capital of a new Province. It is surrounded by extensive suburbs, but it has a peaceful historic centre which preserves some beautiful monuments, all within its medieval walls.

■ Practical information
Information office. APT, 38 Via Luigi Muzzi (north of the Duomo (☎ 0574-35141), with information office at No. 48 Via Cairoli (☎ & fax. 0574-24112).

Getting there
By rail. *Centrale*, east of the town across the Bisenzio, for all trains on the main Florence–Bologna line. Services on the Florence–Lucca–Viareggio line stop also at *Porta al Serraglio*, 200 metres north of the cathedral.

By bus. Half-hourly services via the motorway in c 30 mins from Florence run by *CAP* and *Lazzi* from the right side of the Florence railway station (Piazza Adua). It stops in Prato at Piazza Santa Maria delle Carceri and in Via de' Tintori (request stop in Via Rinaldesca for the return services from Prato to Florence).

Parking. The centre is closed to traffic: parking (with hourly tariff) in Piazza Mercatale, Piazza Santa Maria delle Carceri, and Piazza San Francesco. Free parking in Piazza Macelli.

Hotels
★★★★ *President*, 20 Via Simintendi (Pl. 1; ☎ 0574-30251, fax 0574-36064).
★★★ *Flora*, 31 Via Cairoli (Pl. 2; ☎ 0574-33521, fax 0574-40289); *Giardino*, 4 Via Magnolfi (Pl. 3; ☎ 0574-26189, fax 0574-606591); *San Marco*, 48 Piazza San Marco (Pl. 4; ☎ 0574-21321, fax 0574-22378); *Milano*, 15 Via Tiziano (Pl. 5; ☎ 0574-23371, fax 0574-27706).
★★ *Il Giglio*, 14 Piazza San Marco (Pl. 6; ☎ 0574-37049, fax 0574-604351).
Rooms to let at *Villa Rucellai (Fattoria di Canneto)* 16 Via di Canneto (☎ 0574-460392).

Restaurants in the historic centre
£££ *Baghino*, 9 Via dell'Accademia; *Osvaldo Baroncelli*, 13 Via Fra Bartolomeo.

££ *La Cucina di Paola*, 16 Via Banchelli.
£ *Pizzerie* and *tavole calde*; *Brogi*, 7 Piazza Duomo; *Chez le crouton*, 51 Via Carraia.
Pasticceria specialising in biscuits (*biscotti di Prato*), Antonio Mattei, 22 Via Ricasoli (opened here in 1858).

Theatres and annual festivals
Teatro Comunale Metastasio, with a renowned theatre season (October to April). *Teatro il Fabbricone*, Viale Galileo. The *Prato Fair* is held in September (with a historical pageant on 8 September). A big general market is held on Mondays at the Mercato Nuovo.

History. Although probably already settled in the Etruscan period, the first recorded mention of Prato is in the 9C. It became a free commune in the 12C and after 1351 came under the influence of Florence. The manufacture of wool in the city had reached European importance by the 13C, and it received further impetus in the following century through the commercial activity of the famous merchant Francesco di Marco Datini. Its textile factories continue to flourish, and it has become the centre of the rag-trade in Europe. As an industrial centre, its population is expanding faster than almost any other city in central Italy.

Piazza del Duomo is a large square (closed to traffic; being repaved in 1998) where many streets converge around the cathedral. The fountain dates from 1863 (by Emanuele Caroni and Ulisse Cambi).

Duomo

The *duomo (closed 12.00–15.30) was founded in the 10C, but the present Romanesque building was begun in 1211 by Guidetto da Como. The unusual **façade** (1385–1457), partly striped in green and white marble, is crowned with a quadrilobe open sculptured frieze. Above the main portal is a *lunette with the *Madonna and Saints Stephen and Laurence* by Andrea della Robbia (1489). The ***pulpit** of the Sacred Girdle, designed by Donatello and Michelozzo (1434–38), is protected by a charming roof. It has a frieze depicting dancing putti by Donatello (replaced by casts in 1972—the originals are kept in the Museo dell' Opera del Duomo, see below). The Holy Girdle (see below) is displayed from the pulpit in a traditional ceremony on 1 May, Easter Day, 15 August, 8 September, and Christmas Day (it is processed three times out of one of the little doors and back through the other). The ***south side** of the cathedral, the oldest part of the building, has beautiful blind arcading and Romanesque inlaid marble decoration, and two fine doorways. The handsome campanile also dates from the early 13C, except for the last storey which was added c 1356 by Niccolò di Cecco del Mercia.

Donatello's pulpit on the exterior of the Duomo at Prato

Interior

The nave is supported by massive shiny green marble columns with good capitals, and the deep arcades are decorated with green and white striped marble. Immediately to the left is the *Chapel of the Sacred Girdle (see below).

The splendid bronze *screen was begun in 1438 by Maso di Bartolomeo and continued by Antonio di Ser Cola and Pasquino di Matteo (1467). On the altar is a statuette of the *Madonna and Child, one of the best works of Giovanni Pisano (1317). The chapel is entirely frescoed by Agnolo Gaddi with scenes from the life of the Virgin and the story of the relic of the Holy Girdle.

Above the west door, Assumption of the Virgin by Ridolfo del Ghirlandaio.In the south aisle is a wooden Crucifix by the bottega of Giovanni Pisano. The *pulpit in the nave is by Mino da Fiesole and Antonio Rossellino. The beautiful transept and east chapels, thought to have been designed by Giovanni Pisano, were added in 1317–68. A balustrade (incorporating some sculpted marble panels by Francesco di Simone Ferrucci, 1487), by Bernardino Radi and Gherardo Silvani (1637) precedes the high altar on which is a bronze Crucifix by Ferdinando Tacca (1653). The fine bronze candelabrum is by Maso di Bartolomeo.

The choir is decorated with celebrated *frescoes by Filippo Lippi (helped by Fra Diamante). This is one of the most beautiful fresco cycles of the early Renaissance (1452–66), and the monumental figures demand and reward close study (coin-operated light). On the right wall: scenes from the Life of St John the Baptist; the Salome in the *Banquet of Herod is supposed to be a portrait of Lucrezia Buti,

---

The Sacred Girdle

The chapel was built in 1385–90 to house the greatly revered relic which is traditionally considered to be the girdle (cintola) which the Madonna gave to St Thomas at her Assumption. Thomas is supposed to have given it for safe-keeping to a friend before he set out on a long sea voyage. When a certain Michele from Prato married a girl called Maria in Jerusalem, he is meant to have received it from her mother as a dowry.

The story goes that when he returned to Prato with it in 1141 (his wife died on the journey) he preserved the relic in secret in the rush basket in which he had received it, and in order to protect it he is supposed to have, irreverently, slept on it. Angels, as a sign of their disapproval, placed it on the floor several times while he slept. On his death bed, Michele presented the relic to the church where it was solomnly installed after an elaborate procession in 1174. (St Francis of Assisi came here to see it in 1212.)

After the attempted theft of the girdle in 1312, its custody was disputed between the church and the Comune, and since its installation in this chapel, built specially for it, in 1395, both the canons and the rulers of the city have kept a key. The pulpit (see above) on the façade, connected to the chapel by an internal corridor, was built for its ostentation in the 15C, when it was also seen by Pope Alexander V, King Louis of Anjou, St Bernardine, and the Byzantine emperor John Paleologus. At this time an exquisite reliquary was made for it by Maso di Bartolomeo (now kept in the Museo dell'Opera del Duomo), but since 1638 it has been preserved in a crystal box. The frescoes in the chapel by Gaddi illustrate (on the right wall) the story of Michele and the relic from the time of his marriage to his donation of it to the church.

the nun who was first Lippi's model and then his wife. On the **left wall**: scenes from the *Life of St Stephen*. Filippo Lippi also designed the beautiful stained glass window (except for the lower register which is modern).

South transept. The tabernacle of the *Madonna dell'Ulivo* (1480), designed by Giuliano da Maiano, contains a statue of the *Madonna and Child* and a bas-relief of the *Pietà* by his brothers Benedetto and Giovanni. The second chapel right of the choir (Cappella Vinaccesi) was frescoed with episodes from the Old Testament by the local painter Alessandro Franchi in 1880 (being restored in 1998). The 13C wooden figure of Christ was part of a Deposition group.

The **Cappella dell'Assunta** (first chapel right of the choir; coin operated light in the choir) is decorated with 15C frescoes of *the life of the Virgin and of St Stephen*. The cycle was begun in 1435 by Paolo Uccello who painted the upper *scenes (the vault, two lunettes with the *Birth of the Virgin and St Stephen*, and the *Stoning of St Stephen*). When Paolo Uccello left the following year to paint the monument to Hawkwood in the Duomo in Florence, the lower scenes were frescoed by Andrea di Giusto.

In the first chapel left of the choir (restored) are more early 15C frescoes; and in the second chapel is the ***tomb of Filippo degli Inghirami** (d. 1480) and a fine stained glass window depicting the Visitation and Nativity. Above the door into the sacristy is a monument to Carlo dei Medici (d. 1494) by Vincenzo Danti. The chapel of the Sacrament in the **north transept** has a carved entrance arch by Giovanni Camilliani (1544), and an altarpiece by Zanobi Poggini (1549).

Museo dell'Opera del Duomo

To the left of the Cathedral, beside **Palazzo Vescovile** with a 15C loggia, is a little courtyard with a 16C fresco in a tabernacle. Here is the entrance to the **Museo dell'Opera del Duomo** (open 09.30–12.30, 15.00–18.30; fest. 09.30–12.30; closed Tues). Work has been in progress since 1994 to enlarge the museum and meanwhile only two rooms are open as well as the cloister and vaults. Some of the masterpieces in the collection are temporarily housed in the Museo di Pittura Murale (see below).

Room I. 14C paintings, including a *Madonna and Child*, and *Evangelists* and *Saints* by Giovanni Toscani. Temporarily displayed here is the *reliquary for the sacred girdle, an exquisite work by Maso di Bartolomeo (1446). **Room II**: Illuminated 15C anthem books, two late 16C embroidered copes, and part of the treasury: reliquaries, chalices, thuribles, reliquary busts, and a pax by Danese Cattaneo. The *panels of dancing putti by Donatello from the Pulpit of the Sacred Girdle (outside the cathedral, see above), is being restored but should be on show again here in another room in 1999.

Part of the old **cloister** is a unique survival from the 12C, with tiny slender columns with exquisite capitals and green and white marble decoration. From here you can visit the medieval arches (*Le Volte*) beneath the transept of the Duomo, with early 15C frescoes, the 14C altar of the Holy Girdle, a small antiquarium, and some remains of the earlier church. A very unusual medieval pavement here is composed of some one hundred pieces of pottery kitchen ware.

Other paintings which belong to the museum which will eventually be on display include: Maestro della Natività di Castello, *Madonna and Child enthroned with Saints* (from the church of Santi Giusto e Clemente at Faltugnano); Michele Tosini, *Portrait of Lapo Spighi*; and Carlo Dolci, *Guardian Angel*.

Piazza del Comune

Opposite the right flank of the Duomo **Via Mazzoni** (called the Corso), the main street of the town, leads to the handsome Piazza del Comune, with a statue (1896) of the Merchant of Prato (see below), and a pretty little fountain by Ferdinando Tacca (1659; the original statue of the young Bacchus and the basin are preserved inside Palazzo Comunale, see below). The main stone façade with its Gothic windows and outside staircase of the splendid **Palazzo Pretorio** was added to a medieval core in the early 14C, and the battlements completed in the 16C. The main hall, with a fine roof, survives from the 14C. The palace houses the *Galleria Comunale and the Museo Civico** founded in 1852 which was closed for long-term restoration work in 1998 (not expected to reopen until after 2000). Meanwhile some of the masterpieces are exhibited at the Museo di Pittura Murale (see below).

The rest of the contents include: a frescoed *tabernacle by Filippino Lippi (1498), restored after severe damage in the Second World War. It was formerly on the corner of a house in Piazza del Mercatale (see below) purchased by Filippino for his widowed mother, who had been a nun at the nearby convent of Santa Margherita. A portrait of *Baldo Magini*, by Ridolfo del Ghirlandaio; *Madonna and Child*, by Lodovico Buti; Fra Bartolomeo, *Madonna and Child* (fresco fragment); Andrea della Robbia, *St Anthony Abbot* (lunette); Battistello, *Noli me tangere*; and works by Gaspare Vanvitelli, Gian Domenico Ferretti (*Annunciation*), Francesco Morandini (*Tobias and the Angel*), Giovanni Battista Naldini, and Bilivert.

Cupboards and jars from the old hospital pharmacy are also preserved here, together with a fine collection of plaster-casts. There is also an alabaster model for the Demidoff monument on Lungarno Serristori in Florence by Lorenzo Bartolini, who was born near Prato at Savignano (1777–1850).

Also in the piazza is the arcaded late 18C **Palazzo Comunale** (by Giuseppe Valentini). A worn Medici stemma of 1550 survives on the corner, by Battista del Tasso. In 1997 the **Museo del Tessuto** opened in a room on the ground floor (**open** Mon 14.30–18.30, Wed–Sun 10.30–18.30; closed Tues).

It contains a collection of textiles (kept for conservation reasons in drawers) including pre-Columbian works, Coptic fabrics, medieval fragments, Renaissance velvet, 17C embroideries and lace, 18C damask and brocade, and 19C cloth produced in the Prato textile manufactories. A section is dedicated to material made in Prato since the Second World War, including silk and synthetic fibres. There are also looms, carders, and spinning-machines, a display illustrating natural dyes, a collection of samples, and some costumes.

At the foot of the stairs of Palazzo Comunale (entrance at No. 2) is the original *fountain with the young *Bacchus* by Ferdinando Tacca, removed from the piazza outside. Upstairs the **Sala del Consiglio** (shown on request 08.00–14.00, except fest.) has a fine ceiling, two 15C frescoes, and a series of portraits in handsome frames (some by Alessandro Allori) of the grand-dukes of Tuscany, and of Cardinal Niccolò of Prato by Tommaso di Piero Trombetto.

Via Cairoli leads out of the piazza through a little square with the 19C façade of Palazzo Buonamici and its hanging garden. No. 19 is the Baroque Palazzo Gatti and beyond is the 16C **Palazzo Novellucci**, recently acquired by the province of Prato, which contains 18C stuccoes and painted decoration. A bit further on, beside a tall medieval tower is Piazza Santa Maria delle Carceri. Palazzo della Canonica by Giuseppe Valentini adjoins the church of ***Santa Maria delle Carceri** (closed 12.00–16.30), a masterpiece of the early Renaissance. It is one of the most important works by Giuliano da Sangallo, begun in 1485 (the exterior was left incomplete in 1506). The Greek-cross plan is derived from the architectural principles of Alberti and Brunelleschi. It was built on the site of a prison wall (hence *Carceri*) on which a painted image of the Virgin was thought to work miracles. The exterior, in green and white marble, recalls the Romanesque buildings of Florence (the last side was completed in the 19C). In the domed centrally-planned **interior** pietra serena is used to emphasise the structural elements. The beautiful enamelled terracotta frieze and tondi of the *Evangelists* are by Andrea della Robbia. The stoup, with a bronze statuette of St John the Baptist, is by Francesco da Sangallo, son of the architect, and the stained glass windows date from the 15C.

On a mound next to the church is the *Castello dell'Imperatore** (restored). The castle was begun by the son of the Emperor Frederick II to protect the route from Germany to Southern Italy, but left unfinished at the death of the Emperor in 1252. It is typical of the simple, austere Hohenstaufen castles of Southern Italy. In the empty interior (**open** 09.30–12.30, 15.00–18.30; fest. 09.30–12.30; closed Tues) three of the eight vaulted towers can be visited. The walkway which provides a good view of the city and countryside has been closed for many years. Concerts and plays are held here in summer.

From Piazza Santa Maria delle Carceri, Via Cairoli leads to the 19C **Teatro Comunale Metastasio** (admission on request at No. 59). The elegant interior was built in 1827–30 by Luigi Cambray Digny. It has a good theatrical reputation. Via Mazzini continues from the theatre towards Piazza San Marco where there is a sculpture (*Square form with cut*; 1969–70) by Henry Moore, known by the inhabitants of Prato since its installation here in 1974 as *Il Buco* (the hole).

Via Verdi skirts the theatre building and forms a crossroads with Via Garibaldi. This road leads (right) to the huge **Piazza Mercatale**, surrounded with a medley of pleasant buildings. Here the modern church of **San Bartolomeo** (the 14C church was destroyed in the Second World War) has a 15C marble tabernacle on the high altar with a painted *Crucifix* of the 14C Pistoian school above. The paintings include a tondo (above the west door) in a fine frame by the school of Botticelli, and works by Santi di Tito, Leonardo Mascagni, Livio Mehus (*Rest on the Flight*, at the end of the left wall), and Empoli. In the crypt is a fine wooden *Crucifix* of the 14C.

In the other direction, Via Garibaldi (see above) passes the oratory of the **Madonna del Buon Consiglio** (No. 53; if closed ask at Santa Maria delle Carceri), with a della Robbian lunette (and other works by the della Robbia inside).

Opposite the entrance to the castle (see above) is the east end of the Romanesque church of **San Francesco**, with a handsome striped marble façade. At the foot of the altar steps is the tomb of Francesco di Marco Datini (see below), by Nicolò Lamberti (1412). On the north wall is the tomb of Gimignano Inghirami (d. 1460), attributed to Bernardo Rossellino. The effigy rests on a comfortable damask catafalque and elaborate cushion. From the charming 15C cloister (planted with olive trees) or from the sacristy is the entrance to the **Chapter House** (or Cappella Migliorati) with good and well-preserved frescoes by Niccolò di Pietro Gerini (c 1395) of the *Crucifixion*, and stories from the life of St Anthony Abbot and St Matthew.

In front of the church (see below) is the **Biblioteca Roncioniana** (1751–66). In the vestibule is a *Tobias and the Archangel*, attributed to Andrea della Robbia).

Via Santa Trínita leads out of Piazza San Francesco. In Via Silvestri (right) is the church of the **Spirito Santo**. In the nave is a *Presentation in the Temple* by

Fra Diamante, possibly to a design of Filippo Lippi, and a *Madonna and Child with St Anne* attributed to Sogliani. The high altarpiece of the *Pentecost* is by Santi di Tito. In the presbytery is a high relief of *St John the Baptist* (15C) and a charming *Annunciation* and a tiny predella by the school of Orcagna. Off the south side there is a pretty little portico with Ionic columns.

Palazzo Datini

Via Rinaldesca leads out of Piazza San Francesco to the huge *Palazzo Datini with unusually large projecting eaves on the corner of Via Ser Lapo Mazzei. This was part of the residence of Francesco di Marco Datini, the famous Merchant of Prato (1330–1410), whose life was described in *The Merchant of Prato* (1957) by Iris Origo. Datini's papers and business documents (including over 140,000 letters), all of which were carefully preserved by him, provide a unique record of medieval life; they are housed in an archive in the palace. During his lifetime the palace was also used by the Comune of Prato to entertain illustrious visitors, among them Leonardo Dandolo, the Venetian ambassador in 1397, Pope Alexander V's representative in 1409, the illegal occupant of the papal chair, the antipope John XXIII, and Louis of Anjou in 1409–10.

The palace was acquired by Datini in 1354 and modifications were made by him between 1387 and 1390 when Niccolò di Pietro Gerini was commissioned to carry out the painted decoration in the courtyard and loggia, part of which survives. Datini left the palace to a charitable institute called the *Ceppo dei Poveri*, and after his death the exterior of the palace was frescoed with scenes from his life by Ambrogio di Baldese, Niccolò di Piero Gerini, and others (some of the sinopie of these frescoes are preserved inside the palace). The present frescoes on the exterior by Giuseppe Catani, replaced the originals in 1910. Part of the ground floor, including the courtyard, is open (09.00–12.00, 15.30–18.30 except Sat afternoon and Sun). At the foot of the stairs is a fresco of *St Christopher* by Niccolò di Pietro Gerini and a room with a painted vault and a portrait of Datini, dressed in red. Another room with a frescoed lunette of the *Redeemer* above the door has delightful painted decoration with woods and animals, and another good vault. Other rooms have frescoes detached from the courtyard.

Beyond is **Palazzo degli Alberti**, the headquarters of the Cassa di Risparmio bank, which owns a particularly interesting art collection (**open** by previous appointment; 08.30–12.30, 15.00–16.00, except Sat and Sun). The works, arranged in a gallery overlooking the banking hall, include: a *Crucifix* (with an interesting landscape), an undocumented work attributed to Giovanni Bellini; a *Madonna and Child* almost certainly by Filippo Lippi; Caravaggio, *Christ crowned with Thorns*. The fine 17C Tuscan paintings are by Matteo Rosselli, Santi di Tito, Alessandro Rosi, Giovanni Battista Vanni, Lorenzo Lippi, Giovanni Bilivert, Carlo Dolci (*Charity*), Cesare, Vincenzo and Pier Dandini, Francesco Furini, Sustermans, and Bernardino Mei. The collection of marble sculptures by Lorenzo Bartolini include *Faith* and some portrait busts. On the stairs are two large paintings by Galileo Chini.

In front of Palazzo Datini, Via Tinaia leads to Via Pellegrino on which is the pretty little 19C church of **San Pier Forelli** (1838). It has a barrel vault and semi-circular apse lit from a semi-dome. Nearby is the huge 18C **Collegio Cicognini**, a well-known school attended by the poet Gabriele d'Annunzio. It has an elaborate façade, and incorporates 18C frescoes, and a theatre built c 1780.

Via Santa Caterina leads up to a little piazza in front of the church and convent of **San Niccolò** (for adm. ring at the convent school), restored in 1994. Chamber music **concerts** are sometimes held here. The Dominican convent founded in 1321, was altered in the 18C. In 1785 the school was founded here and a neo-classical wing was added by Giuseppe Valentini.

The **church** has an 18C interior with frescoes attibuted to Rinaldo Botti. It preserves two 14C frescoes on the right wall, including a fragment of the story of the life of San Nicola by Pietro di Miniato and the high altarpiece of the *Assumption* is by Alessandro Gherardini. In the **sacristy** is a fine enamelled terracotta lavabo (1520) attributed to Benedetto and Santi Buglioni, and a 15C *Crucifix*.

The interesting **convent** has an 18C **nuns' choir**, with rococo decorations by Niccolò Nannetti, and stuccoes, and wooden choirstalls. Two 15C frescoes survive here, including a lunette with the *Madonna of the Holy Girdle* attributed to Pietro di Miniato. The altarpiece of the *Madonna of the Rosary* is by Luigi Crespi (1732). In a corridor is displayed the *Mystical Marriage of St Catherine* by Tommaso di Piero del Trombetto and a 16C *Crucifix*. The delightful **pharmacy**, with its original cupboards painted with blue-and-white landscapes, dates from 1764. There are similar cupboards in the **Stanza dei Padri**. The **chapter house** has a 14C wooden ceiling and a large fresco (1509) attributed to Girolamo Ristori. The **large refectory** has a fresco attributed to Tommaso di Piero del Trombetto, and its wood furnishings dating from the late 16C, and the **small refectory** has a 15C fresco of the *Supper of St Dominic* attributed to Bartolomeo Bocchi In a chapel on the upper floor is a *Nativity with Saints Stephen and Catherine* attributed to Zanobi Poggini. Other works of art belonging to the convent include a 15C terracotta relief of the *Nativity* and a painting of *Tobias and the Angel* attributed to Giovan Pietro Naldini.

From Palazzo Alberti, Via Banchelli leads right and Via Guasti left to the 13C–14C church of **San Domenico**, which has an arcaded flank. Founded in 1283 it was finished by Giovanni Pisano before 1322. It contains a 17C organ, on which the composer Domenico Zipoli (born in Prato in 1688 and died in Argentina in 1726) probably played. Over the high altar is a Baroque baldacchino. **South aisle**. Second altar, *Crucifix* by Niccolò Gerini; **third altar**, *St Vincent Ferrer* attributed to Pier Dandini; **fifth altar**, *Madonna and Saints and Angels* by Camillo Sagrestani. **North aisle**. Second altar, *Madonna appearing to St Philip Neri*, by Matteo Rosselli; **fourth altar**, *Crucifix before St Thomas Aquinas*, by Francesco Morandini; **fifth altar**, *Annunciation*, signed by Matteo Rosselli. In the **Chapter House** (off the cloister) interesting early 15C frescoes of the *Life of St Dominic* attributed to Pietro di Miniato were uncovered in 1984.

Museum of Mural Painting

In the adjoining convent is a Museum of Mural Painting (entered from No. 8 in the piazza) which has a permanent exhibition of detached frescoes from buildings in the town and surrounding area (**open** 10.00–13.00, 15.30–19.00; fest. 10.00–13.00; closed Tues).

In 1998 the museum hosted an exhibition called *I Tesori della Città* with works from the Museo Civico and Museo dell'Opera del Duomo (both closed for restoration, see above). As these works are expected to remain here until at least the year 2000 this new arrangement is described below.

At the top of the stairs is a stained glass fragment with the *Annunciation* by Fra Paolo di Mariotto da Gambassi (1509).

First section. *Predella by Bernardo Daddi, illustrating the story of the *Sacred Girdle* (see p. 158), and a polyptych of the *Madonna and Saints* by the same artist. A polyptych of the *Madonna and Saints* with a double predella by Giovanni da Milano is still being restored.The polyptych, also with a double predella, with the *Coronation of the Virgin and Saints* (two of them missing) was commissioned by the merchant Francesco di Marco Datini from Pietro di Miniatoin 1410. Beyond a *Madonna and Four Saints* by Lorenzo Monaco are two works by Andrea di Giusto. On the opposite wall sinopie by Paolo Uccello are displayed, detached from the chapel of the Assunta in the Duomo of Prato in 1964, and *Jacopone da Todi*, a fresco detached in 1871 from the same chapel and also attributed to Paolo Uccello (or the Master of Prato).

Room A displays a detached fresco and a sinopia by Agnolo Gaddi, and a fresco of the *Madonna and Child with angels and Saints Catherina of Alexandria and Mary Magdalene* with its sinopia commissioned from Niccolò Gerini by Francesco Datini for his garden.

Second section. **Works by Filippo Lippi**, including the *Madonna del Ceppo* (with Francesco di Marco Datini presenting members of the confraternity of the Buonomini del Ceppo to the Madonna), the *Death of St Jerome* and stories from his life (from the Duomo), and a *Nativity* (with the help of assistants). The *Madonna of the Holy Girdle with Saints* was begun by Filippo but probably finished by his assistant Fra Diamante, to whom the predella, also displayed here, is attributed, showing the *Presentation in the Temple*, the *Adoration of the Magi*, and the *Massacre of the Innocents*.

In **Room B** is a painting of *St Dominic* attributed to Bernardo Daddi, a choir book with miniatures by Rossello Franchi, works by Domenico di Michelino and the 'Maestro di Pratovecchio', and two small paintings of the *Annunciation with St Julian* derived from a work by Filippo Lippi.

Third section.15C works: Francesco Botticini, Madonna enthroned with four Saints; Filippino Lippi, Madonna and Child with Saints Stephen and John the Baptist (in its original frame); 15C Florentine master (formerly attributed to Filippino Lippi), *St Lucy. The two tondi are by Raffaellino de' Carli, and Luca Signorelli. In the side corridor are 15C *graffiti decoration of courtly scenes by Girolamo Ristori detached from the garden of Palazzo Vaj in Prato. Room C has late 15C works, including a Crucifix painted by the bottega of Botticelli.

Opposite the façade of San Domenico is the 18C church of **San Vincenzo e Santa Caterina de' Ricci** (open at 17.00), with a fine interior of 1733. In the Dominican convent are mementoes of St Catherine de' Ricci (1522–90) who lived here from the age of 15. She became prioress and was famous for her visions and saintliness. She was canonised in 1746. In Via San Vincenzo, at No. 24 is the church of San Clemente in another convent (closed order; service at 18.00).

Via Convenevole leads from Piazza San Domenico past the little church of **San Michele** (the church of the Misericordia) with an altarpiece of the *Assumption* by Alessandro Allori (1603) and a Romanesque *Crucifix*.

At the end of Via Convenevole Via della Stufa leads left to a piazza in front of the church of **Sant'Agostino**, erected in 1271, but considerably altered since then.

The **interior** contains 16C–17C altarpieces, including, in the **north aisle** (second altar), a *Madonna* designed by Vasari (and executed by Giovanni Battista Naldini), and (third altar) *St Thomas of Villanova*, by Lorenzo Lippi. In the chapel at the end of the north aisle, *Sacred Conversation*, by Empoli (who also painted the *Immaculate Conception and Saints* on the second south altar). A door in the north wall leads into the garden of the cloister; to the left is reached the **Cappella di San Michele** with a damaged frieze of saints (14C) and a relief of a *Madonna and Child* by the school of Ghiberti. The **Chapter House**, beyond, has a fine cross-vault and a 14C fresco of *Christ in Pietà*.

Nearby is the church of **San Fabiano** (entrance on request at No. 28 Via del Seminario; see the Plan). Interesting fragments of the pre-Romanesque monochrome mosaic pavement with figures of animals, sirens, and birds, are displayed in the cloister and on the west wall (the façade can be seen from Via Giovanni di Gherardo which skirts the walls).

In front of San Michele (see above), Largo Carducci leads back to Piazza del Duomo.

Over 2km south-east of the centre (bus 7 or 8 from Viale Piave near the Castello dell'Imperatore) between the motorway exit (Prato-est) and Viale della Repubblica, is the **Centro per l'Arte Contemporanea Luigi Pecci**, designed by Italo Gamberini (1907–90), and opened in 1988 (**open** 10.00–19.00 except Tues). The huge, well illuminated galleries are used for contemporary art exhibitions. There is also an open-air theatre, library, auditorium and snack bar.

The province of Prato

■ Practical information
Information office. APT of Prato, 48 Via Cairoli, Prato (☎ 0574–24112).

Getting there
By bus (*COPIT* or *CAP*) from Florence (9 Largo Alinari) every half hour (in c 30 mins) to Poggio a Caiano. From Poggio a Caiano bus via Comeana to Artimino in 20 mins, and via Seano to Carmignano (in 20mins).

Hotels
Artimino. ★★★★ *Paggeria Medicea* (☎ 055–8718081, fax 055–8718080).

Restaurants
Artimino. ££ *La Delfina*.
Bacchereto. ££ *La Cantina di Toia*.

Villa di Poggio a Caiano
The village of **Poggio a Caiano** at the foot of Monte Albano, is visited for its Medici *villa, rebuilt in 1480 by **Giuliano da Sangallo** for Lorenzo il Magnifico. It was then used by later members of the Medici dynasty, and in subsequent centuries the Austrians and French rulers, and the kings of Italy all stayed here. Since 1996 work has been in progress to restore the furnishings of the villa to the appearance it had during the Savoy period in 1911. The top floor is now used for exhibitions.

Open every half hour on the half hour, 09.00–15.30; March and Oct

09.00–16.30; Apr, May & Sept 09.00–17.30; June–Aug 09.00– 18.30; closed on the 2nd and 3rd Mon of the month.

PROVINCIA DI PRATO

The fine rectangular building stands on a broad terrace surrounded by a colonnade. A classical Ionic portico on the first floor with the Medici arms in the tympanum bears a beautiful polychrome enamelled terracotta frieze (a copy of the original, which is now kept inside the villa). The semicircular steps were added by Pasquale Poccianti in 1802–07.

On the **ground floor** is a little **theatre** built in the 17C by Marguerite-Louise of Orléans, wife of Cosimo III. When Elisa Baciocchi, Napeolon's sister, was Grand-duchess of Tuscany at the beginning of the 19C it was restored, and the famous violinist Niccolò Paganini often played here. The theatre was redecorated after 1860. The **billiard room** has charming 19C painted decorations. A room in Bianca Cappello's apartment has a 16C fireplace and stone staircase (closed for restoration).

First floor

A room with 19C grisaille decorations by Luigi Catani overlooking the loggia, adjoins another room where the original polychrome enamelled **terracotta *frieze**, once on the façade, is displayed. A classical representation of a Platonic myth (or philosophical interpretation of the Golden Age with representations of classical heroes and myths; apparently an allusion to the good government of Lorenzo the Magnificent), it was designed to celebrate the Medici dynasty. It is thought by some scholars to be the work of Andrea del Sansovino (c 1490–94), with the help of a collaborator, but others consider it a later work (it is also attributed to Bertoldo di Giovanni). The pretty little 19C living room has wallpaper decorated with the Florentine iris.

The decoration of the ***salone**, was designed by Lorenzo's son Leo X in 1513–21 to celebrate the return of the Medici to Florence (after Lorenzo's eldest son, Piero, had been exiled in 1494 and a Republican government established in Florence). It has a carved and gilded barrel vault with the Medici arms by Andrea Feltrini and Franciabigio. The **frescoes** were begun by Franciabigio, Andrea del Sarto and Pontormo (1519–21) and completed by Alessandro Allori (1579–82). The subjects were designed by Paolo Giovio and illustrate incidents in Roman history paralleled in the lives of Cosimo il Vecchio and Lorenzo il Magnifico, as well as mythological scenes celebrating

The Medici Villa at Poggio a Caiano

the return of the Medici dynasty in the 16C as rulers of Florence.

On the **left of the entrance**: *Julius Caesar receives the Tributes from Egypt* (recalling Lorenzo il Magnifico receiving gifts from the Sultan of Egypt in 1487), by Andrea del Sarto (Allori added the child with the turkey, the figures with the horse on the right-hand side, and the man with the parrot on the left). The numerous animals include a parrot and a giraffe. Opposite, *Scipio received by Syphax, King of Numidia after his victory over Hasdrubal in Spain* (in memory of Lorenzo il Magnifico's visit to Naples whre he was entertained by Ferdinand of Aragon) by Alessandro Allori. On the other side of the door, the *Return of Cicero from exile* (alluding to the return of Cosimo il Vecchio to Florence in 1434) is by Franciabigio (the four figures on the right-hand side, and the statue of a river-god, as well as the obelisk and rostrum were added by Allori). On the **entrance wall**: *the Consul Flaminius at the council of the Achaean league* (alluding to Lorenzo il Magnifico's intervention at the Diet of Cremona which reversed the plans of the Venetian Republic), also by Allori.

The decorative scheme culminates in the remarkable **lunette* illustrating the story of *Vertumnus and Pomona* as told by Ovid, a very fine work by Pontormo (c 1520). The harmonious idyllic scene was probably intended as a celebration of the new members of the Medici family. On the right are three female figures with white stoles: the splendid figure of Pomona, goddess of fruits, in green, with Ceres seated above her on the wall and Summer dressed in lilac. On the left, on either side of a dog, are Vertumnus in two disguises (as an old man and as a young man), with Bacchus seated above. Above and round the oculus (which looks towards Florence) putti play in the sacred laurel tree, above this idealised rustic scene. Bernard Berenson commented: "as design, as colour, as fancy, the freshest, the gayest, most appropriate mural decoration now remaining in Italy". The lunette opposite, illustrating the *Garden of the Hesperides*, and the frescoes above the windows were added by Allori.

Beyond a room with red silk hangings and Medici portraits by Sustermans, is Vittorio Emanuele II's bedroom. Other rooms include an Empire bathroom added by Elisa Baciocchi.

Beneath the loggia on the façade (with a fine barrel-vault) are remains of a fresco by Filippino Lippi, part of Lorenzo's original decoration.

Medici Villas

Villa di Poggio a Caiano is the most important of the **Medici villas** surrounded by parks and gardens in the environs of Florence, nearly all of which are open to the public. There are long-term plans to arrange a Museum here, encompassing the history of all the Medici villas. These country houses were used by the Medici to entertain artists and poets and as summer retreats from the heat of Florence. Leading architects of the time, including **Michelozzo** and **Buontalenti** were employed to enlarge or design these luxurious residences which were decorated with fine paintings (most of them now dispersed).

In the 15C, Cosimo il Vecchio employed Michelozzo to build **Cafaggiolo** (in 1451) and **Trebbio** (in 1461), both villas in the Mugello valley. Cosimo's grandsons Lorenzo and Giuliano spent their childhood at Cafaggiolo (which was sufficiently far from Florence to be safe during outbreaks of the plague in the city). Cosimo also employed Michelozzo to enlarge the villa of **Careggi**, nearer to Florence, which became the literary and artistic centre of the Medicean court in the 15C and is traditionally taken as the meeting place of the famous **Platonic Academy** which saw the birth of the Renaissance Humanist movement. Among its members, who met in the gardens, were Marsilio Ficino, Angelo Poliziano, Pico della Mirandola, and Greek scholars including Gemisthos Plethon and Argyropoulos, who came to Florence after the fall of Constantinople. Cosimo spent the last years of his life here (both his son, Piero di Cosimo, and Lorenzo il Magnifico also died here). Cosimo also had Michelozzo design the Medici villa outside Fiesole in 1458–61.

Lorenzo il Magnifico enjoyed hunting at Cafaggiolo, and he employed Giuliano da Sangallo to build **Poggio a Caiano**. Surrounded by a large park it became his favourite country residence, and he kept a large stud here. His younger cousins, Giovanni and Lorenzo di Pierfrancesco de' Medici acquired the **Villa di Castello** in about 1477 (and Botticelli's *Birth of Venus* and *Primavera* were hung here until the 18C).

The Medici grand-dukes in the 16C also took an interest in the villas. Cosimo I had Buontalenti design the villa at **Cerreto Guidi**, and he renovated the villas of Careggi and Castello (where he took a particular interest in the garden). Francesco I commissioned Buontalenti to build the villa at **Pratolino** (now Demidoff) and he took up residence with Bianca Cappello at Poggio a Caiano. They both died here on the same day in 1587, apparently of tertian fever (although there were rumours that they had been poisoned). Ferdinando I, who often stayed at Cafaggiolo, ordered Buontalenti to design the **Villa della Petraia**. He also built the hunting lodges of **Artimino** (known as 'La Ferdinanda') and the **Ambrogiana** (not open to the public).

In the 17C Cosimo III lived at **La Topaia** above the Villa di Castello beneath Monte Morello (now privately owned). After 1696 he commissioned the large paintings from Bartolomeo Bimbi (some of which are now kept at Poggio a Caiano) which document the numerous fruits and vegetables he grew there.

Top floor

This was reopened in 1998 for exhibitions. There are also long-term plans to open a Museum here to exhibit the numerous still lives collected by the Medici and Lorraine grand-dukes. Of particular interest are those by Bartolomeo Bimbi from the Villa La Topaia (see above), with numerous different types of grapes, lemons, citrons, apples, and cherries (in their splendid original Dutch frames). For the time being this part of the villa will probably be accessible only by appointment. In 1987 a large wooden merry-go-round which dates from 1799 was found in the villa.

The delightful **garden** and **park**, which descend behind the villa to the River Ombrone, contain numerous fine trees. The huge orangery was built by Poccianti in 1825.

Etruscan tombs at Comeana and Montefortini

Southwest of Poggio a Caiano is **Comeana**. Just outside the village, beside the cemetery (signposted), is the Etruscan tomb of **Boschetti** (7C BC), discovered in 1955 and formerly inside a mound or tumulus. It is now covered for protection. Nearby is the **Tumulus of Montefortini** now covered with oak trees, beside the road (entrance gate on the left; usually **open** 09.00–17.00; Sat & fest. 09.00–13.00). Inside the mound an **Etruscan chamber tomb** was found in 1962, with an entrance corridor (or dromos) open to the sky. The antechamber and rectangular funerary chamber both have interesting 'false vaults'. The huge monolith which sealed the entrance survives. The stone shelf which runs round the walls of the inner chamber probably served for the illustrious defunct's possessions. The tomb dates from c 620 BC. Next to it excavations have been in progress since 1980 of a second tomb in the same tumulus, with a longer dromos, and a circular inner chamber supported by a central column 6m high. This seems to have been the more important tomb, built some 30 years earlier. The vault may have collapsed in an earthquake.

Villa di Artimino

The beautiful Villa di Artimino (also known as 'La Ferdinanda'), stands in attractive woodland surrounded by superb Tuscan countryside about 2km from Comeana. It was designed by Bernardo Buontalenti (1594) for Ferdinando I.

This is one of the finest Medici villas. A singular feature of this villa are its numerous different chimneys. Galileo was a guest here in 1608. The Paggeria Mediea or service wing, also by Buontalenti, is now a hotel. The empty rooms of the villa are used for conferences and parties (for **adm**. enquire at the Paggeria, ☎ 8718081).

The basement of Villa di Artimino houses the **Museo Archeologico Comunale** (**open** 09.00–13.00; fest. 09.00–12.30; closed Wed), which displays Etruscan finds from excavations (still in progress) of the Etruscan-Roman settlement of Artimino and its necropoli.

The museum is beautifully arranged and well labelled. **Cases 1–8** contain material from Etruscan dwellings including Bucchero vases, ceramics, spindles and weights for looms and cooking pots. The rest of the collection comes from the necropoli. In **case 9** are ointment jars (7C BC). Displayed on its own in **case 10** is a rare *incense burner in Bucchero ware (7C BC) with an elegant stand, found at Prato di Rosello. In **case 11** are ivories (including small winged lions), bronze harnesses, and jewellery from the Boschetti tumulus. In **case 12** are Bucchero and impasto vases from the same tomb.

Cases 13 and **14** contains objects (ivory plaquettes and bronze objects) from the Montefortini tumulus. In **case 15** is a well-preserved bronze service for use at banquets (4C BC), including a splendid bronze situla with two handles. Displayed on its own in **case 16** is a large red-figure crater (4C BC) with dionysiac scenes found at Grumaggio. **Case 17** contains a beautiful Etruscan *amphora found at Prato di Rosello dating from the end of the 6C BC or beginning of the 5C BC. Also displayed here are cippi, a 6C stele, and three Volterra urns. The adjoining room has a fine display of 14C–15C ceramics from Bacchereto.

This hilltop site between the Ombrone and Arno rivers was once occupied by an Etruscan settlement from the 7C BC. Remains of a sacred area, probably part of the acropolis, were excavated in 1972 behind the Paggeria. A huge necropolis, known as **Prato di Rosello**, with some ten tumuli dating from the 7C BC, has come to light on the eastern slopes of the hill above the tumuli of Montefortini and Boschetti.

On the little hill in front of the villa is the charming medieval borgo of **Artimino**, and the fine Romanesque church of San Leonardo (only open for services on fest.). Imbedded in the outer walls of the church are casts of urns (the originals of which are in the Archaeological Museum of Artimino). Near the church, tombs from around 300 BC and later have been found.

At **Carmignano** (reached cross-country from Artimino in about 7km, or direct from Poggio a Caiano in 5km) the church of San Michele contains a remarkable altarpiece of the *Visitation* by Pontormo (c 1530) on the second south altar. At the east end are two detached frescoes by Andrea di Giusto. This area has been famous since the 14C for its wine (produced with the addition of cabernet grapes), in particular at Bacchereto and Capezzana.

A few kilometres below Artimino is the little town of **Seano**. Beside the road an attractive sculpture park was opened in 1988 with a fine collection of 36 bronzes by the sculptor Quinto Martini (1908–90), who was born here.

The road continues across Monte Albano, past the Romanesque church of San Giusto to descend to Vinci (see Ch. 7).

The Apennines above Prato

The road from Prato to Bologna (100km; N325) follows the main railway line across the Apennines. It ascends the Bisenzio valley passing through the wide upland basin of **Vaiano**, with its 13C campanile. There is a small archaeological and liturgical collection (15C–19C) in the Badia di San Salvatore, founded by the Benedictines in the 9C–10C, and restored in 1997. Nearby is **Figline di Prato** with the Romanesque Pieve of San Pietro (14C–15C frescoes; and a small museum of 14C–17C paintings and church silver). In the hills to the right of Vaiano is **Savignano**, the birthplace of the painter Fra Bartolomeo della Porta (1475–1517) and the sculptor Lorenzo Bartolini (1777–1850).

Near the ruined 12C–13C castle of **Cerbaia** is **San Quirico di Vernio** (278m), a substantial village with two residences (16C and 18C) belonging to the Conti Bardi family. The Oratory of San Niccolò dates from 1706. The mountain pass is just before **Montepiano** (700m), a summer resort. Here the 11C–12C

Badia di Santa Maria contains 13C–14C frescoes. The region of Emilia (see *Blue Guide Northern Italy*) is entered near Castiglione dei Pepoli.

In the other direction, the old road from Prato to Pistoia passes **Montemurlo**, where the medieval Guidi castle was the scene of the last attempt of the partisans of the Florentine Republic to overthrow the Medici dynasty (1537).

9 · Pistoia

Pistoia (93,200 inhab.) is a lively old Tuscan town with an unusual number of beautiful churches, whose character reflects its position between Florence and Pisa. Many of the churches contain good sculptures. It is an important horticultural centre, particularly noted for the cultivation of ornamental plants. There are extensive nurseries on the surrounding plain.

■ Practical information

Information office. APT Abetone, Pistoia, Montagna Pistoiese in Palazzo dei Vescovi, 4 Piazza Duomo (☎ 0573–21622).

Getting there

By rail. Piazza Dante Alighieri, with services on the Florence–Viareggio line (from Florence, 34km in 35–45 mins).

By bus. From Florence run by *Lazzi* via the motorway in 45mins, to Piazza Dante Alighieri; and by *COPIT* in 1 hour to Piazza San Francesco. *COPIT* services from Pistoia to Abetone, Cutigliano and San Marcello Pistoiese *Lazzi* services to Prato, Montecatini Terme, Lucca and Pisa.

Parking. The centre is closed to traffic: car parks at the ex-Officine Meccaniche Breda, off Via Pacinotti, or east of the Fortezza Santa Barbara, between Via del Bastione Mediceo and Via Cellini.

Hotels

★★★ *Patria*, 8 Via Crispi (Pl. 1; ☎ 0573-25187; fax 0573-368168); *Milano*, 12 Via Pacinotti (Pl. 2; ☎ 0573-975700; fax 0573-32657).
★★ *Firenze*, 42 Via Curtatone (Pl. 3; ☎ 0573-21660; fax 0573-23141).
4km east at Pontenuovo, *Il Convento* ★★★, 33 Via San Quirico; (☎ 0573-452651, fax 0573-453578).

Restaurants in the centre

££ *San Jacopo*, 15 Via Crispi; *La Vela*, 12 Piazza dell'Ortaggio.
£ *Trattoria dell'Abbondanza*, 10 Via dell'Abbondanza; *Trattoria Lo Storno*, 8 Via del Lastrone; *Tonino*, 159 Corso Gramsci.

Restaurants on the outskirts of the city

££ *La Cugna*, Località La Cugna, 238 Via Bolognese and *Rafanelli*, Località Sant'Agostino, 47 Via Sant'Agostino.

Café. *Valiani*, Via Carducci (in a 13C oratory next to the church of San Giovanni Fuorcivitas).

Picnics. The public gardens in Piazza della Resistenza and in the Fortezza di Santa Barbara (closes at 13.30) are both pleasant.

Markets. Piazza Duomo and Piazza Spirito Santo (on Wed and Sat mornings).

Annual Festival. The *Giostra dell'Orso* (Tournament of the bear, the heraldic symbol of the city which supports its coat of arms), a medieval jousting tournament in which the mounted participants have to hit a wooden bear with their lance, is held on 25 July in Piazza del Duomo.

History. Pistoia is first mentioned as the scene of Catiline's defeat in 62 BC. It was a republic in the 12C but was seized by the Florentines in 1306 and in 1315 by Castruccio Castracani (d. 1328), a military and political adventurer. From 1329 it existed under the protection of Florence, whose fortunes it shared, as the Medici arms on the walls testify. As an ironworking town in medieval times, it gave its name to the pistol (originally a dagger, afterwards a small firearm).

The town became well known in the 18C for its organs constructed here by the Tronci and Agati families. The **Breda works** here are famous for the production of railway carriages and buses; a new factory was built in 1973 on the outskirts of the town between the railway and the motorway (the huge old *officine*, off Via Pacinotti, have been abandoned and are at present used as a car park).

Guittone Sinibaldi, called Cino da Pistoia (1270–1337), friend of Dante, was born here; also Clement IX (Giulio Rospigliosi), Pope in 1667–69.

If you are approaching the town from Florence (or from the station) you will enter it on the site of the south gate; from here Via Vannucci and Via Cino lead to Piazza Gavinana.

San Domenico

Corso Fedi, on the right before the piazza, leads to the church of **San Domenico** built c 1280, probably to the design of Fra Sisto and Fra Ristoro, with 14C alterations.

The **interior** is particularly interesting for its sculptured **funerary monuments**. The fine stained glass in the east window dates from 1930. **South side**. Tomb of the lawyer and teacher Filippo Lazzari, by Bernardo and Antonio Rossellino; third altar, *St Sebastian* by Giacinto Gimignani. In a niche below 14C fresco fragments is the beautiful sculpted **tomb effigy** of Beato Lorenzo da Ripafratta (the friar, acclaimed for his generosity to those in need, died in the convent in 1457). Beyond the fourth altar, Gothic tomb of Andrea Franchi; fifth altar, *Assumption* by Matteo Rosselli.

South transept. Empoli, *St Charles Borromeo* with members of the Rospigliosi family, and 17C Rospigliosi funerary monuments (the busts are attributed to Bernini). In the chapel to the left of the presbytery, Cristofano Allori, *St Domenic receiving the Rosary* (with a portrait of the artist discussing his payment for the painting with the sacristan of the convent) and more 17C monuments. The organ, by Rovani da Lucca, dates from 1617.

In the **sacristy** (usually shown on request) are some interesting detached frescoes: the *Journey of the Magi*, attributed to the school of Benozzo Gozzoli; *St Jerome kneeling*, thought to be an early work by Verrocchio (also attributed to Domenico Veneziano and Antonio del Pollaiolo); and *St Mary Magdalene* (14C Sienese). Also here is a painting of the *Marriage of St Catherine*, by Fra Paolino.

A door in the south aisle leads into the **cloister** where in an unknown spot, the body of Benozzo Gozzoli, is buried. He died here in 1497 during the plague (commemorative plaque). Some of the lunettes are frescoed with scenes from the *Life of Mary Magdalene* by Giovanni di San Giovanni and Matteo Rosselli.

The **chapter house** here has a damaged fresco of the *Crucifixion* by an unknown master of the mid-13C, with its *sinopia, thought to be the oldest known in Italy.

On the other side of Corso Fedi is a little garden with palm trees, an equestrian statue of Garibaldi (1904) and amusing Art Nouveau lamp-posts. The **Chapel of Sant'Antonio Abate (del Tau)** (open 08.00–13.00 except Sun) was built in 1360 by the monks who cured the sick and disabled (who wore a T or Greek *Tau* on their cloaks, probably symbolising a crutch). The fine Gothic vaulted **interior** is entirely frescoed with *scenes from the life of St Anthony Abbot* and the *story of the Sacred Girdle*, and, in the vault, the *Creation*. These are by Niccolò di Tommaso (1372), probably with the help of Antonio Vite (formerly attributed to Bonaccorso di Cino and Masolino).

In the adjoining **Palazzo del Tau** the **Centro Marino Marini** was opened in 1990 (open 09.00–13.00, 15.00–19.00 except Sun pm and Mon; **cumulative ticket** with the Museo Civico and Museo Rospigliosi). Here, well arranged in the numerous small rooms of the former convent are graphic works and plaster-casts by the sculptor, who was born in Pistoia (1901–66).

Farther along Corso Fedi, on the left, is the church of **San Paolo**, with a fine façade of 1291–1302. Over the later door are statues of *St Paul between two angels* by Jacopo di Mazzeo, and, (high up on the pinnacle) a figure of *St James*, attributed to Orcagna. Inside is a 14C woodrn *Crucifix* (left wall).

Via Porta Carratica and Via Campo Marzio lead to Piazza della Resistenza where there is a public park beside the 14C city walls. The impressive **Fortezza di Santa Barbara** is open 09.00–13.30 exc Mon. Originally a 14C fort, it was strengthened for the Grand-duke Cosimo I by Nanni Unghero and protected by bastions designed by Bernardo Buontalenti.

San Giovanni Fuorcivitas

Via Crispi leads north from Piazza Garibaldi to the 12C–14C church of San Giovanni Fuorcivitas. The handsome striped north side, with a blind arcade surmounted by two blind galleries, serves as a **façade**. The fine portal bears a relief of the *Last Supper* by Gruamonte (1162).

In the dark **interior** (light on right side), with stained glass of 1908, the *pulpit* is by Fra Guglielmo da Pisa, a follower of Nicola Pisano (1270; restored in 1998). The *stoup, with the theological and cardinal Virtues in the middle of the church is by Giovanni Pisano. On the west wall is a large Cross (13C–14C; removed for restoration). Over the altar on the right side, tondo of the *Madonna and Child*, a good work by the 15C Florentine school. The high altar is composed of 12C intarsia panels from the Duomo. On the right wall of the sanctuary, *St John the Evangelist* and stories from his life, by Giovanni di Bartolomeo Cristiani (1370); on the opposite wall, polyptych by Taddeo Gaddi (1353–55), and *St Roch* by Bernardino di Antonio del Signoraccio. On the altar on the north side of the nave, *Visitation* in white glazed terracotta, a particularly moving work by Luca della Robbia (c 1445). Above the door, 15C wooden statue of *St Lucy*.

Near the west end of the church, through the entrance to the Cinema Verdi, the charming cloisters can be seen.

Farther along Via Cavour, Via Roma leads left past (right) the **Palazzo della Cassa di Risparmio**, an interesting building of 1905 by Tito Azzolini (with interior decorations by Galileo Chini) which stands opposite the old **Palazzo del Capitano del Popolo** (1283), on the corner of Via di Straccieria. The low medieval buildings here (which now have interesting old shop fronts) were used by the workmen who constructed the Baptistery (see below). Beyond is **Piazza della Sala,** a delightful medieval market square, with the Pozzo del Leoncino, a well (1453) surmounted by the Florentine *Marzocco* (1529).

The large **Piazza del Duomo** has two handsome Gothic public buildings, as well as the Duomo, Baptistery, and Campanile. Above the far corner rises the tall medieval **Torre di Catilina**.

Duomo

The *Duomo (closed 12.00–16.00; Chapel of St James **opened** by the sacristan 10.00–12.00, 16.00–17.45; fest. 11.20–12.00, 16.00–17.30; fee) has an arcaded Romanesque Pisan façade. The porch was added in 1311, and the high arch in the barrel vault is beautifully decorated by Andrea della Robbia, as is the *lunette above the central door. The separate ***Campanile** (being restored in

1998) was originally a watch tower, and is thought to have been adapted to its present use, with the addition of the three tiers of arches, in 1266 by Fra Guglielmo of Pisa, or in 1301 by Giovanni Pisano. The clock dates from 1712.

A cathedral in Pistoia is documented as early as the 5C. The present church, dedicated to the Lombard Saint Zeno, erected c 1220 was drastically altered at the end of the 16C, but work in 1951–66 restored it as far as possible to its Romanesque form. At this time the fine wooden ceiling, decorated in 1388, was exposed.

Bishop Atho, who was a Benedictine and writer, and became known for his unselfish charity in the city, successfully engineered the removal of the relics of St James the Greater by a group of pilgrims from his famous shrine at Santiago de Compostela to Pistoia in 1144. He was canonised after his death in 1153. In 1145 he built the **Chapel of St James**

The 13C Duomo and campanile at Pistoia

in part of the south aisle (with a separate entrance), to conserve the precious relics of the apostle, who became patron saint of the city. For this chapel the silver altar was commissioned in 1287 which since 1953 has been displayed in a chapel in the south aisle. Bishop Atho's chapel was demolished in 1787. Next to the chapel was the sacristy which was robbed by Vanni Fucci in 1293, recorded by Dante in his *Divina Commedia*, (*Inferno*, XXIV) as the *Sagrestia dei belli arredi* (the sacristy with beautiful furnishings). This is now incorporated in part of the Cathedral Museum (see below).

Interior
West wall. Funerary monument of St Atho, (see above), with reliefs showing the Bishop receiving the reliquary of St James, attributed to Cellino di Nese (1337). The bishop's body, first buried in the Baptistery, was translated to the cathedral in 1337 on which occasion legend relates that a wonderful scent of roses emanated from his coffin (roses are still blessed in the cathedral on his saint's day). The *font is by Andrea Ferrucci da Fiesole, on a design by Benedetto da Maiano. In the lunette above the door, fresco of St Zeno (12C?).

South aisle. On the west wall is a Gothic window surrounded by beautiful fragments of 14C frescoes, attributed to Bonaccorso di Cino, all that remains of the famous Chapel of St James (demolished in 1787; see above). On the aisle wall, *tomb of Cino da Pistoia, thought to be by Agostino di Giovanni on a design by Cellino di Nese (1337). The painted *Crucifix* is by Coppo di Marcovaldo (and his son Salerno, 1275).

Formerly called the Chapel of the Crucifix, the chapel, which since 1953 has contained the ***Altar of St James** (for adm. see above), was decorated in 1839. The famous altar is a masterpiece of medieval goldsmiths' work. It is decorated with numerous silver and partially gilded bas-reliefs and statuettes. It was commissioned in 1287, and remodelled and added to during successive genera-tions (up to 1456). It is made up of a dossal—the earliest part—attributed to Pace di Valentino, with a statue of *St James enthroned*, which was added by Maestro Giglio in 1353. The altar frontal below, with fifteen scenes from the New Testament was completed in 1316 by Andrea di Jacopo di Ognabene. The two panels on either side of the altar are the work of Francesco di Niccolò and Leonardo di Ser Giovanni (1361–71). The panel on the left flank, with stories from the life of St James, includes two half figures of prophets which were added in 1400 by Brunelleschi (who may also have executed the standing figure of St Augustine, and the seated figure of an Evangelist). Behind the altar is a charming 15C Flemish tapestry.

The crypt. Beside the steps down to the crypt, in a Gothic niche, are fine 14C frescoes and a triptych with the *Crucifixion* (1429). Two sides of the Romanesque crypt survive, and fragments from the earlier church can be seen here including panels from the pulpit by Guido da Como (1199; dismantled in the 17C). On a lower level is the 17C crypt.

In the chapel at the end of the south aisle is a good altarpiece of the *Corona-tion of the Virgin with Saints Baronto and Desiderio* by Mattia Preti, and *Moses receiving the tables of the law* by Luigi Sabatelli and the *Entombment* by Giuseppe Bezzuoli (1845–6).

The **choir** was designed in the early 17C by Jacopo Lafri. The frescoes are by Passignano and the high altarpiece of the *Resurrection* is by Cristofano Allori. The colossal statues of *Saints James* and *Zeno* are by a certain Vincenzo (1603), a pupil of Giambologna. To the right, at the top of the sanctuary steps, stands a bronze candelabrum by Tommaso di Bartolomeo (1442). At the entrance to the choir, on the north wall, is a fresco fragment of the *Madonna* attributed to Coppo di Marcovaldo.

North aisle. At the end of the north aisle is the **Chapel of the Sacrament**. Here (south wall) is the *__Madonna di Piazza__ with Saints John the Baptist and Zeno*, an extremely beautiful painting which is the only documented work left by Verrocchio (1485), probably with the help of Lorenzo di Credi. It is protected by a red curtain, but it is usually possible to see it on request. Opposite is a *half-length bust of Archbishop Donato de' Medici, variously attributed to Antonio Rossellino or Verrocchio. The ciborium on the altar dates from 1662.

In the **north aisle** are a frescoed 14C *Madonna* and a seated statue of *Pope Leo XI*. At the west end of the aisle is the *__tomb of Cardinal Niccolò Forteguerri__ projected by Verrocchio (1476–83) with Christ in Glory surrounded by angels and statues of Faith and Hope. The figure of Charity (on the left) was added by Lorenzetto in 1515, and the bust, two putti, and sarcophagus and the frame added in 1753.

The *__Baptistery__ (open 09.30–12.30, 15.00–18.00; closed Mon) is a beautiful octagonal building entirely decorated on the outside by bands of green and white marble. It was started in 1337 by Cellino di Nese, traditionally thought to be on a design by Andrea Pisano, and finished in 1359. The capitals and reliefs above the main entrance and the Madonna (attributed to Tommaso and Nino Pisano) in the tympanum are particularly fine. On the right is a tiny Gothic pulpit of 1399. The wooden doors are the work of Pier Francesco di Ventura (1523).

In the bare brick **interior** is a **font** with fine intarsia panels by Lanfranco da Como (1226). The statue of *St John the Baptist* is by Andrea Vaccà (1724).

Palazzo dei Vescovi

Palazzo dei Vescovi, founded on this site at the end of the 11C and finished in the 12C (and enlarged in the 14C) was beautifully restored in 1982 by a bank (which now owns it and uses part of it as offices). It contains two museums: an archaeological section and the *Museo della Cattedrale di San Zeno.

Admission to both museums by guided tour on Tues and Thur at 08.30, 10.00, 11.30 and 15.30 and Fri at 08.30, 10.00, 11.30, 14.30, 15.30 and 16.45.

The archaeological section. In the **basement** is displayed material found during excavations in the area of the palace, from the Roman period onwards. Highlights include two Etruscan cippi used in the foundations, and a hoard of medieval ceramics found in a well. Details of the excavations themselves including a Roman villa and part of a road are shown and explained.

Museo della Cattedrale di San Zeno

In the **first room** there is a Roman cinerary urn (2C AD) with a carriage drawn by four horses, found during excavations in the Duomo. The 15C illuminated choirbooks are displayed in rotation. In the 12C **Sacristy of St James** (which was attached to the Chapel of St James, formerly in the Duomo, see above) is the *reliquary of St James**, by Lorenzo Ghiberti and his bottega (1407). In the **Sala dell'Udienza** is a fresco of the *Crucifixion* is by Giovanni di Bartolomeo Cristiani (1387). Displayed here are two 14C marble statuettes (Sienese or French); the *reliquary of San Zeno**, made by the local goldsmith Enrico Belandini while in Aix-en-Provence in 1369; the so-called Cross of St Atho (c 1280), and the so-called chalice of St Atho, attributed to Andrea and Tallino d'Ognabene (1286). In the **Corte Vescovile** two *reliquaries are displayed, one by Rombolus Salvei (1379), and the other by Maestro Gualandi (1444). Also displayed here: octagonal ebony and ivory coffer by the bottega degli Embriachi (late 15C); chalice of 1384 signed by the local goldsmith Andrea di Pietro Braccini; and a polychrome wooden statue of an *Angel with the head of the Baptist*, an interesting work thought to be by a French sculptor (c 1361).

A spiral staircase leads up to the **Torre Vescovile** displaying 17C vestments, and 18C church silver. Another room has been reconstructed to contain *tempera murals by Giovanni Boldini (1868), with scenes of pastoral life and of the sea at Castiglioncello. They were detached from the Villa La Falconiera near Pistoia, where the Falconer family entertained Boldini and other painters of the Macchiaioli school, including Telemaco Signorini, who were at work in Tuscany at this time (the name comes from their characteristic use of *macchie* or 'patches' of colour). Beyond a room with two 16C carved panels by the local sculptor Ventura Vitoni (1442–1522) which survived the fire in 1641 which destroyed the choir in the Duomo, is more 17C church silver. The 12C **Cappella di San Nicolò**, the Bishop's private chapel, contains 14C fresco fragments. Steps lead up to the top of the Romanesque façade of the cathedral (now closed in), above the present loggia. Another room has 17C reliquaries, including the reliquary of St Bartholomew (1663). The **Sala Sinodale** contains fragments of battle scenes, among the oldest medieval frescoes in Tuscany, and a triptych by Giovanni di Bartolomeo Cristiani.

On the west side of the piazza is **Palazzo Pretorio**, a Gothic building of 1367 and later, which has a good courtyard, with painted and sculptured armorial bearings of magistrates.

Museo Civico
On the opposite side of the piazza is **Palazzo del Comune**, another fine Gothic building of 1294, with later additions. On the façade is a curious black basalt head which has probably been here since 1305. The palace houses the Museo Civico. **Open**. 10.00–19.00; fest. 09.00–12.30; closed Mon; cumulative ticket with Palazzo del Tau and Museo Rospigliosi.

Piano nobile
Stairs lead up to the piano nobile. On the left is the **Sala dei Donizelli**. 13C *panel of *St Francis*, with stories from his life; a lovely 14C painting of *Mourning over the dead Christ* attributed to Lippo di Benivieni; Master of 1310 (attributed), polyptych of the *Madonna and Saints*; 14C Tuscan statues; Mariotto di Nardo, *Madonna enthroned with four angels*; chalice by the local goldsmith Andrea di Jacopo d'Ognibene or Piero Braccini; Francesco di Valdambrino, *Angel*; Mariotto di Nardo and Rossello di Jacopo Franchi, *Annunciation and Saints*; three paintings of the *Madonna enthroned and Saints* by Lorenzo di Credi, Ridolfo del Ghirlandaio, and Gerino Gerini; 15C marble relief of the *Madonna and Child*.

Sala dei Priori. Bernardino di Antonio Detti, *Madonna della Pergola*, a very unusual work full of strange symbols and unusual iconographical references; Agnolo di Polo, bust of the *Redeemer*; a 15C and a 16C statue of *St Sebastian*; Fra' Paolino, *Annunciatory Angel* and *Virgin Annunciate*; and a *Rest on the Flight into Egypt*, by the 16C Florentine school.

Stairs lead up past the **Centro Michelucci**, with drawings and models of works by the architect Giovanni Michelucci (1891–1991), born in Pistoia, and a section of 20C Pistoian paintings, to three rooms on the top floor.

Top floor
The **Salone** contains late 16C and 17C paintings, including works by Gregorio Pagani, Matteo Rosselli, Il Cigoli, Empoli, Francesco Curradi, Carlo Saraceni (*Madonna and Child*, attributed), Giacinto Gimignani, Antonio Domenico Gabbiani, Lo Spagnoletto (*portait of Lanfredino Cellesi of Pistoia*), Giuseppe Gambarini, and a contemporary copy of Carlo Maratta's *portrait of Clement IX*. The decorative arts displayed here include Venetian glass, and Italian majolica.

The **Puccini Collection** was left by the last descendant, Niccolò, in the 19C to a charitable institute, and part of it was acquired by the Museo Civico in 1913 and 1977. It includes: Giovanni di Bartolomeo Cristiani, *Madonna enthroned with angel musicians*; Frankfurt Master, triptych; Maso di San Friano (bottega), *Angels and the Madonna*; Giovanni Battista Naldini, *Holy Family*; Il Cigoli, *Marriage of St Catherine*; Mattia Preti, Susannah and the Elders; Pietro Dandini, portrait of the doctor *Tommaso Puccini* (1669–1727), and a marble bust of him by Giovanni Battista Foggini.

The **last room** contains 18C and 19C works by Luigi Sabatelli, Anton Raphael Mengs (portrait of *Cardinal Francesco Saverio de Zelada*), and Gilbert Stuart Newton, and historical canvases by Enrico Pollastrini and Giuseppe Bezzuoli (and Puccini portraits).

Palazzo Rospigliosi

A 17C covered passageway links Palazzo Comunale with the Duomo high up above the narrow Ripa del Sale which descends to Palazzo Rospigliosi (No. 3; **open** Tues–Sat, 10.00–13.00, Tues, Thur, and Fri also 16.00–19.00; cumulative ticket with Palazzo del Tau and Museo Civico). The **Museo Rospigliosi** and the **Museo Diocesano** can be visited here. The palace was left to the cathedral by the last member of this branch of the Rospigliosi family in 1981. Pope Clement IX (Giulio Rospigliosi) probably stayed in the sumptuous bedroom in the apartment on the piano nobile. The four rooms contain original furnishings and 17C and 18C frescoes. The interesting 17C paintings (with fine frames) include numerous works by Giacinto Gimignani (1606–81, a native of Pistoia) and his son Ludovico, as well as works by Jacopo Vignali, Lorenzo Lippi, and Felice Ficherelli.

In other rooms the **Museo Diocesano** (well labelled) is displayed. The first room (which overlooks the hanging garden) contains 12C–13C Crosses, a 14C Cross in silver by a local craftsman, and chalices. The second room has a 14C painting of the *Madonna enthroned*, and reliquary busts and church silver. The third room has 17C–18C church silver. The fourth room has paintings of the *Sacred Conversation*: three of them by Fra Paolino (Paolo di Bernardino del Signoraccio) and one by Leonardo Malatesta. Beyond the fifth room displaying 18C vestments, the sixth room contains an exquisite small polychrome terracotta figure of the *Kneeling Virgin* (c 1460). The last two rooms contains a series of six paintings by Alessio Gimignani and 17C local works.

Via Pacini (at the end of Ripa del Sale) and Via San Pietro lead to the disused 12C church of **San Pietro**, with a characteristic façade. A relief of Christ giving the keys to St Peter, the Madonna, and the Apostles can be seen over the main portal.

San Bartolomeo in Pantano

Crossing Via Pacini at the bottom of Ripa del Sale, Via San Bartolomeo leads to the eponymous disorderly piazza in front of the church of *San Bartolomeo in Pantano. This was the church of a famous Benedictine monastery founded c 761. Count Ugo of Tuscany died here in 1001. The church was enlarged in 1159 and has a fine **façade** with a relief (1167) over the door of Christ and the Apostles, probably by Gruamonte.

The beautiful basilican **interior** with large capitals has a 13C Tuscan fresco of *Christ in majesty* in the apse. On the walls other fresco fragments have been exposed. The *pulpit by Guido da Como (1250), still Romanesque in spirit, has one of its columns resting on a crouching figure thought to represent the sculptor. It has four bas reliefs showing scenes in the life of Christ and at the corners, symbols of the Evangelists. On the wall behind are exhibited four more bas reliefs from the pulpit with scenes from the life of the Virgin. The altarpieces include (south aisle) works by Ignazio Hugford and Giovanni Maria Butteri, (south transept) Alessio Gemignani, and (north transept) Matteo Rosselli.

Via Pacini leads north to the **Ospedale del Ceppo**, founded in 1277, and still in use. The fine portico has recently been attributed to Michelozzo, with modifications by Giovanni Battista di Antonio di Gerino (c 1480). It is decorated with a colourful **enamelled terracotta *frieze** (1514–25), excellently carved and very well preserved (cleaned in 1984). It depicts the *Seven Works of Mercy* by Giovanni della Robbia, with the help of Santi Viviani Buglioni; the seventh was added by Filippo di Lorenzo Paladini in 1584–86. Between the scenes are the cardinal and theological Virtues, also by Giovanni della Robbia. Beneath are medallions with the *Annunciation*, *Visitation*, and *Assumption* and the arms of the hospital, of the city, and the Medici, by Benedetto Buglioni and Giovanni della Robbia. To the left of the hospital, above the door of the adjoining church, is a *Coronation of the Virgin* by Benedetto Buglioni (1512), the oldest work of the series.

To the east of the hospital in Piazza San Lorenzo, is the church of **Santa Maria delle Grazie** or *del Letto*. It was built in 1451 and was formerly attributed to Michelozzo, but the fine presbytery is now generally considered to be the work of the local architect Ventura Vitoni. The high altar has a fine silver tabernacle (1641). The 14C bed, held to be miraculous (legend relates that a patient was miraculously healed when he had a vision of the Madonna while lying in this bed), which gave its name to the church, is preserved in a chapel on the left.

Sant'Andrea

From the Ospedale del Ceppo, Via delle Pappe and Via del Carmine (left) lead to Via Sant'Andrea in which is the church of *Sant'Andrea, with another good 12C **façade** by Gruamonte and his brother Adeodato who signed the relief of the Journey and Adoration of the Magi (1166). The polychrome marble decoration was beautifully restored in 1996.

In the long narrow **interior** (similar to San Bartolomeo in Pantano; coin-operated light) is a 14C font of the Pisan school, and a hexagonal *pulpit signed by Giovanni Pisano (1298–1301), perhaps his masterpiece. He was probably helped by Tino da Camaino. Slim porphyry columns, held up by lions, eagles, and a crouching figure support Gothic arches with reliefs and statuettes of prophets and sibyls. Above, five dramatic reliefs show the *Annunciation* and *Nativity*; *Adoration of the Magi* and *St Joseph being warned to leave Bethlehem*; *Massacre of the Innocents*; *Crucifixion*; *Last Judgement*. Between the scenes are prophets, symbols of the Evangelists and the angels of the Apocalypse. In the apse is a fresco of *God the Father* by Fra Paolino (Bernardino di Antonio del Signoraccio), 1506. In the south aisle, in a 15C tabernacle, a wooden *Crucifix* by Giovanni Pisano and a statuette of *St Andrew* from the school of Giovanni Pisano (formerly on the façade). At the end of the north aisle, *Madonna of Humility*, by Niccolò di Mariano (15C Sienese). The little organ dates from 1888.

At the end of Via Sant'Andrea is Piazza San Francesco, with the church of **San Francesco** (formerly known as *San Francesco al Prato*) begun in 1289, with a façade completed in 1717. The wide open-roofed nave with damaged remains of frescoes (and an altarpiece of the *Raising of Lazarus* by Alessandro Allori on the fourth left altar), ends in a wide vaulted transept with **five east chapels**. Behind the high altar (lights to right switched on by request) are 14C frescoes showing strong Giottesque influence, possibly the work of a pupil, Puccio Capanna. In the chapel to the left is a splended **fresco cycle** of the *allegory of the triumph of St Augustine*, by the Sienese school. 14C frescoes also decorate the second chapel to the right of the choir. In the south transept are interesting remains of a huge frescoed *Crucifix*, attributed to the Master of 1310. A door in this transept leads through the **Sacristy** to the **Chapter House** (not always open) both of which retain good late 14C frescoes, notably on the east wall of the latter, the *Tree of Life* with a *Crucifixion*, possibly by Pietro Lorenzetti. The 14C cloister is beyond.

In Corso Gramsci, south of the church, is the **Teatro Manzoni**, inaugurated in 1694, and altered in the mid-18C by Il Bibbiena.

From Piazza San Francesco Via Bozzi and Via Montanara e Curtatone lead back towards the centre of the town. To the left is the church of the **Spirito Santo**, founded by the Jesuits in 1647 with a good Baroque **interior* by the Jesuit father Tommaso Ramignani, beautifully restored, with its contents, in 1988. Cardinal Giulio Rospigliosi, on becoming Pope Clement IX in 1667, commissioned Gian Lorenzo Bernini to design the **high altar**, and Pietro da Cortona to paint the high altarpiece of the *Apparition of Christ to St Ignatius*. The ciborium in *pietre dure*, ebony, and gilded bronze, also dates from this time. **North side**. First **chapel**, Ottaviano Dandini, *Deposition* (and the two small works on either side); **second chapel**, 17C wooden, robed statuette of the *Madonna of Loreto*, and early 18C paintings of the *Nativity* and *Conception*. The little organ on the left (and its decorative counterpart opposite) are by the Flemish organ-maker Willem Herman (1663). The contemporary carved confessionals have also been preserved.

Nearby, in Piazza Sapienza is the **Biblioteca Forteguerriana**. The library occupies a palace completed in 1534 by Giovanni Unghero for the Scuola della Sapienza, the school founded by Cardinal Niccolò Forteguerri in 1473. The library was founded in 1696 as an adjunct to the school. The main room on the first floor was designed for the library in 1776 by Giuliano Gatteschi.

In Via della Madonna, which leads right off Via Montanara e Curtatone, is the 15C basilican sanctuary of the **Madonna dell'Umiltà**, built by Ventura Vitoni (1495), a pupil of Bramante. The **dome**, a conspicuous feature of the city when viewed from the plain, was added by Vasari in 1562. The main portal dates from the 17C. The fine barrel vaulted **vestibule** contains 18C frescoes illustrating the history of the basilica. The octagonal centrally planned **interior** is an interesting example of High Renaissance architecture. **South side**. On the **first altar**, Lazzaro Baldi, *Rest on the Flight into Egypt*; **second altar**, Francesco Vanni, *Adoration of the Magi*; **third altar**, Il Poppi, *Assumption*. On the first altar left of the high altar, Lodovico Buti (on a design by Vasari), *Annunciation*; second chapel on the left, Passignano, *Adoration of the Shepherds*. The marble **high altar** by Pietro Tacca (with two angels by Leonardo Marcacci) encloses a miraculous 14C fresco of the *Madonna of Humility*, attributed to Bartolomeo Cristiani, around which the sanctuary was built.

10 · The province of Pistoia

■ Practical information

Information offices. APT *Montecatini Terme–Valdinievole*, 66 Viale Verdi, Montecatini (☎ 0572-772244) for **Montecatini** and **Pescia**. *Società delle Terme*, 41 Viale Verdi (☎ 0572-778451) where tickets for the mineral water can be purchased.

APT Abetone-Pistoia-Montagna Pistoiese, 28 Via Marconi, San Marcello Pistoiese (☎ 0573-630145) for the mountain areas above Pistoia. *APT* information offices at **Abetone** (502 Piazza Piramidi, ☎ 0573-60231) and **Cutigliano** (Via Roma 25, ☎ 0573-68029).

Getting there

By rail. The Florence–Viareggio line has stops at Montecatini Terme and Pescia. Montecatini has two stations: *Centrale*, Piazza Italia, and *Succursale*, Piazza Gramsci (the most convenient to visitors, as the nearest to Viale Verdi). All trains on the Florence–Viareggio line stop at both stations; from Florence local trains in 50mins to Montecatini Terme, and in 1hr to Pescia (which has a railway station c 1km south of the town).

By bus (*Lazzi*) from Florence to Montecatini (Via Toti) and Pescia. From Florence and Pistoia to Abetone. Bus Services (*COPIT*) from Pescia to Collodi (in 25mins), and Uzzano, Castelvecchio, and the other small villages in the vicinity.

By road. The A11 motorway from Florence to the sea follows the main road with exits at Montecatini (for Montecatini, Buggiano, and Monsummano) and Chiesina Uzzanese (for Pescia and Collodi).

Hotels

Montecatini Terme. There are two ★★★★★, thirteen ★★★★, about seventy ★★★, and over ninety ★★ hotels, most of them open only from March or April to October or November. The most famous hotel (with a **£££** restaurant) is the ★★★★★ *Grand Hotel e la Pace*, 12 Corso Roma (☎ 0572-75801, fax 0572-78451). Information and booking service at the *Associazione Provinciale Albergatori* (*APAM*), 2 Via Palestro (☎ 0572-70124).
Montecatini Alto. ★★★★ *Park Hotel-Le Sorgenti* (☎ 0572-951116, fax 0572-952731), at Pieve a Nievole.
Monsummano Terme. ★★★★ *Grotta Giusti*, swimming pool (☎ 0572-51165, fax 0572-51269).
Pescia. ★★★ *Villa delle Rose*, Via del Castellare, near the railway station (☎ 0572-451301, fax 0572-444003).
San Marcello Pistoiese. ★★★ *Il Cacciatore*, with restaurant (☎ 0573-630533, fax 0573-630134). **Cutigliano** has numerous ★★★ and ★★ hotels. At **Abetone** two ★★★★ hotels, and numerous ★★★ and ★★ hotels.

Campsite

Near **Montecatini Alto** at Vico: ★★★ *Belsito* (☎ & fax 0572-67373).

Restaurants

Environs of Pistoia. **£** *Bischio*, at La Verginina zoo.
Montecatini Terme. All categories all over the town including **£££** *Enoteca da Giovanni*, 25 Via Garibaldi. **££** *San Francisco*, 112 Corso Roma.
Montecatini Alto. **££** *Le Pietre Cavate* and *Uno Più* at Pieve a Nievole
Pescia. **££** *Cecco*, 84 Via Forti. **£** *La Buca*, 4 Piazza Mazzini. At **Monte a Pescia**, *Monte a Pescia* (**££**).
Cireglio. **££** *Da Ildo* at Castagno di Piteccio.
Cutigliano. **££** *Fagiolino*, 1 Via Carega.
Abetone. **££** *La Capannina*, 254 Via Brennero.

Environs of Pistoia

At **La Verginina**, northwest of Pistoia, is a small **zoo** (**open** daily 09.00–dusk), created in 1970 on a pleasant hillside. In the Valle del Vincio is the pretty village of **Serra Pistoiese**, with an 11C Romanesque pieve. A few kilometres east of Pistoia, at the **Fattoria di Celle** on the Santomato road, is an interesting private collection of modern and contemporary art made since the Second World War by Giuliano Gori. A sculpture park was inaugurated in 1982 (**adm**. by written appointment to the Fattoria di Celle, 51030 Santomato, Pistoia, ☎ 0573-479907). The villa (owned by the Gori since 1970) was built at the end of the 17C, and the park enlarged in the 19C by Giovanni Gambini.

There is a fine road, in parts lined with pine trees, which leads due south from Pistoia across the Albano hills with spectacular views to Vinci (see Ch. 7).

Montecatini Terme

Montecatini Terme (20,600 inhab.) is the best known of Italian spas, with an international reputation (open to all). It became famous at the beginning of the 20C, when the monumental thermal buildings were built. They are spaciously laid out and surrounded by attractive well-kept parks. The warm saline waters are taken, both internally and externally, for digestive troubles. The season runs from May to October.

> **History**. Ugolino Simoni (1348–1425), born in Montecatini, made a fundamental study of the mineral waters of Italy, including those of Montecatini. Although probably known in Roman times, and used by the Medici, they were first developed on a grand scale by the Austrian Grand-duke Pietro Leopoldo in 1773–82. By the beginning of this century, Montecatini was one of the most famous spas in Europe. Giuseppe Verdi often stayed at the *Locanda Maggiore*, and wrote the last act of *Otello* here (1887). Most of the thermal buildings were built in 1928 on a project drawn up in 1915–18 by Ugo Giovannozzi for the Società delle Terme.

The centre of Montecatini is **Viale Verdi** on which are all the most important buildings; at the upper end is a view of Montecatini Alto (or Montecatini Valdinievole). From the unattractive Piazza del Popolo (the church of Santa Maria Assunta was built in 1962) the avenue ascends past the Gambrinus café in a piazza with a colonnade and decorative lamp-posts. The monumental **Town Hall** (and post office) built in 1919, stands opposite the **Società delle Terme** which runs the spas. The spas, used for drinking water and bathing, are all in the fine park beyond. The elaborate **Terme Excelsior** (open all year) was built in 1909 by Bernardini in a florid mixture of styles. The handsome extension was added in 1968. The **Terme Leopoldine** (which probably cover the most ancient spring) was rebuilt in 1926 by Ugo Giovannozzi in a classical style (the temple bears a dedication to Asculapius, the god of healing).

At the end of the Viale rise the splendid buildings of the **Terme Tettuccio**, the most famous thermal establishment in Montecatini, whose waters were mentioned as early as 1370. It was also rebuilt by Giovannozzi in 1925–28, although it preserves an inner façade by Gaspare Paoletti (1779–81). The café, reading room, and drinking gallery are all sumptuously decorated with ceramics, murals, statuary, and wrought-iron work by Galileo Chini, Ezio Giovannozzi (brother of Ugo), and many others.

Beyond the Terme Regina, on Viale Diaz, is the **Accademia d'Arte Dino Scalabrino** (at present closed) with a gallery containing works by Galileo Chini, Giovanni Fattori, Lorenzo Viani, Pietro Annigoni, and others, and a small historical museum. Also on Viale Diaz is the Funicular Station for Montecatini Alto (see below). In the extensive well-kept park beyond the Tettuccio are the Terme Tamerici and the Terme Torretta both built at the beginning of the century by Bernardini in a neo-Gothic style. On the hillside above is the Parco della Panteraie with fine woods (and a swimming pool). The central Railway Station, with handsome marble decoration, dates from 1937. The huge Kursaal, once the Casinò, was sold in 1989 and again in 1994, and may one day be restored.

Montecatini Alto

Montecatini Alto (or *Montecatini Valdinievole*) is reached from Montecatini Terme by funicular railway from Viale Diaz to Montecatini Alto (usually **open** May–Oct 10.00–13.00, 15.00–19.30; in Aug 10.00–midnight; services c every half hour) or by road (5km). It is an old hill town (290m) in a spectacular position. Here the men of Lucca were defeated in 1315 by Uguccione della Faggiola, leader of the Ghibellines of Pisa.

The attractive piazza has several cafés and the Teatrino dei Risorti, an amusing building dating from the early 20C. Above it, on a hill planted with cypresses and ilexes, is the Prepositurale of San Pietro (open only for services). A small museum of vestments, reliquaries, and paintings here has been closed indefinitely.

Walks may be taken in the pleasant surroundings, especially in the Val di Nievole, to the north.

Monsummano Terme

On the other side of the motorway is the little spa of Monsummano Terme, at the foot of the hill. Its vapour baths were once visited by the wounded Garibaldi. In the large piazza with a statue of the Tuscan poet, Giuseppe Giusti (1809–50), who was born here, is the parish church of **Santa Maria della Fontenuova** (1605). It is surrounded by a portico with frescoed lunettes by Giovanni da San Giovanni (1630). In the pretty **interior** there is a fine ceiling and organ. In the **south transept**, Piero Dandini, *Madonna with St Joachim and Anne*. Over the high altar, venerated fresco of the *Madonna and Child*. In the **north transept**, Matteo Rosselli, *Adoration of the Magi*. A delightful **museum** (**open** on request) contains works by Matteo Rosselli, Cristofano Allori, and a *Cross* in ivory attributed to Giambologna.

At the end of the piazza is the **Osteria dei Pellegrini**, a fine building of 1609–16, with a portico in travertine. Just out of this end of the piazza, at the corner of Viale Martini, is **Casa Giusti**, which houses a museum relating to the poet. From the piazza various grotte are signposted; these are caverns in the hillside once used as spas.

A narrow road (also signposted) leads up round the hill with chestnut woods (disfigured by quarries) to **Monsummano Alto**, a fortified medieval village. Its strategic position enabled it to defend the pass between the plain of Lucca and the valley of Pistoia. The road enters the ruined hamlet beside the tallest pentagonal tower. A path leads straight on to the 12C church with its campanile beside a picturesque group of houses, most of them abandoned. Another gate can be seen at the end of the ridge on the hillside below. There is a fine view of the plain stretching towards the sea.

South of Monsummano is **Montevettolini** where the parish church contains an *Assumption* signed and dated 1599 by Santi di Tito and a *Madonna and Saints* by Piero di Cosimo.

Buggiano

West of Montecatini is Borgo a Buggiano, outside which is the huge **Villa di Bellavista**, built at the end of the 17C by Antonio Ferri, with frescoes by Pier Dandini. It is owned by the State and has been partly restored as an exhibition centre (and is also sometimes used for concerts).

The parish church (**Santissimo Crocifisso**) of Borgo a Buggiano was rebuilt in 1771. **Interior** (all the works are labelled). On the nave pilasters are four paintings by Fra Felice da Sambuca (1777). On the first altar on the south side, Fra Paolino da Pistoia, *Madonna enthroned with Saints*, and in the south transept, Bernardino del Signoraccio, *Madonna of the Rosary with Saints Dominic and Francis* (1500–10). Behind the high altar, wooden *Crucifix* thought to date from the early 14C and two terracotta statues of the *Madonna* and *St John the Evangelist* attributed to the workshop of the Buglioni. On the north side (second altar), Giacomo Tais, *Madonna and Saints*, and (first altar), Alessandro Allori, *Martyrdom of St Agatha*. A charming small **museum** (opened on request) contains church silver, vestments, a 14C painted reliquary and numerous

Crosses, some from Buggiano Castello. Two paintings (15C and 16C) from the pieve of Stignano may also be exhibited here.

A by-road leads up through olive groves past a large tabernacle on the right of the road with 15C frescoes of the *Madonna and Child and two angels* (restored in 1991) to **Buggiano Castello**, a charming old village, extremely well preserved. Many of the handsome houses, have attractive red plaster finish. It is best to leave the car on the road below, and walk up through the castellated gateway. Beyond the **ex-convent of Santa Scolastica** with a pretty loggia with tiny columns high up on its façade, in the delightful little piazza (below the church), there stands **Palazzo Pretorio** (recently well restored) with numerous coats of arms including some in della Robbian enamelled terracotta. Through an arch there is a view of the plain and the church tower of Stignano.

The **Pieve** (Madonna della Salute), also in the piazza, was founded in 1038. The wide **interior** has fine capitals. At the west end are a *font and lectern (c 1250). **South side**, second altar, Giovanni del Brina, *Madonna and four Saints* (1571); third altar, Bicci di Lorenzo (or his school), *Annunciation*. Over the high altar is a small wooden *Crucifix* (possibly dating from the 14C). In the chapel to the left of the sanctuary, the *Madonna and Saints* in the style of Andrea del Castagno (1498) has been removed for restoration. **North side**, second altar, Giovanni del Brina, *Madonna of the Rosary*. The terracotta statue of the *Madonna and Child* in the niche is a Tuscan work c 1530. On the first altar, 16C painting of the *Baptism of Christ* (in very poor condition). At the top of the hill are remains of the medieval **Rocca**.

At **Ponte Buggianese**, south of Borgo a Buggiano, in the church of San Michele Arcangelo, are frescoes of the *Passion cycle* by Pietro Annigoni (1910–88), including a striking *Last Supper* in the apse.

Near Borgo a Buggiano is **Stignano**, a hamlet in a fine position where Coluccio Salutati (1331–1406), Chancellor of the Florentine Republic, was born (plaque). The church of Sant'Andrea, with a Romanesque campanile, is usually locked. Two paintings have been removed and are in store in the church of Borgo a Buggiano.

Pescia

Pescia (18,200 inhab.) is a busy town which has expanded to the south. It has a very unusual plan, laid out longitudinally on both sides of the Pescia river: on the left bank is the cathedral and on the right bank the exceptionally long market square (Piazza Mazzini) with the town hall. The town became established in the Middle Ages when it was governed by a Vicario. As an ally of Florence, it suffered a severe defeat by Lucca and the Guelf party in 1281.

The town expanded in the 16C and 17C, and since the Second World War it has become an important horticultural centre particularly noted for its asparagus, carnations, lilies, and gladioli. The striking **flower market** built in 1951 by Giuseppe Gori was superseded by an even larger one in 1980 (by Leonardo Savioli) on the southern outskirts of the town where a flower show (the Biennale del Fiore) is held in early September (next in 2000).

*Piazza Mazzini, at the centre of the town is a huge, long, narrow square which characterises the general layout of the town. At the upper end is the town hall—**Palazzo del Vicario**—covered with coats of arms (restored in the 19C). In the loggia (seen behind an iron grille) is a war memorial by Libero Andreotti.

A neo-Gothic outside staircase connects the palace to the Cancelleria and the Torre Civica. Among the fine palaces in the piazza is Palazzo Della Barba (No. 79) on a design traditionally attributed to Raphael. The Renaissance church of the **Madonna di piè di Piazza** closes the southern end of the square. It was built in the 15C by Buggiano and preserves its exterior, although the interior dates from 1605 (the wood ceiling is by Giovanni Zeti). Over the high altar is a venerated 15C fresco of the *Madonna* in the centre of a painting by Alessandro Tiarini which includes a view of Pescia. The last palace on the west side of the piazza was built c 1530 by Baccio d'Agnolo (but was reduced in size at the beginning of this century).

Ruga degli Orlandi runs parallel to the Piazza on its west side. Among the handsome palaces here is the decorative Palazzo Forti (No. 42). Farther north is the church of the **Santissima Annunziata** (closed), built in 1713–20 by Antonio Ferri. It contains a painting of *St Charles Borromeo* by Volterrano. In Piazza Santo Stefano (left) there is a view of the Castello di Bareglia on the hillside (now the convent of San Francesco di Paola).

The church of **Santi Stefano e Niccolao** is approached by a pretty outside staircase (thought to be by Agostino Cornacchini). Founded in 1068 the church was reconstructed in the 18C. **Interior**. South aisle, first altar, two wooden statues of the *Annunciatory Angel* and the *Virgin Annunciate*; the Virgin is attributed to Matteo Civitali. On either side of the second altar are two paintings of *St Sebastian* and *St Michael* by Agostino Ciampelli. In the sanctuary, *Madonna and four Saints* by Ercole Bazzicaluva (17C), and, on the right wall, *Madonna and Child with angel musicians* (and the *Epiphany* below), a fine 15C painting.

In front of the church is the 18C Palazzo Galeotti, seat of the Biblioteca Comunale and the **Museo Civico**. The works are unlabelled. **Open** Wed, Fri, and Sat 10.00–13.00; Thur 16.00–18.00; or by request at the Library.

Lower floor. **Room 1**: Neri di Bicci, **Annunciation and two Saints*; Lorenzo Monaco (attributed), triptych of the *Madonna and two Saints* (1464). **Room 2**: lunette of the *Madonna and Child with a bishop saint and St Dorothy*, attributed to Benedetto Pagni da Brescia (a pupil of Giulio Romano). **Room 3**: Neri di Bicci, *Coronation of the Virgin*; Santi di Tito, *Christ and St Mary Magdalene*. Beyond, a room of the Galeotti palace has been furnished with 18C decorations.

The first room of the **upper floor** displays a garland by the della Robbia; Benedetto Pagni, *Resurrection of Christ* (restored in 1991). and Giovanni da San Giovanni (attributed), *St John the Baptist in the desert*. Beyond it is a room with mementoes of the musician Giovanni Pacini who lived in Pescia from 1855 to 1867. There is also a library containing the papers of the historian Giovan Carlo de' Sismondi who lived in Pescia in the early 19C. The last room has a collection of local material belonging to the Comune, and a plan of the city dating from 1621.

On the right of Santo Stefano a short road leads up to another quiet little piazza in front of the **Palazzo del Podestà**, a handsome 13C building altered over the centuries. Here is a gallery of plaster casts (a **Gipsoteca**) with the works of the sculptor Libero Andreotti who was born in Pescia (1875–1933) (**open** Wed & Fri 16.00–19.00; Sat 10.00–13.00; last Sun of month 16.00–19.00; winter: Fri 15.00–18.00, Sat 10.00–13.00, last Sun of month 15.00–18.00).

On the left, by the campanile of Santo Stefano (restored in 1388) Via San

Policronio leads up beneath an archway to a bridge over a stream. From here a charming country lane continues uphill, past a tabernacle and skirting the town walls, to the **Castello di Bareglia**. It was converted into the convent of San Francesco di Paola in 1674 and has a pretty loggia. The church (1713) contains paintings by Giacomo Tais. On the other hill (left of the stream), called Colle dei Fabbri, in the church of an ex-convent (now a hospice) is a painting of *St Philip Neri* by Carlo Maratta.

Ponte San Francesco leads across the Pescia torrent to Piazza San Francesco and the **Teatro Pacini**, founded in 1717 (altered in the 19C and reopened in 1991).

San Francesco

Also on the piazza is the church of San Francesco, first built in the 13C, but later altered. A number of paintings have recently been restored.

Interior. **South wall**, frescoed lunette, detached from the exterior; second altar, painting of the eleven thousand Martyrs (1577; removed for restoration); third altar, *St Francis* with six stories from his life signed and dated 1235 by Bonaventura Berlinghieri. Painted only nine years after the saint's death, it is considered to be one of the most faithful images of him. **South transept**, *St Charles Borromeo* by Rodomonte Pieri and Francesco Nardi. In the **Sacristy** is a large fresco of the *Crucifixion* attributed to Puccio Capanna. In the chapel to the right of the sanctuary are remains of frescoes attributed to Nicolò Gerini or Bicci di Lorenzo, and other frescoes dated 1431. In the **Sanctuary** with fresco fragments, on the left wall is an interesting painting of *A Miracle of St Anthony* by Giovanni Martinelli. In the chapel to the left of the sanctuary, triptych of *St Anne* by Angelo Puccinelli (1335), and on the left wall, *Deposition* by Passignano. The altarpiece in the **North transept** of the *Martyrdom of St Dorothy* is a fine work by Jacopo Ligozzi. **North wall**, Lodovico Cigoli (attributed), *St Louis of Toulouse*, *St Elizabeth of Hungary*, and *St Anthony before St Francis*. In the large Chapel of the Immacolata (early 16C) there is a 15C wooden statue of the *Madonna and Child*, and a *Pietà* attributed to Cristofano Allori. Also off this side is the *Cappella Cardini**, a beautifully designed architectural work considered to be an important work of the early Renaissance, derived from Brunelleschi and attributed to Buggiano. It is in urgent need of structural repair and restoration; the 15C *Crucifix* has been temporarily removed to another part of the church. The frescoes are by Neri di Bicci.

Via Battisti leads out of the piazza past the hospital of **Santi Cosma e Damiano**, built in 1762, with a coat of arms on its façade, and modern hospital buildings. Set back from the road on the left is the little church of **Sant'Antonio Abate** (1361; **open** Apr–Nov on Sat 10.00–13.00, 16.00–19.00; or by request at the hospital), which contains fine early 15C frescoes with scenes from the *Life of St Anthony Abbot* attributed to Bicci di Lorenzo, and a wood *Deposition* group dating from the 13C. At a crossroads by a bridge (left) **Palazzo Ricci** (1635) can be seen with a pretty little marble fountain at the foot of its façade.

Via Cavour (beware of traffic) leads on to the **Duomo**, with a massive Gothic campanile (the top was added in 1771), once a tower in the walls. Founded in the 10C, it was rebuilt in 1726 and has a façade dating from 1895 in the Renaissance style. The **interior** was designed in 1693 by Antonio Ferri. Off the **South side** opens the **Cappella Turini** built by Baccio d'Agnolo. The funerary monument of Baldassare Turini has two male figures by Raffaello da Montelupo and an awkward effigy by Pierino da Vinci. The painting of the *Madonna del Baldacchino* by Pietro Dandini is a fine copy of the original by Raphael, removed to the Pitti by Ferdinando dei Medici in 1697. Beside the high altar (by Vaccà) is a lectern composed of Romanesque sculptures from the ambone of the old church. **North side**, third chapel, altar by Andrea Pozzo and an altarpiece of the *Martyrdom of St Lawrence* by Antonio Domenico Gabbiani; second altar, *Madonna and Saints* by Antonio Franchi.

The little Romanesque church of **San Michelino** is closed.

Beneath the campanile of the Duomo an arch leads into a courtyard. Here is the entrance (at the top of outside stairs) to the **Biblioteca Capitolare**, the Cathedral Chapter library (**open** on request in the mornings). In the **Cappella del Vescovado** is a lovely small enamalled terracotta *triptych of the *Madonna between Saints James and Blaise*, a late work of Luca della Robbia, with the help of his nephew Andrea (1455–60). Over the altar is a painting of the *Madonna and Saints* by Domenico Soldini (1592).

In front of the cathedral is the 18C church of **Santa Maria Maddalena** with a pretty dome. A venerated carved *Crucifix* is kept in the sacristy.

Via Giusti continues out of the town, passing beneath the **Porta Fiorentina** erected in 1732 by Bernardo Sgrilli in honour of Gian Gastone dei Medici.

In Piazzale Leonardo de Vinci, in the southern part of the town, is a small civic **Museum of Archaeology and Natural History** (open 09.00–13.00; Tues also 15.00–17.30), with finds from the Valdinievole (the mountain valley north of Montecatini Terme), and a zoological section.

From behind San Francesco (on Piazza San Francesco), a road (unsignposted) leads up through olive groves to **Uzzano**, a charming, quiet little village, extremely well preserved, with pretty gardens and orchards. The entrance is through a narrow medieval archway. It is best to park in Piazza Umberto where the **Palazzo del Capitano del Popolo** has a loggia on the ground floor. From the terrace there is a view of the plain, crowded with greenhouses.

Via Barsanti leads up to the **church** with a decorative little façade and massive campanile. The interior has two vaulted chapels at the west end with worn 15C frescoes, a 13C stoup, a font with a rare 16C wood cover, and (in a niche) a lifesize della Robbian statue in polychrome terracotta (in very poor condition) of *St Anthony Abbot*.

In the two attractive green valleys of the River Pescia are numerous old paper mills (interesting monuments of industrial architecture) and picturesque villages: **Pietrabuona**, **Medicina**, **Fibbialla**, above the Val di Torbola, **Aramo**, **San Quirico**, and **Castelvecchio**, with the fine Romanesque pieve of San Tommaso. **Pontito** is the highest village in the valley with an interesting fan-shaped plan. It was the birthplace of Lazzaro Papi (1763–1834) who translated Milton's *Paradise Lost*. Another road from Pietrabuona leads up to **Vellano**, with the pieve di San Martino founded in 910.

Collodi

Collodi is famous for its Baroque gardens and children's park dedicated to Pinocchio. On the right of the road is the entrance to the spectacular ***Gardens of Villa Garzoni**, now situated in disappointing surroundings.

The villa or castello is closed indefinitely for renovation; **gardens open** 09.00–dusk; from Nov–Mar the park closes on weekdays between 12.00 and 14.30; **children's park open** daily 08.30–dusk.

The grounds, much visited by tourist groups, are administered in a pretentious fashion. The terraced gardens were laid out on this steep hillside c 1650 and embellished in 1786. They are decorated with yew hedges, fountains and statues. From the hemicycle, beyond a sloping parterre, a double staircase leads to an upper terrace at the foot of a theatrical cascade, bordered by two water staircases. At the left end of the terrace is the green theatre laid out with box hedges. At the top is a colossal statue of *Fame*, and, beyond, enclosed by cypresses, an 18C bath-house with separate enclosures for men and women, near a screened gallery intended for an orchestra.

Paths lead up through the ilex woods to the Villa or **Castello** (closed indefinitely for restoration), bought by the Garzoni in the early 17C and altered in 1652. It contains frescoed architectural perspectives attributed to Angelo Michele Colonna and 18C furniture. The peaceful old village of **Collodi** climbs up the hill behind the villa. It is best approached on foot by the stepped lane which leads up beside the wall of the villa. The picturesque hamlet (no cars) has incredibly steep stepped lanes. There are splendid views of the valleys on either side of the ridge.

Across the river is the entrance to the **children's park** commemorating Pinocchio. *Le Avventure di Pinocchio, Storia di un burattino* is the famous book written by Carlo Lorenzini (1826–90) who took his pen-name from Collodi, the birthplace of his mother. It was first published in 1880–83 and later translated into 63 languages. The careful character portrayal and the trying situations in which the boy puppet often finds himself have a universal appeal so that this delightful book is also widely read and acclaimed by adults.

The children's park, built in 1956 and much visited by school trips, has a bronze monument to the puppet hero by Emilio Greco and a piazza with mosaics illustrating the life of Pinocchio by Venturino Venturini. The *Osteria del Gambero Rosso* restaurant was designed by Giovanni Michelucci in 1963. A garden was laid out in 1971 with sculptured tableaux recalling episodes from the book, and an exhibition hall, also designed by Michelucci was opened in 1987.

In the valley beyond Collodi a by-road left is signposted for **Villa Basilica**. The ancient **Pieve** has a delightful exterior and fine interior (12C–13C). In the apse is an unusual painted *Cross by Berlinghiero Berlinghieri. The font now serves as a fountain in the piazza outside.

To the south of Collodi is **San Gennaro** on a hill surrounded by olives, pine trees, and cypresses, with open views. The domed campanile (1840) stands between a large villa and the interesting Romanesque façade of San Gennaro. The church (usually locked) contains an ambone of 1162 and two 15C terracotta statues of the *Annunciation*. In front is a little terrace with lime trees.

Apennines above Pistoia

A road constructed in 1776–78 by Leonardo Ximenes from Pistoia crosses the *Montagna Pistoiese* or Pistoian Apennines. It climbs steeply through woods and several villages through the small resorts of Cireglio, Maresca and Gavinana. The defeat of the Florentine army by Imperial troops at Gavinana in 1530, in which both commanders, Francesco Ferrucci and Philibert, Prince of Orange were killed, sealed the fate of the Florentine Republic and led to the firm establishment of Medici rule over Florence and Tuscany (a fine equestrian monument of 1920 by Emilio Gallori and the Museo Ferrucciano here both commemorate the battle).

The road reaches a summit level of 820m before descending to **San Marcello Pistoiese** (623m), the most important summer resort on the Pistoian Apennines. There are several old dams across the River Lima.

Cutigliano (670m) is a well-kept little resort. The 14C Palazzo Pretorio is covered with coats of arms. In the nearby church of the Compagnia is an enamelled terracotta high altarpiece of the *Madonna between Saints Anthony and Bernardine of Siena* by the della Robbia family.

On the edge of the village, beside two horse- chestnut trees is the **parish church**. In the light interior is a high altarpiece of a *Miracle of St Bartholomew* by Sebastiano Vini, and on the left wall of the sanctuary a *Circumcision* by Giovanni da San Giovanni. At the end of the left aisle is a fine wooden altarpiece which encloses the *Birth of the Virgin* by Nicodemo Ferrucci.

Winter sports facilities include a funicular to **Doganaccia** (1540m), another ski resort, and to Croce Arcana (1730m).

Above **Pianosinatico** (948m) a splendid forest still covers the Tuscan slope of the mountains. **Rivoreta**, north of Pianosinatico, has an Ethnographical Museum which illustrates peasant life in the area.

The **Passo dell'Abetone** (1388m) takes its name from a huge fir-tree which has long disappeared. Round the road summit, still on the Tuscan side of the boundary with Emilia, is **Abetone**, one of the best-known ski resorts in the Apennines, specially favoured by Florentines. Numerous ski-lifts and chair-lifts ascend to the snow fields. It is also much visited in summer (swimming pools, tennis courts, etc.). Across the border in Emilia is Monte Cimone, the highest peak in the northern Apennines (2165m).

The Palazzo Pretorio at Cutigliano

The main road to Bologna, leads north from Pistoia over the Passo della Porretta (or *della Collina*; 932m) in the Apennines. Next to it runs the *Porrettana* railway which until 1934 was the main line across the Apennines. The mountain stretch between Pistoia and Porretta Terme, opened in 1863 is particularly fine. **Pracchia** (616m), above the Reno valley was a summer resort, fashionable between the Wars, at the mouth of a long railway tunnel on the border of Emilia.

11 · Lucca

Lucca (86,600 inhab.) is one of the most beautiful small towns in Italy. It is surrounded by magnificent 16C–17C ramparts which are its most remarkable feature. It conserves much of its Roman street plan, and is especially rich in Romanesque churches. There are also an unusual number of private walled gardens within the walls. Lucca produces large quantities of olive oil.

■ Practical information

Information offices. APT, 2 Piazza Guidiccioni; Information Office, Vecchia Porta di San Donato, Piazzale Verdi (**open** daily 09.30–18.30; ☎ & fax: 0583-419689).

Getting there

By rail. The station at Lucca is in Piazzale Ricasoli, a few hundred metres south of the Baluardo di San Colombano. Services on the Florence-Viareggio line, slow trains stopping at numerous stations (from Florence, 78km in 70–90 mins). A footpath leads directly from the piazza in front of the station across the lawn at the foot of the walls through the bastion of San Colombano and up over the walls to the piazza, beside the apse of the Cathedral.

By bus. Terminus in Piazzale Verdi. *Lazzi* (☎ 0583-584877) from Florence (direct via the motorway in 1hr). Services also to Bagni di Lucca, Montecatini, the coast, Pisa, and Livorno. *CLAP* (☎ 0583-587897) for numerous places in the province, including the Garfagnana.

Car parking is not allowed inside the walls for longer than 90 mins except with an hourly tariff. Visitors are therefore strongly advised to park outside the walls in one of the free car parks (the most convenient of which is *Le Tagliate*, outside Porta San Donato). Limited space is sometimes available off the Viali Carducci, Margherita, del Prete, and Giusti, or outside the station or Piazza Risorgimento. There is a special car park for caravans (with facilities) in Via Luporini outside Porta Sant'Anna.

Bicycles can be hired at the Casermetta San Donato, near the tourist office.

Hotels within the city walls
★★★ *Universo*, 1 Piazza Puccini (also known as Piazza del Giglio; Pl. 1; ☎ 0583-493678, fax 0583-954854); *La Luna*, 12 Corte Compagni (Pl. 2; ☎ 0583-493634, fax 0583-490021); *Piccolo Hotel Puccini*, 9 Via di Poggio (Pl. 3; ☎ 0583-55421, fax 0583-53487).
★★ *Diana*, 11 Via del Molinetto (Pl. 6; ☎ 0583-492202, fax 0583-47795).

Hotels outside the city walls
★★★★ *Napoleon*, 536 Viale Europa (☎ 0583-316516, fax 0583-418398).
★★★ *Rex*, 19 Piazza Ricasoli (Pl. 4; ☎ 0583-955443, fax 0583-954348); *Celide*, 27 Viale Giusti (Pl. 5; ☎ 0583-954106, fax 0583-954304).

Hotels in the environs
★★★★ *Villa la Principessa*; swimming pool, at Massa Pisana, 3.5km outside the town on the N12 for Pisa (☎ 0583-370037, fax 0583-379136); *Villa San Michele* at San Michele in Escheto (☎ 0583-370276, fax 0583-370277).
★★ *Villa Casanova*; swimming pool, at Balbano, 10km west of Lucca towards Massaciuccoli (☎ 0583-548429, fax 0583-368955).

Youth Hostel: *Il Serchio* (open Mar–Oct), 673 Via Brennero, località Salicchi (☎ & fax 0583-341811).

Restaurants within the city walls

£££ *Antico Caffé delle Mura*, 4 Piazzale Vittorio Emanuele; *Buca di Sant'Antonio*, 1 Via della Cervia; *Antica Locanda dell'Angelo*, 21 Via Pescheria.

££ *Il Giglio*, 3 Piazza del Giglio; *All'Olivo*, 1 Piazza San Quirico.

£ *Da Giulio*, 47 Via delle Conce; *Trattoria Gli Orti*, 17 Via Elisa; *Trattoria Leo*, 1 Via Tegrini; *Vecchia Trattoria Buralli*, Piazza Sant'Agostino; *Trattoria Baralla*, Piazza Anfiteatro.

Restaurants outside Lucca

££ *La Mora* at Sesto di Moriano (about 10km north).

Places to picnic. The ramparts (described below) provide a delightful setting.

Pasticcerie. *Taddeucci*, Piazza San Michele (for *buccellato*, a delicious simple cake made with fennel and raisins); *Cioccolateria Caniparoli*, Via San Paolino.

Markets. An **antiques market** is held in Piazza San Martino on the third Sunday of every month (and on the preceding Saturday).

History. Stone implements discovered in the plain of Lucca show that it was inhabited some 50,000 years ago. The Roman colony of *Luca* was the scene in 56 BC of the the the meeting of Caesar, Pompey, and Crassus which led to their political alliance two years later, known as the First Triumvirate. The town is reputed to have been the first place in Tuscany to have accepted Christianity and its first bishop was Paulinus, a disciple of St Peter. In 552 the Goths were besieged here by the Byzantine general Narses who two years later, after the defeat of the Goths, was appointed prefect of Italy by Justinian. In the Middle Ages it was an important city under the Lombard marquesses of Tuscany, and later was constantly at war with Pisa and Florence. Under the rule of Castruccio Castracani, in 1316–28, Lucca achieved supremacy in western Tuscany, but his death was followed by a period of subjection to Pisa (1343–69). Charles IV then gave the Lucchesi a charter of independence, and it maintained its autonomy, often under the suzerainty of noble families, until 1799. In 1805 Napoleon presented the city as a principality to his sister Elisa Baciocchi, and in 1815 it was given to Marie Louise de Bourbon as a duchy.

The Romanesque churches were greatly admired by John Ruskin who spent much time here (at the *Hotel Universo*) studying them. The sculptor Matteo Civitali (1435–1501) was born in Lucca, and nearly all his works remain in the town. Pompeo Batoni (1708–87), also born here, painted fashionable portraits, mainly in Rome. The city also is the birthplace of the musicians Francesco Geminiani (1687–1762), Luigi Boccherini (1743–1805) and Giacomo Puccini (1858–1924).

The city centre

The delightful ***Piazza San Michele**, on the site of the Roman Forum, is still the centre of city life. The pavement and columns date from 1699–1705. The statue of Francesco Burlamacchi is by Ulisse Cambi (1863). When podestà of the city in 1546 Burlamacchi (1498–1548) led a rebellion against Medici rule, but was beheaded for his daring. In the portico of **Palazzo Pretorio** (1492; enlarged 1588) is a statue by Arnaldo Fazzi (1893) of Matteo Civitali, traditionally thought to be the architect of the original building.

San Michele in Foro

*San Michele in Foro is typical of the Pisan Romanesque style which developed in Lucca. Mentioned as early as 795, the present church was largely constructed in the 11C and 12C, though work continued until the 14C. The imposingly tall *façade is richly decorated with coloured marbles, carved columns, and capitals. The upper part and lateral arcading date from the 14C when it was intended to raise the height of the nave (the project was abandoned because of lack of funds). On the tympanum is a huge statue of *St Michael Archangel*. On the southwest corner is a copy of a *Madonna* by Civitali (see below). The façade was often sketched by Ruskin.

Interior (closed 12.30–15.00). The vaulting, which covers a traditional beamed roof, was carried out in the early 16C. On the **west wall** are 14C frescoes of the *Madonna and Child* and other fragments, the *Madonna* by Civitali (from the façade), and an organ dating from 1804. In the apse hangs a *Crucifix* painted in the late 12C.

South aisle. First altar, white enamelled terracotta relief of the *Madonna and Child*, attributed to Luca della Robbia. Beyond a *Martyrdom of St Andrew* by Pietro Paolini, on the second altar is a little sculpted figure of *St*

The upper façade of San Michele

Michael (1658). **South transept**. Monument to Bishop Sylvester Giles (see below) by Vincenzo Consani (1876); painting of *St Filomena* (1867); and a beautiful painting of *Saints Helena, Jerome, Sebastian, and Roch*, by Filippino Lippi.

North transept, *Marriage of the Virgin* by Agostino Marti, and a *Madonna and Child* by Raffaello da Montelupo (1522), a high relief that formed part of the tomb (destroyed in the 19C) of Sylvester Giles, Bishop of Worcester, who died in Italy in 1521. In the north aisle, between the second and first altars, *St Catherine*, by Antonio Franchi.

Puccini's birthplace

Opposite the west door, Via di Poggio leads to Corte San Lorenzo and, at No. 9, the birthplace of Giacomo Puccini (**open** daily except Mon: mid-March–mid-Nov 10.00–13.00, 15.00–18.00 or 19.00; mid-Nov–Dec, 10.00–13.00; Jan & Feb by appointment, ☎ 0583-584028).

The flat, on the second floor, was owned by Puccini's family, many of whom were also musicians, from the beginning of the 19C. The composer (1858–1924) spent his youth here. His forbears had for four generations been organists of San Martino, though he himself was only a chorister at San Michele. His first great success after he moved to Milan was *Manon Lescaut* (1893). His other famous operas are *La Bohème*, *Madama Butterfly*, *Tosca*, and *Turandot*, left unfinished on his death in Brussels in 1924. The house contains interesting mementoes of the composer including portraits of his family, two of his early musical scores composed in 1880–83, letters, and the Steinway piano on which he composed *Turandot*. The Centro Studi Giacomo Puccini was founded in 1996 to promote the study and perfomance of his works, and provide a research centre with a specialised library.

⸰   In Piazza Cittadella a monument to Puccini, by Vito Tongiani, was erected in 1994.

Via San Paolino leads west to the church of **San Paolino**, by Baccio da Montelupo and Bastiano Bertolani (1515–36), with a fine façade. The **interior** has small early 16C stained glass windows.

   South side. **First altar**, Il Riccio, *Holy Trinity* (1566); **third altar**, 15C polychrome wooden statue of *St Ansano*, by Francesco di Valdambrino; **fourth altar**, Pietro Testa, *St Theodore*. The two small cantorie in the nave are by Nicolao and Vincenzo Civitali; Giacomo Puccini often played on the 19C organ.

   South transept. In the right chapel is the *Burial of St Paulinus and three other Saints*, a very unusual 14C painting attributed to Angelo Puccinelli. In the chapel opposite, Gerolamo Scaglia, *Miracle of St Paulinus*, and *Madonna and Child with Saints* by Lorenzo Zacchia (1585). In niches on either side of the presbytery, 14C wooden statues of the annunciatory angel and St Paolino. In the chapel to the left of the presbytery, *Coronation of the Virgin*, with a view of Lucca beneath, an unusual 15C work. In the chapel opposite, Lorenzo Castellotti, *St Joseph*, and a 16C *Madonna and Child*.

   North side. **Fourth altar**, Paolo Guidotti, *Martyrdom of St Valerio* and a rare stone statuette of the *Madonna and Child* dating from the end of the 13C, brought from Paris by merchants in the Middle Ages. **Second altar**, Francesco Vanni, *Madonna and Child*; **first altar**, Giovanni Domenico Lombardi, *Deposition*. The stoup is by Nicolao Civitali.

Museo Nazionale di Palazzo Mansi

Nearby, in Via Galli Tassi, is the Museo Nazionale di Palazzo Mansi (**open** 09.00–19.00; fest. 09.00–13.00; Mon closed).

   The *piano nobile* of the 17C palace has rooms decorated in the 17C–19C and the Pinacoteca is especially interesting for its 17C paintings (many with good frames), and Medici portraits. A fine staircase leads up to the impressive loggia with Tuscan columns, and (left) the **Sala da Pranzo** (dining room) with mirrors, and 18C painted decorations by Francesco Antonio Cecchi. The **Salone del Ballo** (ballroom) has late 17C frescoes by Giovanni Gioseffo dal Sole. In the little **chapel** is a copy of a *Madonna* by Mabuse.

   The **Pinacoteca** is arranged in the four rooms beyond (the pictures are not all labelled but there is a hand-list in each room). **Room I** (the Salone): Leandro Bassano, *Winter Landscape*; Jacopo Ligozzi, *Madonna appearing to St Giacinto*; Paolo Veronese, *St Peter the Hermit before the Consiglio Veneto*; Luca Giordano, *St Sebastian*; Beccafumi, **Scipio*; Domenichino, *Samson*; Carlo Dolci, *St John the Baptist, St Anthony Abbot*; Giovanni Battista Naldini or Giovanni Balducci, *Prayer in the Garden*; Orazio Marinari, *David*; Jacopo Vignali, **Tobias and the angel*; Ventura Salimbeni, *Portrait of a lady as St Catherine of Alexandria*; Rosa da Tivoli, two landscapes; Salvator Rosa, two battle scenes; Federico Zuccari, *self-portrait*; Rutilio Manetti, **Triumph of David*; Orazio Gentileschi, *Mary Magdalene*; Francesco Furini, *Circe*.

Room II contains a fine collection of *portraits: Sustermans, *Portrait of a Young Woman*, Cardinal Gian Carlo de Medici; Bronzino, *Cosimo I in armour* (one of several versions of this well-known portrait), *Ferdinando de' Medici as a boy*; Pontormo, **Portrait of a boy* (once thought to be Alessandro de' Medici); Bronzino, *Don Garzia de' Medici as a child*; Federico Barocci, *Federico Ubaldo della*

Rovere at the age of two; Sustermans, Maria Maddalena d'Austria; Alessandro Allori, *Bianca Cappello*; Sustermans, *Cardinal Leopoldo, Vittoria della Rovere*.

Room III. Andrea Schiavone, *St Mary Magdalene*; Vincenzo Catena, *Holy Family*; Sodoma, *Christ carrying the Cross*; good copy of a *Madonna and Child with St Anne* and the *Young St John* by Andrea del Sarto; Jacopo Bassano, *Adoration of the Shepherds*; Tintoretto, two male portaits; Francesco Avanzi, *Madonna and Child* (the only known work by this 16C Milanese artist).

Room IV. Battle scenes by Salvatore Rosa, Bergognone, and Rosa da Tivoli; Paul Brill, landscapes; Michel Sweerts, *Portrait of a boy*.

Off the Salone del Ballo (see above) are three **small drawing rooms** hung with 17C Flemish tapestries. The pretty **bedroom**, with an alcove, has 18C hangings made in Lucca. Beyond another room with a *Holy Family with St Anne* attributed to Van Dyck, is a room with a portrait of *Antonio Santini as a boy* by the 17C Flemish school. On the left are two 19C rooms with 18C still lifes and a painting of *Danae* by Denis Calvaert.

The 19C paintings have been arranged on the **top floor**. In the first room are three works by the native artist Pompeo Batoni (1708–87) including a portrait of *Archbishop Giovan Domenico Mansi*, and works by Bernardino and Pietro Nocchi (including the *Orsucci family* by Pietro), and Stefano and Agostino Tofanelli. The second room has works by Michele Ridolfi. Other rooms have court portraits including one of *Elisa Baciocchi* by Marie Guillemine Benoist (1806), bas reliefs by Vincenzo Consani made for the base of the monument to Marie Louise de Bourbon in Piazza Napoleone, and late 19C paintings including works by Edoardo Gelli.

Via San Paolino ends in **Piazzale Verdi** with the old **Porta San Donato**, described with the ramparts at the end of this chapter.

Piazza San Martino

The attractive **Piazza San Martino** and the adjoining **Piazza Antelminelli** have a delightful miscellany of buildings from different periods: the Romanesque cathedral, the 14C building of the Opera del Duomo (now restored as the Museo della Cattedrale) next to a 13C tower house and the 16C Oratory of San Giuseppe, the 16C Palazzi Sanminiati (on either side of a little garden with palm trees), and the fine Palazzo Micheletti (1556) with a charming walled garden, by Bartolomeo Ammannati (above which can be seen the roof of the Baptistery). The circular fountain dates from 1835.

The cathedral of San Martino

The *cathedral was consecrated in 1070 by Pope Alexander II, who had begun the rebuilding while bishop of Lucca. The asymmetrical **façade** is decorated with delightful sculptures in the Pisan-Lucchese Romanesque style. The statue of St Martin is a copy of the original 13C work, now inside the cathedral. The upper part, with three tiers of arcades, is signed by Guidetto da Como (1204). The columns are beautifully designed. The lower part of the embattled *campanile dates from 1060, the upper from 1261.

The three wide Romanesque arches (the one on the right smaller to accommodate the campanile) lead in to the **portico**, again beautifully decorated with sculptures, begun in 1233, and partly the work of Guido Bigarelli da Como, recently restored. The exquisite decorative details are carried out in pink, green, and white marble. On either side of the central door, bas-reliefs depict the story of *St Martin* and the months of the year. Over the left doorway is a relief of the *Deposition*, and under it an *Adoration of the Magi*, perhaps early works by Nicola Pisano. Over the right doorway, in the architrave, is the *Meeting of St Martin with the Arians*, and in the lunette, the *Beheading of St Regolus*. On the right pier of the portico is a symbolic labyrinth (12C). The sides of the building are also beautiful, as well as the exterior of the *apse, with its arcades and carved capitals, surrounded by a green lawn.

The tall *interior (closed 12.00–15.00 or 15.30) was rebuilt in the 14C–15C in a Gothic style, with a delicate clerestory, and a beautiful inlaid pavement designed by Matteo Civitali. The east end and roof are being restored (1998). On the entrance wall, the sculpture of *St Martin dividing his cloak* was removed from the façade. It dates from the 13C or possibly the early 14C. The two stoups are by Matteo Civitali (1498).

South aisle. first altar, Passignano, *Nativity*; **second altar**, Federico Zuccari, *Adoration of the Magi*; **third altar**, Tintoretto (and his school), *Last Supper*; **fourth altar**, Passignano, *Crucifixion*; **fifth altar**, Michele Ridolfi, *Resurrection* (1825). The pulpit is by Matteo Civitali.

A door leads into the **sacristy** (cumulative entrance ticket with the Museo della Cattedrale, and San Giovanni) where the celebrated *tomb of Ilaria del Carretto Guinigi**, was moved in 1995 during restoration work on the north transept. The serene effigy is the masterpiece of Jacopo della Quercia (1407), and one of the most original works of the very early Renaissance. The sarcophagus may be the work of Francesco di Valdambrino. Ilaria, who died in 1405, was the second wife of Paolo Guinigi (1376–1432) ruler of the city from 1400–30, who built Villa Guinigi (see p 205). The tomb was placed in the north transept in 1842 and it has not yet been decided where it will be definitively installed.

The tomb of Ilaria del Carretto Guinigi in the cathedral of Lucca

The altar in the sacristy was designed in 1835 and incorporates an early 15C bas-relief of *St Agnello*. The fine painting of the *Madonna and Saints*, with a good predella, is by Domenico Ghirlandaio, and the lunette of the *Dead Christ* attribued to a follower of Filippino Lippi.

South transept. The 17C organ is the work of Domenico Zanobi. The *tomb of Pietro da Noceto (1472) is a beautiful Renaissance Humanist work, by Matteo Civitali, who also sculpted the tomb of Domenico Bertini here. Bertini was papal secretary to Sixtus IV; he commissioned the monument in 1479 before he became podestà of the city in 1487. The two angels flanking the tabernacle in the chapel of the Holy Sacrament, and the altar of St Regulus (1484), right of the sanctuary, are also the work of Civitali. The modern bronze **high altar** was installed in 1987, and part of the marble screen, by the school of Civitali moved to the side chapels, despite local protest. The stained glass in the apse is the work of Pandolfo di Ugolino of Pisa (1485), and the choir stalls by Leonardo Marti (1452). On the high altar is a 14C Sienese triptych.

North transept. Altar with figures of the *Risen Christ* and *Saints Peter and Paul*, by Giambologna (the predella with a view of Lucca is of slightly later date). In the Cappella del Santuario, **Virgin and Child enthroned with Saints* by Fra Bartolomeo (1509). In the middle of the north aisle is the octagonal marble **Tempietto, also by Civitali (1484), built to house the famous **Volto Santo*, a wooden likeness of Christ, supposed to have been begun by Nicodemus and miraculously completed. According to tradition, it was brought to Lucca in 782. It was greatly revered for centuries (and many copies made of it); the favourite oath of the English King, William Rufus is said to have been *Per Vultum de Lucca*. The effigy is usually assigned stylistically to the 13C, probably a copy of an 11C work (in its turn perhaps modelled on a Syrian image of the 8C). On the outside of the Tempietto is a statue of *St Sebastian* by Civitali.

North aisle. **fifth altar**, Stefano Tofanelli, *Assumption* (1808); **fourth altar**, Jacopo Ligozzi, *Visitation*; **third altar**, Giovanni Battista Paggi, *Annunciation* (1597); **second altar**, Alessandro Allori, *Presentation of Maria in the Temple* (restored in 1989); **first altar**, Giovanni Battista Paggi, *Birth of the Virgin*.

Museo della Cattedrale

The Museo della Cattedrale in Piazza Antelminelli was reopened in 1992 in modernised rooms on four floors (**open** daily 10.00–14.00; summer 10.00–18.00; cumulative ticket with San Giovanni and the sacristy of the Duomo).

To the right of the ticket office is a room with elaborate goldsmiths' work made to decorate the Volto Santo, including a *frieze of 1382–84, a 17C crown, a huge jewel made in France in 1660, and a sceptre of 1852. *The Evangelists* by Domenico Fancelli (1663) were used to decorate the tempietto. **Room I** has illuminated codexes, including some by Martino di Bartolomeo. The **Oratory of San Giuseppe** has fine 17C gilded wood decorations.

Upper floor. **Room II** has a tiny wood pyx (1174), a Limoges *reliquary coffer showing the martyrdom of St Thomas Becket, and an ivory diptych from Constantinople (506). The famous **Croce dei Pisani* is an elaborate Crucifix almost certainly commissioned by Paolo Guinigi in 1411 from Vincenzo di Michele da Piacenza. The 15C reliquary of *St Sebastian* is by Francesco Marti. **Room III** displays a 15C wood cupboard, part of the marble screen from the Duomo by Matteo Civitali, paintings by Vincenzo Frediani, and an early 16C crozier by Francesco Marti. **Room IV** has three paintings by Leonardo Grazia da Pistoia, Agostino Marti, and Zacchia il Vecchio. The two carved tondi of the head of *John the Baptist* are by Masseo Civitali and Vincenzo Consani. **Room V** has goldsmiths' work of the 16C and 17C.

On the **top floor Room VI** has late 17C–early 19C church silver. The sculptures in **Room VII** include the head of a bishop or a Pope (late 11C), Fra Fazio, a quaint 14C work, 14C–15C sculpted heads from the cathedral, the head of a man and a colossal statue of **St John the Evangelist* by Jacopo della Quercia, two statuettes of prophets by Francesco di Valdambrino, and two classical female heads dating from c 1480. Also displayed on this floor is a very colourful 17C

Sicilian carpet. The **Torre Belevedere** can be visited and the outside walkway with a view of the piazza.

Santi Giovanni e Reparata

In nearby Piazza San Giovanni, with a pretty walled garden, is the church of *Santi Giovanni e Reparata (cumulative entrance ticket with the sacristy of the Duomo, and the Museo della Cattedrale), whose fine portal of 1187 was preserved when the façade was erected in 1589. The **interior** (1160–87) has Roman columns with Romanesque capitals, a late 16C coffered ceiling, 19C funerary monuments, and frescoes of the *Madonna enthroned with Saints* attributed to Giuliano di Simone. At the east end the 9C crypt of San Pantaleone (which preserves his relics) can be seen.

Off the north side is the **Baptistery** with a remarkable roof of 1393. The excavations here show the 12C font above a square 9C font which partially covers the early Christian font. The **excavations** (separate ticket) carried out in 1969–92 below the church revealed five building levels. Here you can see a fragment of the mosaic pavement of a Roman house (1C BC), traces of Roman baths (2C AD), and the remains of the huge geometric mosaic pavement of the first church (4C–5C) on this site which was the cathedral of Lucca until 715. Its nave is occupied by conspicuous round kilns used during the construction of the present church.

From Piazza San Giovanni a short road leads north across Via del Battistero (with numerous antique shops) to the 12C church of **San Giusto** (left), with a pretty façade and finely carved portal.

Adjoining Piazza San Giovanni is **Piazza del Giglio** (also called Piazza Puccini), with the neo-classical façade of the **Teatro del Giglio**, built in 1817 by the local architect Giovanni Lazzarini. It was one of the most important opera houses in Italy in the early 19C, and here in 1831 was given the first performance of Rossini's *William Tell* (with Niccolò Paganini playing in the orchestra).

Palazzo Ducale

The adjoining **Piazza Napoleone** was laid out in 1806 in front of the Napoleonic residence, and planted with plane trees. The statue of Marie Louise de Bourbon, Duchess of Lucca in 1815–24, is by Lorenzo Bartolini.

Here is the huge Palazzo Ducale, in part designed by Bartolomeo Ammannati in 1578 and enlarged by Filippo Juvarra in 1728. The palace stands on the site of a much bigger castle (which occupied almost a fifth of the town) built for Castruccio Castracani (see p. 194), probably by Giotto, in 1322. Most of this was demolished by the populace in 1369 in anger against the Pisans who had occupied it. The palace became the seat of the Lords of Lucca until 1799, and then the ducal residence. It is now used as Provincial government offices, and by the Prefecture (undergoing restoration).

Behind the building (reached through Ammannati's Cortile degli Svizzeri) is the huge Dominican church of **San Romano** (closed many years ago), which contains the tomb of St Romanus by Matteo Civitali (1490). The church was reconstructed before 1281 and enlarged in the 17C. Opposite the façade is a neo-Gothic stable block.

San Frediano

In the northern part of the town is the church of *San Frediano (1112–47), with a conspicuous tall **campanile**, with crenellations, restored in 1853. The **façade** is unusual for its large mosaic on a gold ground, possibly the work of Berlinghiero Berlinghieri (13C; restored in the 19C). It represents the *Ascension* (with the Apostles below). The church replaced an earlier basilica and has its apse at the west end.

In the splendid basilican *__interior__ the columns of the nave have handsome classical capitals. At the beginning of the **south aisle** is a magnificent *__font__ (probably dating from the mid-12C), in the form of a fountain covered by a small tempietto, sculpted with reliefs of the *Story of Moses*, the *Good Shepherd*, and the *Apostles*. Behind the font is a lunette of the *Annunciation* by Marco (Fra 'Mattia) della Robbia. Nearby are two interesting frescoes detached from behind the organ on the west wall. In the corner is the *Virgin Annunciate*, a polychrome wooden statue by Matteo Civitali. Above the entrance is the organ, attributed to Domenico di Lorenzo. Beneath it are two framed detached frescoes: Amico Aspertini, *Madonna and Child with Saints*, and a *Visitation*.

Near the font is the 17C **Chapel of Santa Zita** (d. 1278), with paintings of *Miracles of the Saint* by Francesco del Tintore. Outside is a high relief of *St Bartholomew* by the della Robbia, and an altar carved by Matteo Civitali. In the next chapel is an interesting painting of the *Deposition* by Paolo Guidotti. In the last chapel (right), a wooden relief of the *Assumption* by Masseo Civitali (in a marble frame), and a detached 13C fresco of the *Crucifixion*. On the left wall of the presbytery is a huge marble monolith, probably from the Roman amphitheatre (see p. 204).

In the **Cappella Trenta** (fourth chapel in the north aisle) is an elaborately carved *altarpiece by Jacopo della Quercia (1422: assisted by Giovanni da Imola) and two pavement tombs by the same artist. Opposite is an *Immaculate Conception and Saints*, by Francesco Francia. Outside the chapel is a statue of *St Peter* by Vincenzo di Bartolomeo Civitali. The second north chapel contains beautiful early *frescoes by Amico Aspertini (c 1508–09) depicting stories of San Frediano, St Augustine, and the bringing of the Volto Santo to Lucca, with interesting local details and classical ruins in the landscapes.

Southwest of the church Via Cesare Battisti, with 17C–18C palaces, leads to **Palazzo Pfanner** (formerly Moriconi-Controni), built in 1667, with a delightful galleried outside staircase. The little 18C *garden, with a charming fountain and fine statuary, is open from March to Oct 10.00–18.00. It can also be seen from the avenue along the city walls (see below). The first floor of the palace, with a collection of 18C–20C local costumes, is not at present open to the public.

Nearby is the 14C church of **Sant'Agostino**, with a plain unfinished façade, and its small campanile resting on arches of the Roman Theatre. Inside, a little Baroque chapel was built in 1620 to house a venerated fresco of the *Madonna del Sasso*.

Across Via San Giorgio, Via del Loreto leads to **Santa Maria Corteorlandini**. The apse and south side of the church reconstructed in 1187 survive; the façade dates from the late 17C.

The pretty **interior** with painted decoration dates from 1715–21. Over the west end is a decorative organ gallery. The east end has painted decoration by Angelo Michele Colonna. Over the first altar in the south aisle, *Madonna and*

Saints attributed to Matteo Rosselli, and over the second altar in the north aisle, *Birth of the Virgin* by Francesco Vanni. A door in this aisle leads to a chapel built in 1662 in imitation of the Santa Casa of Loreto. Outside is a fresco by Filippo Gherardi. A wooden statue of *St Nicholas of Tolentino* by Francesco da Valdambrino has been removed to the Museo Nazionale di Villa Guinigi since its restoration. A precious collection of silk altar frontals (17C–18C) made in Lucca belongs to the church (occasionally exhibited).

Also south of Via San Giorgio is **San Salvatore**, a 12C church with a charming architrave over its south portal, showing a *Miracle of St Nicholas*: the Saint as a baby stands up in the bath in which he is being washed by two women. On either side are observers in towers and domed buildings. On the bath is the signature of the sculptor Biduino. On the façade, the right door has another carved architrave with another story from the *life of St Nicholas*, showing a royal banquet. In the piazza is a pretty fountain by Lorenzo Nottolini (1842).

Via Buia leads from Piazza San Salvatore to cross the picturesque Via Fillungo with two old towers, one, with a bell, dating from the 13C. Next to it is the 13C church of **San Cristoforo** with a fine interior (now used for exhibitions). It is the burial place of the sculptor, Matteo Civitali (d. 1501) and also serves as a War memorial (the walls are covered with the names of soldiers killed).

The Guinigi Tower

Via Sant'Andrea continues to the Guinigi Tower (**open** daily 09.00–19.30; winter 10.00–16.30), 41m high, famous because of the trees which grow on its summit (staircase to the top).

During the rule of Castruccio Castracani in the 14C, the Guinigi were one of the richest families in Lucca, particularly involved in the silk trade. The family continued to take an active part in the government of the city up to the 19C. The last descendants of the family left the tower to the Comune of Lucca.

The upper part of the tower is reached by an iron staircase and on the top is a delightful little garden of seven ilex trees. The view offers a panorama of the city and its tree-planted walls, and the hills beyond. To the south is the side of the cathedral and the curious dome of the baptistery (San Giovanni); farther to the right is the campanile of San Michele, behind which can just be seen

The Guinigi Tower, Lucca

the rear of its tall façade (with an outside staircase). Nearer at hand is the high medieval bell-tower in Via Fillungo. To the north is the campanile of San Frediano which stands beside the conspicuous mosaic on the church façade. Nearby, the oval shape of the amphitheatre, and the campanile and white colonnaded façade of San Pietro Somaldi can be seen; farther round is the white façade and rose window of San Francesco, near the castellated roof of Villa Guinigi. To the east, the top of Santa Maria Forisportam with its campanile is visible.

Adjoining the tower on Via Guinigi (Nos 29, and Nos 20–22) are the **Case dei Guinigi**, two large brick Gothic palaces facing each other. They were both built in the 14C and remodelled in the 16C.

Via Guinigi leads north to Via Mordini which continues right to Via Fratta. Just beyond is the church of **San Pietro Somaldi**, founded in 763. The church was rebuilt at the end of the 12C, and work continued up to the 14C. The grey and white banded façade dates from 1248, although the relief above the central door by Guido da Como and assistants is a little earlier (1203).

Interior. **South aisle**. First altar, Zacchia da Vezzano, *Assumption* (an unusual painting dated 1532); second altar, a good 17C painting of the *Annunciation*; third altar, Giovanni Marracci, *St Bona*; at the end of the aisle, 14C frescoed lunette of the *Madonna and Child*. **North aisle**. On the altar at the east end, Nicolau Landucci, *Holy Family* (1840); third altar, Antonio Franchi, *St Peter*; second altar, highly venerated *Madonna and Child* by Sebastiano Conca; first altar, *Saints Anthony Abbot, Bartholomew, Francis, Domenic, and Andrew*, a good painting attributed to Raffaellino del Garbo.

Via Busdraghi and and Via del Portico lead to the **Roman Amphitheatre**. The medieval houses which follow the ellipse of Via dell' Anfiteatro incorporate some of the brick arches of the amphitheatre. Its arena, where public spectacles were held in Roman days now forms a delightful *piazza, created in 1830–39 by the local architect Lorenzo Nottolini.

The eastern district

In the eastern district of the town at a crossroads by Via del Fosso on a pretty canal (formerly the moat outside the medieval walls) is the **Madonna dello Stellario**, a statue set up in 1687 on an ancient column. Carved on its base is an interesting view of Lucca from outside the walls, at Porta San Donato. Nearby is a neo-classical fountain by Lorenzo Nottolini.

The church of **San Francesco** was rebuilt in the 14C (the upper part of the façade was finished in 1930).**South side**: **second altar**, Sebastiano Conca, *Madonna and Saints*; between the **second** and **third altars**, unusual monument to Giovanni Guidiccioni (1500–41), with a fine statue of the *Madonna and Child* attributed to Vincenzo Civitali; in the chapel to the right of the high altar, a *lunette of the *Presentation of the Virgin in the Temple* and the *Marriage of the Virgin*, a detached fresco of remarkably high quality by the 15C Florentine school (but very damaged) has been removed.

North side: **fifth altar**, Passignano, *Noli me tangere*; **fourth altar**, Federico Zuccari, *Nativity*; between the fourth and third altars, funerary monuments to the musicians Luigi Boccherini (1743–1805) and Francesco Geminiani (1687–1762). In the cloister is the tomb of Bonagiunta Tignosini (1274) with a ruined fresco by Deodato Orlandi.

The Museo Nazionale Guinigi

Nearby, in Via della Quarquonia, is the unusual brick Villa Guinigi, a castellated suburban villa built in 1418. The austere building was restored to house the **Museo Nazionale Guinigi** which contains a fine collection of sculpture and paintings from Lucca and its province, as well as an archaeological collection. In the garden is a Roman mosaic (1C–2C AD), and a group of carved Romanesque lions from the medieval walls (**open** 09.00–19.00; fest. 09.00–14.00; closed Mon).

Ground floor

The archaeological collection and medieval sculpture is arranged here. **Room I** (left of the portico) displays Bronze Age and Villanovan finds from near Lucca, and material from the Etruscan settlement of Serchio. **Room II**: four Ligurian tombs (reconstructed); Etruscan tomb with gold jewellery and an Attic krater (3C BC). Beyond are Roman finds from the city, including an altar of 40 BC–30 BC found in Piazza San Michele, mosaics and marble heads. **South portico**: medieval architectural fragments. **Room III**: fine examples of Lucchese sculpture (8C–14C) including a transenna with a relief of Samson and the lion; fragment of a statue of *St Martin* (12C–13C) from the Duomo; bas-reliefs from the church of San Jacopo in Altopascio; statuette of the *Madonna and Child* attributed to Biduino (late 13C); finds, including gold jewellery from a Lombard tomb (600 AD–650 AD).

Upper floor

On the upper floor are the paintings and later sculpture, mostly by artists born in Lucca or who worked here. **Room X**: marble statuette of the *Madonna and Child* by Tino da Camaino; 'Ugolino Lorenzetti', *Madonna and Child* and *St John the Evangelist*; Francesco Traini, *St Michael Archangel*; Paolo da Siena, painted *Crucifix*; Deodato Orlandi, *Crucifix* (1288) and *Madonna and Child*.

In the next part of the room: Angelo Puccinelli, *Madonna enthroned*, *Mystical marriage of St Catherine and Saints*; Andrea Pisano, wooden statue of the *Madonna and Child*; Giuliano di Simone, polyptych; marble statue of the *Virgin Annunciate* by the early 14C school of Lucca.

In the last part of the room: Gherardo Starnina, *Saints*; polychrome wooden statue of the *Madonna and Child* (early 15C); and, at the end of the room: Priamo della Quercia, polyptych (c 1430), enclosing marble statuettes. The very damaged pavement tomb of Balduccio degli Antelminelli is by Jacopo della Quercia, and that of Caterina Antelminelli by his bottega. The stalls from the Duomo, dating from 1452, are the work of Leonardo Marti.

Room XI: Borghese di Pietro Borghese, painted Cross; Zanobi Machiavelli, *Madonna and Child with Saints*; Giuliano di Simone (attributed), detached fresco of the *Nativity*; two high reliefs in terracotta of the *Madonna and Child* by the bottega of Donatello; Jacopo della Quercia, wooden statue of *St Ansano*; Francesco di Valdambrino, wooden statue of *St Anthony Abbot*.

Room XII: late 15C Flemish painter, *Annunciation*; Vecchietta and Neroccio di Bartolomeo di Landi, *Dormition* and *Assumption of the Virgin* (in polychrome wood); intarsie by Cristoforo Canozzi da Lendinara; terracotta relief of the *Madonna and Child* and marble *relief of the *Annunciation*, by Matteo Civitali; Masseo Civitali, wooden intarsia of *St Martin* from the Cathedral; *Visitation* by a 15C painter from Lucca; wooden statue of *St Nicholas of*

Tolentino (1407) by Francesco di Valdambrino (from the church of Santa Maria Corteorlandini).

Room XIII: late 15C altarpieces of the *Madonna and Child with Saints* by Bernardino del Castelletto, Michele di Pietro Membrini, Vincenzo di Antonio Frediani, and Amico Aspertini. The marble *Ecce Homo* is by Matteo Civitali, and the statue of *Christ in Pietà* (1478) by Masseo Civitali . Also displayed here is a very fine 15C processional Cross in gilded silver, made in Lucca.

Room XIV: Zacchia il Vecchio, *Assumption* and *Madonna with Saints*; Fra Bartolomeo, **Madonna della Misericordia* (1515), and **God the Father with Mary Magdalen and Catherine of Siena*. Above the marble tomb of St Silao by Andrea di Giovanni da Carrara are two putti by Marco della Robbia.

Room XV: intarsia views of Lucca by Ambrogio and Nicolao Pucci (1529) from the Cappella degli Anziani in the Duomo. Works by Riccio, Daniele da Volterra (*Deposition*), Francesco del Brina, and Vasari (*Immaculate Conception*). **Room XVI**. Works by Aurelio Lomi, Jacopo Ligozzi, Domenico Passignano, Ludovico Cigoli, and Federico Zuccari. **Room XVII**. Works by Pietro da Cortona, Guido Reni, Giovanni Lanfranco, and Rutilio Manetti. **Room XVIII–XX** contain 17C–18C works by Pietro Paolini, Girolamo Scaglia, and others.

From Piazza San Francesco, Via del Fosso follows the line of medieval walls leading south between a canal (formerly the moat) and the garden wall of **Villa Bottini** (*Buonvisi*; entrance on Via Elisa). This is a fine building (1566) with two façades, surrounded by a pretty walled garden (**open** 09.00–14.00), with beautiful magnolia trees, and a nymphaeum attributed to Buontalenti. The interior, with many rooms frescoed by Ventura Salimbeni, has been restored by the Comune and it is now used for conferences. It also contains a newspaper library. In July and August concerts are usually held in the garden.

Opposite the entrance in Via Elisa is the church of the **Santissima Trinità** (1589; key from the adjoining convent) which contains a sentimental statue of the *Madonna della Tosse*, by Matteo Civitali. **Porta San Gervasio** (1255) is the best of the medieval gates remaining from the earlier fortifications of the city.

To the south of the gate, entered from Via San Micheletto are the **Botanical Gardens** designed in 1820 by Bernardino Orsetti (**open** 09.00–13.00 except Mon; fest 09.00–13.00, 15.30-18.30). An extremely interesting garden for specialists, it includes medicinal plants, a huge cedar of Lebanon (1820), a sequoia, a camphor tree, and a three-stemmed ginkgo tree.

Santa Maria Forisportam

Inside Porta San Gervasio Via Santa Croce continues to the piazza in front of *Santa Maria Forisportam, named from having been outside the city gates until 1260. It is another fine church with a marble **façade** in the 13C Pisan style. Above the left door is a fine architrave with a lion and a griffin and a cast of a 12C statuette of the *Madonna enthroned* (the original is to be exhibited in the museum when it is restored). In the lunette above the right door is a 13C statuette of a bishop saint. Above the central door is a 17C relief of the *Coronation of the Virgin*.

The pleasant grey **interior** was altered in 1516 when the nave and transepts were raised. On the west wall an early Christian sarcophagus has been adapted as a font. **South aisle**: first altar, Gerolamo Scaglia, *Coronation of the Virgin* (with a 15C fresco fragment below); fourth altar, Guercino, *St Lucy. The ciborium in *pietre dure* and bronze in the south transept dates from c 1680. The handsome **High Altar** was designed by Vincenzo Civitali (and finished in the 18C). In the **north transept** is a neo-classical monument to Antonio Mazzarosa by Vincenzo Consani (1870) and an altarpiece of the *Assumption* by Guercino.

In the **sacristy**, off the south transept, is a *Dormition* and *Assumption of the Virgin* by Angelo Puccinelli (1386) and a *Madonna and Child* by Pompeo Batoni. There is a charming small **museum** (opened on request) in some adjoining rooms with sculpture (including the 12C Madonna from the façade, and a 13C wooden statuette of the *Madonna and Child*), church silver, altar frontals, vestments, a missionary museum, fossils and Roman material.

Via della Rosa leads south to the charming little oratory of **Santa Maria della Rosa** (locked), built in 1309–33 in the Pisan Gothic style. Inside are some traces of the original Roman wall.

The ramparts
A walk around the top of the 16C–17C *ramparts (4195m in circumference) which enclose the town completes a visit to Lucca. The road has been completely closed to traffic and some of the bastions have been restored, while others are being restored. They have been planted with trees since the 16C (although some of these are now diseased and are being replanted) and provide delightful views of the town and of the Apuan Alps. The avenues and parks are beautifully maintained. The earliest circle of walls, of which traces have survived, date from the Roman period; new walls were built in 1198. The present fortifications, extremely well preserved, were carried out in 1544–1650.

The walls are 12m high and 30m wide at the base, and have eleven bastions, on many of which guardhouses survive. The interiors of some of the bastions have been restored, with their complicated defence works, armouries, ammunition stores and passages. Outside the walls are grassy fields on the site of the moat (the recent construction of a car park at the foot of the Baluardo di San Martino has been justly criticised). In medieval times there were only three gates. The walls were never put to use but must have served as an effective deterrent to Lucca's enemies. They were built on a system afterwards developed by Vauban, and recall the ramparts of Berwick-on-Tweed in Scotland and Verona.

The **Baluardo di San Paolino** (see the Plan) dates from 1594–1642. In the delightful park is a monument to the musician Alfredo Catalani by Francesco Petroni. The guardhouse at No. 21 is the seat of *CISCU* (*Centro Internazionale per lo Studio delle Cerchia Urbane*, an International Centre for the Study of Urban Enceintes), founded in 1967 (when the bastion was restored) with a photo archive and library. A tour of the bastion is courteously granted by appointment. It has an interesting interior which incorporates the remarkable vaulted central hall of the 15C defensive tower on this site, as well as various corridors, an armoury, a well and drinking trough for the horses.

A splendid double avenue of plane trees planted by Marie Louise de Bourbon in the early 19C leads along the ramparts to the **Baluardo di Santa Maria** designed by Francesco Paciotti and constructed by Matteo Civitali in 1562. Here is a 19C piazzale with a statue of Vittorio Emanuele II by Angelo Passaglia, and two 13C lions from the medieval walls. The *Antico Caffè delle Mura* (now a restaurant; see listing on p. 194) was built in 1840 by Cesare Lazzarini.

The avenue passes beneath a loggia above the florid **Porta San Pietro**, the most important entrance to the town (1566; by Alessandro Resta), which preserves its original doors and portcullis (the side gates were added in 1846). From here there is a view of the campanile of San Giovanni and the roof of the Baptistery. Beyond you can see the side and apse of the Duomo beneath a bank planted with magnolia trees.

On the **Baluardo di San Colombano** (being restored) are two more 13C lions, and the ruins of a medieval tower. From the **Baluardo di San Regolo** there is a view down Via del Fosso with its canal which runs along the line of the walls, built in 1198. On the bastion there is a children's playground and an ilex grove around a bust of Mazzini on a column. The ramparts (here planted with ilexes) now skirt the wall of the Botanical Gardens (see above). The **Baluardo La Libertà** (or *Cairoli*) is asymmetrically placed at the southeast corner of the fortifications.

There is a view of the Torre Guinigi from the avenue as it crosses above the neo-classical **Porta Elisa**, opened in 1809. At the end of Via Elisa, Porta San Gervasio can be seen in the medieval walls. The **Baluardo di San Salvatore** is walled off for restoration. Remains of a medieval fortification (a rectangular enclosure with four wells on the left of the path) can be seen here. From the **Baluardo di San Pietro** (or *Cesare Battisti*) there is a splendid view of the Apuan Alps. The ramparts pass above **Porta San Jacopo** (opened in 1930) to reach the **Baluardo di San Martino**, the foot of which has recently been disfigured by a car park. The interior was restored in 1967, and ruins of a medieval tower can be seen here. The avenue passes beneath the loggia above **Porta Santa Maria** (1593), one of the three original gates.

The **Baluardo di San Frediano** is a small rectangular bastion protected by grassed earthworks (1554). Many trees have had to be felled here because of disease. From the walls there is a splendid view across fields (crossed by paths) and trees to the mountains beyond. Inside the walls stand the campanile and apse of San Frediano, and the pretty garden decorated with statues of Palazzo Pfenner. The viale skirts a prison wall as far as the **Baluardo di Santa Croce** with remains of a medieval tower. The guardhouse here has two columns and is vaulted below.

The walk now passes beneath the loggia of the handsome **Porta San Donato** (1639) with two statues of San Paolino and San Donato by Giovanni Lazzoni. This replaced the **old Porta San Donato**, built in the medieval walls in 1591, which is conspicuous nearby in Piazzale Verdi. This area of the town, formerly called Prato del Marchese was used from the 18C onwards for football games, horse races and other public spectacles. The gateway, on a design by Ginese Bresciani, was beautifully restored in 1976 and is now the *APT* information office. The line of the old walls can also clearly be seen here, and the foundations of the drawbridge outside the gate. A handsome stable block of 1876, at the foot of the ramparts, is being restored and may one day be used as a conference centre. The **Baluardo di San Donato** (being restored) is beautifully planted with trees. The bastions pass above **Porta Sant'Anna** (or *Vittorio Emanuele*), opened in 1910 to return to the Baluardo di San Paolino.

Environs of Lucca

The environs of Lucca are noted for their fine villas and gardens built between the 16C and 19C, although only three of them are at present open to the public (many others are being studied and may be restored and opened to the public).

In the foothills, northeast of the town, is the late 17C **Villa Reale** at **Marlia** (8km from Lucca), once the home of Napoleon's sister, Elisa Baciocchi. Niccolò Paganini, Metternich and John Singer Sargent all stayed here. It was bought in 1923 by Anna Laetitia (Mimì) Pecci-Blunt (1885–1971). She opened the *Galleria La Cometa* in Rome in the 1930s, and became a well-known collector of Italian art. The house is not open to the public, but the 17C Orsetti *garden, with notable statuary and a theatre, is (open 1 Mar–30 Nov at 10.00, 11.00, 15.00, 16.00, 17.00, 18.00 except on Mon).

Nearby at **San Pancrazio** are two more villas: The 16C **Villa Oliva Buonvisi**, built by Matteo Civitali (the park is open from 15 March–15 November daily 09.30–18.30); and the neo-classical **Villa Grabau**, with a large English park and orangery. The ground floor of the villa and the park are open from Apr–Oct 10.00–13.00, 15.00–19.00 except Mon and Tues morning.

At **Segromigno** (10km) is the 17C **Villa Mansi** (open 10.00–12.30, 15.00–17.00; summer 09.30–13.00, 15.00–19.00; closed Mon). Part of the garden, altered by Juvarra in 1742 survives near the house, with a pescheria (fish pond), the *Bagno di Diana*, and fine statues. The English park was created in the 19C. The villa has late 18C decorations, including frescoes of the *Myth of Apollo* in the Salone by Stefano Tofanelli.

At **Camigliano**, nearby, is the **Villa Torrigiani** (open Mar–Nov except Tues 10.00–12.30, 15.00–dusk) with a rococo façade, and fine park. It contains 17C and 18C paintings and a collection of porcelain.

A few kilometres south of Lucca, in località Vicopelago (off a by-road to Pozzuolo), is the **Villa Bernardini** built in 1600–15 by Bernardo Bernardini with a (modern) garden which includes an 18C green theatre (open daily except Mon morning, 10.00–12.00, 14.30–17.00; summer: 09.30–12.00, 15.00–19.30).

Five kilometres east of Lucca is **Lunata**, with its tall Romanesque campanile, which lies 2km south of **Lammari**, where the parish church contains a tabernacle, Matteo Civitali's last work. Farther east (17km from Lucca) is **Montecarlo**, well known in Tuscany for its production of good wine (red and white, including *Michi* and *Buonamico*). On the other side of the motorway is **Altopascio**, where Castruccio beat the Florentines in 1325. The Order of the Knights of Altopascio (*del Tau*) ran a hospice for pilgrims here in 1084, and it has since been famous for its hoteliers. It is also well known for its bread.

At **Badia di Cantignana**, south of Lucca, The African explorer Carlo Piaggia (1827–82), was born. Together with Romolo Gessi he was the first to circumnavigate Lake Albert. A camellia festival is held at **Pieve di Compito** on three weekends in March (for information ☎ 0583-90624).

On the plain to the south of Lucca is a monumental aqueduct built by Lorenzo Nottolini, c 1823, to bring water to the town from Monte Pisano.

12 · The Garfagnana

The beautiful upper valley of the Serchio north of Lucca is known as the **Garfagnana**. It is well-wooded and richly cultivated. Lying between the Apennines and the Apuan Alps the scenery is spectacular in the side valleys and on the higher ground. In the centre of the valley is Castelnuovo di Garfagnana, situated between the Parco delle Alpi Apuane and the Parco dell'Orecchiella in the Apennines. In the lower valley is the interesting village of Barga.

■ Practical information

Information offices. **Castelnuovo di Garfagnana**. *Comunità Montana della Garfagnana*, 9 Via Vittorio Emanuele (☎ 0583-644911); *Pro Loco*, 10 Loggiato Porta (☎ 0583-644354). **Bagni di Lucca**: *APT*, 139 Via Umberto I, La Villa (☎ 0583-805508). For information about the spa, ☎ 0583-86404. **Borgo a Mozzano**: *Comunità Montana della Media Valle del Serchio*, 100 Via Umberto I (☎ 0583-88346). **Barga**: *Pro Loco*, Piazza Angelio (☎ 0583-723499).

Getting there

By rail. A magnificent railway line, with fine scenery, follows the valley from Lucca to Aulla (91km in c 2hrs 15mins). It is served by local trains stopping at all stations including Bagni di Lucca, Barga, and Castelnuovo di Garfagnana (in c 1hr).

By bus. From Piazzale Verdi in Lucca (*CLAP*, ☎ 0583-587897) to Bagni di Lucca, Barga, Castelnuovo di Garfagnana, Vagli, etc. Services run by *Lazzi* (☎ 0583-584877) also to Bagni di Lucca.

Hotels

Castelnuovo di Garfagnana. ★★★ *Da Carlino*, 15 Via Garibaldi (☎ 0583-644270, fax 0583-65575).
Near the **Parco dell'Orecchiella**. At **Corfino** (Villa Collemandina) ★★★ *California* (☎ 0583-660173) and *Panoramico* (☎ 0583-660161, fax 0583-660159); ★★ *La Baita* (☎ 0583-660084).
San Romano Garfagnano (Villetta). ★★★ *Il Grotto* (☎ 0583-612392, fax 0583-612243).
Passo Radici, Casone Profecchia near Castiglione di Garfagnana: ★★★ *Il Casone* (☎ 0583-649090, fax 0583-649048).
Near the **Parco delle Alpe Apuane**. ★★★★ *Lo Scoiattolo*, Passo Carpinelli (Minucciano) (☎ 0583-611071; fax 0583-611072). ★★★ *Mini Hotel*, Gramolazzo (Minucciano) (☎ 0583-610153; fax 0583-610668); *Belvedere*, Carpinelli (Minucciano) (☎ 0583-611043), and at Vagli Sotto, *Le Alpi* (☎ 0583-664057; fax 0583-664347).
Near **Barga**. ★★★ *Villa Libano*, 6 Via del Sasso (☎ 0583-723774; fax 0583-724185); *La Pergola*, Via Sant'Antonio (☎ 0583-711239, fax 0583-710433).
Bagni di Lucca. ★★★ *Bridge*, Piazza Ponte a Serraglio (☎ 0583-805324); *Corona*, 78 Via Serraglio (☎ 0583-805151; fax 0583-805134); *Bernabò*, Bagni Caldi (☎ 0583-805215). ★★ *Svizzero*, 30 Via Casalini (☎ 0583-805315). ★ *Roma*, 110 Via Umberto I (☎ 0583-87278).

Campsites

Giuncugnano. ★★ *Argegna* (open mid-June–mid-Sept; ☎ 0583-611182).
Minucciano. ★★ *Lago Paradiso* (☎ 0583-610662).

Restaurants

There are numerous *trattorie* in the Garfagnana, especially good in the mountain areas around the Parco dell'Orecchiella, including Casone di Profecchia, and Castelnuovo di Garfagnana.

Bagni di Lucca. ££ *Vinicio* and *Circolo Forestieri*.

Ponte a Moriano. ££ *La Mora*.

Hiking and horse riding are organised along some 350km of nature trails in the Apuan Alps and the Apennines (with overnight stays in mountain refuges). Information from the *Comunità Montana* in Castelnuovo di Garfagnana.

The lower Serchio Valley

At the southern end of the Serchio valley, some ten kilometres north of Lucca (reached from Vinchiana) is **San Giorgio di Brancoli**, in beautiful countryside, where the Romanesque church has an *ambone and a font, both 12C, a *St George* by Andrea della Robbia, and a 14C painted *Crucifixion*. On the west bank of the Serchio is **Diecimo** (at the tenth Roman mile from Lucca), with its 13C Romanesque church. To the west, on the by-road for **Pescaglia** is **Celle dei Puccini**, the home of Puccini's ancestors (their house can be visited; Saturday and Sunday, 15.00–19.00; or by appointment, ☎ 0583-359154). Near Pescaglia is the tiny village of **Vetriano** where a theatre, built in 1890 and reputed to be the smallest public theatre in the world, was donated to the *FAI* (Fondo per l'Ambiente Italiano, founded in 1975 modelled on the British National Trust) in 1998 and is to be restored.

Borgo a Mozzano on the bank of the Serchio, 4km north of Diecimo, has a church which contains expressive 16C sculptures and a wooden figure of *St Bernardine* by Matteo Civitali. The conspicuous **Ponte della Maddalena** is a remarkable ancient footbridge over the Serchio. There are many Romanesque churches in the vicinity.

Bagni di Lucca

A by-road on the east bank of the river leads to Bagni di Lucca, a little spa with warm sulphur and saline waters (**open** to the public), somewhat off the main valley. It is divided into several districts including Bagni Caldi and Bagno alla Villa. Noted for its waters since the 12C, it was particularly fashionable as a residence of the nobility of Lucca and foreigners from the 17C up until the end of the 19C. Its famous visitors have included Shelley, Byron, Browning (who advised Tennyson, Poet Laureate, to stay here in 1851), and Walter Savage Landor. The novelist Francis Marion Crawford (1854–1909) was born here, and in the little Protestant cemetery the romantic novelist Ouida (Marie Louise de la Ramée, born in England in 1839) was buried in 1908.

The town is entered by **Ponte a Serraglio**, from which the lower road leads left along the river overhung with pretty trees to the **Casinò** built by Giuseppe Pardini and founded in 1837 as the first licensed gaming house in Europe. A plaque on the house beside it records Alphonse de Lamartine's stay here in 1825. The upper road leads through woods to the pretty spa of **Bagni Caldi**, with the **Stabilimento Jean Verraud** (early 20C; being restored. The thermal building next door is **open** from around 15 Apr–15 Nov).

In the other direction a road leads from the bridge to **La Villa**, a typical little spa. The **Palazzo del Circolo dei Forestieri** here was built in 1923–24, and the **Teatro Accademico** in 1790 (restored 1986). The old English Chemist still has the royal coat of arms. Here, in the public gardens, is the neo-Gothic **English Church** built in 1839 by Giuseppe Pardini and on the hillside above the royal stables built in 1811.

A road leads up to the tiny hamlet of **Bagno alla Villa**, once an elegant residential district, but which now has an air of decadence. **Villa Buonvisi** was built in Piazza di Sopra in 1570, and Montaigne stayed here in 1581. The village was restored in 1669 for the visit of the Grand-duchess Vittoria della Rovere, and more houses, including the **Casa Mansi** were built at that time. In 1722 James Stuart, the Old Pretender came here with his wife Clementina Sobieska and stayed at the Villa Buonvisi. In 1811 Elisa Baciocchi, having received the principality of Lucca from her brother Napoleon, transformed **Palazzo Orsetti** into her summer residence, and this period of splendour for Bagno alla Villa continued during the Bourbon duchy. In 1818 Shelley and Mary Wollstonecraft lived in the Casa del Chiappa, and in 1822 Byron stayed with his friend John Webb who owned the Villa Buonvisi. The baths here were rebuilt in the 17C (but are now closed).

The by-road continues up the Lima river to **San Cassiano di Controne**. The church owns a remarkable polychrome wood sculpture of *San Cassiano* (or San Martino) on horseback, now attributed to Francesco da Valdambrino, which is one of the earliest equestrian groups produced in the Renaissance (c 1406–07). It was restored in 1995.

In the main valley of the Serchio is the village of **Ghivizzano** with the castle and tombs of the Castracani family who were lords of this district. The village of **Coreglia Antelminelli**, reached by a by-road, contains an interesting church and a museum of 18C–20C figurines (**open** weekdays 08.00–13.00; fest. in summer, 08.00–13.00, 16.00–19.00) for which the locality is famous. Traditionally made in plaster, the statuettes include animals, Greek gods, works by Canova, peasants, and figures for a crib. There are also numerous busts of the famous including Garibaldi, Napoleon, Wellington and Franklin. Although local artisans still practice this craft, they now usually use alabaster or plastic.

Barga

Barga (11,000 inhab.) is the most important place in the lower Serchio valley. It has expanded at the foot of its hill (410m) leaving the little old village remarkably peaceful. Cars can be parked by the bastion, where there is a war memorial, a monument to Antonio Mordini (1819–1902) and a huge cedar of Lebanon. Beyond the old **Porta Reale** (or *Mancianella*) the narrow **Via di Mezzo** winds up and down through the centre of the village. It passes the church of the **Santissima Annunziata** built in 1595 with decorative stuccoes, beside Palazzo Mordini.

Beyond Palazzo Cordati which follows the curve of the street, is a little piazza in front of the **Teatro dell'Accademia dei Differenti**. A theatre was first built here in 1689 and the present building dates from 1795. Above the piazza is a view of the Duomo and its campanile (described below). Piazza Angeli is named

Barga

after the Humanist, Pietro Angeli (1517–96), whose bust is on the corner of his house here. Concerts are often held in this attractive piazza. Via di Mezzo continues to **Piazza del Comune** (or Salvi) with a picturesque loggia (once a market place), with a stone lion, the heraldic *Marzocco*, symbol of the political domination of Florence. Palazzo Pancrazi houses the town hall. In the adjacent Piazza Garibaldi is the handsome 16C **Palazzo Balduini**, perhaps on a design by Bartolomeo Ammannati.

From Piazza Comune a steep flight of steps lead up to the church of **Santissimo Crocifisso** with a pleasant façade. It contains wooden stalls and a decorative gilded wood high altar. Via della Speranza leads out of the village through Porta Machiaia and over the interesting old **Ponte dell' Acquedotto**. Steps continue up from the Santissimo Crocifisso to the grassy terrace in front of the Duomo. From here there is a splendid view which takes in the snow-capped Apuan Alps and the Apennines.

The Romanesque *****Duomo** (restored in 1920 after earthquake damage) has a fine exterior built in the local white stone (*alberese*), and an embattled campanile. It dates from the 9C–14C with later alterations. The side of the earliest church serves as the façade which has an interesting main door. The north doorway has a carved architrave.

In the dark **interior** is a handsome stoup beneath a 14C fresco of *St Lucy*. The painting of *St Christopher* dates from the 18C (probably by Stefano Tofanelli). The sculpted 13C *pulpit is attributed to Guido Bigarelli of Como (or his pupil). In the main apse is a huge imposing figure of *St Christopher* in polychrome wood (early 12C). The stained glass tondo above is on a cartoon attributed to Lorenzo di Credi. In the chapel to the right of the high altar is a terracotta altarpiece of the *Madonna with Saints Sebastian and Roch* (restored), and della Robbian works. In the chapel to the left of the high altar is a large painted *Crucifix* (15C), and a 16C painting of *St Joseph* with a view of Barga (in an elaborate frame), with a Byzantine *Madonna and Child* inserted into the top part of the painting. The contents of the rich treasury, which include a chalice by Francesco Vanni, are at present kept in the Canonica.

Across the grass is the **Palazzo Pretorio** with a loggia and a small archeological museum. Steps lead down past a pretty garden to the **Conservatorio di Sant'Elisabetta** (ring for admission). In the church is a fine high altarpiece in enamelled terracotta attributed to Benedetto Buglioni. A large 15C *Crucifix* has been removed for restoration.

Via del Pretorio returns to the Porta Reale. Outside the gate, below Via Marconi by the hospital, is the church of **San Francesco**, with fine polychrome enamelled terracottas: the *Nativity and Saints* is attributed to Luca della Robbia 'il giovane', great nephew of Luca, and *St Francis receiving the Stigmata* to his brother Giorolamo.

The by-road which leads south from Barga to Fornaci di Barga passes a farm and cemetery next to the pieve of **Loppia**, founded in the 9C, with a worn Romanesque façade. A pretty road continues east beyond Barga to **Tiglio Alto** where the church contains 14C statues of the *Annunciation*, reminiscent of those in the cathedral of Carrara (see p. 226).

On the west bank of the Serchio, opposite Barga, is **Gallicano**, where a by-road leads up to the hermitage of **Calomini**, excavated from the rock in the

12C (the double loggia dates from the 18C). It is opened by Capuchin monks from Lucca in May–September.

Another road continues along the river Turrite from Gallicano to the **Grotta del Vento**, above **Fornovolasco**, a huge **cave** extending for hundreds of metres below the Apuan Alps (guided tours every hour, 10.00–12.00, 15.00–18.00; in winter only on fest. days).

In the main valley above Barga is **Castelvecchio Pascoli**. Nearby, on the hill of Caprona is the house where Giovanni Pascoli (1855–1912) lived from 1895 until his death (**open** 10.00–13.00, 14.30 or 15.00–17.00 or 18.30; closed Mon).

Giovanni Pascoli

One of the best known Italian poets, Pascoli was born in Romagna and had a sad childhood. When he bought this house with his sister Maria he was known as a poet and Latinist. He succeeded Giosuè Carducci in the chair of Italian literature at Bologna University. His *I Canti di Castelvecchio* were published in 1903. One of his last public appearances was in 1911 when he talked at the theatre in Barga about the war in Libya. The house has remained as it was at the time of his death with its original furnishings carefully preserved by his sister who survived him by many years and left their house to the Comune of Barga. It contains mementoes and some of the poet's manuscripts. Pascoli and his sister are buried in the chapel in the garden (the tomb was designed by Leonardo Bistolfi).

Castelnuovo di Garfagnana

Castelnuovo di Garfagnana (6500 inhab.) is at the centre of the Garfagnana, situated where the Turrite river meets the Serchio. In Piazza Umberto I are remains of the 13C **Rocca** or governor's palace, the residence in 1522–25 and in 1640–42 of the poets Ludovico Ariosto and Fulvio Testi when they were governors of the district (now used as the town hall).

Via Fulvio Testi leads up past a little piazza—where you can see the recently restored façade of the Rocca—past the local tourist office to the **Duomo**, rebuilt in 1504. In the interior (left wall), *St Joseph and angels*, a beautiful enamelled terracotta altarpiece (attributed to Verrocchio, or the della Robbia); *Madonna and two Saints* attributed to Michele di Ridolfo Ghirlandaio and an *Assumption* by Santi di Tito. In the chapel to the right of the sanctuary, 14C *Crucifix*.

Via Castracani leads down to the old **Porta Miccia** with a bridge (1324) over the Serchio. On the other side of the river, in Via Marconi, is the **Teatro Alfieri**, dating from 1860, by Giovanni Carli), now used as a cinema. There is a street market in Castelnuovo on Thursdays. Near the village is the **Fortezza di Monte Alfonso** (1579). From Castelnuovo a spectacular mountain road leads over the Apuan Alps via Arni (where the road passes through an unpaved tunnel under Monte Altissimo; 1589m) to Massa on the coast (see Ch. 14).

The Parco Regionale delle Alpi Apuane

Castelnuovo is the starting point for excursions to the **regional park of the Apuan Alps**, a protected area since 1985 and interesting for its spectacular mountain scenery between Versilia and the Serchio valley. You can also go hiking and horseback riding (map and information from the Park Office in

Castelnuovo di Garfagnana, ☎ 0583-644242). Most of the hotels are in the comune of Minucciano in the northern part of the park (see listings above). On both sides of the mountain chain are marble quarries. The fauna include wild boar, deer and mountain goats. The highest peak is Monte Pisanino (1946m).

At **Vagli** (about 18km from Castelnuovo) is a large lake formed by the dam of a hydro-electrical plant (1946). Every 10 years or so when the lake is drained (last time in 1994) the borgo of **Fabbriche di Careggine**, founded in the 13C, re-emerges. Near **Campocatino** (*LIPU* wildlife office) are interesting shepherds' huts built with dry-stone walls and slate roofs, once characteristic of this area. Some of them date from the 17C and are being restored. The hermitage of **San Viviano** is perched on an isolated rock nearby.

The Parco dell'Orecchiella

On the other side of the valley is the Parco dell'Orecchiella in the Apennines with meadows in the green upland plains and extensive woods. For hiking and horse-back riding, information and map from the *Comunità Montana* in Castelnuovo di Garfagnana. There are some hotels near **Corfino** (see listings, above).

A road from Castelnuovo follows the left bank of the Serchio past **Sambuca**. Beyond **San Romano in Garfagnano** is **Verrucole** with the spectacular ruins of a castle which belonged to the Gherardenghi. The walls and a tower survive and are being restored. From **Vibbiana** the road continues up to Orecchiella where there is a Visitor's Centre. From here a path leads to a little **botanical garden** with Alpine plants on the **Pania di Corfino** (1300m) (**open** July–Sept 09.00–12.30, 14.30–18.00, or by appointment, ☎ 0583-644911).

From Castelnuovo a road leads north across the Apennines towards Modena and Pievepelago (see *Blue Guide Northern Italy*). It passes **Pieve Fosciana** with a 14C church which contains an enamelled terracotta *Annunciation* by Benedetto Buglioni and **Castiglione di Garfagnana** with its 14C walls. The church preserves a *Madonna* (1389), the only signed work by Giuliano di Simone of Lucca. **Villa Collemandina** has a Romanesque church with two altars by Matteo Civitali.

Another mountain road leads north from Castelnuovo to **San Pellegrino in Alpe** with an interesting local ethnographical **museum**. It occupies 14 rooms of the 12C hospice which served travellers crossing the Apennines, and illustrates peasant life in the area (**open** 09.30–13.00, 14.30–19.00; Oct–May 09.00–12.00, 14.00–17.00; closed Mon). The church has more fine works by Matteo Civitali. A few kilometres above San Pellegrino is the **Focedelle Radici Pass** (1529m), with winter sports facilities.

Higher up the main valley (10km north of Castelnuovo) is **Camporgiano**. The 15C castle contains a museum with an archaeological section and a collection of medieval and Renaissance ceramics (**open** by appointment, ☎ 0583-618888).

A picturesque road continues past **Giuncugnano** beside the pretty upland plain of **Argegna** to the Foce di Carpinelli Pass (842m). It enters the Aulella Valley at Casola in Lunigiana which, with Aulla, is in the province of Massa-Carrara (described in Ch. 14).

13 · Versilia

Versilia, in the province of Lucca, is the name given to the narrow coastal plain at the foot of the splendid Apuan Alps, famous for its beaches which stretch north from the well-known resort of **Viareggio** all the way to **Forte dei Marmi**. In summer the coast is crowded with holiday-makers, many of them from Florence. The little inland town of **Pietrasanta**, as well as **Camaiore** and **Seravezza** are attractive and have buildings of interest.

■ Practical information

Information offices. APT *Versilia*, 10 Viale Carducci, Viareggio (☎ 0584-962233), with information offices at Forte dei Marmi, Lido di Camaiore, and Marina di Pietrasanta, and the railway station of Viareggio (open in summer). The *Comunità Montana Alta Versilia* has its headquarters at Seravezza, where a *Pro Loco* office is also open in summer.

Getting there
By rail. The area is on the main Pisa–Genoa line with stations at Viareggio and Pietrasanta (slow trains only). In Viareggio the railway station is in Piazza Dante.

By bus. A comprehensive network (run by *Lazzi*) serves all the towns in the area. In Viareggio buses from the station (circular service) along the sea-front (Viale Carducci) to Lido di Camaiore and Forte dei Marmi; also inland to Camaiore; from Giardino d'Azeglio to Pisa; to Lucca and Florence; to La Spezia; and to Torre del Lago Puccini. *Lazzi* service in summer to Pisa airport.

By road. The A12 **motorway** follows the coast from Viareggio with exits at Versilia (for Pietrasanta, Forte dei Marmi, and Seravezza).

Hotels
Viareggio has eight ★★★★, eighteen ★★★, and about fifty ★★, and fifty ★ hotels (some of them seasonal). Numerous hotels of all categories in the coastal resorts of Versilia. Information from *APT* offices and *Associazione Albergatori Viareggio*, 1 Via Leonardo da Vinci, Viareggio (☎ 0584-48385).
Forte di Marmi. ★★★ *Astoria Garden*, 10 Via Leonardo da Vinci (☎ 0584-787054; fax 0584-787109).
Pietrasanta. ★★★ *Palagi*, 23 Piazza Carducci (☎ 0584-70249; fax 0584-71198); and numerous hotels of all categories at the coastal resort of Marina di Pietrasanta.

Campsites. Several near Torre del Lago Puccini.

Restaurants
There are restaurants in and around **Viareggio** of all categories, including **£** *La Darsena*.
Forte di Marmi. **££** *Lorenzo* and *Tre Stelle*.
Camaiore. **££** restaurants in the environs include: *Emilio e Bona* at Lombrici; *La Dogana* and *Cavallino Bianco* at Capezzano Pianore, and *Il Vignaccio* at Santa Lucia.
Pietrasanta. **££** *Il Gatto Nero*, *Da Sci* and *Il Fico*.

Golf course. 18-hole *Versilia* at Pietrasanta.

Viareggio
Viareggio (60,000 inhab.) is the main town of Versilia, and the most popular seaside resort on the west coast of Italy. It first became fashionable in the early 19C and it retains an old-fashioned air with its esplanade planted with palm

trees, Art Nouveau houses, and huge old grand hotels and cafés. The **Carnival**, held in the Lenten period preceding Easter (usually at the end of January or in February) is one of the most famous in Italy. The parade of allegorical floats (many of them topical) takes place on Shrove Tuesday and usually the first and second Sunday of February at 14.30, and on the third Sunday of February at 17.30.

Shelley drowned offshore near Viareggio in 1822 (see p. 286). In this century regular visitors to Viareggio have included the poet D'Annunzio, Isadora Duncan the American dancer, the great actress Eleonora Duse, the painters Carlo Carrà and Felice Carena, the writer and philosopher Giovanni Papini, the playwright Luigi Pirandello, and the art historian Roberto Longhi. Since 1929 the **Premio Viareggio** has been awarded annually here for a work of Italian literature.

The town retains its regular plan from the early 19C when it was laid out by Lorenzo Nottolini on a chessboard pattern with long avenues parallel to the seafront and numerous parks. After Paolina Bonaparte built her villa (now the Villa Paolina, see below) on the edge of the sea in 1820 it became one of the first seaside resorts in Europe. Numerous decorative buildings (in Viale Carducci, Via Michelangelo Buonarroti, Via Ugo Foscolo, Via Antonio Fratti, etc.) survive from the Art Nouveau and Art Deco periods, many with frescoes and graffiti as well as external ceramic decoration (much of it by Galileo Chini). Among the architects who worked here were Giovanni Lazzarini, Alfredo Belluomini, and Roberto Narducci.

A splendid double promenade, with a road and a footway, leads along the shore from the **Giardini d'Azeglio** to **Piazza Puccini**. Some old *bagni* (bathing establishments) survive here. At the inner corner of the Giardini d'Azeglio is Piazza Shelley, with a bust of the poet by Urbano Lucchesi (1894). At 2 Via Machiavelli, in the 19C **Villa Paolina** (see above) is the **Museo A.C. Blanc and Pinacoteca Lorenzo Viani** (open 09.00–13.00 except Mon; fest 16.00–19.00; July & Aug 18–24). It contains a prehistoric and archaeological collection, paintings by Lorenzo Viani (1882–1936), born in Viareggio, and the Lucarelli collection of 20C Italian artists, including De Pisis, De Chirico, Guttuso and Carrà.

In Piazza Mazzini the first **Ospizio Marino** survives, built in 1854–61 by Giuseppe Barellai as a model hospital. Beautiful pine-woods extend along the shore in either direction from the town, and there is a distant view of the Apuan Alps. The outer harbour is busy with boat-yards and a 16C tower guards the inner basins where there is a port.

Coastal resorts north of Viareggio

On the coast to the north is **Lido di Camaiore**, another extended bathing resort. It is the first of a series of more or less exclusive resorts which stretch for some thirty kilometres all the way along the coast to Marina di Carrara. They are extremely crowded (mostly with Florentines) in summer. They are laid out on regular plans with long straight roads parallel to the shore and consist of elegant villas and hotels surrounded by gardens. The sea and wide beaches, separated from the road by colourful beach huts, are not as clean as they once were. All the resorts have spectacular views inland to the Apuan Alps (often snow-capped) and white marble quarries.

The most elegant bathing resorts along this stretch of coast are **Forte dei Marmi** and **I Ronchi**, with numerous villas and small hotels set in thick vegetation (although the pine-woods were severely damaged in a tornado in 1977). The beaches are mostly private and have splendid views of the mountains.

In Forte dei Marmi Aldous Huxley wrote *Crome Yellow* in 1921, and two years later, *Antic Hay*. The Molo, a low pier, is the scene of the evening passeggiata. The only high building on the shore is the round Torre Fiat, a skyscraper built as a holiday colony for Fiat employees.

Lago di Massaciuccoli

Torre del Lago Puccini, on the Lago di Massaciuccoli has recently been developed as a holiday resort with numerous campsites. It can be reached from Viareggio along the Viale dei Tigli, a fine avenue of lime trees which borders the **Macchia Lucchese**, a protected area of woods. It can also be reached from Piazza d'Azeglio by bus, or, in summer by boat from Largo Risorgimento.

Torre del Lago Puccini adopted Giacomo Puccini's name because he made his bohemian home on the lake here where he enjoyed shooting waterfowl. The little lakeside resort is now somewhat disturbed by the close proximity of the motorway. On the waterfront, surrounded by a garden, is the **Villa** which Puccini built (guided tours every half hour, 10.00–12.00, 15.00–19.30; winter 10.00–12.00, 15.00–17.30; closed Mon). All his operas except the last, *Turandot*, were, to a great extent, written here. The house preserves mementoes of Puccini (1858–1924) and his tomb is in the chapel. An **opera festival** is held on the lakeside in summer in an open-air theatre. Outside is a bronze statue of Puccini by Paul Troubetzkoy (1925).

It is possible to take **boat trips** (30 minutes; enquire locally) on the lake to visit the marshes. Since 1979 the lake has been part of the **Parco Naturale Migliarino-San Rossore-Massaciuccoli** which protects the coast from Viareggio to Livorno (information from the *Ente Parco Regionale*, 4 Via Aurelia Nord, Pisa, ☎ 050-525211; see also Ch. 16).

The other side of the lake, which is prettier, is reached by the road from Viareggio for Lucca via **Massarosa**. At Quiesa a by-road leads right for the village of **Massaciuccoli**. By the right side of the road, marked by two cedars of Lebanon (yellow signpost) are the unenclosed remains of a **Roman villa** discovered in 1935. It belonged to the Venulei, a Pisan family, in the 2C AD. Above the excavations is a small Antiquarium. A mosaic pavement with fantastic animals made of stone tesserae was lifted and restored in 1987 (for adm. ☎ 0584-93296). On the other side of the road a path (signposted) leads up through olive groves (five minutes' walk) to remains of small **Roman baths** (unenclosed) on the hillside below the church (which can also be reached by car from the Lucca road). There is a fine view of the lake from here.

At the entrance to the village (a few hundred metres from the Roman villa) a road (not signposted) leads down to a canal from the lake beside two picturesque old houses. Beyond two bridges a walkway raised on stilts (beware of broken planks!) continues across the marshes to the lakeside where there are hides and fishing huts.

From Massaciuccoli a roads signposted to Lucca crosses a hill with some disused quarries, and then descends through woods. It passes the conspicuous 14C castle of **Nozzano** (see Ch. 11) Nearby is **Arliano**, with a very ancient pieve, possibly dating from the 8C.

Camaiore

Inland from Viareggio (reached by a road alongside a canal) is Camaiore, a pleasant little town in a fine position, surrounded by the foothills of the Apuan Alps. It is built on a regular plan with long straight streets. The **Collegiata** (1278) has been much altered. In the presbytery is an *Assumption with Saints Peter and Paul* by Benedetto Brandimarti (late 16C). At the end of the left aisle, *Communion of the Apostles* by Piero Dandini, and on the third left altar, 14C wooden *Crucifix*. In the baptistery the font dates from 1387.

Next to the tiny little Romanesque church of **San Michele** are the 17C premises of the Confraternità del Santissimo Sacramento which now houses a **Museo di Arte Sacra** (open in winter on Thurs & Sat 15.30–18.00; fest. 09.00–12.00; in summer, Tues, Thurs & Sat 16.00–19.30, and fest. 09.00–12.00; if closed ring at No. 71). It contains a Flemish *tapestry with the *Last Supper and scenes of the Passion*, dated 1516, on a cartoon by Pieter Pannemaker; fine vestments, church silver, and a wooden statue of the *Virgin Annunciate* (restored) attributed to the 15C Lucchese school (Matteo Civitali?).

Off the Corso is the **Badia di San Pietro**, founded by the Benedictines in the 8C, and rebuilt in the 11C. Outside, a 14C portal survives from the convent walls. The church contains a Baroque altar and remains of a 14C fresco. The approach road from the sea passes the prominent church of the **Francescani**, with an 18C choir and a marble statue over the high altar dating from 1689.

In the environs of Camaiore is the Romanesque **Pieve di San Giovanni Battista e Santo Stefano** which contains a Roman sarcophagus (2C AD), used as a font, and a triptych by Maestro Gerio (1443). In the village of **Nocchi** the church contains a 15C wooden *Crucifix* and a painting of the *Nativity* attributed to Piero Dandini. Other churches worth a visit in the environs towards Viareggio include **Mommio**, **Corsanico** (with a precious organ built by the Venetian Vincenzo Colonna in 1602–06), **Conca di Sotto**, and **Stiava**.

Towards the sea on the road to Massarosa is **Pieve a Elici**. The restored 11C church stands in a beautiful position and contains a sculpted high altar, a stoup and ciborium attributed to Lorenzo Stagi, and a 13C fresco of the *Madonna and Child*.

Pietrasanta

Pietrasanta is the main inland town of Versilia (23,000 inhab.), which has long been famous for its highly skilled marble workers, and for its bronze foundries. Numerous artists come here to study the techniques of sculpture. A pleasant small town, it has retained its interesting plan with four long straight parallel streets which run at right angles through Piazza Duomo. On the outskirts of the town are some old marble works (some dating from the Art Nouveau period).

History. The town was founded by Guiscardo da Pietrasanta, the Podestà of Lucca in 1255, and thrived under the lordship of Castruccio Castracani in 1316–28. In the following centuries its possession was disputed between Genoa, Lucca, and Florence. From the 16C up until c 1820 it declined because of the presence of malaria in the surrounding marshes. Famous natives include the sculptors Lorenzo and Stagio Stagi (1455–1506 and 1496–1563) and Eugenio Barsanti (1821–64), inventor (with Felice Matteucci) of the internal combustion engine.

*Piazza Duomo** has a fine group of buildings and a splendid view of the castle
and town walls climbing a wooded hillside. Behind the monument to the
Grand-duke Leopoldo II (by Vincenzo Santini, 1843) is a column bearing the
Florentine *Marzocco* by Donato Benti, and a wall fountain.

The **Duomo** (or Collegiata di San Martino), first built in 1256 and enlarged in
1330, has a white marble façade with a beautiful rose *window by the Riccomanni, a local family of sculptors. Above the three portals are unusual sculpted
lunettes. The 16C bas-relief of *St John the Baptist* is by Stagio Stagi, and the coat
of arms (1513) is that of the Medici Pope, Leo X. The unfinished brick campanile
is attributed to Donato Benti.

The **interior** has fine marble altars and confessionals. The frescoes in
grisaille are by Luigi Ademollo (1825). The two stoups are by Stagio Stagi, and
the *pulpit** is by Lorenzo Stagi (1504), with a staircase by Andrea Baratta. The
interesting 17C altarpieces in the aisle are in poor condition. At the end of the
south aisle, 15C statue of the *Virgin Annunciate*. In the south transept, *Nativity*
by Piero Dandini. In the handsome chapel to the right of the sanctuary a late
Gothic painting of the *Madonna and Child with Saints John the Evangelist and John
the Baptist* (exhibited only on certain religious festivals) is preserved. On either
side of the sanctuary are two candelabra by Sergio Stagi and two bronze angels
by Ferdinando Tacca. Over the high altar is a *Crucifix*, also by Tacca. The carved
marble *stalls** are also by Stagi. In the north transept, *Madonna of the Rosary*,
by Matteo Rosselli. At the end of the north aisle is an unfinished statuette of *St
John the Baptist* by Stagio Stagi, who also carved the two capitals on the
pilasters of the crossing. The sacristy and baptistery, with an 18C interior,
(opened by the sacristan) are also interesting: one font is by Donato Benti
(1509), the other dates from 1389; a processional Cross dating from 1509 is
kept in the sacristy.

Beyond the campanile is the 16C **Palazzo Moroni** with a pretty staircase. It
houses the **Museo Archeologico Versiliese** (temporarily closed, ☎ 0584-
795288) with local finds from the Neolithic to Roman periods. Another section
has medieval and Renaissance ceramics found since 1970 during the restoration of the convent of Sant'Agostino. The 14C church of **Sant'Agostino**, with
a handsome façade, has been closed for many years. It has been deconsecrated
and is being restored as a hall for concerts and lectures.

The ex-convent and cloisters (entrance to the right) have been restored as a
cultural centre and the seat of the Biblioteca Comunale. Here is the **Museo dei
Bozzetti** (open in summer 18.00–20.00, 21.00–24.00 except Mon; winter
14.30–19.30, except Mon & fest.), with plaster models by various sculptors,
notably Leone Tommasi (1903–65).

Via della Rocca leads up past a few palm trees and the domed bell tower of
Sant'Agostino to the **Rocca di Sala**, on a hillside planted with olive trees. The
fortress was originally built by the Longobards, and reconstructed in 1324 by
Castruccio Castracani. It contains a 15C palace built by Paolo Guinigi. On the
other side of the square is the 18C **theatre**, and at the far end of the square the
Rocca Arrighina can be seen inside the Porta Pisana, near the Torre delle Ore.
A house here has a plaque recording Michelangelo's stay in 1518.

In Via Mazzini (where a plaque marks the house of Stagio Stagi) is the Misericordia, next to the church of **San Biagio**. It contains an altarpiece of the

Madonna enthroned by the local painter Lorenzo Cellini. A statue of *San Biagio* by Francesco da Valdambrino has been removed for restoration.

On the outskirts of Pietrasanta, near the hospital, is the church of **San Salvatore**, founded in 1523. In the cloister are lunettes of the *life of St Francis* by Luigi Ademollo. The long straight Viale Apua leads directly to the sea at Marina di Pietrasanta. It passes the park (right) of **La Versiliana** in Fiumetto, where D'Annunzio stayed at the beginning of the century. Built in 1886, it is now used for plays, concerts and exhibitions.

On the southern outskirts of the town (signposted off the Lucca road by the cemetery) is the by-road for **Valdicastello Carducci**. It passes the **Pieve di Santi Giovanni e Felicità** a very ancient church amid olive trees. It has a fine rose window, and contains an early sarcophagus and 14C frescoes. In the courtyard is a well by Giuseppe Stagi (1559). Valdicastello was the birthplace of the poet Giosuè Carducci (1835–1907). The house can be visited (**open** Sat 09.00–12.00, Sun 15.00–18.00, in summer: Tues–Sun 17.00–20.00). The church contains a marble tabernacle by Stagio Stagi.

Seravezza

Seravezza is attractively situated in a narrow ravine surrounded by high mountains, with numerous quarries and marble works. Michelangelo stayed here while looking for marble suitable for his sculptures in 1517. The tree-lined streets are built along the Versilia river (its waters white from marble) between two bridges.

The **Duomo** (1503; finished in the 17C), on the right bank of the river beside a group of handsome houses, has a castellated campanile and a dome. The wide **interior** has fine marble altars and confessionals. The high altar has a picture of *St Laurence* on the grille in marble inlay. Behind and above it is a marble reliquary and a Cross. In the chapel to the left of the high altar is a font by Stagio Stagi (recently restored).

On the left bank of the river, some way upstream, is **Palazzo Mediceo** built for Cosimo I in 1555 by Ammannati (recently restored). It is now the seat of the **Museo del Lavoro e delle Tradizioni popolari** (open in winter 15.00–19.30 exc Mon; in summer 16.00–22.00 except Mon), with a collection illustrating local crafts, including the extraction and working of marble. The courtyard has a well with a charming fish above it. Opposite the palace is an old marble works.

On the road which leads to the coast is **Vallecchia** with the pieve of Santo Stefano, another ancient church with interesting sculptures including a pulpit by Andrea Baratta (1681), a bas-relief attributed to Donato Benti, and a 14C *Madonna and Child*.

A road leads east from Seravezza along the floor of the Vezza valley past numerous small quarries and some waterfalls. At Ponte Stazzemese a road leads right and climbs through Mulina for **Stazzema**, a climbing centre, in a splendid position at the foot of oddly-shaped mountains. Disastrous flooding and landslides occurred here in 1996.

Just before reaching the village, the road passes the church of **Santa Maria Assunta** (if closed ring at the canonica) on the edge of the hill, preceded by a charming paved forecourt with a porch overlooking the valley. The first church on this site dates from the 9C; it was enlarged in the 13C and 14C. The façade has a fine 15C rose window and interesting old carvings around the door.

The columns in the **interior** have fine capitals, Gothic on the left, and Renaissance on the right. The wood ceiling dates from after 1630. The organ at the west end is attributed to Filippo Tronci (1775). On the west wall is a 16C bas-relief of the *Baptism of Christ*. At the end of the right aisle is a marble statue of *St Anthony Abbot*, attributed to Nicolao Civitali or Leonardo Riccomanni. The high altar dates from 1649 and bears an altarpiece of the *Assumption* attributed to Matteo Rosselli. The tabernacle on the right wall of the sanctuary and fine portal of the sacristy are both attributed to Lorenzo Stagi. On the left wall of the sanctuary is a very unusual painting of the *Assumption*, with angels, saints, and apostles, attributed to a Catalan painter of the 14C–15C.

From outside the church a cobbled path (300m) leads down through woods to the **Santuario del Piastraio** (open only for occasional services, but visible through an open window), with an 18C interior and a painting of the *Madonna del Bell'Amore* (Madonna and Child with the Host and two Evangelists) attributed to a certain Guglielmo Tommasi (1772).

The road ends at the quiet little village of Stazzema, situated on a ridge, with a clock tower of 1739. The people of Stazzema showed particular courage during the German occupation in the last War when 561 civilians were killed by German soldiers in 1944 in the nearby village of **Sant'Anna** (most easily reached from Camaiore). Here the **Museo Storico della Resistenza** (usually **open** 15.00–19.00) is both a memorial to them and a documentation of the Italian Resistance movement.

A by-road leads north from Seravezza via Fabbiano for the hamlet of **Azzano**, passing the 13C pieve of the **Cappella**, in a panoramic position, with a fine rose window on its facade, and an hexagonal ciborium inside. From the terrace there is a view of the marble quarries and Monte Altissimo. Michelangelo is known to have used marble from quarries in this area, and a road and bridge believed to have been constructed in 1518 by the sculptor for the transportation of the marble from the Valle del Serra were identified in 1996.

A by-road off the Stazzema road leads to **Retignano**, where there is another ancient church which contains a font attributed to Donato Benti and carved altars by Lorenzo Stagi (1486) and Benti (1532). The road continues to **Levigliani**, an ancient village and a centre for climbing in the Apuan Alps.

14 · The province of Massa Carrara

The marble quarries above Carrara are world famous. The inhabitants of the small towns of **Massa** and **Carrara**, although they live only a few kilometres apart, are proudly independent of each other. Their province incorporates the whole of the northeast corner of Tuscany, and includes the **Lunigiana** district in the Magra river valley, with a number of castles (many of them being restored) built to defend the Apennine passes and the Via Francigena, as well as the interesting town of Pontremoli, although this area has perhaps more in common with Liguria than with Tuscany.

■ Practical information

Information office. APT *Massa-Carrara*, 24 Lungomare Vespucci, Marina di Massa (☎ 0585-240046), with an information office at Marina di Massa, 77 Via delle Pinete, località Partaccia (☎ 0585-633115), and at Carrara, Viale XX Settembre, località Stadio (☎ 0585-844403).

Getting there
By road. The A12 motorway follows the coast north from Viareggio with exits at Massa and Carrara. It continues through a corner of Liguria to a junction with the motorway spur to La Spezia and the A15 motorway which branches right up the Magra valley in Tuscany for Parma (exits at Aulla and Pontremoli). **Car parking** in Carrara off Via Cavatore, or (with an hourly tariff) in the main squares.

By rail. On the main Pisa–Genoa line with stations at Massa and Carrara (and Sarzana). From Sarzana a secondary line diverges up the Magra valley via Aulla and Pontremoli.

By bus. (*CAT*) **from Carrara** (Via del Cavatore) to Marina di Carrara and the railway station (every 10mins); **to the Fantiscritti quarries** and Colonnata; and to Massa, Fosdinovo, and Pontremoli.

Hotels
Carrara. ★★★ *Michelangelo*, 3 Corso Fratelli Rosselli (☎ 0585-777161; fax 0585-74545). ★★ *Da Roberto*, 5 Via Apuana (☎ 0585-70634); and many more at Marina di Carrara.
Fivizzano. ★★ *Il Giardinetto* (with restaurant), 151 Via Roma (☎ 0585-92060).

Restaurants
Carrara. £ *Roma di Prioreschi*, 1 Piazza Cesare Battisti.
Colonnata. ££ *Locandapuana* and *Venanzio*.
Caniparola. £ *Trattoria dell'Arca*.
Pontremoli. £ *Da Bussè*.

Massa

Massa is a provincial capital at the foot of the narrow Frigido valley, below the Apuan foothills. It has greatly expanded since the Second World War and now has a largely modern aspect (68,000 inhab.). Founded in the Middle Ages, it was the capital of the duchy of Massa-Carrara from 1442 to 1790 ruled by the Malaspina.

Numerous orange and lemon trees were planted here in the early 19C, notably in the central **Piazza degli Aranci**. Here also is a grandiose marble monument with lions and an obelisk dating from 1861, and the huge **Palazzo Cybo Malaspina** with a delightful red façade by Alessandro Bergamini (1701). The courtyard is by Gian Francesco Bergamini (1665).

Duomo

The Duomo, reached by Via Dante Alighieri has an imposing marble façade of 1936. The 18C **interior** was decorated at the end of the 19C. **Right aisle**. The baptistery has an early 15C font by Riccomanni. First altar, Matteo Rosselli (attributed), *Coronation of the Virgin*; third altar, Luigi Garzi (school of Maratta), *Saints John the Evangelist, John the Baptist, Peter, and James*.

Stairs lead down from the right aisle to the funerary **chapel of the Cybo Malaspina** with tomb-slabs of the ducal family and two funerary monuments.

The tomb of *Eleonora Malaspina (d. 1515) by Pietro Aprili (influenced by the monument to Ilaria del Carretto by Jacopo della Quercia in the Duomo of Lucca) was beautifully restored by local craftsmen. The monument to Lorenzo Cybo is by the school of Stagio Stagi.

Right transept. Marble altarpiece in high relief by Andrea and Tommaso Lazzoni (1672). The **Chapel of the Holy Sacrament** (by Giovanni Francesco Bergamini) dates from 1675–94. The fine *altar (1694) was designed by Bergamini to preserve the fresco fragment of the *Madonna and Child* by Pinturicchio (from the Cybo chapel in Santa Maria del Popolo in Rome). Also here is a triptych attributed to Filippo Lippi and a *Nativity* in enamelled terracotta by Benedetto Buglioni. On the **High Altar**, bronze Crucifix and six candlesticks by Ferdinando Tacca. In the **left transept** is a highly venerated wood *Crucifix* of the early 13C. **Left aisle**, third altar, Carlo Maratta, *Immaculate Conception*. There is also an interesting **Museum** containing vestments, church silver and a *Crucifix* by Ferdinando Tacca (**open** only by appointment, ☎ 0585-42643).

The **Rocca** or **Castello Malaspina**, on a high hill, is reached by a narrow (signposted) road. It was first built in the 11C–12C, and the Renaissance palace of the Malaspina family was enlarged in the 16C–17C. A building of the highest architectural interest, it has been closed for many years for restoration (☎ 0585-44774). At its foot, Rocca is the oldest district of Massa, with very narrow streets (but few old houses) and the church of **San Rocco** which has an interesting 16C *Crucifix*, attributed to the local sculptor Felice Palma.

In the modern part of town, towards the sea is the church of **Santa Maria degli Uliveti**. A wooden sculpture of *St Leonard* by Jacopo della Quercia has been removed to the Canonica. There is an **Ethnological Museum** illustrating peasant life over the centuries in the Apuan Alps at No. 85 Via Uliveti (☎ 0585-251330). The church of **San Giacomo Maggiore** in Via Piastronata contains an interesting 15C painting of the *Madonna del Carmine* by the Lombard School. The church of **San Sebastiano** (1957) contains a 17C *Pietà* by Felice Palma.

From Massa, a spectacular mountain road leads over the Apuan Alps via Antona and Arni to Castelnuovo di Garfagnana (see Ch. 12). This was constructed in 1880 to provide access to the quarries on Monte Altissimo.

Just to the south of Massa is the village of **Montignoso** with fine views. Higher up is **Sant'Eustachio** where the church contains a fine small seated statue of the *Madonna and Child* (in wood) attributed to Tino da Camaino, and a beautiful painting by the Florentine school (dated 1424) at the east end of the *Madonna and four saints* and the story of the patron saint in the predella. A marble statue of *St Eustachio* dates from 1906. The marble mosaic high altar and confessionals were made by local people in the 1950s.

A pretty secondary road (the *Strada del Foce*) connects Massa to Carrara across the hills. It crosses woods and quarries and has good views of the mountains.

Carrara

Carrara (67,700 inhab.) is a flourishing town, world famous for its white marble. The earliest record of Carrara's existence dates from 963 when it was given to the bishops of Luni. It then passed into the hands of Lucca and Genoa before becoming part of the duchy of the Malaspina family with Massa in 1442.

It has been known for its marble since Roman times, and is now one of the main centres in the world for marble production. Carrara has also been well known in Italy since the 19C as a centre of the Anarchist movement. A number of interesting old-fashioned shop fronts are preserved in Carrara.

Duomo

The most interesting part of town is around the good Romanesque *Duomo, altered in the 13C when the attractive Gothic storey was added to its façade. In the handsome south wall is a 13C portal; this is the usual entrance. The charming apse and campanile can be seen in the courtyard of the Canonica from which there is a view of the marble quarries in the Apuan Alps.

The well proportioned **interior** has rough marble walls and huge capitals. There are 13C–16C fresco fragments all over the church. **South aisle**. Beyond the first altar is the Arca di San Ceccardo, supported by two 17C putti. Farther on are two charming 14C *statues of the *Annunciation* showing French influence. At the end of the aisle is the altar of the Holy Sacrament, with a *Madonna and Child* by Clemente da Reggio (16C) and in niches on either side, two statues (in very high relief) of *Saints John and Thomas*. The vault is frescoed by Acquilio Bernardino (1518).

On either side of the **presbytery** are fine carved screens. Over the high altar is a painted 14C *Cross by Angelo Puccinelli. The pulpit, decorated with local coloured marbles, dates from 1541. At the end of the **north aisle** the altar of the Assumption has a statue of the *Madonna* attributed to Moschino (17C) and two statues of *Saints Catherine* and *Jerome*. On the north wall, recomposed marble ancona with seated statues of the *Madonna and Child with four saints*, and an interesting 15C bas-relief beneath. Beyond is a small bas-relief which may represent *Countess Matilda of Canossa* crowned as marquis of Tuscany by Pope Gregory VII.

A door leads into the **baptistery** (if closed, admission on request through the sacristy) which contains a large 16C hexagonal font for total immersion, with an unusual little cupola in polychrome marble on top. The other font is another good work of the 16C. At the west end of the north aisle is a fine carved arch over the altar (perhaps by Giroldo da Como) and a *Crucifix* made as a model by Pietro Tacca flanked by two Baroque statues of the *Annunciation*. At the west end of the south aisle is an altar carved in 1869 by Pietro Lazzerini di Tommaso.

The fountain in the piazza with a statue of Andrea Doria was left unfinished by Baccio Bandinelli. Also in the square is a red house (plaque) believed to have sheltered Michelangelo on his visits to buy marble.

The pretty, narrow **Via Santa Maria** leads away from the Duomo passing some interesting old doorways; at No. 14, the unusual **Casa Repetti** has animal reliefs and little slender columns. It ends in front of the 17C church of the **Carmine** by a monument to Mazzini (1892) and the pink 17C façade of a palace, now the seat of the **Accademia di Belle Arti**, entered from the other side, where it incorporates the medieval Malaspina castle (restored). On the lawn outside is a small statue of *Pietro Tacca* by Carlo Fontana (1900). A carved Roman marble relief (now very worn) found in the quarries of Fantiscritti with the signatures of Giambologna (1598) and Canova (1800) is at present in the courtyard (**adm**. sometimes on request). The pleasant Piazza Gramsci, adjoining the Accademia, has trees (including palms) and views of the hills and quarries.

Via Giorgi leads down to the handsome **Piazza Alberica** with some fine red 17C palaces, and a white marble pavement. An interesting old road runs along the Carrione stream, just out of the square. In the nearby Piazza Garibaldi is the neo-classical **Teatro degli Animosi** by Giuseppe Pardini (1840).

From Piazza Gramsci Via Roma leads straight down to the 19C **Piazza Matteotti** with evergreen trees, and the monumental **Politeama Verdi** (1892). In Via Verdi, on the corner of Via Pelliccia, is an amusing mushroom coloured Art Nouveau building (No. 16). In Via Mazzini is the delightful marble **post office** designed in 1932 by the local architect Giuseppe Boni (with decorations by Sergio Vatteroni).

A long straight avenue (Viale XX Settembre) connects Carrara with **Marina di Carrara** a marble shipping port and resort. It passes a modern building which houses the **Museo Civico del Marmo** (open 08.30–13.30; 10.00–17.00 or 20.00 in summer), an exhibition illustrating marble quarrying and craftsmanship. Outside the cemetery of Turigliano, in a pleasant little garden, a colossal white marble monolith by Sergio Signori (left unfinished at the sculptor's death in 1990) bears a dedication to Gaetano Bresci from the Anarchists. Bresci assassinated King Umberto I in 1900 and died a year later in prison.

Carrara marble

Up until the end of the last century marble was extracted from the mountainside by hand. Wooden wedges were inserted along the natural fissures in the marble. By keeping these wet they would swell and eventually the block of marble would fracture. A handsaw was also used, together with water and sand, by two workers, who were able to cut into the marble at a rate of about 5cm a day. A radical change in quarrying methods occurred at the end of the last century when steel wire, several hundred metres long, was introduced. This, still with the help of sand and water, can cut into the marble at a rate of c 10–20cm an hour. Diamond wire and diamond point saws are now also widely used. The dangerous quarrying techniques used in the last twenty years, which pay little attention to the geological structure of the mountains, have been criticised, and fatal accidents, caused by landslides occur every year.

In the past, once the blocks were extracted, they used to be sent down the mountainside on a slide using ropes and wooden rollers, and then transported by wagons drawn by up to ten bullocks in pairs. A railway was constructed between 1876 and 1891 from the quarries to Marina di Carrara. This is no longer used, but the track which traverses tunnels and the high Ponte di Vara has been converted into a road which is now used by the lorries which climb up into the quarries on rough roads to pick up the marble. It is then transported either to Marina di Carrara for shipping, or to one of the numerous saw mills in and around the town which cut up the marble into slabs and polish it before exportation.

The marble quarries

The famous marble quarries in the Apuan Alps which have been worked for over 2000 years are well worth a visit (information from the Carrara *APT* office, ☎ 0585-844403). They produce about one-and-a-half million tons of white marble a year, and over 95 quarries are now in use. They are situated in three valleys: **Colonnata**, **Fantiscritti** and **Ravaccione**. They can all be reached by road (signposted from Carrara). There is a bus from Carrara to Colonnata six times a day (three on fest.), and to Fantiscritti (Ponte di Vara) on weekdays (four times a day). The quarries of Fantiscritti are perhaps the most interesting, since they are approached past the Ponte di Vara, the old railway bridge, and there is a good museum (see below).

There is a delightful private outdoor **museum** (open daily) by the Fantiscritti quarries which illustrates the history of marble quarrying by means of instruments and tools and remarkable life-size sculptures in marble. From here rough roads lead up through the quarry, and another road follows the old railway tunnel to the Ravaccione quarries.

A beautiful minor road connects Carrara with Fosdinovo, traversing wooded hillsides with views towards the Apuan Alps, and then towards the sea. A by-road leads further inland to **Campo Cecina** (1300m), in the Apuan Alps with a fine panorama of the marble quarries.

Fosdinovo

Fosdinovo is a medieval fortified borgo on the border between Tuscany and Liguria. It is in a beautiful position on a hill top with views of the Apuan Alps, the valley of the Magra, and the gulf of La Spezia. It became a feudal stronghold of the Malaspina family in 1340 and they remained here until 1820.

Since 1867 the **castle** has been owned by the Malaspina-Torrigiani family. It probably dates from before the 13C, and was well restored in 1997 (usually **open** for a guided tour of c 30 mins 10.00–12.00, 15.00–17.00 except Tues ☎ 0187-68891). In 1981 much of the furniture was stolen. The most interesting rooms are the tiny **Camera di Dante** where the poet is supposed to have stayed as a guest in 1306, which has a frescoed niche of *Christ in Pietà* with the kneeling figure of a Malatesta crusader, and the **great hall** with frescoes illustrating Dante's visit by Gaetano Bianchi (1882). From the enclosed loggia there is a fine view of the village and the plain which extends towards the sea. The **battle-ments** can also be visited. Exhibited in various rooms of the castle are: 16C–19C arms and armour, a peacock from a 17C merry-go-round, Montelupo ceramics, and coins minted in Fosdinovo in 1661–69.

From the castle a narrow paved street runs through the borgo to the parish church of **San Remigio**, which has a pleasant grey-and-white interior with colourful Baroque marble altars. On the right side, *Madonna* (second altar) and a bas-relief of the *Liberation of Souls from Purgatory* (last altar), both by Giovanni Baratta. The choir has carved wooden stalls, and on the east wall, high up in a niche, is a seated *statue of *St Remigio* (c 1300). At the end of the left side, funerary monument to Galeotto Malaspina (d. 1367) with his effigy (fully armed) beneath a Gothic canopy. On the west wall are two interesting small bas-reliefs, and near the door the 16C font. A few steps lead down from the east end to the **Oratorio del Santissimo Sacramento**, with more elaborate, well-carved marble altars and a 17C wooden *Crucifix*.

Just beyond San Remigio, preceded by a marble balustrade and pavement, is the unusual white marble façade (1666) of the **Oratorio dei Bianchi**. The 14C polychrome wood statue of the *Virgin Annunciate* which belongs to the church is at present shown in San Remigio only on 25 March and 8 September.

The road which winds down past olive groves from Fosdinovo towards the sea passes through an ancient archway at **Caniparola** where the handsome Villa Malaspina, with a pretty garden, dates in its present form from 1724. Places of great interest nearby which form part of Lunigiana, include Castelnuovo Magra, Luni, and Santo Stefano di Magra, all described, together with Sarzana, the gulf of La Spezia and the rest of Liguria, in *Blue Guide Northern Italy*.

Northeast of Fosdinovo is the valley of the Aulella with the ancient **Pieve di Codiponte**, **Casola in Lunigiana** with a local ethnographical museum (**open** 09.00–12.00, 16.00–19.00 except Mon; winter 09.00–13.00), and the little spa of **Equi**. Beyond **Giuncugnano** is the valley of the Garfagnana, described in Ch. 12.

Farther north is **Fivizzano** a small town enclosed in ramparts by Cosimo I de' Medici. Nearby is the 14C castle of Verrucola. It is on the road via the Passo del Cerreto (1261m) which leads to Reggio Emilia (see *Blue Guide Northern Italy*).

Aulla is in the Magra valley, in the district known as the **Lunigiana**, named after the Roman city of Luni, in Liguria (it now covers the province of Massa Carrara and most of that of La Spezia). The town lies at the foot of the picturesque 16C fort of **Brunella**. At the beginning of this century the castle was bought by Lina Duff Gordon, the journalist, and her husband Aubrey Waterfield, painter and gardener. Waterfield created a remarkable roof-garden on the ramparts. They were visited here by D.H. Lawrence and Rex Whistler. They had to restore the castle after its occupation in the Second World War by German forces. A vivid description of life at the castle is given by Kinta Beevor, the Waterfields' daughter, in *A Tuscan Childhood* (1993). The ground floor now contains a natural history museum and botanical garden related to the Lunigiana (**open** 09.00–12.00, 15.00 or 16.00–18.00 or 19.00, except Mon). **Villafranca in Lunigiana** has a local ethnographical museum in an old mill (**open** 09.00–12.00, 15.00 or 16.00–18.00 or 19.00 except Mon).

Pontremoli

Pontremoli, a pleasant little town with some 17C and 18C palaces, lies in a strategic position among the chestnut-clad foothills of the Apennines. There was a castle here in 990, and a medieval borgo grew up between the Magra and Verde rivers.

Via Cavour and Via Mazzini cross the town from the Porta Parma to the Porta Fiorentina on the line of the ancient Via Francigena to Rome (see p. 423). The central **Piazza della Repubblica** is separated from Piazza Duomo by a clock tower. Here is the Municipio with a portico (and the tourist information office in the courtyard), and the fine **Palazzo Pavesi** (No. 1; 1734–43) attributed to Giambattista Natali. Opposite the town hall is the 18C Pretura (local magistrate's court).

The **Duomo** was built by Alessandro Capra in 1636–87. The **façade** by Vincenzo Micheli dates from 1881, with a lunette mosaic by Annibale Gatti and two statues by Antonio Bucci of Seravezza. The bronze doors are by Riccardo Rossi of Carrara (1965).

The elaborate **interior**, hung with chandeliers, has gilding and stuccowork, and marble altars and confessionals. The first north chapel has a 17C altarpiece and a 16C painting of the *Madonna enthroned*. In the sanctuary are four 18C paintings by Giuseppe Bottani, Giuseppe Peroni, Giovanni Domenico Ferretti, and Vincenzo Meucci. In the south transept is an elaborate carved altar by Lorenzo Franzoni (1808) and in the north transept, an altar dating from 1654 and a painting by Pierre Subleyras (in very poor condition). On the left wall is a 19C *Deposition* by Giuseppe Collignon. In the spandrels of the dome are 19C frescoes of the *Evangelists* by Giovanni Gaibazzi. The chapel of the Holy Sacrament, on the right of the presbytery, is a fine work of 1828.

Opposite the Duomo is the neo-classical **Palazzo del Vescovo** (bishop's palace), with an outside staircase. The winding Via Garibaldi leads gently up to Porta Parma past a series of handsome doorways and several Baroque palaces.

On the left, Vicolo del Piagnaro, a lovely old lane, continues up past some old houses to the **Castello del Piagnaro** with the **Museo delle Statue-Stele** (open 09.00–12.00, 14.00–17.00; summer 09.00–12.00, 16.00–19.00; closed Mon), a museum of menhirs found in the Lunigiana. The castle, founded in the 10C was enlarged in the 14C and destroyed several times. In the Middle Ages it was of fundamental importance to the defence of the Via Francigena (or *Strada della Cisa*; see p. 423) on the stretch of the road across the Apennines from Emilia into Tuscany. It contains a collection of remarkable menhirs of the Lunigiana cult found over the last two centuries in the Magra valley. Fifty-nine of these megaliths, which date from prehistoric times up to the Roman era (but mostly from the Bronze Age), have been found in Lunigiana in the last 100 years or so, and the museum provides a complete documentation of them all. These stone cult images, most

A menhir in the museum at Pontremoli

in the form of warriors with arms or female figures, were found scattered over a large area, not in stone circles nor alignments, nor near burials, and their origins are still being studied. The original ones are displayed in Room III, while rooms V and VI contain casts of the others.

Just out of Piazza Duomo (see above), off Via Garibaldi, Via della Cresa leads beneath some arches to the narrow old **Ponte della Cresa** across the Verde river. Via Ricci Armani continues from Piazza della Repubblica past (left) **Palazzo Dosi** dating from the early 18C by Giovanni Battista Natali, with a courtyard, to Via Cavour with a Baroque palace at No. 15. At the end are some fortifications by the Ponte del Casotto. The bridge leads across the Verde river to a lane which continues to the church of **San Francesco** (marked by its Romanesque campanile). The unusual and attractive entrance portico is by Giovanni Battista Natali (1740). The church contains a fine painting of the *Ecstasy of St Francis* by Gianbettino Cignaroli (18C) on the east wall, and a lovely relief on the second left altar attributed to Agostino di Duccio. The unusual composition shows a half-figure of the *Madonna* with the Child lying in front of her, and a frame of cherubs' heads.

From the end of Via Cavour, opposite a palace with a pretty double loggia in the courtyard and a palm tree, Ponte Battisti (rebuilt after the War) leads across the Magra beneath an arch which connects the the old stone **Castelnuovo** (12C–14C) to the bright orange church of **Nostra Donna**, a fine rococo building built by Giovanni Battista Natali (1738) at present closed for restoration. It contains frescoes by Sebastiano Galeotti, and altarpieces by Alessandro Gherardini and Giuseppe Galeotti. In the piazzetta is the Teatro della Rosa.

Via Mazzini runs parallel to the Magra past a pink palazzo with statuary on the balconies. At No. 30 is the office of the *Comunità Montana della Lunigiana*.

Beyond Piazza Dodi begins Via Pietro Cocchi where at No. 7 is Palazzo Damiani (18C; in very poor repair) and at No. 24 is a neo-classical palace (1807).

On the southern outskirts of the little town is the church of the **Annunziata** (for adm. ring at priest's house nearby), with an unusual tall façade (1937). It contains an octagonal tabernacle attributed to Jacopo Sansovino (1527), and paintings by Luca Cambiaso. The chapel of San Niccolò is decorated by Giovanni Battista Natali, and the sacristy has a vault painted by Francesco Natali and carved benches and cupboards by Francesco Battaglia (1676).

15 · Pisa

Pisa (104,300 inhab.), standing on the Arno a few miles from its mouth, is famous for its beautiful Piazza del Duomo, with the Cathedral, Leaning Tower, and Baptistery. The building of these splendid monuments was begun in the 11C and 12C when Pisa was a great maritime Republic. In the 13C and early 14C Nicola Pisano and his son Giovanni decorated both the inside and outside of the Duomo and Baptistery with their remarkable sculptures. Pisa has a flourishing university (founded in the 14C) as well as the renowned Scuola Normale university college. The Lungarni along the two banks of the river, lined with some fine palaces, are still a special feature of the town (and the seagulls on the Arno are a reminder of its proximity to the sea).

■ Practical information
Information offices. APT (Pl. 15), 26 Via Benedetto Croce (☎ 050-40096). Information offices beside Piazza del Duomo (Pl. 2: ☎ 050-560464), and at the main railway station, and the airport.

Airport. *Galileo Galilei*, 3km south of the centre of the city, for flights to London Gatwick, Manchester, Glasgow, Dublin, Munich, Barcelona, and Paris (and, since 1999, New York via Venice) and internal flights to Rome, Milan, Naples, Sardinia, Sicily, and Elba (☎ 050-500707).

Airport railway station (*Pisa Aeroporto*) with express **train** services (1 hr) via *Pisa centrale* station to Florence (where there is an air terminal in the station).

SITA **bus services** also from the airport to Florence in 1 hr. Bus no. 7 from the airport to *Pisa centrale* station.

Railway stations. *Centrale* (just beyond Pl. 15), Viale Gramsci for all services, one of the main railway junctions in central Italy, with services to Florence, Genoa, Turin, and Milan, and to Grosseto and Rome. For buses to the centre of the city, see below. *Pisa Aeroporto* with services via *Pisa centrale* to Florence. *San Rossore* (Pl. 1) served by all trains on the Lucca line and a few slow trains on the La Spezia line.

Town buses. **No. 1** from the central railway station via Ponte Solferino, Lungarno Simonelli, Via Bonanno Pisano and Piazza Manin to Piazza del Duomo. From the Duomo it returns to the Station via Via Santa Maria, Lungarno Pacinotti, Ponte di Mezzo, and Via Mazzini. **No. 7** from the central railway station to the airport.
From the railway station, the most pleasant route **on foot** to Piazza del Duomo (a walk of about 30 minutes) is via Viale Gramsci, Corso Italia, Ponte di Mezzo, Borgo Stretto, Via Ulisse Dini, Piazza Cavalieri, Via dei Mille, and Via Santa Maria.

Country buses run by the *Consorzio Pisano Trasporti* from Piazza Sant'Antonio (Pl. 14) for Volterra, the coast, and places within the province of Pisa. *Lazzi* from Piazza

Vittorio Emanuele for Lucca, Florence, Livorno, Versilia, and other places in Tuscany.

Hotels

★★★★ *Grand Hotel Duomo,* 94 Via Santa Maria (Pl.2;*1*: ☎ 050-561894, fax 050-560418); *Jolly Hotel Cavalieri,* 2 Piazza della Stazione (south of Pl. 15: ☎ 050-43290, fax 050-502242); *D'Azeglio,* 18 Piazza Vittorio Emanuele (Pl.14;*3*: ☎ 050-500310, fax 050-28017).

★★★ *Villa Kinzica,* 4 Piazza Arcivescovado (Pl. 3; 4: ☎ 050-560419, fax 050-551204); *Royal-Victoria,* 12 Lungarno Pacinotti (Pl.11;*2*: ☎ 050-940111, fax 050-940180).

★★ *Amalfitana,* 44 Via Roma (Pl. 6;*6*: ☎ 050-29000, fax 050-25218); *Villa Primavera,* 43 Via Bonanno Pisano (Pl. 5;*7*: ☎ 050-23537, fax 050-27020).

Campsite. *Torre Pendente,* 86 Viale delle Cascine (☎ 050-561704; beyond Pl 1: open Apr–Oct).

Restaurants

£££ *Il Ristoro della Faggiola,* 1 Via della Faggiola (☎ 050-552725); *Ristoro dei Vecchi Macelli,* 49 Via Volturno (☎ 050-20424).

££ *Kostas,* 39 Via del Borghetto (Greek food), (☎ 050-571467); *Osteria dei Cavalieri,* 16 Via San Frediano (☎ 050-580858); *Alle Bandierine,* 4 Via Mercanti (☎ 050-500000); *La Mescita,* 2 Via Cavalca (☎ 050-598667); *Turiddo,* 12 Piazza S. Frediano (☎ 050-580600); *Salza,* 44 Borgo Stretto (☎ 050-580144); *Bruno,* 12 Via Luigi Bianchi (☎ 050-560818); *La Grotta,* 103 Via S. Francesco (☎ 050-578105).

£ (including self-service restaurants and pizzerie): *Ambarabà,* Via Cavalca; *Il Montino,* 1 Vicolo del Monte (☎ 050-598695); *Castelletto,* 12 Via del Castelletto; *Da Matteo,* 46 Via l'Arancio.

Places to picnic include the Giardino Scotto in the Fortezza Nuova (Pl. 16), Piazza San Paolo a Ripa d'Arno (Pl. 14), the area near the Cittadella and Arsenal (Pl. 9), and Piazza Martiri della Libertà (Pl. 7).

Annual Festival. In June, the *Festa di San Ranieri*, commemorating the patron saint of the city, St Ranieri (1117–60), is celebrated with candle-light festivities on the Arno and the *Gioco del Ponte*, a sham fight on the Ponte di Mezzo between the people living on either side of the Arno (the *Tramontana* and *Mezzogiorno*). Formerly the contestants were protected in armour for the fight to gain possession of the bridge, but since 1947 it has become a battle of strength with a cart in the centre of the bridge which is pushed from one side to the other. The combatants wear 16C–17C costumes and the day ends with a procession of both parties. As one of the historic Italian Marine Republics, together with Genoa, Venice, and Amalfi, a *Regatta* is held here every four years.

History. The origins of the city are uncertain, but the site near the sea seems to have been settled by at least 1000 BC. An Etruscan town, it expanded in the 4C BC and became a Roman colony from the 2C BC, when, situated on a lagoon, it was a naval and commercial port. Roman boats were excavated near the station of San Rossore in 1999. It continued to flourish under the Lombards in the 7C and 8C. By the 11C Pisa had become a maritime republic, rivalling Genoa, Amalfi, and Venice. Constantly at war with the Saracens, Pisa captured from them Corsica, Sardinia, and the Balearic Isles (1050–1100), and at the same time combined war and trade in the East. The wealth of the Pisans was proverbial. In 1135, assisting Pope Innocent II against Roger of Sicily, Pisa destroyed Amalfi. It subsequently joined the Ghibelline party, and remained proudly faithful to it, even though surrounded by Guelf republics such as Florence, Lucca and Genoa. The 12C was the period of her greatest splendour when she was one of the most important cities in Europe.

But in 1284 Pisa was defeated by the Genoese in the naval battle of Meloria and lost her maritime supremacy; from then onwards the city had to submit to a succession of lordships, including those of the Gherardesca family (1316–41) and of Gian Galeazzo Visconti of Milan (1396–1405). The Florentines gained possession of Pisa in 1406, and after one or two unsuccessful efforts at rebellion it became a quiet refuge of scholars and artists, a university having been established in the city in 1343 by Pope Clement VI. When Charles VIII entered Italy in 1494 he was expected to restore Pisa's liberty, but he broke his promise, and Florence took final possession of the city in 1509.

In 1944 the town was bombarded by both German and Allied artillery; the Camposanto and the area near the station suffered worst, and further damage was caused when all the bridges were blown up. Disappointing and disorderly reconstruction work resulted in an unusually high number of unattractive buildings in various parts of the town.

The most illustrious native of Pisa is Galileo Galileo (1564–1642), physicist and astronomer. The mathematician Leonardo Fibonacci (1165–1235) and Titta Ruffo (1877–1953), the famous baritone, were also born here.

British writers in 19C Pisa

In the 19C, the mild marine climate of the town was thought to have been good for those suffering from tuberculosis, and a small English colony was established here. In 1814 Margaret Jane King (Lady Mountcashell) from Ireland, settled here with George William Tighe whom she had met in Rome on the Grand Tour, and they lived for the rest of their lives under the assumed names of Mr and Mrs Mason. Her governess had been Mary Wollstonecraft (1759–97), author of *Vindication of the Rights of Woman* (1792) and mother of Mary Godwin, future wife of Shelley, and she became known for her educational and childrens' books. She also founded the *Accademia dei Lunatici* in Pisa, which was attended in 1927 by the famous Italian poet Giacomo Leopardi when he spent a happy year in the town. Mrs Mason saw much of the Shelleys when they were staying in Pisa at Palazzo Scotto in 1820–22. Shelley wrote *Epipsychidion*, inspired by the Contessa Emilia Viviani, and *Adonais* during his stay here. A descendent of the Tighes discovered an unknown manuscript by Mary Shelley in the attic of her house in 1998 (*Maurice or the Fisher's Cot*, published in the same year).

Mary Wollstonecraft's husband, William Godwin, subsequently married Mrs Clairmont whose daughter Claire, by her first marriage, bore a daughter, Allegra, to Lord Byron in 1817. In 1821 Byron also took up residence in Pisa, in the Palazzo Lanfranchi, with his last mistress Countess Teresa Gamba Guiccioli. In 1822 Leigh Hunt brought his family to stay at Palazzo Lanfranchi and together with Byron and Shelley they published the radical journal called *The Liberal*. An English literary periodical called *The Ausonian* was issued in Pisa in 1827–28 (but was soon repressed because of its radical social views). In 1846 Browning brought his bride to Pisa, before they settled in Florence.

Piazza del Duomo

**Piazza del Duomo, or *Campo dei Miracoli* (Pl. 2), with its bright marble monuments, is one of the most remarkable sights in Italy. The splendid Romanesque buildings of the Cathedral, Baptistery, and Campanile (Leaning Tower) are spaciously laid out in a rational arrangement and superbly set off by the green lawns between them. They are enclosed to the north by the Camposanto and the crenellated city walls in an almost rural setting. The piazza lies well northwest of the centre of the city and, unlike most other Italian cathedral towns, it does not provide the focus of city life.

■ Admission. The **Baptistery, Camposanto, Museo delle Sinopie** and **Museo dell'Opera del Duomo** remain open throughout the day, 09.00–dusk (08.00–19.40 in summer). The **Duomo** is open 10.00–12.45, 15.00–dusk. The **Campanile** is not at present open to the public.

There are admission charges for all of the above (except for the Duomo in Nov–Feb, when it is free), and there are **inclusive tickets** for 5, 4 or 2 of them. The ticket for the Duomo has to be bought in one of the museums or at the offices of the Opera del Duomo, just north of the Duomo.

In the vicinity of the piazza are a **tourist information office**, **WCs**, and numerous souvenir stalls.

Duomo

The *Duomo (Pl. 2), begun by a certain Buscheto in 1063, and continued by Rainaldo (both of them only known as working on this building), is one of the most celebrated Romanesque buildings in Italy, and the prototype of the Pisan style of architecture in which a strong classicism survives. It was restored in 1602–16 after a serious fire in 1595.

The building stands on a white marble pavement and is covered inside and out with black-and-white marble, toned on the exterior to a delicate grey and russet. The *façade* shows four tiers of columns with open galleries, with a row of seven tall arches below. In the left-hand arch is the tomb of Buscheto.

The bronze doors were remodelled after the fire by various sculptors of the school of Giambologna. Outside the south transept is a copy made in 1930 of a beautiful Greek vase (original in the Camposanto). The entrance is usually at the east end near the Leaning Tower, through the **Portale di San Ranieri** which has bronze *doors by Bonanno da Pisa (1180). Above is a lunette with a 15C *Madonna and Child and two angels* by Andrea di Francesco Guardi.

The cruciform **interior** (admission, see above) is over 94.5m long and 32m wide (72m across the exceptionally deep transepts). The 68 pillars have 11C capitals in imitation of classical ones. The coffered, gilded ceiling of the nave was remodelled after 1596. Some of the small stained glass windows (restored in 1947–48) are attributed to Alesso Baldovinetti.

The two stoups (1) bear statues by Felice Palma (1621), perhaps on a design by Giambologna. **West wall**. The tomb of Archbishop Matteo Rinuccini (d. 1852; 2) incorporates a *Crucifix* by Pietro Tacca. The 14C fresco of the *Crucifixion* (3) is attributed to Bernardo Falconi. The Frosini funerary monument (4) has a bas-relief of the *Deposition* by Giovanni Battista Vaccà (1702).

On the walls of the **south aisle**, between the altars, are hung a series of large 18C canvases, all of them labelled. Some of the altarpieces in this aisle have been removed for restoration. First altar (5), Cristofano Allori, *Madonna and Saints* (1610; perhaps completed by Zanobi Rosi in 1626); **second altar** (6) Francesco Vanni, *Disputation of the Holy Sacrament* (with a figure on the left attributed to Annibale Carracci); **third altar** (7) Andrea del Sarto and Giovanni Antonio Sogliani, *Madonna delle Grazie.* Beyond a historical painting (8) by Sebastiano Conca, the **fourth altar** (9) has a carved lunette of *God the Father* by Bartolomeo Ammannati.

South transept. On the first altar (10), carved by Stagio Stagi, *Madonna and Child with Saints* by Giovanni Antonio Sogliani and Perin del Vaga. The two early 18C paintings (11, 12) are by Domenico Muratori and Benedetto Luti. The **Chapel of San Ranieri** (13) Pisa's patron saint (1117–60) has 17C sculptures by Francesco Mosca, and a marble and bronze coffer by Giovanni Battista Foggini which contains the remains of the saint. The *tomb of the Emperor Henry VII (14) was sculpted by Tino da Camaino (1315) with a fine effigy (it has been partly reassembled here; other statues are in the Museo dell'Opera del Duomo). The Renaissance altar (15) was carved by Pandolfo Fancelli. On the altar right of the choir (16), *Christ on the Cross* by Giovanni Bilivert.

Beneath the oval dome, frescoed by Orazio Riminaldi (1627) are remains of a Cosmatesque pavement with marble inlay; another fragment, discovered near the high altar in 1977, may date from the end of the 11C. In the centre of the outside face of the triumphal arch is a large 14C fresco of the *Madonna and Child* attributed to the Master of San Torpè. The balustrade at the entrance to the **choir** bears two bronze angels by Giambologna and assistants (1602). The wooden throne and benches have good marquetry work. The stalls (15C) were reconstructed in 1616 from what survived of the fire. On the entrance piers, in rich frames, are a delightful *St Agnes (17) by Andrea del Sarto and a *Madonna* by Giovanni Antonio Sogliani. The marble lectern and candelabra are by Matteo Civitali. On the walls beneath the cantoria are paintings by Andrea Del Sarto: *Saints John, Peter, Margaret* and *Catherine.* The *Crucifix* on the high altar is by Giambologna; the angel on the column to the left is by Stoldo Lorenzi (1483).

Round the **apse** (admission only with special permission, but now well lit):

PISA DUOMO

20 19
17 16
Entrance
Portale di San Ranieri
15 14
21 13
22
10 11 12
23 18 9
8
7
24
6
25
1 1
5
26 2 3 4

0 metres   100   200

Sodoma, *Descent from the Cross* (1540) and *Sacrifice of Abraham* (1542); works by Sogliani, and Beccafumi. On the intrados of the apse arch are frescoed angels by Domenico Ghirlandaio (restored). In the apse is a fine **mosaic**, the *Redeemer enthroned between the Madonna and St John the Evangelist*, a 13C work completed by Cimabue in 1302.

The ***pulpit** in the nave (18) by Giovanni Pisano (1302–11; perhaps with the assistance of Tino da Camaino), removed in 1599 after the fire, was reconstructed in 1926. It is a masterpiece of Gothic sculpture. The columns, on plain

Detail of the Portale di San Ranieri, the Duomo, Pisa

bases, resting on lions, or carved into figure sculpture, have statues of sibyls above the capitals, and florid architraves. Above, deeply carved relief panels representing scenes from the New Testament are separated by figures of prophets. The bronze *lamp hanging over the nave, supposed to have suggested to Galileo the principle of the pendulum, was in fact cast by Battista Lorenzi in 1587, six years after the discovery. It was restored in 1998 and exhibited temporarily at the beginning of the nave.

On the altar to the left of the presbytery (19) is a much venerated 13C painting of the *Madonna* to which the Pisans are traditionally supposed to have turned in times of trouble since 1225. The painting of the *Birth of the Virgin* (20) is by Corrado Giaquinto.

North transept. Funerary monument of Archbishop d'Elci by Vaccà (1742). In the Cappella del Sacramento (21), bronze and silver ciborium by Giovanni Battista Foggini (1685), and sculptures by Chiarissimo Fancelli (1625) and Francesco Mosca (c 1563). In the arch high above (difficult to see) is a mosaic of the *Annunciation* attributed to Gaddo Gaddi. On the altar (22), carved by Stagio Stagi is a Miracle of Christ by Aurelio Lomi.

The **north aisle** is hung with more large 18C paintings (all labelled). Fourth altar (23), 16C bas-relief in the lunette of the *Madonna appearing to St Ranieri*; third altar (24), Ventura Salimbeni, *God the Father and Saints*; second altar (25) Passignano, *Holy Spirit and martyrs*; first altar (26), Giovanni Battista Paggi, *Christ on the Cross and Saints*.

The Campanile

Superbly sited at the east end of the cathedral rises the *campanile, the famous **Leaning Tower** (Pl. 2). It is a beautiful work, circular in plan with eight storeys of round arches, six open galleries, and a bell-chamber of smaller diameter. The tower, 54.5m high, leans 4.5m out of the perpendicular. It is one of the most original bell-towers in Italy, apart from its marked inclination which has accounted for its world-wide fame. It has been closed to the public since 1990 for safety and conservation reasons.

Begun in 1173, the tower was only 10.5m high when a subsidence of the soil threw it out of the perpendicular. During the 13C the architect in charge appears to have been Giovanni di Simone, who endeavoured to rectify the inclination as the building proceeded. By 1301 the building had risen as far as the bellchamber, and Tommaso di Andrea da Pontedera completed the tower in the late 14C as it now stands. A spiral staircase (294 steps) leads to the top (splendid *view). Up until a few years ago the lean had been increasing by c 1mm a year, so in 1992 steel cables were inserted around the base of the tower, and between the first and second galleries. In 1998, after years of debate, it was decided to 'anchor' the tower with two steel cables and carry out a complicated operation on the subsoil in an attempt to stabilise the foundations. Excavations at the foot of the tower since 1980 have revealed remains of Etruscan and Roman buildings.

Galileo, according to his pupil Vincenzio Viviani, carried out experiments from the tower to provide an ocular demonstration to members of Pisa university that all falling bodies independent of their size, descend with equal velocity.

Sculptors of Pisa

Nicola Pisano (c 1200–80) had a profound influence on the development of sculpture in Italy. His works mark a break with medieval art and contain a new Gothic realism and narrative style which point the way forward to the Renaissance.

Nicola was probably a native of Puglia in Southern Italy but lived most of his life in Pisa where his first known work is the Baptistery pulpit. The only other two sculptures certainly by his hand are the pulpit in Siena cathedral (1268) and the Fontana Maggiore (the fountain outside the cathedral) in Perugia (1278).

For these last two commissions he was assisted by his son **Giovanni Pisano** who later carved two more splendid pulpits of exquisite workmanship, one in the church of Sant'Andrea in Pistoia (1301), and the other, the most sumptuous of all, in the Duomo of Pisa (1302–11). Giovanni, who also worked for some ten years as a sculptor for Siena cathedral, is also recognised as having had a fundamental influence on Italian sculpture.

Later in the 14C two more important sculptors were at work, also called Pisano (but no relation to Nicola and Giovanni): Andrea (1290/95–1349) who produced masterpieces for the campanile and baptistery of Florence, and his son Nino (d. 1368) who worked mostly in Pisa.

The Baptistery

The *baptistery (Pl. 2), west of the Duomo, is a noble circular building begun in 1152 by Diotisalvi. The Gothic decoration was added to the Romanesque building in the 13C by Nicola Pisano (1270–84) and his son Giovanni (1297).

The Gothic dome and cusped arches were added in the 14C by Cellino di Nese. There are four portals, of which the most elaborate, facing the Duomo, is embellished with foliated columns and a Madonna by Giovanni Pisano (copy; original in the Museo dell' Opera).

The handsome **interior** (admission, see above) has a two-storeyed ambulatory, and is decorated with bands of black-and-white marble. A staircase leads up to the gallery, and another flight continues up to the top of the dome where the vaulting can be seen. The beautiful octagonal *font of white marble, carved and inlaid in mosaic, is by Guido da Como (1246). The statue of *St John the Baptist* is by a local artist, Italo Griselli (1880–1958). The 13C altar stands on a raised mosaic pavement. The *pulpit, by Nicola Pisano, is signed and dated 1260. Resting on slender pillars bearing figures of the *Virtues*, it bears panels sculptured in bold relief (*Nativity, Adoration of the Magi, Presentation, Crucifixion*, and *Last Judgement*).

The Baptistery, Pisa

The Camposanto

The *camposanto (Pl. 2), or ceme-tery, (**adm.**, see above) was begun in 1278 by Giovanni di Simone, and completed in the 15C. The bright marble exterior wall has handsome blind arcading and a Gothic tabernacle over one door with statues attributed to the bottega of Giovanni Pisano.

The **interior** is in the form of an oblong cloister, lit by graceful traceried windows (never filled with glass), around a lawn. Tradition has it that this is the site of an earlier burial ground for which Archbishop Ubaldo Lanfranchi (1108–78) brought five shiploads of earth from the Holy Land. It was used as a cemetery for illustrious Pisan citizens up to 1779. It was deco-rated with extremely important **frescoes** in the 14C and 15C by Taddeo Gaddi (1300), Andrea Bonaiuti, Antonio Veneziano, Spinello Aretino, Piero di Puccio (1377–90), and Benozzo Gozzoli (1468–84).

From the 14C onwards Roman sculptures were brought here, including a huge collection of sarcophagi. All these works were severely damaged in the Second World War, when the roof fell in. The frescoes (also ruined by exposure to the elements) have now all been detached for reasons of conservation, and some are displayed in a gallery here (although there are long-term plans to return them to their original positions). The sinopie are preserved in the Museo delle Sinopie (see below). In the walks, bitterly cold in winter, are numerous pavement tombs.

The **Roman sculpture and sarcophagi** in the Camposanto made up one of the most important classical collections in Europe in the early Renaissance. Many of these have been destroyed or removed, but a remarkable series of 84 sarcophagi, most of them dating from the 3C AD, remain (although many of them are very damaged). Some of them were re-used by Pisan citizens in the Middle Ages. Over the centuries funerary monuments were also erected here, some of which were later removed. The monuments have been in the process of cleaning and re-arrangement for a number of years.

South walk. Left of the entrance. **outer wall**: sarcophaghi of the 2C and 3C, and **inner wall** two neo-classical monuments and two Roman statues. The large wall tomb at the end of this walk is that of the physicist, Francesco Algarotti (d. 1764).

The west walk was rearranged in 1991 (when the monuments were cleaned). The oval sarcophagus with two male figures in togas, dating from the mid-3C AD, was re-used in the 14C by the Falconi family. On the wall, funerary monument of Francesco Vegio by Francesco Ferrucci (Il Tadda) with remains of 16C frescoes by Agostino Ghirlanda around it. Behind a Roman sarcophagus with figures of Genii (3C) is the wall tomb of Counts Bonifazio and Gherardo della Gherardesca attributed to a Pisan sculptor and dated 1330–40. The sarcophagus is decorated with arcaded niches with the *Pietà and Saints*, and the figure of the defunct is flanked by the *Annunciatory angel* and the *Virgin Annunciate*. Beyond the small funerary monument of Selvaggia Borghini with her profile by Enrico Van Lint (1829), in the centre of this walk is the large wall momument to Bartolomeo Medici (1573), with a bust and an obelisk attributed to Niccolò Tribolo.

The harbour chains of the ancient port of Pisa, displayed here, were carried off by the Genoese in 1342 (and returned by them in 1860). On two plinths, busts of *Carlo Metteucci* by Giovanni Duprè (1869) and of *Giorgio Regnoli* by Reginaldo Bilancini (1860). On the wall is a bust of *Amedeo of Savoy* by Cesare Zocchi (1897). The sarcophagus with festoons (one of the earliest in the Camposanto) was the tomb of Bellicus Natalis, Consul in AD 87. On the wall is the funerary monument of the painter Giovanni Battista Tempesti, with a seated female figure by Tommaso Masi (1804), and at the end of the north Walk is the large monument to Francesco Sanseverino Murci by Francesco Mosca decorated with coloured marbles. At the end of the wall, funerary monument of the physicist, Lorenzo Pignotti (d.1817), with a good relief by Stefano Ricci. A granite column serves as a base for a marble crater of the 1C BC. The frescoes (late 16C–early 17C) are by Aurelio Lomi (*Esther and Assuero*) and Paolo Guidotti (*Story of Judith and Holofernes*).

North walk. Outer wall: two 3C sarcophaghi, and that of Larcius Sabinus (mid-2C AD); **inner wall**: tomb of Rafidia, a freedwoman (1C AD). A door in the outer wall leads into the Cappella Ligo degli Ammannati, with the tomb of a Pisan doctor who died in 1359.

On the left is a huge room built in 1952 to house some of the frescoes detached from the south walk of the Camposanto, including **Triumph of Death*, *Last Judgement*, and *Stories of the Anchorites*. These have been variously attributed to Orcagna, Francesco Traini, Vitale da Bologna, and Buffalmacco. but are now generally held to be by an unknown 14C master named from these frescoes the Master of the Triumph of Death (1360–80). In 1839 Franz Liszt, the pianist and composer, was inspired by these scenes to create his *Totentanz* (he lived for a period with his mistress Countess d'Agoult near Pisa on the sea at Il Gombo.) Also here, *Crucifixion* by the Maestro della Crocifissione di Camposanto (c 1380), and Taddeo Gaddi, *Patience of Job*.

The gallery (at present closed) on the other side of the Cappella degli Ammannati contains photographs of other frescoes formerly in the Camposanto (and some of them totally destroyed in the War) by Buffalmacco, Francesco Traini, and Benozzo Gozzoli. In the centre, Greek *vase (2C–1C BC), with dancing nymphs and satyrs and Dionysiac scenes carved in low relief, a superb work which was studied by sculptors of the Renaissance. It was formerly outside the Cappella di San Ranieri of the Duomo (and replaced there by a copy in 1930).

North walk (right of the door into the Cappella Ammannati). **Outer wall**; 2C and 3C sarcophagi, re-used in the Middle Ages. A large one illustrating the myth of Phaedra and Hippolytus was used again in 1076 for Beatrice, mother of Countess Matilda of Canossa. The Cappella Aulla has a polychrome terracotta *Assumption* attributed to Giovanni della Robbia (damaged). To the right of the door, beyond three 3C sarcophagi is one decorated with Satyrs and Meanads and Dionysiac scenes on the cover, and one showing the myth of Meleager hunting the Caledonian boar. On the **inner wall**: several small sarcophagi for children. Beyond two steps, two fine large sarcophagi, one with a battle scene between Romans and barbarians (very damaged), and one with niches with the figures of the·Muses (and on the cover a marriage bed with a husband and wife).

East walk (still being rearranged). Tomb with an effigy of Filippo Decio (d. 1535) by Stagio Stagi; seated female statue (1842) by Lorenzo Bartolini for the tomb of Count Mastiani; tomb of the scientist Mossotti (d. 1863), with a reclining female figure by Giovanni Duprè. The Cappella del Pozzo (closed) with a dome, was built at this end of the Camposanto in 1594. On the wall here can be seen the nails and part of the preparation used for the *intonaco* for the frescoes.

South walk (being rearranged). **Outer wall**: inscribed decrees ordaining honours for Gaius and Lucius Caesar, nephews of Augustus; Roman milestones (2C). On the **inner wall**: the second sarcophagus right of the door has winged Victories holding a medallion (on which was later carved a medieval coat of arms). **Outer wall** (beyond the door): sarcophagus with winged Victories inscribed with the name of Aelius Lucifer, a Roman freedman (former slave); two oval sarcophagi with lions attacking their prey; sarcophagus with an open door symbolising the entrance to the after-life; sarcophagus with hunting scenes illustrating the myth of Meleagar and the Seasons, with a marriage bed and husband and wife on the cover.

Museo delle Sinopie

On the south side of the lawn is the former Ospedale Nuovo di Misericordia (13C–14C), where the *Museo delle Sinopie del Camposanto Monumentale (Pl. 2; **adm**. see above) was opened in 1979. A *sinopia* is the name given to the sketch for a fresco made on the rough wall (prepared with *arriccio*) in a red earth pigment (called *sinopia* because it originally came from Sinope on the Black Sea). The sinopia was then gradually covered with *grassello*, another type of wet plaster, as work proceeded day by day on the fresco itself. By detaching a fresco from the wall it has been possible in many instances to recover the *sinopia* from the inner surface. The 14C–15C frescoes of the Camposanto (see above) were severely damaged in the last War and had to be detached: the *sinopie* were then restored and are now displayed together here.

A platform provides a view of three huge *panels with *Stories of the Anchorites*, the *Last Judgement and Hell*, and the *Triumph of Death*, all generally attributed to the Master of the Triumph of Death (but thought by some scholars to be by Buffal-macco). On the far (end) wall, *Crucifixion* by Francesco Traini and *Ascension*, attrib-uted to Buffalmacco. On the north wall, *Theological Cosmograph* by Piero di Puccio. On the last wall are smaller *sinopie* (very damaged) by Spinello Aretino, Antonio Veneziano, Andrea Bonaiuti, and Taddeo Gaddi. On the upper level are frescoes and *sinopia* fragments by Buffalmacco (including *Incredulity of St Thomas* and *Resurrec-tion*). On the ground floor the *sinopie* are by Piero di Puccio and Benozzo di Lese.

Museo dell'Opera del Duomo

The *Museo dell'Opera del Duomo (**adm**. see above), in Piazza dell'Arcivesco-vado, was opened in 1986, using the latest methods of security and display, in the former chapter house of the Cathedral behind the Leaning Tower. The collection includes works of art from the Duomo, Baptistery, and Camposanto. The fine building, with a double loggia, overlooking a little garden, has good views of the Leaning Tower. Handlists are supplied.

Ground floor

Room 1 displays 19C models in wood and alabaster of the monuments in Campo dei Miracoli, and casts of their foundation stones. **Room 2** contains casts of the first pulpit made for the Duomo by Guglielmo Pisano in 1162.

Room 3: 12C sculpture from the Duomo, showing Islamic and French influences. The intricately carved transenna (probably an altar frontal) is attributed to Rainaldo. On the left wall are capitals and inlaid marble panels from the façade of the Duomo (their original postitions are shown on a diagram). In front is a long transenna from the presbytery by the school of Guglielmo Pisano, carved on the back of a Roman panel with a frieze of dolphins. The striking polychrome wood *Crucifix* is attributed to a Burgundian artist. The splendid bronze *griffin (11C) and the basin and capital (10C) are Islamic works brought from the East as war booty. The statue of *St Michael* is attributed to Biduino, and the seated statue of David playing the cithern shows the influence of Provence sculptors.

The small **Room 4** displays a late 12C *capital from the Campanile. **Room 5** contains 13C heads from the exterior of the Baptistery (their original positions are shown on a diagram) and fragments from the transenna. **Room 6**, a pretty barrel vaulted room with wall paintings, displays the Gothic statues (very worn) from the summits of the triangular tympanums on the exterior of the Baptistery. They are by **Nicola and Giovanni Pisano**, and assistants. Facing them are busts of *Christ blessing*, by Nicola Pisano, between the *Madonna and St John the Evangelist*, originally above the main entrance of the Baptistery facing the Duomo.

In the **corridor** and Room 7 are parts of the late 13C frieze with carved rectangles which ran round the base of the exterior of the Duomo. **Room 7** displays **sculptures by Giovanni Pisano**, including a (headless) *Madonna and kneeling figure* representing Pisa, formerly part of an allegorical group with the Emperor Henry VII. The *Madonna and Child and Saints John the Evangelist and John the Baptist* were removed from the main door of the Baptistery. The half-length *Madonna del Colloquio* is a beautiful composition.

Room 8 contains **works by Tino da Camaino**: fragments of the font from the Duomo; statues of the *Annunciation* and two deacons from the tomb of the Emperor Henry VII in the south transept of the Duomo; the tomb of St Ranieri (his first work, 1301–06); and the seated Henry VII between dignitaries of the state. **Room 9**. Funerary monuments of two archbishops by Nino Pisano. **Room 10**. Funerary monument of Archbishop Pietro Ricci by the Florentine sculptor Andrea di Francesco Guardi; architectural fragments by Matteo Civitali, and the workshop of Lorenzo and Stagio Stagi.

The **Cathedral *treasury** is displayed in **Rooms 11 and 12**: 12C Cross, known as the *Croce dei Pisani* in bronze and silver; two 12C Limoges enamelled caskets; Tuscan embroidered altar-frontal (1325); and a cope, also dating from the 14C. The *girdle with five reliefs decorated with enamels and precious stones dates from the end of the 13C or beginning of the 14C. Also displayed here: 15C reliquary of St Clement, and an 11C ivory casket. The ivory statuette of the *Madonna* *and Child*, is a superb work by **Giovanni Pisano** (1299–1300), originally over the main altar in the Duomo. The *Crucifix* is also by Giovanni Pisano. In the 17C chapel (Room 12) are displayed 17C reliquaries and the service of gilded church silver (French, 1616–17) given by Maria de' Medici to Archbishop Bonciani.

First floor

Stairs lead up to **Room 13**: paintings by a follower of Benozzo Gozzoli (*Madonna and Child, four Saints, and patrons*), and by Battista Franco and Aurelio Lomi. Marble angels by Tribolo and Silvio Cosini. **Room 14**: 18C paintings by Giuseppe and Francesco Melani and Giovanni Domenico Ferretti.

Room 15 displays wood intarsia (fragments from furnishings made for the Duomo); allegories of Faith, Hope, and Charity, by Baccio and Piero Pontelli (1475) are displayed opposite two works by Cristoforo da Lendinara. Also here are panels from choir-stalls by Guido da Seravallino. **Room 16**: two liturgical parchment scrolls, known as *Exultets* (12C and 13C), with illuminations, 14C illuminated choirbooks, and a 16C wooden lectern.

Rooms 17–19 retain their neo-classical decorations (including a charming alcove) from the time when the palace was the home of Giovanni Rosini (1776–1855), writer and publisher, and curator of the Camposanto. He befriended Giacomo Leopardi when the poet was staying in Pisa in 1827. The Church vestments now displayed here date from the 16C–19C. **Room 21**: engravings and watercolours by Carlo Lasinio (1759–1838) responsible for the restoration of the Camposanto. The delightful copies in watercolour of the frescoes of the Camposanto provide a precious record of them before their almost total destruction in the Second World War.

Rooms 22–24 contains an archaeological collection displayed by Lasinio in the Camposanto in 1807: cinerary urns, sarcophagi, busts, including one of Julius Caesar, Etruscan urns, and Egyptian antiquities.

The exit from the museum is along the **portico** on the **ground floor** where the colossal *half-figures of *Evangelists*, *Prophets*, and the *Madonna and Child*, by **Nicola** and **Giovanni Pisano** from the exterior of the Baptistery (1269–79) are displayed.

The handsome Renaissance **Palazzo Arcivescovile**, also in Piazza Arcivescovado, has a bright yellow façade and an attractive 16C courtyard (with a statue of Moses by Andrea Vaccà, 1709). A flying bridge connects the palace with its walled garden across Via Capponi. At the end of Via Corta is the church of **San Ranieri** (often closed) which contains a fine painting of the *Madonna and Saints* by Aurelio Lomi.

The 12C castellated **walls** which enclose the north and west side of Piazza del Duomo were pierced by the **Porta del Leone** (opposite the west end of the Camposanto) in the 13C. The gate was named after the Romanesque lion which survives here. Through the closed wooden gates can be seen part of the **Jewish Cemetery** which was moved here in the 16C, and surrounded in 1801 by a high wall. The **Porta Nuova**, the present exit from the piazza, replaced the Porta del Leone in 1562.

From Piazza del Duomo, Via Santa Maria runs south. Opposite the end of Via dei Mille the short Via Luca Ghini leads to the entrance of the **Botanical Gardens**

(Pl. 6; **open** 08.00–13.00, 14.00–17.30; Sat 08.00–13.00; fest. closed; ring at the door on the left). Founded in 1543 by Luca Ghini, and on this site since 1591, this is the oldest university botanic garden in Europe. The large building which houses the Botanic Institute was built in 1890, and in the same year the two fine palm trees from Chile were planted here. The old garden is laid out in rectangular beds (well labelled) in front of the Institute. At the end on the left is the original building which housed the Botanic Insitute, its façade decorated in imitation of a grotto with shells and pebbles. The gardens (damaged in a hurricane in 1994) contain notable examples of palm trees, ginkgos, magnolias, and camphor trees.

Via dei Mille continues left, passing the end of Via della Faggiola where (on the corner of Via dei Preti, now called Via Leopardi) the Italian poet Giacomo Leopardi took lodgings in 1827–28. The pretty Romanesque church of **San Sisto** has a fine interior, with good capitals and has been beautifully restored. The high altar was designed by Giuseppe Vaccà in 1730. The aisles are decorated with banners and in the corners of the west wall are 14C–15C ships' masts, and a 14C Arab inscription from the Koran.

Piazza dei Cavalieri

Once the centre of the city, (Pl. 7), the Piazza was named after the Knights of St Stephen, an Order founded by Cosimo I in 1561 to combat the Turkish infidel, in imitation of the Knights of Malta.

Santo Stefano dei Cavalieri (Pl. 7; **open** 09.00–12.30; also Sat and Sun pm), their church, has a handsome façade by Giovanni de' Medici (1594–1606), son of Cosimo I, and an unusual campanile by Vasari (1572).

The fine **interior** (**open** 09.00–12.30, Sat also 16.00–19.00) by Vasari (1565–69) is usually decorated with the banners captured from the infidel (these have been removed for restoration since 1990). The ceiling (1604–13) has six scenes of *Cosimo I as Grand Master of the Order*; the *return of the fleet after the battle of Lepanto*; *Maria de'Medici setting out to marry Henri IV of France*; and three naval battles (1602–13) over the Turks in which the Knights were victorious. These are good paintings by Cigoli, Jacopo Ligozzi, Cristofano Allori, and Empoli. 17C carved wooden ornaments (attributed to Santucci) and lanterns (also removed for restoration) from the Knights' galleys are displayed in various parts of the church. The two fine organs date from 1734 and 1569. The high altar, with a statue of the patron saint, is by Giovanni Battista Foggini.

The two stoups were designed by Vasari and carved by Fancelli. The five tempera paintings (late 16C) of scenes from the life of St Stephen in grisaille (on the north, south, and west walls) are attributed to Empoli, Alessandro Allori, Vasari, and Ligozzi (or Stradano). The pretty pulpit by Chiarissimo Fancelli (1627; restored in 1930) has *pietre dure* inlay. At the end of the south side is a painting of the *Madonna and Child* by Aurelio Lomi, in an elaborate frame.

In the monumental side aisles are white marble confessionals. On the south side: first altar, Vasari, *Stoning of St Stephen*; second altar, Crucifix attributed to Tacca. On the north side: second altar, Bronzino, *Nativity* (restored in 1997); first altar, Lodovico Buti, *Miracle of the Loaves and Fishes*.

To the left of the church is **Palazzo dei Cavalieri**, formerly della Carovana, modernised in 1562 by Vasari, with spectacular graffiti decoration, designed by

him (much restored). It is now the seat of the **Scuola Normale Superiore**, a university college of extremely high standing, founded by Napoleon in 1810, and modelled on the Ecole Normale Supérieure in Paris. It incorporates a large medieval hall of the old Palazzo del Popolo, now used as a lecture hall. Concerts are given here from December to May. Outside is a statue of Cosimo I by Francavilla (1596).

The **Palazzo dell'Orologio**, closing the north side of the square, occupies the site of the old Torre dei Gualandi also called the Torre della Mula when it was used as a mews for eagles (emblems of the city as incorporated into the Pisan coat of arms) which were confined here at moulting time. The tower continued its function as a small prison when in 1288 Count Ugolino della Gherardesca, who was suspected of treachery at the battle of Meloria, and his sons and grandsons were starved to death here. The episode is described by Dante (*La Divina Commedia, Inferno*, XXXII) who notes that since that time the tower came to be known as the Torre della Fame (the Tower of Famine). The building is now used as a library by the Scuola Normale, and the tower can be seen from the entrance, incorporated in the structure.

Borgo Stretto

Via Ulisse Dini leads down to Borgo Stretto (Pl. 7), a pretty arcaded shopping street in the centre of the town (closed to private traffic), with wide pavements. Some of the porticoes date from the 14C–15C. Off the narrow old Via Notari (parallel to the right) a daily **market** is held in **Piazza delle Vettovaglie**, with porticoes dating from 1544 (but damaged in the War).

In Borgo Stretto is the church of **San Michele in Borgo**, built in the 11C, with a lovely 14C façade by Fra Guglielmo Agnelli, follower of Nicola Pisano and typical of the Pisan Gothic style. Over the central door are statues of the *Madonna and Child with two Saints* in a Gothic tabernacle. The curious red lettering dates from the 16C–17C when the lower part of the façade was used for propoganda in the elections for a rector of a local school. Above is pretty arcading with a great variety of capitals and masques in the spandrels between the arches. In the **interior** (damaged in the last War) are high arcades with good capitals. Over a door on the west wall (at the end of the north aisle) is a detached 13C fresco of *St Michael*. At the end of the south aisle are four paintings of the *Virtues* by Aurelio Lomi (1605; restored in 1997), and a *Presentation in the Temple* also painted by him (1611). The high altarpiece of the *Madonna and Saints* is by Baccio Lomi. At the end of the north aisle are two paintings by Matteo Rosselli (1627), and, over an altar, a 14C Pisan *Crucifix*.

Borgo Stretto ends at the central Piazza Garibaldi on the Arno (described below).

From Borgo Stretto, opposite Via Ulisse Dini (see above), the narrow Via San Francesco leads to the church of **Santa Cecilia** (1103) with a façade and campanile decorated with majolica plaques (replaced by copies). Inside, a handsome Romanesque column at the west end supports a corner of the campanile. Over the high altar, *Martyrdom of St Cecilia* by Ventura Salimbeni.

Santa Caterina

To the north, across the huge Piazza Martiri (planted with plane trees), stands the large church of Santa Caterina (Pl. 4), built for the Dominicans in the 13C, with a façade of 1330. The **interior** has a colourful east window (1925). **South side**. Tomb of Gherardo di Compagno (1419), and St Catherine of Alexandria by Aurelio Lomi. A chapel off this side, which serves as a war memorial, contains a *Pietà* by Santi di Tito.

In the chapel to the right of the high altar, polychrome 15C relief of the *Madonna and Saints*. On either side of the **presbytery**, *statues of the Annunciation* by Nino Pisano. In the north transept, Fra Bartolomeo, *Madonna and Saints*.

North side. Francesco Traini, **Apotheosis of St Thomas Aquinas*; second altar, Cesare Dandini, *St Vincent Ferrer*; tomb of Archbishop Simone Saltarelli (d. 1342) by Nino Pisano; first altar, Raffaello Vanni, *St Catherine of Siena receiving the stigmata*.

To the northeast of the church (see the Plan) are vestiges of **Roman baths,** uncovered in 1942. From Via Cardinale Maffi there is a dramatic view of the Leaning Tower. In the other direction, Via San Zeno leads northeast to (c 400m) the little Romanesque chapel of **San Zeno** (Pl. 4; propped up with scaffolding and usually closed). Of ancient foundation it shows various architectural styles from the 10C and incorporates a few Roman fragments in its façade. It has been deconsecrated and is now sometimes used for exhibitions and concerts. There are plans to open a research centre and small museum here called the *Giardino di Archimede*, dedicated to mathematics. Outside Porta San Zeno, Via Vittorio Veneto skirts a fine stretch of the city walls.

San Francesco

Via San Francesco (see above) continues east to the Gothic church of San Francesco (Pl. 8), with an elegant Gothic campanile. The handsome plain façade was finished in 1603. The well illuminated **interior** is typical of Franciscan churches, with a wide aisless nave and Gothic chapels at the east end. **South side**: first altar, Empoli, *Baptism of Christ*; **second altar**, Giovanni Battista Paggi, *Resurrection*; **third altar**, Passignano, *St Peter receiving the keys from Christ*; **fourth altar**, Santi di Tito, *St Francis receiving the stigmata*. In the Gothic chapel of St Filomena is a tomb of 1414.

On the **high altar** is a large marble reredos by Tommaso Pisano. In the vault, frescoes of the Apostles, friars and monastic virtues by Taddeo Gaddi (1342). The east window has good stained glass dating in part from the 14C; the other windows at the east end also have pretty stained glass. In the second chapel to the right of the high altar, *Crucifixion and Saints* by Spinello Aretino. In the third chapel left of the high altar are remains of 14C frescoes. The vaulting in the north transept bears the weight of the campanile.

In the **Sacristy** a chapel is frescoed by Taddeo di Bartolo, and on the walls are *sinopie* by Niccolò di Pietro Gerini of the frescoes by him in the chapter house.

North side; **fifth altar**, Francesco Vanni, *St Francis*; **third altar**, Ventura Salimbeni, *Assumption*.

On the south side of Via San Francesco is Piazza San Paolo, with the deconsecrated church of **San Paolo all'Orto**. It retains the lower part of its beautiful, delicately carved facade with polychrome marble inlay and sculptures by Biduino (c 1180), carefully restored in 1992. Farther south is **San Pierino** (1072–1119; closed), which has a large crypt (seen from the outside). Via Palestro, with the **Teatro Verdi** (1867; small museum), and **Synagogue** (1648; restored in 1865 by Marco Treves), leads east to **Sant'Andrea**, another good 12C church (closed; used by a cultural society). Beyond the huge **Palazzo di Giustizia** (1938–58) Via Giusti and Via del Giardino lead to Piazza delle Gondole, built on a canal, with a 16C fountain. Here is the end of the **Aqueduct** built by the Medici in 1601–13 to bring water to the city from Asciano (c 6km away). The low brick arches are very well preserved. South of the Piazza, in Via Santa Marta, is the church of **Santa Marta**, with a harmonious 18C interior.

Several streets lead south from San Francesco to the Lungarno Mediceo, on which is the Museo Nazionale di San Matteo (described below).

Museo Nazionale di San Matteo

The ex-convent of San Matteo (used as a prison in the 19C) has been occupied since 1947 by the Museo Nazionale di San Matteo (Pl. 12), which contains works of art from Pisan churches and convents. The later works belonging to the city collections are now exhibited in Palazzo Reale (see below; **open** 09.00–18.00; fest. 09.00–13.00; closed Mon).

In the entrance hall, sarcophagus with the Good Shepherd (4C AD). Off the attractive brick **cloister**, with sculptural fragments, are four rooms which display 16C pottery and the Tongiorgi *collection of majolica tondi from Pisan church façades and ceramics (10C–18C), including numerous Islamic pieces. Another room contains high reliefs from San Michele.

First floor

Room 1 (left). Early Tuscan painted *Crucifixes* (13C), including one signed by Giunta Pisano (believed to be the earliest painter whose name is inscribed on any extant Italian work), and one (recently restored) signed by Berlinghiero; and early Pisan panel paintings including *St Catherine* with stories from her life (13C). Room 2: panels by Deodato Orlandi and the Maestro di San Torpè (early 14C); Francesco Traini, *polyptych of *St Dominic* with stories from his life (signed), *Madonna and Child with Saints*; Lippo Memmi, polyptych. At the end of the room: Simone Martini, *polyptych (signed 1319–21); works by Giovanni di Nicola, and a wooden statue of the *Virgin Annunciate* by Agostino di Giovanni.

Room 3 (right): 14C and 15C Pisan wooden sculptures; works by Francesco di Valdambrino; *Madonna del Latte*, a half-length polychrome marble gilded statue from Santa Maria della Spina by Andrea and Nino Pisano; Nino Pisano, *Christ in pietà*, wooden high relief of the *Madonna and Child*, and marble statuette of the *Madonna and Child* (the last two from Santa Maria della Spina); Andrea and Nino Pisano, *Annunciatory angel*, a wooden statue from San Matteo.

In the **long gallery** (**Room 4**) overlooking the cloister are sculptural fragments, which were arranged in the 19C in the Camposanto. They include French and Pisan statuettes (including two by Tino da Camaino and Nicola Pisano) and capitals carved by Giovanni di Balduccio.

Room 5. Displayed on stands to the left: Barnaba da Modena, *Madonna enthroned*, *Madonna and Child*; Antonio Veneziano, *Assunta*, and processional standard with the Crucifixion and St Ranieri. Also in Room 5: works by Jacopo di Michele; polyptychs by Martino di Bartolomeo; Taddeo di Bartolo, Processional standard with the Crucifixion and St Donnino; Cross in rock crystal decorated with miniatures (Venetian, early 14C; removed); Maestro di Barga, processional standard (Crucifixion and St Ursula). On the stands opposite: Taddeo di Bartolo, *Madonna and Saints and two angels*; Spinello Aretino, *Coronation of the Virgin*, fragment of a polyptych, six frescoed heads; Agnolo Gaddi, two fragments of a polyptych; works by Luca di Tommè, Cecco di Pietro, and Francesco Neri da Volterra.

In the short gallery (**Room 6**), are four polychrome wooden statues by Francesco di Valdambrino. **Room 7**. Works by Turino di Vanni. **Room 8** Masaccio, **St Paul*; Michelozzo, stucco relief of the *Madonna and Child*; Fra Angelico, *Madonna of Humility*; Donatello, reliquary **bust* of *St Rossore* (or St Luxorious), a splendid work in gilded bronze (1424–27) from Santo Stefano dei Cavalieri; Master of the Castello Nativity, *Madonna and Child with angel musicians*; Neri di Bicci, *Coronation of the Virgin*; Zanobi Machiavelli, *Madonna and Saints*. **Room 9** contains three paintings by Benozzo Gozzoli.

In the last long gallery (**10**): **Madonna of Humility* by Gentile da Fabriano and two altarpieces of the *Madonna and Saints* by Domenico Ghirlandaio. The painted terracotta bust of the *Redeemer* is by the circle of Verrocchio, and the bronze bust of a saint attributed to Michelozzo. Also here are an enamelled terracotta tondo by Benedetto Buglioni, and a *Madonna in Adoration* by Andrea della Robbia. The last room (**11**) has 15C and 16C works in poor condition. A tempera **painting* on canvas of *Christ blessing* attributed to Fra Angelico has been removed for many years for restoration.

In the little piazza outside the museum is the church of **San Matteo**, founded in 1027. The pretty blind arcading and the east end of the Romanesque church can be seen along the Lungarno. The church (and façade) was reconstructed after a fire in 1607. The handsome Baroque **interior** with paintings in marble frames, marble stoups and confessionals, was damaged in the War but beautifully restored in 1990. It contains fine 17C and 18C paintings. The 18C vault fresco of the *Glory of St Matthew* is by the local painters Giuseppe and Francesco Melani. **South side**: stories from the *life of St Matthew* by Jacopo Zoboli and Marco Benefial on either side of the south altar, which has a painting of *Christ in Judgement with the Madonna and Saints* by Clemente Bocciardi. The high altarpiece of the *Calling of St Matthew* by Francesco Romanelli is flanked by two oval paintings by Giuseppe Melani. **North side**: stories from the *Life of St Matthew* by Sebastiano Conca and Francesco Trevisani on either side of the north altar which has a 13C Pisan painted *Crucifix* (the head is ruined) and the *Madonna and St John the Evangelist and angels* painted by Stefano Marucelli. Beneath the nuns' choir, *Madonna and Child with angels and Saints*, by the 16C Florentine school.

Palazzo Medici (now the Prefecture), on the left of the piazzetta, was built in the 13C–14C and owned by the Medici from 1446. Lorenzo il Magnifico often stayed here with his friend Politian. It was restored to its medieval aspect in 1879 by Ranieri Simonelli. In Piazza Mazzini is a statue of Mazzini by Giuseppe Andreoni (1883).

The attractive **Lungarno Mediceo** continues along the river. Next to **Palazzo Roncioni** (No. 16) with a handsome façade by Giovanni Stefano Marucelli (1630), where Madame de Stael stayed in 1815–16, is **Palazzo Toscanelli** (formerly Lanfranchi), with a fine 16C façade. It was occupied by Lord Byron in 1821–22, and is now the seat of the State Archives. Via delle Belle Torri runs parallel to the Lungarno here; fragments of some of the 12C–13C tower houses survive incorporated into unattractive new buildings. In Piazzetta Cairoli is a column surmounted by a pretty statue of *Abundance* by Pierino da Vinci (1550).

The small but busy **Piazza Garibaldi** (Pl. 11), at the end of Ponte di Mezzo, is at the centre of the city. The bronze statue of Garibaldi is by Ettore Ferrari (1892). The 18C Palazzo del Casino dei Nobili has three high arches. The arcaded Borgo Stretto (described above) leads north from the piazza. **Ponte di Mezzo** (Pl. 11), rebuilt in 1950, is on the site of the Roman bridge over the Arno. It has been the scene of the annual *Gioco del Ponte* (in June) since it was first celebrated under the Medici in 1596 (see practical information, above).

Lungarno Pacinotti

Lungarno Pacinotti continues along the river past Hotel Victoria opened in 1842 (where Charles Dickens stayed in 1845). **Palazzo Agostini** (or dell'Ussero; No. 26) has early 15C terracotta decoration on its façade. Here is the **Caffè dell'Ussero** opened in 1794, and famous as the meeting place of writers during the Risorgimento (it preserves mementoes of its famous patrons, including Giuseppe Giusti, and Renato Fucini).

Via Curtatone e Montanara leads away from the river to the **University**, on this site since 1473. The present façade dates from 1907–11. The splendid courtyard survives from 1550. A Studio existed in Pisa as early as the 12C, and the university was founded in 1343. It has a high reputation. Beyond the university, in Via Cavalca (right) can be seen the high Torre del Campano (13C).

On the opposite side of Via San Frediano is the 11C church of **San Frediano** (Pl. 7), with a good façade. It preserves columns and capitals in its altered **interior** which has delightful 17C confessionals. In the first chapel in the south aisle is a 13C painted *Crucifix, and on the right wall, an *Adoration of the Magi* by Aurelio Lomi. In the chapel to the right of the high altar is an amusing Baroque altar. In the chapel to the left of the high altar are three paintings by Alessandro Tiarini illustrating stories from the *Life of Santa Brigida*. On the north wall, Ranieri Borghetti, *Saints Paul and Bartholomew*; third and first chapels, paintings by Ventura Salimbeni.

On Lungarno Pacinotti (see above) the tiny church of the **Madonna dei Galletti** has an attractive 17C–18C interior and a fresco of the *Madonna and Child* by Taddeo di Bartolo over the high altar, flanked by two wooden 18C angels. At No. 43 is **Palazzo Lanfreducci** (or Upezzinghi), also known as the **Palazzo alla Giornata**, with a fine white marble façade by Cosimo Pugliani (1594). **Palazzo Mazzarosa** (No. 45) dates from the 19C. In Piazza Francesco Carrara is a good statue of the Grand-duke Ferdinando I by Pietro Francavilla (1594).

Museo di Palazzo Reale

At No. 46 is the huge **Palazzo Reale** (Pl. 10), built in 1583–87 by Bernardo Buontalenti for Francesco I de' Medici. It is on the site of a medieval building and incorporates an old tower house, but it was severely damaged in the last War. It now houses the Museo di Palazzo Reale (**open** 09.00–14.00, except fest).

The museum contains part of the city's art collections, illustrating the period of the Medici and Lorraine grand-dukes of Tuscany, as well as the Royal House of Savoy, and important private donations made to the city by Pisan citizens in the 19C. The contents of the rest of the civic museum, with works of art from

Pisan churches and convents, is housed in the Museo di San Matteo (see above).

On the stairs is an 18C bust of the Lorraine Grand-duke Pietro Leopoldo I by Giovanni Antonio Cybei and paintings of the last Grand-dukes wearing the uniform of the Knights of Santo Stefano, the order founded by Cosimo I.

In the first two rooms thirty-five 16C tapestries made in the Medici workshops, and 16C costumes, are to be displayed. Other rooms display portraits of the Medici by Bronzino (*Eleonora di Toledo and her son Francesco*), Tiberio Titi, and Alessandro Allori (*Ferdinando I as Cardinal*, before he became grand-duke). In a room where the early 18C grisaille decoration by the workshop of Luigi Ademollo dating from the period of the Lorraine grand-dukes survives, there is a display from the huge collection of armour (dating from the 15C onwards) originally kept in the Cittadella della Rocca and afterwards adapted for use in the Gioco del Ponte (see above). Another room contains the *bozzetti* for the large 18C paintings which are in the aisles of the Duomo. In a room decorated with yellow damask are more court portraits, three of them by Giuseppe Maria Crespi, and oval paintings in pretty frames of ladies of the court commissioned in the late 17C by Vittoria della Rovere from Antonio Franchi. In the room with red furnishings: Rosso Fiorentino (attributed) *Rebecca at the well*; a tiny early work by Raphael, part of a predella; and a *Madonna* signed by Giusto de' Menabuoi (removed for restoration).

The important **Ceci collection** donated to the town by the surgeon Antonio Ceci (1852–1920) is displayed in the last four rooms. The first room contains 18C–19C ivory miniatures, part of the richest private collection in Italy. In the next room is a painting by Guido Reni of *Sacred and Profane Love, small bronzes, and medals. Ceci's collection of porcelain includes fine examples from France and the far East. The last room has numerous paintings from his collection by Valerio Castello, Francesco Francia (*Madonna and Child*), Andrea Boscoli, Michele di Matteo (*Coronation of the Virgin*), Magnasco, Bernardo Strozzi, and Frans Francken. The exquisite little *Holy Family* is thought to be a 16C copy of a work by Jan Brueghel, and the small painting of the *Crucifixion* is attributed to Herri met de Bles. The drawings and watercolours include works by Elisa Toscanelli and a bozzetto is attributed to Canova. The gipsoteca, with works by the local sculptor Italo Griselli (1880–1958) is still being arranged. Other private collections are to be exhibited in other rooms of the palace.

Behind the palace, in Via Santa Maria, is the church of **San Nicola** (Pl. 10), founded c 1000, but much altered over subsequent centuries. In the 13C ***campanile** is a remarkable spiral staircase on which Bramante (according to Vasari) modelled his Belvedere staircase in the Vatican.

Interior. South side. First altar, Francesco Traini, *Madonna and Child*, and a polychrome wooden *Madonna* attributed to the school of Jacopo della Quercia. Second chapel (on the wall) *St Charles Borromeo* by Giovanni Bilivert; fourth chapel, *St Nicholas of Tolentino* protecting Pisa (clearly depicted) from the plague, c 1400. The 17C chapel to the right of the high altar was decorated by Matteo Nigetti, who also designed the high altar (flanked by two statues by Felice Palma). In the chapel to the left of the high altar, *Crucifix* attributed to Giovanni Pisano. **North side. Fourth chapel**, *Madonna and Child*, a statue attributed to Nino Pisano (removed since 1996 for restoration); second chapel, altarpiece of the *Annunciation* by Giovanni Bilivert (in very poor condition).

At No. 26 Via Santa Maria is the **Domus Galileiana**, opened in 1942 to commemorate the famous scientist Galileo, born in Pisa. It has a fine library (admission granted to scholars). Next door is the birthplace of the scientist Antonio Pacinotti (1841–1912). Farther on, the modern Palazzo Da Scorne incorporates a large Romanesque capital into its unattractive façade.

Lungarno Pacinotti ends at **Ponte Solferino**, rebuilt in 1974 after its collapse in the flood of 1966. Lungarno Simonelli continues to the **Arsenal**, a boatyard built by the Medici Grand-dukes in 1548–88. On the façade (in very poor repair) are marble masques and five inscriptions. The buildings are now used as stables for horses by the Ministry of Agriculture. Beyond rises the tall medieval **Cittadella** or Fortezza Vecchia (Pl. 9), with the Torre Guelfa, enlarged in the 15C. Ponte della Cittadella (1957; first built in the 13C) leads to the south bank of the Arno (see below).

The south bank of the Arno

At the south end of Ponte della Cittadella is the 13C **Porta a Mare** (Pl. 13), and abandoned ruins of a bastion in the walls. On the river can be seen the old gate of the Navicelli canal (now covered over) which was begun by Cosimo I in 1541 to connect Pisa with Livorno. Inside the Porta a Mare is a large Art Nouveau villa with a tower (No. 12), with good wrought-iron work and palm trees in its garden.

In this remote part of the city a spacious piazza with trees (and an excellent view of the tall Cittadella across the river) opens out in front of the church of *San Paolo a Ripa d'Arno** (Pl. 14), founded in 805. The splendid **façade** (restored in 1944) probably dates from the 13C and the north flank has fine blind arcading. The solemn bare interior (closed) has a handsome Roman sarcophagus, and a fine Romanesque capital (second on left). Behind the east end, surrounded by a lawn with a few trees, is the unusual Romanesque chapel of **Sant'Agata**, a tiny octagonal brick building (after 1063). On the other side of Via San Paolo is the wall of the **ex-Convent of San Benedetto** (1393), the courtyard of which has been restored in an incongruous style by a bank. The façade on the Lungarno, beyond the little church (closed) has terracotta decoration carried out in 1850 by Domenico Santini.

Lungarno Sonnino leads along the river to Ponte Solferino, just beyond which is the charming little church of *Santa Maria della Spina** (Pl. 10), named after a thorn of the Saviour's crown, is a gem of Pisan Gothic architecture (1230 finished in 1323), the gift of a Pisan merchant. It was restored after War damage (usually **open** Mon, Wed & Fri 10.00–12.00, Tues, Thurs & Sat 17.00–19.00).

From the bridge Via Crispi leads south towards Piazza Vittorio Emanuele II and the Station. It ends in front of the church of **Sant'Antonio** (1341; reconstructed after the Second World War).

Nearby, at No. 71 Via Mazzini is the **Domus Mazziniana** (open 08.00–13.00 except Sunday), built in 1952 on the site of a house (destroyed in the War) where Giuseppe Mazzini died in 1872, while visiting his friends the Rosselli under the false name of John Brown. It contains mementoes of Mazzini and a library specialising in the Risorgimento. In Piazza Sant'Antonio is a mock-Gothic tram station (now used as a bus station) near a stretch of the city walls.

Across Piazza Vittorio Emanuele II, with a bronze statue of the king by Cesare Zocchi (1892) is the church of San Domenico (closed) in Corso Italia.

Corso Italia (Pl.11, *15*; closed to traffic), the main street on the south bank of the Arno, returns north towards the river and Ponte di Mezzo past the church of **Santa Maria del Carmine** (Pl. 15) It was founded in 1325 and enlarged in 1612 (restored). In the pretty **interior** with attractive confessionals, on the right of the entrance is a painting of *St Teresa* by Crescenzio Gamberelli. On the south side, *Annunciation* by Andrea Boscoli, *Madonna and Child with two Saints* by Antonio Sogliani (and beyond a pretty pulpit of 1705, *Madonna and Saints* by Baccio Lomi. The altarpieces on the north side are by Alessandro Allori (*Ascension*), and the school of Aurelio Lomi (*Saints*).

Lungarno Gambacorti continues to the handsome **Palazzo Gambacorti** (No. 1), built by Pietro Gambacorti in 1370–80, and now the town hall. In Piazza XX Settembre, at the south end of Ponte di Mezzo, is the **Loggia dei Banchi** built by Cosimo Pugliani (1603–05), on a design by Bernardo Buontalenti, as a market place. From here Corso Italia leads due south to Piazza Vittorio Emanuele II.

Lungarno Galileo continues along the river to **San Sepolcro** (Pl. 11), an octagonal church with a very unusual pyramidal roof built in the 12C by Diotisalvi, probably for the Knight Templars, and restored in 1975. It is now below the level of the road. The striking interior lit by small windows, has tall pilasters forming a high Gothic arcade around the brick pyramidal roof. The font has stone reliefs by Mario Bertini (1956).

Lungarno Galileo continues to **Palazzo Lanfranchi** (now owned by the Comune) dating from the Middle Ages but rebuilt in the 16C. It has recently been drastically restored (only two rooms with 19C ceilings have been preserved) and is now used for exhibitions.

Via Lanfranchi leads south to **Via San Martino**, a handsome street with a number of 16C–18C palaces, and one of the best preserved in the city. Here is the church of **San Martino** (Pl. 16), begun in 1332 and consecrated in 1477 (restored in 1969–75). On the façade is a copy of a relief of St Martin (the original is now inside the church).

The **interior** has an open timber roof. At the west end are detached frescoes of the *Life of Mary* by Giovanni di Nicola. **South side**. The 13C painted *Crucifix* with stories of the Passion is by Enrico di Tedice. **First altar**, Aurelio Lomi, *St Andrew*. Above the entrance into the side chapel, 14C relief of *St Martin and the beggar* by Andrea da Pontedera. The chapel, with a pretty barrel vault, has two detached frescoes and *sinopie* attributed to Antonio Veneziano. **Second altar**, Palma Giovane, *St Benedict*; **third altar**, Passignano, *Madonna and Child* (removed). **North Side**. **Second altar**, Jacopo Ligozzi, *Mary Magdalene in front of the Crucifix*; **first altar**, Giovanni Sordo (Mone), *Annunciation*.

At No. 19 Via San Martino is a Roman relief of a female figure, a fragment of a 3C sarcophagus (restored in 1988). Known as *Kinzica*, it is named after a legendary Pisan heroine who saved Pisa from the Saracens in 1004.

At the end of Ponte della Fortezza (1959; first built in 1286) is the ruined **Palazzo Scotto** to the right of which is the 17C Palazzo Chiesa. Shelley lived here in 1820–22 (plaque). Lungarno Fibonacci follows the wall of the ruined **Fortezza Nuova** built in 1512 by Giuliano da Sangallo. It now encloses a public garden known as the **Giardino Scotto**.

16 · The province of Pisa

The province of Pisa is very extensive and takes in part of the coast as well as a large area south as far as Volterra and the metalliferous hills (both described in Ch. 17), and localities along the Arno towards Florence. On the plain just outside Pisa is the huge **Certosa di Pisa** with its 18C monastic buildings. Towards the sea is the Romanesque **basilica of San Piero in Grado**. The coastline is protected by the nature reserve of San Rossore. The most interesting town inland is **San Miniato** with some fine churches and a diocesan museum. In the attractive countryside to the south are the pretty little-known villages of Montopoli in Val d'Arno, Palaia, Peccioli, Casciana Alta, and Lari.

■ Practical information

Information offices. APT **Pisa**, 26 Via Benedetto Croce (☎ 050-40096). At **San Miniato**, information office in Piazza del Popolo (☎ 0571-42745).

Getting there
By bus. From Pisa, the *Consorzio Pisano Trasporti* runs buses from Piazza Sant'Antonio (Pl. 14) to towns in the province and to the coast.

By train. On the Florence-Pisa line to *San Miniato-Fucecchio* in San Miniato Basso for San Miniato (slow trains only in 40 mins from Florence).

Hotels
Of all categories at the resorts of **Marina di Pisa** and **Tirrenia**.
San Giuliano Terme. ★★★ *Villa di Corliano*, at Rigoli (☎ 050-818193, fax 050-818897).
San Miniato. ★★★ *Miravalle*, with first-class restaurant, 3 Prato del Duomo (☎ 0571-418075, fax 0571-419681).
Casciana Terme. Small hotels (★★★ and ★★).

Campsites at Marina di Pisa and Tirrenia.

Restaurants
Marina di Pisa. ££ *Da Gino*, 2 Via delle Curzolari.
San Miniato. ££ *Canapone*, Piazza Bonaparte; *Collebrunacchi*, 12 Via Collebrunacchi (in the environs).

The coast near the mouth of the Arno
A road from Pisa, lined by a long straight avenue of plane trees, follows the Arno to its mouth, past boat building yards and fishing huts.

San Piero a Grado
The church of *San Piero a Grado was built on the site where St Peter is said to have landed on his journey from Antioch to Rome. Excavations have confirmed the existence of a building here in the 1C AD. In Roman times this was the site of the last ferry across the Arno. The present Romanesque basilica dates from the 10C–12C.

The pretty **exterior** has blind arcading and incorporates Roman and medieval architectural fragments and friezes. The 11C ceramic basins (some of them from Tunisia, Morocco, and Spain) have been replaced by copies (the originals are displayed in the Museo Nazionale di San Matteo in Pisa). The 13C campanile was destroyed in 1944. The entrance is through a central lateral door.

The **interior** (usually open in the mornings) is unusual in having apses at both the east and the west ends. The re-used columns have a great variety of Roman capitals. At the west end a ciborium covers an area of excavations of earlier churches on this site including two apses, one dating from the 3C–4C and one from the 8C–9C. Here a granite half-column (which formerly supported the ancient altar) marks the spot where St Peter is supposed to have preached. The 16C loggia was built in the apse at the west end to support a cantoria. Against the walls of the church are numerous ancient architectural fragments found in the excavations, and four inscriptions in *pietra serena* (formerly part of the 17C high altar) which recount the story of St Peter. Also here is an interesting carved wood 16C confessional. The *fresco cycle (being restored) in the nave is attributed to Deodato Orlandi (1300–12). Above portraits of popes from St Peter to John XVII (1003) are scenes from the life of St Peter and St Paul.

Marina di Pisa is a pleasant old-fashioned bathing resort (with several Art Nouveau houses) at the mouth of the Arno, first developed in 1869. It is backed by dense pinewoods, whose seeds are used in making confectionery.

The nature reserve of San Rossore

The coast to the north and south has been protected since 1979 as the **Parco Naturale Migliarino–San Rossore–Massaciuccoli**, although there are still problems over the administration of the park. Between the Arno and the Serchio rivers is the **Tenuta di San Rossore**, a summer estate of the President of the Republic was donated to the State in 1988. Camels were kept here in the 19C but its bird and animal sanctuaries now house less exotic animals including wild boar and deer which were first introduced for hunting. To the south is the **Tenuta di Tombolo**, and to the north (beyond the Serchio) **Migliarino** and **Massaciuccoli** (see Ch. 13). Although the area has fine pinewoods, wetlands, and birdlife, in some parts of the park the trees are threatened with disease, the rivers are still polluted, and the coastline has been eroded.

■ Information on the nature reserves from the *Ente Parco Regionale*, Via Aurelia Nord 4 (☎ 050-525211). Part of the Tenuta di San Rossore is **open** on Wed, Sat, & fest. 08.00–19.30; **bus** No. 11 from Pisa, Piazza Vittorio Emanuele (three times a day on fest.). The entrance for those with **cars** is from Ponte alle Trombe on the Gombo road which also passes the Cascine Vecchie. **Guided tours** (for information, ☎ 105-525211 or 0330-778623) are organised from the Cascine Vecchie near the restaurant called *Da Poldino* for those on foot, with bicycles, or on horseback. These provide access to areas of the park not otherwise open, including the River Arno, Gombo (north of the mouth of the Arno), and the rivers Morto Nuovo and Serchio.

Shelley's body was washed ashore on the beach of Gombo in 1822 (see Ch. 13). Allan Ramsay, the painter, was more fortunate and escaped with his life from a shipwreck here in 1736 on his first jouney to Rome. The mouth of the Serchio at **Marina di Vecchiano** is one of the most beautiful parts of the coastline with interesting bird life.

To the south of Marina di Pisa the modern resort of **Tirrenia** extends towards Livorno (see Ch. 18). **Stagno** in the midst of the former marshes of the Arno, drained (c 1620) by Sir Robert Dudley, is now occupied by a huge oil refinery.

The province north of the Arno

The road to Lucca from Pisa, which follows a canal constructed by Cosimo I lined with ancient plane trees, passes **San Giuliano Terme**, a small spa at the foot of Monte Pisano, whose spring waters have been known since ancient times. New thermal buildings were constructed here in 1744 by Francesco Pecci for the Grand-duke Francesco I. A bust and plaque mark the Casa Prinni where Shelley stayed in the summer of 1820.

A road continues up Monte San Giuliano past olive groves (with a view back of Pisa), through a tunnel, and then descends towards Lucca (see Ch. 11). The old road to Lucca, slightly longer, passes between the 14C castle of **Nozzano**, a Luccan outpost and the Pisan castle of **Ripafratta**.

To the east is the straggling unattractive village of **Calci**. From the piazza with four palm trees a road leads shortly to the **Pieve**, founded in 1088–98, marked by its massive, square, unfinished campanile. The attractive façade in the Pisan style has decorations in two shades of grey. The basilican **interior** has fine columns and capitals. The large monolithic rectangular *font has an interesting sculpted front (mid-12C) by an artist influenced by Biduino. Beside the unusual robed figure of Christ in the centre is a gnome, symbolising the river Jordan. On the right is *St John the Baptist*; the other figures represent the Madonna and two angels. The pretty marble confessionals date from 1757. On a pilaster of the church is a 13C head of Christ which has been adapted as a copy of the Volto Santo of Lucca (see p. 200). On the altar right of the high altar, *Madonna and Child with Saints* signed by Aurelio Lomi (who may also have painted the *Adoration of the Shepherds* in a chapel off the right side of the church). In the sacristy is kept a beautiful late 14C painting of the *Madonna and Child.

The Certosa di Pisa

Nearby is the huge *Certosa di Pisa on low ground, now in a disappointing setting. This is one of the largest monumental monasteries in the country. The Charterhouse was founded in 1366 and reconstructed in the 18C. It was built to house 60 Carthusian monks, but the monastery was closed in 1973.

Guided tours are given every hour: winter 09.00–16.00; summer 09.00–18.00; fest. 09.00–12.00; closed Mon.

In the **first courtyard** is the monumental façade (1718) of the church and the two wings of the monastery. To the right, an elaborate gateway (1768), decorated in the form of a grotto with shells and pebbles, leads into the garden. The **Church** has colourful frescoes by Giuseppe and Pietro Rolli and a marble lectern in the form of an angel by the school of Bernini. The east end has a high altarpiece by Volterrano. The side chapels contain altarpieces including a *Crucifix* by Bernardino Poccetti, and *St Bruno* by Jacopo Vignali. The Cappella del Rosario and Cappella della Sacra Famiglia have decorations by Giuseppe Maria Terreni.

The **large Cloister** has an elaborate fountain and white marble porticoes by Giovanni Battista Cartoni (1636–51). It is surrounded by the spacious monks' cells, one of which is shown. The smaller **Chapter Cloister** survives from the 15C (the well dates from 1614). Beyond the Cappella del Capitolo is the **Refectory** with a *Last Supper* by Bernardino Poccetti and 18C frescoes of *Supper at Emaus* and the *Marriage at Cana* by Pietro Giarrè. The elaborate **Grand-ducal Apartments** where distinguished guests stayed in the 18C, have period furniture and stuccoes by Angelo Maria Somazzi and more frescoes of a pilgrim on his way to the Certosa and other scenes by Pietro Giarrè. The 17C **Prior's Cloister** has an unusual double well. A **terrace** looks out over the monastery garden and fish tanks (and to the right, in the distance, can be seen the Leaning Tower and Baptistery of Pisa). A grand staircase (by Michele Fossi) leads down to the courtyard and vestibule.

In a wing of the monastery (and in a covered loggia, once used by the monks to take their exercise) the University of Pisa has recently arranged the **Museo di Storia Naturale**, a collection founded at the University in 1591 by Ferdinando I and enlarged in the 18C and 19C (usually **open** 09.00–13.00, 14.30–19.00 except Mon; summer 09.00–21.00 except Mon). The natural history collections are extremely interesting and some are still displayed in showcases dating from 1752. The zoological section includes mammals, cetaceans, molluscs and birds, and there is a comparative anatomy display. Another section is dedicated to

The Certosa di Pisa at Calci

Tuscan minerals and marble from the Apuan Alps, and ammonites and Triassic fossils from the Veneto.

Nearby is the little spa of **Uliveto Terme** (well known for its mineral water) and the conspicuous Torre degli Uperrighi at Caprona on the very edge of a quarry.

The little town of **Cascina**, a centre of the furniture trade, lies beneath Monte Verruca (563m), a prominent peak of Monte Pisano. In 1364 it was the scene of a Florentine victory over the Pisans. The environs are no longer attractive, with numerous small factories, but the main street of the town, **Corso Matteotti**, is lined with porticoes.

At the beginning on the left, behind a railing, is the little 14C **Oratory of San Giovanni** (if closed, ring at the convent school next door at No. 9). The Gothic vaulted interior contains a cycle of frescoes by Martino di Bartolomeo (1398) in extremely poor condition, including saints in Gothic niches and scenes from the Old Testament above. The altarpiece of the *Annunciation* by Luca di Tommè was removed to Florence many years ago.

Farther along the main street, between the town hall and a palace with an attractive balcony, Via Palestra leads to **Piazza della Chiesa** with three churches and a 15C tower. Only the 12C **Pieve di Santa Maria** is open regularly. It has a fine basilican interior with handsome columns and a seated terracotta statue of the *Madonna and Child* (early 16C; in the chapel to the right of the apse). The church of **San Benedetto**, a short distance west of Cascina on the main road, has a splendid English alabaster relief (14C).

To the north of Cascina is **Vicopisano**, a village built on a little hill which still has a number of towers and part of its fortifications, restored by Brunelleschi after it was taken by the Florentines in 1407. It is bordered on the south by a canal built by the Medici grand-dukes to deviate the course of the Arno which now flows 2km south.

At the foot of the hill is the **Torre del Brunelleschi** (c 1406) in the walls which mount the hillside. Near it is the **Torre delle Quattre Porte** resting on a vault which once had four open arches. On the other side of the hill, a narrow road can be followed up on foot past the Municipio, with a tower, to the 14C **Palazzo Pretorio**, with numerous coats of arms. It is in very poor condition and part of it is privately owned, but it is being restored. Above, on top of the hill, is the castle tower (now enclosed in a private garden) and a number of other towers can be seen below.

Outside the village (near Piazza Cavalca) on flat ground by the main road is the fine 12C Romanesque **Pieve**. It contains a sculptured wood group of the *Deposition* (12C–13C) and (in a niche on the left side) a large statue of *St John the*

Baptist, a fine work dating from before 1390 and recently attributed to Nino Pisano. It was restored in 1990 and the arms and head probably date from the 17C. The little baptismal font dates from the 15C.

Farther east is the village of **Santa Maria a Monte** which has an interesting circular plan—all its streets are curved. Its castle was of strategic importance in the Middle Ages and was contested by Florence, Lucca, and Pisa. From Piazza della Vittoria, where a large yellow palace houses the town hall, Via Carducci leads down and continues right round the village. It passes a terrace with a view of the built-up plain of the Arno beside a fine palace and the church of **San Giovanni Evangelista**. In the **interior** the baptismal font has fine sculptures by Domenico di Giovanni Rosselli (1468). On the right of the high altar (behind glass; difficult to see) is a *statue of the *Madonna and Child* enthroned in polychrome wood of 1255. At the east end is a 14C *Crucifix*. Over the side door is an unusual dark stone ambone supported by two lions, with carvings and (unfinished) inlaid marble decoration. Above the attractive east end are worn frescoes by Luigi Ademollo. The **Canonica** next door has a large (but damaged) della Robbian tondo over the door. Via Carducci continues back to Piazza della Vittoria past another pretty curving street with a nice row of little houses. Various winding streets lead up around the top of the hill and the site of the castle which was never repaired after severe damage in the Second World War.

Farther east is **Castelfranco di Sotto**, on low ground beside the Arno, severely damaged in the Second World War, and by the Arno flood of 1966. It preserves its rectangular plan. Beyond an old gate, a road leads to the main piazza with the 15C Palazzo Comunale with a portico facing the flank of the church of **San Pietro**, which contains a painting by Alessandro Allori, a fine 13C statue of *St Peter*, and a 14C *Annunciation* group.

On the eastern border of the province is **Santa Croce sull'Arno** with some 430 tanneries which produce 35 per cent of Italian leather. Fucecchio and the towns further east are in the province of Florence (see Ch. 7).

The province south of the Arno

San Miniato

San Miniato is an interesting little town in a fine position, formerly known as *San Miniato al Tedesco*. It is roughly equidistant between Pisa and Florence (45km from both). On the site of an 8C church dedicated to the Florentine martyr St Minias, the Lombard town became the seat of the Imperial Vicariate in Tuscany. Here Countess Matilda was born in 1046. Its name 'al Tedesco' is supposed to have been derived from the fact that is was often visited by emperors in the 12C and 13C. From 1369 San Miniato came under Florentine dominion.

At the highest point of the town was the **Rocca**, built by Frederick II in 1240 and used by him as a prison for Pier delle Vigne in 1247. Vigne, formerly his most trusted minister ('*io sono colui, che tenni ambo le chiavi del cor di Federico*'—'I am he who kept both the keys of Federico's heart'; Dante *La Divina Commedia, Inferno*, 31–108) fell into disgrace in 1247 (perhaps because he had plotted against the Emperor with Pope Inncoent IV) and was blinded and held here. He is supposed to have committed suicide by throwing himself from the tower in 1249. Only two towers remain of the castle; the highest one, conspicuous for miles around, was rebuilt after its destruction in the Second World War. Paths lead up to the gardens around it. The second massive square tower now serves as the belfry for the Duomo, in the **Prato del Duomo** with pretty trees.

The **Duomo** was built c 1195, but later altered and restored in 1860. The Romanesque brick façade was decorated, like a number of other Pisan church façades at this time, with 31 blue and brown ceramic bowls, probably manufactured in North Africa. Some of these were removed in 1979 to be exhibited in the Museo Diocesano.

Interior. The pulpit and funerary monuments in the aisles are by Amalia Duprè. On the first altar in the south aisle is a *Nativity* by Aurelio Lomi. Over the high altar is a 17C wooden *Crucifix*. In the north transept, Francesco di Angelo Lanfranchi (Lo Spillo), *Deposition* (1528), restored in 1988. Over the first altar in the north aisle, Cosimo Gamberucci, *Raising of Lazarus*.

Next to the Duomo is the **Museo Diocesano** which displays works of art that have been collected from churches in the region. The works are all labelled (**open** 09.00–12.00, 14.30–17.30, except Mon; in winter open only on Sat and Sun).

Room 1: sculptural fragments; detached fresco fragment of a *Maestà* by the Maestro degli Ordini. **Room 2**: Neri di Bicci, *Madonna and Child with Saints*; Rossello di Iacopo Franchi, *St Catherine of Alexandria*, and a scene of her martyrdom; Cenni di Francesco di Ser Cenni, *St Jerome translating the Bible* (which was signed and dated 1411) and a predella scene with the saint being fed by the angel); school of Orcagna, *St Michael Archangel* (and a scene of his fight with the devils). Giovanni da San Giovanni (attributed), detached fresco of the *Annunciation and prophets*, and two frescoed heads. Cases display liturgical objects and church silver. **Room 3**: two drawings by Lodovico Cigoli; Master of Santi Quirico e Giulitta (attributed; formerly thought to be by Filippo Lippi), small *Crucifixion* (c 1430); Francesco Granacci, *Madonna enthroned with Saints*; Jacopo di Michele (*Il Gera*), processional standard, painted on both sides, with the *Flagellation* and *Crucifixion*; Antonio Maria Ferri, wooden model of the church of the Crocifisso (see below); circle of Andrea del Castagno (or an early work by Andrea), *Madonna of the Holy Girdle*; Fra Bartolomeo (with assistants), *Circumcision*. The terracotta bust (with traces of polychrome) of the *Redeemer attributed to Andrea del Verrocchio has been removed for restoration.

The two rooms upstairs display paintings by Matteo Rosselli, Il Poppi, and Lodovico Cigoli (including the *Sacrifice of Isaac*). The two large paintings of the *Deposition* and the *Way to Calvary* are unusual 17C works by the Tuscan-Flemish school.

Opposite the Duomo is the 12C **Palazzo dei Vicari dell'Imperatore**, and the handsome 17C **Palazzo Vescovile** with an angled façade. Three flights of steps lead down beneath the palace to Piazza della Repubblica where the big 17C **Seminario** has a fine façade (the painted decoration and the medieval shop-fronts beneath have been restored). Via Vittime del Duomo leads out of the piazza beneath an arch down to the old **Palazzo Comunale**, the town hall. The Council Chamber on the first floor (admission on request) has a fresco of the *Madonna and Child between Saints* by Cenni di Francesco di Ser Cenni. On the ground floor (entered from the street; unlocked on request at the town hall) is the 15C **Oratory of the Madonna di Loreto** with delightful frescoes probably

SAN MINIATO · 263

dating from 1413 and attributed to Arrigo di Niccolò and others, and a fine wood ancona with 16C Florentine paintings. A theatrical staircase leads up the **Sanctuary of the Crocifisso**, an unusual builing on a Greek-cross plan by Antonio Maria Ferri (1705–18; restored in 1990, open Sat & Sun). It contains 18C frescoes by Antonio Domenico Bamberini. The statues outside include (in a niche) the *Risen Christ* by Francesco Baratta.

Farther on a road climbs left to the huge church of **San Francesco** built in 1276 on the hillside below the Rocca (and completed in 1480). In the interior on the left wall is a fresco fragment of St Christopher by the school of Masolino.

From Piazza della Repubblica (see above) Via Conti descends to **Piazza del Popolo**, the centre of San Miniato, with the church of **San Domenico**. Of ancient foundation, the **interior** has 18C frescoes depicting the *Life of St Dominic* on the upper walls attributed to Antonio Domenico Bamberini. In a chapel at the end of the right side (left of the door into the sacristy) is the tomb of Giovanni Chellini, a Florentine doctor who died in 1461, with a fine effigy, now attributed to Pagno di Lapo Portigiani (on a model by Donatello, who was Chellini's patient). It was recomposed here in the 19C. The altarpiece of the *Madonna and Child* is by Domenico di Michelino and the Master of the Johnson Nativity. In the adjacent chapel (right of the sanctuary) are restored 14C frescoes of the *Life of the Virgin* and (on the pilaster) *St Lawrence*, a fragment attributed to the bottega of Masolino. The *Madonna and Child* is by the Master of San Miniato. The Sanctuary was frescoed in 1900 by Galileo Chini. In the chapel opposite the one with the Chellini monument is a *Deposition and two Saints* in a fine ancona by Il Poppi (recently restored). In other parts of the church are interesting frescoes by the 15C Florentine school and altarpieces by Francesco Curradi, Giovanni Battista Vanni, and Antoniazzo Romano.

Via IV Novembre continues past a number of handsome palaces. In a little piazza the 16C **Palazzo Grifoni** (with a loggia), attributed to Giuliano di Baccio d'Agnolo, is being restored after it was half destroyed in the War. Via Carducci continues past the church of the **Santissima Annunziata** (1522), centrally planned, with an octagonal cupola (over the altar is a worn 14C fresco of the *Annunciation*), and farther on (left; No. 15 Via Roma) is the Conservatorio and church of **Santa Chiara** (closed) which contains a *Crucifix* by Deodato Orlandi and a *Noli me tangere* by Lodovico Cigoli.

West of San Miniato, close to the Arno, is **San Romano**, scene of the indecisive battle of 1432 between the Florentines and the Sienese. The Florentines, led by the condottiere Nicolò da Tolentino, considered it their victory, and a painting of it in three episodes was commissioned by the Medici c 1456 from Paolo Uccello. Considered his masterpiece, the three scenes are now divided between the Uffizi Gallery, the Louvre and the National Gallery in London. There is a good collection of old pharmacy jars in the Farmacia Mannelli in San Romano.

Nearby is **Montopoli in Val d'Arno** in San Romano in pleasant farming countryside. There was a fortress here by the 8C. On the approach road (preceded by a portico and a palm tree) is the church of **Santa Marta** (usually closed) which contains a *Raising of Lazarus* by Lodovico Cigoli and a *Madonna with Souls in Purgatory* by Santi di Tito.

The road leads up past the large church and campanile (formerly a tower of the castle) of **Santo Stefano** (if closed; ring at No. 5). In the pleasant interior (**south side**) the baptistery has a large 16C oval font, and a chapel contain a 14C *Crucifix*. Beyond the second altar, with a *Madonna of the Rosary* by Francesco Curradi, is a *Resurrection* by Orazio Fidani. **North side**. Ludovico Cigoli (attributed), *Prayer in the Garden*; second altar, Jacopo Vignali, *Madonna with Adam and Eve*, a striking painting, signed and dated 1664. On the wall is an interesting small painting of the *Annunciation* (1513), and, above, a lunette with *God the Father*. On the first altar, fresco of the *Holy Family* (1519).

The road continues to Piazza Michele da Montopoli from which a short road leads to a remarkably high and wide arch at the foot of a hill on which the castle was built. The road continues to ascend, and beyond the town hall facing a little piazza with a view and an old tower, it narrows into a track.

From Montopoli a pretty country road leads south up through woods to **Palaia**, first mentioned in 980. There are views of the distant hills to the south towards Volterra and north towards the Apennines. The approach road leads left around the little hill, with a view of the large 13C **Pieve di San Martino** outside the village. It is approached by a signposted road but is usually closed (it was over-restored in the 19C). Porta Fiorentina leads into the long Piazza della Repubblica (closed at the far end by another gate). Above Porta Fiorentina is the campanile of the little 12C church of **Santa Maria** with a plain façade (closed). Via del Popolo leads out of the piazza under a gate with a clock and up past (left) the inconspicuous church of **Sant'Andrea** with a brick façade and small tower. In the interior are two fine statues of the *Madonna and Child* on the right and left of the high altar: the one on the right in painted wood is signed and dated 1403 by Francesco da Valdambrino and the one on the left in terracotta has recently been attributed to Luca della Robbia (c. 1435). On the left wall are parts of a terracotta ciborium with figures of saints, by Andrea della Robbia. On the east wall is a *Crucifix* attributed to the school of Giovanni Pisano. There is a fine view from the Rocca at the top of the village.

To the southwest is **Peccioli**, a pleasant little village in the Era valley. A road leads up from the market square in front of the church of the *Carmine* (closed) to the central piazza. Here is the unusual east end of **San Verano**, next to an amusing bell-tower crowned with circular battlements. The church is entered by the side door. It was founded in the 12C, but later altered and restored after the Second World War. The Romanesque Pisan façade looks out over the plain. In the interior on the right side is a 13C Madonna and Child attributed to Enrico di Tedice. The Oratory (1580) off the left side has a fine carved wood ceiling (the paintings from it by Jacopo Vignali have been removed for restoration). Here is hung a Madonna and four saints by Neri di Bicci. A 14C Crucifix and a 13C painting of St Nicholas of Bari also belong to the church. In the piazza, opposite the east end of the church, is the restored **Palazzo Pretorio** (No. 5) with coats of arms high up on the façade, some in enamelled terracotta.

Outside the village (well signposted) is a small park with life-size models of dinosaurs and a children's playground (open daily).

To the west is **Casciana Terme**, an attractive little spa town surrounded by low hills planted with olives and vineyards. It has tree-lined streets and some Art Nouveau houses. It was known for its curative waters in Roman times and in the

Middle Ages (when they were taken by Countess Matilda). In 1311, the Pisans built baths here and it became well known again in the 18C. It has warm anti-rheumatic waters used for both bathing and drinking. The season runs from April to November.

In the central Piazza Garibaldi is the handsome neo-classical façade of the **Terme** by Giuseppe Poggi (1870). Behind are the new spa buildings (being enlarged) and a park. Just off the piazza is the tourist information office (called the Ritrovo del Forestiero). There are numerous small furniture factories in the area.

A pretty by-road leads up to **Casciana Alta**, a hamlet with a spacious piazza with plane trees, and a terrace overlooking lovely countryside. Here the church of **San Niccolò**, with a cupola, has a heavily decorated neo-classical interior with orange-painted Corinthian columns. The painting of the *Hospitality of St Julian* is by Orazio Fidani.

To the north is **Crespina**. The Macchiaioli artist Silvestro Lega often stayed and painted in this area. Above the village is the church of **San Michele** with a statue of the saint on the façade. A painting of *St Michael Archangel* by Bernardo Daddi belongs to the church.

From the church, Via Montegrappa (signposted *La Guardia*), Via San Rocco, and Via Belvedere lead to the beautiful 18C **Villa di Belvedere**, with a monumental flight of steps on the façade, approached by an ancient cypress avenue and preceded by a handsome garden (not open to the public). The elegant little 18C domed chapel was built by Mattia Tarocchi in 1775–84 and decorated by Giovanni Battista Tempesti. It contains a painted *Cross* by the Master of San Torpè. The countryside here is particularly lovely.

A narrow road which crosses pretty countryside where the vineyards produce good wine, passes a neo-classical oratory on its way east to **Lari**. A little village of Etruscan origins, it was built in a circle around the foot of a huge Medici fortress with splendid brick bastions designed by Francesco da Sangallo in 1530. A gate leads through the outer walls and then steps (signposted) lead up round the bastion to the entrance to the **castle** (**open** Oct–Apr on fest. 15.00–18.00; May–Sept on fest 15.30–19.30; or ☎ 0587-684126). Founded in the 11C the castle became the property of the Pisan family of Upezzinghi in the 13C and in the 15C of the governors of Florence. Inside is a little paved courtyard with a well and numerous coats of arms on three walls including many in enamelled polychrome terracotta. The ground floor can be visited. There is a *Madonna and Child* by the bottega of Andrea della Robbia, as well as the prisons, and it is possible to walk around the ramparts.

The **church** at the foot of the castle was restored in 1910. On either side of the choir, the two marble statues of the *Annunciation* are attributed to Andrea Guardi. On the left wall is a beautiful tabernacle with a *Madonna and Child* in enamelled terracotta surrounded by a garland, by Giovanni della Robbia (1524). In a niche off the right side is a painting of the *Madonna* by Francesco Melani, highly decorated.

Cevoli, nearby, has a conspicuous church beside a cemetery with a large semicircular apse which contains the only known painting signed by Andrea de Pisis (who helped Benozzo Gozzoli with the frescoes in the Camposanto in Pisa), dated 1490.

Due north, on the south bank of the Arno is **Pontedera**, a busy market well known for its large Piaggio motor-scooter factory. In 1998 a Museum dedicated to the *Vespa* was opened here in one of the factory warehouses erected in the 1920s. The exhibits include the first model designed in 1946 (some 20 million vespas will have been manufactured by the year 2000), and other vehicles produced by Piaggio since 1884.

17 · Volterra and environs

Volterra lies in a magnificent position on a precipitous hill (531m) with open views in every direction across a splendid yellow and grey landscape of rolling clay hills. It is an austere medieval walled town (12,600 inhab.), the successor to an Etruscan city of much greater extent. Almost all the buildings are constructed out of *panchina*, a kind of limestone which is the matrix of alabaster, and which is found here in abundance. The town has for long been famous for the traditional skill of its craftsmen in working alabaster, and some two hundred workshops here still produce objets-d'art.

■ Practical information
Information office. IAT, 2 Via Turazza (☎ 0588-86150).

Getting there
By road. The fastest route by road to Volterra from Florence is via the Florence–Siena superstrada as far as the exit *Colle Val d'Elsa Nord*. Here N68 continues west past Colle Val d'Elsa (described in Ch. 29). The beautiful road runs along a pretty ridge of hills with distant views, including the towers of San Gimignano to the north (see Ch. 28). The road then climbs through magnificent countryside to reach the distinctive open landscape around Volterra.

By bus. Services run by *SITA* from Florence via Castelfiorentino in 2hrs 40min. Other services from Florence and Siena via Colle Val d'Elsa, where a change is necessary. There are also buses to Volterra from Pisa, Massa Marittima, and San Gimignano.

By rail. The nearest station for Volterra is Saline di Volterra, 11km southwest in the valley. It is on a branch line to Cecina (in 30 mins; some trains are substituted by buses), which is on the main line from Pisa to Rome (slow trains only). Bus connection with trains runs to Piazza XX Settembre in Volterra.

Parking. Large underground car park at the entrance to the town just before Piazza Martiri della Libertà. Other car parks outside the walls.

Hotels in Volterra
★★★★ *San Lino*, 26 Via San Lino (☎ 0588-85250; fax 0588-80620).
★★★ *Etruria*, 32 Via Matteotti (☎ & fax 0588-87377); *Villa Nencini*, 55 Borgo Santo Stefano (outside Porta San Francesco; ☎ 0588-86386; fax 0588-80601); *Sole*, 10 Via dei Cappuccin (☎ & fax 0588-84000).

Hotels in the environs
Pomarance. ★★★ *Pomerancio*, 18 Via Roncalli (☎ & fax 0588-64616).
Castelnuovo di Val di Cecina. ★★★ *Il Castagno*, località Piana (☎ 0588-20540).
Larderello. ★★★ *La Perla*, località La Perla (☎ 0588-67287).

Youth hostel. *Ostello della Gioventù*, 2 Via del Poggetto (☎ 0588-85577).

Campsite. ★★ *Le Balze*, Via Mandringa, open Apr–Oct (☎ 0588-87880).

Restaurants in Volterra

Volterra. ££ *Etruria*, 8 Piazza dei Priori.

£: *Il Pozzo degli Etruschi*, 28 Via delle Prigioni; *La Pace*, 29 Via Don Minzoni; *Pizzeria il Rifugio*, Piazza XX Settembre; *Da Badò*, 9 Borgo San Lazzaro; *Lo Sgherro*, Borgo San Giusto (beyond Porta San Francesco).

Lovely places to **picnic** include the Parco Archeologico and the outskirts of the town, near San Giusto or overlooking the Balze.

Annual festivals. *Astiludio* on 1st Sun in September, with flag-throwing and processions. Theatre Festival in July.

A large **market** is held in the town on Saturday mornings (near the Roman Theatre in summer).

History. Velathri was the northernmost of the 12 cities of the Confederation of Etruria Propria and one of the most prominent. In the 3C BC it became the Roman Volaterrae. In the late 2C BC it supported the cause of the democratic consul Marius against the dictator Sulla during the Civil Wars which preceeded the collapse of the Roman Republic. Volterra was besieged for two years before falling to Sulla's troops. It gained some importance under the Lombards and was for a time the residence of the Lombard kings.

After bitter struggles, it was subdued by Florence in 1361, and again in 1472 in the the **War of Volterra**, waged by Lorenzo il Magnifico for control of its alum deposits, which culminated in the sacking of the city by the Florentines under the command of Federico da Montefeltro. Lorenzo is said to have asked for forgiveness on his deathbed for this brutal act. Another rebellion was crushed by Francesco Ferrucci in 1530 and Volterra remained under Florentine dominion, and later under the Grand-duchy of Tuscany, until the unification of Italy in 1860.

Natives of Volterra include the satirist Persius Flaccus (AD 34–62), St Linus, the reputed successor of St Peter in the papal chair, Pope Leo the Great (440–461), and the painter Daniele Ricciarelli da Volterra (1509–66).

Piazza dei Priori

Piazza Martiri della Libertà forms the southern entrance of the town; at the north end of the piazza, Via Marchesi leads left to Piazza dei Priori, bordered either by medieval buildings or ones built in the medieval style. Immediately to the left is the austere **Palazzo dei Priori** (open weekdays 10.00–13.00, 15.00–16.00; winter 10.00–13.00), with its battlemented tower, now the town hall, the oldest building of its kind in Tuscany. It was begun in 1208 and completed in 1257 by Riccardo da Como; the windows on the first floor were altered later and the upper part of the tower was rebuilt and modified in 1846.

The vestibule is decorated with coats of arms, and steps lead up to the first floor and the **Sala del Consiglio Comunale** (admission when not in use), the town council chamber since 1257. The original timber ceiling was replaced by the present double cross-vault in 1516. On the end wall is a fresco of the *Annunciation* by Jacopo di Cione (1383), and to the right, the *Marriage Feast at Cana* by Donato Mascagni; the remaining decoration is modern. In the next room, the **Saletta della Giunta**, are several paintings: *Job and his wife* by Donato Mascagni, the *Birth of the Virgin* by Ignazio Hugford, and the *Adoration of the*

VOLTERRA

CECINA

S. GIUSTO E LE BALZE

⊕→N

0   200 yards
0   200 metres

Porta
S. Francesco
V. PISANA

Porta
S. Felice
S. Dalmazio
PIAZZA
INGHIRAMI
S. Francesco

VIA S. LINO
S. Lino

VIA MAZZINI
VIA LANDINI

Battistero
Arco Etrusco
Mus. Arte Sacra
Duomo
Torre Buomparenti

S. Alessandro
PIAZZA
MARTIRI
LIBERTA
Underground
Car Park
PIAZZA
DEI
PRIORI
Palazzo
d. Priori
Palazzo Minucci-Solaini (Pinacoteca)

Roman Theatre
& Baths

Palazzo Pretorio
Palazzo Viti

V. DI PORTA DIANA

VIALE CESARE BATTISTI
VIALE GARIBALDI
VIALE DEI PONTE

Piscina
Romano
Parco
Archeologico

V. GRAMSCI
V. GUARNACCI
Porta
Fiorentina

V. DI SOTTO
S. Michele

S. Antonio
PIAZZA
D. BASTIONE

Rocca Nuova

VIA DI CASTELLO

PIAZZA
XX SETTEMBRE
S. Agostino

Porta
Docciola
VIALE G. D'ANNUNZIO

Fortezza

V. DON MINZONI
Museo
Etrusco
Guarnacci
Porta
Marcoli

Rocca
Vecchia
Porta a Selci

Medieval Walls

VIALE DEI FILOSOFI

V. CARDUCCI
V. PORTA A SELCI
PIAZZA DELL
UNITA ITALIANA

Etruscan Walls
S. Andrea

VIA S. LAZZERO
VIALE DEI FILOSOFI

COLLE VAL D'ELSA (N68)

Magi by Giovanni Domenico Ferretti. Steps lead up to the bell-tower from which there is a magnificent view, stretching as far as the sea.

To the right of Palazzo dei Priori is **Palazzo Vescovile**, originally the town granary, which was begun in the 14C. In between, set back from the piazza, is the north transept of the cathedral, decorated with horizontal bands of black-and-white marble.

Across the piazza is a remarkable sequence of 13C architecture. Begin on the right with **Palazzo Pretorio**, surmounted by the Torre del Porcellino, which derives its name from the sculpted boar on a bracket to the right of the top window. The vertical emphasis of the building is underlined by the narrow windows flanking the tower. The adjacent **Palazzo del Podestà** has three large rounded arches on the ground floor and two-light windows on the three upper storeys. The crenellated tower to the left, formerly a prison, adds to the variety of forms, openings, and use of stone. At the end of the piazza is the former **Palazzo Incontri**, now used as a bank, which has been considerably modified through the centuries. Facing it, at the opposite end of the piazza, is the modern **Palazzo Demaniale**, designed to harmonise with the older buildings.

Via Turazza leads out of the piazza to the left of Palazzo dei Priori. It passes the remains of the Romanesque transept and nave of the cathedral, and the late 18C **Oratorio della Misericordia**. This chapel contains a *Crucifixion* by Donato Mascagni (1602) over the altar, and paintings by Giovanna Forzoni (*Agony in the Garden*, 19C), Giuseppe Nicola Nasini (*Birth of the Virgin*), and Giuseppe Arrighi (*St Anthony of Padua*).

In the beautiful **Piazza San Giovanni** is the baptistery, opposite the cathedral façade, and, at the far end, the Hospital of Santa Maria Maddalena.

The Duomo

The Duomo, or Basilica of Santa Maria Assunta (open all day) dates from the 12C, and the **façade** is a fine example of 13C Pisan architecture, with blind arches beneath the roof and three small round windows. The lower part was modified in the 16C with the addition of the three larger windows and the doorway, decorated in the lunette with green and white marble.

The **interior**, which was rebuilt in the later 16C, has a Latin-cross plan with five apse chapels and an additional chapel at the end of each transept. The nave and aisles are divided by columns of painted stucco and capitals by Leonardo Ricciarelli. The long nave has a magnificent coffered ceiling designed by Francesco Capriani, and executed by Jacopo Pavolini (1580).

South aisle. First altar, Pieter de Witte (also known as Pietro Candido; 1578), the *City of Volterra presented to the Madonna by her patron Saints Giusto and Ottaviano*; second altar, Francesco Curradi, *Birth of the Virgin*; third altar, Giovan Battista Naldini, *Presentation of the Virgin* (1590).

South transept. Outside the Chapel of San Carlo Borromeo, which preserves the wall of its Romanesque structure, is a *Crucifixion* by Francesco Curradi (1611). Inside are paintings by Matteo Rosselli (*St Carlo*), Camillo Incontri (*St Mary Magdalen*), Alessandro Gherardini (*St Francis of Paola*)and Francesco Brini (*Immaculate Conception*). The Holy Sacrament chapel at the end of the transept has a fine ceiling with stucco decoration by Lionello Ricciarelli and two scenes from the life of Christ by Giovanni Balducci; the altarpiece of the *Raising of Lazarus* is by Santi di Tito (1592) and the painted niches have 18C frescoes of saints by Agostino Veracini The Chapel of the Deposition has a monumental Deposition (1228), composed of life-size figures in gilded and painted wood, by a Pisan sculptor. Behind is a small chapel of the original Romanesque church, with fresco fragments representing Christ's Passion, attributed to Taddeo di Bartolo.

To the right of the choir is the **Chapel of St Ottaviano**, whose body is preserved in a marble urn by Raffaello Cioli of Settignano (1522–25). St Ottaviano, a 6C hermit and one of Volterra's venerated patron saints, saved the city from a terrible plague in 1522.

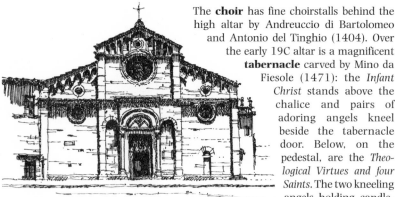

The Duomo, Volterra

The **choir** has fine choirstalls behind the high altar by Andreuccio di Bartolomeo and Antonio del Tinghio (1404). Over the early 19C altar is a magnificent **tabernacle** carved by Mino da Fiesole (1471): the *Infant Christ* stands above the chalice and pairs of adoring angels kneel beside the tabernacle door. Below, on the pedestal, are the *Theological Virtues and four Saints*. The two kneeling angels holding candlesticks are by Andrea Ferrucci of Fiesole. Flanking the high altar are two angels, also by Mino da Fiesole, kneeling on two elegant Gothic columns. The fresco of *God the Father* in the vault is by Niccolò Cercignani.

The first chapel off the **north transept** contains the marble tomb of St Ugo (1644), bishop of Volterra. In the next chapel is a polychrome statue of the *Madonna* by Francesco di Valdambrino. The end chapel, dedicated to St Paul, has frescoes in the vault depicting the *Life of St Paul*, by Giovanni da San Giovanni. The altarpiece of the *Conversion of St Paul* is by Domenichino (Domenico Zampieri), the *Decapitation* by Francesco Curradi, and *Paul's mission to Damascus* by Matteo Rosselli.

Outside the sacristy is a holy water stoup by Andrea Sansovino and, over the door, the *Immaculate Conception* by Cosimo Daddi. The **Sacristy** has 15C choirbooks and cupboards. An impressive Baroque reliquary cupboard contains fine silver busts of the patron saints of Volterra.

North aisle. **Third altar**, Niccolò Cercignani, *Immaculate Conception* (1586). The 13C Pisan pulpit supported on columns borne by lions was put together in 1584 using various sculptural fragments. The reliefs represent the *Sacrifice of Isaac*, the *Annunciation* and *Visitation*, and the *Last Supper*. **Second altar**, *Annunciation*, a painting of great harmony and beauty, full of light and space, with a landscape extending far into the distance. Formerly attributed to Mariotto Albertinelli, it is now generally accepted as the work of Fra Bartolommeo (1497). **First altar**, Francesco Cungi, *Martyrdom of St Sebastian* (1588).

A little chapel, dedicated to Our Lady of Sorrows, has two niches containing painted terracotta scenes of the *Adoration of the Magi* and the *Nativity*, attributed to Luca and Andrea della Robbia c 1474), the latter with a charming frescoed background by Benozzo Gozzoli. On the west wall is the tomb of Monsignor Mario Maffei attributed to Giovanni Angelo Montorsoli (1537) and a Romanesque altar frontal.

The Baptistery

Facing the cathedral is the elegant, octagonal baptistery, the restoration of which has just been completed. It is built in the local stone with a façade decorated with horizontal bands of black-and-white marble. The doorway is framed with clusters of slender columns supporting a rounded arch above the architrave, which is carved with heads of Christ and the Madonna and the twelve apostles, and inscribed with the date 1283. The dome was added in the 16C when the walls had to be heightened to counteract the thrust.

The **interior** is simple and unadorned. Inside the entrance is a holy water stoup made from an Etruscan funerary stone. The large octagonal font in the centre is by Giuseppe Covo, and the statue of *St John the Baptist* by Giovanni Cybo (1759). Above the altar is an altarpiece representing the *Ascension* by Niccolò Cercignani (1591) the upper part of which was destroyed in the Second World War. To the right of the altar is the original baptismal **font** by Andrea Sansovino (1502), with marble bas-reliefs of the *Baptism of Christ* and four seated figures of *Faith*, *Hope*, *Charity*, and *Justice*.

To the left of the cathedral façade is a lunette containing statues of *Saints Giusto, Lino,* and *Ottaviano* by the contemporary sculptor Raffaello Consortini. Beyond is the tall, square **Campanile**, dated 1493, which towers over the piazza.

Closing the piazza on the left is the ex-hospital of **Santa Maria Maddalena** (restored as a study centre in 1990), with an elegant Renaissance portico. The **Oratorio** in Via Franceschini has 17C frescoes.

Museo d'Arte Sacra

The **Palazzo Vescovile** in Via Roma houses the Museo d'Arte Sacra (**open** summer 09.00–12.30, 15.00–18.00; winter 10.00–13.00; combined ticket with the Pinacoteca and Museo Etrusco). The collection comprises works of art and objects from the cathedral and from other churches of the diocese. In the vestibule are bells (11C–15C) and bas-reliefs with scenes from the life of *St Vittore* attributed to Giovanni di Agostino, Roman and Romanesque reliefs and four 14C Pisan sculpted angels.

In the **first room**: sculptures by Giovanni di Agostino, a bust of *St Lino* by Andrea della Robbia, and a silver reliquary bust of *St Ottaviano* by Antonio del Pollaiolo, a painted wooden tabernacle attributed to Bartolomeo della Gattaand other paintings by Taddeo di Bartolo and Neri di Bicci and a fine Pisan 13C *Crucifix*. There are numerous liturgical objects, inlaid wood panels and reliquaries. The most celebrated painting is a small panel of the *Madonna and Child with St John the Baptist and St John the Evangelist* (1521) by Rosso Fiorentino.

In **room 2** is a gilded bronze *Crucifix* attributed to Giambologna and church silver and several paintings including a *Madonna and Child with Saints* by Daniele da Volterra of (1545), a *Madonna* attributed to Giusto d'Andrea, and an *Annunciation* by Benvenuto di Giovanni and two *Saints* by Cosimo Daddi. **Room 3** contains illuminated choir books and vestments.

The Pinacoteca and Museo Civico

Via Roma crosses Via Ricciarelli, off Piazza dei Priori, and passes under the lofty archway of the 13C Buomparenti and Buonaguidi tower houses. The medieval Via Buomparenti leads into Via Sarti. On the corner (No. 1) is **Palazzo Minucci Solaini** which was restored in 1982 to house the **Pinacoteca e Museo Civico** (**open** daily, in summer 09.00–19.00; winter 09.00–14.00; combined ticket with Museo d'Arte Sacra and Museum Civico).

The small, elegant Renaissance palace with a loggia surrounding the courtyard is traditionally attributed to Antonio da Sangallo il Vecchio. The collection, consisting mainly of paintings by Tuscan artists formerly exhibited in Palazzo dei Priori, is small but choice. The works are arranged chronologically.

First floor. Room 1: 13C Tuscan *Crucifix*; Romanesque capitals and a sculptured lunette. **Room 2**: 14C and early 15C works and a chapel with a small altarpiece, attributed to Francesco Conti. **Room 3**: magnificent polyptych, signed and dated 1411 (from the Palazzo dei Priori), and the *Madonna of the Rose* by Taddeo di Bartolo. **Room 4**: polyptych by Cenni di Francesco (1408) and works by Francesco Neri da Volterra and Jacopo di Michele. **Room 5**: triptych by the Portuguese painter Alvaro Pirez (c 1423). **Room 6**: two polychrome wood statues of the *Virgin* and the *Angel Gabriel* by Francesco di Valdambrino (c 1410), originally in the cathedral. **Room 7**: several paintings by Priamo della Quercia. **Room 8**: altarpiece by Neri di Bicci. **Room 9**: *Nativity* and predella scenes, signed and dated 1470, by Benvenuto di Giovanni. **Room 10**: an impressive altarpiece representing *Christ in glory worshipped by Saints Benedict, Romualdo, Attinia, and Greciniana*, in a beautiful landscape (1492), by Domenico del Ghirlandaio; so-called Master of Santo Spirito (recently identified as the brothers Agnolo and Donnino di Domenico Mazziere), *Madonna enthroned with Saints*; Leonardo Malatesta, *Madonna and Child with Saints*. **Room 11** displays the gallery's most famous work, the *Deposition* by **Rosso Fiorentino**, signed and dated 1521, one of the masterpieces of Florentine Mannerist art. Also here are two fine works by Luca Signorelli, both dated 1491, an *Annunciation and Madonna and Child enthroned with Saints John the Baptist, Francis, Anthony of Padua, Bonaventura, and Jerome*. **Room 12**: two paintings by Pieter de Witte (Pietro Candido) and a *Nativity* by Domenico Mascagni and three works by Pomarancio. **Room 13**: Fragments including a *Head of the Madonna* by Giuliano Bugiardini, and some small 15C–16C Florentine and Flemish paintings. **Room 14**: Baldassare Franceschini (called Il Volterrano), *Madonna and Child in glory with Saints Francis, Clare, John the Evangelist, Stephen, Mary Magdalen, and Paul* (1639). More rooms are to be opened to display 17C and 18C silver, and the collection of coins and medals from the Museo Guarnacci. The loggia provides beautiful views over the valley.

Via Sarti

In the spacious Via Sarti are several fine palaces including Palazzo Tortora Salvetti (on the left) and Palazzo Ruggieri Buzzaglia with two balconies (on the right).

Farther down is the fine 16C façade of **Palazzo Viti** (originally Incontri), attributed to Bartolomeo Ammannati. In the early 19C the ground floor and courtyard, which had remained unfinished, were bought by the Accademia dei Riuniti and rebuilt as a **theatre** (now a cinema). The palace was acquired in 1850 by Benedetto Giuseppe Viti, an alabaster merchant, who had the interior redecorated for a visit of Vittorio Emanuele II in 1860. The entrance staircase (at No. 41) by Giovanni Caccini was decorated with a bust of the King and a plaque commemorating his visit. The **piano nobile** (which may be visited on request) has elegant period furniture and a unique collection of works in alabaster, as well as Indian and Chinese objects acquired by Viti during his trading expeditions in the East.

Via Sarti leads into the small Piazza San Michele. Here is a 13C medieval tower and the church of **San Michele Arcangelo** which has a fine Pisan-Romanesque façade decorated with blind arches on two levels, divided by striped black-and-white marble decoration. In the lunette over the doorway is a 14C statue of the *Madonna and Child*. The interior was altered in 1827. To the left of the altar is a glazed terracotta *Madonna and Child* attributed to Giovanni della Robbia in a marble tabernacle. The church also has an unglazed terracotta statue of *St Michael Archangel* by Andrea Della Robbia.

Via Guarnacci leads north from the piazza to **Porta Fiorentina**, which preserves its old wooden doors. Just outside the gate is the entrance to the ***Roman theatre** (usually **open** 11.00–16.00), built at the end of the 1C BC and one of the best preserved in Italy. Excavations, begun in 1952 by Enrico Fiumi, revealed part of the cavea and scena, with Corinthian columns over 5m high. Numerous coins (3C BC–4C AD) found here are now in the Museo Guarnacci (see below). Inside the portico, which was added a century later, are remains of Roman baths. When closed, the theatre can be viewed from above.

From Piazza San Michele, Via di Sotto passes the Romanesque flank of San Michele and Via Docciola, a picturesque street with steps leading down between cypress trees to the **Fonti di Docciola**, a fountain protected by a brick vault supported on two large Gothic arches, dating from 1245. Nearby is the 13C **Porta di Docciola**. Via di Sotto broadens as it reaches Piazza XX Settembre. To the right is the 15C **Oratory of Sant'Antonio Abate**, inside which is a painting of the titular saint by Priamo della Quercia (1442).

On the left is a war memorial and the church of **Sant'Agostino**, founded in the late 13C, but rebuilt in 1728. It has a basilican plan with a nave and two aisles divided by Corinthian columns. Inside, on the right, is the tomb of Alessandro Riccobaldi (d. 1523), decorated with skulls and cross-bones. In the south aisle is a 13C painted *Crucifix* (damaged) and a 14C fresco of the *Madonna and Child* in a marble tabernacle. A chapel to the right has monochrome frescoes, all copies after famous paintings, dating from 1912, and over the altar is a 14C fresco of the *Madonna* and beneath it is a painted terracotta *Pietà*. In the chapel to the left of the high altar is a *Madonna with Saints Thomas of Villanova and Clare of Montefalco* by Volterrano (1669), and, in the north aisle, the *Madonna del Soccorso* by Ulisse Giocchi (1614). On the entrance wall are fresco fragments of a large *Crucifixion*, detached from the Badia, attributed to a follower of Giotto.

The Guarnacci Etruscan Museum

The lovely building, with a garden, at No. 15 Via Don Minzoni houses the *Museo Etrusco Guarnacci, one of the most interesting Etruscan collections in Italy, and extremely well displayed (also labelled in English; **open** daily in summer, 09.00–19.00; winter, 09.00–14.00).

The nucleus of the collection was donated in 1732 by Canon Pietro Franceschini who was the first to discover Etruscan urns in the area. It was subsequently enriched by the important bequest of Monsignor Mario Guarnacci (1701–85), a wealthy prelate of Volterra who financed local excavations and bequeathed his archaeological collection and library to his native city.

The arrangement begins on the **ground floor** with a prehistoric section demonstrating the existence of primitive communities in this territory, with finds from excavations, and maps. The Roman section includes portrait heads, reliefs, fragments of murals, and several mosaic floors from the theatre and baths.

The Etruscan civilisation, from the 10C BC onwards, is magnificently documented.

An Etruscan urn in the Museo Etrusco Guarnacci, Volterra

Entire finds from local tombs dating from the 8C–7C BC are exhibited, with arms, household objects, fibulae and bronzes. From the 6C BC there are stele and fragments with inscriptions. The collection is particularly famous for its **Etruscan cinerary urns**, in alabaster or terracotta, mostly dating from the 3C BC, found locally and numbering over 600. The terracotta urns are probably the oldest. Many are sculpted with fine reliefs and the lids generally bear the recumbent figures of the dead, with the cup of life reversed.

On the staircase walls are Roman inscriptions and Romanesque fragments. **First floor**. Rooms XIII–XIX contain cinerary urns arranged according to the subjects of the reliefs: Theban and Trojan cycles, Amazons, Ulysses, mythological themes. Room XX: terracotta *tomb cover with strikingly realistic portraits of a husband and wife (early 1C BC). Room XXII contains lamps and works in bronze, including the famous bronze votive figure of the early 3C BC, known as the 'Shadow of the Evening' on account of its immensely elongated proportions. Room XXIII displays coins. Room XXIV: bronze figurines, bone and ivory objects, and jewellery.

Second floor. Room XXVII: fragments of a pediment. Room XXIX contains examples of tools used for sculpting marble and alabaster. Room XXX (with a fine view) has chosen examples of alabaster urns dating from the 3C–2C BC. Room XXXI has examples of urns, illustrating various themes. Room XXXII: portraits and large-scale reclining figures. Room XXXIII: mirrors. Room XXXIV: bronze objects. Room XXXV: marble statues, stele, and inscriptions. Room XXXVI: contains Etruscan pottery.

Opposite the museum, Vicolo Marchi leads to Via di Castello, which has a magnificent view of the **Fortezza**. This massive structure is composed of the Rocca Vecchia to the left, built by the Duke of Athens in 1343, joined by a double rampart to the Rocca Nuova on the right, which was added by Lorenzo il Magnifico in 1472–75. The Rocca Nuova forms a square, with circular towers at each corner, surrounding the battlemented tower known as *Il Maschio*. The Rocca Vecchia has a semicircular tower called *La Femmina*, and another tower next to the Porta a Selci beside the entrance. The Fortezza has always been a prison, and is still used as such.

Via di Castello leads back to the town centre via the **Parco Archeologico Fiumi**, a beautiful public garden (ideal for picnics) on the site of the Etruscan and Roman acropolis. There are fine views from the park which overlooks excavations of a Roman piscina or reservoir.

From Piazza San Giovanni (see p. 269) Via Persio Flacco (beside the Baptistery) leads to Via Lungo Le Mura which continues downhill overlooking the valley to the south, ending at the famous **Porta all'Arco**, the main gateway to the Etruscan town, dating from the 4C–3C BC, partly rebuilt by the Romans in the 1C BC.

The splendid, impressive round arch is decorated with three monumental heads, supposed to be of Etruscan divinities. It has miraculously survived despite sieges and modern warfare. A plaque to the right records how the citizens of Volterra saved it from destruction in 1944 by undertaking to fill it with paving stones overnight: *Ospite, quest'opera grande dei nostri maggiori minacciata dal furore di una barbara guerra fu serbata alla tua ammirazione soltanto da noi Volterrani* (Know, O Visitor, that this arch, one of the greatest of our monuments, was preserved for your admiration from the threat of a barbarous war by citizens of Volterra singlehanded).

From beneath the arch the pretty Via Porta all'Arco winds back uphill to Piazza dei Priori.

The historic centre

The centre of the old town has a maze of winding streets which run up and downhill, with narrow alleys, many of which are arched. From Piazza dei Priori, Via Ricciarelli leads west past the Buomparenti and Buonaguidi tower-houses (see above), and other interesting houses including a fine rusticated palace, to the little **Oratory of San Cristofano**, inside which is a fresco of the *Madonna* attributed to Mariotto d'Andrea da Volterra. Via San Lino continues downhill. On the right is the church of **San Lino**, with a façade of 1513. The **interior** has a series of lunettes with scenes from the *Life of Christ* by Cosimo Daddi (1618). On the south altar, Cesare Dandini, *Birth of the Virgin*; on the high altar, Francesco Curradi, *Madonna in Glory with St Lino and other Saints*. On the north altar is a *Visitation* by Cosimo Daddi. The tomb of Beato Raffaele Maffei, the founder of the church, is by Silvio Cosini (1522) and the statues of *Beato Gherardo* and the archangel *Raphael* in the side niches are by Stagio Stagi.

The street ends at Piazza Inghirami, inside Porta San Francesco. To the left is the small church of **San Dalmazio**, which is still owned by the Inghirami family, with a Renaissance doorway (1516). It contains an altarpiece of the *Deposition* signed and dated 1551 by Giovan Paolo Rossetti, a native of Volterra. The ceiling fresco of the *Glory of St Dalmazio* is by Ranieri del Pace. The two ovals with stories of *St Benedict* by Giovanni Camillo Sagrestani, the *Vision of St Dominic* by Jacopo Vignali and the *Noli me Tangere* by Giovanni Balducci.

San Francesco

Opposite, above a slope, is the 13C church of San Francesco, which has been extensively rebuilt. **Inside**, on the south side of the nave: Giovan Battista Naldini, *Immaculate Conception* (1585); Niccolò Circignani, fresco of the *Pietà*; Alessandro Gherardini, *Hermits* (1748).

A door leads into the **Cappella della Croce di Giorno**, built in 1315 next to the church by the Tedicinghi family, with its own entrance facing the piazza. The chapel was entirely painted with **frescoes** by Cenni di Francesco in 1410, representing the *Legend of the True Cross and the Infancy of Christ*, commissioned by the subsequent owners, the Conti Guidi. This is not only a rare and fascinating example of a narrative cycle, but it is also a description, in countless details, of the architecture and costumes of the period.

On the main entrance wall, in a lunette: *Seth receives the branch of the Tree of Sin and plants it on Adam's grave*; and below: *the Queen of Sheba predicts the future of the miraculous wood*; **left wall**: *the wood is used to make the Cross*; next bay: *St*

Helena identifies the True Cross; below: *St Helena carries away the Cross*; to the left: on the pilaster, *St Francis receiving the stigmata*; *Chosroes, King of Persia, steals the Cross*; *Vision of the Emperor Constantine*, and the *Battle of Maxentius at the Milvian bridge*; left of the door: *the idolatry of Chosroes*; **right wall**: *Chosroes beheaded, and Heraclius, barefoot, brings the Cross back to Jerusalem*; on the right pilaster: *St John the Baptist*. The second bay of the right wall represents *the Nativity and Adoration of the Shepherds* in the lunette, and a large, dramatic scene of the *Massacre of the Innocents* below. In the apse, from left to right, the *Holy Sepulchre*, above the *Flight into Egypt*; *Death of the Virgin* (damaged); *Annunciation*, above the *Circumcision*. The spandrels of the vault are frescoed by Jacopo da Firenze with figures of the *Evangelists and Saints* standing on clouds against a blue sky. On the altar a *Crucifixion* attributed to Bartolomeo Neroni replaces Rosso Fiorentino's *Deposition*, now in the Pinacoteca.

Passing from the chapel into the church there is a tomb (1719) of a member of the Guidi family over the doorway.

The marble Baroque **high altar** contains a 15C image of the *Madonna*. In the crossing (left) is the tomb of Bishop Jacopo Guidi who died in 1588. On the left side of the nave is a *Madonna and Child with Saints* by Vincenzo Meucci. At the entrance to the sacristy there is a holy water stoup in the form of a marble, prow-like, female figure of the vestal virgin Tuccia, holding a sieve, dated 1522. In the **sacristy** is a group of terracotta figures by Zaccaria Zacchi, representing the *Pietà*. Farther down the nave are a *Crucifixion* by Cosimo Daddi, the tomb of Mario Guarnacci (after whom the museum is named) in yellow and white marble with reclining figures of *Justice* and *Contemplation* beside his portrait bust, and a *Nativity* by Giovanni Balducci.

Outside the 14C **Porta San Francesco**, one of the grandest and best preserved gateways of the town, Via del Borgo di Santo Stefano leads down past the ruined church of that name to the church and convent of **Santa Chiara**, which has a portico attributed to Ammannati. Nearby is an impressive stretch of **Etruscan walls**.

Borgo San Giusto continues downhill to (c 15 minutes) the church of **Santi Giusto e Clemente**, its eccentric tall façade rising above a grassy slope planted with cypresses. It was founded in 1627 to replace an earlier church which disappeared into the Balze (see below), but only completed in 1775. In front of the **façade** are terracotta figures of the patrons and protectors of Volterra, *Saints Giusto* and *Clemente* (right), the titular saints (brother missionaries who came from Africa in the 6C), and (left) *Saints Ottaviano* and *Lino*. They stand on monolithic stone columns with Romanesque capitals.

The grandiose **interior** has a Latin-cross plan with a single nave. **South side.** Cosimo Daddi, *Visitation*; Giovanni Domenico Ferretti, *St Francis Xavier preaching*; *Martyrdom of Saints Attinia and Greciniana* (1642). In the south transept there is a photographic reproduction of a *Madonna and Child* by Neri di Bicci. On the main altar, flanking a marble urn, are the statues of *Saints Giusto and Clemente*. In the Cappella della Compagnia, ceiling fresco of *Elisha and the angel* by Volterrano (1631). On the north side is a painting of the *Martyrdom of St Ursula, and Saints surrounding the Madonna* by Pietro Dandini,

The road continues past a small gate (view) and ends beside the restored Etruscan walls overlooking the formidable precipice of **Le Balze**, formed by the natural erosion of the Pleistocene clay. Erosion and several earthquakes have not only engulfed the greater part of the earliest necropolis of Volterra and buildings of subsequent periods, but continues to be a threat. Off Via Pisana, on a hill, are the ruins of the **Badia** which was abandoned after the earthquake of 1846 and subsequent landslides.

Environs of Volterra

Below the Fortezza (see above) Viale dei Ponti, a beautiful panoramic road built by the Grand-duke Leopoldo II, runs beneath the medieval walls overlooking the Cecina valley. It passes close to the 15C church and monastery of **San Girolamo**, possibly designed by Michelozzo. Beneath the portico are two chapels with reliefs, representing *St Francis giving the Tertiary Rule to St Louis of France* and the *Last Judgement*, both by Giovanni della Robbia, and dated 1501. In a chapel to the right of the entrance is the *Immaculate Conception* by Santi di Tito. Flanking the high altar are a *Madonna enthroned with Saints* by Domenico di Michelino and the *Annunciation with Saints Michael and Catherine of Alexandria* signed and dated 1466 by Benvenuto di Giovanni, a work of great charm and refinement. The two statues representing *St Francis* and *St Jerome* are by a follower of Cieco da Gambassi. In the four niches on the sides are stucco figures of saints by Mazzuoli. Not far from the church are remains of the few surviving Etruscan ipogee tombs (their contents are in the Museo Guarnacci, Volterra).

West of Volterra is the medieval castellated village of **Montecatini Val di Cecina** (416m) surrounding a monumental castle tower. It commands a beautiful view above the Cecina valley. On the opposite side of the valley is **Montegemoli**, another medieval castle in a fine position, which was partially rebuilt in the Renaissance period.

South of Volterra the main road descends through rolling hills and white chalk hillocks (*crete*), to **Saline di Volterra**, a small industrial town, named after its underground salt deposits which have been systematically mined since the 9C. Here a beautiful winding road diverges left (there is a spectacular view of Volterra in the distance).

Pomarance

The road follows a ridge overlooking the Cecina valley, characterised by the *crete*, and then climbs towards the medieval town of Pomarance (370m). Of Etruscan and Roman origin, it owed its prosperity to the wealth of minerals mined locally and later to the exploitation of vapour jets. In 1472 it came under the dominion of Florence and exercised control over a vast area comprising the upper Cecina valley and most of the surrounding metalliferous hills. It was the birthplace of two painters called Pomarancio: Cristoforo Roncalli (1552–1626) and Niccolò Cercignani (c 1517–96).

Parts of the old walls survive and the **Porta Volterrana**, on the north side of the town, was built in 1326. In the central piazza is the clock tower and the **Palazzo Pretorio**, first built in the 12C, with a Florentine *Marzocco* lion on the corner and numerous coats of arms.

Beyond an archway is the parish church of **San Giovanni Battista** which was rebuilt in the 18C but preserves its Romanesque façade with blind arches. Inside are frescoes covering the nave and apse, including a large *Last Supper* by Luigi Ademollo behind the altar. On the altars in the nave, *Annunciation* by

Roncalli and *Madonna of the Rosary* by Cercignani. In the south transept chapel is a *Madonna and Saints* by Vincenzo Tamagni (1525). The baptistery chapel has a charming Nativity group of painted terracotta figures attributed to Zaccaria Zacchi with a background fresco of the *Magi* by Tamagni. A *Madonna and Child enthroned* and scenes of the *Infancy of Christ* by a 13C artist and a *Madonna* by a Sienese painter, dated 1329, have been removed to the nearby Canonica.

There are several palaces belonging to the Larderel and other local families and some medieval houses and towers in the older part of the town. On the south side is a natural rocky terrace.

Four kilometres south of Pomarance, a by-road leads off eastwards to **San Dalmazio**, an attractive little town on a hill, which was originally a monastery before being transformed into a fortified castle, parts of which still survive. A little beyond San Dalmazio is a turning, past the ruins of a Romanesque church, for the **Rocca di Sillano** (530m), reached by a steep climb on foot. This 12C castle, which was a stronghold of Volterra, preserves ruins of three circles of walls around a polygonal tower. A short distance further on is another hill-top town, **Monte-castelli** (494m) which still has its medieval walls, two towers and a Romanesque church. Inside are interesting, carved capitals and an altarpiece by Cosimo Daddi.

The main road to the south (N439) continues uphill past chimneys and pipelines, with a distinct smell of sulphurous springs, to **Montecerboli** (386m), with some medieval houses and a Romanesque church built in brick. In the new parish church is a 13C triptych of the Madonna and Child flanked by the two St Johns and a 14C Sienese *Crucifix*.

Just beyond the town is the industrial town of **Larderello** (390m), noted for the production of boric acid. François De Larderel began to extract boric acid from the nearby natural vapour jets (known as *lagoni* or *soffioni*) in 1818. A German scientist, Franz Hoefer, discovered its presence here in 1777. The small town built for the workers near the original industrial plant was named Larderello in 1846 by Grand-duke Leopoldo II.

The National Electrical Company (*ENEL*) has opened the **Museo della Geo-termia (open** daily on request, ☎ 0588-67724) on its premises. It documents the scientific exploitation of the steam jets which was continued by Larderel's son and grandson, initially for the production of boric acid and later for electricity. Guided tours also include a visit to a boric acid spring and a power station. Today there are 14 power stations fed by over 60 kilometres of pipelines. The museum will eventually be housed in the De Larderel palace. In front of the palace are busts of François de Larderel and his wife on two columns. Another column commemorates a prize received at the Paris Exhibition of 1867.

The residential area, rebuilt after damage from bombing in 1945, has a church by Giovanni Michelucci. There is also a late Renaissance church dedicated to the *Madonna of Montenero* with a Gothic bronze pulpit. The bare landscape, with its pipelines, furnaces, and power stations covering some 170 sq km, with clouds of steam bursting from the ground, has been called the 'Valley of Hell'.

After a steep climb, the road descends to **La Perla** where there are baths recommended for the treatment of rheumatism, and continues to **Castelnuovo di Val di Cecina** (612m). This is a small industrial and agricultural town, also popular as a summer resort on account of its location near ancient chestnut woods. The town was extended beyond the medieval castle in the 16C. A pretty by-road diverges left towards Radicondoli (see Ch. 29).

18 · Livorno

Livorno is a busy and lively town with a maritime air, which, since the 1970s has become one of the biggest container ports in Italy (169,000 inhab.). As well as a commercial port with important ship repair yards it also has numerous car ferry services to Sardinia and Corsica. It was laid out on a polygonal plan in 1576 by Bernardo Buontalenti for the Medici who constructed the fortifications and surrounded it by a deep moat (the Fosso Reale). In the 19C the city expanded on open symmetrical lines. Although it suffered systematic destruction from bombing in 1943, part of the Medici defence works survive, as well as numerous monumental 19C buildings, and the town was well reconstructed. The spacious seaboard is particularly attractive. It has a well-known street market where American goods are sold (Camp Darby, a US army base is nearby). In the 17C and 18C the town, as a free port, was much frequented by British merchants and sailors who called it *Leghorn*. On the first Sunday of every month museums and churches are often specially opened and street markets and boat excursions organised.

■ Practical information

Information offices*. APT*, 6 Piazza Cavour (☎ 0586-898111); information offices open in summer at the Molo Mediceo, and at the passenger terminal (Calata Carrara), near the Stazione Marittima.

Getting there
By rail*.* The station is inPiazza Dante, c 1km east of Piazza Grande (Bus No. 1). Frequent train service to Pisa in 10–20 mins, and local trains to Florence via Pisa and Empoli in 1hr 20 mins. Express services to Rome and Genoa on the main line along the coast. Local trains on this line serve Castiglioncello, Cecina, San Vincenzo, and Piombino.

By bus*.* **Town buses.** No. 1 from the railway station to Piazza della Repubblica, Piazza Grande, the Darsena Vecchia, and Viale Italia (for the Museo Civico; Bagni Pancaldi stop); several others buses (including No. 2) from the station to Piazza Grande (some going on to Antignano and Montenero).

   Country buses. Although most places in the province, and Florence and Pisa are best reached by train from Livorno, there are also *Lazzi* bus services from Piazza Manin to Empoli, Florence, Pisa, Viareggio, and Lucca; and *ATL* services from Piazza Grande to Bibbona and Castagneto Carducci (as well as Castiglioncello, Cecina, and Piombino).

Car parking*.* Much of the centre of the city has restricted access for motorists (except residents) from 07.30–19.30. Car parking best off Viale Carducci (and bus No. 1 to the centre). Car park (with hourly fee and reduction for long-term parking), 5 Scali Bettarini.

Maritime Services*.* **Boats** from Porto Mediceo run by *Toremar* (☎ 0586-896113) to **Capraia**, daily in 3 hrs (once a week via Gorgona in 3½ hrs), and in summer to **Elba**. In summer *Fratelli Rossignoli* (☎ 0336-582413) also run a boat service to **Capraia**, **Elba**, and the **Cinque Terre**.

Car ferries from Calata Carrara for **Corsica** (Bastia) run by *Corsica Ferries* (☎ 0586-881380) and *Corsica Marittima* (☎ 0586-210507). For **Sardinia**. *Sardinia Ferries* (☎ 0586-881380) to Golfo Aranci and *Moby Lynes* (☎ 0586-826823) to Olbia. Services to Olbia and Cagliari from Calata Assab, Porto Nuovo run by *Lloyd Sardegna Compagnia di Navigazione* (☎ 0565-222300). For **Palermo** *Grandi Navi Veloci (Grandi Traghetti*; ☎ 010-589331*)* from Calata Tripoli.

Hotels
★★★ *Gran Duca*, 16 Piazza Micheli (☎ 0586-891024; fax 0586-891153); *Gennarino*, 301 Viale Italia (☎ 0586-803109, fax 0586-803450); *Atleti*, 50 Via dei Pensieri, near the Hippodrome, off Viale Italia, towards Antignano (☎ & fax 0586-502409).

At **Antignano** on the sea (6km south): ★★ *La Capinera*, 32 Via del Castello (☎ 0586-580508, fax 0586-580814).

Campsite. ★★ *Miramare*, 220 Via del Littorale (open April–Sept; ☎ 0586-580402).

Youth Hostel. *Villa Morazzana*, 68 Via di Collinet (☎ 0586-500076, fax 0586-502426).

Restaurants
Livorno is famous for its fish restaurants (fish is always more expensive than meat).
££ *La Barcarola*, 63 Viale Carducci; *Il Sottomarino*, 48 Via Terrazzini.
£ *Carlo*, 43 Via Caprera; *Da Galileo*, Via della Campana (off Via Garibaldi); *Enoteca Doc*, 42 Via Goldoni.

At **Antignano**. ££ *La Capinera*, 32 Via del Castello.
Montenero. ££ *Montallegro*, 3 Piazza di Montenero.

Local speciality. The characteristic *Torta*, a delicious and cheap savoury snack made from chick peas, is sold from small *pizzerie* all over the town (to be eaten standing up or taken away).

Sea-bathing south of the town beyond Antignano at Il Romito (rocks) or at Quercianella (private beaches; fee), or further south along the coast between Cecina and Piombino.

History. Though a fortress here was the subject of a dispute between Pisan, Genoese, and Florentine overlords from the early Middle Ages, Livorno's rise dates from 1571, when the new port was begun by decree from Cosimo de' Medici. Numerous British sailors came to the town during this period.

Ferdinando I (1587–1609) continued the work and employed Sir Robert Dudley (see below) to construct the great mole (1607–21) as a breakwater, build warships, and administer the port. Ferdinando, by his proclamation of religious liberty, made the town a refuge for persecuted Jews, Greeks who had fled from the Turks, converted Moslems expelled from Spain and Portugal under Philip III in 1609, and Roman Catholics driven from England under the penal laws against papists (1606) proclaimed by James I. They were joined by many Italians fleeing from the oppression of their own states, and by exiles from Marseilles and Provence. During the 17C the port was used to import large quantities of red herring from Great Yarmouth and wheat from King's Lynn. In the 18C the 'British Factory' was established in Livorno by a group of British merchants and factors to assist the numerous British families in the town. Ferdinando's policy was pursued by his successors, and Livorno became a great port, now the third largest in Italy.

As a neutral port it was able to supply numerous ships for the naval battles against Napoleon, and Lord Nelson came here in 1793. In 1749 Sir Joshua Reynolds landed here on his only visit to Italy, and Tobias Smollett, Byron, and Shelley all lived for a time at Montenero on the outskirts of the town (see below). In the mid-19C Livorno became a well-known bathing resort. Robert Stephenson built the railway line from Pisa to Livorno which was opened in 1844; it terminated at the neo-classical Stazione Ferroviaria Leopoldo (San Marco; see the Plan), now closed. A regular steam-ship service was introduced in 1872 between Livorno and Great Britain.

Giovanni Fattori (1825–1908), the Macchiaioli painter and Pietro Mascagni (1863–1945), composer of *Cavalleria Rusticana* were both born here. Another native was the artist Amedeo Modigliani (1884–1920). In 1984 two sculptures were dredged up from the Fosso Reale and acclaimed by numerous art critics to be lost masterpieces by Modigliani. They were soon proved to be fakes made by a group of young students, and the incident was recognised as one of the most successful hoaxes of recent years.

The reef of *Meloria* rises nearly 5km off Livorno, where the maritime power of Pisa was crushed by the Genoese in 1284. An English trading fleet was also routed hereabouts by the Dutch in 1653.

The **railway station** is a fine Art Nouveau building (1910) by Pietro Via. Beside it, in Piazza Dante, are the remains of a spa hotel built in 1905 by Angelo Badaloni. The long, wide **Viale Carducci**, with an avenue of trees and pretty lamp posts, leads due west towards the centre of the city. Beyond an old factory building of 1906 are the **public gardens** laid out in 1854, and the monumental **Cisternone**, a water cistern built in 1829–32 by Pasquale Poccianti, with a classical portico and exedra (the semi-dome recalls the Pantheon in Rome).

Via de Larderel continues past the large neo-classical **Palazzo De Larderel** (1832–50). The French Larderel family came to live in Livorno in 1799 and became wealthy through the extraction of boric acid south of Volterra (see Larderello, p. 278). Inside are plaster casts of the statues of illustrious Tuscans which can be seen in the niches of the loggia of the Galleria degli Uffizi in Florence. Beyond is the huge **Piazza della Repubblica**, known as the *Voltone* since it rests on a wide vault over the Fosso Reale (which still flows beneath it; see below). It was laid out in 1834 by Luigi Bettarini: on the great expanse of pavement rise well-designed lamp-posts and two statues, one of Ferdinando III by Francesco Pozzi (1837), and one of Leopoldo II by Emilio Santarelli (1885). To the north is a good view of the moated Fortezza Nuova (described below).

Via Grande continues past the handsome **Cisternino**, another fine neo-classical building designed by Poccianti in 1827. In Via Madonna (right) three Baroque façades survive among the unattractive modern buildings: the former churches of the **Annunziata** (1605), and of the **Concezione** (1599), both by Alessandro Pieroni, and the 18C façade of **San Giorgio degli Armeni**.

Piazza Grande, in the centre of the city, was a huge square laid out in the 16C–17C and formerly surrounded by porticoes by Alessandro Pieroni (only a fragment survives at the southwest corner). It was greatly reduced in size when a much criticised modern building was built in the centre, so that it is now divided from Largo Municipio to the north.

The **Duomo** was begun in 1587, modified in 1606 by Alessandro Pieroni, and completed in 1609 by Antonio Cantagallina. It had to be virtually rebuilt in 1954–59, after severe damage in 1944, when only the south wall was left standing. The Doric portico which precedes the façade (and which was an integral part of the design of Piazza Grande) is also probably by Pieroni. Although the traditional attribution of the piazza and portico to Inigo Jones is now discredited, it may be that the famous architect saw the square if he docked at the port of Livorno on the second of his two trips to Italy when he accompanied the Earl and Countess of Arundel on their Grand Tour in 1613–14. The huge square with porticoes and the church of St Paul, which he designed for Convent Garden, London in 1631–39 are certainly reminiscent of an Italian piazza.

Interior. Although the ceiling was destroyed the paintings were salvaged and were reinstalled here after restoration: Passignano, *Assumption*; Empoli, *Madonna and Child with St Francis of Assisi*; and Jacopo Ligozzi, *Triumph of St Giulia*. Among the funerary monuments on the south wall, the most notable is that of Alessandro del Borro by Giovanni Battista Foggini. On either side of the high altar are two small heads of angels by François Duquesnoy, killed in Livorno by his brother in 1643. On the right wall, *Translation of the body of St Giulia* by the local painter Tommaso Gazzarrini (1834) opposite a *Miracle of St Francis* by Giuseppe Bezzuoli. The transepts were added in the 18C (reconstructed after the Second World War).

In Largo Municipio, north of Piazza Grande, is **Palazzo Municipio** by Giovanni del Fantasia (1720), with a bell tower and a double staircase added by Bernardino Ciurini. On the left is the 17C **Palazzo di Camera di Commercio**, designed with three large arches by Annibale Cecchi. On the corner of Via della Posta is **Palazzo Granducale** (now Palazzo della Provincia) designed in the 17C by Antonio Cantagallina (and reconstructed after the War).

Nuova Venezia

Via San Giovanni (once the main street of the old town, but now without character) leads out of the west side of the piazza past the 17C church of **San Giovanni** (restructured) which contains a handsome ciborium by Ferdinando Tacca incorporated in the high altar. Behind the church a road leads across a bridge to an area, laid out in 1629–44, and known as **Nuova Venezia**, because of its numerous canals used as moorings for small boats. **Via Borra** was one of the most important streets in the city in the 18C (the most interesting palace here is Palazzo delle Colonne at No. 29, designed by Giovanni Battista Foggini). Beyond the next pretty bridge is the 18C octagonal church of **Santa Caterina** (undergoing a lengthy restoration; it contains interesting *trompe l'oeil* frescoes and a *Coronation of the Virgin* behind the high altar by Vasari).

There is a good view from the bridge of the wall of the **Fortezza Nuova** built in 1590 on a design by Giovanni de' Medici, Vincenzo Bonanni, and Bernardo Buontalenti (altered in 1696). It is surrounded by a moat, and the interior has been laid out as a pleasant **public park** (open daily 08.00–dusk; the entrance is near a palm tree). It is sometimes used for exhibitions.

Just beyond the church of Santa Caterina Via San Marco crosses the interesting Via dei Floridi with houses built above the old bastions, to the façade of the former **Teatro di San Marco**. A worn plaque here records the founding of

LIVORNO

the Italian Communist Party in 1921. A modern school building has recently been built behind the façade.

On the other side of Santa Caterina the Scali del Rifugio skirts the canal past the ex-convent of Santa Caterina where Sandro Pertini (1896–1990; elected President of the Republic in 1978) was held as a political prisoner during the

Fascist regime (plaque set up in 1977). To the right a roadway leads down over an archway giving access to the canal to the **Bottini dell'Olio** (1705–31) which were the last important buildings constructed in Livorno by the Medici, on a project by Giovanni Battista Foggini. The warehouse could store some 24,000 barrels of oil; the fine vaulted hall has been restored and is now used for exhibitions. Amidst evident signs of bombing from the last War is the church of **San Ferdinando** (still undergoing a lengthy restoration), with a good 18C interior (also by Foggini) and excellent marble sculptures by Giovanni Baratta.

The port

Via della Venezia leads back from San Ferdinando to Via San Giovanni which continues right to the **Darsena Vecchia** (1591), the main harbour for the fishing fleet. In the harbour is the wall of the crumbling **Fortezza Vecchia**, the most important of the Medici defence works in the city. It was built to the design of Antonio da Sangallo in 1521–34, and embodies part of a small Roman fortress, the so-called Matilda Tower (11C), and remains of a Pisan fort of 1377. The road skirts the Darsena Vecchia past a theatrical piazza with a colossal equestrian statue of Vittorio Emanuele II by Augusto Rivalta (1882) facing the huge **Palazzo del Governo** (now the Prefecture), a Fascist building of 1942 with monumental white marble bas-reliefs (1954). In Piazza Micheli, is the famous **Monumento dei Quattro Mori*, a monument to Ferdinando I with a statue of him by Giovanni Bandini (1595), and four colossal Moorish slaves in bronze (1623–26), the masterpieces of Pietro Tacca chained to the pedestal. On the wall of the Medici fortifications here (restored as part of a hotel) is a plaque which Sir Robert Dudley's biographer, John Temple Leader, placed here in 1896.

From Piazza Micheli a bridge leads to the ferry quay in the Porto Medicео, and on the other side of the Fortezza Vecchia is another ferry quay (Calata Carrara) near the Stazione Marittima. Some way farther north, at the entrance to the port, is the tall **Torre del Marzocco**, attributed to Lorenzo Ghiberti (1439).

From Piazza Micheli the ugly **Via Grande**, with monotonous square arcades, leads past two copies of the fountains made by Tacca for the monument to Ferdinando I (see above) but instead installed in Piazza Santissima Annunziata in Florence, back to Piazza Grande (described above).

The apse of the Duomo faces **Via Cairoli** which leads south towards Piazza Cavour. At the beginning on the left is the church of **Santa Giulia** (1603) with attractive benches and confessionals in the interior. Over the high altar is a painting of the patron saint with stories from her life, attributed to the Maestro di Varlungo. Beyond an 18C courtyard is the Cappella di San Ranieri (1696–1701), with interesting pavement tombs. Off Via Cairoli, behind the Post Office, in Via del Tempio is the **Synagogue**, built in 1962 on a design by Angelo Di Castro, after the destruction of the old synagogue in the Second World War.

The Fosso Reale

Via Cairoli ends in **Piazza Cavour** (statue by Vincenzo Cerri, 1871) across two branches of the attractive Fosso Reale, built as a defensive moat around the town by the Medici c 1559. In the centre of the Scali Aurelio Saffi which skirts the left-hand canal, is the huge russet-coloured building of the **Central Market** set up in 1894 by Angelo Badaloni. It has eight caryatids by Lorenzo Gori in its impressive interior. On the opposite side of the canal is the large Benci school building in a similar colour, also by Badaloni, and the neo-Gothic façade of the **Dutch Church** (1864). Off this side of the canal (see the Plan) is Piazza XX Settembre, laid out in 1819 by Poccianti around the neo-classical portico of the church of **San Benedetto** built in 1819 on a design by Angelo Pampaloni. Since 1944 the piazza has been the site of the famous **Mercatino** where American goods are sold (**open** all day except Mon morning) in iron sheds.

Via Verdi leads to the right out of Piazza Cavour, past the neo-Gothic **Waldensian Church**, built in 1845 by Rumball as the Presbyterian Church of Scotland. Beyond is the entrance (No. 59) to the **Old British Cemetery** (for the key to the gate apply at the offices of the Misericordia, **open** 09.00–12.00, 15.00–18.30; fest. 09.00–12.00). Probably opened in the 16C, this was for many years the only Protestant cemetery in Italy. Numerous British merchants, sea captains, and Anglican clergymen, with their families, were buried here. Also some Swiss and French Huguenots and Americans, including Elizabeth Seton, a Roman Catholic convert who became a missionary in America and was canonized in 1977. Many of the monumental tombs, pyramidal in form, date from the 1660s. Tobias Smollett (see below) was buried here in 1773 (the tomb, with an obelisk and Latin inscription, is to the right of the centre). The cemetery was visited by Shelley, Longfellow, and Fenimore Cooper and was closed in 1840 when the new cemetery was opened in the northern suburbs. The **Anglican church** outside, with a classical temple façade, was built by Angiolo della Valle in 1840. It is now used by the Misericordia as a chapel.

Sir Robert Dudley

Sir Robert Dudley (1574–1649) was the son of Sir Robert Dudley, Earl of Leicester, Elizabeth I's favourite. Famous as a navigator and mapmaker, he sailed to the West Indies and was knighted by Elizabeth I. However in 1605 when he failed to prove he was Dudley's legitimate son he decided to move to Italy and lived in Tuscany for the rest of his life. Although he had already married three times, he took with him to Italy his cousin Elizabeth Southwell, Elizabeth I's lady-in-waiting and after their conversion to Roman Catholicism he gained a dispensation from the Pope to marry her (and they went on to have twelve children).

He became a naval engineer and administered the port of Livorno for the Medici Grand-dukes. He also built warships, the first of which he launched in 1608 armed with 64 large cannon, and he supervised the draining of the marshes between Livorno and Pisa. In 1608 he was recognised as the Duke of Northumberland by the Habsburg Emperor. Some of his nautical instruments and guages to measure the ebb and flow of tides are preserved in the Museo della Storia della Scienza in Florence. He was lent Villa Corsini on the outskirts of Florence near the Villa della Petraia by the Medici Grand-dukes and died there.

The southern part of town

Off Via Rossi, the other side of Piazza Cavour, Via Goldini leads to the **Teatro Goldoni** (1843–47 by Giuseppe Cappellini) where in 1921, at a Congress of the Socialist Party, a schism resulted in the founding of the Italian Communist Party (see above). The theatre was acquired by the Comune of Livorno in 1987 and is being restored. A short way further east, across Corso Amedeo, is the church of **Santa Maria del Soccorso** (1835) by Gaetano Gherardi, with a painting of *St Lawrence* by Enrico Pollastrini (1862) in the first south chapel.

In Via Calzabigi (see plan) is the entrance (No. 54) to the **Museo Mascagnano**, opened in 1985 in a 19C Castelletto to commemorate Pietro Mascagni (1863–1945), the Livornese musician (**open** 10.00–13.00 except Mon; Thurs and Sat also 16.30–19.30). Among numerous mementoes are Mascagni's musical scores, his piano, photographs and manuscripts. In the park of Villa Maria (entered from No. 22 Via Redi) is a modern art gallery.

The 19C **Villa Fabbricotti**, over 1km south of Piazza Cavour, approached along the unattractive, straight Via Marradi and Via della Libertà (best reached by Bus No. 2 from Piazza Cavour) is surrounded by a public park (**open** daily 08.00–dusk). A new building in the park houses the **Museo Provinciale di Storia Naturale** (usually **open** 09.00–12.30, 16.00–19.00 except Sat afternoon & fest.). Founded in 1929 it has sections dedicated to geology, botany and zoology, and a large collection of finds from the district of Livorno dating from the Palaeolithic era onwards. There is an exit from the park on Via Roma, where, at No. 234, is the **Villa Henderson**. This was built in 1780 by John Webb and purchased

The Shelleys in Italy

The poet **Percy Bysshe Shelley** sailed to Leghorn in 1818 with his second wife, Mary Wollstonecraft (author of *Frankenstein*, and daugher of his friend the philosopher William Godwin) and their two children William and Clara. While in Italy they stayed in Milan, Bagni di Lucca, Venice, Padua, Este, Pisa (see p. 234), Florence, and Rome (where William died in 1819). They then settled at Villa Valsovona in Montenero where Shelley finished his tragedy *The Cenci*. While in Livorno he bought a little schooner, the *Ariel*, which he used to sail up the Arno to Pisa with his friend Lieutenant Edward Williams.

In 1822 the Shelleys moved to the Casa Magni at Lerici, on the Gulf of La Spezia in Liguria with Lieut. Williams and his wife, where they continued to enjoy sailing in the *Ariel*. Byron, who spent a holiday at the 18C Casa Dupuy in Montenero, may have sailed from Livorno in his boat, the *Bolivar*, to visit them at the Casa Magni. In the same year Shelley and Williams sailed from Lerici back to Livorno to meet the essayist, poet and philosopher Leigh Hunt on his arrival from England. It was on their return to the Casa Magni on 8 July 1822 that they were drowned when the *Ariel* sank off Viareggio. Their bodies, washed ashore ten days later on the beach of Gombo, north of the mouth of the Arno, were cremated there in the presence of Byron, and Leigh Hunt. Shelley's ashes were collected and buried in the Protestant cemetery in Rome. He was 30 years old.

As both his prose and poetry show Shelley was deeply inspired by Italy and the cause of Italian liberty. He wrote *Lines written among the Euganean Hills* in Este in 1818, and *Ode to the West Wind* in Florence in 1819. *Prometheus Unbound* was completed in Rome in 1820. When in Pisa in 1821, a year before his tragic death, he wrote *Epipsychidion*, inspired by Contessina Emilia Viviani whom he had met at the Terme di San Giuliano the previous summer, and *Adonais*.

from the Webbs in 1917 by George Henderson (it now belongs to the Province). The Hendersons founded a sailors' mission (known as 'The Bethel') in Livorno and George built a Seamen's Institute with funds provided by British merchants.

Villa Mimbelli

Towards the sea, in Via San Iacopo in Acquaviva, the remarkable 19C **Villa Mimbelli** surrounded by a fine park (open daily) has housed the **Museo Civico Giovanni Fattori** since 1994.

■ The museum is usually **open** 10.00–13.00, 17.00–23.00; winter 10.00–19.00; closed Mon.
It is best reached by Bus No. 1 from the station or Piazza Grande to Viale Italia (Bagni Pancaldi stop), from which it is a 5 minute walk along Via Forte dei Cavalleggeri to Via San Jacopo in Acquaviva.

The villa, completely restored in 1994, was built in 1865–70 for Francesco Mimbelli, a rich merchant, by Giuseppe Micheli and decorated in elaborate neo-Renaissance style. It includes an unusual staircase with the bannister supported by majolica putti, exotic fireplaces, trick mirrors, stencilling and frescoes (some by Annibale Gatti), and a domed 'cabinet' (or fumoir) in Moorish style. At present (while the stable block in the park is being restored) exhibitions are also held here so the arrangement is subject to change.

A modern staircase (with busts of Byron by Pietro Tenerani and Vittorio Alfieri by Luigi Pampaloni, and a bronze statuette by Ettore Ximenes) leads up to the **second floor** where some of the 135 *paintings by the Macchiaioli painter Giovanni Fattori born in Livorno are usually on display. These include battle scenes at Montebello and the *Madonna della Scoperta*, country scenes in the Maremma and Roman Campagna, and portraits (including a *Peasant Woman* and *Signora Martelli at Castiglioncello*).

Other Macchiaioli painters represented include Silvestro Lega (*Peasant Girl*), Vincenzo Cabianca, Telemaco Signorini, Serafino da Tivoli, Giovanni Boldini (including a portrait of Cabianca), Cristiano Banti, and Angiolo Tommasi. There are also good works (not always exhibited) by Enrico Pollastrini (1871–76) and Plinio Nomellini.

The civic collection also includes important earlier works but there are no plans at present to exhibit these. They include: Maestro della Natività di Castello, *Adoration of the Child*; Borgognone, *Battle scene*; circle of Botticelli, *Madonna and Child*; Neri di Bicci, *Crucifixion*; Carlo Cignani, *Deposition*; Beato Angelico, *Head of the Redeemer crowned with thorns* (an unusual and striking work); and Greek and Russian icons with interesting examples of the Cretan School (16C–17C).

The pleasant **Viale Italia** (see plan) skirts the shore with a wide promenade passing ship-building yards, then gardens and elegant seaside houses, and 19C hotels and bathing establishments, including the Bagni Pancaldi. On Piazzale Mascagni, a pretty terrace built out into the sea with a Doric gazebo (recently restored), is the **Aquarium** (open 10.00–12.00, 16.00–19.00 or 14.00–17.00 in winter; closed Mon) and, farther on, the huge **Naval Academy**, founded in 1879. Next to it is the 17C church of **San Jacopo in Acquaviva**, sited where St James the Greater is supposed to have landed on his way to Spain; St Augustine also is said to have stayed here after his baptism. The Viale continues past Art Nouveau houses and the attractive suburbs of **Ardenza** (with a neo-classical crescent, built in 1840, overlooking the sea), and **Antignano**, built as bathing resorts.

Montenero

Above Antignano is Montenero (193m). A funicular railway opened in 1909 (or a winding road) ascends the hill. The little village, with fine views of the coast, is built round a sanctuary. Tobias Smollett (born in 1721) lived here for the last two years of his life and finished *Humphrey Clinker*. The villa where he died, surrounded by a large garden towards Antignano, has a plaque (Villa del Giardino, now Villa Niccolai Gamba). He described it then as being in 'a most romantic and solitary situation'. Shelley took up residence here in 1819.

The pilgrimage **church** (1676) contains a miraculous painting of the *Madonna*, supposed to have sailed by itself in 1345 from the island of Negropont (Euboea) to the shore at Ardenza. The painting was formerly attributed to Margaritone di Arezzo, but is now thought to be by Il Gera of the Pisan school. Beneath the loggia (1866) are the funerary monuments of illustrious natives of Livorno including Enrico Pollastrini, Giovanni Fattori and Pietro Mascagni. In the **interior** the ceiling is frescoed by Filippo Galletti and the dome by Giuliano Traballesi. The high altar is a fine work in *pietre dure*. In rooms near the sacristy is a huge collection of 19C and 20C ex votos including some charming seascapes, and the Turkish costume of a little girl who was saved by her brother in 1800 after she had been carried off to a harem from Livorno by the Turks (the story was the inspiration for Rossini's opera *L'Italiana in Algeri*).

19 · The coast south of Livorno

The name **Maremma** was originally given to the marshy coastal plain which stretched from Cecina, some 35km south of Livorno, to the Argentario and beyond to the border with Lazio. It has come to refer to much of south-west Tuscany: the Maremma Pisana, which includes the coast between Pisa and Piombino and the metalliferous hills *(colline metallifere;* Ch. 17) further inland, and the Maremma Grossetana (see Ch. 20) covering the area between Piombino to the north, the promontories of the Uccellina (Ch. 22) and Monte Argentario (Ch. 23) to the west and Monte Amiata to the east.

The typical vegetation in this area, known as **macchia mediterranea**, comprises a variety of evergreen plants, shrubs and trees. Along the coast, growing out of the sand, are lilies, honeysuckle, rosemary, heather, juniper, myrtle and wild olive, backed by maritime and domestic pine trees. Further inland are thick woods of cork, ilex and oak trees with bushes of broom, arbutus, gorse and briar spreading over the hilly slopes. The fertile plains have extensive stretches of wheat and oat crops, sunflowers and corn. Fruit trees, especially peach trees abound and, of course, the traditional vines and olive trees.

There has been increasing awareness in recent years of the need to protect the natural, archaeological and wildlife environment of the Maremma. The Parco Naturale della Maremma was created in 1975 (see Ch. 22), followed by the bird sanctuaries along the coast (Bolgheri, Orbetello, Lake Burano). Other sites, combined with archaeological and walking itineraries have recently been opened in the Val di Cornia (see below).

The swamplands were for centuries abandoned until the development of modern industrial towns along the coast (Vada, Rosignano Solvay, Cecina) as a result of the building of the railway, connecting Pisa to Rome, the rebuilding of the Via Aurelia and the draining of the marshland.

■ Practical information

Information offices. APT Livorno, 6 Piazza Cavour (☎ 0586-898111). Information offices open in summer at **Castiglioncello**, 967 Via Aurelia (☎ 0586-752017); **San Vincenzo**, Via B. Alliata (☎ 0565-701533); **Cecina**, Piazza Carducci (☎ 0565-611111); **Piombino**, località Fiorentina (☎ 0565-276478); and **Suvereto**, Via Matteotti (☎ 0565-829304).

Getting there
By road. Via Aurelia (N1) is now a busy road, recently realigned and made into dual carriageway. It still follows the line of the ancient **Via Aurelia** built c 241 BC to link Rome with the Etruscan towns on the Tyrrhenian coast. It left Rome at Porta Aurelia (now Porta San Pancrazio) and reached the shore at Alsium (Palo Laziale), a port of the Etruscan city of Caere (Cerveteri), then followed the coastline to Cosa. In c 109 BC it was extended to Populonia, Pisa and Genoa. It ended in Gaul at Forum Julia (Fréjus, on the French Riviera). The modern road follows roughly the same line, although in places it now runs further inland and by-passes the towns.

By rail. The main railway line from Pisa to Rome follows the above route. Only slow trains stop at the coastal towns: Castiglioncello, Rosignano, Vada, Cecina, Bolgheri, Castagneto Carducci, San Vincenzo, Campiglia Marittima. A branch railway runs from Piombino to Campiglia in 20mins.

By bus. Buses run by ATL from Livorno along the coast to Castiglioncello, Cecina, and Piombino.

For the best places to **swim**, see p. 43.

Hotels on the coast
The coast south of Livorno has numerous seaside resorts, which are extremely crowded in summer. Detailed up-to-date information about hotels, apartments, and campsites is available from the *APT* of Livorno (☎ 0586-898111).

Castiglioncello. Numerous hotels of all categories (most of them closed in winter), including ★★★ *Atlantico*, 12 Via Diego Martelli (☎ 0586 752440; fax 0586 752494) and *Martini*, 3 Via Diego Martelli (☎ & fax 0586 752140). Hotel residences: ★★★★ *Villa Godilonda*, 12 Via Biagi (☎ 0586 752032; fax 0586 751177); ★★★ *San Domenico*, 22 Via Diego Martelli (☎ 0586 752116).

Quercianella. ★★★ *Villa Margherita*, 44 Via M. Puccini (☎ 0586 491023; fax 0586 491622).

Donoratico (Rosignano Marittima). Near the Aurelia. ★★★ *Nuovo Hotel Bambolo* (☎ 0565 775206; fax 0565 775346) with restaurant.

San Vincenzo. Numerous hotels of all categories include the ★★★★ *Park Hotel I Lecci*, 116 Via della Principessa (☎ 0565 704111; fax 0565 703224).

Cecina. ★★★ *Palazzaccio*, on the Aurelia (☎ 0586 682510; fax 0586 686221).

Cecina Mare has numerous ★★★ hotels, including *Il Gabbiano*, 109 Viale della Vittorio (☎ 0586 620183; fax 0586 620867) and ★★ hotels, including *Azzurra*, 3 Viale della Vittorio (☎ & fax 0586 620595).

Marina di Bibbona and **Forte di Bibbona** have numerous ★★★ and ★★ hotels.

Piombino. ★★★★ *Centrale*, 2 Piazza Verdi (☎ 0565 220188; fax 0565 220220); and ★★★ *Collodi*, 7 Via Collodi (☎ 0565 224272; fax 0565 224382).

Campsites

At **San Vincenzo** sites include ★★ *Park Albatros* (☎ 0565 701018) and ★★★★ and ★★★ sites at **Cecina Mare**, ★★★ sites at **Marina di Bibbona**, **Vada**, and **Forte di Bibbona** and (all categories) at **Piombino**.

Restaurants

Castiglioncello. £ *La Baracchina*, Punta Righini; ££ *Nonna Isola*, 556 Via Aurelia.
Rosignano Marittimo. £ *La Gattabuia*, 32 Via Gramsci; ££ *San Marco* in località San Marco; ££ *Bagnoli*, at Bagnoli; ££ *Il Cacciatore* at Castagneto.
San Vincenzo. Famous luxury-class restaurant £££ *Gambero Rosso*, 13 Piazza della Vittoria, one of the best places to eat in Italy. ££ *Il Bucaniere*.
Cecina. £££ *Scacciapensieri*, 22 Via Verdi; £ *Antica Cecina*, 17 Via Cavour.
Casale Marittimo. ££ *Le Volte*; £ *Vecchio Frantoio*, 28 Via Marconi.
Suvereto. ££ *Ghigo*, 45 Via Matteotti.
Campiglia Marittima. £ *Il Canovaccio*, 1 Via Vecchio Asilo.
Piombino. ££ *Osteria Carugi*, 10 Via Francesco Ferrer.

Castiglioncello is a large resort on a promontory. It was a favourite place of the *Macchiaioli* painters who drew inspiration from the beautiful scenery and used to stay with the writer and art critic, Diego Martelli (1838–96) in his villa here. The **Museo Archeologico Nazionale**, designed to look like an Etruscan temple, is being rearranged to house the rich finds, excavated at the beginning of this century in a nearby Etruscan necropolis dating from the 4C–1C BC.

Just beyond Castiglioncello to the south at **Rosignano Solvay** factories process the soda from the salt-works of Saline di Volterra (see Ch. 17). The old town of **Rosignano Marittimo** is a few kilometres inland. It was originally just a castle and its medieval walls were reinforced with towers in the 17C by Grand-duke Cosimo II. The **Civico Museo Archeologico**, in Palazzo Bombardieri (**open** 09.00–13.00, 16.00–19.00, excluding Mon; ☎ 0586-799232) documents the history of the lower Cecina Valley and the coast south of Livorno. It has a collection of Etruscan and Roman material excavated in the neighbourhood. This area is known for its excellent wine (*Montescudaio*).

To the north of Castiglioncello is **Quercianella**, a little seaside resort with beaches backed by pine woods. **Vada**, to the south of Castiglioncello has numerous campsites near the beaches, which are less crowded than those of Castiglioncello.

On the north bank of the river Cecina, on the outskirts of **Cecina**, a small modern industrial town, at San Pietro in Palazzi, is the early 18C **Villa La Cinquantina** (**open** Sat & Sun 10.00–19.00; Tues–Fri 15.00–19.00 (winter); 10.00–19.00 (summer), ☎ 0586-680145). On display is an Etruscan and Roman collection comprising objects discovered in two ships wrecked off the nearby coast. A recently excavated necropolis near Casale Marittimo has yielded interesting weapons, a helmet and shield, and objects in bronze dating from the 6C BC. There is also a local ethnographical museum here. Inland is the pretty little medieval village of **Casale Marittimo**. Just south of Cecina, at San Vincenzino, a Roman villa has been excavated and there are plans to create an archaeological park here with an Antiquarium.

On the coast south of Cecina are the resorts of **Marina di Cecina**, **Marina di Bibbona** and **Forte di Bibbona**, and **Castagneto-Donoratico**.

At **San Guido** the Via Aurelia is lined by a splendid avenue of cypresses, nearly 5km long, planted in 1801 by Camillo della Gherardesca, whose family had been feudal lords in this area since the early 13C. It leads up to the castle (restored) and little village of **Bolgheri**. Here the poet Giosuè Carducci spent his childhood (1838–49) and the cypress avenue is the subject of a famous poem by him. The white and rosé wines of Bolgheri are particularly good, and *Sassicaia* is considered the best Cabernet wine of Italy.

Just south of the road to Bolgheri is a turning for the wildlife sanctuary, **Rifugio faunistico padule di Bolgheri** (2100 hectares), administered by the WWF (**open** 15 Oct–15 Apr, Fri and 1st and 3rd Sat of the month, 09.00–12.00, 14.00–16.30; *bookings only*, ☎ 0565-777125). The landscape, typical of the Maremma, includes umbrella pines, ilexes, cork trees, and dunes covered with vegetation known as the *macchia*. This was once a hunting reserve of the Della Gherardesca family, and the wild animals here include deer and wild boar. The marshland attracts a great variety of migratory birds.

A few kilometres further south, there is a turning inland for the pretty village of **Castagneto Carducci**. The Gherardesca castle dominates the medieval village. The little 17C oratory of the SS Crocifisso has a Pisan *Crucifix* above the high altar. The road winds uphill to Sassetta, another picturesque village. Nearby, the wooded slopes of **Poggio Neri** have been equipped for trekking, cycling and horseriding. Nearer the coast are the remains of the 10C castle of **Donoratico**.

San Vincenzo and Rocca San Silvestro

San Vincenzo is a well known large seaside resort extended to the south by the **Riva degli Etruschi**, a vast bungalow colony. Around San Vincenzo are six protected areas, of archaeological, historical and naturalistic interest, that have been grouped together to form the **Parchi della Val di Cornia**. They include Poggio Neri, San Silvestro and Montioni inland, and the coastal parks of Rimigliano, Populonia and Baratti and La Sterpaia. All have parking facilities (info. Piombino 57025, via G. Lerario 90, ☎ 0565-49430; fax 0565-49733, also for public transport). East of San Vincenzo is the **Parco archeologico-minerario di San Silvestro**. This area has been mined for almost three thousand years, and is one of the most important medieval mining sites in Europe.

■ There are various itineraries for visiting the Rocca San Silvestro, the mining areas, the Temperino underground gallery (360m long) and the museum (**open** Sat and Sun 11 May–16 June, 09.00–19.00; 22 June–29 Sept, Tues–Sun 09.00–20.00; **guided tours only in certain areas**, ☎ 0565-49430). **Car parks** (*Madonna di Fucinaia* and *Il Temperino*, off SP 20, about 6km from San Vincenzo on the road to Campiglia Marittima) and information office.

The **Rocca San Silvestro**, a medieval fortified village and castle in a striking position, now in ruins, was still inhabited well into the 15C by the miners who extracted silver, copper and lead for the mints of Lucca and Pisa. The park has been called an 'open-air archive' which documents mining in the Etruscan, medieval and Renaissance periods. The mines were abandoned in the mid-15C for technological reasons and ceased to be viable. An attempt on the part of Cosimo I to reactivate the mines and furnaces was soon abandoned and the last to exploit the mines were some English and French companies in the 19C.

Campiglia Marittima (231m) is a picturesque little town, about 10km inland, spread over two hills with wide views. The medieval district round the **Rocca** preserves parts of its walls including several of its city gates. At the centre is the **Palazzo Pretorio** which displays numerous coats of arms of the 15C–16C governors, or *Podestà,* on the façade. The surrounding streets and alleyways offer charming vistas. Outside the Porta Fiorentina gate is the cemetery and the **Pieve di San Giovanni,** a fine example of Pisan Romanesque architecture of the 11C–12C. It is built of beautifully cut stone and the doorways are decorated with geometrical and animal carvings. A boar hunt is represented in the architrave over the side door. The interior has a timber roof and a single apse with a stone vault. An **annual festival**, the *Maggio Campigliese,* with a procession and joust, is held in the town in May.

Due west of Campiglia is the coastal nature reserve of Rimigliano stretching along 4km of coast, with beautiful walks in ilex and pine woods.

Inland is the charming little town of **Suvereto**, one of the first medieval towns in the area to become a free commune. Much of the castle survives and the circle of walls, though restored, is almost intact. The Romanesque church of **San Giusto** dates from the 12C and has columns and figures of lions decorating the doorway. Many of the medieval buildings and winding streets are well preserved, as is the **Palazzo Comunale** with its 12C tower, loggia and staircase. The church of **Santa Maria** has a relief of *Christ blessing* over the doorway, attributed to Vittorio Ghiberti.

Continuing south over the hills (approximately 12km) you reach Montioni and the nearby **Parco di Montioni** which may be explored on mapped footpaths.

Populonia

The ancient Etruscan town of Populonia is situated high on the Massoncello promontory, originally an island, from which there is a magnificent view stretching from the Apuan Hills to Punt'Ala and the islands of Elba, Corsica and Capraia. It is reached from the little port of **Baratti**, on the south side of the Gulf of Baratti near a beautiful beach, backed by pine trees.

Populonia was one of the most important ports of ancient Etruria. Iron from Elba and perfumes, amulets and objects from Syria, Egypt, and Greece were traded here as early as the 8C BC in exchange for tin and copper mined in the nearby hills known as the *Colline Metallifere* (metalliferous hills). Its importance was also due to its furnaces for smelting metals. In 1974 the wreck of a Roman ship, 20m long, was discovered at a depth of 18metres. It was carrying goods from the Middle East, and the finds are now exhibited in various museums in Tuscany.

The **Necropolis of Populonia** and the archaeological sites document settlements in the area from the Iron Age to Roman times (information office and car park; **open** daily 09.00–dusk; guided tours also available, ☎ 0565-29002). Excavations of the necropoli of **San Cerbone**, **Casone** and **Poggio della Porcareccia** were begun in 1919 and in certain areas are still taking place. There are several interesting large tumulus tombs dating from the 7C–5C BC as well as one in the form of an edicola. Remains found here of two iron chariots, bronze figurines etc., are now in the Archaeological Museum in Florence. Some tombs were discovered under enormous slag heaps.

Further uphill, on the south-eastern slope of **Poggio della Guardiola** is the extensive Hellenistic necropolis of **Le Grotte** (mid-4C–2C BC) with numerous

An Etruscan tumulus tomb at Populonia

underground tombs, two of which have simple painted decoration. Two itineraries have recently been created in the woods, an archaeological walk among the tombs and stone quarries and a nature tour illustrating the different species of trees and plants. Off the main road, about half way up the hill to Populonia, is another necropolis known as **Bucche delle Fate** (3C–1C BC), reached from a footpath through the woods. The path terminates in a beautiful cove (Cala San Quirico) with rocks and a small beach. There are footpaths continuing along the south side of the promontory towards Salivoli, with a beach and car park, which may also be reached from Piombino.

Continuing up the road to Populonia there is a splendid view over the bay of Baratti. Enormous blocks of stone forming the outer walls of the Etruscan acropolis are visible. Today, **Populonia** is a typical medieval hill-top town, encircled by its walls and dominated by its castle. In the 5C it had its own coinage but with the Roman conquest and the siege of Sulla the town began to decline. In 546 it was sacked by Totila and given by Charlemagne to Pope Hadrian I c 780.

The **Castle** (open 09.30–12.30, 14.30–dusk, except Mon), which has two impressive towers and ramparts, commands a magnificent view. Outside the circle of the medieval walls on the west side excavations, begun in 1980, have brought to light the foundations of a temple of the 2C BC. There are plans to create an Archaeological Museum near the site. The medieval town has three parallel streets. Near the Castle is the little church of Santa Maria della Croce, remodelled in the 18C. There is a little private museum, **Museo Archeologico Gasparri** (open daily ☎ 0565-29512). Here are assembled objects in bronze and terracotta from the surrounding necropoli and a number of Attic, Apulian and Etruscan vases. Photographs record the most interesting finds, which are kept in Florence.

Piombino

On the other side of the Massoncello promontory, once an island, is **Piombino** (39,600 inhabitants). It is an important seaport and one of the major steelworks in Italy. It is also the port for Elba (see Ch. 42).

In Roman times it was a port and in the 12C–13C it was fortified by the Pisans.

It came under the dominion of the Appiani family and was extensively rebuilt by the Florentine architect and sculptor Andrea Guardi. Most of its city walls have been destroyed but the towered gateway and oval fortification known as the **Rivellino** still stands in the main piazza.

The old town is divided by **Corso Vittorio Emanuele II** which leads to the 13C **Palazzo Comunale** (largely reconstructed) and the clock tower of 1598. The marble tabernacle of the *Madonna and Child* (a copy) above the entrance is by Ciolo and Marco da Siena (the original is preserved inside). The church of **Sant'Antimo**, an Augustinian church dating from the late 14C, has tombs of the Appiani family, a baptismal font by Andrea Guardi (1470) and an altarpiece of the *Holy Trinity and Saints* by Francesco Vanni. Beside the church is a fine Renaissance cloister.

Via Canonica leads to steps down to Via del Popolo which overlooks the sea and proceeds to the **castle**, which incorporates a 13C tower and was provided with fortifications by Cosimo I in 1552.

From Piazza Bovio there are steps down to the little **harbour**, which has existed since medieval times and which is used by fishing boats.To the right is the **Fonti dei Canali**, a fountain beneath an arch decorated with fine animal heads attributed to Nicola Pisano and the carved date 1248. **Palazzo Appiani** in the piazza is to become the Museo del Mare and it is here that archaeological finds from the Gulf of Baratti will be exhibited.

Near the little harbour (at 5 via Mazzini) the Istituto di Biologia has an **aquarium** (open Mon–Fri 09.00–12.00, 16.00–19.00).

From Piazza Bovio a street leads up towards the **Citadel**, past the former hospital and Romanesque church of **Sant'Antimo sopra i Canali**. In Piazza Manzoni there is the church of the Misericordia and a public garden which overlooks the canal of Piombino. Uphill is **Piazza Citadella**, where the Appiani family established themselves in 1465. Although considerably altered, there is still a well and the family chapel with a classical façade by Andrea Guardi. Inside is a glazed terracotta *Madonna* attributed to Andrea della Robbia.

Northeast of Piombino on the Vignale road, there is a bird sanctuary, *Oasi WWF Orti-Bottagone*, with a salt-water marshy area (**Orti**) and another of soft-water (**Bottagone**) where, besides a rich variety of reeds and acquatic plants and flowers, as many as 150 species of bird may be found (**open** throughout the year, fax 0565-49430).

Another park in the Val di Cornia is **La Sterpaia**, covering an area of c 2.5km (at present **open** in summer only, ☎ 0348-3415649), where thick oak and pine woods stretch down to the dunes and beautiful beaches.

20 · Grosseto and its northern province

Grosseto, although little visited by tourists, has fine ramparts, an interesting cathedral, and a museum with a good archaeological collection (due to reopen soon). The province covers a wide area of the Maremma known as the *Maremma Grossetana*. In the northern part are the important **Etruscan sites** of Roselle and Vetulonia, and a number of lovely little villages in beautiful countryside, including **Montepescali** and **Roccatederighi**, and the medieval town of **Paganico**.

On the coast there is the attractive resort of **Castiglione della Pescaia**, and other stretches of sea which are easily accessible from Grosseto, include some very pretty bays with sandy beaches.

■ Practical information

Information offices. **Grosseto**. *APT*, 206 Via Monterosa (☎ 0564-454510), with information office in Via Fucini (☎ 0564-454510). *APT* information offices also at **Castiglione della Pescaia**, Piazza Garibaldi (☎ 0564-933678) and Follonica, Viale Italia (☎ 0566-40177).

Getting there

By rail. Grosseto railway station (☎ 0564-22331) is on the Pisa–Rome main line (services from Pisa in 1hr 30min). **Follonica** also has a station on this line (slow trains only).

By bus. Buses from Grosseto run by *RAMA* (☎ 0564-25215) from all places of importance in the province. **Buses** run by *TRA-IN* from Siena (Piazza San Domenico) via Paganico to Grosseto.

Parking in Grosseto outside the ramparts.

Hotels

Grosseto. ★★★★ *Bastiani Grand Hotel*, 64 Piazza Gioberti (☎ 0564-20047; fax 0564-29321). ★★★ *Leon d'Oro*, 46 Via San Martino (☎ 0564-22128; fax 0564-22578) and *San Lorenzo*, 22 Via Piave (☎ 0564-27918; fax 0564-25338).

Marina di Grosseto. ★★★ *Lola Piccolo*, Via XXIV Maggio (☎ 0564-34402; fax 0564-34011).

Castiglione della Pescaia has numerous hotels of all categories, including ★★★ *Miramare*, 35 Via Vittorio Veneto (☎ 0564-933524; fax 0564-933695) and ★★★ *Corallo*, 1 Via N. Sauro (☎ 0564-933668; fax 0564-936268), both with restaurants.

Punta Ala. ★★★★ *Piccolo Hotel Alleluja*, Via del Porto (☎ 0564-922050; fax 0564-920734) and ★★★ *Gallia Palace*, 70 Via delle Sughere (☎ 0564-922022; fax 0564-920229), both with restaurants. ★★★ *Punta Ala*, 5 Via del Pozzino (☎ 0564-922646; fax 0564-922636).

Tirli. ★★ *Tana del Cinghiale*, Via del Deposito (☎ 0564-945810; fax 0566-55873), with restaurant.

Follonica has numerous ★★★ and ★★ hotels on its popular sandy beach, including ★★ *Miramare*, 84 Via Lungomare Italia (☎ & fax 0566-41521).

Paganico. ★★ *La Pace*, 1 Via della Madonnina (☎ 0564-905046).

Bagni di Petriolo. ★★★★ *Grand Hotel Terme di Petriolo*, with sulphur pools (☎ 0564-908871; fax 0564-908712).

Campsites of all categories at Marina di Grosseto, Castiglione della Pescaia and Le Rocchette. At Follonica ★ *Pineta del Golfo*, 3 Via delle Collacchie (☎ 0566-53369).

Restaurants

Grosseto. £££ *La Buca di San Lorenzo*, 1 Via Manetti.

Near **Badiola** at Macchiascandona. £ *Macchiascandona*.

Follonica. ££ *Leonardo Cappelli* (*da Paolino*), Piazza XXV Aprile.

Portiglione. £ *Vittorio*.

Castiglione della Pescaia. £ *Taverna Osteria del Buco*, 11 Via del Recinto.

Tirli. ££ *Tana del Cinghiale*.

Grosseto

Grosseto (62,000 inhab.) is capital of the province of the same name. It is the chief town of the Tuscan Maremma, a district ravaged by malaria throughout the Middle Ages. Reclamation work was begun by the Lorraine grand-dukes of Tuscany, and the marshes were gradually drained. A drainage scheme (*bonifica*) on a large scale was undertaken after 1930 and Grosseto is now the centre of a rich agricultural zone. The town suffered considerable damage in the Second World War.

History. Grosseto probably had Etruscan origins. In the 10C it was a castle ruled by the Aldobrandeschi and strategically situated where the Ombrone river was bridged. The seat of the Bishop of Roselle was transferred here in 1138 following a Saracen raid on Roselle. After a century of conflicts, Grosseto was subjected to Siena in the 14C, and eventually came under the dominion of the Medici in 1559. The town derived its wealth from its port on the Ombrone, and the nearby salt deposits.

The old town, which has a few medieval remains, is entirely enclosed in hexagonal brick **ramparts**, incorporating the 14C Sienese keep or *cassero*. These fortifications were built by the Medici in 1564–93, and also served as a defence against pirate attacks from the nearby coast. The Sienese keep, originally a tower and courtyard with a gateway, was later roofed over and transformed into the governor's headquarters. It is now used for exhibitions. Five of the bastions were laid out as public gardens by Leopoldo II in 1835.

The main road which enters Grosseto from the west passes the railway station on the right, and terminates at the circular Piazza Fratelli Rosselli. Here are the Prefettura, with a classical colonnade, and the **Palazzo delle Poste** (1930), a fine example of Fascist architecture. From **Porta Nuova** Corso Carducci leads through the old town past the 11C façade of **San Pietro**, to Piazza Duomo, onto which face the **Palazzo Comunale** (1870) and the cathedral.

The **Duomo**, dedicated to St Lawrence, was founded, probably on the site of an earlier church, in 1294 (the date is recorded in the curious circular palindrome to the right of the main entrance). After Grosseto fell to Siena in 1336 Sienese craftsmen were employed here under the architect Sozzo di Rustichino, recorded in an inscription on a pilaster.

The sculpture on the **façade**, including the symbols of the Evangelists, and a number of the capitals and columns of the unusual arched gallery, date from the mid-14C and are by Giovanni di Agostino. The same sculptor was responsible for the first two windows and the carvings on the jambs of the doorway on the south side. The lunette and remaining decoration were added by Leopoldo Maccari in 1897. The exterior of the cathedral underwent modifications in the 16C and was completed in neo-Gothic style in the 19C, using the same Carrara marble.

The **interior** was also considerably remodelled: the transept, side chapels and vault in the 16C, the high altar and choirstalls in the 17C and an overall restoration was carried out in the mid-19C. The baptismal font and marble frame surrounding the *Madonna delle Grazie* by Matteo di Giovanni are by Antonio Ghini (1470) and the holy-water stoup by a Sienese sculptor close to Antonio Federighi (1506). On the west wall is a lunette with Christ blessing attributed to Giovanni d'Agostino and two 15C stained glass windows. The large altarpiece in the choir is attributed to Ventura Salimbeni.

To the right of the cathedral is **Piazza Dante**. It has a portico running along two of the sides and at the centre a monument to Leopoldo II by Luigi Magi (1846). **Palazzo della Provincia**, in neo-Gothic Sienese style, dates from the beginning of this century and probably stands on the site of the original Aldobrandeschi castle. Beyond is the Piazza del Mercato off which is Via Mazzini. At No. 61 is the **Museo di Storia Naturale** (open daily except Mon 09.00–13.00, 15.00–19.00; fest. 09.00–13.00). It contains an interesting collection of mammals, birds and insects native to the region, as well as prehistoric remains and Neolithic finds, and a large collection of shells.

The town centre is small and easy to explore. Off Piazza Indipendenza is the late 13C church of **San Francesco**, which has a simple Gothic façade with a rose window and a modern lunette over the doorway. The interior has a single nave with a timber roof and rectangular apse. There are remains of 14C–15C frescoes, including a *Madonna*, *St Anthony Abbot* and a large *St Christopher*. The large painted *Crucifix* hanging above the high altar is attributed to Duccio, an early work strongly influenced by Cimabue. To the right of the choir is the chapel of St Anthony with a fresco cycle illustrating the saint's life and virtues, by Francesco and Antonio Nasini (1683). The sacristy has an *Annunciation* by Francesco Curradi. To the left of the church is the cloister (much restored) with 14C fresco fragments. The fine well in travertine was built by Ferdinando I dei Medici in 1590.

The Archaeological and Art Museum of the Maremma

In the contiguous Piazza Baccarini is the **Museo Archeologico e d'Arte della Maremma** and the **Museo d'Arte Sacra della Diocesi di Grosseto**, re-opened in March 1999 and beautifully arranged on three floors (**open** daily 09.00/10.00–13.00; weekends and in summer also 16.00/17.00–18.00/20.00, closed Mon; ☎ 0564-488750). The fine archaeological collection, founded in 1860 by Canon Giovanni Chelli, has objects ranging from prehistoric to the Etruscan and Roman eras. The Chelli collection (**Room 1**) comprises mostly objects from the districts of Chiusi and Volterra, including cinerary urns and early Etruscan pottery. **Rooms 2–12** document the history and excavations of Roselle, the Etruscan city situated on the east side of Lake Prile, from the archaic to the medieval period. Of particular interest are the monumental statues of Augustus and his family, dating from the time when Roselle became a Roman colony, and other statues of the Bassus family recently discovered in their private basilica. Excavations from the Grosseto district (**Rooms 13–23**) are arranged systematically according to sites and are well labelled. The exhibits range from votive offerings to objects of daily use, Etruscan pottery and examples from Greece, the cargo of a Roman ship discovered off the island of Giglio.

The section covering the diocese of Grosseto (**Rooms 24–34**) comprises many paintings and liturgical objects removed from the cathedral. The final section (**Rooms 35–40**) covers the medieval and later periods and the history of the city of Grosseto. There are several interesting early Sienese paintings including a *Last Judgement* by Guido da Siena, a *Madonna and Archangel Michael* by Segna di Bonaventura and works by Ugolino di Nerio and the Master of Ovile. There is a charming *Madonna of the Cherries* by Sassetta and other 15C paintings by Pietro di Domenico, Girolamo di Benvenuto and a charming little *Madonna* by Sano di Pietro. Among the later paintings is an altarpiece of the *Madonna in Glory* above a view of Grosseto by Alessandro Casolani of 1631. There are also sculpture fragments from the cathedral façade, sculptures and illuminated choirbooks.

Environs of Grosseto

Roselle

Northeast of Grosseto are the excavations of **Roselle**, reached by a well-signposted by-road. One of the most important Etruscan cities in northern Etruria, probably founded in the 7C BC on the southeastern side of Lake Prile (see below), it came under Roman dominion in the 294 BC and most of its major buildings dated from the Imperial era. A bishopric was founded here in the Middle Ages. In 935 it was pillaged by the Saracens, and abandoned after 1138 when it became a quarry for the nearby villages.

The pretty drive up Poggio Moscona through a wood passes several tombs (car park at the top). A footpath to the right continues along a stretch of the impressive cyclopean walls (6C BC), reaching 5m in height, which formed a ring over 3km long around the Etruscan town. **Open** to the public daily (summer 07.30–20.30; winter 09.00–17.30) and leaflets are provided in English.

The Maremma Grossetana

The numerous rivers and streams in this area attracted settlements long before the Etruscans, who arrived in the 8C BC and founded the cities of Vetulonia, Populonia, Marsiliana and Roselle. Necropoli, traces of houses and remains of walls composed of huge blocks of stone dating from this time are a constant and evocative presence. Following the destruction of the Etruscan settlements and their colonisation by the Romans, the population declined, the consular roads fell into disrepair, and canals and land were neglected. The few inhabitants withdrew to the towns and villages in the hills. After the Lombard invasions in the 10C the area came under the dominion of the Aldobrandeschi family and other feudal lords, who erected strongholds in defence against attacks, mostly from Siena and Orvieto.

From the 13C onwards sieges, conflicts, pirate raids and malaria caused destruction and depopulation until the final capitulation to Sienese rule. When Siena in turn fell to the Medici of Florence in 1555, and became part of the Grand Duchy of Tuscany, Cosimo I was obliged to cede parts of the Sienese territory to Spain and these were provided with impressive fortifications (these can still be seen at Orbetello and Porto Ercole). The poverty was such that many villages were all but totally abandoned.

Radical reforms did not begin until the 19C under Grand-duke Leopoldo II, who promoted better living conditions by draining the marches, promoting an agricultural programme and introducing a few industries. However, it was only in the 20C, after the First World War, with land development, the introduction of industries along the railway and the building of the acqueduct which supplied water from the Fiora river to the Argentario, that modernisation was achieved. Today with the disappearance of malaria, the increased ownership of cars and the development of tourism, there has been a real transformation in the standard of living. This explains why so many of these villages survive almost intact and why the landscape preserves its wild and mysterious character.

The footpath leading uphill overlooks the Roman road (formed of large flag-stones) and the area comprising the Roman forum and basilica. Nearby are remains of a house with mosaic floors, a paved street, and drains. Towards the hill on the right, large statues of the Emperor Claudius and the Imperial family were discovered in a rectangular chamber; they are now in the museum of Gros-seto. Beyond further excavations (still in progress) is the amphitheatre, 37m x 27m, with four entrances, in *opus reticulatum* of the 1C AD. On the adjacent hill traces of the earlier Etruscan settlement have been brought to light, together with remains of household objects, pottery, tiles, and unbaked bricks. There is evidence from wells found here that the Etruscans used a system of collecting rain water similar to the Roman *impluvium*. The view over the plain (formerly Lago Prile) is particularly beautiful.

Near the modern village of Roselle were thermal baths known since Roman times and still in use until the early 20C.

On the other side of the main road is **Nomadelfia**, a Christian community, founded in 1947 by Don Zeno Saltini (d. 1981) to create a family, especially for young people in need: there are now over 300 members.

East of Grosseto in the Ombrone valley is **Istia d'Ombrone**, a pretty village situ-ated on a bend of the river. Parts of its walls survive, and an arched gateway leads to the interesting 14C church of **San Salvatore.** It has a simple brick façade in the Sienese style. The interior contains a late medieval capital trans-formed into a holy-water stoup; a 14C fresco fragment of *St Anthony Abbot* worshipped by three women; the *Meeting at the Golden Gate* by Vincenzo Tamagni (1528); a charming *Madonna and Child*, formerly the central panel of a polyptych, by Giovanni di Paolo, and a statue of the *Madonna and Child* in poly-chrome wood by Domenico di Niccolò dei Cori, dating from the early 15C.

The coast near Grosseto

The nearest places to the provincial capital on the sea, both with extensive beaches, numerous hotels and camping sites are **Marina di Grosseto** and **Principina a Mare**, a resort in pine woods, which has been greatly developed in the last 20 years.

To the north is a lovely wood of umbrella pines known as the Pineta del Tombolo with a beautiful sandy beach. Inland is a marshy area called Le Mazze, privately owned but protected by the WWF, which may be visited on request (☎ 0564-26588). A short distance to the north is **Castiglione della Pescaia**, the most famous and attractive resort on the Maremma coast. It is very crowded in summer, but extremely pleasant in other seasons. Its small harbour, which was strategically important in Etruscan and Roman times, is now crowded with yachts and boats. It belonged to Pisa in the 12C and later came under the rule of Alfonso of Aragon, Siena, and Florence. The Medici Grand-duke Ferdinando I rebuilt its walls in 1608 around the Aragonese fort on the hill overlooking the harbour.

The old town, restored in recent years, is entered through an arched gateway and a street leads up to the **castle** (private) from which there are extensive views along the coast and inland across the plain to the hills. A pretty street winds round inside the walls which are well preserved. The church of **San Giovanni Battista**, originally Romanesque but remodelled in the 16C, has a large bell-tower added in the 19C, which dominates the sky-line. There is a medieval relief on the architrave over the doorway and a carved stone font. The paintings are of the baroque period. A silver reliquary containing relics of the local saint Guglielmo (see below) dates from 1668. In the nearby cemetery is the tomb of the writer Italo Calvino (1923–85) who lived nearby from 1972 until his death.

Just outside Castiglione, beyond the Giorgini bridge, a footpath leads along the

PROVINCIA DI GROSSETO

0   10 miles

0   20 kms

canal to the **Casa Rossa**. This interesting building in brick and travertine, with three arched sluices, was designed in 1767 by Leonardo Ximenes, a Spanish Jesuit and an expert in hydraulics, for Grand-duke Pietro Leopoldo of Lorraine. It served as a dam to control the waters between the Ombrone and to catch fish and was part of one of the earliest projects to reclaim the Grosseto plain. The bridge was added in the 1830s. The building was recently restored and there are long-term plans to open a museum to document the fauna and flora of the surrounding marshland. The swamp which gradually developed as a result of the silting up of the canal at Castiglione and periodical floods of the Ombrone and other rivers, was the primary cause of malaria and the consequent poverty and decline of the population in the district.

A road runs inland from Castiglione to Grosseto alongside the Bruna river, which marks the northern boundary of the former **Lago Prile**, the salt lake of Etruscan and Roman times which gave access to the harbours of Vetulonia and Roselle. At **Ponti di Badia** an unsurfaced road crosses the Bruna and leads to a hillock with remains of the **Badia al Fango**, a Benedictine monastery on the site of the Roman Villa Clodia, where Catullus' beloved Lesbia is said to have resided. Formerly a small island or peninsula, it served as the port of the Lake of Castiglione during the Medici period. It commands an extensive view over the plain of Grosseto (standing out across the marshes to the west is the Casa Rossa, described above). Nearby, beside an avenue of cypress and pine trees which leads to the estate of **La Badiola**, is a simple stone with a Cross erected in 1989 to commemorate Leopoldo II who used to stay here, and whose love and concern for the Maremma were fundamental in bringing this area back to life after it had suffered centuries of neglect.

Along the coast known as Riva del Sole, to the north of Castiglione, there are numerous beaches and resorts. Exclusive holiday villas at **Roccamare** are set among pine trees, with private beaches beyond low sand dunes.

On the point at the southern end of the gulf of Follonica, is **Punta Ala**, surrounded by thick pine woods. Formerly a natural beauty spot, with only a watch tower, it became the property of Italo Balbo, the Fascist politician and pilot, in 1929 and since the Second World War it has been transformed into a luxury holiday resort equipped with its own harbour, a golf course (18 holes) and other sports facilities.

To the north of Punta Ala a road runs inland along the Alma river and uphill to the village of **Tirli** (410m), first recorded in the 9C. The parish church (17C) has altars and stucco decoration by Andrea Ferrari of Lugano (1674). The high altar contains various relics of San Guglielmo (St William of Aquitaine) who died here in 1157 and who, together with St George, is traditionally venerated in the Maremma. At the north end of the village is a beautiful chestnut wood. On the opposite side is a path which leads to the ruins of the Guglielmite hermitage of **Malavalle**, which may also be reached from a country road on the outskirts of Castiglione. A procession is traditionally held at Tirli on Good Friday.

Follonica, 20km north of of Punta Ala, now an unattractive industrial town on the coast, has popular sandy beaches. From here there are good views of Elba and the promontory of Piombino.

Iron furnaces, supplied from the iron mines of Elba, have existed here since ancient times. Under the Medici the furnaces became a state monopoly for the production of arms and ammunition (cannon balls). The iron foundry created by Leopoldo II in 1834 was bombed in 1947 and abandoned in 1962: only the impressive iron entrance gate by Carlo Reishammer survives. The same architect also built the parish church of San Leopoldo, in an interesting combination of cast iron, stone, plaster, and wood.

South of Follonica is the little harbour of **Portiglione**. A footpath just off the main road leads through beautiful evergreen vegetation, known as *macchia mediterranea* along the cliffs and down to the little bay of **Cala Martina**. It was from here that Garibaldi, following his defeat in Rome and subsequent flight across Italy, escaped by boat in 1849 (commemorated by a bronze bust on a column). A little further on is **Cala Violina**, a small bay famous for its clear water and sandy beach. Another road to these beaches is from a turning off the Collacchie SS 322 on the north side of Pian d'Alma towards the Torre della Civetta.

From Portiglione a road goes inland to **Scarlino** (229m), a particularly attractive hill-top town in a beautiful position overlooking the sea and the surrounding countryside. Parts of the 13C fortress, including an impressive round tower and some of the defence walls, are well preserved, as are many of the medieval streets and houses. The Palazzo Comunale (partially rebuilt) also dates from the 13C, the tower is a 17C addition. Nearby is the *Centro di documentazione del Territorio* (☎ 0566-37052) which provides a complete historical survey of the town and the surrounding district (open most weekdays, otherwise on request). In the main square in the upper town is a marble monument to Garibaldi, represented half-length in a declamatory pose, with an inscription recording how five young men of Scarlino courageously helped the hero at the time of his escape.

The church of **San Donato** and its cloister, at the lower end of the town, date from the late Romanesque period but have been greatly altered over the centuries. In the chancel are carved choirstalls dating from 1713. There is also the fine tomb of Vanni and Emanuele Appiani, sons of Jacopo III Lord of Piombino, who died in 1471, by a Tuscan sculptor influenced by the great humanist tombs in Florence. A number of paintings and frescoes, some fragmentary, of various dates and varying in quality are also of interest.

Vetulonia and environs

The little hill-top town of **Vetulonia** (335m), northwest of Grosseto, is built on the site of the city of Vetulonia or Vetluna, one of the richest and most flourishing of Etruscan cities. The discovery of several necropoli has confirmed the documented description of Vetulonia as an important member of the Etruscan Confederation. Its identification was officially established in 1887 when the name was changed from Poggio Colonna. The earliest tombs date from the late 9C BC. The period of greatest prosperity was in the 8C–7C BC and the numerous tombs excavated at the end of the last century, some of them outstanding in size, were particularly rich in terracotta vases and objects in bronze, silver, and gold. These are now to be found in various museums, principally in Florence and Grosseto.

The Romans defeated the Gauls here in 224 BC, and are said to have borrowed from Vetulonia the insignia of their magistrates—the fasces, curule chair, and toga praetexta—and the use of the brazen trumpet in war.

Before entering Vetulonia, after the turning for the Via dei Sepolcri, are the ruins of a Romanesque abbey. Outside the town is an excavated area with interesting Roman remains of streets, houses and other buildings, drains and cisterns.

The archaeological areas and the tombs are **open** daily, summer 08.00–19.30, winter 09.00–16.30; ☎ 0564-931811).

The remains of the **citadel walls**, visible in various stretches, originally made a 5km circuit. At the top of the town is another stretch of walls probably dating from the 6C–5C BC and there are several medieval houses built out of older stones. The parish church, originally Romanesque, has an impressive bell-tower. There are several points around the town which offer splendid views.

Off the main street is the former school which has now been transformed into the local Antiquarium (due to re-open in the near future). Objects excavated in the nearby tombs will be exhibited here.

The Via dei Sepolcri leads down to the domed **Tumulo della Pietrera** and the **Tumulo del Diavolino**, the most remarkable tombs in the 8C–7C necropolis.

At the foot of the hill of Vetulonia, the road to the south passes another necropolis, and then branches right to the picturesque village of **Buriano** (239m), which is dominated by the massive ruins of its 10C Rocca. The church, built in 1302, has a fine tower. Inside is a 15C stained glass window representing the *Birth and Assumption of the Virgin*, a fresco fragment of an *Epiphany* dated 1524, and a wooden statue of *St Guglielmo*. A road encircles the whole village and there are beautiful views in all directions.

North of Vetulonia, across the Rigo valley, is **Caldana**, a village in a beautiful natural setting which preserves its medieval walls. The church of San Biagio has a fine 16C travertine façade is in the style of Antonio da Sangallo il Vecchio. The simple and elegant interior has arched bays, windows, and cornices picked out in grey stone against the white plaster. The fresco of St Biagio (Blaise) and St Guglielmo is by Giuseppe Nicola Nasini and the 17C baptismal font is carved out of the locally quarried *portasanta* marble.

Nearby is **Ravi**, a former castle, now a village, in a fine position on a slope of Monte Calvo. This mountain which rises to 469m can be explored on foot, and offers spectacular views stretching from Massa Marittima to Monte Amiata and the Argentario.

Gavorrano (273m) is another small fortified town in lovely surroundings. There was originally a double circle of elliptical walls with towers—now incorporated into the houses—and an arched gateway. The Palazzo Comunale was largely reconstructed in the 19C. Nearby is the parish church, of Romanesque origin but later enlarged and provided with a façade in 1927. It preserves an exquisite statue of the *Madonna del Carmine* by Giovanni di Agostino (c 1336).

Beyond the modern Aurelia (5km and then a turning to the right) are the ruins of **Castel di Pietra** (172m) where Pia de' Tolomei was allegedly murdered by her husband, Nello de'Pannocchieschi (Dante, *Divina Commedia*, 'Purgatorio' V, 130–136). Dante's story became a favourite theme with poets, playwrights and artists in the Romantic period and was also used by Donizetti in his opera *Pia de'Tolomei* of 1837. Situated on private property, it may be reached via a footpath by previous request at the nearby *Azienda agricola di Castel di Pietra.*

Roccastrada and environs

Roccastrada (475m), originally a small walled town built round its castle, has expanded considerably in recent years thanks to various industries. The old medieval district has picturesque streets, many of which are joined by steps and archways. The old castle, built onto a spur of rock and the two churches preserve very little of their original character and are much restored.

The road from Roccastrada to the Aurelia by-passes the village of **Sticciano**, nestling on the top of a hill behind which rises Monte Leoni (614m). A pretty road leads up to the former medieval castle, which was demolished when it was taken by Siena in the 14C. The Romanesque church is well preserved and has an altarpiece of the *Madonna del Rosario* by a local painter, Giovan Giuseppe Mattei, dated 1700. There are beautiful views across the plain towards the hills round Vetulonia and the sea. The nearby woods have good footpaths.

Farther south is **Montepescali** perched high up above the plain which, in Etruscan times, was filled with the salt Lake Prile. It is a small medieval town surrounded by olive groves. The old walls survive in part and there are terraces with panoramic views towards the sea and towards Monte Leoni.

The small 14C church of **San Lorenzo**, at the entrance to the town, has a fresco of the *Assumption* by the school of Bartolo di Fredi on the left wall. Picturesque streets lead up to the castle tower, with a large clock, and the pretty stone façade of the Romanesque church of San Niccolò. Inside are numerous fragmentary frescoes and four charming scenes of the *Life of the Virgin* dated 1389, by a close follower of Bartolo di Fredi. *The Madonna and Child enthroned with Saints and Angels* by Matteo di Giovanni was originally in San Lorenzo. Over the high altar is a fine 14C painted *Crucifix* of the Sienese school.

To the northwest of Roccastrada is the village of Sassofortino from which a road leads into the woods of **Monte Sassoforte** (787m). A footpath, signposted to

Roccatederighi

the *Castello*, crosses a wild wood with enormous rocks and age-old trees. There is a splendid view from the impressive castle ruins at the summit. **Roccatederighi** (520m) is a picturesque town situated on a rocky spur of Monte Sassoforte. The castle was extensively rebuilt at the beginning of this century. The parish church of **San Martino** was given a new façade in the late 15C and was modified inside over the centuries. It contains a little *Madonna with St Augustine* by a Sienese artist and a finely carved reliquary, both dating from the 17C. The streets and houses still preserve their medieval character and offer picturesque views.

To the south is the impressive castle of **Montemassi**. The village, with its towering ruins, dominates a cone-shaped hill surrounded by olive groves. The castle, a stronghold of the Aldobrandeschi, fell to Guidoriccio da Fogliano commander of the Sienese troops in 1328, a victory celebrated by Simone Martini in his famous fresco in the Palazzo Pubblico in Siena (see p. 344). There is a particularly fine view from the castle ruins. The church of **Sant'Andrea Apostolo** contains a few paintings, including a fragmentary *Madonna* close in style to Matteo di Giovanni and various furnishings and liturgical objects. The little church of **Santa Maria delle Grazie** is surrounded on three sides by a portico; inside is a 19C copy of a Madonna by Matteo di Giovanni. The medieval village and parts of the walls are still partially preserved.

· The main road north of Roccastrada winds down the hillside through woods of oaks and chestnuts passing beneath the fortified village of **Torniella** (441m), from which there are fine views. Steps lead past the church of San Giovanni Battista to the castle overlooking a small piazza.

Just north of Torniella is a footpath (approx. 10km) along the Farma Valley which leads to Bagni di Petriolo (see below).

Paganico and environs

Paganico is the principal town on the fast, busy road between Grosseto and Siena. Although called a superstrada the road is not dual-carriageway and passes through beautiful and varied scenery, perhaps at its most lovely in spring when the yellow broom is in flower. The little medieval town of **Paganico**, on a loop of the river Ombrone, was in a strategic position for defending Siena from the south. Its walls and gates which survive almost intact were built in the mid-14C by Lando di Pietro, the architect of Siena Cathedral.

The church of **San Michele**, in the piazza, dates from the same period. On the right wall of the nave is a giant figure of *St Christopher*. On the left, is an altarpiece of the *Madonna and Child with Saints* by Andrea di Niccolò (c 1480). Over the high altar is a *Madonna and Child enthroned worshipped by Saints* by Guidoccio Cozzarelli. Nearby is a very expressive painted *Crucifix* of the late 15C.

The **frescoes** in the choir are a masterpiece of 14C Sienese painting. When they were restored, the name of the artist, Biagio di Goro Ghezzi and the date (1368) were discovered. On the soffit of the arch are half-length figures of *Saints* and in the vault, the *Evangelists*. On the end wall, around the window, is the *Annunciation*. The artist has made use of the window jambs to make the perspective of his composition more convincing (note the presence of the Infant Jesus and the Dove on the left). On the north wall is the *Nativity*, with angel choirs, and other charming details. Below are three scenes from the *Legend of St Michael*. On the opposite wall is the *Epiphany* above a scene with *St Michael dividing the Damned from the Blessed*, who are received by the Queen of Heaven.

North of Paganico, the main road passes close to **Civitella Marittima** (329m). On the other side of the main road an unsurfaced road winds down to a cypress avenue and the Romanesque abbey church of **San Lorenzo al Lanzo**, in a particularly beautiful position in the Lanzo valley. The only authentic part of the church is the façade. The doorway is flanked by two half-columns supporting capitals with strange animal heads, similar in style to those of Sant'Antimo (see p 408). The interior is heavily restored and the former monastic buildings are now private.

The road runs along a viaduct high above the Farma valley. A by-road branches off towards the hill-top village of **Pari** again in a beautiful position. Far below the main road is **Bagni di Petriolo**, a rare example of a medieval fortified spa. A little loggia on the edge of the river, a chapel and parts of the peripheral 15C walls still survive from the time when Pope Pius II came here to benefit from the sulphurous water springs. The modern baths are **open** in summer on weekdays (06.30–13.30, 15.30–20.00).

To the south of Paganico, on the other side of the Ombrone, is **Sasso d' Ombrone**. A very pretty road climbs up to the picturesque village which is beautifully situated overlooking the valley. The church of San Michele, dating from the early 20C, has a fine early 15C polychrome wooden *Crucifix* by a Sienese sculptor.

Further south is **Campagnatico** (275m), a pretty village on a ridge with remains of its old castle. At the entrance to the village on the left is the church of the Misericordia (closed for restoration). The main street leads to a small piazza onto which faces the former church of Sant'Antonio, now transformed into a public hall and containing some 14C and 15C frescoes. Further up is the Romanesque church of **San Giovanni Battista**. It has an elegant façade with a perforated rose window. The bell-tower is built onto the earlier fortifications. The interior has a single nave and three apses with some frescoes. In addition, other frescoes representing the *Life of the Virgin* (from the Misericordia) are signed and dated 1393 by Meo di Piero and Cristoforo di Bindoccio.

In the 19C, horse breeding was encouraged here and several elegant houses have stables decorated with horses' heads. A *palio* or donkey race is held every summer. There is a very pretty road (towards Grosseto) through beautiful countryside from Campagnatico to Istia d'Ombrone.

Opposite Campagnatico, on the other side of the superstrada, is the hill-top village of **Montorsaio** (384m), on the edge of thick woods. The parish church has a copy of a *Madonna* by Sano di Pietro (now exhibited in the museum of Grosseto) and a late Renaissance sacristy cupboard. In the nearby confraternity chapel of Santa Croce is a fine *Crucifix* (1629). From Montorsaio a footpath leads (in 1 hr, or 1hr 30min.) to the summit of **Monte Leoni** (614m), passing remains of the convent of San Bernardino (suppressed in 1751), with panoramic views. Roselle, further south on the outskirts of Grosseto, is described above.

21 · Massa Marittima

Massa Marittima is an ancient mining town in beautiful countryside. Mining has taken place in the surrounding metalliferous hills (rich in iron, copper, and lead ores) since Etruscan times. It was a flourishing industry in the Middle Ages (when the earliest known Mining Code was drawn up here), and again in the last century. The town's period of greatest glory was from 1225 to 1335 when it was an independent Republic: its splendid Duomo, with its remarkable sculptural works, dates from this time. Massa Marittima remains one of the most fascinating and enchanting towns in southern Tuscany.

■ Practical information
Information office. 22 Via Norma Parenti (☎ 0566-902756).

Getting there
By rail. The nearest railway station is at Follonica, 17km southwest on the main line from Pisa to Grosseto.

By bus. Buses run by *Autolinee Società Ferrovia Massa-Follonica* (☎ 0566-902016) from Follonica. Services also from Grosseto (*RAMA*), and Volterra.

Parking. Outside the old town.

Hotels
★★★ *Il Sole*, 43 Corso della Libertà (☎ 0566-901971; fax 0566-901959).
★★ *Duca del Mare*, with restaurant, Piazza Dante Alighieri (☎ 0566-902284; fax 0566-901905).

Restaurants
££ *Taverna del Vecchio Borgo*, 12 Via Parenti. £ *Osteria Da Tronco*, 5 Vicolo Porte.
Bar *Le Logge*, Piazza Garibaldi (specialising in Panforte).

Annual festival. *Il Girifalco*, a cross-bow contest between the districts (or *Terzieri*) of the town, in traditional costume, takes place twice a year on the **Feast of St Bernardine** (20 May or the following Sunday), and on the second Sunday in August.

History. Massa Marittima flourished as an independent republic from 1225–1335, before falling under Sienese rule. From 1317 it minted its own silver coin, the grosso, which bore the figure of St Cerbone. The famous Mining Code drawn up at this time is one of the most important legislative documents to have survived from the Middle Ages in Italy. St Bernardine of Siena (1380–1444) was born in Massa, and it was here that he preached his last Lenten Sermons. His family, the Albizzeschi, were nobles. He became a Franciscan friar and was famous as a preacher throughout northern and central Italy. Many of his sermons and writings have survived. He had a particular devotion to the Name of Jesus and he is represented as an old, ascetic friar holding a tablet with rays surrounding the letters IHS and a cross.

The town is divided into two distinct parts, the **Città Vecchia** around the cathedral, and the **Città Nuova** on a hill above. Both districts were enclosed in the 13C circuit of walls, the extent of which reflects the prosperity of the medieval town prior to Sienese dominion in 1335. The Città Nuova and the Città Vecchia were then divided by the Sienese who erected an immense fortified wall which incorporated Porta alle Silici.

The Città Vecchia

You can enter the Città Vecchia either through the 13C Porta Salnitro, from which a road leads steeply up along the side of the Duomo, or from Porta dell'Abbondanza (or *delle Formiche*), behind the Duomo. The main square, **Piazza Garibaldi** (usually called Piazza del Duomo), is triangular in shape and presents beautiful and varied views in every direction.

Duomo

The Duomo was begun in the early 13C and is magnificently positioned at a strange angle above an irregular flight of steps with the north side creating a monumental perspective, counterbalanced by the bishop's palace, and the towering campanile at the centre. Dedicated to St Cerbone, whose relics were transferred to Massa from Populonia in the 9C, the cathedral has a splendid Romanesque **exterior** in travertine with blind arcading. The upper part of the **façade**, with exquisitely carved arches and capitals, symbols of the Evangelists, and a kneeling telamon, was added in the Pisan Gothic style in 1287–1314. Bas-reliefs sculpted above the main doorway in a single marble block, probably by a 12C Pisan sculptor, illustrate stories from the life of St Cerbone (see below): the saint is miraculously saved from shipwreck; he is thrown into the bears' den; he performs a miracle with two deer; he presents the Pope with a flock of geese; and he celebrates Mass in the presence of the Pope.

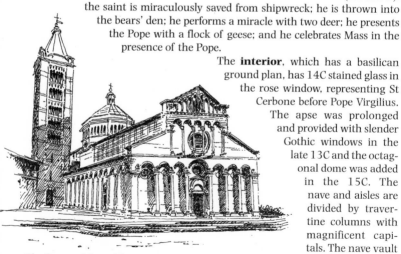

The **interior**, which has a basilican ground plan, has 14C stained glass in the rose window, representing St Cerbone before Pope Virgilius. The apse was prolonged and provided with slender Gothic windows in the late 13C and the octagonal dome was added in the 15C. The nave and aisles are divided by travertine columns with magnificent capitals. The nave vault dates from 1626.

To the right of the

The Duomo, Massa Marittima

entrance is a series of reliefs, thought to be pre-Romanesque, representing *Christ with angels*, the *Apostles*, and the *Massacre of the Innocents*. The splendid rectangular **font**, carved in a single square block of travertine resting on three lions and a lioness, with reliefs of the *Life of the Baptist and Christ Blessing*, is by Giroldo da Como (1267). The 15C tabernacle which rises from its centre, with carved figures of prophets in niches and crowned by a marble statue of the Baptist is dated 1447 but the sculptor is not known. The paintings in the **south aisle** include the *Virgin in glory with Saints* by Giuseppe Nicola Nasini and the *Birth of the Virgin* by Rutilio Manetti. Beyond is a side chapel with a 14C Sienese fresco of *Saints Lucy, Margaret and Agatha*, and some illuminated choirbooks in a case. The Chapel of the Crucifix has a painted *Crucifix*, attributed to Segna di Bonaventura, and an *Immaculate Conception* by Rutilio Manetti.

The **high altar**, designed as a triumphal arch, is by Flaminio di Girolamo del Turco (1623) and its polychrome wooden *Crucifix*, recently restored, is now universally regarded as an autograph work by Giovanni Pisano.

Behind the high altar is the **Arca di San Cerbone**, a marble urn signed and dated 1324 by Goro di Gregorio, a masterpiece of Sienese Gothic sculpture. The sculptor reveals great gifts as a storyteller and his reliefs are full of charming details, spontaneity and poetry.

St Cerbone

The story of St Cerbone, who was probably born in Africa in 493, is illustrated in the following scenes: he escapes from vandals to the Maremma, where he leads a hermit's life; he is condemned by Totila to be devoured by bears for giving shelter to enemy soldiers, but instead the bears only lick his feet; after becoming Bishop of Populonia, his parishioners object to his saying Mass before dawn and, since he will not change his ways, denounce him to Pope Virgilius; the Pope sends a delegation summoning the bishop to Rome; the envoys refuse Communion from Cerbone and are overcome by thirst; in answer to the saint's prayers two female deer allow themselves to be milked; three sick men he meets on the way to Rome are miraculously cured; at the gates of Rome, Cerbone summons a flock of geese to accompany him, as a gift for the Pope; he is received by Virgilius whom he invites to assist at Mass before dawn; at the service the Gloria is sung by angels which is the reason why he insisted on saying Mass so early, a fact that his humility prevented him from divulging.

Along the walls of the choir are eleven small marble statues of the Apostles by the Sienese sculptor Gano di Fazio (early 14C).

In the chapel to the left of the high altar is the **Madonna delle Grazie**, a majestic icon of the *Madonna and Child* (1316), by a close follower of Duccio and probably executed in his workshop, but which has been attributed also to the young Simone Martini. The panel, which has been cut down, also has the Crucifixion and Passion scenes painted on the back by the same hand. Fragments of a *Presentation in the Temple* by Sano di Pietro, which was sawn into pieces and stolen in 1922, are on the adjacent wall.

Steps lead down to the **undercroft** in which are displayed a silver-gilt reliquary *Cross* decorated with enamels by Andrea Pisano, a reliquary of two thorns of Christ's crown in crystal, silver and enamels by Goro di Ser Neroccio, and two wooden angels attributed to Vecchietta. The fresco of the *Crucifixion* in a lunette is by a 15C Sienese artist.

In the **north aisle** of the church are an *Annunciation* by Raffaello Vanni (1643); a fragmentary fresco of the *Adoration of the Magi* by Biagio di Goro and some 14C frescoes. Beside the entrance is a 14C frescoed triptych above a 3C Roman sarcophagus relief.

The tall bell-tower is probably contemporary with the church, but the upper part is restored. Beside it is Palazzo Vescovile, the Bishop's Palace.

Palazzo del Podestà ~ the Archaeological Museum

Opposite the cathedral to the left of the piazza is the 13C **Palazzo del Podestà**, with steps leading up to the entrance. Its austere façade in travertine has four double windows on two levels and numerous coats of arms recording the governors of the town from 1426 to 1633. The palace houses the **Museo Civico Archeologico** (open 10.00–12.30, 15.30–19.00, in winter 15.00–17.00; closed Mon). The collection documents the various settlements in the district from prehistoric times to the Roman era and has a particularly rich Etruscan section.

In a room on the ground floor a selection of the most important paintings from the **Pinacoteca** are exhibited provisionally. The most important work is the **Maestà** by Ambrogio Lorenzetti of c 1330, showing the *Madonna and Child enthroned surrounded by saints, angels, and the theological virtues.* Other fine works include a small *Madonna* by Sano di Pietro, and the *Angel Gabriel* by Sassetta (the companion panel with the *Virgin* is in New Haven, USA).There are also some later paintings on the upper floor.

The interesting archaeological material on the ground floor was excavated in the vicinity of Massa Marittima. The earliest dates from the Paleolithic age. Of particular interest are the unusual funerary stele carved in stylised human form, reminiscent of those of Luni (see p. 231), dating from the 3rd millenium BC. There is pottery from the early Bronze age. The **Etruscan section** documents the excavations in recent years of the necropoli and settlements near Lake Accesa which have brought to light objects ranging from the 9C–6C BC. There is a fine collection of ceramics, including imported Hellenistic works. The 19C Galli collection comprises interesting Etruscan pieces from Tarquinia and Vulci.

To the right of Palazzo del Podestà is the small 13C palace of the Conti di Biserno (the first-floor windows were added in the 16C), beside Palazzo Comunale with two robust crenellated towers (extensively restored). From the corner of Palazzo Vescovile, Via Ximenes leads to **Palazzo dell'Abbondanza**, a 13C public fountain with three large pointed arches, over which a granary was built in the 15C. From Piazzale Mazzini there is a fine view of the cathedral apse and tower.

In Via Corridoni, a short distance away, is the **Museo della Miniera** (guided visits daily, every half hour: **open** winter 10.00–12.00, 15.00–16.00; summer 10.00–12.30, 15.30–19.00; closed in Feb; ☎ 0566-902289). Situated in an abandoned mine, it demonstrates mining techniques and exhibits equipment, machinery and mineral specimens.

The Città Nuova

From Porta dell'Abbondanza two streets lead uphill to Piazza Matteotti in the Città Nuova. Here parallel intersecting streets create a quite different plan to the lower town. **Porta alle Silici**, part of the vast and impressive fortifications erected by the Sienese after their conquest of Massa in 1335, is connected to the older **Torre del Candeliere** by an immense flying arch. The clock tower, which was reduced to two-thirds of its original height by the Sienese, may be climbed (**open** 11.00–12.30, 17.00–19.00; closed Mon; **open** in winter only on request). The Sienese **fortress** (on the site of the former Bishop's Palace) was partly destroyed in the 18C–19C to make room for the hospital. From the adjoining parapet there is a splendid view over the roofs of Massa and the surrounding countryside.

Downhill from Piazza Matteotti is the **Porta San Francesco**, near the 13C Franciscan church, which was reduced in length after a landslide. On the north side of the Piazza is Palazzo delle Armi, with an arched portico, where ammunition was stored. It now contains the **Museo di Storia e Arte delle Miniere**. **Open** 16 July–31 Aug 10.00–12.00, 16.00–19.00; 1 Apr–15 July and Sept, 10.00–11.00, 15.00–17.00; Oct–March, Sat and Sun, 10.00–11.00 or on request. The museum documents excavations in the district, with reliefs, diagrams and photographs illustrating the development of mining from Etruscan to modern times. The **Mining Code** document of 1310 is also kept here. On the upper floor are a selection of minerals, instruments, and tools, and a cast of an ape skeleton (*Oreopithecus Bambolii*), discovered in a lignite mine.

The Church of St Augustine

Corso Diaz leads to the church of **Sant'Agostino**, founded in 1299. The simple **façade** has an oculus above an elegant doorway. The polygonal apse, pierced by arched Gothic windows (with modern glass), was designed by Domenico di Agostino (1348), who completed the Cathedral of Siena.

The **interior** has a single nave, divided into bays by grandiose pointed arches. The paintings include: *St Guglielmo* attributed to Antonio Nasini; *Flight into Egypt* by Lorenzo Lippi; *Madonna and Saints* by Rutilio Manetti; *Annunciation* by Jacopo da Empoli. The tomb of the Augustinian theologian Michele Bellucci (d. 1479) is by Urbano da Cortona. In the **St Lucy Chapel**, right of the choir, is a reclining effigy of *St Lucy* (the 15C original is in the Musée des Arts Decoratifs in Paris) and frescoes, one of them representing the presentation of the Mining Code of Massa, attributed to Vincenzo Tamagni. In the **choir** is a *Nativity* by Bartolomeo Ponti (1627) and frescoed angels on the left wall flanking a 15C marble tabernacle.

The *Adoration of the Shepherds with Saints Bernardine and Anthony of Padua*, behind the high altar, is by Pietro di Francesco Orioli (c 1480). In the chapel on the left is a painted terracotta *Madonna and Child* by Zaccharia Zacchi. The *Visitation* is by Rutilio Manetti (1639). The **sacristy** has showcases with liturgical objects and choirbooks. A door opens from the church into the elegant cloister and conventual buildings. The tall slender bell-tower rises behind. It was built onto one of the towers on the city walls in 1627.

Next to Sant'Agostino is the façade of the former church of **San Pietro all'Orto,** now the premises of the *Terziere della Città Nuova*, which houses the paraphernalia for the annual Girifalco contest (see above). The rooms also contain a small collection of pottery and coins found locally, and some 14C frescoes recently discovered under whitewash. The beautiful stepped Via Moncini returns downhill from Porta alle Silici to the cathedral.

Environs of Massa Marittima

South of the town is the **Lago dell'Accesa**, a small lake (580m long, 400m wide), set in a beautiful, tranquil landscape. It is next to the source of the river Bruna. Nothing remains of the Medici and Lorena iron foundry (another one was in the nearby village of **Valpiana**), but there is evidence that the fusion of metals here dates back to Etruscan times. Settlements and necropoli, excavated on the southwestern side of the lake, date from the 7C BC (the excavations are described in detail, and the finds exhibited, in the Archaeological Museum of Massa Marittima, see p. 310).

A road leads north of Massa Marittima towards the metalliferous hills (see Ch. 17). It winds up through oak and chestnut woods onto a high ridge above the Pavone valley through very wild countryside. **Monterotondo Marittimo** is built on a hill in a natural ravine. It preserves part of its 13C castle, a crenellated tower (restored) of the Palazzo Comunale and picturesque medieval streets and alleyways. A *Madonna and Child* by the so-called Master of Monterotondo, an artist close to Duccio has been removed from the parish church of San Lorenzo to the Pinacoteca in Siena. This was the birthplace of the writer Renato Fucini (1843–1921) who wrote stories set in the Maremma, charmingly told but mostly very sad. The hills around are covered with thick chestnut woods and there is a splendid view over the hills to the sea.

To the west are the **Terme di Bagnolo** (550m) a spa, with hot springs (43° C). Towards the sea, on the road for Piombino, is the village of **Frassine** which has ruins dating from the Lombard (early medieval) period. It has a Sanctuary of the Madonna (restored) containing a carved wooden *Madonna and Child* by the 14C Pisan school, and an interesting collection of painted ex-votos (16C–19C).

Suvereto, and the coastal area beyond are described in Ch. 19.

East of Monterotondo, in the heart of the metalliferous hills, is the little town of **Montieri** (704m), important for its silver mines. In the medieval village, which is well preserved, is the church of **Santi Paolo e Michele** and an impressive Romanesque bell-tower. It has a number of 16C–17C paintings and an 18C terracotta *Via Crucis*. Above the high altar are the remains of Beato Giacomo Papocchi of Montieri, a 13C hermit whose saintly life is illustrated in the surrounding paintings. Opposite the church is a medieval tower-house and other interesting buildings. A short rise leads up to the 13C **castle** beyond which is the church of **San Giacomo** and the cell inhabited by Beato Giacomo. Off Via Roma is the church of **San Francesco** which has 17C paintings and furnishings.

There are plans to map itineraries for **walking tours** in the neighbourhood, which is rich in areas of archaeological and mining interest, in beautiful natural surroundings.

South of Montieri is a turning for **Boccheggiano** (664m), reached by a winding road through woods. It was important for its pyrite mines. Although the village has been completely changed over the centuries, it has a certain charm and is beautifully situated. In the church of **San Sebastiano** is a marble statue of the saint by Bartolomeo Cennini of 1650, a gift of the 17C antiquarian, Leonardo Agostini, who was born here.

22 · The Parco Naturale della Maremma

The **Parco Naturale della Maremma**, a coastal area of some 70 sq. km just south of Grosseto, was designated a national park in 1975. It extends from Alberese south across the beautiful wooded and roadless **Monti dell'Uccellina** (417m) to Talamone. The fifteen kilometres of coastline here are perhaps the best preserved in Italy.

■ Practical information

Park information office at Alberese (☎ 0564-407098). *Tourist information*, APT Grosseto (☎ 0564-454510).

Getting there

By bus. There is a *RAMA* bus service from Grosseto to Alberese (☎ 0564-404169).

By car. At the **northern entrance** of the park cars have to be left at Alberese, where a bus takes visitors to the entrance. The **southern entrance** to the park (car park) is on the Talamone road from Fonteblanda. The coast can be explored along the beach from the car park at Marina di Alberese.

Hotels

Talamone. ★★★★ *Talamonio*, 4 Via Garibaldi (☎ 0564-887008; fax 0564-887380). ★★★ *Capo d'Uomo*, 7 Via Cala di Forno (☎ 0564-887077; fax 0564-887298).

Alberese. *Agriturismo accommodation*. There are no hotels here, but some 26 farms offer generally excellent Agriturist accommodation (all listed in the Grosseto *APT* hotel list): information about these can also be had by enquiring locally.

Campsite at Talamone ★★ *Talamone* (☎ 0564-887026).

Restaurants

Alberese. ££ *Da Remo*, at Rispescia

Talamone. ££ *La Buca di Nonno Ghigo*, 1 Piazza Garibaldi and *Da Flavia*, Piazza IV Novembre.

Alberese

North of Alberese a road leads to the coast, past farms where the Maremma white long-horned cattle are grazed and then through pine woods to **Marina di Alberese**; a beach with a car park. This unspoilt stretch of coast (although suffering from erosion) with sandy dunes, and backed by thick pinewoods planted in the mid-19C, begins at the estuary of the Ombrone river (the Classical *Umbro*, one of the chief rivers of Etruria). This marks the northern limit of the park. On the right bank of the river is the remarkably well preserved **Palude della Trappola**, a marsh area and bird sanctuary. The beach extends south as far as **Cala di Forno**, at the foot of Monti dell'Uccellina, where there are natural grottoes. Farther on, the rocky slopes of the Uccellina plunge straight into the sea: here the beautiful coastline and distinctive vegetation, which includes dwarf palm trees, can only be seen from the sea.

   Alberese is a small pleasant village built on a spacious plan in 1951 near the northern entrance to the park. **Tickets** must be purchased here at the information office in order to visit the park. A bus leaves on the hour every hour (09.00–dusk) on Wed, Sat, and Sun (numbers are limited during the summer months) for the entrance to the park (10mins) from which various itineraries are indicated along marked footpaths (most of them require a minimum of three hours; children are welcome).

The vegetation in the park varies from woods of pine trees, ilexes, elms, and oaks to marshlands, and the typical Mediterranean *macchia* of myrtle and juniper bushes. Animals which run wild here include the famous white long-horned cattle, deer, foxes, goats, wild cats, horses, and wild boar. The cattle and horses are herded by cowboys known as *butteri* (rodeo at Alberese in August). Migratory birds and numerous aquatic species abound.

Behind the church is the entrance (pedestrians only; open daily) to the *Itinerario Faunistico*, a beautiful walk of less than an hour through a protected area, where deer and other wild animals can usually be seen. The Museo della Cultura Popolare Grossetana at Alberese is at present closed.

The **Monti dell'Uccellina** offer splendid views and walks through a natural setting of great variety and beauty, with a few towers and romantic ruins. The **Torre della Bella Marsilia** is the lonely remnant of the castle of Collecchio, home of the Marsili family of Siena. In 1543 the castle was destroyed by the corsair Barbarossa and the entire household murdered except for the lovely Margherita, who was carried off to the harem of the Sultan Suleiman the Magnificent, soon to become his legitimate sultana and the mother of Selim II.

Nearby are the ruins of **San Rabano**, an 11C Benedictine abbey later occupied by the Knights of St John of Jerusalem. The apse of the Romanesque church survives in part with some of its original decoration. The octagonal dome was probably a 14C addition and the tall tower is still standing. There are also remains of the walls built around the monastery.

The towers of **Castelmarino** and **Collelungo** are near some natural caves and rocks, facing onto the beach. The walk to **Cala di Forno** and its tower, at the far end of the beach, ends in a charming little bay.

The Via Aurelia skirts the park as far as **Fonteblanda** where a road leads towards Talamone, at the southern boundary of the Park. The road passes olive groves and the cemetery, on the right. A short way beyond, an unsurfaced road to the right (500m; signposted *Parco Naturale della Maremma*) leads past the site of a Roman villa and baths, to the south entrance to the Park.

Cars may be parked outside an enclosure with a stile. No ticket is required but visitors must leave the park before dusk.

There are two footpaths (the longer walk takes approximately 2–2½hrs) which lead through the thick *macchia* vegetation and woods, and emerge on the coast overlooking the sea. These walks are especially beautiful towards sunset.

Talamone

The approach to Talamone, a summer resort, is particularly striking with the castle silhouetted against the sky. The original Etruscan city and port, said to have been founded by the Argonaut Telamon c 1300 BC stood on the south side of the bay, but was abandoned for its present position by the Romans in the Imperial era. The medieval town developed on the rocky promontory overlooking the bay and in the 14C Talamone became the port for Siena. Here also Garibaldi and the Thousand put in on their way to Sicily in 1860 to collect arms and ammunition and to land a party for a feigned attack on the Papal States.

The picturesque harbour with yachts and fishing boats at their moorings, lies at the foot of the steep village. Although damaged in the Second World War, Talamone retains its charm and the walk up along the walls to the Rocca offers splendid views of the Argentario and island of Giglio. The 15C **Rocca**, an impressive block-like construction with tower, was rebuilt by the Sienese on the site of an Aldobrandeschi family castle. Lower down is Piazza Garibaldi (with a bronze bust of the hero) with the parish church (1953) which contains modern paintings and stained glass windows. A terrace overlooking the harbour dominates the entrance to the village, with the War Memorial at the centre of a parapet.

The origins of Talamone go back to the late Bronze Age. The Etruscan settlement occupied the nearby hill of **Talamonaccio**, north of the Osa estuary, and excavations have identified the acropolis and necropolis. The temple (4C BC) was later rebuilt and provided with a splendid pediment (150 BC), which was recently restored and is now exhibited in Orbetello (see below).

23 · Orbetello and Monte Argentario

Orbetello was the most important harbour south of Livorno, protected by one of the many fortresses along the coast. The town is situated on the central strip of land linking the Argentario promontory to the mainland, with a lagoon on either side enclosed by two sand bars (or *tomboli*), the Tombolo di Giannella and the Tombolo di Feniglia, which have extensive beaches. The Monte Argentario is very beautiful, especially in the wilder southwestern parts and there is a magnificent view from Monte Telegrafo (635m). There are two important WWF sanctuaries, one in the lagoon of Orbetello and the other further south, near the station of Capalbio, on Lake Burano. Although the Argentario is known for its rather exclusive and fashionable summer resorts, there are also campsites along the Tombolo della Giannella. The islands of Giglio and Giannutri can be reached by regular boat services from Porto Santo Stefano. The mild climate of the promontory is not only ideal for the winter quarters of numerous migratory birds but it also favours a luxuriant and unusual flora, including wild orchids and dwarf palm trees. As well as the typical *macchia mediterraneo* (see p. 288), there are also citrus fruit trees, olive groves and vineyards. The archaeological site of Cosa combines the fascination of ruins with a beautiful natural setting.

■ Practical information

Information offices. APT Grosseto (☎ 0564-454510); **Orbetello**, Piazza della Repubblica (☎ 0564-861226); **Porto Santo Stefano**, 55 Corso Umberto (☎ 0564-814208).

Getting there
By car. The Via Aurelia between Pisa and Rome skirts the lagoon of Orbetello.

By rail. There is a railway station at Orbetello Scalo on the main line between Pisa and Rome (slow trains only).

By bus. Bus services (*RAMA*) from Grosseto and Follonica to Orbetello.

Hotels
Orbetello. ★★★ *I Presidi*, 34 Via Mura di Levante (☎ & fax 0564-867601) and *Sole*, 2 Via Colombo (☎ 0564-860410; fax 0564-860475). ★ *Piccolo Parigi*, 169 Corso Italia (☎ 0564-867233; fax 0564-867211).

Porto Ercole. ★★★★ *Il Pellicano*, località Sbarcatello (☎ 0564-833801; fax 0564-833418).

Porto Santo Stefano. ★★★ and ★★ hotels, including ★★★ *Villa Domizia* at Santa Liberata (☎ & fax 0564-812735).

Campsites
On the **Tombolo di Feniglia**. ★ *Feniglia* (☎ 0564-831090), and on the Tombolo di Giannella ★★★ and ★★ sites.

Restaurants
Orbetello. ££ *Il Nocchino*, 64 Via dei Mille; £ pizzeria *Da Gennaro*. On the Tombolo di Giannella *Il Tramonto* £.

Capalbio. ££ *Da Maria*, 3 Via Comunale and *Da Carla*, 33 Via Emanuele; and £ *Trattoria La Toscana*, 2 Via Emanuele.

The Lagoon of Orbetello

The extensive Lagoon of Orbetello is enclosed between the *Tombolo di Giannella* and the *Tombolo di Feniglia*, two tongues of sand which extend to the Argentario promontory. At the centre of the lagoon, on another isthmus, is the small town and harbour of Orbetello. The lagoon has a bird sanctuary in the Laguna di Ponente for some 200 species, protected by the World Wide Fund for Nature (WWF). Access is from Cariolo on the Via Aurelia, two kilometres south of the railway station of Albinia. There are several walks, nine bird-watching stations and two towers, besides a special botanical walk in the Patanella woods.

Open Sept–Apr, Thurs and Sun, 10.00 and 14.00; guided tours for groups, Sat (☎ 0564-820297). It is possible to book overnight accomodation (☎ 06-854892).

Orbetello

Orbetello, on a sandy isthmus, is an old-fashioned resort (considerably damaged in the Second Word War) in a beautiful site in the middle of the lagoon with palm trees on the waterfront.

The position of Orbetello favoured settlements in ancient times. It was an Etruscan colony (remains of the town walls are still visible) and a place of importance in the Middle Ages. It became the capital of the *Stato dei Presidi* (or 'garrison state'), formerly ruled by Siena, in this coastal area of the Maremma, which included Ansedonia, Porto Ercole, Porto Santo Stefano, and Talamone. This was created by Philip II of Spain when he entered into an alliance with Cosimo I in 1557 by which Siena and her territories were ceded to the Medici. Later, in 1646 the town held out against a two-month siege by the French. After the war of Spanish Succession the area came under Austrian control, and was part of Napoleon's Kingdom of Etruria in the early 19C. All these coastal towns were incorporated into the Grand Duchy of Tuscany after the Congress of Vienna (1815).

On the approach to the town the road passes the former airfield from which Italo Balbo (see p. 302) led a formation flight of seaplanes across the Atlantic to celebrate the tenth anniversary of Fascism at the World Fair of Chicago in 1933.

The road leads through one of the elegant gateways, built by the Spaniards when they fortified the town to a piazza with a large public garden, partly surrounded by fortifications. There is a large car park on the waterfront to the right. Via Dante leads to the **cathedral** (Santa Maria Assunta). The beautiful

façade of travertine stone has an upper triangular section containing a rose-window, above which is a niche with a statue of Christ blessing. The arched doorway, dated 1376, has finely carved decoration. The church was almost entirely rebuilt in the 17C, incorporating the original façade. Inside, the decoration and floor tiles are Spanish in taste. The pretty chapel of St Biagio has an early Romanesque marble altar-frontal carved with Biblical symbols, peacocks, and vine branches.

On the opposite side of the piazza is the former **convent of the Clarisse** which houses the Municipal Library (it contains a well documented section on the Maremma and its history) and the tourist information office. The celebrated Etruscan **Pediment of the Temple of Talamone**, of the 2C BC, is temporarily exhibited here (**open** daily in summer, 10.00–12.30, 16.00–20.00; in winter afternoons only Thurs–Sun, ☎ 0564-868010). The pediment is a grandiose relief in terracotta, with figures modelled partly in the round. Although fragmentary, it is a moving representation of the story of Oedipus and the death of his two sons, Polynices and Eteocles. The foundations of the temple may be visited on the site of the Etruscan city excavated on the hill of Talamonaccio (see Ch. 22).

Via Solferino, to the right of the cathedral, leads to Piazza Garibaldi. Here is the **Palace of the Spanish Governor** with a porticoed façade and clock-tower, at the foot of which is a bust of Garibaldi. Left of the palace the Corso leads to Piazza del Plebiscito onto which faces the Palazzo del Municipio, decorated with coats of arms. Along the sea front are impressive walls of Etruscan origin. On the south side is the **Polveriera Guzman**, a rectangular building with three defence towers, built in 1692 by the architect Ferdinando de Grunenbergh. Inside are two spacious rooms which will house the Archaeological Museum (due to open soon).

In the lagoon around Orbetello are various towers and one surviving windmill. To the south of Orbetello the **Tombolo di Feniglia** a beautiful sandy isthmus, 6km long and 1km wide, joins the peninsula to the mainland. The woods felled here at the beginning of the 19C have been replaced by a forest of pine trees, planted at the beginning of this century. It is now one of the most beautiful stretches of pine trees along the coast and is a protected area with a vast sandy beach. It is crossed by a footpath (also open to cyclists) some 7km long. A port for private boats recently constructed at Cala Galera nearby has eroded the coastline.

The Monte Argentario peninsula

A dyke, 1.5km long, built by Leopoldo II in 1842, joins Orbetello to **Monte Argentario** (635m), usually known simply as the Argentario, a roughly circular peninsula once covered with thick woods of ilexes and oaks and still beautiful despite deforestation and extensive building in some areas. It is covered with wild flowers in spring. The beauty of the promontory can best be appreciated from the sea. Porto Santo Stefano and the smaller Porto Ercole are now famous as holiday resorts with harbours for yachts and lively fish markets.

Porto Ercole

Porto Ercole is a well-known resort. It has a particularly sheltered port above which are situated impressive fortifications of the Spanish period (16C). Etruscan in origin, it was known as *Portus Herculis* by the Romans, and thrived until the 15C when, through poor administration and the threats of pirates, it fell into decline. Porto Ercole then became an important military and naval base of the Spanish *Stato dei Presidi* (see p. 316).

At the entrance to the old town, surrounded by walls, is an elegant gate with a plaque commemorating the painter Caravaggio who died offshore here in 1610. Steep steps lead up to the Piazza Santa Barbara with the parish church of **Sant'Erasmo**. Inside are interesting tombstones of some of the governors and a fine marble altar. The nearby **Palazzo Consani**, built for Agostino Chigi in the early 16C, was the residence of the Spanish governors. It is attributed to the architect Baldassare Peruzzi.

The towering **Rocca**, now a ruin, is a vast citadel with powerful fortifications and moats. Its earliest parts date from the 13C but it was considerably rebuilt in the 15C and 16C. There is a little Renaissance church with a portico designed by Bernardo Buontalenti. (Permission to visit the Rocca may be obtained from the *Delegazione Comunale* at Viale Caravaggio No.6.) A passage connects the fort to the bastion of Santa Barbara by the harbour across which is the modern district of Le Grotte.

On the hill facing the Rocca is the **Forte Filippo**, built in 1558 to a design by Giovanni Camerini. The fort has four enormous bastions with defences on various levels. Below, by the coast, is the **Forte Santa Caterina** surrounded by tall defence walls and a moat with a drawbridge. Both these forts are private.

South of the town, opposite the small island of Isolotto a footpath leads up to the **Forte Stella**, the third fortress surrounding Porto Ercole. It was built by Florentine architects sent by the Medici Grand-duke Cosimo I and financed by King Philip II of Spain. It derives its name from the star-shaped fort surrounded by high walls with four projecting bastions.

On the north side of the Argentario peninsula, the road skirts the lagoon and meets the road from Albinia which runs along the Tombolo di Giannella. At Santa Liberata there are excavations of a large Roman villa and fish farm. The road winds along the coast down to the harbour of **Porto Santo Stefano**. Originally a fishing village, the port was first developed in the 15C and the massive Spanish fort dates from 1560. It is now a popular summer resort but its charm has been greatly impaired by War damage and excessive rebuilding. This is the port for the Isola del Giglio (see below).

A *strada panoramica*, beginning at the harbour encircles the promontory through beautiful and varied scenery with splendid views. From Porto Santo Stefano it passes along the coast high above cliffs planted with vineyards, olive groves, and orange and lemon trees. The Cala Grande is one of the most beautiful bays along the coast. A parapet faces the island of Giglio and provides an ideal point from which to enjoy the sunset. The road becomes more tortuous (there is an unsurfaced stretch of c 4km) on the south side of the promontory and passes through wilder areas overlooking steep cliffs, rocky bays and grottoes, rocks emerging from the sea and two small islands. As it approaches Porto Ercole the road passes the bays and sandy beaches of villas and hotels.

Near the turning for the Tombolo della Giannella a road climbs inland to the summit of **Monte Telegrafo** (635m). It passes the mother-house of the Passionist Order, founded by St Paul of the Cross (Paolo Danei, 1694–1775). Eight monks now live here; the small church (1735) has altarpieces by Sebastiano Conca and Pietro Aldi. The road continues through thick vegetation, characteristic of the *macchia mediterranea*, to the peak where there is a splendid view.

Isola del Giglio

■ Practical information

Information office. *APT* Porto Santo Stefano (☎ 0564-814208).

Navigation services (car ferries and hydrofoils). Frequent service in c 1hr run by *Toremar*, at Porto Santo Stefano, (☎ 0564-810803); on Giglio (☎ 0564-809349) and *Maregiglio*, at Porto Santo Stefano (☎ 0564-812920); on Giglio, ☎ 0564-809309).

Hotels
★★★ and ★★ hotels at Campese and Giglio Porto (including ★★ *Pardini's Hermitage*, Cala degli Alberi (☎ 0564-809034; fax 0564-809177).
Campsite. ★ *Baia del Sole*, at Sparvieri (☎ 0564-804036).
Rooms to let at Campese, Castello and Giglio Porto.

The pretty island of Giglio, 17.5km west of Porto Santo Stefano, has an area of 21 sq. km and a little grey granite fortess-village (bus from the port), and vineyards. Pathways lead down to the sandy beach from the village. The island is crowded at weekends in summer, and new buildings are spoiling its natural beauty, although about half of the island has been protected since 1996 as part of the *Parco Nazionale dell'Arcipelago Toscano* (see Ch. 42).

In 1961 a boat was discovered offshore in the bay of Campese some 50m below the surface, shipwrecked c 600 BC. Its cargo of Greek and Etruscan ceramics, including numerous aryballos and Corinthian ware, wooden flutes, and a rare bronze Corinthian helmet, has mostly been recovered, and in 1985 part of its keel, 3m long, was salvaged. Oxford University has been in charge of the project.

The **island of Giannutri**, to the southeast, was also threatened with tourist development, but became part of the *Parco Nazionale dell'Arcipelago Toscano* in 1996. It has ruins of a Roman villa belonging the Domizi Enobardi family. A **boat service** from Porto Santo Stefano via the Isola del Giglio in summer is run by *Maregiglio* (see above).

Ansedonia and Cosa

At the southern end of the Orbetello lagoon is the modern fashionable resort of **Ansedonia** with elegant villas surrounded by pines and oak trees on the slopes of a beautiful promontory. On the top of the hill (114m) are the ruins of the Roman town of **Cosa**. There are two turnings off the Via Aurelia for Ansedonia: the one to the north leads to Cosa, the one further south to the harbour.

Excavations in the area have revealed that there have been settlements here since prehistoric times. The Etruscan settlement became a Roman colony in 273 BC. By the 2C BC, Cosa was a flourishing town with its Capitol and Forum, and the city gates and walls are still partially preserved. Beneath the cliffs on the south side, was a small harbour, the *Portus Cosanus*.

Extending south was an extensive lagoon rich in fish, separated from the sea by sand dunes, with a canal leading to a deep natural passage, 260m long, linking the lagoon to the sea, called the '**Spacco della Regina**'. This passage provided for the ebb and flow of the tides and prevented the harbour from silting up. When parts of the passage collapsed causing it to block up, another shorter passage, the **Tagliata**, was cut through the cliffs nearer the harbour. The hewing out of this passage, with walls some 15–20m high and other parts tunnelled through the rock, was an amazing feat and it was also engineered to control the waters and the catching and farming of fish. There are steps and a walkway on the cliffs from which one may see the Tagliata. Some remains of the Roman harbour are still visible in the little bay and there is a fine view of the promontory and cliffs from the beach.

The particularly interesting excavated site of **Cosa** extends over a considerable area amidst magnificent olive trees and ilexes (**open** daily, Oct–Apr 09.00–sunset; May–Sept 08.00–20.00, explanatory panels, also in English. The Antiquarium is **open** May–Sept 09.00–19.00, Oct–Apr 09.00–14.00).

The site includes several stretches of walls constructed of enormous stone blocks. On a slight rise are remains of two temples and the forum, from which there is a splendid view stretching from the Orbetello lagoon and Monte Argentario to the lake of Burano, over dunes and marshland. More excavations are in progress on another slope on the south side of the promontory.

The little **Antiquarium**, installed in a reconstructed house, was opened to the public in 1997. It contains interesting pieces of sculpture, terracotta ornaments from the temples, pottery, oil jars, glass, bronze objects and coins. There are texts (also in English) explaining the history and excavations of Cosa and its port. There is also a section on the medieval monastery on the site and the later castle of Ansedonia which was raised to the ground by Siena in 1328.

On the beach is a house and a medieval defence tower built on the site of a Roman villa. Puccini composed part of his opera *Tosca* here. There were several large Roman villas in the area on estates which produced wine and oil.

On the other side of the Aurelia a by-road (signposted *Villa Romana*) leads inland past the ruins of a Roman villa (**Villa delle Colonne**) whose interesting perimeter wall has unusual cylindrical towers. The road continues for c 1km; the second road on the left (unsurfaced) climbs a small hill (not signposted; keep left) to a house in pine trees, beside which a sign for the *scavi archeologici* (archaeological excavations) indicates the overgrown ruins of the Roman villa of **Settefinestre** in a romantic setting (on the hillside below, beside a fence). Excavations (some of them since covered over) in 1976–81 revealed remains of a large villa of the 1C BC (probably abandoned by the mid-2C AD), with farm buildings attached. Numerous rooms with geometric mosaic floors were identified, and part of its front wall (3.5–4.5m high), as well as wall-paintings.

The farm (with wine and olive presses, and buildings thought to have been used as pigsties) appears to have been run by slaves whose modest quarters have also been found. The visible remains, now abandoned, include the high wall with buttresses and arches.

Capalbio

Inland, at the southernmost end of Tuscany, is Capalbio, a charming little medieval village, visible from the main road, which has recently become fashionable as an exclusive summer resort. It is in a beautiful position on a low hill above thick ilex, cork, and oak woods once typical of the vegetation in the Maremma, in the centre of a game reserve. The area is famous for its wild boar (*cinghiale*; fair in September).

The double circle of medieval walls and the entrance gateway and tower are well preserved. The **Castello** has a tall tower which dominates the town. The streets are picturesque and there are charming views from the walkways above the walls overlooking houses and gardens. The church of **San Nicola**, remodelled in the 15C, has some Romanesque capitals and remains of 15C–16C frescoes. The little oratory of the **Madonna della Providenza** has an interesting chapel decorated with frescoes in the style of Perugino (c1500).

Domenico Tiburzi, the most famous brigand of the Maremma, died here. A legendary figure, and the terror of upper Lazio and the Maremma, he was finally caught and shot in 1896 aged 60, having been on the run for 24 years.

At **Pescia Fiorentina**, to the east on the border with Lazio, an old iron foundry survives, of great interest to industrial archaeologists (there are long-term plans to restore it). It also has a modern sculpture garden known as the **Giardino dei Tarocchi** by Niki de Saint-Phalle, containing gigantic compositions of glass, ceramics and coloured enamels.

On the other side of the Via Aurelia is Capalbio station, and across the railway line, a short distance along a by-road to the left, is the entrance to the lovely **bird sanctuary** of the **Lago di Burano**, a marshy lagoon 4km long administered by the Word Wide Fund for Nature (WWF) (**open** Sept–Apr for guided tours of 2–3 hours on Sun, at 10.00 and 14.30; ☎ 0564-898829).

Standing above the lake is the Torre di Buranaccio (private), a small well-preserved fort similar to that of Porto Santo Stefano. Visitors may walk down as far as the lake on a path between tall rushes. There are posters illustrating the variety of local fauna and flora, including butterflies.

There is a fine beach at **Chiarone** to the east.

24 · Pitigliano and Saturnia

This is an area of great natural beauty in the south eastern corner of Tuscany near the border with Lazio. The landscape is immensely varied: at times dramatic and austere, at others inviting and serene. Dense woods and coppices alternate with rolling hills and fertile valleys scattered with farmhouses. Characteristic are the ruined castles and hill-top villages, built out of the underlying rock or stone, many of them still enclosed in their medieval walls. Important Etruscan necropoli have been found in the area (especially around Sovana and Saturnia) and excavations continue. The finds are exhibited in the local museums of Pitigliano, Manciano and Scansano.

■ Practical information

Information office. APT of **Grosseto** (☎ 0564-454510). Local information office in **Sovana** in Palazzo Pretorio (☎ 0564-614074).

Getting there

By bus. Buses run from the railway station in Grosseto (run by *RAMA*) to Scansano, Saturnia, Manciano, Pitigliano and other towns.

Hotels

Pitigliano. ★★ *Guastini*, 4 Piazza Petruccioli (☎ 0564-616065; fax 0564-616652).

Sovana. ★★★ *Taverna Etrusca*, with restaurant (☎ 0564-616183; fax 0564-614193).
Saturnia. ★★★★ *Terme di Saturnia*, Via della Follonata (☎ 0564-601061; fax 0564-601266); ★★★ *Villa Clodia*, 43 Via Italia (☎ 0564-601212; fax 0564-601305).
Scansano. ★★★★ *Antico Casale*, at Castagneta (☎ 0564-507219; fax 0564-507805).
Manciano. ★★★ and ★ hotels.

Restaurants
Sorano. £ *Da Fidalma*, 6 Via Busatti.
Saturnia. ££ *I Due Cippi-da Michele*, Villa Pensiero, 26 Piazza Vittorio Veneto.
Semproniano. £ *La Posta*, 6km south at Catabbio.
Manciano. £ *Da Paolino*, 41 Via Marsala.
Montemerano. £ *Locanda Laudomia*, località Poderi di Montemerano.
Montorgiali. £ *Franco e Silvana*.
Pereta. £ *Da Wilma*.
Magliano in Toscana. ££ *Da Guido*, 18 Via Roma.

Pitigliano

Pitigliano (4500 inhab.) is spectacularly situated on a rocky spur overlooking a gorge on all sides, excavated by three torrents (the Lente, Meleta, and Prochio). Its clustered medieval stone houses, dominated by the cathedral bell-tower and two other towers, give the impression that they are growing out of the rocks amongst the wild vegetation. The area is known for its excellent white wine (Bianco di Pitigliano).

> **History.** Etruscan in origin, Pitigliano later came under Roman rule and was subsequently a feud of the Aldobrandeschi family of Sovana. In 1293 it passed by marriage to the Orsini who enlarged the fortress in the first half of the 16C and rebuilt the city defence walls. When the Orsini family became extinct, Pitigliano passed to Cosimo I Medici and became part of the Grand Duchy of Tuscany in 1608. A Jewish colony, protected by the Medici, was established in Pitigliano in 1570. Leopoldo II, commemorated by a bust on an obelisk in the piazza, restored the town and built the church of Santa Maria Assunta and the bridge over the Meleta.

The arched aqueduct was built in 1545 by Gian Francesco Orsini, who also commissioned Giuliano da Sangallo to enlarge the 13C castle. **Palazzo Orsini** is partly a medieval castle and partly a Renaissance palace. Sangallo added the fine entrance doorway and the elegant courtyard with a well, bearing the family arms. It houses the **Museo Diocesano di Arte Sacra** (open daily, 10.00–13.00, 15.00–19.00/20.00, closed Mon except in Aug, ☎ 0564-615568). The collection comprises fine liturgical objects from the local cathedral and other churches and includes some 15C sculptures, a *Madonna and Child* enthroned by Guidoccio Cozzarelli and two altarpieces by Francesco Zuccarelli (1702–88) who was born here. There is also a 15C wooden ceiling and fragments of a frescoed frieze of the same period representing members of the Orsini family and famous historical figures. A precious reliquary of St Flora and St Lucilla was recently transferred here from Santa Fiora.

There is also a small **Museo Civico e Archeologico** (open daily, Oct–Mar 10.00–16.00; Apr–Sept 10.00–19.00, closed Wed except in Aug, ☎ 0564-617019) containing an interesting collection, mostly of objects excavated in the nearby necropoli of Poggio Buco with some fine examples of Etruscan pottery.

The palace faces onto Piazza della Repubblica, which is decorated with two 18C fountains and opens at either end to the surrounding countryside.

Via Roma leads into the old town whose narrow streets and darkened stone houses, with their outside staircases, preserve its medieval character. **Piazza del Duomo** has an impressive monument, erected in 1490 to celebrate the Orsini family (the bear, or *orso* is the family emblem). The **cathedral**, medieval in origin, has a Baroque façade, but the interior has been modernised. There is a *Madonna of the Rosary* by Francesco Vanni (1609). Two other paintings commemorating *Pope Gregory VII* are by Pietro Aldi (1885). The massive bell-tower has a bell weighing three tons.

In Via Orsini is the Renaissance church of **Santa Maria**, built to a strange trapezoidal ground plan. A Romanesque sculptural relief of a figure with two winged animals is inserted in the wall under the tower. A small piazza here has a fine view over the Meleta valley. Steps lead down to the **Porta di Sovana**, built into an Etruscan section of the walls (4C BC). Via Zuccarelli leads back to Piazza della Repubblica through the old Ghetto. The **Synagogue** dates from 1589 and has recently been restored (open Sunday morning, also Wednesday and Friday in summer). It documents the presence of a large Jewish community in the town from the 15C (their cemetery was on the road to Sovana).

Outside the town, near the ruins of the monastery of San Francesco, on the road to Sorano, is a gateway which formed the entrance to **Poggio Sterzoni**, once a famous park, similar to that of Bomarzo, near Viterbo in Lazio, where gigantic sculptures of monsters and animals decorate the garden of another Orsini palace built in 1525 by Vignola. It was created by Niccolò IV Orsini in the 16C. It is now a wilderness containing remains of carved statues, steps and niches carved out of the tufo rock. Here Count Orso Orsini strangled his wife, Isabella degli Atti, in 1575.

Sovana

Sovana, eight kilometres north of Pitigliano, is now a village with little more than a single street running from the castle ruins to the cathedral. It is in a beautiful position on a ridge overlooking a wide panorama. It is traditionally reputed to be the birthplace of Hildebrand, later Pope Gregory VII (1026/8–1085).

> **History.** An important Etruscan settlement and later a Roman municipium, Sovana became a bishopric in the 5C. Its period of greatest importance was in the 13C when it was the seat of the Sovana branch of the Aldobrandeschi family, after it had separated from the Santa Fiora branch. It then passed under the Orsini and was conquered by Siena in 1410. Attempts to repopulate the village under subsequent Medici rule were doomed on account of malaria.

At the entrance to the village are the impressive ruins of the Aldobrandeschi **castle** (13C–14C), and remains of the Etruscan walls. Facing onto the small brick piazza is the former Palazzo del Comune, dating from the 12C, with a clock and bell-cot, which has been the local archive since the 17C. To the right is the **Palazzo Pretorio**, which was largely rebuilt by Siena in the 15C and has nine coats of arms of the Sienese governors on the façade. It now houses a recently installed **Museo Comunale Etrusco e Medievale** (open daily in summer, 10.00–13.00, 15.00–18.00; in winter, Fri–Sun, ☎ 0564-633023). On the adjacent Loggia del Capitano is a large Medici coat of arms carved in marble.

On the opposite side of the piazza is the church of **Santa Maria Maggiore**, the interior of which has large round arches dividing the nave from the aisles. Frescoes of the Umbrian or Sienese school of the late 15C or early 16C have recently been discovered under the whitewash. The high altar stands beneath a carved marble ciborium of the 9C, which was probably removed from the cathedral in the 18C. The workmanship is superb and it is a unique example of its kind in Tuscany: the elegantly carved baldacchino, terminating in an octagonal spire, rests on four slender columns with elaborate capitals. Beside the church is the **Palazzo Bourbon del Monte** which dates from the mid-16C when the Medici restored the town.

At the end of the village, in a stone-flagged piazza surrounded by cypresses, is the Romanesque **cathedral** of Santi Pietro e Paolo (☎ 0564-616532). The original church was probably begun during the papacy of Gregory VII, but its present structure is thought to date from the 12C–13C. It has a semicircular apse and a polygonal dome. The doorway on the south side, probably removed from the façade and put together with pre-Romanesque fragments, is decorated with stylised figures, animals, and plants.

Interior. Compound piers divide the nave from the aisles and some of the capitals are finely carved, several of them with biblical scenes. The paintings include a *Martyrdom of St Peter* by Domenico Manenti. The 15C urn, possibly Sienese, has a carved image of *St Mamiliano*, whose body it contains. He was long venerated as the evangeliser of the district in the 6C. There are remains of 15C frescoes in the crossing and the baptismal font is dated 1494. The small crypt (11C) has seven simple columns. The nearby **Canonica** was the bishop's palace until the bishopric was officially transferred to Pitigliano in 1843, together with reliquaries and an altarpiece by Cozzarelli (now in the museum of Pitigliano).

Near Sovana are many interesting **Etruscan necropoli** (identifiable with maps obtainable locally, for information, ☎ 0564-633023), mostly rock tombs of the 3C–2C BC, which were first excavated by George Dennis in 1844. Some, of impressive dimensions among thick vegetation, are visible from the road, such as the arched niche of the Tomba della Sirena.

Off the road heading out of Sovana to the west are the necropoli of **San Sebastiano** (reached by an Etruscan passage through rock) and **Poggio Felceto** where you can see the **Tomba Ildebranda** (3C BC), originally an impressive temple-like structure named after Hildebrand, and the Pola tomb, with remains of columns which supported a pediment. Another passageway connects this necropolis to that of **Poggio Starziale** containing the Tifone tomb, a large niche with a pediment, and the 'Cavone', an Etruscan passage with wall tombs and inscriptions.

Sorano

Sorano (374m), to the east, is in an area well known for its white wine. This small medieval town, largely derelict but beautiful nonetheless, has a modern suburb. The approach from Sovana, passing Etruscan rock tombs, is particularly spectacular. The town is dominated by the old Orsini fortress called the **Masso Leopoldino** (guided tours only). The district below it is the oldest part of the town and the buildings, many of them in ruin, are intricately wedged together and built into the rock. On the south side of the town is the **Fortezza Orsini e Museo** (open daily 10.00–18.00, ☎ 0564-633023). There are guided tours around the bastions and defences of the fortress which was built by Anton Maria Lari in 1552 onto the earlier fortress. It is a fine example of Renaissance military architecture. There is a small collection of medieval and Renaissance ceramics and glass.

There are several ruined castles in panoramic positions, in the area, including **Montorio** and **Ottieri**, which were also strongholds of the Aldobrandeschi and Orsini families.

Saturnia

The **Terme di Saturnia** is a well-known spa of sulphurous water (37°C), known since Roman times. Nearby are the **Cascate del Gorello** next to an old mill, where hot water falls in cascades over whitened rocks, creating natural pools. This uniquely beautiful spot has unfortunately suffered from neglect, and the waters have been partially diverted in recent years.

The village of **Saturnia**, west of Pitigliano and Sovana, was built on a travertine spur overlooking the Albegna valley. It was an Etruscan town of some importance, and there are several necropoli nearby (at Pian di Palma and Puntone). In the 3C BC it became a Roman colony. The Porta Romana, through which ran the Via Clodia, and the adjacent walls are well preserved (the arch is medieval). There are still remains of foundations and floors in the village dating from the 2C–1C BC. In 1299 Saturnia was sacked by the Sienese, who later built the fortifications and rebuilt the medieval castle. There is a large pleasant piazza with a public garden off which is the church of S. Maria Maddalena. The church (of Romanesque origin) has a *Madonna and Child* attributed to Benvenuto di Giovanni. An antiquarium of excavated Etruscan and Roman objects has been transferred to the Archaeological Museum of Grosseto.

A short distance north of Saturnia is the excavated site of **Puntone** which may be visited.

About 15km north of Saturnia is **Semproniano**, a small hill-top town situated high up (600m) and clustered around the ruins of its castle. From here a by-road leads to the picturesque village of **Rocchette di Fazio**. Built on a rock overhanging the Albegna valley it commands a magnificent view. At its centre, surrounded by trees, are the ruins of the 12C castle. The small Chiesa della Madonna on the village square has a 14C–15C wooden statue of the *Madonna*. There are a number of interesting medieval buildings including the Romanesque Pieve di Santa Cristina, reached by a flight of steps, which has some damaged early 15C frescoes.

Manciano

Manciano (444m), south of Saturnia, dominates the surrounding countryside. Largely modern in aspect, it nevertheless preserves its medieval centre. Picturesque streets and houses surround the 15C **Rocca** and its impressive tower, which, like the town walls, have been considerably restored. In Piazza Garibaldi is a monument to the local painter, Pietro Aldi (1852–1888), who designed the fountain (only built in 1913). The clock tower was erected by the Sienese in the 15C.

In Via Corsini is the **Museo di Preistoria e Protostoria della Valle del Fiora** (**open** in summer, 10.30–13.30; 14.30–17.30; in winter, Tues and Fri morning and Sat until 16.30; closed Sun and Mon, ☎ 0564-629204). It contains a well organised arrangement of material from excavated sites in the Fiora valley north-east of Manciano and adjacent areas, including prehistoric finds (it is particularly rich in artefacts from the Bronze Age). The collection of paintings by the two artists born in Manciano, Pietro Aldi and Paride Pascucci (1866–1954), has been transferred to the Comune next to the museum and may be seen on request. There are also works by these painters in the local churches.

In the neighbourhood of Manciano are a number of ruined castles in romantic settings.

North of Manciano is **Montemerano** (303m), a picturesque walled village on a hill of ancient olive trees. On the north side of the hill is a gateway, opening onto a beautiful view, and part of the old walls enclosing a small piazza. The church of **San Giorgio** has a simple stone façade dating from the late 14C. Inside are several important works: a monumental polyptych by Sano di Pietroof 1458, complete with its predella and pinnacles; a painted wooden statue of *St Peter* by Vecchietta; a *Virgin of the Annunciation* by the Master of Montemerano; a carved relief of the *Assumption* attributed to Vecchietta and various frescoes of the 15C Sienese school. It is worth exploring the village to enjoy its charming vistas.

Scansano

Scansano (500m) is an agricultural town with a well-preserved medieval district at its centre. Today it is well-known for its red wine, *Morellino di Scansano*. There is a large **car park** at the entrance to the town.

Via XX Settembre leads into Piazza Garibaldi, in the centre of which is a marble statue of Garibaldi. Opposite the two cast-iron fountains, an arched gateway with a clock-tower leads to the old town.

From the path which skirts the outside of the walls, overlooking the country-side, there is a striking view of the tower and apse of the church of **San Giovanni Battista**, soaring high above the walls. The church, which was extensively remodelled in the 17C, has several attractive altarpieces and minor works of the 16C Sienese school.

In the Comune in Via XX Settembre there is a small antiquarium, the **Mostra Archeologica della Media Valle dell'Albegna** (which may be visited on request, ☎ 0564-507122). Here one may also obtain information on the excavated sites in the neighbourhood of Scansano (notably at Ghiaccioforte, a hill on the right bank of the Albegna, and the remains of the Roman Villa Degli Anili).

The road north of Scansano towards Roccalbegna by-passes **Poggioferro**, where there is a *Madonna* by Giovanni di Paolo in the parish church, and **Murci** (572m), overlooking an extensive landscape.

On the road to Grosseto, which winds through beautiful, hilly countryside, there is a turning at Pancole for the castle of **Montepò** (451m), an early 16C fortress (private) with four corner towers, in a splendid position, and the ruined medieval castle of **Cotone**. The road also passes near **Montorgiali**, a grey stone village with a castle at its centre, perched on a hill.

South of Scansano another scenic road passes **Pereta**, a charming little medieval village, which preserves its walls and a very tall tower. The entrance is through a gateway with battlements, and the main street is lined with picturesque houses. The square tower stands on its own near the former castle. There is a fine view from the piazza in front of the pretty church of San Giovanni Battista.

Magliano in Toscana

Further south (on the same road) is **Magliano in Toscana** which has splendid 14C and 15C fortifications with seven semi-circular towers and three gates. Originally this was an Etruscan and later a Roman town. In the Middle Ages it became a stronghold of the Aldobrandeschi and was subsequently conquered by Siena.

Inside Porta San Martino is the Romanesque **church** of the same name dating from the 11C. It has a fine façade of travertine stone and the side entrance has carvings of a figure and dragons. In Corso Garibaldi on the left is **Palazzo dei Priori**, built in 1425, decorated with coats of arms. A little further on to the right is the church of **San Giovanni Battista**, Romanesque in origin but with an elegant Renaissance façade, dated 1471. Inside are frescoes and paintings from the 15C–17C and four Baroque altars. There is a fine baptismal font inscribed with the date 1493.

Further along the Corso is the Gothic Palazzo di Checco il Bello and at various points there are views over the surrounding countryside.

Outside the walls is the church of the **Annunziata** in which there is a charming *Madonna and Child* by Neroccio, unfortunately cut out of a larger altarpiece. The interior of the church is largely covered with 15C frescoes of the Sienese school, some of them in fragmentary state.

In the olive grove beyond the church is a remarkable, ancient, gnarled olive tree, known as the 'witch's olive tree', which is alleged to be well over a thousand years old.

Outside the town, just past the cemetery, a by-road (signposted for Sant'Andrea) leads to the imposing ruins of the 11C church of **San Bruzio**, among olive trees. Originally the church of a Benedictine monastery, now only the apse and the great arches opening towards the transepts and nave survive. There are beautifully carved capitals supporting the arches, on which rests an octagonal drum with squinches, open to the sky. The force conveyed by the structure and the luminous quality of

The ruins of 11C San Bruzio

the stone enhance the romantic effect of these extraordinarily beautiful ruins.

25 · Monte Amiata

Monte Amiata, the highest mountain in Tuscany (1738m), was originally a volcano. This explains its interesting geological formation, rocky spurs and ravines, mineral deposits, and sulphurous springs. The rich mercury (cinnabar) deposits were known to the Etruscans and they have been systematically mined since 1860.

The mountain is encircled by a road which runs through magnificent woods of chestnuts, beeches, oaks, and fir trees, which are at their most beautiful in autumn. The peak (signposted at various points) is marked by an enormous iron Cross by Luciano Zalaffi (1910). The view embraces the Orcia, Fiora, and Paglia valleys, and, on a fine day, it is possible to see the Tyrrhenian coast and the islands of Elba and Corsica, as well as the towns of Siena, Cortona, and Orvieto, and the lakes of Trasimene and Bolsena.

All the roads towards the mountain are inviting and varied: those from the south are perhaps the most spectacular. Picturesque small towns and villages are prettily situated on the slopes. Modern suburbs, which have developed conspicuously in recent years, testify to the growing importance of the area as a summer and winter resort. There are numerous ski lifts, hotels and restaurants.

■ Practical information

Information offices. APT dell'Amiata, 97 Via Mentana, **Abbadia San Salvatore** (☎ 0577-778608). *Pro-Loco* offices at Santa Fiora, Piancastagnaio, Arcidosso, and Castel del Piano. *Comunità Montana del Monte Amiata*, località Colonia, **Arcidosso** and 1 Via Grossetana, **Piancastagnaio**.

Getting there
By car. Monte Amiata is close to the Via Cassia (N2), and approximately one hour's drive from the Siena–Grosseto road (turning at Paganico).

By bus. Buses to **Abbadia San Salvatore** from Siena, Grosseto, Buonconvento, and Chiusi. Abbadia San Salvatore is connected by bus to Santa Fiora and Arcidosso.

Hotels
Castel del Piano. ★★★ *Impero*, 7 Via Roma (☎ 0564-955337; fax 0564-955025).
Seggiano. ★★★ *Silene* (with restaurant), 8 Via Capo Vetra, località Pescina (☎ & fax 0564-950805).
On **Monte Amiata**. ★★★★ *Contessa*, Prato della Contessa, **Castel del Piano** (☎ 0564-959000; fax 0564-959002); ★★ *Lo Scoiattolo*, Prato della Contessa (☎ 0564-959003) and *Le Macinaie*, località Pozzo Stella (☎ 0564-959001; fax 0564-959013).
Abbadia San Salvatore. ★★★ *Adriana*, 76 Via Serdini (☎ 0577-778116); *Giardino*, 63 Via Primo Maggio (☎ 0577-778106); and *Kappadue*, 15 Via del Laghetto (☎ 0577-778609). ★★ *San Marco*, 19 Via Matteotti (☎ 0577-778089) and numerous others.
Piancastagnaio. ★★★ *Del Bosco*, 41 Via Grossetana (☎ 0577-786090).
Bagnolo. ★★ hotels including *Il Fungo*, 10 Via dei Minatori (☎ 0564-953025).
Santa Fiora. ★★ *Eden*, 1 Via Roma (☎ & fax 0564-977033).
Arcidosso. ★★★ *Toscana*, 39 Via Lazzaretti (☎ 0564-967486; fax 0564-967000); ★★ *Gatto d'Oro*, Aia dei Venti (☎ 0564-967074).

Campsite at Castel del Piano ★★★ *Amiata*, località Montoto (☎ 0564-955107).

Restaurant ££ *Sala Carli*, 46 Via Pinelli, Abbadia San Salvatore.

Skiing. There are facilities at Abbadia San Salvatore, Castel del Piano and, località Macinaie, Contessa.

Annual fair at Piancastagnaio, celebrating the chestnut harvest, takes place at the beginning of November.

The approach to Monte Amiata from Paganico, along the Orcia valley, passes a turning to the left for **Montenero**, a medieval village situated on a hill (338m). Behind the little church of the Madonna, a narrow street leads up through an arched gateway to a piazzetta with a 16C well built by the Medici. Opposite, in the parish church of Santa Lucia, is a large *Crucifix* attributed to Ambrogio Lorenzetti behind a Baroque altar supporting a graceful glazed terracotta statue of *St Lucy*. Outside the old walls is a public park from which the view opens to the west.

On the main road is **Montegiovi**, another typical medieval village built in grey stone, with remains of a polygonal tower and parts of the walls. At the foot of the village is the church of San Martino with an early 14C façade flanked by a tall square tower. Inside there are elegant Baroque altars.

A road to the south leads to **Monticello Amiata** (734m) a fortified village with picturesque streets, in a splendid position surrounded by hills. The church of San Michele has a tall tower silhouetted against the sky. The 13C interior, rebuilt in the 19C, contains an altarpiece by Riccio. A 17C house at no. 21 Via Grande has a small museum devoted to local traditions and peasant life.

Montelaterone (685m) is also perched in a panoramic position facing Castel del Piano and Arcidosso across a narrow valley. This village is composed of a network of steps and alleys on various levels within its walls, dominated by a castle. There are many remains of its medieval past in the steep streets and stepped alleyways climbing up to the Romanesque church of San Clemente and the ruins of the Rocca. The Chiesa della Misericordia, the façade of which was rebuilt in 1907, has frescoes by Francesco Nasini (see below). There are beautiful views in all directions.

Castel del Piano

Castel del Piano, on the west side of the mountain, is one of the largest towns (4600 inhab.) on the slopes of Monte Amiata, and shares the history of most of the neighbouring towns and villages. In the late medieval period it came under the dominion of Abbadia San Salvatore, and subsequently passed to the Aldobrandeschi and Siena before becoming part of the Grand Duchy of Tuscany under the Medici in the mid-16C. It was the birthplace of the Nasini family which produced three generations of painters, the most important being Francesco (1621–95) and his son Giuseppe Nicola (1657–1736). In the 15C Pope Pius II admired Castel del Piano for its situation and charm. It is in a beautiful position overlooking the Orcia and Ombrone valleys and surrounded by woods. It is well organised as a holiday resort in all seasons.

If you need to park, follow the main road which enters Piazza Garibaldi. The Piazza was created in the 19C around a fountain and a monument to Garibaldi. Corso Nasini, the main street, divides the medieval town on the north side from the modern suburb, which is spacious and attractive.

In Piazza Madonna is the church of **Santi Niccolò e Lucia**, with an elegant bell-tower and 18C façade. Inside are four Baroque altars on either side of the nave. The neo-Gothic ceiling was painted by Francesco Notari, a local 19C artist. The second altar on the right has a *Miracle of St Cerbone* by Domenico Manetti (c 1642). In the right transept, the Cappella del Crocifisso has carved wood figures and an altar by Amato and Benedetto Amati of Arcidosso (1670). In the same chapel is a *Pietà* by Giuseppe Nicola Nasini, who also painted the *Agony in the Garden* and *St Francis receiving the stigmata*. The high altar is attributed to the Mazzuoli brothers of Siena; the *Birth of the Virgin* is by Giuseppe Nicola Nasini, who also painted the *Mystic Marriage of St Catherine of Alexandria* and the *Martyrdom of St Agnes* (second and first altars on the left).

The nearby **Oratory of the Madonna delle Grazie** has a fine stone façade (19C). The altarpiece of the *Madonna del Carmine* is by Francesco Nasini (1652). The elaborate Baroque high altar contains a venerated image of the *Madonna and Child* in the manner of Sano di Pietro.

Further down is the **Town Hall**, in a palace formerly owned by the Ginanneschi family, some fine houses and the **Oratory of the Misericordia**.

Opening onto Corso Nasini are three gateways leading into the picturesque, walled medieval town. The first is under the clock-tower, beyond which is a 16C loggia on the corner of the Piazzetta degli Ortaggi. The medieval streets also have several Renaissance houses. Via delle Chiese leads from the church of San Leonardo (with a few remains of 15C frescoes inside) to the small church of the Santissimo Sacramento. The 18C interior houses a polychrome wooden statue of the *Madonna of Loreto*. At the end of Corso Nasini is Piazza Panorama. Here a road leads up to the Parco dei Daini (deer park).

To the northwest is **Seggiano** surrounded by chestnut woods and pretty scenery. Just outside the village is the **Santuario della Madonna della Carità**, a small church with a Greek-cross plan crowned by a dome and an elegant façade, which was built by the inhabitants of Seggiano after a terrible famine in 1603. The interior is also simple and elegant. Since all the altarpieces were stolen they have been replaced by modern works. The road winds uphill outside the medieval walls, some built on impressive rocks, to a piazzetta with fine views and the church of Corpus Domini. From the square a street leads downhill to the church of **San Bartolomeo** with a simple Romanesque façade (restored). Inside is a polyptych representing *Saints Bartholomew, Michael, and John the Evangelist*, attributed to Bartolomeo Bulgarini.

On the outskirts of the village, in a picturesque position, is the small **Oratory of San Rocco**, dating from 1486. The choir has frescoes representing the *Deposition* and the *Madonna enthroned with Saints* by Girolamo di Domenico (1493).

Pescina (747m) is a modern resort in chestnut woods (beautiful walks). There is a charming *Madonna and Child* by Luca di Tommè in the parish church.

Abbadia San Salvatore

Abbadia San Salvatore (8500 inhabitants) lies on the edge of extensive chestnut woods covering the eastern side of Monte Amiata. The **abbey** is one of the oldest monasteries in Tuscany and had control over a vast area. It was an important station in the Middle Ages on the Via Francigena, the pilgrim route from northern Europe to Rome (see p. 423). The modern suburb which has developed round the monastery, has become a popular summer and winter resort.

The picturesque medieval borgo or **village** preserves intact its outer walls and streets, with medieval and Renaissance houses of local grey stone. San Leonardo is a small Gothic church, and Santa Croce retains part of its Romanesque façade, although it was rebuilt in the 18C.

The Benedictine Abbey, which was immensely rich and powerful, enjoyed numerous privileges under the protection of popes and emperors, and exercised feudal jurisdiction over much of southern Tuscany. It was founded, according to tradition, in 743 by the Lombard king, Ratchis, on the spot where he saw a vision. At the peak of its temporal and spiritual powers in 1035 the Abbey was rebuilt and reconsecrated by Abbot Winizzo. There followed a period of decline when it came under the dominion of Siena in 1347, and eventually was incorporated into the Medici state in 1559. The monastery was suppressed by Grand-duke Leopoldo II in 1783, and most of its treasury and archives were removed to Florence. A Benedictine community was reinstalled here in 1939.

A gateway leads into the piazza, with a fountain at the centre, opposite the abbey **church**, restored c 1930, when the Baroque altars were demolished, and again in the 1960s and 1980s when an attempt was made to reconstruct its 11C appearance. The narrow **façade**, with its three-light window over the arched entrance, is flanked by two towers, a tall square crenellated bell-tower on the left, and an unfinished tower on the right; it is a rare example of Romanesque west-work in Italian architecture.

The **interior** is one of the earliest churches to have a Latin-cross plan. The nave has a timber roof and the elevated choir is framed by three rounded arches spanning its entire width. A late 12C carved wooden *Crucifix* (right) shows *Christ Triumphant* (with open eyes). On the opposite wall is a fresco of the *Martyrdom of St Bartholomew* by Francesco Nasini (1694).

Steps lead up to the **choir** which was decorated with frescoes in the 17C by Francesco and Antonio Annibale Nasini. The same artists painted the right-hand chapel with frescoes illustrating the legend of King Ratchis and his vision of Christ above fir trees during a hunt, allegorical figures and saints, and the *Pietà* with angels beneath the altar. The corresponding chapel on the left, dedicated to the Madonna, has stories of the *Life of the Virgin* and the contiguous chapel has scenes of *Christ's Infancy* (damaged), also by the Nasini brothers.

The **crypt,** which probably dates from the 10C–11C, is one of the largest and earliest in Tuscany. There are 32 columns with beautifully carved capitals supporting a stone vault. The capitals present a variety of leaf, figure, and animal motifs comparable to early Lombard sculpture in Northern Italy.

The **monastery**, on the left of the church, has a cloister dating from the 16C (restored), with a well. Steps lead up to two newly installed rooms containing the precious monastic **treasury**. The collection includes a tiny 8C Irish reliquary, and a unique 8C–9C **red silk cope**, probably of Persian origin, woven with a pattern of simurghs (legendary birds) in roundels and once decorated with pearl embroidery. This was for long associated with the cult of the 4C Pope St Mark, but during its restoration in 1991, an inscription relating to Pope John VIII (872–82) was discovered. The hem was lined with strips of silk, woven in four colours, with roundels containing pairs of ballerinas. This is an extraordinarily rare Byzantine textile dated to the 8C. A copper-gilt reliquary bust of Pope St Mark (also recently restored), decorated with enamels and dated 1381 is attributed to Mariano d'Agnolo Romanelli.

Piancastagnaio

Piancastagnaio (772m), overlooks the Paglia valley. Outside the village, on a hill, is the church of **San Bartolomeo**, which was part of a Franciscan monastery. The simple stone façade is half covered by a large porch. Inside, are various frescoes of the 14C–15C and works by members of the Nasini family. In the chapter house, off the cloister, frescoes of the *Life of the Virgin* have been recently discovered under whitewash.

At the entrance to the village, with narrow, very picturesque streets, is a fortified gateway beside the impressive Aldobrandeschi **fortress**, one of the best preserved examples of 14C military architecture in the district, with a great tower. It now houses a small local museum. Beyond is the Romanesque church of **Santa Maria Assunta**, which contains some 17C paintings. Beautifully sited on the main square is **Palazzo Bourbon del Monte**, built by the Perugian architect Valentino Martelli (1611) in a sadly neglected state. An annual fair is held in the piazza at the beginning of November coinciding with the chestnut harvest. On the road encircling the village to the left of the gateway is the church of **Santa Maria delle Grazie** with a recently discovered fresco cycle attributed to Nanni di Pietro (15C).

On the Santa Fiora road, a short distance from Piancastagnaio, is the sanctuary of the **Madonna di San Pietro**, with an elegant 17C façade and bell-tower. The interior, recently restored, is covered with frescoes by Francesco Nasini, illustrating the *Four Last Things* (1640), in a lively and personal style.The fresco with the venerated image of the *Madonna* is by Martino d'Urbano da Celia (1583). The road which winds across the southern slopes of Monte Amiata has splendid views.

Santa Fiora

The village of Santa Fiora is named after its patron saint. It originally belonged to Abbadia San Salvatore but subsequently came under the dominion of the Aldobrandeschi who ruled over much of southern Tuscany. In 1274 their territorial possessions were divided between two branches of the family: the Santa Fiora branch ruled over Monte Amiata and the northern part of the Maremma and the Sovana branch over southern Maremma and the coastal area. Santa Fiora then passed through the female line to the Sforza Cesarini, until it was incorporated in the Grand Duchy of Tuscany under Pietro Leopoldo in the late 18C.

The entrance to this picturesque and well-preserved little town is via an archway through **Palazzo Sforza Cesarini**. This grandiose, late Renaissance palace (now the town hall) shows the family arms with a lion rampant and a quince tree. Only the clock tower dominating the rectangular Piazza Garibaldi and a small stretch of the fortifications survive from the original Aldobrandeschi castle.

Via Carolina leads down past the Misericordia and Piazza XII Giugno (which commemorates an air-raid during the Second World War) to the **Pieve delle Sante Fiora e Lucilla**, dedicated to the two saints, whose relics were brought here in the 11C. The **façade** preserves a fine Romanesque rose-window, but the doorway dates from the 15C–16C when the church was renovated. The **interior** has rounded arches on piers dividing the nave from the aisles and the simple whitewashed structure, outlined in grey stone, is filled with light from the large windows. The altarpieces and pulpit in glazed terracotta are by Andrea della Robbia and his workshop (c 1480–90). On the right wall is a triptych representing the *Coronation of the Virgin* between *St Francis receiving the Stigmata*, and the *Penitent St Jerome*, with a predella showing the *Annunciation*, the *Nativity*, and the *Adoration of the Magi*, in a frame decorated with fruit, flowers, and classical motifs. Beyond is a *Crucifix* in a niche, also in glazed terracotta, decorated with geometrical and floral designs and a frieze of quinces. The **pulpit** represents the *Last Supper*, *Resurrection*, and *Ascension*. The largest and most elaborate work is the altarpiece, complete with lunette, predella and ornate frame, representing the *Assumption of the Virgin with Angels and Saints*, in which the white figures are set against a simple blue ground. Above the baptismal font is a lunette in polychrome glazed terracotta representing the *Baptism of Christ*, and the *Last Supper* beneath the altar.

A steep road, terminating in steps, leads down from the medieval district to the church of **Sant'Agostino**, which preserves its fine 14C bell-tower. The church contains a number of interesting polychrome wood statues, in particular a fine *Madonna and Child* by Jacopo della Quercia, and a few paintings.

The road continues through a gateway, past gardens with vines and roses, to a large public fountain, to the right of which is the little oratory of the **Madonna delle Nevi**. Over the entrance is a della Robbia relief representing Fiora and Lucilla. The interior has a rather damaged series of saints frescoed in oval frames by Francesco Nasini. Next to the chapel is a public fountain fed from the Fiora spring.

Behind the chapel is the entrance to the garden of **La Peschiera** (open weekends June–Sept, 10.00–13.00, 15.30–18.00, or by appointment, ☎ 0564 977571). This delightful garden was created in the Renaissance, but later suffered from neglect until it was restored by Lorenzo Sforza in 1851. Wonderfully cool in summer, the garden surrounds a fishpond and bubbling rivulets which collect the spring waters of the river Fiora. Further uphill is a public park with a chestnut wood and a childrens' playground. The Fiora provides the water supply for much of the province of Grosseto.

Arcidosso

Arcidosso (679m) lies on a ridge between Monte Amiata and Monte Labbro. It is now primarily a holiday resort, with a large modern district which has developed towards the southeast. From the car park it is a short walk to Corso Toscana, leading to the old town. The cast-iron fountain, known as the **Fonte del Poggiolo**, was made in Follonica in 1833 and transferred here from Piazza del Duomo in Grosseto.

The **Porta di Mezzo**, a triple-arched gateway surmounted by a clock-tower, was largely rebuilt in the mid-19C. The gateway leads uphill to the winding streets of the old fortified town and downhill to the little piazza and church of San Leonardo. Inside is a holy-water stoup by a local 17C sculptor, Pietro Amati, who also carved the frame surrounding the altarpiece (1589) by Francesco Vanni, representing the Beheading of John the Baptist.

Another gateway, the **Porta di Castello**, with the Medici arms, leads steeply up to the Aldobrandeschi **Rocca**, a severe block-like construction with an impressive tower. Nearby is the church of San Niccolò which overlooks a vast panorama. At the far end of the medieval town is the Romanesque church of Sant'Andrea built against the walls beside another arched gate.

> ### *Davide Lazzaretti*
> In 1868 Davide Lazzaretti, the 'Messiah of Monte Amiata', founded a Christian community on Monte Labbro which aimed at instructing and helping the poor. A prophet and visionary, he was regarded with suspicion and condemned by the Church, and his republican ideals were interpreted as a threat by the local authorities. He was shot by carabinieri as he led a throng of followers down from Monte Labbro to Arcidosso in 1878.

On a hill, facing Arcidosso from the west, above a flight of steps, is the sanctuary of the **Madonna delle Grazie** (also known as **L'Incoronata**). The church was first built to house a venerated image of the Madonna after the plague of 1348 and was rebuilt and enlarged over the centuries and provided with a portico and a bell-tower. The interior has a rich Baroque high-altar containing an oval Madonna, of the early 15C Sienese school, and other paintings. On the terrace outside the church is a fountain in local stone, with the Medici arms.

On the road to Montelaterone, just over 2 kilometres from Arcidosso, is the church of **Santa Maria ad Lamulas**, recorded since the 9C. Although largely rebuilt in imitation Romanesque style, it preserves some fine Lombard capitals and its three original apses. The fine painted and gilt wooden statue of the *Madonna and Child* is by a mid-15C Sienese sculptor.

On the road between Arcidosso and Castel del Piano is the monastery and church of the **Cappuccini**, founded by Ferdinando I de'Medici in 1590. Over the high altar is the *Madonna enthroned with Saints Bernardine, Francis and Leonard* by Francesco Vanni (1593), one of the Sienese artist's finest works. The *Annunciation*, on the right-hand altar, is attributed to Giuseppe Nicola Nasini.

Monte Amiata Wildlife Park
On the road going south from Arcidosso towards Roccalbegna, at l'Aiole is a turning signposted for the **Parco Faunistico del Monte Amiata** (open daily, except Mon 07.15–sunset, ☎ 0564–966867), a wildlife reserve which extends over the northeast slopes of Monte Labbro. Wild animals and birds live in protected areas which are equipped with footpaths and hides for visitors. At the summit of the mountain (1193m) are the ruins of the tower and church built by Davide Lazzaretti and his followers.

Roccalbegna
Near the picturesque castle of **Triana** is the turning for the small town of Roccalbegna (522m) which is perched on the southern slopes of Monte Labbro, high above the Albegna valley. It is dominated by a tall, cone-shaped rock 40 metres high, known as **Il Sasso**, on top of which are the remains of an Aldobrandeschi castle. The view from here is worth the climb up the steep steps. Remains of the town walls incorporating the Porta Maremma formerly connected the castle with a fortress on the south side, now an overgrown ruin.

The streets of Roccalbegna are laid out on a regular grid plan with the church of **Santi Pietro e Paolo** at the centre. Its **façade** of beautifully cut stone has a large oculus above a richly carved arched doorway, flanked by spiral columns. The **interior** has been restored to its medieval appearance. On the high altar is a triptych by Ambrogio Lorenzetti (c 1340), which has unfortunately been reduced in size. The central panel of the *Madonna and Child* is a very beautiful work. Typical of the artist is the meditative, slightly sad expression of the Madonna and the refined attention to detail. On either side are two stately seated figures of *St Peter* and *St Paul* with their attributes. Other works include a *Deposition* attributed to Casolani, besides a few frescoes and a late 14C *Crucifix*.

Behind the church steps lead up to the **Oratorio del Crocifisso** (open on request), which has been converted into a museum for works of art and liturgical objects from the local churches. The contents include a fine large painted *Crucifix* by Luca di Tommè (c 1360), a number of paintings by 17C Sienese artists and several by Francesco Nasini.

Beyond the Porta di Maremma is a pleasant public park with tall trees. Steps lead down to the bank of the Albegna river which flows amongst huge boulders and acquatic plants.

From the Grosseto road, which winds uphill, there is a particularly spectacular view over Roccalbegna and the surrounding countryside.

26 · Siena

Siena (59,000 inhabitants), is not only one of the most fascinating towns in Tuscany but is also in a particularly beautiful position, with lovely environs. The town is the capital of the Tuscan province of the same name. It preserves its medieval character to a remarkable degree, and has been largely unspoilt by new buildings. Its beautiful Gothic buildings include the Cathedral and Palazzo Pubblico, as well as numerous churches. The delightful Sienese school of painting produced, in the first half of the 14C, masterpieces by Duccio di Buoninsegna, Simone Martini, and Pietro and Ambrogio Lorenzetti, all of whose work is well represented in the Pinacoteca, Palazzo Pubblico, and Museo dell'Opera del Duomo. The Campo is one of the most remarkable squares in Italy. The seventeen *Contrade* or wards into which the town is divided still manage to play an active part in the life of the city, culminating in the famous Palio horserace which has survived as perhaps the most spectacular annual festival in Italy, in which the whole city participates.

The town is built on a Y-shaped ridge and spreads into the adjacent valleys; the streets are consequently often steep, and to pass from one part of the city to another it is often necessary to cross a deep valley. For this reason, and also because its treasures are unusually scattered, several days are needed for an adequate visit. From the town there is an extensive and varied panorama which includes Monte Amiata and the metalliferous hills, as well as the clay downs of Asciano and the wooded district of Montagnola. To the north, the scenery changes once again, with the densely cultivated hills of the Chianti. The particularly beautiful environs of the town are described in Ch. 27.

■ Practical information

Information offices. APT, 43 Via di Città (Pl. I; 6); information office at No. 56 Piazza del Campo (Pl. I; 6; ☎ 0577-280551).

Getting there
By rail. The station (beyond Pl. I; 1) is c 1.5km north of the town at the bottom of the hill.

Buses connect from the piazza opposite the station to Piazza Gramsci (Pl. II; 6) in 7mins.

By bus. Long-distance buses run by *SITA* from Piazza San Domenico (Pl. I; 1) to Florence (Piazza Stazione) c every hour in 1hr 15mins (via the superstrada). Also to Grosseto, Lucca, and Arezzo. *TRA-IN* town buses (for the environs) from La Lizza (Pl. II;5).

Parking. The centre has been entirely closed to traffic. Parking areas are clearly indicated at the entrances to the town. For **access to hotels and garages**, permission to enter the centre of the city can be obtained from the *Vigili Urbani* (town police) at San Domenico or No. 7 Viale Tozzi.

Sometimes **free parking space** can be found near the Fortezza and La Lizza (Pl. II; 5), except on market day (Wednesday) and on Sunday (when football matches are held). **Car parks with an hourly tariff** (Lire 1300) in Via Fontanella, near Porta Tufi (Pl. II; 14) called *Il Campo*, and near Porta San Marco (Pl. II; 13) called *Il Duomo* and by San Domenico in Viale dello Stadio (Pl.I; 1), called *Lo Stadio*.

Park and ride. There is a car park at **Fontebranda** (Pl. II; 9), with a mini-bus service to the centre. **Free car parking** (with minibus service every 15mins) on the outskirts of the town at: **Due Ponti** (beyond Porta Pispini; Pl. II; 12; bus to Logge del Papa, Pl. I; 7), and at **Coroncina** (beyond Porta Romana, Pl. II; 15; bus to Piazza del Mercato Pl. I; 11).

Hotels
★★★★ *Park Hotel*, 18 Via Marciano (beyond Pl. II; 1; towards the Florence superstrada), with swimming pool (☎ 0577-44803, fax 0577-49020); *Athena*, 55 Via Mascagni (Pl. II; 13; *1*: ☎ 0577-286313, fax 0577-48153); *Jolly Hotel Excelsior*, 1 Piazza La Lizza (Pl. II; 6; *2*; ☎ 0577-288448, fax 0577-41272).

★★★ *Santa Caterina*, 7 Via Piccolomini (Pl. II; 15, 16; *8*: ☎ 0577-221105, fax 0577-271087); *Palazzo Ravizza*, 34 Pian dei Mantellini (Pl. I; 13; *3*; ☎ 0577-280462, fax 0577-221597); *Minerva*, 72 Via Garibaldi (Pl. II; 2; *4*; ☎ & fax 0577-284474); *Duomo*, 38 Via Stalloreggi (Pl. I; 13; *5*; ☎ 0577-289088, fax 0577-43043); *Chiusarelli*, 9 Via Curtatone (Pl. I; 1; *6*; ☎ 0577-280562, fax 0577-271177).

★★: *Lea*, 10 Viale XXIV Maggio (Pl. II; 9; *7*; ☎ 0577-283207).

Hotels on the outskirts
★★★★ (all with swimming pools): *Certosa di Maggiano*, 82 Via Certosa (beyond Pl. II; 16; ☎ 0577-288180, fax 0577-288189); *Villa Patrizia*, 58 Via Fiorentina (beyond Pl. II; 1; ☎ & fax 0577-50431); *Villa Scacciapensieri*, 10 Via di Scacciapensieri (near the Osservanza; beyond Pl. II; 4; ☎ 0577-41441, fax 0577-270854).

★★★ *Castagneto*, 39 Via dei Cappuccini (beyond Pl. II; 9; ☎ 0577-45103, fax 0577/283266).

Youth hostel. *Guidoriccio*, 89 Via Fiorentina, località Stellino (on the northern outskirts towards the Florence superstrada; bus No. 15 from La Lizza; ☎ 0577-52212, fax 0577-56172).

Campsite ★★★: *Siena Colleverde*, 47 Via di Scacciapensieri (**open** mid-March–mid-Nov; bus No. 8 from Piazza del Sale; Pl. I; 6; ☎ 0577-280044, fax 0577-333298).

Restaurants
£££: *Alla Speranza*, 33 Piazza del Campo (Pl. I; 6); *Da Enzo*, 49 Via Camollia (Pl. II; 2).
££: *Da Mugolone*, 8 Via dei Pellegrini (Pl. I; 6); *Medioevo*, 40 Via dei Rossi (Pl. I; 2); *Grotta del Gallo Nero*, 67 Via del Porrione (Pl. I; 7, 11); *Grotta Santa Caterina*, 26 Via Galluzza (Pl. I; 5, 6); *L'Angolo*, 13 Via Garibaldi (Pl. II; 2); *Renzo*, 14 Via delle Terme (Pl. II; 6, 10); *Spadaforte*, 13 Piazza del Campo (Pl. I; 6); *Il Ghiottone*, 68 Via Massetana (Pl. I; 13, 14).

£: *La Vecchia Osteria*, 8 Via San Marco (beyond Pl. II; 13); *Il Carroccio*, 32 Via Casato di Sotto (Pl. I; 10); *La Speranza*, 35 Piazza del Campo (attached to a luxury-class restaurant; see above; Pl. I; 6); *Pizzeria il Riccio*, 44 Via Malta (Pl. II; 1); *Pizzeria O'Pazzariello*, 22 Via Curtatone (Pl. II; 6); *Pizzeria Roberto*, 26 Via Calzoleria (Pl. I; 6); *Quattro Venti*, 68 Via San Pietro (Pl. I; 14).

Restaurants in the outskirts

£££: *Antica Trattoria Botteganova*, 29 Via Chiantigiana (beyond Pl. II; 4). **£**: *La Colombaia*, 99 Strada Chiantigiana, località Malafrasca.

Pasticcerie. *Panforte* and other traditional Sienese sweets are sold in *pasticcerie* and cafés all over the town, including *Nannini*, 24 Via Banchi di Sopra (Pl. I: 6).

Picnic places. The Botanical Gardens (Pl. II; 14); the Fortezza (Pl. II; 5); near Fontebranda (Pl. II; 10); below San Domenico (Via Camporegio; Pl. I; 1, 5); outside Porta San Marco (Pl. II; 13) and Porta Tufi (Pl. II; 14); Prato Sant'Agostino (Pl. I; 14); and in front of the Basilica of Santa Maria dei Servi (Pl. I; 16).

Theatres. *Dei Rinnovati*, Palazzo Pubblico. Chamber music concerts in the *Accademia Musicale Chigiana*, 89 Via di Città (Pl. I; 10). **Music week** in August.

English church. St Peter's, Via Garibaldi (Pl. II; 2), open for occasional services.

History. Siena appears in history as *Saena Julia*, a **Roman colony** founded by Augustus. Although not an important Roman centre, the Roman she-wolf feeding Romulus and Remus was adapted as an emblem of the city in the Middle Ages; her rulers wished to increase her prestige by emphasising her glorious past. In the early Middle Ages the Lombards took control of the town, then on the pilgrimage route from France to Rome (see Via Francigena, p. 423). Under Charlemagne the town was governed by counts, but during the 12C it became a **self-governing commune**; the noble families and bishops became less powerful and a rivalry with Florence began, which was to last for centuries.

In the 13C Siena expanded and became an important banking centre in Europe. Rivalry with Florence reached a peak in 1260 when Siena, now head of the Tuscan Ghibellines who supported the Emperor (including Florentine exiles from the Guelf or pro-papal regime of the *Primo Popolo*), defeated Florence at the **battle of Montaperti**, still a celebrated victory in Sienese history and a constant source of pride for the smaller town. However, when Manfred was killed and his Imperial German army defeated at Benevento in southern Italy by Charles of Anjou in 1266, the merchant families and bankers of Siena decided it was in their interest to support the Pope instead (their support of the Ghibelline cause and subsequent excommunication had damaged their trade in Europe).

In 1287 a Guelf middle class (*popolo grasso*) oligarchy, ruled by a **Council of Nine**, was established in Siena. These councillors, often rich merchants, held office for only two months, and provided an exceptionally stable form of government which lasted until 1355. They accepted the supremacy of the Guelf city of Florence, and, deciding on a policy of peace with their neighbour, created a climate in which the town could prosper. It was at this time that the greatest works of art were executed by the Sienese school of painting. However, in 1348, the town was devastated by the Black Death and over three-quarters of the population died.

The government of the Council of Nine was overthrown by Charles IV of Bohemia in 1355. There followed a long period of instability, with a revolt by the wool workers in 1371. In 1399 Siena came under the power of Gian Galeazzo Visconti of Milan for a few years (as part of an alliance against Florence). The period of unrest continued throughout the 15C although the commune survived despite an attempt by the nobleman Pandolfo Petrucci in 1487 to take over autocratic control of the government.

In the 16C the town made an alliance with the Habsburg Emperor Charles V, but when he sent a Spanish garrison to occupy it the Sienese revolted and switched their allegiance to France. As a result the Emperor combined forces with the Medici Duke Cosimo I of Florence and Siena was taken in 1555 after a disastrous 18-month siege. The Sienese showed great courage, and some 700 families, refusing to live beneath the Medici yoke, migrated to Montalcino, where they maintained a Sienese republic until 1559 when that too was handed over to Florence by the Treaty of Cateau-Cambresis. From then on Siena shared the history of **Florence** and **Tuscany**. The town suffered little damage in the Second World War since it was entered unopposed by French Expeditionary Forces in 1944.

Sienese art

The town has superb Gothic buildings including the Palazzo Comunale, the Cathedral, and numerous palaces. The Renaissance was late in influencing Siena (chiefly through Bernardo Rossellino and Giuliano da Maiano). The architects Lorenzo Maitani (1275–1330), Francesco di Giorgio Martini (1439–1502), and Baldassarre Peruzzi (1481–1537) were natives of the town. **Sculptors** who worked here in the 13C and early 14C included Nicola and Giovanni Pisano, Tino da Camaino, Agostino di Giovanni, and Goro di Gregorio. Later, Jacopo della Quercia (1371–1438) and his pupils produced fine works, and the school renewed its splendour (c 1450–1550) in Neroccio di Bartolomeo, Il Vecchietta, Giovanni di Stefano, Francesco di Giorgio Martini, Giacomo Cozzarelli, Lorenzo di Mariano (Il Marrina), and Bartolomeo Neroni (Il Riccio). From the 13C to 15C many sculptors, including Francesco di Valdambrino, Mariano d'Agnolo Romanelli, and Domenico di Niccolò dei Cori, produced splendid painted wooden statues, for which Siena is particularly famous.

The justly famous **Sienese school of painting**, which flourished from the second half of the 13C to the first half of the 14C, began with Guido da Siena. The most important painter was Duccio di Buoninsegna (c 1260–1319), contemporary with Cimabue, who painted his celebrated *Maestà* in 1311 (now in the Museo dell'Opera del Duomo), which was for a long period the inspiration of the school. His art was carried on by Simone Martini (1284–1344), a friend of Petrarch, and by Lippo Memmi (fl. 1317–47). It reached maturity in Pietro and Ambrogio Lorenzetti (fl. 1306–50). Later, came Taddeo di Bartolo, Domenico di Bartolo, Sano di Pietro, Matteo di Giovanni (the most unusual painter of the school), Benvenuto di Giovanni, Lorenzo di Pietro (see above), Stefano di Giovanni (Sassetta), Francesco di Giorgio Martini (see above), Giovanni di Paolo, Bernardino Fungai, Pietro di Francesco Orioli, and Girolamo del Pacchia.

At the beginning of the 16C Sodoma, influenced by the art of Leonardo da Vinci, introduced a new spirit among the artists already mentioned and their immediate successors (Fungai, Domenico Beccafumi, Brescianino). In the later

16C and early 17C artists active in the city included Francesco Vanni, Ventura Salimbeni, Rutilio Manetti, and Bernardino Mei. In the 19C the town produced the painter Cesare Maccari (1840–1919), and sculptor Giovanni Duprè (1817–82).

The Palio

Every year 10 Contrade are selected to compete in the famous *Corsa del Palio*, a horserace which takes place twice a year in the Campo: on 2 July (Visitation) and 16 August (the day after the Assumption). The later and more important contest was first run in 1310; the earlier race was established in 1659. Rivalry between the Contrade is strong, and provides an extraordinary atmosphere of excitement in the city throughout the summer. The prize is the *Palio* (also known as the *drappellone* or *cencio*), a banner designed anew each year which goes to the winning Contrada, not an individual, and celebrations continue for many weeks after the victory, in which the horse is the main protagonist.

Three days before the *Palio* the horses are drawn by lot by each Contrada. Jockeys are chosen in advance (and paid for) by each Contrada. There are six dress rehearsals, the last one on the morning of the race called the *provaccia*. At 14.30 or 15.00 the horse and jockey are blessed in the church of each Contrada, a remarkable ceremony in which everyone is invited to keep silent (flash photography forbidden) in order not to disturb the horse; not until it is well outside the church does the cheering and singing erupt. At 16.30 or 17.00 in Piazza Duomo (well seen from Via del Capitano) a parade forms, led by the dignatories of Siena and members of each Contrada in Renaissance costume, drummers, knights, and horses. It then proceeds round the Campo to the accompaniment of the tolling bell from the Torre del Mangia, and with two flag throwers performing the *sbandierata* for each Contrada. At the end of the procession a triumphal chariot drawn by four white oxen bearing the *Palio*, with eight buglers and three Sienese dignatories enters the Campo from Casato di Sotto, ringing a bell. The crowds wave flags as it passes. The *Palio* is hung up at the corner of the Campo near Via dei Pellegrini (beside the starting posts).

The horses and jockeys (riding bare back) enter from the courtyard of Palazzo Pubblico, lining up behind a rope. Another horse (drawn by lot) canters up from behind outside the rope: when he is level with the rope the *mossiere* lets the rope fall so that they all start together (*la mossa*). The timing is extremely difficult so there are usually a number of false starts (which are signalled by a loud bombarda or cannonshot which recalls the jockeys to the starting point). It can take some 40 minutes to start the race (after three false starts the order of horses is changed). The *mossiere* is rushed out of the Campo as soon as the race starts as his decision is often contested. The race consists of three laps of the Campo, and it is the horse that wins (even if it is riderless).

Celebrations by the winning Contrada last all night (and the horse eats at the head of the table at the banquet held in its honour). The following morning the Captain, flag throwers, drummers, and horse of the winning Contrada parade around the city with the Palio visiting the headquarters of each Contrada (except that of their traditional enemies). Each Contrada honours the winners by joining them in flag throwing. The banner of the winning Contrada is flown from Palazzo Pubblico. There has been criticism in recent years that the Palio is too dangerous for the horses; it is quite common for one of the horses to be put down after breaking a leg.

Siena is closed to traffic for several days before the Palio. Tickets (not cheap) are sold in advance for the stands or terraces or for the area inside the railings of the fountain, but they are very difficult to find (enquire at the *APT*). The most exciting way to see the race is from the centre of the Campo (free standing room only) which is crowded with spectators. All entrances to the Campo are closed some time before the ceremony begins; the last one to close is at Via Duprè. The Campo can hold about 30,000 people.

The Contrade

Aquila (eagle)	*Nicchio* (scallop shell)
Bruco (caterpillar)	*Oca* (goose)
Chiocciola (snail)	*Onda* (wave)
Civetta (owl)	*Pantera* (panther)
Drago (dragon)	*Selva* (wood)
Giraffa (giraffe)	*Tartuca* (tortoise)
Istrice (porcupine)	*Torre* (tower)
Leocorno (unicorn)	*Valdimontone* (*montone*,
Lupa (she-wolf)	mountain goat)

Since the 13C the city has been divided into three **Terzi**: *di Città, di San Martino*, and *di Camollia*, and each Terzo subdivided into wards, or **Contrade** by the Comune for administrative purposes. In the 14C there were 42 Contrade, reduced in the 16C to 23. Since 1675 there have been 17, each with a headquarters and small museum beside its oratory, run by an assembly elected by all those born in the Contrada over 18 years old.. Children are baptised at an open-air font in the Contrada. The oratories and museums are only open on certain days of the year (enquire at the *APT* office) or by appointment in advance.

Siena's **city walls** survive almost entire (good views from Via Girolamo Gigli, Via Peruzzi, etc, Pl. II; 16, 12, 8, and 7) but, of the original 38 gates, only eight are extant. These are (from the northwest clockwise): *Porta Camollia, Porta Ovile, Porta Pispini, Porta Romana, Porta Tufi, Porta San Marco, Porta Laterina*, and *Porta Fontebranda*.

The Campo

Steep alleys lead down from the main streets of the town, Via di Città and Via Banchi di Sotto, to the ****Campo** (Pl. I; 6), the main piazza of Siena and centre of civic life, laid out in the 12C. First paved in red brick and marble in 1327–49, it has the remarkable form of a fan or scallop-shell and slopes down to the Palazzo Pubblico on the flat southeast side. Occupying the site of the Roman forum, it is the scene in summer of the famous Palio. It is enclosed by a picturesque medley of palaces (with restaurants, cafés, and shops); the only survivor of the original 14C buildings, besides the splendid Palazzo Pubblico, is Palazzo Sansedoni

The Torre della Mangia, Siena

which follows the curve of the piazza at the northeast end of the semicircle. Although it was reconstructed in 1767, it dates from 1340, with three stories of Gothic windows and a tower asymmetrically placed. The Fonte Gaia is a tame reproduction (1858; by Tito Sarrocchi) of the original fountain by Jacopo della Quercia (see p. 353).

Palazzo Pubblico ~ The Museo Civico

The *Palazzo Pubblico (Pl. I; 6, 10) is a very fine Gothic town hall built in 1297–1310 to house the Council of Nine, government offices and Council chambers. The ground floor is still used as municipal offices, while the top floor, with its splendid frescoes, is open to the public.

Exterior. The higher central block was the first to be built with characteristic Sienese stone arches at ground level and brick upper storeys. The two wings on either side were heightened with a third storey in Gothic style only in 1681. But the most remarkable feature is the slim, tall tower (102m high), known as the *Torre del Mangia, which can be seen from many miles around. It was built by Muccio and Francesco di Rinaldo in 1338–48 in ruddy brown brick. The beautiful stone cresting, probably designed by Lippo Memmi, is thought to have been constructed by Agostino di Giovanni. The tower may be climbed (see below). At its base is the **Cappella di Piazza** (1352–76), an open loggia built to commemorate the deliverance of the city from the plague in 1348. Most of the statues are by Mariano d'Agnolo Romanelli (1376–80). The chapel was heightened above the four pilasters with arches and a beautiful carved architrave by Antonio Federighi in 1463–68.

The door beside the loggia leads into the **Cortile del Podestà** (14C). On the left is the entrance to the tower (see below), and on the right is the **ticket office** and an iron staircase (1979) which leads to the **upper floor**. On the landing is a case of Sienese ceramics, mostly 17C–18C. The museum is **open** daily 10.00–17.15; fest 09.30–12.45 (separate ticket for the tower).

Interior

The upper floor, now the Museo Civico, is remarkable for its superb frescoes by the Sienese school dating from the early 14C to the 16C (by Simone Martini, Ambrogio Lorenzetti, Sodoma and others).

The first four rooms of the museum were opened in 1985 to display paintings which form part of the municipal collections (diagrams are provided in each room). **Room 1**: 16C–18C non-Sienese and foreign schools, including works by Felice Brusasorci, Johann Heinrich Schonfeld, and Il Bamboccio. **Room 2** (right) and **Room 3** contain 16C–17C Sienese paintings including works by Alessandro Casolani, Il Pomarancio, Ventura Salimbeni, and frescoes and sinopie by Sodoma detached from the Cappella di Piazza. **Room 4**: 17C–18C Sienese paintings (Domenico and Rutilio Manetti) and a case of church silver.

The **Sala del Risorgimento** was designed in 1878–90 and decorated under the direction of Luigi Mussini to illustrate the life of Victor Emmanuel II by Sienese painters including Amos Cassioli and Cesare Maccari. Here are 19C busts of famous Sienese, and sculptures by Tito Sarrocchi (Flora) and Giovanni Duprè (reclining figure of a child).

A flight of stairs leads up to the spacious **loggia** with a view of the covered market building and orchards beyond. It has a restored timber ceiling. The **Sala della Signoria** is the seat of the Consiglio Comunale. The 16C lunettes are decorated with frescoes illustrating events in Sienese history.

The **Sala di Balia** is entirely frescoed with *scenes from the life of Pope Alexander III by Spinello Aretino and his son Parri (1407–08), including a splendid naval battle. The entrance wall has been badly damaged by rising damp. Also here is an inlaid seat by Barna di Turino.

The **Anticamera del Concistoro** contains some detached frescoes (one attributed to Ambrogio Lorenzetti), a 14C painted *Crucifix*, *Madonna and Child* attributed to Matteo di Giovanni, and wooden statues attributed to Jacopo della Quercia and his workshop.

The **Sala del Concistoro** has a marble doorway by Bernardo Rossellino (1448). The *vault is frescoed by Beccafumi (1529–35), illustrating heroic deeds of ancient Greece and Rome. Three large Gobelins tapestries (removed) represent the elements *Earth*, *Air* and *Fire*; five other tapestries also usually exhibited here are 16C Florentine works. Above the door, *Judgement of Solomon* attributed to Luca Giordano.

In the **vestibule** is a ruined fresco of the *Madonna* from the loggia by Ambrogio Lorenzetti, and the gilded bronze she-wolf (part of the arms of Siena, evincing pride in her Roman origin), by Giovanni di Turino (c 1429), removed from the exterior of the palace.

The **Anticappella** is decorated with frescoes by Taddeo di Bartolo illustrating the Virtues and famous Roman and Greek heroes and divinities, and a colossal *St Christopher*. Two 15C intarsia panels and a case of goldsmiths' work (12C–17C) are also displayed here.

The **Cappella** has a fine wrought-iron screen (1435–45) on a design attributed to Jacopo della Quercia. It is also frescoed by Taddeo di Bartolo, with scenes from the *Life of the Virgin* (1407–08). The altarpiece is by Sodoma. The 15C chandelier in wrought iron and gilded polychrome wood is by Domenico di Niccolò dei Cori (1420–30) who also carved the *stalls (1415–28).

Upper Floor

PALAZZO PUBBLICO

Sala del Mappamondo

The Sala del Mappamondo was named after a circular map of the Sienese state painted for this room by Ambrogio Lorenzetti, now lost (see below). The Council met here before 1342. Here is the famous ***Maestà**, the earliest work of Simone

Martini (1315; partly repainted by him in 1321), depicting a beautiful Madonna seated beneath a baldacchino borne by apostles and surrounded by angels and saints. It was restored in 1990–93.

On the opposite wall is the famous fresco of *Guidoriccio da Fogliano*, Captain of the Sienese army, setting out for the victorious siege of Montemassi, a delightful work (partly repainted, but cleaned in 1981), traditionally attributed to Simone Martini (1330). Since 1977 it has been the subject of a heated debate among art historians, some of whom suggest it may be a later 14C work, and therefore no longer attributable to Simone Martini. The fresco beneath, discovered in 1980, and thought to date from 1315–20, which represents the deliverance of a borgo (with a castle) to a representative of the Sienese Republic has been variously attributed to Duccio di Buoninsegna, Pietro Lorenzetti, or Memmo di Filippuccio. The traces of a circular composition here are thought to mark the position of the lost fresco of the Sienese state which gave its name to the room (see above). On either side are *Saints Victor and Ansanus*, by Sodoma.

On the long wall: *Victory of the Sienese at Poggio Imperiale* by Giovanni di Cristoforo Ghini and Francesco d'Andrea (1480), and *Victory at Val di Chiana*, by Lippo Vanni, both predominantly in burnt sienna. On the pilasters below (left to right): (in the angle) *Blessed Bernardo Tolomei* by Sodoma (1533); *St Bernardine* by Sano di Pietro (1450), and *St Catherine of Siena* by Vecchietta (1461).

The *Sala della Pace* was the room of the Council of Nine who ruled Siena from 1287 until 1355. The remarkable allegorical *frescoes* by Ambrogio Lorenzetti (1338) are considered the most important cycle of secular paintings left in Italy from the Middle Ages. On the wall opposite the window is an *Allegory of Wise Government*: on the entrance wall are illustrated the effects of *Good Government* in the town and countryside. The city represents Siena. Opposite is an *Allegory of Evil Government* (very damaged) with its effect on the town and countryside (very damaged).

The **Sala dei Pilastri** contains 13C–15C paintings including a 13C *Crucifix*, part of a polyptych by Martino di Bartolommeo, a stained glass window with *St Michael Archangel* by Ambrogio Lorenzetti; an *Annunciation* by Niccolò di Ser Sozzo; and some carved wooden painted and inlaid coffers. The *Massacre of the Innocents* by Matteo di Giovanni (1482) belongs to the church of Sant'Agostino.

The Torre del Mangia

The entrance to the tower, the *Torre del Mangia is on the left-hand side of the Courtyard.

Stairs lead up to the ticket office, and then out onto a little roof terrace at the foot of the tower. A stone staircase continues up past the mechanism of the clock. Higher up there is a view of the church of Santa Maria dei Servi, before the two bells are reached. Narrow wooden stairs continue right up to the top of the lantern with another bell. There is a splendid view: to the northwest are the Campo and San Domenico with the tree-covered Fortezza; to the northeast in the foreground the domed church of Santa Maria Provenzano and San Francesco, and a stretch of walls enclosing fields beyond. On the hill behind is the Osservanza. To the southeast can be seen the church of Santa Maria dei Servi with its tall brick campanile, and orchards, and to the southwest the church of Sant'Agostino and the Duomo, with the tall nave of the *Duomo Nuovo*.

The Duomo

■ There is a cumulative ticket for the Piccolomini Library in the Duomo, the Museo dell'Opera del Duomo, and the Baptistery. The **Duomo** is **open** 07.30–13.20, 14.30–16.50. The **Piccolomini Library** is **open** every day 10.00–13.00, 14.30–16.45. The **Baptistery** is **open** March–Oct. 09.00–19.30; winter 10.00–13.00, 14.30–17.00. The **Museo dell'Opera del Duomo** is **open** daily 09.00–13.15; mid-March–Oct 09.00–19.15.

In Piazza del Duomo is the ****Duomo** (Pl. I; 9) dedicated to the *Assumption*. It is the earliest of the great Tuscan Gothic churches, despite certain Romanesque elements. It is known that Nicola Pisano was involved as architect in the 13C.

The first church on this site probably dates from the 9C, and a second building is traditionally thought to have been consecrated in 1179. The present cathedral was under construction from c 1215 and the cupola was completed in 1263. In 1316 it was enlarged under the direction of Camaino di Crescentino. After 1285 the façade, designed by Giovanni Pisano was begun and in 1339 there was a scheme to build an even bigger cathedral: an immense nave was to be constructed south of the original church, which was to be turned into a transept (see plan on p. 349). Lando di Pietro and Giovanni di Agostino began this herculean task, but the plague of 1348 and the political misfortunes of the city compelled its abandonment. The original plan was resumed, leaving the huge unfinished nave to record the ambition of the Sienese.

The building measures 89m by 24m (52.5m across the transepts). The apse was completed in 1382. The upper part of the façade, in the style of the Cathedral of Orvieto, was added by Giovanni di Cecco after 1376.

Exterior

Marble steps, flanked by columns bearing the she-wolf of Siena (the originals, attributed to the workshops of Giovanni Pisano and of Urbano da Cortona are now in the Museo dell' Opera del Duomo (see below) ascend to a plinth of white marble inlaid with black, on which the cathedral stands. The ****façade**, in polychrome marble, is remarkable for its magnificent statuary, now mostly replaced by copies (originals in the Museo dell'Opera). The lower part, with three richly decorated portals of equal height and size, with

Siena Duomo

SIENA I - CENTRE

PIAZZA S. FRANCESCO

S. Francesco

Oratorio di S. Bernardino

3

4

VIA DELLE VERGINI

VIA DE' BARONCELLI

A DEL FOSSO

IRAFFA

VIA BALDASSARRE PERUZZI

CIVETTA

VIA SALLUSTIO BANDINI

M. VIGILIO

S. Vigilio

Università

S. Giovanni d. Staffa

7

PIAZZETTA GRASSI

LEOCORNO

Fonte di Follonica

8

Palazzo ccolomini

Logge del Papa

S. Martino

VIA DEL PORRIONE

VIA DI PANTANETO

nagogue

SCOTTE

S. Spirito

DI SALICOTTO

IAZZA DEL ERCATO

VICOLO DELLA FORTUNA

VIA DEL RIALTO

TORRE

S. Giorgio

VIA DEI PISPINI

VIC DEL SASSO

VIA DELL'OLIVIERA

11

VIA S. MARTINO

12

S. Giacomo

VIA DI SALICOTTO

VIA DEL ORO

VIA ROMA

Palazzo di San Galgano

I PORTA GIUSTIZIA

VIA DEL SOLE

VIA S. GIROLAMO

Palazzo Bianchi

VIA DELLE CANTINE

S. Girolamo

VIA DEI SERVI

15

VIA PORTA GIUSTIZIA

VALDIMONTONE

16

S.M. dei Servi

VIA FONTANELLA

0   100 yards

0   100 metres

triangular pediments, was designed by Giovanni Pisano in 1284–85 and 1296–97 who, together with his pupils, was responsible for the sculptures of prophets, philosophers, and patriarchs. The architrave of the main portal bears stories from the *Life of the Virgin*, an early work by Tino da Camaino. The two carved columns on either side of the main door were removed in 1970 and are now exhibited in the Museum. The upper part of the façade, with a great rose window, was added in the second half of the 14C in a less harmonious design; in the three gables are bright 19C Venetian mosaics.

On the east side the **campanile** (1313) rises from the transept (on the base of an earlier tower). Its six storeys, banded in black and white, are pierced by windows whose openings increase in progression from single to sixfold. The **Porta del Perdono** which leads into the south transept bears the cast of a tondo of the *Madonna and Child*, almost certainly by Donatello (original in the Museum). On the roof of the nave and south transept are copies of 14C statues of the Apostles (originals in the Museum) placed here in 1681 when they were removed from the interior and replaced there by statues by Giuseppe Mazzuoli (in turn removed to the Brompton Oratory, London in the 19C). On the left flank of the Cathedral is the lapidary stone of Giovanni Pisano who was buried here.

Interior

The dichromatic style of the exterior, familiar from many Tuscan Romanesque churches, is repeated with greater emphasis in the *interior. Here the elaborate use of bands of black and white marble on the walls and columns provides a magnificent effect. The round arches of the nave support a pointed vaulting. The interior contains numerous important sculptural works.

The *pavement

The floor of the whole church is ornamented with a remarkable series of over 50 exquisite marble figures, designs and scenes, of which the oldest (1373) are in simple graffiti (black outlines on the white marble), while the others are inlaid with black, white, or coloured marble, or (in the 16C) marbles of different tones. Many of the panels have been restored or remade over the centuries, particularly in 1860. Many of them are covered by protective flooring and are shown only from 7–22 August. More than 40 artists, most of them Sienese, worked at this pavement: the most original and productive of whom was Beccafumi who executed 35 scenes from 1519 to 1547.

The scenes in the **nave** (the letters below refer to the plan of the Duomo) are as follows: *Hermes Trismegistus* (A; Giovanni di Stefano); Sienese wolf with symbols of her allies (B; 14C); *Wheel with the Imperial eagle* (C; 14C); *Hill of Virtue* (D; Pinturicchio); *Wheel of Fortune and Power* (E; attributed to Domenico di Niccolò dei Cori). In the **side aisles** (F–P) are figures of ten *sibyls* (1481–83), designed by Guidoccio Cozzarelli, Neroccio di Bartolomeo, Benvenuto di Giovanni, Matteo di Giovanni and Antonio Federighi (*Erythraean Sibyl* in the south aisle).

The thirteen scenes beneath the dome (X) are by Domenico Beccafumi (1519–24) some remade in 1878. In the transepts (Q, S, W) are scenes by Beccafumi, Benvenuto di Giovanni, Matteo di Giovanni, Francesco di Giorgio, Antonio Federighi, Neroccio di Bartolomeo, Domenico di Bartolo and Pietro del Minella (*Death of Absalom*, 1447). In the north transept is the splendid scene of the

SIENA DUOMO

Massacre of the Innocents by Matteo di Giovanni (R; 1482). In front of the altar steps is a tondo (T) with *David* by Domenico di Niccolò dei Cori, 1423), near two scenes (Y and Z) by Beccafumi with *Moses* (1525–47).

The nave. The carved columns of the main west door are attributed to Giovanni di Stefano (1483). The reliefs of the pedestals are by Urbano da Cortona. The glass in the rose window represents the *Last Supper* (1549; by Pastorino de' Pastorini, a pupil of Guglielmo de Marcillat). The monument (1) to Paul V (Camillo Borghese) in a fine niche by Flaminio del Turco has a statue by Domenico Cafaggi (1592). The two stoups (2, 3) are beautifully carved by Antonio Federighi. Above the nave arches are a monotonous series of busts of popes produced from 1495 onwards by means of terracotta moulds.

South aisle. **First altar** (4) Domenico Maria Canuti, St Gaetano (1681); **second altar** (5) Annibale Mazzuoli, *Ecstasy of St Jerome* (1725); **third altar** (6) Raffaello Vanni, *St Francis of Sales* (1654); **fourth altar** (7) Pier Dandini, *Mystical Marriage of St Catherine* (1671). Above the doorway to the campanile (8) is the tomb of Bishop Tommaso Piccolomini, a fine work (1484–5) by Neroccio di Bartolomeo Landi. Beneath it are six bas-reliefs by Urbano da Cortona. The hexagon of the **dome** was decorated at the end of the 15C with gilded statues of saints attributed to Giovanni di Stefano, and figures of patriarchs and prophets in chiaroscuro, by Guidoccio Cozzarelli and Benvenuto di Giovanni. During restoration work in 1982 on the dome, sculptures were discovered on the capitals and brackets of one of the windows and attributed to Nicola Pisano.

South transept. The circular Baroque **Cappella Chigi** (9) was built for Alexander VII in 1659–62, almost certainly on a design by Bernini to house the Madonna del Voto. The statues are by Antonio Raggi (*St Bernardine*), Ercole Ferrata (*St Catherine*), and Bernini: *St Jerome* (10) and *St Mary Magdalene* (11). Above the statues are marble bas-reliefs of 1748. Maratta painted the *Visitation* (in very poor condition) and the *Flight into Egypt* is a mosaic after a painting by the same artist.

> The **Madonna del Voto**, a fragment of a larger painting, is by a follower of Guido da Siena. This venerated painting has been the traditional focus of entreaty for the Sienese in times of crisis. On six occasions in their history the inhabitants have placed the keys of their threatened city before it and prayed for deliverance. The first occasion was before the battle of Montaperti in 1260; the latest on 18 June 1944, a fortnight before the liberation of Siena. It is surrounded by gilded bronze angels by Ercole Ferrata. The bronze statue in the chapel is by Arturo Viligiardi (1918).

The organ (12) was designed by Bernini. The Roman Baroque monument to Alexander III (13) was completed by Ercole Ferrata. On the altars: (14) Luigi Mussini, *St Crescenzio* (1867) and (15) Mattia Preti, *St Bernardine* (1670). On the wall, monument to Alexander VII (16) by Antonio Raggi, on a model by Bernini. The marble pavement tomb of Bishop Carlo Bartoli (d. 1444) was designed by Pietro del Minella and carved by Federighi. The **Chapel of the Sacrament** (17) has a fine altar by Flaminio del Turco (1585) and an altarpiece of the *Adoration of the Shepherds* by Alessandro Casolani.

Choir. The marble high altar (18) is by Baldassarre Peruzzi (1532); the huge bronze *ciborium is by Vecchietta (1467–72). At the sides, the uppermost angels carrying candles are by Giovanni di Stefano (1489), the lower two are by Francesco di Giorgio Martini (1490). The Cross and candelabra are to a design of Riccio (1570). The eight candelabra in the form of angels (19) on brackets against the pillars of the presbytery are fine works by Domenico Beccafumi (1548–51). In the apse (20), is a fresco of the *Ascension* by Beccafumi (altered in 1812), and, on either side (21) frescoes by Ventura Salimbeni. The round window in the apse contains 13C *stained glass** (1288) from cartoons by Duccio, probably the oldest existing stained glass of Italian manufacture. It shows the *Burial, Assumption*, and *Coronation of the Virgin*, together with the four patron saints of the town, and the four Evangelists. The glass was removed for restoration in 1997. The intarsia *choir-stalls are of varying dates: 1362–97, by several artists under Francesco del Tonghio; 1503, by Giovanni da Verona; and those by Riccio and his school, 1567–70.

To the left of the altar is the entrance to the **Sacristy** and **Chapter house** (22; sometimes shown on request). The sacristry contains frescoes (1412) now attributed to Benedetto di Bindo. Beyond a vestibule with a fine bust of *Alexander*

VII by Melchiorre Caffà, a follower of Bernini, is the Chapter house, with a *Madonna and Saints* by Pietro di Francesco Orioli.

The octagonal **pulpit* (23) is a remarkable Gothic work by Nicola Pisano (1265–68), completed six years after his famous pulpit in the Baptistery of Pisa. He was assisted by his son Giovanni, and by Arnolfo di Cambio. Around the base of the central column are the figures of Philosophy and the seven Liberal Arts, and at the top of the columns, the Christian Virtues, Evangelists, and Prophets. The seven panels beautifully carved in high relief symbolise the Redemption, with scenes from the life of Christ and two scenes of the Last Judgement. They are divided by another series of carved figures, including a beautiful Madonna and Child. The elegant staircase was added in 1543 to a design of Riccio.

North transept. The altar (24) has an altarpiece by Francesco Vanni. The *tomb of Cardinal Riccardo Petroni (25; d. 1313) is by Tino da Camaino, the design of which was frequently copied throughout the 14C. In front (26) is the bronze pavement *tomb of Bishop Giovanni Pecci, signed by Donatello (1426). The monument to Pius II(27) is by Giuseppe Mazzuoli (1694); that of Pius III (28) is by Pietro Balestra (1703).

The ****Cappella di San Giovanni Battista** (light; 29) is a graceful Renaissance structure probably by Giovanni di Stefano (1492). The elegant portal is by Marrina (and the classical bases to the columns by Antonio Federighi); the wrought-iron gate is the work of Sallustio Barili. In the interior are (restored) frescoes by Pinturicchio including three scenes from the *Life of St John the Baptist*, and portraits of two kneeling figures (the one shown in the robes of the Order of St John is Alberto Aringhieri, the founder). The statue of *St Ansanus* is by Giovanni di Stefano; that of *St Catherine* is by Neroccio. The bronze statue of **St John the Baptist* (removed many years ago for restoration) is one of Donatello's later works (1457) which is similar, in some ways, to his *St Mary Magdalene* (now in the Museo dell'Opera del Doumo in Florence). The font (c 1460) is beautifully carved by Antonio Federighi. Outside the chapel (30) is the monument to Marcantonio Zondadari by Giuseppe and Bartolomeo Mazzuoli.

The Piccolomini Library

In the **north aisle** is the entrance to the *Libreria Piccolomini (31) one of the most delightful creations of the Renaissance. It was founded in 1495 by Cardinal Francesco Piccolomini (afterwards Pius III) to receive the library of his uncle Aeneas Silvius Piccolomini (Pius II). Its marble façade is by Marrina (1497). Above the altar (right) was placed a relief of *St John the Evangelist* attributed to Giovanni di Stefano. The large fresco above it, by Pinturicchio, shows the *Coronation of Pius III*.

The bright interior consists of a hall decorated with colourful and highly decorative **frescoes* by Pinturicchio and his pupils (1502–9) in an excellent state of preservation. Raphael is thought to have contributed to the design of some of the scenes. They represent ten episodes from the life of Pius II (beginning at the right of the window): 1. *Aeneas Silvius goes to the Council of Basle*; 2. *He presents himself as envoy to James II of Scotland*; 3. *He is crowned as poet by Frederick III* (1442); 4. *He is sent by the Emperor to Eugenius IV* (1445); 5. *As Bishop of Siena, he is present at the meeting in 1451 of the Emperor Frederick and his betrothed Eleonora of Portugal outside the Porta Camollia*; 6. *He is made Cardinal by Calixtus III* (1456); 7.

He becomes Pope (1458); 8. He proclaims a crusade at Mantua (1459); 9. He canonises St Catherine of Siena (1461); 10. He arrives, dying, at Ancona (1464).

The beautiful vault decoration is also by Pinturicchio and his pupils. In the centre is the celebrated group of the *Three Graces*, a Roman copy of an original by Praxiteles, acquired in Rome by Cardinal Francesco Piccolomini. It served as model to Pinturicchio, Raphael, and Canova. Here are exhibited the 15C ***choir books** of the cathedral and the Scala hospital, illuminated by Liberale da Verona, Girolamo da Cremona, Sano di Pietro, and others. The ceramic floor has a beautiful design.

The great ***Piccolomini altar** (32) in the north aisle, is by Andrea Bregno (c 1480). The statuettes in the four lower niches of *St Peter, St Pius, St Gregory,* and *St Paul* are documented early works by Michelangelo (1501–4), who may also have worked on the figure of *St Francis* above, which was begun by Pietro Torrigiani. The *Madonna and Child* at the top, traditionally attributed to Giovanni di Cecco, is thought by some scholars to be Jacopo della Quercia's earliest work (c 1397–1400). The painted *Madonna and Child* over the altar (framed by marble reliefs) is attributed to Paolo di Giovanni Fei (c 1385). **Third altar** (33) Pietro Sorri, *Epiphany* (1588); **second altar** (34) Francesco Trevisani, *Christ between Saints James and Philip*; **first altar** (35) Francesco Trevisani, *Martyrdom of the Four Soldier Saints.*

Beside the façade of the Duomo is the long Gothic façade of **Palazzo Arcivescovile** (Archbishop's Palace), with marble black-and-white decoration on the ground floor and brickwork above (probably reconstructed in 1665).

Ospedale di Santa Maria della Scala

Opposite the façade of the cathedral is the irregular Gothic façade (modified over the centuries) of the Ospedale di Santa Maria della Scala (Pl. I; 9), a hospital founded in the 9C for pilgrims travelling down the Via Francigena (see p. 423) on their way to Rome (the oldest document to have survived which mentions the hospital dates from 1090). Its name *Scala* comes from its position in front of the 'steps' which lead up to the cathedral. It was at first administered by the Cathedral but after 1195 became progressively a lay institution. Up until a few years ago it was still a hospital, but this has now been transferred and the huge group of buildings is slowly being restored. It will be transformed into an important cultural centre and museum (and the Pinacoteca Nazionale will one day be transferred here). Only a small part is so far open to the public but in the next few years more and more will become accessible. Temporary exhibitions are also held here. The areas at present open, described below, are **open** 11.00–16.30.

The **Cappella del Manto** (chapel 'of the mantle', named after a fresco of the Madonna della Misericordia, protecting the Sienese with her mantle, see below), preserves a lovely frescoed lunette by Domenico Beccafumi showing the *Meeting at the Golden Gate*. The **Sala del Pellegrinaio**, the 14C pilgrims' hall, has delightful ***frescoes** illustrating the history of the hospital and life within it, carried out in 1440–44.

The **first two bays** are ruined. **Over the two doors**: Vecchietta, *Story of the Blessed Sorore*, mythical founder of the hospital, and, opposite, Domenico di Bartolo, *Feeding the poor in the hospital*. In the **third two bays**: Domenico di Bartolo, *Reception and education of orphans in the hospital* and the *Marriage of an* *orphan*, and (opposite) *Building work to enlarge the hospital*. **Fourth two bays**: Priamo della Quercia, *Investiture of the Rector of the hospital by the Blessed Agostino Novello*, and (opposite) Domenico di Bartolo, *Distribution of Alms*. In the **last two bays**: Domenico di Bartolo, *Healing of the sick*, and (opposite) *Celestine III granting rights to laymen for running the hospital*. In the **two bays on either side of the windows**, *Payment of the wet nurses of the hospital* painted in the 16C by Giovanni di Raffaello Navesi and Pietro d'Achille Crogi.

The **Cappella del Sacro Chiodo** (the Chapel of the Holy Nail or Sagrestia Vecchia) was built before 1444 for the precious hospital treasury (not at present on view) most of which was acquired in 1359 in Constantinople. It included the relic of the 'Holy Nail' (for which a reliquary was made in Siena in the 14C), and an exquisite Greek Evangelistery with late 11C Byzantine miniatures and a gilded silver cover, probably made in Venice in the late 13C and incorporating cloisonné enamels, many of them from Constantinople. Later pieces include an arm reliquary signed by Goro di Ser Neroccio, and three 15C reliquary busts.

The chapel was entirely decorated by Vecchietta in 1446–49, illustrating the articles of the Creed. The scenes are particularly interesting for their iconography but are unfortunately very ruined. Beneath a handsome marble tabernacle is a fresco of the *Madonna del Manto* by Domenico di Bartolo (1444), with the *Madonna of the Misericordia* (detached from the Manto chapel in 1610).

In another room of the hospital the damaged **Fonte Gaia**, one of the masterpieces of Jacopo della Quercia (1409–19), is exhibited. It was removed from the Campo (see p. 341) in 1844, dismantled in 1858 and is being slowly restored.

Downstairs, a long vaulted corridor with pretty paving leads to the charming **Oratorio di Santa Caterina della Notte**, the oratory of a confraternity which survives with its 17C furnishings virtually in tact. It contains paintings by the school of Rutilio Mannetti and Francesco Rustici, late 17C stuccoes, a marble statuette of the *Madonna and Child* dating from the late 14C (on the altar), and, in the last room, a painting of the *Madonna and Child with angels, and Saints John the Baptist and Andrew* by Taddeo di Bartolo, and four small early 16C paintings used to decorate coffins.

Off the vestibule of the hospital church is the **Cappella della Madonna** with frescoes by Giuseppe Nicola Nasini, and a painting of the *Madonna* over the altar by Paolo di Giovanni Fei.

The **hospital church**, dedicated to the **Annunziata**, was rebuilt in 1466. The fine hall **interior** has been attributed to Guidocco d'Andrea, Vecchietta, or even Francesco di Giorgio Martini. The carved and painted wooden ceiling is by Benvenuto di Giovanni, Pellegrino di Mariano, Agostino d'Andrea and Domenico di Cristofano. On the south wall, on the first altar, is an *Assumption* by Pietro Locatelli, and on the second altar is a painted Crucifix of c 1330. The organ was built by Piffaro of Siena (1514–19); the organ case is traditionally attributed to Peruzzi and is decorated with two polychrome reliefs in roundels attributed to Ventura Turapilli. Raised high above a flight of steps is the main altar, with a relief on the altar frontal of the *Dead Christ* by Giuseppe Mazzuoli, on top of which is a bronze statue of the **Risen Christ* by Vecchietta (1476). Two candle-bearing angels are by Accursio Baldi (1585). In the huge apse is a fresco by Sebastiano Conca (1732). On the north wall (second altar) is a *Vision of St Teresa* by Ciro Ferri, and (first altar) an *Annunciation* attributed to Giovanni Maria Morandi. By the door is a stoup by Urbano and Bartolomeo da Cortona (1453).

Museo Archeologico Nazionale

In another part of the hospital (entered from the south end of the piazza) the Museo Archeologico Nazionale (**open** 09.00–14.00; fest. 09.00–13.00; closed on 1st, 3rd, and 5th Sun of the month) was temporarily arranged in 1993. Founded in 1933 and formerly exhibited in Palazzo della Sapienza, it contains Etruscan and Roman material. The first section, the Antiquarium, is devoted to private collections. The **Bonci Casuccini collection** has material from Chiusi, including a terracotta canopic vase and throne (6C BC). The large **Bargagli Petrucci collection** has finds from Sarteano (including numerous cinerary urns). The **Chigi Zondadori collection** includes a carved Roman sarcophagus front (2C AD). At the end of the hall is the **Mieli collection** with bucchero ware and bronzes from Chiusi. The material from the **Accademia dei Fisiocritici** includes coins, small bronzes, and lamps.

The **topographical collection** opens with material from Siena, including finds from the Roman villa at Pieve al Bozzone. Upstairs is displayed material from the surroundings of Siena, and in the last section of the hall finds from Murlo (including a terracotta frieze of horses in bas-relief), Valle d'Elsa, Chianti, Monteriggioni, Colle and Casole d'Elsa.

Opposite the south flank of the Duomo is Palazzo del Governatore dei Medici (Palazzo Reale), now the Prefecture, rebuilt in 1593.

Museo dell'Opera del Duomo

Piazza Jacopo della Quercia occupies the site of the unfinished nave of the Duomo Nuovo (see p. 345): the marble arcades survive as well as the façade and side portal which give some idea of the size and beauty of the projected building. Its south aisle has been converted into the *Museo dell'Opera del Duomo (Pl. I; 10). This is a beautifully kept museum with important works of art from the cathedral (for admission, see p. 345).

Top floor

The **Sala della Madonna dagli Occhi Grossi** is named after the *Madonna dagli Occhi Grossi*, by a Sienese painter known as the Maestro di Tressa (1220–30). It adorned the high altar of the cathedral before Duccio's *Maestà* (and has temporarily been removed for restoration). The other paintings here include: Ambrogio Lorenzetti, *Four Saints*; Giovanni di Paolo, *St Jerome*; and four small works by Sodoma (removed for restoration). The painting of *St Bernardino of Siena* by Sano di Pietro is flanked by two paintings showing the Saint preaching in the Campo and in Piazza San Francesco; Gregorio di Cecco, polyptych; Sano di Pietro, *Madonna and Child with Saints*.

The **Sala dei Conversari** (so called because Vittorio Alfieri read his tragedies to the public here in 1777) displays works by Matteo di Giovanni; Beccafumi, *St Paul* and two statues of the *Annunciation*; Il Pomerancio, *Madonna and Child with Saints*; altar frontals. The **Sala dei Parati** contains vestments and a marble statue of a child by Giovanni Duprè. From here can be reached the **Scala del Falciatore**, a stair which winds up to the façade of the new cathedral (extensive views of the city and countryside).

Off the stairs is the **Sala del Tesoro** which contains the *treasury of the cathedral including croziers, reliquaries (including the reliquary of St Galgano from the end of the 13C), and paxes. The Crucifixes include *Christ on the Cross (in wood) by Giovanni Pisano, an early masterpiece (c 1280; restored in 1987). Sculptural works include three busts (from statues) of saints, by Francesco di Valdambrino in polychrome wood (1409), and 12 statues of saints attributed to Giuseppe Mazzuoli (models for the marble statues now in the Brompton Oratory, London). In a small room off the treasury is displayed the *treasury from the Chigi chapel which has beautiful Roman and French works of the early 17C.

First floor

The **Sala di Duccio** is filled with the celebrated *Maestà* by Duccio di Buoninsegna, one of the most beautiful and important works of art in Italy. The main panel depicts the *Virgin and Child enthroned surrounded by angels and saints* (the four patron saints of Siena are shown kneeling in the foreground). The Latin inscription on the throne is an invocation: 'Oh Holy Mother of God bring peace to Siena and life to Duccio since he has painted you thus'! On the opposite wall is the *Story of Christ's Passion* in 26 scenes, formerly on the back of the main panel, and along the wall between them are panels from the predella and cimasa with *Scenes from the life of Christ* and the *Last days and death of the Virgin*. This huge painting was commissioned for the high altar of the Duomo in 1308 (the contract is preserved in the Archivio di Stato, see p. 367) where it remained until 1505, but it was dismantled in 1771 when the original frame was destroyed and a few of the panels from the predella and cimasa were dispersed (some of them are now in the Washington and London National Galleries) or lost at this time so that it is still not known exactly how the great painting was composed.

Duccio took some three years to paint it and it was at once recognised as a masterpiece by the Sienese who were so pleased with it that they declared a

Duccio di Buoninsegna

Duccio di Buoninsegna (c 1260–1319) was greatly admired by his contemporaries, although little else is known about his life, and very few works definitely by his hand have survived. His bottega was in Via di Stalloreggi just inside the Arco delle Due Porte, where from 1313 he lived with his wife Taviana and eight children. He is recorded as having worked as a young man for the Commune of Siena decorating their statute-books and store chests, but his earliest surviving painting is the Madonna di Crevole, also exhibited in this room, from the church of Santa Cecilia in Crevole. His first important commission was in 1285 when the Laudesi confraternity in Florence ordered a Madonna from him for their chapel in Santa Maria Novella. This Maestà, known as the Rucellai Madonna (and for long attributed to Cimabue), is now exhibited in the Galleria degli Uffizi. His masterpiece was the Siena Maestà which established him as the greatest painter of his time. Another exquisite work by him is preserved in Siena, the Madonna 'dei Francescani' which is a tiny painting (now in the Pinacoteca Nazionale). The cartoon for the round stained glass window in the Duomo is also attributed to his hand. Nothing is known of his life after 1313, and it seems that he never worked in fresco. There are works, mostly Madonnas and Child, all over Tuscany attributed to his school. Simone Martini was his greatest follower. Although Lorenzo Ghiberti mentions him with great admiration he was later forgotten and his importance ignored in the 18C when the Maestà was divided up.

public holiday and processed it through the streets from his studio in Via di Stalloreggi and round the Campo accompanied by the Council of Nine, prelates, and the populace to the accompaniment of the ringing of the church bells and a municipal fanfare. It shows numerous Byzantine influences endowed with a new Gothic spirit which was to be developed from this work by the great Sienese school of painters. It is embued with a calm beauty and rich colour and extraordinary narrative power.

Also exhibited in this room are the *Madonna di Crevole* by Duccio, and the *Birth of the Virgin* by Pietro Lorenzetti.

A room to the right displays gilded wood statuettes of the *Madonna and Child and four Saints* (from the church of San Martino), generally attributed to Jacopo della Quercia and Giovanni da Imola, but possibly by Antonio Federighi. The statue of *St John the Baptist* from the church of San Giovanni is attributed to Jacopo della Quercia or his bottega. In the small room beyond are polychrome wood statues: beside a late 14C carved *Crucifix* is the *Madonna and St John the Evangelist* by Domenico di Niccolò dei Cori (1415). The statue of *St John the Baptist* is by Francesco di Giorgio Martini (1464) and that of *St Savino* is by Guido di Giovanni (1393–95), painted by Paolo di Giovanni Fei.

A room to the left of the Sala di Duccio contains illuminated MSS., drawing projects related to the cathedral and Piazza del Campo, and a drawing of the cathedral pavement by Giovanni Paciarelli (1884).

Ground floor

The **Sala delle Statue** contains the original *statues and sculptural fragments from the façade of the cathedral, by Giovanni Pisano and his school, constituting one of the most important groups of Italian Gothic sculpture.

In the centre, bas-relief of the *Madonna and Child with St Anthony Abbot and Cardinal Antonio Casini*, by Jacopo della Quercia, and a tondo of the *Madonna and Child*, almost certainly by Donatello (from the Porta del Perdono of the Duomo). Works by Urbano da Cortona (*St Peter, St Bernardine in Glory*); (left wall) fragments of four symbolic animals sculpted by Giovanni Pisano; (near the grille) two wolves nursing twins, from the columns outside the Duomo, one attributed to the workshop of Giovanni Pisano and one to the workshop of Urbano da Cortona. In the floor are fragments of the original Duomo pavement. At the end, altarpiece of the *Baptism of Christ*, by Andrea del Brescianino (1524).

Off the gallery, steps lead down to the **Sala del portale centrale del Duomo**. Here are displayed the two columns and lions carved c 1290 by Giovanni Pisano and an assistant for either side of the main door of the Duomo (and removed from there in 1970). The statues of the twelve apostles by the school of Giovanni Pisano were originally inside the Duomo where they were replaced by statues by Giuseppe Mazzuoli in 1680–89 and 1717–21 and put on the roof of the cathedral. The statues by Mazzuoli are now in the Brompton Oratory in London. Three of the statues are now attributed to Tino da Camaino (1317–18). The angel from the cusp of the façade is by Tommaso Redi. The seated statue of the *Redeemer and two angels in adoration* by Giovanni d'Agostino (c 1345) come from the lunette of the side door of the Duomo Nuovo (they have been replaced in situ by copies).

Another door leads out of the gallery to a flight of stairs (decorated with gargoyles from the baptistery) which leads down to the church of **San Niccolò**

in Sasso which retains its early 17C interior virtually intact. The delightful barrel **vault** was decorated in 1622 with stuccoes and paintings by Ludovico di Antonio Chiappini and Il Francesino. The **high altarpiece** of the *Madonna enthroned with Saints* is by Francesco Vanni (1608), and the wooden 15C statue of *St Nicholas of Bari* is attributed to Antonio Federighi. The gilded statues at the east end of angels and the *Annunciation* are by Domenico Cavedon and Lodovico Chiappini. The altarpiece on the **south side** of the *Crucifix* is by Niccolò Tornioli, and on the left of it is a *Resurrection* by Rutilio Manetti and on the right of it a *Nativity* by Astolfo Petrazzi. **North side**. The altarpiece of the *Pentecost* is by Rutilio Manetti and the *Ascension* on the right of it is by Astolfo Petrazzi. On the left is the *Last Judgement* by Raffaello Vanni. At the west end are two stucco statues, *Augustus* (?) and a *Sibyl* by Chiappini.

The museum can be left by the main door of the church which emerges on Via del Poggio. The side door of the Duomo Nuovo, between the incomplete nave and the cathedral, is a beautiful Gothic *portal (the sculptures by Giovanni d'Agostino have been removed to the Museo dell'Opera del Duomo and replaced by casts). From here a steep flight of steps, constructed in 1451 descends to the Baptistery. Half-way down is the entrance (usually closed) to remains of the **Duomo crypt** where there are some primitive fresco fragments with scenes from the *Passion* by the school of Guido da Siena (c 1270–80) the earliest known frescoes of the Sienese school. Part of the exterior wall of the Duomo before it was enlarged can also be seen here.

The Baptistery

At the bottom of the steps is the *Baptistery (Pl. I; 5; beneath part of the cathedral) with a noble but unfinished Gothic façade by Domenico di Agostino (1355). The **interior** (for admission, see p. 367), finished c 1325 probably by Camaino di Crescentino has a beautiful hexagonal *font*, one of the most interesting sculptural works of the early Renaissance (1417–30). The gilded bronze panels in relief illustrate the Life of St John the Baptist: the *Angel announcing the birth of the Baptist to Zacharias*, by Jacopo della Quercia; *Birth of the Baptist*, and his preaching, by Turino di Sano and Giovanni di Turino; *Baptism of Christ* and *St John in prison*, both by Lorenzo Ghiberti; *Herod's Feast* by Donatello. The six statues at the angles are by Donatello (Faith and Hope), Giovanni di Turino (Justice, Charity, and Prudence), and Goro di Ser Neroccio (Fortitude). The marble tabernacle above was designed by Jacopo della Quercia who carved the five statues of prophets in niches and the crowning statue of the Baptist. The four bronze angels are by Donatello and Giovanni di Turino.

The 15C *frescoes were restored in 1993. On the two lateral vaults nearest the entrance are figures of the *Apostles and Saints* attributed to Agostino di Marsiglio. The four *Apostles* in the central bay are by Vecchietta, who also frescoed the three vaults nearest the altar with the *Articles of the Creed*, the apsidal arch with the *Assumption of the Virgin and a glory of angels*, and the three lowest scenes in the apse of the *Annunciation, Flagellation*, and *Way to Calvary*. The three Passion scenes above in the apse are by Michele di Matteo Lambertini (c 1451–55). In the large lunette to the left of the apse are scenes of the *Miracles of St Anthony of Padua* by Benvenuto di Giovanni (c 1460) and in the large lunette right of the apse, *Washing of the Feet* by Pietro di Francesco Orioli (1489).

Immediately east of the Baptistery is the **Palazzo del Magnifico**, built for Pandolfo Petrucci from the plans of Cozzarelli, who also designed the bronze ornaments on the façade (1504–08).

The Pinacoteca Nazionale

The **Pinacoteca Nazionale (Pl. I; 14) is the most important gallery for the study of the great Sienese masters, including Duccio di Buoninsegna, Ambrogio and Pietro Lorenzetti, and Sassetta, all of whom are well represented. The collection also includes fine works by Sodoma. The Pinacoteca has been housed since 1932 in the handsome 14C *Palazzo Buonsignori, in Via San Pietro, restored in 1848. The display is strictly chronological (**open** daily Tues–Sat 09.00–19.00; Mon 09.30–13.30; fest. 08.00–13.00; winter daily 08.30–13.00).

Many of the paintings have been restored; others are in the course of restoration. There are long-term plans to move the collection to the ex-Ospedale di Santa Maria della Scala (see above), and a number of rooms have a provisional arrangement, and are not very well kept. The first floor is often used for exhibitions so that the permanent collection has to be temporarily re-hung or closed.

Second floor

The first two rooms illustrate the **origins of the Sienese school of painting**. **Room 1**: Maestro di Tressa (attributed), *altar frontal, partly in relief, representing *Christ blessing* between symbols of the Evangelists, and scenes from the *Legend of the True Cross*, the first securely dated work (1215) of the Sienese school; 2. Margarito d'Arezzo (attributed; c 1270–80), *St Francis*; 597. *Crucifix*, with Passion scenes (first years of the 13C); 8. **Guido da Siena**, three scenes from the *Life of Christ*, one of the first paintings known on canvas. **Room 2**: Guido da Siena (attributed), *16. *Madonna and Child* (dated 1262). 7. Reredos with *Madonna and Saints*; 15. Guido da Siena, or a follower of the late 13C (known as the Maestro del Dossale di San Pietro), *St Peter enthroned* with stories from his life; works attributed to Guido da Siena or his followers, including (9–13) scenes from the *Life of Christ*; 313. Maestro del Dossale di San Pietro, *St Francis* and stories from his life (from the church of San Francesco in Colle Val d'Elsa).

Rooms 3 and 4 contain **works by Duccio** and his followers. **Room 3**: *28. Duccio di Buoninsegna and assistants, polyptych of the *Madonna and Saints*; 39. Ugolino di Nerio (attributed), dossal; Niccolò di Segna, 38. *Four Saints*, 46. *Crucifix* (1345); 47. Duccio di Buoninsegna and assistants, polyptych, *Madonna and Saints*, a late work; 21. Circle of Segna di Bonaventura, *Crucifix* (from the church of San Giusto in Siena). **Room 4**: *20. Duccio, the *Madonna dei Francescani*, a tiny work of jewel-like luminosity, considered to be one of his masterpieces (c 1285; much ruined); 18. School of Duccio (attributed to the Maestro di Città di Castello), *Madonna and Child* (from the church of San Pellegrino, Siena); 40. Segna di Bonaventura, *Four Saints*; works attributed to the Maestro di Città di Castello; Ugolino di Nerio (attributed), 36. *Crucifix*; 34. *Crucifixion and St Francis*.

Rooms 5–8. Paintings by **Simone Martini** and **Ambrogio** and **Pietro Lorenzetti**. **Room 5**: minor painters of the 14C, including Bartolo di Fredi (104. *Adoration of the Magi*), and Luca di Tommé. **Room 6**: Simone Martini, *Madonna and Child* (from the Pieve of San Giovanni Battista in Lucignano d'Arbia), *Pala di Beato Agostino Novello* (from the church of Sant'Agostino,

First Floor

Second Floor

PINACOTECA NAZIONALE

formerly in the Museo dell'Opera del Duomo); Lippo Memmi, 595. *Madonna*, 19. *Madonna and Child with Saints* (fresco fragment).

Room 7. Main part: 76. Maestro di Ovile, *Madonna and Child*; 598. Ambrogio Lorenzetti, *Crucifix* (very damaged); Paolo di Giovanni Fei, 116. *Birth of the Virgin and Saints*, 300. *Madonna and Child with Saints*; Maestro di Ovile, 61. *Assumption*, *St Peter enthroned between Saints* (from the church of San Bartolomeo a Sestano); 317. Maestro di San Lucchese (attributed to Cennino Cennini), *Birth of the Virgin.*

In a **side room (7A)**: Ambrogio Lorenzetti, 77. *Madonna and Child between Saints Mary Magdalene and Dorothy*, 77A. *Lamentation*, 90, 314. (by a follower of Ambrogio) *Saints Peter* and *Paul* (from the church of San Michele a Sant'Angelo in Colle, Montalcino); Pietro Lorenzetti, *Madonna and Child* (from the Pieve di Santi Leonardo e Cristoforo at Monticchiello, near Pienza) and *Madonna and Child* from the pieve of Castiglione d'Orcia; Ambrogio Lorenzetti, 605. *Madonna and Child*, 92. *Allegory of the Redemption*; 147. Pietro Lorenzetti, *Crucifixion.*

In the other side room (**7B**): Ambrogio Lorenzetti, 70–1. Two small landscapes (a city by the sea, and a castle on the edge of a lake), perhaps part of a larger decoration for a cupboard door, 88. *Annunciation*, the last dated work by Ambrogio Lorenzetti (commissioned in 1344), 65. *Madonna between Saints and doctors of the church*; Pietro Lorenzetti, **Madonna enthroned* (from the church of Sant'Ansano a Dofano, near Monteaperti), 578–9. *Saints Agnes* and *Catherine of Alexandria*, two panels from a polyptych. **Room 8**: Pietro Lorenzetti, 50. *Madonna and Child with Saints.*

The first side of the loggia (**Room 9**). Works of the **14C Sienese and Florentine schools**, including: 607. Niccolò di Pietro Gerini *Crucifixion with St Francis*; 67. Angelo Puccinelli, *St Michael enthroned with Saints*; 119–125. Spinello Aretino, *Coronation and Dormition of the Virgin*, parts of a polyptych.

Beyond the Chapel (**10**) is **Room 11** which displays **the late 14C Sienese school**. Taddeo di Bartolo, 55. *Crucifix*, **128. Triptych*, **131. Annunciation, Dormition, and Saints Cosmas and Damian* (signed and dated 1409).

The second side of the loggia (**Room 9**): 60. Bernardo Daddi, triptych, dated 1336; 157. Lorenzo Monaco, *Madonna and Saints*; **164.* Domenico di Bartolo, *Seated Madonna with angel musicians* (dated 1433); 171. Michelino da Besozzo, *Marriage of St Catherine* (the only signed work by this artist).

Rooms 12–19. 15C Sienese painting. Room 12 is devoted to **Giovanni di Paolo**: 173. *St Nicholas of Bari and other Saints* (signed and dated 1453), **200. Crucifixion* (signed and dated 1440), inside the polyptych of San Galgano. A *Madonna and Child* from the church of San Simeone at Rocca d'Orcia is also temporarily displayed here. **Room 13**: Giovanni di Paolo, 206. *Madonna dell'Umiltà*, 172. *Last Judgement*; Sassetta, 9. *Presentation in the Temple*, 95, 87. *Prophets*, 168–9. *Saints*, 167. *Last Supper*, 166. *Temptation of St Anthony* (all from an altarpiece painted in 1423–26). **Room 14**: Neroccio di Bartolomeo, 295, 285, 281. Three paintings of the *Madonna and Child with Saints*; Matteo di Giovanni, **286. Madonna and Child with angels* (signed and dated 1470); Francesco di Giorgio Martini, 288. *Madonna and Child with an angel*, 277. *Annunciation*; 400. Matteo di Giovanni, *Madonna and Child with Saints and angels*; 437. Francesco di Giorgio Martini, *Nativity and Saints*; 280. Matteo di Giovanni,

Madonna and Child; 282. Neroccio di Bartolomeo, *Madonna and Child* (signed and dated 1476); 432. Matteo di Giovanni, *Maestà*. 278. Neroccio, *Madonna and Child*. 274–6. Francesco di Giorgio Martini, *Story of Joseph* (very damaged).

Room 15 (temporarily closed): **late 15C works** including three paintings of the *Adoration of the Shepherds*: 414b. by Matteo di Giovanni, 390, and 279. by Pietro di Domenico. In the **corridor**: Maestro dell'Osservanza, 218. *Martyrdom of St Bartholomew* and *Christ in Pietà* (very damaged), 216. Predella of the altarpiece in the Basilica of the Osservanza. **Room 16** (being re-arranged): **Sano di Pietro**, 265. *St Jerome in the desert*; 246. *Polyptych*, signed and dated 1444; 227. *Assumption*; 240, 272. *Saints*. **Rooms 17–18**: Sano di Pietro, 233, 255. Predelle, 241. *Madonna appearing to Pope Calixtus III* (with a view of Siena). **Room 19**: Vecchietta, 210. *Madonna and Child with Saints*, (in the centre), *204. Painted cupboard for reliquaries (from Santa Maria della Scala) with scenes from the Passion and lives of the saints; Francesco di Giorgio Martini, 440. *Coronation of the Virgin*, and a detached fresco of the *Madonna enthroned with angels* from the Villa Piccolomini di Vignano; kneeling figure in terracotta of *Mary Magdalene* by Cozzarelli.

On the **stairs** down to the first floor are fresco fragments by Domenico di Bartolo from the Ospedale di Santa Maria della Scala.

First floor

Room 20: 309. Girolamo da Cremona, *Annunciation*; 581. Benvenuto di Giovanni (attributed), *Noli me Tangere*. **Room 22** has two paintings by the Maestro di Volterra. **Room 23**: **Umbrian and Umbrian-Sienese schools**. In one part of the room (**23A**): 379, 381, 393. Girolamo del Pacchia (attributed), *Charity, Fortitude,* and *Justice*; 495. Pinturicchio, *Holy Family with the young St John*; 503. Girolamo Genga, *Madonna and Child*; 407. Umbrian-Sienese painter of the early 16C, *Nativity*. There are also a number of works by Pietro di Francesco Orioli including a *Visitation* from Campiglia d'Orcia. In the other part of the room (**23 B**): 333, 334. Girolamo Genga, *Ransom of prisoners*, and *Flight of Aeneas and Anchises from Troy* (frescoes detached from Palazzo del Magnifico). **Room 26** is an enclosed loggia with a splendid view of the Torre della Mangia, the cathedral bell tower and Duomo Nuovo and the open countryside. Sculptured panels are exhibited here including 14C marble reliefs, some by Gano di Fazio from the church of Santa Maria dei Servi, a relief of *San Galgano*, and six reliefs in *pietra serena* by a Sienese sculptor from Jacopo della Quercia's circle.

Room 27. Works by Brescianino (650–2. *Charity, Hope,* and *Fortitude*) and **Beccafumi** (420. *St Catherine receiving the Stigmata*). **Room 29**. Works by Marco Pino and Beccafumi (*Birth of the Virgin*, and *Coronation of the Virgin from Santo Spirito*). **Room 30** contains the splendid large *cartoons by Beccafumi for the Duomo pavement (restored). **Room 31**. Girolamo della Pacchia, *Annunciation* and *Visitation* (from S. Spirito); *352. **Sodoma**, *Scourging of Christ*, a superb work (1511–14). Beyond **Room 32** (closed) with more works by Sodoma is **Room 37** with two masterpieces by Beccafumi (*427. *Descent into Hell* and *423. *St Michael and the rebel angels*). Sodoma, 443. *Christ in limbo* and 413. *Deposition*. Also here are statues by Marrina (*Annunciation, Madonna in Adoration*, and the *Risen Christ*). Other works not at present on view include paintings by Francesco Maffei, Giuseppe Bazzani, Rutilio Manetti, Simondio Salimbeni, and Francesco Vanni.

In a room on the **third floor** the small paintings of the **Collezione Spannocchi,** formed in the 17C, are arranged. Dürer, *St Jerome* (a signed work); Lorenzo Lotto, *Nativity*; Francesco Furini, *Mary Magdalene*; Flemish works; Giovanni Battista Moroni, two portraits of gentlemen; Bernardo Strozzi, *St Francis*; Paris Bordone, *Annunciation, Holy Family*; Bartolomeo Montagna, *Madonna and the Redeemer* (two fragments of a larger work); Palma Giovane, the bronze serpent (signed and dated 1598); Padovanino, *Rape of Europa*; 16C Flemish school, portrait of a jeweller; Girolamo Mazzola Bedoli, portrait of a young man.

Via di Città and the contrade of Aquila and Pantera

From the west side of the Campo *Via di Città (Pl. I; 10, 6), bordered by handsome mansions, winds upwards to the south. To the left (No. 89) is the 14C **Palazzo Chigi-Saracini** (Pl. I; 10), a characteristic Sienese Gothic fortified palace with splendid three-light windows. The charming courtyard is usually open. It houses the renowned **Accademia Musicale Chigiana**, founded in 1932 by Count Guido Chigi Saracini. The academy holds international courses in July and August and concerts are given in the theatre built in 1923 in 18C style.

Exhibitions are held in the palace periodically of parts of the famous *Chigi-Saracini Art Collection. The huge collection was formed at the end of the 18C by Galgano Saracini, and is particularly important for its Sienese works, ranging from the 13C–17C. Most of it is now owned by the Monte dei Paschi bank (the Accademia Chigiana owns the remaining part of it). Admission to scholars is sometimes granted by previous appointment at the head office of the Monte dei Paschi bank in Piazza Salimbeni (see below).

The paintings include: Maestro di Tressa (early 13C), *Madonna and Child*; Margarito d'Arezzo, painted *Cross*; Pisan follower of Francesco Traini, *St Paul*; works by Mariotto di Nardo, Sano di Pietro, and Matteo di Giovanni; a tabernacle by the Maestro dell'Osservanza, a tondo by Botticelli and his bottega; and fine works by Sassetta, including the *Adoration of the Magi. Later masters represented include Bernardino Mei. There is also a collection of small sculptures, drawings and archaeological material.

To the right (No. 128) is the splendid Renaissance **Palazzo Piccolomini delle Papesse**, built by Caterina Piccolomini, sister of Pius II, from the plans of Bernardo Rossellino (1460–95); it is now occupied by a bank. Then comes **Palazzo Marsili** built in brick in 1444–50 (restored). Next to it is the 15C **Palazzo Marsilli-Libelli** (seat of the *Soprintendenza per i Beni Ambientali e Architettonici*) which bears the Piccolomini coat of arms, attributed to Urbano da Cortona or Vecchietta.

Parallel to Via di Città, **Casato di Sotto** (Pl. I; 10) leads gently uphill from the Campo past a number of fine palaces. On the left is **Palazzo Chigi** (No. 15), constructed in the early 16C, and the birthplace of Alexander VII (plaque). Palazzo dei Conti della Ciaia (No. 23) has a façade designed by Francesco Brandini (1715). From Vicolo del Salvatore (left) there is a fine view of the Basilica dei Servi di Maria (see below). Beyond is the beige-coloured **Palazzo Ugurgeri** (No. 39) with graffiti decoration. On the right, Vicolo di Tone leads up to Via dei Percennesi, a very narrow street with flying arches and tall medieval houses in the heart of the *Contrada dell'Aquila* (Pl. I; 10). Off the left side of Casato di Sotto two flights of steps in Vicolo della Fonte lead down to a handsome public fountain beneath the road, protected by a high arch (1359). Near the end of Casato di Sotto is the **Oratorio dei Tredicini**, the oratory of the district called the Contrada dell'Aquila (see p. 340), built in 1630. The high altarpiece is by Bernardino Mei. Costa Larga leads back uphill to Piazza Postierla (see below).

Via di Città ends in **Piazza Postierla** (or I Quattro Cantoni; Pl. I; 10). Here a column with a fine iron standard-holder is surmounted by a she-wolf (1487 recently replaced by a disappointing copy). Off the piazza, in Via del Capitano (right), are the 16C Palazzo Piccolomini Adami (on the left, at the corner) and the late 13C Palazzo del Capitano (No. 15). In Piazza Postierla is a chemist's shop with furniture dating from c 1830.

Via di Stalloreggi begins in Piazza Postierla and leads up through the **Contrada della Pantera** (Pl. I; 13, 14), the oldest part of the city, with numerous medieval houses. In Piazza del Conte is the fountain used for baptisms in the contrada.

The ex-**Palazzo dei Bisdomini** (No. 43) is one of the best Gothic palaces to survive in the city. It stands on the corner of Via di Castelvecchio, at the beginning of which is a pretty tabernacle protecting a fresco of the *Pietà* (called the Madonna del Corvo) by Sodoma. Via di Castelvecchio branches left through an interesting medieval part of the town. Some way along on the left, two arches lead to a little fortified piazza on a hill. Via di San Quirico is wider and ends at the little church of San Quirico. Via di Stalloreggi continues down to the Arco delle Due Porte (see below).

From Piazza Postierla, Via di San Pietro leads past Palazzo Bonsignori, seat of the Pinacoteca Nazionale (described above), next to which is the church of **San Pietro alle Scale** (Pl. I; 14), rebuilt in the 18C with a pleasant interior (usually closed). On the north wall are a fragment of a fresco of *St Catherine* in very poor condition, attributed to Liberale da Verona, and five panels by Ambrogio Lorenzetti. On the high altar, *Flight into Egypt*, by Rutilio Manetti.

The church of Sant'Agostino

Via di San Pietro continues down past (left) the Casato di Sopra (Pl. I, 14; a winding old street), to the Arco di Sant'Agostino, beyond which is the church of Sant'Agostino (Pl. I; 14), dating from 1258. From the terrace there is a good view of the town and countryside. The church was reopened in 1997 (it had been closed since 1982), and can now be visited from mid-March to the end of October, 10.30–13.30, 15.00–17.30. It is also sometimes used for concerts.

The attractive bright **interior** was remodelled in 1749 by Vanvitelli. It has particularly interesting early 17C altarpieces. **South side**. First altar, Astolfo Petrazzi, *Communion of St Jerome*; **second altar**, Perugino, **Crucifixion*.

The ***Piccolomini Chapel**. The chapel was founded in 1596 by Ascanio Piccolomini, Archbishop of Siena, in the chapter house of the Augustinian convent. It contains an altarpiece of the **Epiphany* by Sodoma (c 1530) and a lunette fresco of the **Madonna seated among Saints* by Ambrogio Lorenzetti. The two other beautiful Sienese works which used to be here are: **Massacre of the Innocents*, by Matteo di Giovanni (1482; removed to the Palazzo Pubblico since its restoration), and the altarpiece of the *Blessed Agostino Novello* by Simone Martini, also painted for the chapel, which is now exhibited in the Pinacoteca

Nazionale. At the entrance to the chapel is a statue of the Piccolomini *Pope Pius II* by Giovanni Duprè. **Fourth altar**: Ventura Salimbeni, *Calvary.*

In the **south transept** the Cappella Bichi has two *frescoes in grisaille of the *Birth of the Virgin* and the *Nativity*, attributed to Francesco di Giorgio Martini (discovered in 1978). Above are two monochrome lunettes by Signorelli. The majolica pavement dates from 1488. In the adjacent chapel, altarpiece painted by Raffaello Vanni. The **high altar** is by Flaminio del Turco. Beneath it is a reliquary of the Beato Agostino Novello.

North transept. In the **first chapel**, painting by Sebastiano Conca; **second chapel**, fresco fragment by Bartolomeo Neroni (Il Riccio) of a sepulchral monument; and Rutilio Manetti, *Temptations of St Anthony*. The funerary monument to Agostino Chigi (d. 1639) has statues by Tommaso Redi.

The wooden statues in the transepts have not yet been returned here since their restoration: the statue of *St Nicholas of Tolentino* is attributed to Giacomo Cozzarelli, another statue is attributed to Jacopo della Quercia, and the seated *Madonna wearing a crown and holding the standing Child* is by Giovanni di Turino (1420; restored in 1986). **North aisle**. **Third altar**, Francesco Vanni, *Baptism of Constantine*; (beyond the door), Carlo Maratta, *Conception*; Giovanni Francesco Romanelli, *Adoration of the Shepherds.*

In the Prato di Sant'Agostino is the entrance (No. 4) to the **Accademia dei Fisiocritici**, a science academy of physio-chemistry and natural philosophy founded in 1691 by Pirro Maria Gabrielli. It has geological, mineralogical, and zoological collections (**open** weekdays 09.00–13.00, 15.00–18.00, except Thurs afternoon).

From Sant'Agostino, Via Sant'Agata leads to the church of **San Giuseppe**, the oratory of the ***Contrada del Capitano dell'Onda.*** The brick façade dates from 1653 and the marble bust of *St Joseph* is by Tommaso Redi. The octagonal cupola was probably designed by a follower of Baldassarre Peruzzi, and it has a centrally planned 16C interior. The walled Via di Fontanella circles the cultivated hillside beside a public fountain beneath the apse of Sant'Agostino. It joins Via Mattioli (see below). Beyond the Arco di San Giuseppe the picturesque Via Giovanni Duprè descends through the Contrada dell'Onda to Piazza del Mercato (Pl. I; 10) from which Palazzo Pubblico with its loggia and tower is seen from the rear. In the other direction are fields and orchards.

To the southeast of Sant'Agostino, on a steep slope, are the **Botanical Gardens** (Pl. I; 14), transferred here in 1856. Via Pier Andrea Mattioli leads past the entrance (No. 4; **open** 08.00–17.00; Sat 08.00–12.00; closed fest.). There are tropical greenhouses, and well labelled and carefully tended plants. Beyond is the neo-classical façade (1839) of the church of the **Maddalena** which contains paintings by Antonio Bonfigli and Raffaello Vanni. Via Mattioli ends at **Porta Tufi** (Pl. II; 14), a fine gateway erected c 1326. Outside the gate is the **Misericordia Cemetery** (1843–74), with tombs decorated by Tito Sarrocchi, Cesare Maccari, Amos Cassioli, Giovanni Duprè and others.

From the Prato di Sant'Agostino, Via della Cerchia leads southwest towards Pian dei Mantellini. It ends beside the church of **Santi Niccolò e Lucia** (Pl. II; 14), with 17C frescoes by Sebastiano Folli and Francesco Bertini and wood carvings in the interior. On the south altar is a venerated *Madonna* in an 18C frame.

The high altarpiece of the *Martyrdom of St Lucy* is by Francesco Vanni (1606); above is a fresco by Ventura Salimbeni. On either side of the presbytery, two 15C polychrome statues: *St Lucy* attributed to a Sienese sculptor close to Francesco di Giorgio Martini and *St Nicola* (with an unusual head, attributed to a follower of Giovanni di Stefano).

San Niccolò al Carmine

Beyond, in the wide Pian dei Mantellini is the Carmelite convent and church of San Niccolò al Carmine (Pl. I; 13; also called Santa Maria del Carmine), founded in the 13C, with a huge campanile.

Interior. **South side**. Bartolomeo Neroni and Arcangelo Salimbeni, *Adoration of the Shepherds*; in the niche, *Assumption* with angels playing musical instruments, and saints, a damaged fresco attributed to Benedetto di Bindo. Over the altar, Domenico Beccafumi, **St Michael*. In the chapel of the Sacrament, off the south side, in a fine 16C frame, *Birth of the Virgin and the Redeemer* by Sodoma. At the end of the south side a painting of *Saints*, signed and dated 1593 by Francesco Vanni, surrounds the *Madonna dei Mantellini* (replaced by a photograph while it is being restored). The 17C **high altar** attributed to Tommaso Redi bears an earlier ciborium. Behind the altar a small Byzantine painting of the *Madonna and Child* has been removed.

On the **north side**, Alessandro Casolani, *Martyrdom of St Bartholomew*, and, over the altar, Girolamo del Pacchia, **Ascension* (in poor condition). At the west end of the wall, Giuseppe Collignon, *Holy Family appearing to Saints* (1825). On the west wall, Stefano Volpi, *Crucifixion*. In the **sacristy** (admission on request), formerly a private chapel, with interesting architectural details, is a statue of *St Sigismondo* by Giacomo Cozzarelli (in polychrome terracotta) and a painting of the *Annunciation* by Raffaello Vanni (recently restored). Part of the Convent is now used by the university; the 16C **cloister** with frescoes by Giuseppe Nicola Nasini (1710) can be seen at No. 44.

Pian dei Mantellini has several handsome buildings which follow its curved shape. To the right of the church, at No. 40, is **Palazzo Incontri**, a good neo-classical palace by Serafino Belli (1799–1804) with pilasters and busts in roundels. Beyond, at No. 28 is the façade of the former church of the **Conservatorio delle Derelitte** (by Riccio, c 1554). Opposite the flank of the Carmine is **Palazzo del Vescovo** (later Celsi Pollini Neri) attributed to Baldassarre Peruzzi. It has a second façade in the narrow lane which leads up to a fine medieval tower next to the little church of **Sant'Ansano** (Pl. I; 13; usually closed), built in 1441 by Pietro del Minella, Antonio Federighi, and others. It contains a precious stained glass tondo of *St Ansano* attributed to Cozzarelli, a high altarpiece by Rustichino, signed and dated 1617, and two 15C frescoes of the *Adoration of the Magi* and *St Ansano*. To the right of the church a religious institute occupies a building erected in 1877–81 in Renaissance style.

In front of Sant'Ansano, Via Tommaso Pendola leads through the **Contrada della Tartuca** (Pl. I; 13, 14), with its oratory, built by members of the contrada in 1682–85. The stucco relief on the high altar is by Giovanni Antonio Mazzuoli. The panel in the pavement, in imitation of that of the Duomo, was designed by Arturo Viligiardi (1891). The two paintings of *Miracles of St Anthony* are by Giuseppe Nicola Nasini. Parallel to the south is Vicolo della

Tartuca, a medieval blind alley with a flying bridge, and Via Tito Sarrocchi, with the house (No. 35) where the artist Beccafumi lived from 1516.

Off the other side of Pian dei Mantellini, Via San Marco leads down through the *Contrada della Chiocciola* (Pl. II; 14). At the beginning of the street, on the left, is the façade of the former church of San Marco next to a relief of the *Lion of St Mark* (1954). Farther on, at No. 37, in a courtyard behind an iron gateway is the 17C church dedicated to **Santi Pietro e Paolo** which serves as the oratory of the Contrada della Chiocciola. Built in 1645 on a design by Flaminio del Turco, it has a high altarpiece by Andrea del Brescianino. Farther down, at the fork with Via della Diana is the delightful 18C chapel of the **Madonna del Rosario**. In front is a Renaissance well. On the right side of Via San Marco is the huge convent of **Santa Marta** with a long façade probably by Il Tozzo, follower of Peruzzi (1535). On the opposite side, at No. 149, is a tabernacle with *Christ on the Cross* by Ventura Salimbeni. Outside Porta San Marco (c 1326) there is a fine view of the countryside.

Pian dei Mantellini ends at a gate in the walls called the **Arco delle Due Porte** (Pl. I; 13). High up on the wall of a house (No. 7) is a tabernacle with an early 14C fresco, thought to be the oldest tabernacle in the town. Just inside the gate is a house (on the right; plaque) where Duccio di Buoninsegna lived. The 16C tabernacle has a fresco attributed to Baldassarre Peruzzi (or Bartolomeo di Davide).

Via di Stalloreggi, which leads up to Piazza Postierla is described on p. 363.

From the gate Via Paolo Mascagni leads downhill to **Porta Laterina** (Pl. II; 13) which preserves its wooden doors. Near it is a huge bastion in the walls designed by Baldassarre Peruzzi. Outside the gate is a delightful view of the walls as far as Porta San Marco with olive groves and orchards outside them and unspoilt countryside beyond.

From the Arco delle Due Porte, Via del Fosso di Sant'Ansano, a narrow pretty road, curves north beneath the huge building of the Ospedale di Santa Maria della Scala (see p. 352) which covers the hill on the right. Beyond the low wall on the left are fields planted with olives and vines.

Via del Fosso di Sant'Ansano ends at Piazza della Selva in the *Contrada della Selva* (Pl. I; 9). Here is **San Sebastiano (in Valle Piatta)**, the oratory of the contrada. This small church is attributed to Domenico Ponsi (1507) or Baldassarre Peruzzi. It contains a *Madonna and Child with Saints* by Benvenuto di Giovanni, and two paintings of c 1630 by Astolfo Petrazzi (*Epiphany*) and Rutilio Manetti (*Crucifixion*). The stepped Vicolo di San Girolamo leads up to Piazza del Duomo (see above).

Palazzo Piccolomini ~ Archivio di Stato

From the northeast angle of the Campo, Via Rinaldini leads to *Palazzo Piccolomini (Pl. I; 7; which faces Via Banchi di Sotto), a handsome building and good example of Florentine Renaissance architecture, probably designed by Bernardo Rossellino and begun by Porrina in 1469. In the courtyard are good suspended capitals by Marrina (1509). The palace contains the **Archivio di Stato**, one of the finest extant collections of archives in Italy (well catalogued). The study room is open to students in the morning (except 15–30 August).

The fascinating little **museum** (**open** Mon–Sat 09.00–13.00) has important medieval documents, particularly well preserved. One room contains the unique series of book bindings known as the **Tavolette di Biccherna*, the painted covers of the municipal account-books, displayed chronologically from 1258. The most famous artists of the day were employed to decorate them, including (in the 14C) Ambrogio Lorenzetti, Paolo di Giovanni Fei, and Luca di Tommè, and (in the 15C) Giovanni di Paolo, Vecchietta, Sano di Pietro, Benvenuto di Giovanni, Francesco di Giorgio Martini, Bernardino Fungai, Guidoccio Cozzarelli, and (in the 16C) Domenico Beccafumi. Some of the scenes give a fascinating picture of medieval life.

Other rooms contain numerous documents (the oldest of which dates from 736), including illuminated statute books, the contract between the Commune and Jacopo della Quercia for the Fonte Gaia in the Campo, the contract drawn up by the Opera del Duomo for Duccio's *Maestà*, a pergamene signed by Frederick I Barbarossa, Boccaccio's will, and the Imperial charter (with its seal intact) by which Montepulciano was ceded to Siena after their victory over the Florentines at Montaperti (20 November 1260).

Opposite are the administrative offices of the **University**, founded c 1240, at the side of which Via San Vigilio leads to the university church of **San Vigilio** (Pl. I; 7). The fine ceiling has paintings by Raffaello Vanni. The third chapel on the south side has a marble altar by Tommaso Redi and Dionisio Mazzuoli and reliefs attributed to Mazzuoli. The high altar dates from 1688; the two paintings on either side are by Francesco Vanni. The third altar on the north side has a bronze *Crucifix* attributed to Pietro Tacca and two sculpted half-figures attributed to Giuseppe Mazzuoli.

This area is part of the ***Contrada della Civetta*** whose oratory is in Via Cecco Angiolieri, and whose headquarters is in the restored Castellare degli Ugurgieri.

Via San Vigilio ends at Via Sallustio Bandini opposite the Renaissance **Palazzo Bandini Piccolomini** (built c 1465 by Antonio Federighi, now used by the University). This characteristic street descends past two more interesting Bandini palaces on the bend of the road, opposite a high wall with two stone 13C lions (perhaps formerly bearing columns on a church façade), and ends in Piazzetta Grassi. Here is the church of **San Giovannino della Staffa**, now the oratory of the ***Contrada del Leocorno*** (Pl. I; 7). It contains works by Raffaello Vanni and Rutilio Manetti, and a 14C *Madonna and Child* by Francesco di Vannuccio.

Via Banchi di Sotto ends at the elegant **Logge del Papa** (Pl. I; 7; being restored). It was built for Pius II by Antonio Federighi (1462). The decorations are attributed to Francesco di Giorgio Martini.

Next to it is the church of **San Martino** (Pl. I; 7) mentioned in an 8C document, with a façade by Giovanni Fontana (1613). The pleasant **interior** by Giovanni Battista Pelori dates from after 1537. **South side**, **second altar**, Guido Reni, *Circumcision*; **third altar**, Guercino, *Martyrdom of St Bartholomew*; **fourth altar**, marble statue of *St Thomas of Villanova* attributed to Giovanni Antonio Mazzuoli. The Baroque **high altar**, with a ciborium, is attributed to Giuseppe Mazzuoli. On the wall of the choir are two sepulchral monuments attributed to Bartolomeo Mazzuoli.

North side. **Fourth altar**, statue of the *Madonna and Child* by Giuseppe Mazzuoli; **third altar**, **Nativity* by Domenico Beccafumi. On the **west wall** is a painting of the *Madonna protecting Siena* (1528)..

On the left of the Logge del Papa, Via di Pantaneto descends to the church of **San**

SIENA II

L'OSSERVANZA

VIA SIMONE MARTINI

VIALE PIETRO TOSELLI

VIA MEMMI

3

4

VIA DUCCIO DI BONINSEGNA

Fonte d'Ovile

VIA B. PERUZZI

S. Francesco

PIAZZA S. FRANCESCO

Oratorio di San Bernardino

7

8

STRADA DI BUSSETO

VIA ANTONIO VIVALDI

S. Giov. d. Staffa

VIA B. PERUZZI

Logge d. Papa

S. Martino

S. Spirito

S. Giorgio

VIA DI PANTANETO

S. Gaetano

VIA DEI PISPINI

VIA DELL'OLIVIERA

Porta Pispini

12

VIA ARETINA

AREZZO

VIA S. MARTINO

NICCHIO

Pal. di San Galgano

S. Raimondo

VIA DI SALICOTTO

VIA ROMA

VIA DEL SOLE

VIA CANTINE

S. Girolamo

Museo della Società Esecutori di Pie Disposizioni

Santuccio

VIA VAL DI MONTONE

SS. Trinità

S.M. dei Servi

VALDIMONTONE

see SIENA I CENTRAL map

15

16

VIA DI PORTA GIUSTIZIA

VIA DI FONTANELLA

Porta Romana

8

VIA GIROLAMO

VIA CERTOSA

VIA GIROLAMO

VIA PICCOLOMINI

0   200 yards
0   200 metres

S. QUIRICO D'ORCIA

CERTOSA DI MAGGIANO

Giorgio (Pl. I; 12) which has a good marble façade (1738) and a much older campanile (1260). The **interior** has white stucco decoration. On the **west wall** is the tomb of Francesco Vanni (1656), with his bust in bronze by his sons Raffaello and Michele, the last of whom carried out the exquisite and very unusual marble panel. **South side**, first altar, Placido Costanzi, *Calling of St Peter*; second altar, Niccolò Franchini, *Death of the Virgin*. In the **south transept**, Pietà with St Carlo by Vincenzo Meucci; *Pietà with St Catherine*, by Francesco Vanni, and a funerary monument by Giovanni Janssens (1748). The **high altarpiece** is attributed to Sebastiano Conca. In the **north transept** is a *Vision of St Filippo Neri* by Raffaello Vanni and another funerary monument by Janssens.

Beyond the church, Via dei Pispini leads left to a piazza with a pretty fountain. Here is the 16C church of **Santo Spirito** (Pl. I; 8, 12). The cupola is attributed to Giacomo Cozzarelli (1508) and the portal to Baldassarre Peruzzi (1519).

Interior. **South side**, **first chapel**: frescoes and paintings by Sodoma. The terracotta *Nativity* group is by Ambrogio della Robbia (1504). **Second chapel**: wooden statue of *St Vincent Ferrer* by Giacomo Cozzarelli. **Third chapel**: Domenico Beccafumi, *Coronation of the Virgin* (removed). On either side of the high altar, *Four Saints* by Rutilio Manetti. In the **north transept** there is a painting of the Madonna and Child by Andrea Vanni. **North side**, **third chapel**: Girolamo del Pacchia, *Coronation of the Virgin*, and a large painted *Crucifix* attributed to Luca di Tommè. In the **second chapel**: terracotta statue of *St Catherine of Siena* by Giacomo Cozzarelli. The two wooden kneeling figures of *St Jerome* and *Mary Magdalen* are by Francesco di Giorgio Martini. In the **first chapel** the *Assumption of the Virgin with Saints Francis and Catherine*, formerly attributed to Matteo Balducci, is now thought to be by Pacchiarotto.

Via dei Pispini descends to a fork with Via dell'Oliviera. Here is the pretty façade of **San Gaetano** (1683), the oratory of the ***Contrada del Nicchio***. Via dei Pispini continues down to the splendid **Porta Pispini** (or Porta San Viene; Pl. II; 12), dating from c 1326–28. The fresco painted by Sodoma above the gate has been detached and removed to the church of San Francesco. To the left of the gate, at an angle of the city walls, is the only surviving bastion of the seven designed by Peruzzi in the 16C to strengthen the earlier defences. On the right of the gate steps lead down to a public fountain. The church of **Sant' Eugenia**, 700m outside the gate (marked by its campanile) contains (on the high altar) a *Madonna*, one of the finest works of Matteo di Giovanni.

Vicolo del Sasso, opposite Santo Spirito, leads shortly to Via Roma. On the right is **Palazzo Bianchi** (1804) with a large garden. A pretty carved tabernacle, dated 1477 by Giovanni di Stefano is on the wall. Opposite is the Renaissance **Palazzo di San Galgano**, built in the style of Giuliano da Maiano (1474). The church of **San Raimondo al Rifugio** (closed many years ago) has a marble façade of 1660. It contains interesting 17C paintings, including works by Francesco Vanni and Rutilio Manetti. A *Virgin Annunciate* in wood by Jacopo della Quercia (1410–20), which belongs to the church, has been restored.

At No. 71 Via Roma are the premises of the **Società Esecutori di Pie Disposizioni** (Pl. II; 12). This 'society of executors of benevolent legacies' is the successor to the medieval lay brotherhood of the Compagnia della Madonna, suppressed by the Grand-duke of Tuscany in 1785. The Society's **museum** is

open on request (ring on the first floor) Mon and Fri 09.00–12.00, Tues and Thurs 15.00–17.00. It includes a painted lunette showing *St Catherine of Siena leading Pope Gregory XI back to Rome*, by Girolamo di Benvenuto; a *Crucifix* by the Duccio school; *Madonna and Child* by Sano di Pietro; *Madonna and Child, Saints Peter and Paul*, by Niccolò di Ser Sozzo, and *Holy Family* by Sodoma. The custodian conducts visitors across the road to another museum opened in 1981, donated by the Bologna-Buonsignori families, which contains an eclectic collection of prehistoric material, Etruscan and Roman ceramics and glass, jewellery, Deruta majolica, Chinese porcelain, a *Portait of a Lady* by Gino Severini, and arms.

Via Roma ends at **Porta Romana** (Pl. II; 15, 16), Siena's largest gate (1328), defended with a barbican.

From Via Roma (opposite No. 71) Via Val di Montone (partly stepped) leads up past the ex-church of San Leonardo, now the headquarters of the ***Contrada di Valdimontone*** (Pl. II; 15), and its church; the **Oratorio della Santissima Trinità**. It has a splendid 16C–17C Mannerist interior. The vault is frescoed by Ventura Salimbeni and the stuccoes are by Brescianino and Lorenzo and Cristoforo Rustici. In the **Sacristy** is a *Madonna and Child* by Neroccio di Bartolomeo who also painted the beautiful frame.

Santa Maria dei Servi

Via Val di Montone ends at the church of *Santa Maria dei Servi (Pl. I; 16), a large church with a massive brick campanile in a peaceful corner of the town. From the top of the steps there is an unusual view of the Duomo Nuovo, the campanile and the Duomo, and Palazzo Pubblico.

The spacious **interior**, with lovely capitals, has numerous interesting works of art from different periods. **South aisle**. Above the **first chapel**: remains of 14C frescoes; **second chapel**: *Madonna del Bordone* by Coppo di Marcovaldo, signed and dated 1261, partly repainted by a pupil of Duccio. On either side, two 16C paintings. **Third chapel**: Rutilio Manetti, *Birth of the Virgin*; **fourth chapel**: Alessandro Franchi, *Madonna and saints*; **fifth chapel**: Matteo di Giovanni, *Massacre of the Innocents* (1491; in very poor condition).

South transept. On the right wall, Francesco Vanni, *Annunciatory Angel*. In the chapel, painted *Cross* attributed to Niccolò di Segna; above the sacristy door, Segna di Bonaventura, *Madonna and Child*. **Chapels at the east end**: second chapel to the right of the sanctuary, especially interesting remains of frescoes (including the *Massacre of the Innocents*) attributed to Francesco di Segna, with the help of Niccolò di Segna and Pietro Lorenzetti. On the **high altar**, Bernardino Fungai, *Coronation of the Virgin*. In the **first chapel** to the left of the sanctuary, frescoed in the 19C, on either side of the altar are small frescoed tondi attributed to Giuseppe Nasini. The **second chapel** to the left of the sanctuary contains more good frescoes (scenes from the *Life of St John the Baptist*) attributed to Francesco and Niccolò di Segna and Pietro Lorenzetti. The altarpiece of the *Nativity* is by Taddeo di Bartolo (1404).

North transept. In the chapel, Giovanni di Paolo, *Madonna of the Misericordia* (signed and dated 1431). On the wall, Rutilio Manetti, *Miracle of the Blessed Gioacchino Piccolomini* (1633). Opposite is a painting of the *Madonna and the plague in Siena* by Astolfo Petrazzi painted to frame a painting of the *Madonna del Popolo* by Lippo Memmi (c 1325), removed several years ago to the Pinacoteca

Nazionale. Also in this transept, *Madonna Annunciate* by Francesco Vanni.

North aisle. Fifth chapel: *Adoration of the Shepherds* by Dionisio Montorselli and a 16C *Dead Christ* in polychrome terracotta. **Fourth chapel**: Francesco Curradi, *Madonna and Saints*, and (left wall), *Adoration of the Shepherds* by Alessandro Casolani; **second chapel**: *Madonna di Belvedere* attributed to Jacopo di Mino del Pelliciaio and Taddeo di Bartolo and (on either side) 16C Sienese paintings. **First chapel**: Francesco Vanni, *Annunciation*. On the west wall, 18C marble statue of the *Immacolata*.

The walk back to the Campo may be made along Via dei Servi, Via San Girolamo (left) and Via di Salicotto (left again). Via di Salicotto runs through the **Contrada della Torre** (Pl. I; 11) whose **Oratorio di San Giacomo** is on the left of the road beside No. 76 (ring for the custodian, 10.00–12.00, except Thurs). It contains a *Crucifixion* by Rutilio Manetti. In the last lane on the right before the Campo, Vicolo delle Scotte (off Via di Salicotto), is the **Synagogue**, a neo-classical building (1756). There was a Jewish community in Siena from 1229 onwards. They were confined to a ghetto in this area by Cosimo dei Medici in 1571, the doors of which were burnt down by French troops in 1796. However, it was not until 1895 that the Jews were given complete freedom to reside in the city.

From the Campo, Vicolo di San Pietro leads up to the **Croce del Travaglio** where the three main streets of Siena, the Banchi di Sopra, the Banchi di Sotto, and Via di Città, meet. Opposite is the **Loggia della Mercanzia* (Pl. I; 6), begun in 1417 on a design by Sano di Matteo; the upper story was added in the 18C. The five statues of saints (1456–63) are by Antonio Federighi and Vecchietta, the former of whom carved the marble bench (right) beneath the portico. The merchants' guild held a commercial tribunal here, famous for its impartiality, to which even foreign States resorted.

Via Banchi di Sopra (Pl. I; 2, 6) leads north to Piazza Tolomei, where from the 11C the Sienese parliament used to assemble. **Palazzo Tolomei* (Pl. I; 2, 6) is one of the oldest Gothic palaces in Siena (now owned by a bank), begun c 1208 and restored some 50 years later.

Opposite is the church of **San Cristoforo** (Pl. I; 2) where the magistrates of the Republic officiated. Dating from the 11C–12C, it is one of the oldest churches in Siena. The neo-classical façade dates from 1800.

Interior. On the first altar on the north side, Girolamo del Pacchia, *Madonna enthroned and Saints* (c 1508). In the north transept is an unusual 15C fresco of the *Pietà* and *Allegory of the Passion* (in very poor condition). In the pretty domed east end, on the high altar, is a statuary group of the *Translation of St Benedict*, attributed to Giovanni Antonio Mazzuoli (1693). In the south transept is a fine statuette of *St Galgano* in terracotta and white glazed enamel, by the della Robbia school. A painting of *St George and the dragon* attributed to the Maestro dell'Osservanza or Sano di Pietro (once on the south wall) is at present replaced here by a photograph. Next to it is a polychrome terracotta *Madonna and Child*.

Santa Maria di Provenzano

Via del Moro, flanking San Cristoforo, descends past an archway into the 13C cloister (restored in 1921) to the quiet Piazza Provenzano Salvani (Pl. I; 2). There is a good view of a stretch of the city walls. Here is **Santa Maria di**

Provenzano (1594) with a pretty exterior. The Mannerist **façade** is by Flaminio del Turco (1604) with four statues (1816) and the dome was designed by Don Giovanni de' Medici.

The **interior** has neo-classical furniture. On the west wall, monochrome painting by Bernardino Mei. **South wall**. Giovanni Bruni, *Birth of the Virgin* (19C). The first elaborate marble altar by Flaminio del Turco encloses an altarpiece of the *Mass of San Cerbone* by Rutilio Manetti (signed and dated 1630). In the spandrels of the dome are 18C frescoes and the marble pavement beneath it dates from 1685. **South transept.** Altarpiece by Francesco Rustici (1612) and, in the centre, *Madonna* by a pupil of Raffaello Vanni. On the **high altar**, designed by Flaminio del Turco, is a highly venerated little 15C terracotta bust of the *Madonna* in honour of which the Palio (see p. 338) of 2 July is run. The prize banner is kept in the church before the race. On either side are two silver statues by Francesco and Giovanni Antonio Mazzuoli. The ciborium dates from 1734. The two organs are by Sebastiano Montese (1728).

North transept. 17C *Crucifix* and two statues by Antonio Manetti (1837–39) and a 17C ciborium. **North wall**. Giovanni Bruni, *Circumcision*; on the altar, Dionisio Montorselli, *Vision of St Catherine* and *Martyrdom of St Lawrence*; Giovanni Bruni, *Coronation of the Virgin*. On the west wall, Bernardino Mei, *Mass of St Gregory the Great*.

To the right of the church, in Via delle Vergini, is the Oratory and headquarters of the **Contrada Imperiale della Giraffa** (Pl. I; 3). Via Provenzano Salvani leads along the left side of Santa Maria to Via del Giglio in which (left) is the church of **San Pietro a Ovile** (Pl. I; 2), probably of ancient foundation but rebuilt in the 18C, now used for lectures and in poor repair. In the **interior**, on the east wall, fragment of an *Annunciation* attributed to Bartolo di Fredi. A painted *Crucifix* by Giovanni di Paolo has been removed. On the altar to the left of the high altar, 14C *Crucifix*, attributed to the Maestro del Crocifisso dei Disciplinati (the two wood figures of the *Madonna* and *St John* by Domenico di Niccolò dei Cori have been removed to the Pinacoteca Nazionale). On the north altar, a photo replaces the *Madonna enthroned and four angels* by the Master of the Madonna di San Pietro a Ovile, now identified as Bartolomeo Bulgarini. The painting has been moved to the Villa di Montarioso (see Ch. 27). On the wall is a fragment of a fresco of the *Annunciation*, a very early Sienese work. On the west wall, Sebastiano Folli, *Holy Family and young St John* (1614).

San Francesco

Via Provenzano continues to Via dei Rossi, and (right) to Piazza San Francesco (good view of the Osservanza) and the large Gothic church of San Francesco (Pl. II; 7). It was built in 1326–1475, all but destroyed by fire in 1655, and afterwards used as a barracks for a long period. In 1885–92 it was heavily restored; the façade is by Vittorio Mariani and Gaetano Ceccarelli (1894–1913), but the pretty campanile survives from 1763.

The cold **interior** has late 19C stained glass (restored after the War). High up on the **west wall** detached frescoes from the Porta Romana by Sassetta and Sano di Pietro, and from Porta Pispini by Sodoma have been placed. Nine paintings which belong to the church were returned here in 1997 and set up on incongruous scaffolding altars (the Baroque side altars were destroyed in the

19C). They are 16C–17C works by Giuseppe Nicola Nasini, Giovanni Battista Ramacciotti, Alessandro Casolani, Jacopo Zucchi, Pietro Sorri, Pietro da Cortona (*Martyrdom of Santa Martina*), and Dionisio Montorselli.

South wall. Two frescoed tabernacles with the *Visitation and Saints* by the 14C–15C Sienese school. An ancient wooden *Crucifix* has been placed in a 14C carved tabernacle. **South transept**. In the chapel, fresco of a polyptych with the *Madonna enthroned and Saints* by Lippo Vanni. The marble statue of *St Francis* (against the wall of the transept) has recently been attributed to a 15C sculptor influenced by Francesco di Valdambrino. **Choir chapels**. Outside the fourth chapel to the right of the sanctuary, pavement tomb of 1541 with graffiti decoration (on a cartoon attributed to Beccafumi). In the **third chapel**: small relief of *Mary Magdalene between two angels*; **second chapel**: funerary monument of Cristoforo Felici, with a very unusual carved effigy by Urbano da Cortona (1462–87); first chapel right of the choir, 14C Sienese *Madonna and Child* (attributed to Andrea Vanni). On the left wall of the sanctuary, two busts of *Silvio Piccolomini* and *Vittoria Forteguerri* (father and mother of Pius II), made for their tomb and probably dating from the 15C. To the left of the choir **first chapel**, detached fresco of the *Crucifixion* by Pietro Lorenzetti; **third chapel**: two fine *frescoes by Ambrogio Lorenzetti, one with the *Martyrdom of Franciscan monks* and one with a scene of *St Louis of Toulouse before Pope Boniface VIII*. **Fourth chapel**, *Madonna and Child enthroned* (restored), attributed to Jacopo di Mino.

In the **north transept** is a chapel with a fine marble pavement by Il Marrina. **North wall**. Detached fresco of the *Crucifix and St Jerome*, sculptural fragments from the ancient church, and the huge monumental doorway by Francesco di Giorgio Martini removed in the early 20C from the façade of the church. The Renaissance **cloisters** house the university's Faculty of Political Science.

Oratorio di San Bernardino

To the right of San Francesco, the 15C Oratorio di San Bernardino (Pl. II; 7) stands on the spot where the saint preached (**open** April–Nov 10.30–13.30, 15.00–17.30). The **lower chapel** has lunettes frescoed with scenes representing the saint's life by 17C Sienese artists including Francesco Vanni, Domenico Manetti, Ventura Salimbeni, and Rutilio Manetti. The painting in the ceiling with a view of Siena (1580) is by Francesco Vanni. The paintings include a *Madonna and Child* by Sano di Pietro, and works by Astolfo Petrazzi and Bernardino Mei. In the vestibule on the **first floor** is a standard by Francesco Vanni and a bas-relief signed by Giovanni di Agostino (1341).

The **upper chapel**, beautifully decorated by Ventura Turapilli (after 1496), contains very fine frescoes of 1518 by Sodoma (*Presentation, Visitation, Assumption* and *Coronation of the Virgin*), Beccafumi (*Marriage of the Virgin, Transition of the Virgin*), and Girolamo del Pacchia. The Museo Diocesano is to be temporarily exhibited here.

Via dei Rossi, arched at either end (Pl. I; 2), returns to Via Banchi di Sopra which ends (right) at **Piazza Salimbeni** (Pl. I; 2), laid out at the end of the last century when the three palaces here were enlarged or restored. In the centre is **Palazzo Salimbeni**, enlarged in neo-Gothic style in 1866 by Giuseppe Partini. On the left is **Palazzo Tantucci** by Bartolomeo Neroni (1548), restored by Partini and, opposite, **Palazzo Spannocchi** which has two fine façades; one by Giuliano da

Maiano in Via Banchi di Sopra, the other by Giuseppe Partini in imitation of the Renaissance style (1881), facing the piazza. These three palaces form the seat of the **Monte dei Paschi di Siena**, a banking establishment founded in 1624, which owns an interesting collection of works of art (admission only with special permission). It includes paintings by Sano di Pietro, Sassetta, Giovanni di Paolo, the Maestro dell'Osservanza, Benvenuto di Giovanni, Domenico Beccafumi, Rutilio Manetti, and Bernardino Mei. The bank also owns most of the Chigi Saracini Collection, see p. 362.

Costa dell'Incrociata descends from Piazza Salimbeni to Via della Sapienza. Here is the church of **San Pellegrino a Sapienza** (Pl. I; 2; usually closed). **Interior**. The vault was frescoed in the 18C by Giuliano Traballesi. On the **south side** (behind glass) is a tiny ivory portable altar known as the *Madonna delle Grazie*, a precious work probably by a French craftsman, and a rare survival from the 14C. On the wall beside it is a small incised marble *Crucifix*, a very unusual work (removed for restoration), recently attributed to Guccio di Mannaia (c 1310). On the south altar, Lorenzo Feliciati, *Madonna of the Misericordia* (1772). On the north and south walls are two fragments of a painting with *St Paul and a bishop Saint* by a follower of Ambrogio Lorenzetti. On the **high altar**, Giuseppe Nasini, *Birth of the Virgin*. The north altarpiece of the *Preaching of St Paul* is by Alessandro Calvi. The six stucco statues in niches are by Giuseppe Mazzuoli the Younger. The beautiful painting, now attributed to the bottega of Simone Martini, of the *Blessed Andrea Gallerani* (founder of the Misericordia) has been restored but not yet returned to the church.

Parallel to Via della Sapienza is the interesting medieval Vicolo della Palla a corda. The **Biblioteca Comunale** (Pl. I; 1, 2; **open** weekdays 09.00–20.00; Sat 09.00–14.00) contains over 100,000 volumes and 5000 MSS., as well as illuminated missals, breviaries, and Books of Hours, St Catherine's letters, a 7C papyrus from Ravenna, drawings by Peruzzi and Beccafumi, a book with illustrations by Botticelli, and fine examples of bookbinding (including an 11C Byzantine work).

Casa di Santa Caterina

Costa Sant'Antonio descends from Via della Sapienza to the Casa di Santa Caterina (Pl. I; 1; **open** 09.00–12.30, 15.30–18.00), the house where St Catherine of Siena was born. It was converted into a sanctuary after its purchase by the Comune in 1466.

The present entrance is through a **portico** erected in 1941. Beyond, the charming little **loggia** was built perhaps by Peruzzi or by his follower Giovanni Battista Pelori (1533). Here is (left) the **Oratorio della Cucina**, the family kitchen converted in the 16C into an oratory, which has the most interesting decorations. On the wall to the left of the entrance: paintings by Alessandro Casolani, Pietro Sorri (St Catherine liberating a woman possessed of the devil), Pomarancio, Lattanzio Bonastri and Gaetano Marinelli (1872). The altarpiece is by Bernardino Fungai, and on either side are two paintings by Riccio. On the wall to the right of the altar: paintings by Pietro Aldi (1872), Riccio and Arcangelo Salimbeni (1578), Pomarancio, and Alessandro Casolani. On the wall opposite the altar, is a curved painting in a niche by Francesco Vanni, and on either side, works by Pietro Sorri, Rutilio Manetti, and Francesco Vanni. The wood stalls date from 1518 and 1555, and the majolica pavement from the 16C.

Opposite is the **Church of the Crocifisso** built in 1623 on the site of the Saint's orchard to house the *Crucifixion* (by the late 12C Pisan school) before which St Catherine received the stigmata at Pisa in 1375, now over the high altar. It is preserved in a cupboard decorated by Riccio. The marble high altar is by Tommaso Redi (1649). In the south transept is an altarpiece by Sebastiano Conca and in the north transept an altarpiece by Rutilio and Domenico Manetti. Stairs lead down to the **Camera della Santa,** St Catherine's cell, frescoed by Alessandro Franchi in 1896. It preserves a small painting of *St Catherine receiving the stigmata* by Girolamo di Benvenuto.

Below is the **Oratorio della Tintoria** or Santa Caterina in Fontebranda, now the oratory of the ***Contrada dell'Oca*** and only open on special occasions. It was built in 1465 on the site of the dyer's workshop (*tintoria*). It contains frescoes of five angels by Sodoma, and St Catherine receiving the stigmata and other scenes from her life, by Girolamo del Pacchia and Ventura Salimbeni. The splendid polychrome wooden *statue of *St Catherine* is by Neroccio di Bartolomeo, sculpted for this oratory in 1475.

St Catherine of Siena

Caterina Benincasa (1347–80), or Catherine of Siena, was the daughter of a dyer and took the veil at the age of eight. Her visions of the Redeemer, from whom she received the stigmata and, like her Alexandrian namesake, a marriage ring, have been the subject of countless paintings. Her eloquence persuaded Gregory XI to return from Avignon to Rome, and her letters (preserved in the Biblioteca Comunale; see above) are models of style as well as of devotion. She died in Rome, where she is buried in Santa Maria sopra Minerva, was canonised in 1461, and in 1939 was proclaimed a patron saint of Italy. She was made a doctor of the Church in 1970, the first female saint, with St Teresa of Avila, to be given this distinction. The only authentic portrait of Catherine can be seen in the nearby church of San Domenico, in the chapel in which she became a Dominican. Another chapel in the same church was built in 1460 to preserve the relic of her head brought back to Siena from Rome in 1383. The chapel is frescoed with scenes from her life by Sodoma.

Fonte Branda

Vicolo del Tiratoio passes under the house of St Catherine and a pretty little lane leads downhill to the *Fonte Branda (Pl. I; 5), the oldest and most abundant spring in Siena. It was mentioned as early as 1081 and covered over in 1248 with brick vaults by Giovanni di Stefano. The water for the public fountain is channelled from a large reservoir. The church of San Domenico is conspicuous on the hill above.

San Domenico can be reached either by Via della Sapienza (see above) or from Costa Sant'Antonio, by taking Vicolo del Campaccio through the first archway on the left, a lane which climbs up above St Catherine's house to Via Camporegio.

San Domenico

At the top of Camporegio hill stands the austere Gothic church of San Domenico (Pl. I; 1, 5), begun in 1226, enlarged, damaged, and altered in successive centuries. The campanile dates from 1340 (altered in 1798). From the edge of the hill there is a view of the Duomo and Palazzo Pubblico above old houses on a hillside. The **interior** is built in the usual Dominican form, with a wide aisleless nave, transepts, and a shallow choir with side chapels. The **Cappella delle Volte**, a chapel at the west end, contains the only authentic portrait of *St Catherine*, by her contemporary and friend, Andrea Vanni. St Catherine assumed the Dominican habit in this chapel. The other paintings here are by Mattia Preti and Crescenzio Gambarelli.

South side. First altar, Alessandro Casolani, *Birth of the Virgin* (1584). Beyond it is the **Cappella di Santa Caterina**. On the entrance arch, *Saints Luke and Jerome*, by Sodoma. The tabernacle on the altar, by Giovanni di Stefano (1466) encloses a reliquary containing St Catherine's head. On the right and left of the altar are celebrated *frescoes by Sodoma (1526), representing the Saint in ecstasy and swooning. The pilasters have good grotesques. On the left wall, the saint interceding for the life of a young man brought to repentance, also by Sodoma; on the right wall, Francesco Vanni, the saint liberating a man possessed. The beautiful pavement is attributed to Giovanni di Stefano.

Above the steps down to the huge **crypt** (begun in the 14C, but usually closed) is a detached fresco of the *Madonna and Child and a Knight* attributed to Pietro Lorenzetti. The *Nativity* is by Francesco di Giorgio Martini and an assistant. The *Pietà* in the lunette above is by Matteo di Giovanni and the predella by Bernardino Fungai.

Over the **high altar** is a fine *tabernacle with two angels, by Benedetto da Maiano (c 1475; difficult to appreciate because of the incongruous stained glass in the east windows designed by Bruno Cassinari in 1982). In the first chapel to the right of the altar fragmentary remains of frescoes detached from the cloister, have been hung. These are by Andrea Vanni and Lippo Memmi, and there is also a triptych of the *Madonna and Child with Saints Jerome and John the Baptist* by Matteo di Giovanni. In the first chapel to the left of the sanctuary, polychrome wood statue of *St Anthony Abbot* attributed to Giovanni di Turino. In the second chapel to the left of the high altar is a *Maestà*, a splendid huge painting by Guido da Siena (second half of the 13C, but dated 1221). On the side walls incongruous 18C frescoes by Giuseppe Nasini surround *St Barbara enthroned between angels and Saints Mary Magdalene and Catherine* by Matteo di Giovanni, opposite a *Madonna and Child with four Saints* by Benvenuto di Giovanni.

On the third altar on the **north side**, *Four saints and God the Father* by Sodoma and (below) 16C *Mysteries of the Rosary* (surrounding a 14C *Madonna and Child*, removed for restoration). On the second north altar, Rutilio Manetti, *Miracle of St Anthony Abbot*.

From Piazza San Domenico Viale dei Mille leads above the Stadium (Pl. II; 5) on the valley floor, to the huge **Fortezza Medicea** (Pl. II; 5), or Forte di Santa Barbara, built for Cosimo I de' Medici by Baldassarre Lanci in 1560. On the bastions are avenues with delightful views. In the vaults is the *Enoteca Italica*, an exhibition of Italian wines (**open** 12.00–midnight for wine tasting and buying), specialising in those from Tuscany.

From San Domenico the unattractive Viale Curtatone (Pl. I ; 1) leads past the neo-classical **Evangelical Church** (1882) to the undistinguished **Piazza Matteotti** with its huge Post Office, built in 1910 (by Vittorio Mariani). Here, the little **Oratorio delle Suore** (or *del Paradiso*) is approached by a double stair-case. This is the oratory of the ***Contrada del Drago***. The interior, decorated in 1693, has paintings by Francesco Rustici, Domenico Manetti, and Raffaello Vanni. The bust of *St Catherine* in polychrome terracotta is by Marrina (1517).

Via Pianigiani leads east out of Piazza Matteotti to the little **Oratorio di Santa Maria delle Nevi** (Pl. I; 2; usually locked), an elegant Renaissance building (1471) attributed to Francesco di Giorgio Martini. The *altarpiece (Madonna delle Nevi) is by Matteo di Giovanni (1477).

Just beyond the church, Via di Vallerozzi descends steeply towards Porta Ovile (Pl. I; 2). Halfway down on the right Via dell'Abbadia leads up to Piazza Abbadia (Pl. I; 2) with the **Rocca di Palazzo Salimbeni** (14C; restored in the Gothic style in the 19C). The Medici coat of arms by Domenico Cafaggi (1570) can be seen high up in the courtyard.

Also in Piazza Abbadia is the church of **San Michele al Monte di San Donato** (Pl. I; 2), consecrated in 1147, but transformed in 1691 and heavily restored. **Interior**. The inner door dates from 1918. **South wall**. Antonio Buonfigli (attributed), *Madonna of the Rosary*, and (above) 13C fresco fragments including the *Raising of Lazarus*; first altar, Annibale Mazzuoli, *Madonna and St Apollonia*. Beyond the second altar, in a stucco frame, *Crucifix and Saints* attributed to Antonio Buonfigli or Francesco Nasini. The **south transept** has 18C paintings by Giovanni Battista Sorbi. Here a small polychrome wooden group of the *Pietà* is displayed. It is a very unusual work (restored in 1986) now attributed to Vecchietta. On the high altar are two marble angels in the manner of Giuseppe Mazzuoli. The **choir**, with frescoes by Luigi Ademollo (1794), is hung with paintings by Andrea Vanni, Benedetto di Bindo and Sodoma. The **north transept** has paintings by Antonio Nasini (1693). On the **north side** is a heavily restored wood statue of *St Anthony*.

Via di Vallerozzi continues down to the church of **San Rocco**, the oratory of the ***Contrada della Lupa*** (Pl. II; 6). A classical column outside bears a bronze copy of the she-wolf of Rome. The interior has fine 17C Sienese paintings by Raffaello Vanni, Rutilio Manetti, and Ventura Salimbeni.

From here it is a short way left, off Via Pian d'Ovile, to the brick **Fonte Nuova di Ovile** (Pl. II; 2; 1303) with two fine Gothic arches, reached by steps below the road. Via Vallerozzi ends at **Porta Ovile** (Pl. II; 2); on the left is a tabernacle with a fresco of the *Madonna and Child with Saints* by Sano di Pietro. The fine gate dates from the 14C; outside is a view of a stretch of the city walls with orchards and old houses and the side of the church of San Francesco. Steps go down to the picturesque **Fonte d'Ovile** (1262). Just inside the gate, in Via del Comune is the headquarters of the ***Contrada del Bruco*** (Pl. II; 6). The inhabi-tants of this district are known for their independent character and spirit of fierce allegience to the Contrada. In the oratory is a *Madonna and Child* by Luca di Tommè. One of the poorest parts of the town in the Middle Ages, there was a revolt here in 1371 of the wool-workers belonging to the Contrada. This was one of the first workers' revolts in medieval Italy (preceding the famous Ciompi insurrection in Florence by seven years). Three hundred members of the

Contrada, with a rag-merchant called Domenico di Lano at their head, took up arms against the Council of Nine and a faction of nobles belonging to the Salimbeni family. After heavy losses, the workers finally gained the upper hand and obtained some benefits and a partial change in the government of the town.

Via Montanini leads north from the Oratorio di Santa Maria delle Nevi (see above) past (No. 92) **Palazzo Ottieri (Costantini),** with a 15C façade attributed to Francesco di Giorgio Martini, with fine ironwork. On the right, is the church of **Sant'Andrea** (Pl. II; 6), approached by steps added in 1755. It was founded in the 12C, transformed in the 18C, and restored in this century. In the **interior** on the **south side** are (first altar), fine 15C frescoes of the *Madonna and Child with St Anne,* and (second altar) a pretty stucco frame enclosing a fresco by Apollonio Nasini. Over the **high altar**, *Coronation of the Virgin,* signed and dated by Giovanni di Paolo (1445). On the **north side** (second altar), another fresco of a saint by Nasini enclosed in a stucco frame, and (first altar) fragments of 15C frescoes. On the west wall is a stucco bas-relief of the *Madonna and Child* by the 15C Sienese school.

Beside the church is the **Oratorio di Sant'Anna in Sant' Onofrio**. Inside is a half-length figure in terracotta of *St Bernardine* (right of the high altar) dating from the end of the 15C (in the manner of Cozzarelli). The stucco statues in the niches date from 1769.

Via Montanini ends at a fork with Via di Camollia and the unattractive Via Garibaldi. On the curve of Via Garibaldi (and considerably below the level of the road) is the church of **San Sebastiano** (locked), which contains early 17C frescoes.

Near San Sebastiano is the Anglican church of **St Peter's** financed by Mrs Georgina Allinson Hignetti in 1908 and built in medieval style in the following year. It is open for occasional services. Via Camollia continues north and Via dei Gazzani diverges left for the church of **Santo Stefano** (closed for restoration), rebuilt in 1671–75. On the high altar is a polyptych by Andrea Vanni (1400) with a predella by Giovanni di Paolo. It also contains paintings by Rutilio Manetti and Antonio Bonfigli.

Santo Stefano is on the corner of **La Lizza** (Pl. II; 5), a small attractive public park laid out in 1778 by Antonio Matteucci and Leopoldo Prucher with two diverging avenues of horse-chestnuts and cedars of Lebanon beside the Fortezza Medicea (see above). The fine statue of Garibaldi is by Raffaello Romanelli. A general street market is held in this area on Wednesdays. The Palazzo di Giustizia was built here in 1986.

Via del Romitorio leads down from the church of Santo Stefano, under a tunnel and past a little garden, to the church of **Santa Maria in Portico a Fontegiusta** (Pl. II; 1), an elegant little Renaissance church. On the brick façade is a fine marble portal (1489) with a frieze attributed to Giovanni di Stefano. The **interior** is in the form of a vaulted hall. The tiny round window on the west wall has restored 15C stained glass. The fresco on the right of the *Visitation* (1522) is attributed to Scalabrino. On the south altar, Bernardino Fungai, *Coronation of the Virgin with Saints.* On the east wall (right of the high altar), Francesco Vanni, *Intercession of the Blessed Ambrogio Sansedoni for the protection of Siena* (Siena is portrayed below). The ***high altar** is a splendid work in marble in the form of a classical edicola by Marrina (c 1517) with a lunette of *Christ in Pietà* (by Michele Cioli da Settignano) and two winged *Victories*. It surrounds the highly venerated

Madonna di Fontegiusta, a late 14C fresco attributed to Cristoforo di Bindoccio (called Malabarba) and Meo di Pero. On either side of the altar are faded frescoes by Ventura Salimbeni and the large lunette above has a fine fresco of the *Virgin in Glory* by Girolamo di Benvenuto (1515). By the door on the north side is a tiny stoup in bronze, signed and dated 1480 by Giovanni delle Bombarde. On the north wall is a fresco (partly repainted) of the *Sibyl announcing to Augustus the Birth of Christ*, attributed to Baldassarre Peruzzi or Daniele da Volterra.

A small **museum** has been arranged in an old tower of the medieval walls, now incorporated in the church. Among the contents are an interesting bronze ciborium, traditionally attributed to Vecchietta, a polychrome wooden statue of *St Sebastian*, attributed to Giovanni di Stefano, and a terracotta bust of *St Bernardine* attributed to Vecchietta.

From the front of the church of Fontegiusta the short Via Fontegiusta leads up beneath a pretty arch to Via di Camollia. On the right is the headquarters and oratory of the *Contrada dell'Istrice* (Pl. II; 2). Via di Camollia continues left to the church of **San Pietro alla Magione** (Pl. II; 1) with a rebuilt façade and a Gothic portal. In the **interior** are numerous remains of detached 14C frescoes, and (in a niche on the right wall) a 15C sinopia of the *Madonna and Child*. The little marble tabernacle on the right of the sanctuary is modelled on the façade of the Duomo. The adjoining 16C chapel contains a fresco of the *Madonna and Child* by Riccio.

Surrounding the church are the restored buildings of the **Magione** (mansion), a medieval pilgrims' hospice founded by the Knights Templar.

Via di Camollia ends at the **Porta Camollia** (Pl. II; 1), rebuilt in 1604 and inscribed *Cor magis tibi sena pandit*—'To you Siena opens her heart (wider than this gate)'—to commemorate a visit of the Grand-duke Ferdinando I. A few steps beyond is a column recalling the meeting on this spot of Frederick III and Eleanora of Portugal in March 1451 (depicted in the frescoes in the Libreria Piccolomini, see above). Beyond the column in Viale Vittorio Emanuele II, is the Antiporto or barbican (1675), in imitation of the Porta Romana. In Via Cavour, c 500m from the antiporta, is the brick **Palazzo dei Diavoli** or *dei Turchi* attributed to Antonio Federighi (1460).

27 · The environs of Siena

In the countryside which surrounds Siena there are often splendid views of the hill-town, from the south in particular. At a short distance from the town on all sides there are many charming country roads and a vast choice of places to visit, often in panoramic positions, including monasteries, villas, formal or romantic gardens, little villages, ruined castles, and country churches in a landscape which varies from farmland and woods to river valleys and the unique clay downs known as *Le Crete* towards Asciano. This district lends itself to exploration, and only some of the most interesting places are mentioned below.

■ Practical information
Information office. APT Siena, Piazza dell Campo 56, Siena (☎ 0577-280551, fax 270676).

Hotels
Near the **Osservanza**: ★★★★ *Villa Scaccia pensieri*, 10 Via di Scaccia-pensieri (☎ 0577-41441; fax 0577-270854). *Certosa di Maggiano*, 82 Via di Certosa (☎ 0577-288180; fax 0577-288189).
Sovicille: ★★★★ *Borgo Pretale* (☎ 0577-345401; fax 0577-345625).

Restaurants
Torri: *Le Torri di Stigliano* (£) at Stigliano, 2 km south.

L'Osservanza church and convent

The convent and church of L'Osservanza is the most important Sienese church outside the city walls. About 2.5km from Porta Ovile (see Ch. 26; Pl. II; 2), it is reached by car along Via Simone Martini and the 16C Madonnina Rossa (beyond the railway crossing). Alternatively take bus No. 3 from Piazza del Sale.

The basilica (**open** 09.00–13.00, 16.00–19.00) was founded in 1423 by St Bernardine (see p. 307). Its aim was to restore the observance of the original Franciscan rule, relaxed by papal dispensations. The convent was enlarged in 1476–90 probably by Francesco di Giorgio Martini and Giacomo Cozzarelli. It was confiscated by the city in 1874, restored in Renaissance style in 1932 but then well rebuilt in 1949 after severe War damage.

Interior. The stucco and terracotta roundels in the vaults and in the sanctuary are attributed to Giacomo Cozzarelli. On the west wall the two roundels with saints surrounded by garlands of fruit are attributed to Andrea della Robbia. On either side of the entrance to the sanctuary are white glazed figures of the *Annunciatory Angel* and the *Virgin* in tabernacles by Andrea della Robbia. **North side**: first altar, Sano di Pietro, *Madonna and Child*, with four angels; **second altar**, Andrea della Robbia, blue and white enamelled terracotta altarpiece of the *Coronation of the Virgin*; **fourth altar**, *Four Saints* by Andrea di Bartolo (1413). In the sanctuary is a fresco with its sinopia by Pietro di Francesco Orioli.

South side: detached fresco of the *Crucifixion* by Bartolomeo Neroni; **third altar**, Sano di Pietro, *Madonna and Child with Saints*. On the right wall, *St Elizabeth of Hungary* by Girolamo di Benvenuto, and, on the left wall, *St Bernardine* by Pietro di Giovanni d'Ambrogio; **fourth altar**, triptych attributed to the Maestro dell'Osservanza, who acquired his name from this painting.

In the **sacristy** is a group of seven polychrome terracotta figures mourning over the dead Christ, by Giacomo Cozzarelli (beautifully restored in 1984). A small **museum** contains a *Head of Christ* by Lando di Pietro (1338), all that remains of a wood *Crucifix* destroyed in 1944, and a *reliquary of St Bernardine by Francesco d'Antonio (1454).

The **Certosa di Pontignano**, also reached from Porta Ovile, is described in Ch.4.

Near Porta Pispini (see Ch.26; Pl. II; 12) the *Strada di Busseto* leads east out of Siena, and beyond the railway is the pretty little hamlet of **Sant'Agnese a Vignano**. The villa of the art historian, Cesare Brandi (1906–88), with a library and art collection, is used by the University of Siena as a Fine Arts Institute.

Outside Porta Romana (see Ch. 26; Pl. II; 16), on the southern outskirts of Siena, is the **Certosa di Maggiano**, probably the first charterhouse to be founded in Tuscany. It was built in 1315 and suppressed in 1782; it is now restored as a hotel. The church has an interesting 18C interior (frescoes by the Nasini) and sculptures by the Mazzuoli brothers.

Outside Porta Camollia (see Ch. 27; Pl. II; 1), Via Caduti di Vicobello and the Strada di Vico Alto lead north towards the **Villa di Vicobello** built on a hill for the Chigi family by Baldassarre Peruzzi. It is surrounded by a large garden, the best preserved private 16C garden near Siena (**adm.** by appointment, ☎ 0577-377184).

West of Siena, outside Porta San Marco (Ch. 26; Pl. II; 13) is the village of Volte Alte (244m), with the **Ville delle Volte**, another 16C villa attributed to

PROVINCIA DI
SIENA

N

Baldassarre Peruzzi. Also outside Porta San Marco (on the N73 signposted for Roccastrada and Grosseto) is the battlemented **Villa di Monastero**, formerly the Benedictine abbey of Sant'Eugenio (suppressed in 1810 and now a home for the aged) surrounded by a large park. There are two cloisters, one of which is fortified. The church has a dome with frescoes in the spandrels by Ventura Salimbeni and Francesco Vanni. There are paintings by Rutilio Manetti, Riccio, Benvenuto di Giovanni and Sodoma (attributed).

Nearby is the 12C **Castello di Belcaro**, in a lovely position (**adm.** weekdays 14.00–16.00 by appointment, ☎ 0577-394237), enlarged in the 16C by Peruzzi.

Lecceto, west of Siena, is a magnificent fortified monastery in dense ilex woods. It was founded on the site of an ancient hermitage by the Augustinians and is still inhabited by Augustinian nuns (Mass on fest. at 17.00). The **church** has a simple Romanesque façade, partly covered by a portico with remains of frescoes.

The **interior** was transformed in the late Baroque period and a marble screen placed behind the altar to separate the nave from the choir. In the nave are the two fine pavement tombs of Niccolò Saracini (1350) and Jacopo Magistri Martini (1499). On the nave wall are some interesting fresco fragments; a figure of *St Michael* is attributed to Ambrogio Lorenzetti, whose famous *Madonna of Lecceto* has been removed (and will one day be displayed in the new Diocesan Museum in San Bernardino in Siena). A rare series of twenty **choirbooks** (14C–15C), with miniatures by Giovanni di Paolo and others, which belong to the monastery, are now preserved in the Biblioteca Comunale in Siena (see p. 375). Next to the church is the entrance to the elegant cloister on two storeys, from which there is a good view of the massive battlemented tower.

A short distance north of Lecceto is the little Romanesque-Gothic church of **San Leonardo al Lago** (reached by a narrow path from the road) is perched on a small hill dominating a valley which was once a lake. It has a fine 14C façade with a rose window over the doorway. Surrounding the church are remains of defence walls. The **interior** is decorated with a number of frescoes, in particular the apse, which is covered is with scenes of the *Life of the Virgin* (with angels in the vault), by Lippo Vanni (1360–70), a follower of Pietro Lorenzetti. To the right of the church (ring the bell) are remains of the former monastery. In the refectory is a *Crucifixion* frescoed by Giovanni di Paolo.

Farmhouses near Siena

The Montagnola Senese

The area further west and southwest of Siena is known as the Montagnola Senese. It comprises extensive woods of oaks, ilexes and chestnuts, cultivated fields where formerly there were marshes, villages and farms—mostly of medieval origin—often well preserved and picturesquely situated, and monasteries and villas of later date with their parks and gardens.

Castello di Celsa

The Castello di Celsa, about 15km west of Siena, owned by the Aldobrandini family, is in a beautiful position, approached by an avenue of umbrella pines. The **garden** can be visited by previous appointment (☎ 0577-317002) or apply to the Aldobrandini administration in Rome (☎ 06-6861138; fax 06-68307326). Standing on a remote hilltop, surrounded by oak forests, it has a superb unspoilt view of Siena and the whole of southern Tuscany.

Dating back to at least the 13C the castle was sacked by the Spaniards in 1554 and restored in the 17C. One of the two wings on the triangular courtyard was rebuilt in the Gothic style in the last century. Baldassarre Peruzzi is said to have designed the circular chapel as well as the original gardens in the early 16C. The gardens now consist of a terrace which overhangs the valley below between two simple pavilions, a semicircular pool. A modern parterre of box and gravel represents the arms of the Aldobrandini. To the east lies a second semicircular pool approached up a staircase which has reliefs of river gods and dolphins. Beyond is an ilex *bosco* (wood).

Villa Cetinale

Close by is **Cetinale**, the most spectacular villa in the area. The grand villa has a 16C core (including the outside stair and portico). It was built in 1680 for

Cardinal Flavio Chigi by Carlo Fontana. The **garden** is **open** to the public by appointment in the mornings (☎ 0577-311147; fee). After many years of neglect the villa and garden were sold by the Chigi family in 1978. Both are now beautifully maintained and the garden has been carefully restored.

In front of the house is a formal garden with topiary and yew hedges, land-scaped in the early 20C. Under the loggia are two Roman statues (4C AD) and an inscription 'welcoming' visitors. On the left side of the villa is another lovely garden, now planted with numerous varieties of rose. The other façade of the house, with an outside staircase, looks towards a densely wooded hill near the top of which is the conspicuous early 18C 'Romitorio' or hermitage.

A broad grassy path runs between two walls decorated with busts and statues (including colossal figures of Dacian prisoners). Cypresses planted at the begin-ning of the 20C line the path leading up to the stone '**theatre**', now surrounded by terracotta urns. The colossal bust on the left is a portrait of *Napoleon*, placed here in his honour when he visited the villa. A gate, flanked by the Chigi arms, admits to a long flight of some 250 steps which leads straight up through dense woods to the '**Romitorio**' (1717), a five storied building, recently carefully restored which has a *Cross of Lorraine* on the exterior (with reliefs of Christ and the four evangelists). There is a church on the ground floor, used by the hermit monks who once lived here, and a delightful little walled garden (recently replanted). From the highest room there is a wonderful view through the little window down to the villa and (on a clear day) to Monte Amiata in the distance. The woods, no longer all part of the estate, stretch from here more or less continuously all the way to the sea.

On the right of the villa is another wood (enclosed by a wall with two gates) known as '**La Tebaide**' (Thebaid), also created by Cardinal Chigi in the late 17C. The seven little chapels in the woods dedicated to the Sorrows of the Virgin and the statues of hermits by Giuseppe Mazzuoli were intended to evoke an atmos-phere of prayer and contemplation for the visitor. Along the winding paths are tortoises, dragons, and various monsters, carved out of the living rock, and the little lake is overgrown with white water lilies.

Ancaiano, just south of Cetinale, is a charming village which has an unexpect-edly large and elegant parish church, built in the 17C, by Pope Alexander VII Chigi, Flavio Chigi's uncle. The interior has a few 16C–17C paintings and two earlier frescoes.

The nearby village of **Sovicille** preserves parts of its medieval walls and some picturesque houses. Facing the main square is the much restored church of San Lorenzo, with an old campanile. Inside, on the right of the nave, is a fresco of the *Madonna and Child with Saints* attributed to Alessandro Casolani.

Outside the village is the Pieve di San Giovanni Battista, better known as **Pieve di Ponte allo Spino**. This small 12C–13C Romanesque church is built of evenly-cut stone that has acquired a beautiful patina over the centuries. Its simple **façade** is dominated by a bell-tower built on to a massive earlier tower. The east end, with its three apses and raised crossing decorated with blind arches may be seen from the footpath along the side of the church. The **interior** has a basilican plan with pilasters dividing the nave from the aisles, which are of equal height and covered by a timber roof. The transept and crossing are vaulted. The capitals are richly carved with both realistic and symbolic figures,

geometrical and plant motifs, showing Lombard and possibly also French influences. An archway to the right of the façade leads into the courtyard which
preserves part of the cloister and remains of the canon's house, with two fine
Gothic windows.

Rosia, another village on a nearby hill, has a 13C Romanesque church with
a tall bell-tower. Steps lead up to the entrance, an arched doorway in an unusually broad façade with three narrow windows. Inside, the nave and two aisles
support a timber roof. To the right of the entrance is a triptych of the *Madonna
and Child with Saints Sebastian and Anthony Abbot* by Guidoccio Cozzarelli, and a
rectangular marble baptismal font, carved with a bas-relief of *Christ and six
angels* (15C).

Continuing eastwards, along the Torrente Rosia with wooded slopes on either
side, the road passes by an old bridge (the Ponte della Pia) and reaches a crossroads marked by a column erected by Leopoldo II. Above, on a hill, are the
ruined walls and towers of castle **Montarrenti**.

Across the Torrente Rosia a cypress avenue climbs uphill to **Torri**,a tiny
medieval village surrounded by its old walls. Beyond an archway in the walls is
a pretty piazza, leading to an enclosure onto which faces the south side of the
Romanesque-Gothic church of **Santissima Trinità e Santa Mustiola**. Built in
beautifully hewn stone, it has a fine carved doorway and three arched windows
decorated with human and animal heads. The **interior**, which was heavily
restored in the 19C, has a *Madonna and Child* by Luca di Tommè. To the left,
under the arms of Pope Pius II with the date 1462, is the entrance to the
cloister (open Mon and Fri 09.00–12.00) of the former Vallombrosan
monastery, now a private villa. This small cloister, built in brick, has loggias on
three levels: the lowest arches are decorated with black-and-white marble and
supported by a variety of columns with fine capitals. The middle loggia has
octagonal brick columns, and the top loggia has slender wood columns. There
are extensive woods above Torri, with fine views of Siena in the distance.

To the south is the village of **Orgia** upon a hill, just outside of which is the
little **Museo del Bosco** (open Fri and Sat 09.30–12.30, ☎ 0577-342097),
which has farm implements and objects used by farm labourers in this district.
Maps of the footpaths in the surrounding area may be obtained from the
Comune in the village (☎ 582336; for a guide (fee) ☎ 0577-342053).

28 · San Gimignano

San Gimignano is a charming hill town of 7000 inhabitants, which has
preserved its medieval appearance more completely than any other town in
Tuscany. It can, however, be uncomfortably crowded with tourists (mostly on
day trips from Florence or Siena) in spring and summer. The town is famous for
its numerous towers which make it conspicuous from a great distance and
provide one of the most remarkable sights in Italy. It is possible to walk along the
13C walls from which there are fine views of the rich agricultural farm land
which surrounds the town, famous for its wine (notably the white *Vernaccia*)
which was already renowned in the 14C. The countryside nearby is remarkably
unspoilt and exploring the by-roads at random can be particularly rewarding.

Practical information

Information office. *APT*, 1 Piazza Duomo (☎ 0577-940008).

Getting there

By car. The quickest route from Florence is via the superstrada, taking the exit for *Poggibonsi*, but a slower and more attractive route is via the Via Cassia.

By bus. There is a frequent service from Florence to Poggibonsi in 50mins (run by *SITA*), and from there services to San Gimignano run by *TRA-IN*.

By train. There are trains to Poggibonsi (on the line from Empoli to Siena, with some through trains from Florence). Frequent bus services from Poggibonsi station to San Gimignano.

Car parks outside the walls.

Hotels in the centre

★★★ *Bel Soggiorno*, 91 Via San Giovanni (☎ & fax 0577-940375); *La Cisterna*, 24 Piazza della Cisterna (☎ 0577-940328; fax 0577-942080); *Leon Bianco*, 13 Piazza della Cisterna (☎ 0577-941294; fax 0577-942123); *L'Antico Pozzo*, 87 Via San Matteo (☎ 0577-942014; fax 0577-942117).

Hotels in the environs

★★★ *Le Renaie* at Pancole, 6km north (☎ 0577-955044; fax 0577-955126) and *Pescille* at Pescille (☎ & fax 0577-940186).

Campsite ★ *Il Boschetto di Piemma*, 3km east at Santa Lucia (closed in winter; ☎ 0577-940352).

Youth hostel Ostello della Gioventù, 1 Via delle Fonti (☎ 0577-941991).

Numerous **rooms to let** and **accommodation in farmhouses**, offering agriturism. (information from Hotels Promotion in San Gimignano at Via San Giovanni, ☎ 0577-940809).

Restaurants

££: *Dorandò*, 2 Vicolo dell'Oro; *La Stella*, 75 Via San Matteo. Numerous trattorie and pizzerie on or near Via San Giovanni.

Beautiful places to **picnic** can be found in the surrounding countryside or near the Rocca behind the Collegiata.

History. The town derives its name from St Gimignano, a 4C bishop of Modena, traditionally venerated here. It was long known as San Gimignano delle belle Torri from the noble towers of its palaces, most of which were constructed in the 12C–13C. Thirteen still survive out of the 76 traditionally thought to have existed. The town has Etruscan origins and was later inhabited by the Romans. In medieval times it owed its prosperity to its situation on the Via Francigena, an important road for commerce and the main pilgrim route to Rome from northern and central Europe (see p. 423). Dante was sent here in 1299 as an ambassador of Florence to try and attach the smaller town to the Guelf League. After the devastation caused by the Black Death in 1348 San Gimignano came under the protection of Florence and there was an artistic revival in the 15C. However, the town declined commercially as a result of the deviation of the pilgrim route further northeast to the Elsa valley. The town suffered some damage in the Second World War.

CERTALDO

VIALE GARIBALDI

S. Agostino

VIA BAGNAIA

S. Iacopo

Porta S. Iacopo

PIAZZA
S. AGOSTINO

S. Pietro

V. CELLOLESE

Porta
S. Matteo

S. Chiara

VIA FOLGORE DA SAN GIMIGNANO

S. Girolamo

VIA VENTI SETTEMBRE

VIALE GARIBALDI

Palazzo
Tinacci

VIA DELLE FONTI

Porta
d. Fonti

VIA SAN MATTEO

VIA CAPASSI

VIA DELLE ROMITE

Fonti

Palazzo
Pesciolini

S. Bartolo

Palazzo d.
Cancelleria

VIA CAPASSI

VIALE DEI FOSSI

Torri
Salvucci

P.O.

Rocca

Collegiata

PIAZZA
DEL
DUOMO

Palazzo
d. Podesta

V. S. STEFANO

Museo
d'Arte Sacra

Pal. del
Popolo

i

S. Lorenzo
in Ponte

Ornithological
Museum

Museo
Civico

PIAZZA
DELLA
CISTERNA

VIA D. CASTELLO

Arco dei Becci

Palazzo Tortoli

Porta
Quercecchio

VIA DI QUERCECCHIO

VIA D. INNOCENTI

Palazzo
Pratellesi

VIA PIANDORNELLA

VIA S. GIOVANNI

VIALE DEI FOSSI

VIA BERIGNANO

S. Francesco

N

0   100 yards
0   100 metres

P

Porta
S. Giovanni

PIAZZA
MARTIRI DI
MONTE
MAGGIO

SAN GIMIGNANO

VOLTERRA, SIENA

The entrance to the town is through **Porta San Giovanni** (1262), the finest of
the town gates. Via San Giovanni, with a good view of the tall tower of Palazzo
del Popolo at the end, continues past the little Pisan-Romanesque façade of the
deconsecrated church of **San Francesco**. Beyond Palazzo Pratellesi (14C), now
the Biblioteca Comunale, is the **Arco dei Becci**, another ancient gate beside

several tall towers, forming part of the first circle of walls (12C). Beyond is the charming triangular **Piazza della Cisterna**, with a well dating from 1287. It is built on a slight slope and is surrounded by 13C–14C palaces, houses and towers (San Lorenzo, described on p. 393, is reached from here by Via del Castello).

Piazza del Duomo

An opening on the north side leads into **Piazza del Duomo**, another handsome medieval square with several spectacular towers. Opposite, above a flight of steps is the Collegiata. To the left is the crenellated **Palazzo del Popolo** with its loggia and massive tower; to the right is **Palazzo del Podestà** built in 1239 and enlarged a century later. Above the wide archway, which served as a passage for loading and unloading grain, rises the **Torre della Rognosa** rising to a height of 51m (in 1255 it was decreed that no tower was to exceed this height in order to diminish rivalry in tower building).

The Collegiata

■ **open** 09.30–12.30, 15.00–17.30. A ticket is required to visit the Capella di Santa Fina; a combined ticket which gives admission to all the town's museums is available.

The Romanesque Collegiata was solemnly consecrated by Pope Eugenius III in 1148 and enlarged in 1466–68 by Giuliano da Maiano.

The **interior** is decorated with important fresco cycles, which were scarred by war damage but are mainly well restored. Right-hand wall: the beautiful **New Testament cycle** composed of 22 episodes on three levels, representing the *Life* and *Passion of Christ* with a large *Crucifixion* scene in the fifth bay, is one of the great works of Italian Gothic painting. For long attributed to Barna da Siena (c 1381) and Giovanni d'Asciano, they are now thought to have been executed in 1333–41 by a master from the workshop of Simone Martini; possibly Lippo Memmi assisted by Federico Memmi and Donato Martini.

Left-hand wall: the **Old Testament cycle**, again on three levels, comprising 26 episodes from the *Book of Genesis*, and relating to Noah, Abraham, Joseph, Moses and Job, are signed and dated 1367 by Bartolo di Fredi. On the west wall are the *Last Judgement, Paradise*, and *Hell* by Taddeo di Bartolo (c 1410), full of details that have re-emerged since they were cleaned in 1990. On pedestals flanking the west door are two fine wooden statues of the Virgin Annunciate and the Angel Gabriel by Jacopo della Quercia (1421) which were painted in 1426 by Martino di Bartolomeo.

The beautifully preserved Renaissance **Cappella di Santa Fina**, off the south aisle, was commissioned from Giuliano da Maiano (1468) to honour Fina, the patron saint of the town. The altar and marble shrine with exquisite bas-reliefs are by Benedetto da Maiano (1472–77). The frescoes decorating the vault and walls of the chapel are by Domenico Ghirlandaio (c 1475): (right lunette) *St Gregory announcing to Santa Fina her imminent death*, and the *miraculous flowering of violets on her wooden bed*; (left lunette) *Funeral of Santa Fina* accompanied by three miracles: the *healing of her nurse's paralysed hand*, the *blind choir boy's sight regained*, and the *ringing of the church bells by angels*. The *saints* and *prophets* are also by Ghirlandaio, possibly assisted by Sebastiano Mainardi. A very rare early 14C reliquary bust of gilded and painted leather decorated with coloured glass inlay, attributed to the Sienese sculptor Manno di Bandino, is preserved in the shrine.

Benedetto da Maiano also made the marble tabernacle over the **high altar**. The choir stalls, pulpit and lectern are by Antonio da Colle (1490) who also made the inlaid wooden door leading to the **sacristy**. In the sacristy are various paintings including a *Deposition* by Jacopo Ligozzi and another *Deposition* by Domenico Passignano both dating from the 1590s.

To the left of the church is an archway, with a niche above containing a statue of San Gimignano (1342), which leads into **Piazza Pecori**. Here, beneath an elegant loggia is the baptismal font by Girolamo di Cecco (1378) and a fresco of the *Annunciation* by Sebastiano Mainardi (1482). The *prophet* frescoed in the vault is by Lippo and Federico Memmi.

The Museo d'Arte Sacra

Also in the piazza is the entrance to the small Museo d'Arte Sacra, with paintings, sculptures, and liturgical objects mostly from the Collegiata, and an Etruscan collection (**open** daily in summer, 09.30–20.00; in winter 09.30–13.30, 14.30–16.30, except Mon).

In the little chapel on the **ground floor** are tomb-slabs, and other sculptural works and fragments. In the adjoining room are paintings by Fra Paolino, Tamagni, Matteo Rosselli, a few sinopie by Benozzo Gozzoli and some very fine **illuminated 14C choir books** by Niccolò di Ser Sozzo and Lippo Vanni.

First floor. In the room to the right is a detached fresco of the *Crucifixion and Saints* by Benozzo Gozzoli and a *Madonna and Child with Saints* (fresco and sinopia) by Tamagni. The room to the left contains a wooden figure of *Christ*, similar to the *Volto Santo* of Lucca, probably an early 13C Sienese work, and other sculptures including 14C polychrome wooden statues of the *Virgin* and *Angel Gabriel* (formerly in the Collegiata). A marble portrait bust of *Onofrio di Pietro* by Benedetto da Maiano, was commissioned by the Commune of San Gimignano in 1493 to honour this distinguished citizen and scholar. There is also a marble bust of the *Redeemer* by Pietro Torrigiani. In the next room is a *Madonna and Child* signed by Bartolo di Fredi, a red velvet antependium, with doves and the monogram of Christ embroidered in gold, made in Florence in 1449, and a wooden *Crucifix* by Benedetto da Maiano. There is also a collection of 15C–18C church silver, and a statue of *St Anthony Abbot* by Francesco di Valdambrino. In the Loggia is a small collection of Etruscan material excavated locally.

Behind the Collegiata is the ruined **Rocca**, forming part of the fortifications built by the Florentines from 1353, surrounded by a public garden and partly enclosed by old walls. The surviving tower commands a remarkable view of the town and of the countryside beyond. Steps lead down to Via Quercecchio (with a fine view of Colle Val d'Elsa, Casole d'Elsa, Radicondoli, and Monte Maggio in the distance). A small deconsecrated church now houses an **Ornithological Museum** (same ticket and admission times as the other museums, see p. 389).

Palazzo del Popolo (1288–1323), also called Palazzo Nuovo del Podestà overlooking Piazza del Duomo, which still serves as the town hall, was restored after War damage. The splendid tower, known as the Torre Grossa (54m) was begun in 1300. Under the loggia is a fresco of the *Madonna and Saints* by a 14C master.

The Museo Civico

A passageway leads into a pretty courtyard with fresco fragments (two by Sodoma) and an outdoor staircase, leading to the Museo Civico (**open** daily in summer, 09.30–19.30; in winter 09.30–13.30, 14.30–16.30, closed Mon, ☎ 0577-940008).

The **Sala del Consiglio**, where Dante is supposed to have delivered his appeal (see p. 387) contains a large fresco of the ***Maestà* by Lippo Memmi** (signed and dated 1317). This superb work, showing the Madonna enthroned beneath a canopy surrounded by angels and saints, with the podestà Mino de' Tolomei kneeling in adoration, recalls the famous work by Simone Martini in the Palazzo Pubblico in Siena. The fresco was subsequently enlarged in the mid-1350s by Bartolo di Fredi who added two saints on each side and Benozzo Gozzoli is known to have repainted and restored parts of the fresco in 1466. The other walls are decorated with Sienese frescoes of hunting and tournament scenes (late 13C) and, on the end wall, the people of San Gimignano swearing allegiance to Charles of Anjou (ante 1292).

The small adjoining room contains a fine polychrome marble bust of *Santa Fina* (c 1498) and a terracotta bust of *St Gregory*, both by Pietro Torrigiani.

The **chapel** has a fresco of the *Holy Trinity* by Pier Franceso Fiorentino, a *Pietà* with symbols of the Passion by a follower of Neri di Bicci, and a *Madonna and Child with five Saints* by Leonardo Malatesta da Pistoia (early 16C).

Stairs lead up to the **Pinacoteca**, with fine views over the town. In the **Camera del Podestà**, a small room off the stair landing (left), are charming frescoes of domestic scenes warning against the wiles of women, including *Aristotle ridden by Campaspe*, by Memmo di Filippuccio (early 14C). The fine reliquary bust of *St Ursula* in polychrome and gilded wood is by the Sienese sculptor Mariano d'Agnolo Romanelli (late 14C), and the painted terracotta bust of Beato Bartolo is attributed to Torrigiani.

The gallery (*Pinacoteca*) contains an important collection of Sienese and Florentine painting from the 13C–15C. Among the earlier works: a *Crucifix with Passion scenes* by Coppo di Marcovaldo, one of the masterpieces of 13C painting in Tuscany; another *Crucifix* attributed to the Maestro delle Clarisse (c 1280–85); a *Madonna and Child enthroned* (c 1280; damaged) by Guido da Siena. The group of 15C works includes a *Madonna and Saints* by Sebastiano Mainardi, a *Madonna of Humility worshipped by two Saints* with a charming predella (1466) by Benozzo Gozzoli, two large circular panels representing the *Annunciation*, early works by Filippino Lippi of 1482, a *Madonna in glory with Saints Gregory and Benedict in a landscape* (1512) by Pinturicchio, one of the artist's last works, a *Madonna and Child with four Saints* by Domenico di Michelino, and a *Madonna and Child with four Saints*, signed and dated 1466, by Benozzo Gozzoli.

Leading off the main hall are two small rooms containing: a *Crucifix* of the Sienese school (c 1290), polyptych of the *Madonna and Child with eight Saints* (c 1310) by Memmo di Filippuccio and female heads by Bartolo di Fredi. The reliquary tabernacle of *Santa Fina* is a charming work painted in brilliant colours on both sides with stories of her life and miracles (c 1402) by Lorenzo di Niccolò. Other paintings include a tondo with the Madonna and Child and two angels by Sebastiano Mainardi, a polyptych by Taddeo di Bartolo(1394), a *Madonna and Child, Saints and angels* by Neri di Bicci, and *St Gimignano*and stories from his life (from the high altar of the Collegiata) by Taddeo di Bartolo.

There is also a polyptych with the *Assumption and Saints* (c 1345) by Niccolò di Ser Sozzo, a polyptych of *San Giuliano* by the Master of 1419, and a triptych of *St Bartholomew* by Lorenzo di Niccolò(1401).

In the passage are various sculptural fragments and reliefs. The **Torre Grossa** (Great Tower) may be climbed for a splendid view.

Beyond the twin Salvucci Towers, the picturesque **Via San Matteo**, lined with medieval buildings, leads towards the 13C Porta San Matteo. It passes Palazzo della Cancelleria, the Romanesque façade of the church of San Bartolo and the 13C Pesciolini tower house, all grouped outside a double arch from an earlier circuit of walls, with Palazzo Tinacci just beyond.

Sant'Agostino

Inside the gate, Via Cellolese leads to **Sant'Agostino**, a large Latin-cross church with three apsidal chapels, consecrated in 1298. The entrance is by a side door. To the right of the main door is the **Cappella di San Bartolo** with the splendid tomb of Blessed Bartolo (1228–1300), another patron of San Gimignano. This elaborate monument was made by Benedetto da Maiano in 1495. It is set in a niche with a marble curtain drawn back on either side. The shrine is composed of an urn with reliefs of two flying angels, above which are the three Theological Virtues seated in niches. At the base of the shrine are three predella scenes representing episodes from the saint's life. Crowning the shrine is a roundel with a beautiful relief of the *Madonna and Child*, surrounded by cherubs and adored by two angels. On the left wall of the chapel are frescoes of *Saints Gimignano, Lucy, and Nicholas of Bari* by Sebastiano Mainardi, who also painted the four doctors of the Church in the vault.

On the **south wall** of the nave are a *Madonna and Child with eight Saints*, predella scenes and saints on the pilasters by Pier Francesco Fiorentino (1494); and above, a fresco of the *Pietà* by Vincenzo Tamagni. Beyond the side entrance, a fresco of *Christ and symbols of the Passion* by Bartolo di Fredi. The same artist also painted the frescoes (c 1374) in the **south apse** of scenes from the *Life of the Virgin* (*Nativity, Presentation in the Temple, Marriage of the Virgin*, and *Dormition*). Over the altar, is the *Nativity of the Virgin* with the donatrix and *St Anthony Abbot* on the right by Vincenzo Tamagni (1523).

The large altarpiece above the **high altar** depicting the *Coronation of the Virgin* worshipped by Fina, Augustine, Bartolo, Gimignano, Jerome, and Nicholas of Tolentino is signed and dated 1483 by Piero del Pollaiolo.

The **choir** is entirely covered with **frescoes by Benozzo Gozzoli** and assistants (1464–5) illustrating the *Life of St Augustine* from his childhood to his death, in 17 scenes on three levels, full of charming details.

The sequence begins on the left from below. **First row**: 1. *Augustine is sent to school in his native town Thagaste*; 2. *at nineteen he goes to Carthage university*; 3. St *Monica prays for her son* (repainted in the 18C); 4. *Augustine sails to Italy*; 5. *his arrival in Italy*; 6. *he studies rhetoric and philosophy in Rome*; 7. *his departure for Milan* (inscribed and dated 1465 by Benozzo Gozzoli who included his self-portrait in this scene—second figure on the right). **Second row**: 8. *Augustine is received by St Ambrose and the Emperor Theodosius*; 9. (left) *he listens to St Ambrose preaching*, (centre) *Monica implores the conversion of her son*, (right) *Augustine discusses Manichaeism with St Ambrose*; 10. *Augustine reads the Epistles* of St Paul; 11. he is baptised by St Ambrose; 12. (left) Augustine and the Infant Jesus on the seashore, (right) Augustine explains the rule to his monks, (centre) he visits the hermits at Montepisano; 13. death of his mother Monica. **Third row**: 14. Augustine, a consecrated bishop, blesses the people of Hippo; 15. he converts the heretic Fortunato; 16. Augustine in ecstasy is inspired by St Jerome; 17. Augustine's funeral. The vault and pilasters are decorated with evangelists and saints, by Gozzoli's workshop.

On the **north wall** is a Mystic marriage of St Catherine by Giovanni Balducci, and a Madonna and Child with Saints by Fra Paolino of Pistoia (1530). Beyond a door which leads into the sacristy and a pretty Renaissance **cloister**, is Sebastiano Mainardi's, fresco of St Gimignano blessing three dignitaries of the city (1487), above an effigy of Fra Domenico Strambi, the patron who commissioned the paintings for the high altar and choir. The marble relief, with four half-length bishops in roundels, has recently been identified as part of the original shrine of San Bartolo and attributed to Tino di Camaino (c 1318). Beyond is a fragmentary fresco of the Madonna delle Grazie by Lippo Memmi, a marble pulpit of 1524, a large fresco of St Sebastian interceding for the citizens of San Gimignano, painted by Benozzo Gozzoli in 1464 after the plague of that year, and a Deposition and Saints by Vincenzo Tamagni.

In Piazza Sant'Agostino is the Romanesque church of **San Pietro** which contains frescoes by Memmo di Filippuccio.

From Piazza della Cisterna (see above) Via del Castello leads down to the church of **San Lorenzo**, which has a Romanesque façade in brick (1240). Inside are frescoes by Cenni di Francesco who also frescoed the contiguous oratory (1413).

All the minor churches are of interest for their architecture or paintings (or both), but nearly all of them are kept locked. Especially noteworthy are **San Girolamo**, in Via. S. Gimignano, which has an altarpiece by Vincenzo Tamagni (1522), and nearby **San Jacopo**, a charming little Pisan-Romanesque building, which has frescoes by Lippo Memmi and Memmo di Filippuccio and an altarpiece representing St James by Pier Francesco Fiorentino.

Outside Porta delle Fonte, just to the south, is an arcaded medieval public fountain, known as **Le Fonti**.

Environs of San Gimignano

The **Pieve di Cellole**, one of the finest Romanesque churches of the Val d'Elsa, is reached from Porta San Matteo along the Certaldo road (left; signposted for Gambassi) and then the second turning right. This charming church, which gave Puccini the setting for his Suor Angelica, is situated on a hill (395m) among cypress trees. It was completed in 1238 and the **façade** of beautifully cut travertine blocks has a simple doorway decorated with two stylised capitals of different shape. Above the lunette is an elegant two-light window.

Interior. Broad stone columns with stylised capitals, support the arches separating the nave from the aisles. The apse is decorated with blind arches and a narrow window. The hexagonal baptismal font is carved out of a single block of travertine. In the sacristy are two altarpieces (c 1500) and an impressive life-size Crucifix of polychrome wood. An Etruscan necropolis has been excavated in the area.

... the pretty road to Poggibonsi is the **Villa di Pietrafitta** reached by an unsurfaced road which winds steeply up along a cypress avenue. The villa, which once belonged to Cardinal Mazarin, has been extensively altered over the centuries. There is a small octagonal chapel next to the house dated 1584. The view extends over vineyards and olive groves to the surrounding hills.

29 · Colle di Val d'Elsa and environs

Colle di Val d'Elsa is a small town built high up on a rocky spur on the left bank of the river Elsa. Although less well known than many other small towns in Tuscany, it is a delightful place with many interesting art treasures. The medieval upper town is particularly well preserved and its position offers magnificent views on all sides. The environs of Colle are also well worth visiting: Badia a Coneo, Casole d'Elsa, Mensano, Radicondoli, Monteriggioni and Abbadia Isola.

Practical information

Information office 43 Via Campana (☎ 0577-922791, fax 0577-922621) Apr–Oct 09.30–13.30, 15.30–19.00, Nov–Mar 10.00–13.00, 15.30–17.30 (closed Sun). *Pro-Loco*: 5 Piazza Arnolfo (☎ 0577-920389).

Getting there

By car. Colle can be reached by road direct from Florence by the *superstrada* to the exit *Colle Val d'Elsa Nord* which is 3km from the town centre. **Car park** beneath the walls with a flight of steps to the upper town.

By bus. From Florence via Poggibonsi in 1hr (run by *SITA*).

By rail. Train services to Poggibonsi (on the line from Empoli to Siena, with some through trains from Florence). Frequent bus services from Poggibonsi station to Colle Val d'Elsa.

Hotels

Colle di Val d'Elsa. ★★★ *Villa Belvedere* (☎ 0577-920966, fax 924128), with restaurant. 2km outside the town at **località Belvedere**; *La Vecchia Cartiera*, 5 Via Oberdan (☎ 0577-921207; fax 0577-923688).
Casole d'Elsa. ★★★★ *Relais La Suvera*, at Pievescola (☎ 0577-960300; fax 0577 960220).
Monteriggioni (località Strove): ★★★★ *Residence San Luigi* (☎ 0577-301055; fax 0577-301167); ★★★ *Casalta* (☎ 0577-301002), both with restaurant.
Near **Poggibonsi**: ★★★ hotel *Europa* on the Via Senese at Calcinaia, 2km south (☎ 0577-933402; fax 0577-936069).

Restaurants and cafés

Colle di Val d'Elsa: ££ *L'Antica Trattoria*, 23 Piazza Arnolfo di Cambio and *Arnolfo*, 2 Piazza Santa Caterina. Café: *Lido*, 4 Piazza Santa Caterina, for ice-creams.
Monteriggioni: ££ *Il Pozzo*; restaurants in the hotel *San Luigi* and hotel *Casalta* at Strove; ££ *Il Piccolo Castello* at Castello di Monteriggioni.
Poggibonsi: £ *Italia*, 34 Via Trento and *La Galleria*, 20 Galleria Cavalieri di Vittorio Veneto.

Annual festivals. Summer festival at Radicondoli, with concerts.

History. In the Middle Ages the exploitation of the river Elsa through a system of canals gave rise to flourishing wool and paper industries. In the 12C Colle was an independent commune. It was repeatedly disputed between Siena and Florence: at the **Battle of Colle**, which was fought on the plain below the town in 1269, the Florentines routed the Sienese, thereby avenging the terrible Battle of Montaperti of 1260. Provenzano Salvani, the valiant veteran of Montaperti, but hated nephew of Sapa (Dante, *Divina Commedia, Purgatorio*, xiii, 100–138), met his end here. The town eventually came under Florentine dominion in 1333. Colle received the title of city in 1592. It is also associated with the manufacture of glass which is still produced here, employing over 800 people. Arnolfo di Cambio (1232–1302), the famous sculptor and architect who built Palazzo Vecchio in Florence was born here.

The Volterra road passes beneath the walls beside a car park, from which a short flight of steps leads to the **Upper Town** (or *Colle Alto*), divided into two districts: *Borgo Santa Caterina* to the west and the *Castello*, the oldest part, to the east. A street runs along a parapet at the back of the houses following the horse-shoe shape of the hill, with a fine view of the valley and countryside beyond.

San Francesco

To the right, across the slopes of the public gardens, is an old stone bridge with irregular arches which leads to the **monastery of San Francesco** from which there is a fine view of the upper town. The adjacent **church**, founded in 1229, is one of the earliest Franciscan churches in Tuscany. It has a Romanesque façade in sandstone with brick mouldings decorating the two-light window above the doorway.

To the left is the entrance to the **monastery** (now a Seminary; ring the bell for admission), with a fine Renaissance **cloister**. It has some interesting frescoes: a charming *Madonna and Child* enthroned by Ghirlandaio's workshop and fresco fragments by an artist similar in style to Duccio.

From the cloister one enters the church, which was rebuilt inside in the 17C–18C. The nave is decorated with elegant plasterwork and its large windows mean that it is full of light. Over the high altar is a polyptych, signed and dated 1479 by Sano di Pietro. It shows the *Madonna and Child enthroned with Saints Benedict, Cyrinus, Donatus, and Justina*; and the *Annunciation* above. Behind the altar is an early 16C Florentine *Crucifix*. The frame also includes saints on the pilasters and predella scenes. There are various fresco fragments which have emerged from under the 18C decoration, including a 14C *Madonna and Child with an apostle* (on the first altar to the right of the main entrance) which has been attributed to Cennino Cennini. On the next altar is a copy of the altarpiece of *St Francis* in Santa Croce in Florence. The *Concert of Angels* is a fragment of a larger work by Astolfo Petrazzi. The Baroque tomb of the organist Antonio Giacobbi is dated 1740. The *Madonna and Child appearing to St Philip Neri* is by Simone Pignoni.

Borgo Santa Caterina

Via di San Francesco leads into Borgo Santa Caterina, the western district of the old town, past a squat, circular brick tower (once a fresh water cistern). To the right is the **Porta Nuova**, an impressive gateway attributed to Giuliano da

Sangallo. It has two powerful round towers and battlements on the outside. From here the main street, **Via Gracco del Secco**, leads towards the upper town past numerous interesting medieval and Renaissance houses. Opposite the hospital of San Lorenzo is the 17C church of **San Pietro** which has an *Assumption* by Pier Dandinion the main altar. The restored conservatory here is used for exhibitions. In a little piazza on the left is the church of **Santa Caterina** inside which is a fine stained glass window representing *St Catherine*, attributed to Sebastiano Mainardi. The adjacent oratory has an impressive group of lifesize figures in painted terracotta, representing the *Lamentation* by Zaccaria Zacchi (early 16C). Via Campana continues past (left) **Palazzo del Municipio** with the Medici arms, to a splendid **bridge** (originally a drawbridge), with a fine panorama on either side. The bridge links Borgo Santa Caterina to the Castello, the eastern (and oldest) district of the upper town, which has very beautiful paving (carefully restored a few years ago).

At the far end of the bridge the road passes beneath an archway incorporated in the fine **Palazzo Campana** (1539) by Giuliano di Baccio d'Agnolo, a stately building with handsome windows, and continues past several picturesque medieval houses.

The Castello

In the pretty **Piazza del Duomo** (which retains its herringbone brick paving) is **Palazzo Pretorio** (1335), decorated with coats of arms. It has recently been restored to house the Museo Archeologico 'R.Bianchi Bandinelli'.

Open April–Sept, Tues–Fri 10.00–12.00, 17.00–19.00; Sat & fest. 10.00–12.00, 16.30–19.30; closed Mon; winter: Tues–Fri 15.30–17.30; Sat & fest. 10.00–12.00, 15.30–18.30; closed Mon.

Remains of 15C–16C frescoes discovered under whitewash inside include an *Annunciation* by Giovanni Maria Tolosani (1514) and coats of arms by Pier Francesco Fiorentino. The museum has a section of Etruscan pottery and bronze objects excavated in the Elsa valley, and other material dating from prehistoric to medieval times. Also exhibited here are the sculptures and ceramics formerly in the *Museo Civico e d'Arte Sacra*. There is a fine well-head with reliefs illustrating rural scenes, and capitals and others Romanesque fragments.

The **Terrosi Collection**, acquired in 1971 and arranged on the first floor, contains fine vases and other objects discovered in the Calisna Sepu tomb, one of the most important Etruscan necropoli of the Hellenistic period.

On the second floor is a section devoted to excavations in the area over the last few decades. The most important finds, dating from the archaic period, come from the Pierini tomb. There is a large quantity of material from the later Hellenistic period, including a collection of cinerary urns from the necropolis of Le Ville.

Duomo

The Duomo was originally Romanesque, as can be seen from the series of blind arcades along its north flank. It was rebuilt in 1603–19 and the façade was completed in 1815. The cathedral was restored inside and out in 1992 to celebrate the city's 400th anniversary. The fine campanile (unfinished) dates from the early 17C.

The elegant and dignified **interior** has a Latin-cross plan. In the nave is a marble pulpit, resting on earlier capitals and supporting columns, decorated with bas-reliefs dated 1465 which are attributed to Giuliano da Maiano.

The altarpieces in the chapels along the nave form an interesting selection of 17C painting. **South side, first chapel**: *Miracle of the St Marziale* and side paintings by Giovanni Paolo Melchiorri (1694); **second chapel**: *Adoration of the Magi* by Vincenzo Dandini (1673), *Baptism of Christ* and *Marriage at Cana* by Deifebo Burbarini; **fourth chapel**: *Nativity* (1635) by Rutilio Manetti, *Conversion of St Paul and Martyrdom of St Peter* by Astolfo Petrazzi. In the **south transept**, behind a wrought-iron railing, is the **Cappella del Santo Chiodo** (Holy Nail) which was built by Pius II for the relic of one of the nails supposed to have been used at the *Crucifixion*. The marble tabernacle is attributed to Mino da Fiesole and the bronze lectern with a palm branch and eagle is by Pietro Tacca. Hanging on the transept wall, to the left of the chapel, is a *Nativity* by Francesco Poppi (1567).

Over the **high altar** is a bronze *Crucifix*, which was presented to the cathedral by the Grand-duchess Maria Maddalena of Austria in 1629. It was designed by Giambologna and cast after his death by Pietro Tacca.

In the **north transept** is the **Chapel of the Holy Sacrament** which has a fine altarpiece of the *Last Supper* by Ottavio Vannini, signed and dated 1636. In the adjacent **baptistery** is an *Annunciation* by Cosimo Gamberucci (1618).

North side. **Fourth chapel**, *Resurrection*, the *Immaculate Conception*, and *Madonna and Child with Saints* by Filippo Tarchiani (1635–42); **third chapel**, *St Gregory interceding for the plague-stricken in Rome* (1643) by Niccolò Tornioli and side paintings of saints by Giovanni Rosi; **second chapel**, *Ascension, Noli me tangere*, and *Doubting Thomas* by Giuseppe Chiari; **first chapel**, *Marriage of the Virgin* by Giovanni Odazzi and *Dream of St Joseph* and *Flight into Egypt* by Paolo de' Matteis.

Also in Piazza del Duomo is **Palazzo Vescovile**, which has a room decorated with frescoes by Bartolo di Fredi. Via di Castello continues alongside the palace, past a large tabernacle on the corner.

Museo Civico d'Arte Sacra

This is next to the former **Palazzo dei Priori**, the façade of which is decorated with graffiti. An outside stairway here leads leads up to the **Museo Civico e d'Arte Sacra**. This interesting little collection with objects from all periods is arranged in three rooms (**open** Apr–Oct 10.00–12.00, 16.00–19.00 except Mon; winter Sat & fest. only 10.00–12.00, 15.30–18.30).

Room 1. Girolamo Genga, *Madonna and Child*; 16C–17C paintings by Bachiacca, Giovanni Battista Naldini, Francesco Rosselli, and Francesco and Giovanni Brini. The *Pietà* by Cigoli is a particularly good example of the artist's work. The Medici coat of arms was painted by Poppi. The marble bust of Lorenzo Usimbardi is attributed to Felice Palma or Ferdinando Tacca. Also here, *St Sylvester baptising the Emperor Constantine* by Giovanni Antonio Galli, called *Lo Spadarino*, and *St Cecilia* by Mario Balassi. In the centre of the room are displayed local 19C paintings by Niccolò Cannicci, Antonio Salvetti, Vittorio Meoni and Ferruccio Manganelli.

Room 2 contains earlier paintings. 15C–16C works by Ventura di Moro, Giovan Maria Tolosani (a follower of Ghirlandaio), and Pier Francesco Fiorentino . The beautiful *★Maestà* is attributed to the so-called Master of Badia a Isola, a late 13C or early 14C painter very close to Duccio. It comes from the Abbadia Isola (see p. 402). The *Madonna and Child* by Segna di Bonaventura is another precious early work of the same period. The *Birth of the Virgin* is by the local 15C painter Cennino Cennini, and the remarkable polychrome wood *Crucifix* (the arms are missing) is by Marco Romano (late 13C or early 14C). The early 16C fresco of the *Adoration of the Magi* from a tabernacle in Colle is by Giovan Maria Tolosani. Also displayed here are illuminated choirbooks once used in the cathedral.

Room 3. Here are assembled a miscellany of works. The *****treasury of Galognano** is composed of four rare silver chalices in four different sizes and a patten, thought to date from the late 6C AD, found in a field near Colle in 1963. The two cases of 14C–19C liturgical objects include a 15C chalice and patten decorated with enamels from Colle cathedral. The 17C works include paintings by Pier Dandini, and a wooden horse's head. At the end of the room is an altarpiece of the *Madonna and Saints* by Simone Ferri (1581) and frescoes by Francesco Rosselli. Also displayed here are a 15C Sienese reliquary of the arm of St Philip Apostle, a carved wooden head of *St John the Baptist*, attributed to the circle of Giambologna, and an *Ecce Homo* by the della Robbia workshop. The large 19C paintings are by Antonio Salvetti, Antonio Puccinelli, and Gennaro Landi.

Opposite the museum is the **Teatro dei Varii**, in a 14C building, formerly the seat of the *Accademia dei Varii*, a literary and theatrical society. The theatre was built to a design by Antonio Galli Bibiena (1760) and reconstructed in 1826. In 1926 Antonio Salvetti restored the façade which has a loggia. The little theatre, which seats just over 200 people, was restored and reopened in 1991.

The street broadens into a charming small square. On the right is the Romanesque church of **Santa Maria in Canonica** with a simple bell-tower. The stone façade has a rose-window and decoration in brick, with small blind arches under the roof. The **interior**, altered in the 17C, has a large tabernacle of the *Madonna and Child with Saints* by Pier Francesco Fiorentino.

At the end of the street are more interesting medieval houses and the **Tower-house of Arnolfo** dating from the early 13C. A long vaulted alley (**Via delle Volte**) returns from here towards Palazzo Campana and the former drawbridge through the oldest part of the town.

The lower town

From a small street to the right a steep footpath (La Costa) paved with bricks descends to the lower town. It meets Via Garibaldi at the Quattro Cantoni onto which face the four fine palaces of the Beltramini–Palazzuoli, Tommasi, and Sabolini families. In a niche on Palazzo Beltramini is a marble relief of the *Madonna and Child* attributed to Tommaso Fiamberti.

Sant'Agostino

An archway leads to the church of Sant'Agostino. The façade (unfinished) dates from the 13C but the bell-tower is modern. The **interior** has beautiful proportions, with columns separating the nave from the aisles. It was rebuilt by Antonio da Sangallo il Vecchio (1521). **South aisle**: *Immaculate Conception* by Francesco Curradi, *Madonna and Child* by Taddeo di Bartolo, *Deposition with Saints* by Ridolfo del Ghirlandaio (1518), *Martyrdom of St Catherine* by Giovanni Battista Pozzo(1589).

In the **Cappella Bertini** (1598), to the right of the choir, is a very fine *Pietà* with *Saints* by Lodovico Cardi, called Il Cigoli, and also a *Nativity* by Giuliano Biagi (1591), and marble busts of *Cosimo I* by Francesco Bordoni, and *Francesco Bertini* by Giovan Battista Caccini. In the **north aisle**, *St Andrew and other Saints worshipped by the donor Andrea Albertani* by Giovan Battista Paggi (1586), and a fresco of the *Pietà with Saints Anthony and Francis*, in a 17C silver frame, known as the '*Madonna di Piano*', surrounded by a marble tabernacle attributed to Baccio da Montelupo

Beyond the church is the chimney of a former glass factory and a 15C paper factory (now a hotel). The attractive main square, **Piazza Arnolfo**, has an obelisk-like War Memorial at the centre, porticoes on two sides and the obsolete railway station at one end. To the northeast is the Banca del Lavoro, a modern building in orange-painted steel and glass by Giovanni Michelucci. Beyond the former railway station, in Via di Spugna, is the **Cappella del Renaio**, with a Giottesque fresco of the *Pietà* over the altar, and, opposite, the 10C church of **Santa Maria a Spugna**, which has a Romanesque façade. Behind the church is the river Elsa, with remains of the Ponte di Arnolfo and a view towards the former Abbey of San Salvatore, now transformed into a farmhouse.

Environs of Colle di Val d'Elsa

On the Volterra road (which passes the impressive Porta Nuova, described above) is the pretty little Renaissance church of **Le Grazie**. The round window on the façade is surrounded by a glazed terracotta garland. The interior has frescoes by Giovanni Maria Tolosani. To the right of the church is a small cloister built of brick.

At the crossroads for San Gimignano on the right, the road to the left towards Casole d'Elsa has a turning to the right for **Badia a Conéo** (open for Mass on Sun at 09.15, or on request), in a beautiful position with panoramic views. This superb 12C Romanesque **church**, once part of a Vallombrosan abbey suppressed in the 16C, combines grandeur and simplicity. Entirely built in light grey stone, it has a plain **façade** with four blind arches and half-columns and two capitals decorated with foliate and animal motifs. The exterior of the apse has blind arcading with small stylised human heads. A wide arch to the right opens on to a courtyard with picturesque farm buildings on the site of the former cloister.

The beautiful **interior**, entirely faced with stone, has a Latin-cross plan with a single nave and three apses, of which only the central apse is visible from the outside. Over the crossing is a dome. The transept and apse are vaulted, while the nave has a timber roof. A transversal arch divides the nave from the transept; another arch has carved capitals. The apse is decorated with small blind arches and carved capitals.

Casole d'Elsa

In pretty countryside further south is the old hill town of Casole d'Elsa (417m) still partially enclosed by its medieval walls. The fortifications were reinforced by the Sienese in the 15C, allegedly by Francesco di Giorgio, who is also believed to have remodelled the Palazzo Pretorio and the Rocca. The town suffered considerably from bombing in the Second World War.

The Romanesque **Collegiata**, which was rebuilt in the later 15C and again in the last century, has been painstakingly restored after war damage. On the arch over the choir, which is divided into five chapels framed by Gothic arches, are remains of 14C frescoes of the *Last Judgement* attributed to Giacomo di Mino del Pellicciaio. To the left of the side entrance is the baptismal font over which is a small statue of the *Baptist* (1485). Along the right wall of the nave are a terracotta relief of the *Nativity* by Benedetto and Santi Buglioni, the tomb of Bishop Tommaso Andrei (d. 1303) by Gano da Siena, and several altarpieces (well labelled). In the south transept is a *Madonna and Child with four standing Saints* by Girolamo del Pacchia. The last chapel to the left of the choir has 15C Florentine frescoes on the vault. In the north transept is a large detached fresco lunette of the *Madonna and Child enthroned with angels* by a close follower of Duccio.

A door leads to a large chapel known as the **Chiesa di Santa Croce**, which has a number of paintings including (flanking the altar) the *Virgin annunciate and angel Gabriel* by Rutilio Manetti. In the nave, against the north wall is the fine cenotaph of Ranieri del Porrina (d. 1315), by Marco Romano, with a full length effigy in a marble niche and two beautiful figures of *Virtues*. Steps lead down to the crypt with remains of the earlier church. The other altarpieces in the nave include the *Immaculate Conception and two Saints* by Amos Cassioli, and *St Augustine washing Christ's feet* by Rutilio Manetti.

To the right of the church is the **Canonica**, an interesting structure in stone and brick, with remains of a cloister, dating from c1500. It is now the **Museo Archeologico e della Collegiata** (open daily except Mon 10.00–12.00, 16.00–19.00; winter: weekdays 15.00–18.00; fest. 10.00–12.00, 15.00–18.00). The collection includes: a *Maestà with Bishop Ranieri of Cremona and his brother Messer Porrina Aringhieri, Lord of Casole*, a detached fresco of the early 14C by a close follower of Duccio; *Madonna and Child* attributed to Segna di Bonaventura; a triptych by the Master of Sant'Ansano; *Madonna and Child enthroned and Saints and angels* by Andrea di Niccolò (1498), *Visitation* by Girolamo del Pacchia, *Madonna and Child and Saints* (detached fresco) by Giacomo Pacchiarotti (1520); a ciborium by Alessandro Casolani; and illuminated manuscripts and liturgical objects. An archaeological section comprises finds from excavations of necropoli in the neighbourhood dating from the 4C BC and later.

Via Casolani passes the 14C **Palazzo Pretorio** (right), alleged to have been redesigned by Francesco di Giorgio Martini in 1487. It now houses the **Antiquarium Comunale** (open Sat and Sun 11.00–13.00, or by appointment) which contains finds, mostly Etruscan, from excavations in the neighbouring district. The 14C **Rocca** dominates the far end of the little town, overlooking an extensive landscape, with hills in the distance. On the outskirts of Casole, on a hillock, is the little Romanesque church of **San Niccolò** next to the cemetery. The frescoes inside are by Alessandro Casolani and Francesco Rustici.

Farther south is the little village of **Mensano** (499m) with its walls and castle still in part extant. The 12C Romanesque church of **San Giovanni Battista** has a simple oblique façade with an oculus and a fine portal. The noble interior (restored in the 1950s) has a basilican plan with impressive monolithic stone columns dividing the nave from the aisles, and three apses. The lovely capitals, unusually large in size, and carved with an intricate assemblage of acanthus and other leaves, heads and fantastic animals, are by Bonamico, whose name is carved on a marble slab on the left side of the altar.

Still farther south, beyond Casone, in a beautiful position (509m), is **Radicondoli**. This little town preserves parts of its medieval fortifications, as well as picturesque streets and a few Renaissance palaces. The 16C **Collegiata** has a very fine altarpiece of the *Assumption and Nativity* by Pietro di Domenico and a *Madonna* attributed to Niccolò di Ser Sozzo in a side chapel. The cemetery has a late 12C funerary chapel (the **Pieve Vecchia**) dedicated to San Simone. It has a Latin-cross plan with a single apse and a projecting transept. In the interior brick and stone are used to obtain a decorative effect. It contains some interesting pre-Romanesque carving.

There is an annual summer festival at Radicondoli, during which concerts and theatre performances are held in the cloister of the Convento dell' Osservanza.

Poggibonsi

North of Colle di Val d'Elsa is Poggibonsi, an unattractive commercial town of 25,000 inhabitants which has developed considerably since the last War (with furniture manufactories). Excavations have ascertained the existence of a village on this site from the 6C until the early 10C. Fortifications were built in the 12C by the Conti Guidi, thus creating the foundations of *Podium Bonizi*, which developed into a small town in the early 13C, soon to be destroyed by the Florentines. By the 13C the town was no longer governed by a feudal system but a free Commune and grew rapidly thanks also to its position on the Via Francigena. In 1220 it was granted the title of Imperial city by Frederick II.

Little remains of the old town except for the restored church of **San Lorenzo** in Piazza Savonarola which has a 14C *Crucifix* attributed to Giovanni d'Agostino. The Gothic **Palazzo Pretorio**, on the corner of Via Repubblica beside a crenellated medieval tower, has coats of arms on the façade. The **Collegiata**, opposite, rebuilt in 1860, has a marble baptismal font of 1341 and, in the apse, a painting of the *Resurrection*, attributed to Vincenzo Tamagni. Dominating the town on a hill is the castle of **Poggio Imperiale** begun in 1488 for Lorenzo il Magnifico by Giuliano da Sangallo and continued by Antonio da Sangallo il Vecchio in the first half of the 16C. From the Colle Val d'Elsa road it is possible to get a good view of the fortifications and of parts of the medieval walls. At the foot of the steep hill is a fountain known as the **Fonte delle Fate**, beneath an arched portico dating from the 13C.

South of Poggibonsi a by-road leads uphill to the monastery of **San Lucchese**, rebuilt and enlarged in the 14C (and damaged in the last War). Parts of the original Romanesque church are visible in the façade and along the left side. The plan follows the style of early Franciscan churches with a nave and three apsidal chapels . On the right wall is a copy of a *Noli me Tangere* by Raffaellino del Garbo (destroyed in the Second World War), a fresco of the *Madonna and Child with Saints* of the Sienese school and another fresco by Bartolo di Fredi of the *Martyrdom of St Andrew*. A door opens onto the cloister with 16C frescoes depicting the story of *St Lucchese*, a holy layman (d. 1260) who spent his life helping the poor. In the sacristy is a 14C cupboard decorated with painted figures of apostles and saints by Memmo di Filippuccio. The apse window is by Rodolfo Margheri (1945). To the left of the transept above the arch of the Chapel of San Lucchese are frescoes (1388) illustrating the *Life of St Stephen* by the Master of San Lucchese who has recently been identified with Cennino Cennini. On the left wall of the transept, *Miracle of St Lucchese* by an anonymous 14C painter. The vault and walls of the chapel were frescoed in the 19C. On the left of the nave is another frescoed lunette with *St Nicholas of Bari* by Bartolo di Fredi and a large della Robbia polyptych dated 1514. From outside the church is a fine view of the surrounding countryside.

To the east of Poggibonsi is **Luco** a picturesque little village and the nearby 14C Castle of **Strozzavolpe** (open on the third Sunday in October for the festival of San Luco). Situated in a romantic position above a deep gorge, it is enclosed by high defence walls with a drawbridge beneath a tall square tower. The view embraces Siena, San Gimignano, and Castellina in Chianti. Nearby, on higher ground, is **Talciona** and the little Romanesque church of Santa Maria. It has an interesting carved relief of the *Magi* over the doorway, dated 1234.

On the Cassia road south of Poggibonsi, near Staggia, is a turning (left) for **La Magione**, a medieval hospice consisting of a charming group of buildings beside the small church of San Giovanni al Ponte (11C–12C). This is one of the best preserved of the many hospices for pilgrims which existed along the Via Francigena (see p. 423).

The little fortified town of **Staggia** still has several of its defence towers and ruined castle. Beside the Romanesque church of Santa Maria Assunta (restored) is a small **museum** (☎ 0577-930901 or ring at the priest's house for the key). It houses an important altarpiece by Antonio del Pollaiolo representing the *Communion of St Mary Magdalen*; a 14C Sienese *Madonna and Child*; and other paintings by Angelo Salimbeni and Giovanni Maria Butteri. There are some fresco fragments and liturgical objects.

Monteriggioni is a beautifully preserved medieval fortified village, built on a hillock. The circle of walls, dating from the 13C and the largest of its kind in Tuscany to have survived practically intact, has fourteen towers. Monteriggioni is mentioned by Dante: *Divina Commedia, Inferno*, xxxi, 41–44 '...*come in su la cerchia tonda Monteriggion di torri si corona* ('like Monteriggioni, whose round circle of walls are crowned with towers'). A main street crosses the village, joining the two gates. A few houses and a pretty Romanesque church face onto the piazza, and other houses surround a small public garden. Inside the walls are other private gardens.

A short distance west is the Cistercian abbey of San Salvatore founded in 1001, traditionally known as **Abbadia Isola** on account of its position in the middle of marshland. In the 14C it was fortified by the Sienese. A small village surrounds the abbey church. The church was largely rebuilt after the octagonal cupola collapsed in the 18C. The basilican **interior**, beautifully proportioned, has alternating piers and columns and three apses, with a simple crypt beneath the raised choir. Two detached fresco lunettes on the right of the nave are by Taddeo di Bartolo and Vincenzo Tamagni. On the left wall is a large fresco of the *Assumption* by Tamagni and a baptismal font with a carved relief, representing the *Baptism of Christ* (1419). The beautiful *Maestà* by the so-called Master of

Badia a Isola has been removed to the museum of Colle Val d'Elsa. The abbey is recorded in Bishop Sigeric's journey on the Via Francigena (see p. 423).

30 · San Galgano and environs

This wild, unspoilt area southwest of Siena has beautiful woods and river valleys. The ruined abbey of **San Galgano**, in the countryside a few kilometres northwest of Monticiano, with its grassy nave open to the sky is one of the most remarkable sites in Tuscany, and the chapel of San Galgano on the hill nearby is exceptionally interesting for its architecture. The little neighbouring villages of **Monticiano**, **San Lorenzo a Merse**, **Frosini**, and **Chiusdino**, although rarely visited, are particularly delightful.

■ Practical information

Information office APT Siena (☎ 0577-280551). Information office at the Comune of Chiusdino (☎ 0577-751055).

Getting there
By bus. Buses (several times a day) run by *TRA-IN* from Siena (Piazza San Domenico) to Massa Marittima via Palazzetto stop at San Galgano.

Hotels
Monticiano. ★★ *Da Vestro*, 4 Via Senese (☎ 0577-756618; fax 0577-756466). Near **San Lorenzo a Merse**, ★★★★ *Locanda del Ponte*, at Ponte a Macereto (☎ 0577-757108; fax 0577-757110).

Restaurants
Scalvaia. **£** *Osteria-pizzeria La Capanna*, at the entrance to the village (☎ 0577-759059). There is also a restaurant (**££**) at **Frosini**.

San Galgano

The ruined **Abbey of San Galgano** (**open** daily 08.00–12.00, 14.00–sunset) is situated between Chiusdino and Monticiano, in beautiful farming country southwest of Siena.

The abbey was built by the Cistercians of Casamari between c 1224–88, in honour of St Galgano who was canonised in 1185. Galgano Guidotti (1148–1181), a native of Chiusdino, of noble birth, decided to abandon a life of pleasure and become a Cistercian monk. He spent his last years living as a hermit on the hill of Monte Siepi where he built a little chapel.

The monastery became extremely powerful and the monks often ruled over disputes between cities such as Siena and Volterra; they also supervised the building of Siena cathedral. Subsequently there was a period of decline and corrupt administration. In the 16C the abbot sold the leading off the church roof which by 1786 had collapsed. The buildings were later abandoned and the church deconsecrated.

The **church** is a remarkable building modelled on the French Cistercian mother-house of Cîteaux. The façade, which remained unfinished, has three arched doorways separated by columns. The entrance to the church is on the right, past the chapter house and a fragment of the cloister. The roofless building, with a grass-grown nave, and a magnificent east end, is one of the most romantic sites in Tuscany. The majestic proportions of the structure and the effect of the windows framing the sky are particularly striking. There are remains of tracery in the smaller rose windows of the transept and in a few of the windows of the nave. The nave is divided by pillars with Gothic arches resting on finely carved capitals. The transept, forming a Latin-cross, is also divided by columns. The exterior of the apse and north flank of the church are built of beautifully cut regular stones, and one of the large gothic windows still preserves its carved mouldings. The little rectangular detached **cemetery chapel** also dates from the 13C.

The spacious **chapter house** is divided into two parts by low columns and has a fine vaulted ceiling and windows. On the upper floor are sixteen cells along the corridor and the monks' chapel.

On Monte Siepi (338m), the little hill above, is the circular **Chapel of San Galgano** (open, as above). It was built in 1182 over the tomb of St Galgano and is unique of its kind. The exterior is built in stone to a height of 4m and then in alternate bands of stone and brick. The **interior**, one of the few centrally planned churches in Tuscany, has a conical-shaped cupola, built of concentric rings of red brick and white travertine. The sword in the stone at the centre commemorates St Galgano's renunciation of knightly pursuits in favour of a life of prayer before the Cross.

A doorway leads into another chapel, added in the 14C, which has frescoes and *sinopie* by Ambrogio Lorenzetti and his workshop (c 1344). In the central lunette is the *Virgin in Majesty adored by Saints and angels* holding baskets of flowers, with the figure of Eve reclining in the foreground. Below, divided by the window, are the *Virgin* and angel *Gabriel*; it is interesting to note the differences in composition between the frescoes and sinopie, or underdrawings, which have been detached and hung on the adjacent wall. On the left wall are scenes from the *Life of St Galgano*: the saint conducted to Heaven and his vision of St Michael in Rome. In the vault are medallions with figures of prophets. There is a splendid view of the abbey from the hill.

Monticiano

To the southeast is the village of Monticiano, which came under Sienese dominion in the 13C. Although damaged in the Second World War, medieval houses survive above the former walls (there is a good view of them from the road leading south). In the piazza, above a flight of steps, is the Romanesque church of **Sant'Agostino**, with a façade in travertine and a fine doorway and oculus. Here is preserved the funerary urn of Blessed Antonio Patrizi (d. c 1311), an important figure in the Augustinian monastic movement in medieval Tuscany. The single-naved interior, re-decorated in the Baroque period, has a 14C frescoed polyptych of the *Madonna and Child with Saints*, and a damaged *Crucifixion*. On the left side of the nave is a painting of the *Death of the Blessed Antonio Patrizi* by Rutilio Manetti (c 1629).

Off the pretty cloister is the **chapter house** which houses a small **museum**. The collection includes an arched stained-glass window with *Christ on the cross between the Virgin and St John*, church silver, bells, vestments, reliquaries, illuminated choir-books and a few paintings. On the walls are interesting 15C frescoes by anonymous artists, including monochrome *Passion Scenes* silhouetted against a red ground, and a *Last Supper*. The *Madonna and Child enthroned between St Augustine and the Blessed Antonio Patrizi*, surmounted by the *Annunciation*, is attributed to a follower of Taddeo di Bartolo.

Farther uphill, in the older district, is the Romanesque church of **Santi Giusti e Clemente** dating from the 12C. The doorway is decorated with a motif of palmettes. Inside is a 14C Sienese *Crucifix*.

The Roccastrada road continues south past by-roads for **Luriano**, a group of farmhouses and villa, near which is a medieval mill, the **Molino della Pile**, and the village of **Scalvaia**. The area further south, in the province of Grosseto, is described in Ch. 20.

A pretty road winds east from Monticiano to join the superstrada between Siena and Grosseto passing **San Lorenzo a Merse**, a small village above the river Merse (rice is cultivated in the valley). The main street leads up to the Romanesque church which has a stone façade decorated with green marble, in the Sienese style. It has a timber roof and an apse pierced by a single lancet window. To the left of the church is a chapel, and beyond is the old castle in a panoramic position.

North of San Galgano is **Frosini**, a medieval castle transformed into a villa stands at the centre of this tiny village which has a pretty Romanesque church. From the public garden situated on a slope facing south there is a fine view of the surrounding countryside.

Chiusdino

West of San Galgano, in beautiful countryside with interesting old farmhouses, is Chiusdino, St Galgano's birthplace. It is a typical hilltop village (564m), with a cluster of grey stone houses on narrow steep and winding streets, often with steps and archways. The simple Romanesque parish church has been extensively modernised. Nearby, in a pretty little piazza, is the **Chapel of the Compagnia**, with a relief of *St Galgano* over the door by Urbano da Cortona dated 1466. Almost next door is **St Galgano's house**, with horizontal bands of brick decorating the façade, and the copy of another relief showing the saint in a wood by Giovanni d'Agostino. The original relief and a *Madonna and Child* by Niccolò di Segna of 1336, together with 12C–13C liturgical objects are kept in the nearby **Casa Parocchiale**. At 2 Via Mascagni is a small **museum** dedicated to the Cetine mines, with photographs, implements and objects relating to the mining industry in the metalliferous hills (☎ 0577-756738; and see Ch. 17).

31 · Montalcino and Sant'Antimo

Montalcino (567m) is a charming little walled town, about 45 km south of Siena, in a beautiful position above vines and olive groves, with a wide panorama of the surrounding countryside. It is famed for its red wine; the remarkable *Brunello*, which keeps well and can be matured for many years, is one of the choicest Tuscan wines, and considered by some experts to be among Italy's finest.

■ Practical information

Information offices. *Ufficio Turistico Comunale*, 8 Costa del Municipio (☎ & fax 0577-849331). *Pro-loco*, same address (☎ 0577-848242).

Getting there
By bus. Buses (*TRA-IN*) from Siena (Piazza San Dominico) via Buonconvento for Montalcino and Sant'Antimo.

Parking. Car parks outside the fortress or outside the walls.

Hotel
★★★ *Il Giglio*, 5 Via Soccorso Saloni, Montalcino (☎ 0577-848167).

Restaurants in Montalcino
££ *Il Moro*, Via Mazzini.
£ *Trattoria Sciame*, Via Ricasoli and £ *Osteria Porta al Cassero*, 9 Via della Libertà.

Restaurants in the environs
££ *La Taverna dei Barbi*, località I Barbi.
££ *Poggio Antico* at **Poggio Antico**.
£ *Trattoria Il Pozzo* at **Sant'Angelo in Colle**.

Annual festivals. A theatre festival is held in Montalcino in July. The *Sagra del Tordo*, on the last Sunday in October, features a bow and arrow competition, dancing and gastronomic regional specialities.

> **History**. This area was already inhabited in the Palaeolithic era and later there were Etruscan and Roman settlements, here. In the Middle Ages, Montalcino became a flourishing and independent town, but was repeatedly attacked by Siena and defended by Florence, finally succumbing to Sienese rule after the Battle of Montaperti in 1260. There followed a period of peace and prosperity and in 1462 Montalcino received the title of city from Pius II. After successfully resisting two sieges in 1526 and 1553, the town was forced to capitulate to Florence, despite a heroic defence lasting four years. In 1559 it became part of the Grand Duchy of Tuscany.

Although particularly famous for its *Brunello*, other excellent wines produced locally include the *Rosso di Montalcino*, and *Moscadello*, a sweet fizzy wine. It is also known for its traditional white-and-turquoise coloured pottery, and for its honey.

Montalcino is usually reached from Buonconvento (see Ch. 32), on the Cassia, the main road south from Siena. On the by-road, just outside Montalcino, above a hill on the right, is the church of the **Osservanza**, founded in the 15C. The interior, which was rebuilt in the 18C, has an early 14C *Crucifix* and a *St Bernardine* by Sano di Pietro. The road climbs steeply, passing under the impressive ramparts dominated by the Medici arms.

The town has numerous medieval houses with gardens and orchards, and steep streets offering picturesque views. The 14C Sienese **fortress** (open daily, except Mon 09.00–13.00, 14.00–20.00; in winter, 14.00–18.00) was provided with its notable ramparts by Cosimo I Medici in 1571. Inside the courtyard is the nave of a former church and, through an arch, a small garden with ilex trees. On the ground floor of the castle is an Enoteca, where it is possible to taste and buy the local wines. There are fine rooms on the upper floors and steps lead up to the towers and ramparts with a walkway from which there are magnificent views in all directions across the Orcia, Ombrone, and Asso valleys.

Via Ricasoli descends from the castle passing (left; No. 44) **Palazzo Pieri Nerli** which has a courtyard with a portico and well. On the right is the monastery of **Sant'Agostino**. The 14C church has a fine marble doorway and rose-window. The interior preserves many of its original 14C frescoes (very worn); those in the choir of the *Life of St Augustine* are by Bartolo di Fredi. The stained-glass windows are modern.

The Museo Civico e Diocesano d'Arte Sacra

To the right, in the cloister, is the Museo Civico e Diocesano d'Arte Sacra which has been beautifully rearranged and all the works restored (**open** daily except Mon, Jan–Mar 10.00–13.00, 14.00–16.00; Apr–Dec 10.00–l8.00). It comprises a small archaeological section from local excavations an important collection of 13C–16C Sienese painting and sculpture and a unique group of polychrome, wooden life-size figures.

The first room has many important works, mostly from the town hall or churches in the town. A magnificent polyptych, signed and dated 1388, by Bartolo di Fredi has been restored and reassembled; the central panel of the *Coronation of the Virgin surrounded by angels* is considered to be the artist's masterpiece. There are several almost life-size figures in polychrome wood including the *Virgin and Angel Gabriel* (1370) by Maestro Angelo and two *Crucifixes* by Angelo di Nalduccio. Another important sculptor, Francesco di Valdambrino is represented by a seated figure of *St Peter* and a *Crucifix*. There is also an *Annunciation* group by Domenico di Niccolò dei Cori.

The collection of gold ground paintings includes a triptych by a close follower of Duccio, a charming *Madonna and Child* by Luca di Tommè, other works by Bartolo di Fredi, a *Madonna and Child* by a master close to Ambrogio Lorenzetti, a *Madonna* by the Master of Panzano and a *Madonna and Child* seated in a rose garden by Sano di Pietro.

Another section displays works from churches in the neighbourhood, which had to be removed since they were no longer sufficiently protected. These include two panels of *St Peter* and *St Paul* by Ambrogio Lorenzetti from Sant' Angelo in Colle (see p. 410), an extremely refined *Madonna and Child with two angels* by Giovanni di Paolo from Rocca d'Orcia (see p. 425), a *Madonna and Child crowned by angels* by Vecchietta from Castiglione d'Orcia (see p. 425), a *Madonna and Child* by Guidoccio Cozzarelli from San Giovanni d'Asso and another *Madonna* by Marco Pino from Argiano.

Two of the earliest works in the museum come from the Abbey of Sant'Antimo (see below): a late 12C *Crucifix*, painted in tempera on wood, showing Christ with open eyes, and two volumes of an illustrated Bible with exquisite miniatures, dating from the second half of the 12C.

The section of 15C–16C paintings includes works by Benvenuto di Giovanni,Girolamo di Benvenuto , Riccio, and Vincenzo Tamagni.

There is also a statue of *St Sebastian* by Andrea della Robbia and a group of della Robbian reliefs, other sculptures, miniatures, liturgical objects and vestments, and a rare collection of local pottery, mostly jugs, dating from the 13C.

A steep street leads down from Sant'Agostino to the triangular Piazza del Popolo above which looms the tall narrow tower of **Palazzo dei Priori** (1292). Numerous coats of arms decorate the front and side of the palace and beneath is a portico with a statue of *Cosimo I* by Giovanni Berti (1564). Inside the palace, which preserves some frescoed and sculpted coats of arms, is an office which provides information about the local wines (**open** daily, except Mon, 10.00–13.00, 15.30–18.30). Also facing the piazza is a grandiose **Loggia**; the two first bays in stone date from the 14C, the four larger brick arches were built in the 15C. Opposite the loggia is an attractive, old-fashioned café.

To the right of Palazzo dei Priori, Via del Municipio leads into Piazza Garibaldi at the end of which is the church of **Sant'Egidio**. It contains a frescoed triptych by an artist close to Luca di Tommé, a *Madonna and Saints* by Francesco Cozza, and a painted *Crucifix* by Francesco di Valdambrino (c 1420).

Via Spagni leads uphill to the cathedral of **San Salvatore**, situated at the highest point of the town. It was built in 1818–32 by Agostino Fantastici to replace the Romanesque church. It has a grandiose brick portico and a spacious neo-classical interior with Ionic columns. The two altarpieces of the *Immaculate Conception* and *St John the Baptist* in the nave are by Francesco Vanni (1588). In the baptistery chapel are interesting reliefs from the Romanesque church representing *Christ and the symbols of the Evangelists*. In front of the church is a small piazza with a view over the town. Via Spagni continues downhill to the **Madonna del Soccorso**, a sanctuary built in the 17C on the site of an ancient chapel. The elegant travertine façade is by Francesco Paccagnini (1829). The Baroque high altar encloses a venerated image of the *Madonna*, possibly 14C. To the right is an *Assumption of the Virgin* by Vincenzo Tamagni. From the terrace next to the sanctuary there is a splendid view towards Siena.

Viale Roma descends along the outside of the walls to Piazza Cavour where there is a little public garden. Here the former hospital of **Santa Maria della Croce** founded in the 13C (now the Comune) still preserves parts of its original structure. The old pharmacy, inside the main entrance, has frescoes of the *Madonna enthroned, Saints Jerome and Augustine*, figures in niches, and trompe-l'oeil cupboards by Vincenzo Tamagni (1510), visible through a window.

Downhill from Piazza Cavour are pretty streets leading to an old mill and public fountain and wash-house. Uphill again is the church of **San Francesco**, in front of which is a terrace with fine views of the town.

The church retains its 14C façade and tall square tower. It has been deconsecrated and is now incorporated into the local hospital, together with the 16C cloister and the remaining monastic buildings. There are two small chapels frescoed with scenes from the *Life of the Virgin* by Tamagni (key from the porter).

From Piazza Cavour the Corso leads back to Piazza del Popolo.

East of Montalcino, on the Cassia, is **Torrenieri**, a small industrial town important in the past for the production of bricks. The castle, remains of which still survive, was a stopping-point on the Via Francigena (see p. 423) mentioned by Bishop Sigeric. The parish church has a small *Madonna and Child* by Domenico di Niccolò and a *Madonna and Child with Saints* by Francesco Bartalini.

Sant'Antimo

South of Montalcino is the picturesque village of **Castelnuovo dell'Abate**, overlooking the abbey church of Sant'Antimo.

Open daily 10.30–12.30, 15.00–18.00; Sun 09.15–10.45, 15.00–18.00. The times of the offices with Gregorian chant are indicated in the church

Abbey church of Sant'Antimo

(☎ 0577-835659). Organ concerts are held in the church in July and Aug.

One of the finest Romanesque religious buildings in Italy, it is in a beautiful setting in the Starcia valley, surrounded by olive groves and hills covered with ilex woods. The original abbey is said to have been founded by Charlemagne in 781, and as a Benedictine foundation it continued to enjoy the protection of the Holy Roman Emperor, as well as receiving Papal privileges. A period of decline began in the 13C, and the abbey was suppressed by Pius II in 1462 and placed under the jurisdiction of the bishop of Montalcino. The present church probably dates from the early 12C (the date 1118 is inscribed on a column of the ambulatory). The style combines French and Lombard elements.

The simple, lofty **façade** was never completed and was probably intended to have a double doorway. Originally, there was a portico supported on two columns resting on lions, which are now inside. The architrave over the doorway has stylised vine branches and other carved decoration. The exterior of the church is of monumental simplicity, its forms outlined by sequences of pilasters, corbels, and pierced openings. There are blind arches running along the nave under the roof. The prow-like choir gives an impression of compactness with its three beautiful apses. The decoration is subdued: two white columns with fine capitals linked by a row of carved corbels emphasise the curve of each apse. The bell-tower, which is divided into four storeys by a cornice and blind arches, is decorated with some stylised reliefs including a *Madonna and Child* on the east side. The stone varies in type and colour and the decorative effect is enhanced by some beautifully veined blocks. The older apse of the Carolingian chapel has an oculus at its base through which can be seen the 9C crypt, a small vaulted chamber with two apses facing each other and four columns, and a baptismal font let into the ground. There is a small finely carved doorway on the north side. The doorway on the south side is decorated with palmettes and interlaced bands beneath an architrave carved with eagles, gryphons, and monsters. Above, in the lunette, are the Sergardi arms and corbels with strange heads on either side.

Interior

The abbey has a basilican plan: the nave is supported on columns and four cruci-form piers, with an upper gallery and a clerestory above. A timber roof covers the nave, whereas the side aisles are vaulted. The aisles become narrower towards the east end, leading into an ambulatory, with three radiating chapels, a feature which is rarely found in Italian architecture. The interior is built of travertine of a particularly warm tonality, quarried locally. The luminous honey-coloured stone, and the numerous windows combine to create a wonderful, tranquil atmosphere. The light changes according to the season and the time of day, and the effect at sunset is particularly beautiful.

The sculptural decoration is of exceptionally high quality: the capitals of the nave present a variety of geometrical and leaf motifs. The finest is that of the second column on the right representing Daniel in the lions' den, which is now attributed to the Master of Cabestany, of French or Spanish origin. The sculptural decoration of the primitive church was subsequently adapted and re-used in some capitals of the ambulatory and gallery, or inserted into the outside walls.

The **gallery**, reached by a spiral staircase next to the sacristy, continues round the entire church. It was partially fitted up with rooms by the Bishop of Montalcino in the 15C one of which has a fireplace and wall paintings. Next to the entrance to the **sacristy** are carved pilasters from the Carolingian period and a stoup with two superimposed Romanesque capitals with the Piccolomini crescent in each corner. The sacristy occupies the primitive church or so-called **Carolingian chapel**, a small rectangular chapel with an apse (the vault was probably added later). It has a 15C cycle of grisaille frescoes of the *Life of St Benedict* by Giovanni di Asciano, and two anonymous 16C frescoes of *Christ on the Cross between Saints Anthony and Sebastian* and a *Pietà*.

The **ambulatory**, the design of which may have been borrowed from French prototypes, is supremely elegant and refined in every detail. There is great harmony in the play of light created by the columns, windows, vaults, and blind arches. Certain stones and the bases of some columns have been carved in onyx or alabaster instead of travertine and, when sunlight falls directly on them, they take on a translucent glow. Columns surround the high altar, on the steps of which is a long inscription referring to a benefactor, Count Bernardo, probably dating from the early 12C.

Over the altar is an impressive 13C painted *Crucifix*. The polychrome wooden statue of the *Madonna del Carmine* (Umbrian, c 1260), recently restored, is now exhibited in a glass case. To the right of the altar are steps leading down to a small rectangular crypt which has a barrel vault and a frescoed *Pietà*. At the foot of the bell-tower, at the north end of the ambulatory, is a small chapel with three niches, tall narrow pilasters in the corners, and three window openings. One of the bells is dated 1219.

Practically nothing remains of the monastic buildings or cloister, except for the well. The fine triple-arched window with cushion capitals, supposedly belonging to the chapter house, is pre-Romanesque.

A lovely road (partly unsurfaced) leads west from Sant'Antimo to **Sant'Angelo in Colle** (also reached by a direct road from Montalcino). This is an enchanting, well-preserved village on the top of a hill, still contained within its circle of walls. In the piazza at the centre is the Romanesque church of San Michele which has a *Madonna of the Rosary* by Francesco Rustici, dated 1625. There is a splendid view from the village across the Orcia valley towards Monte Amiata.

To the southwest is **Poggio alle Mura**, a former castle (now Villa Banfi) where a **Museo del Vetro** (open in summer 11.00–13.00. 15.30–19.00, in winter 10.00–13.00, 15.30–19.00) has been installed, which exhibits glass, together with a collection of farming implements.

32 · Asciano & Monte Oliveto Maggiore

Asciano is a delightful and interesting small town, with a good museum. **Monte Oliveto Maggiore**, one of the most important monasteries in Tuscany in a beautiful isolated position, is famous for its frescoes by Luca Signorelli and Sodoma. Both these places are approached from the Via Cassia, the old Roman road between Siena and Rome which runs through a remarkable landscape of bare clay hills known as *Le Crete*. Beneath their deeply eroded slopes are clusters of trees. There are relatively few scattered farmhouses and the crests of the hills are often marked by pines and cypresses.

This chapter also describes some lovely small villages including **Buonconvento**, whose museum has a fine collection of paintings, and **Murlo**, which has an interesting archeological collection.

■ Practical information

Information office. APT of **Siena** (☎ 0577-280551). **Asciano** information office, open in summer, 18 Corso Matteotti (☎ 0577-719510).

Getting there

By car. Asciano can be reached direct from Siena on the N438; an alternative approach is by the Cassia (N2) as far as Monteroni d'Arbia where a particularly beautiful by-road diverges east for Asciano. **Monte Oliveto Maggiore** can either by reached from Asciano or by another by-road from Buonconvento.

By bus. Buses run by *TRA-IN* from Siena (Piazza San Domenico) to Asciano and Buonconvento (with a few services to Monte Oliveto Maggiore).

By rail. The branch railway line (some trains are substituted by buses) from Siena to Chiusi has stations at Asciano and Rapolano Terme. Another branch line from Siena to Grosseto has stations at Isola d'Arbia, Monteroni d'Arbia and Buonconvento.

Hotels

Asciano: ★★★ *Il Bersagliere*, 41 Via Roma (☎ & fax 0577-718629). Accommodation is available at the abbey of **Monte Oliveto Maggiore** (☎ 0577-707017).
Buonconvento: ★★ *Roma*, 14 Via Soccini (☎ 0577-806021; fax 0577-807284).
Murlo: ★★★ *L'Albergo di Murlo*, Via Maritiri del Rigosecco, Vescovado (☎ 0577-814033; fax 0577-814243).
Rapolano Terme has four hotels.

Campsite: ★★★ *Le Soline* at Casciano di Murlo (☎ 0577-817410).

Restaurants

Near **Asciano**: ££ *Osteria della Pievina*, 5km northwest on the SS438 and at **Sante Marie** (7km north) £ *Da Ottorino*.
Near **Murlo** (8km south) at La Befa £ *Osteria La Befa*.

Asciano

Asciano is a little town in the *Crete* region southeast of Siena. The countryside here is particularly beautiful in spring, covered with yellow broom and red poppies. Access to the town is through the Porta dei Bianchi, but by car one should follow the road to the right, along the walls built by the Sienese in the 14C, to the gateway at the opposite end where there is a car park. There is a splendid view of the apse and tower of Sant'Agata from outside the walls.

The piazza within the walls is dominated by the façade of the collegiate church of **Sant'Agata**, rising above a flight of steps. The original church dates from the 11C but it was rebuilt and enlarged in the following centuries. The geometrical simplicity of the **exterior** enhances the beauty of the travertine stone. The façade probably dates from the later 14C, at the time of the transition between the Romanesque and Gothic styles. It is composed of three slender blind arches, forming a triumphal arch, above which is a large oculus with blind arcading along the roof, separated by a string-course that creates the effect of a pediment. The decoration is confined to the inner arch surrounding the doorway and to the capitals of the pilasters.

The **interior** is unique to the district: a Latin cross plan with a single nave, with two side apses leading off the transept and a larger central apse. Above the crossing is a hemispherical dome resting on a drum, decorated with small columns and corbels, which is supported by four large arches springing from the piers. At the summit is an elegant lantern. On the right of the nave is a fresco of the *Madonna and Child with St Michael, Tobias and the angel* by a follower of Sodoma, on the left is a *Pietà* by Riccio. A 15C *Crucifix* hangs over the altar.

To the left of the church is the **Oratorio di Santa Croce** where the remarkable collection of art treasures belonging to Asciano is temporarily exhibited, while the new **museum** in Casa Corboli is being completed. The Oratory is open on request (tourist office in Corso Matteotti nearby).

This small collection contains several masterpieces of Sienese art. There is a large altarpiece representing *St Michael slaying the dragon between two standing Saints*, with a *Madonna and Child* in the central pinnacle, by Ambrogio Lorenzetti, from the ruined abbey of Rofeno. One of the most fascinating works is the triptych representing the *Birth of the Virgin*, with the *Madonna of Humility* flanked by two smaller panels above, by the Master of the Osservanza, an artist close to Sassetta. The unusual *Nativity*, with *St Augustine* and *St Galgano* on either side, by Pietro di Giovanni d'Ambrogio is a somewhat naïf but charming rendition of the story, and the landscape in the background is clearly inspired by the *Crete* in this district. The polyptych with the *Madonna and Child enthroned*, surrounded by Saints James, Augustine, Bernardine and Margaret, with the *Annunciation and God the Father blessing* above, is by Matteo di Giovanni and comes from the church of Sant'Agostino. Other works include a *Madonna and Child* by Segna di Bonaventura, an *Annunciation* by Taddeo di Bartolo, an *Assumption of the Virgin* by Giovanni di Paolo and a charming *Madonna and Child* attributed to Lippo Memmi. Among the sculptural works are two polychrome wooden *Annunciation* figures of the *Virgin and Angel Gabriel* by Francesco di Valdambrino. The Oratory has some frescoes and an altarpiece by the Nasini family.

About half-way down Corso Matteotti on the right is the little church of San Bernardino which provisionally houses the **Museo Etrusco** (open daily, except

Mon, 10.00–12.30, and 16.30–18.30, June–Sept). The collection, which dates from 1959, has material from the excavations at Poggio Pinci (c 7km east of Asciano; there are plans to open the site to the public) and the Molinello tomb, dating from 7C–1C BC. There are interesting Etruscan ceramics, urns and bronze objects. When the collection is moved to its new premises, it will be enriched with material from other sites in the neighbourhood.

Further along the Corso to the left is the municipal tower crowned with battlements, beneath which is a fountain. At the pharmacy opposite, which has elegant 19C cupboards displaying old jars, one may ask to see the large mosaic pavement belonging to a Roman villa.

Further down on the right is the church of **Sant'Agostino**, a Gothic church with a simple brick façade. The interior has transversal arches and altars of grey stone; the first two enclose damaged 16C frescoes. Behind the high altar (the *Madonna and Child* by Matteo di Giovanni is a reproduction) is the marble tombstone of Giacomo Scotti by Urbano da Cortona (1487).

Immediately beyond the church is **Casa Corboli**, a medieval building where the city museum of paintings and sculpture (described on p. 412) is soon to be opened. The house preserves some 14C allegorical frescoes.

A little street between Sant'Agostino and Casa Corboli leads to the walls which overlook the Bestima river. Further up is a view of the cascades, near which is a public park.

In Via Mameli nearby is the **Museo Cassioli** (open as for the Museo Etrusco) which contains paintings, oil sketches and drawings by Amos Cassioli (1832–91), who was born in Asciano, a purist and romantic painter, best known for his frescoes representing scenes of the Risorgimento in Palazzo Pubblico in Siena. His son Giuseppe (1865–1942) was primarily a sculptor.

Off the far end of Corso Matteotti a pretty road (La Peschiera) runs left along the walls to Piazza del Grano. At the centre is a large marble fountain by Antonio Ghini (1450). The Palazzo del Podestà is studded with coats of arms. There are several charming medieval streets near the piazza.

From the piazza outside the walls, behind the Collegiata, a road leads uphill to **San Francesco**, in a panoramic position. The Gothic church was completely remodelled inside in the 17C. Beneath the whitewash on the walls frescoes by Sienese artists of the 13C–15C are gradually coming to light. There is also a della Robbia relief of the *Madonna and Child with angels* and a marble holy-water stoup attributed to Antonio Ghini.

Northeast of Asciano is **Rapolano Terme**, a medieval town with spa waters and travertine quarries.

The Abbey of Monte Oliveto Maggiore

Eight kilometres south of Asciano is the Abbey of Monte Oliveto Maggiore, on a promontory in a dense cypress wood. It is one of the best known monasteries in Tuscany (**open** daily 09.15–12.15, 15.15–17.00 or 18.00). There is a car park outside the gate (and a bar and restaurant). Hospitality is available at the guest house.

The monastery was founded in 1313 by Giovanni Tolomei of Siena, a wealthy professor of law, who withdrew at the age of forty to this area on his family property called the Desert of Accona. Here he settled with his companions, founding the Olivetan order (a branch of the Benedictine order) which was approved by the bishop of Arezzo, Guido Tarlati, in 1319, and confirmed by Pope Clement VI in 1344. Giovanni Tolomei, who assumed the name of Bernardo, was later beatified. The order grew rapidly and by the early 15C there were already thirty houses in Tuscany and Umbria.

Pius II and Charles V sojourned here, the latter with 2000 followers. The monastery was suppressed by Napoleon in 1810. It was restored and made a National Monument in 1866. The Abbot General usually resides here and a number of monks work on the restoration of rare books.

The **entrance** is past a drawbridge and through a fortified building with an arched passage above which is a large niche with a glazed terracotta statue of the *Madonna and Child, crowned by two angels*, by Giovanni della Robbia. In a corresponding position on the other side is a seated figure of *St Benedict* also by Giovanni della Robbia. A path leads down to the **monastery** through an avenue of cypress trees. The huge monastic buildings extend beyond the church. In the surrounding cypress woods are small 18C chapels, dedicated to founder members of the Order and various saints. The large fish reservoir was built by the Sienese architect Giovan Battista Pelori (1533).

The frescoes in the great cloister

The **great cloister** (1426–74), with two storeys of loggias, is famous for its frescoes illustrating the *Life of St Benedict*. The nine frescoes on the west wall are by **Luca Signorelli** (1497–98) and the others are by **Sodoma** (Giovanni Antonio Bazzi, 1505–08). The cycle is a masterpiece of fresco painting combining a picturesque and lively narrative style with charming naturalistic detail in a variety of landscape and architectural settings. In between the episodes are painted pilasters, several of which are decorated with grisailles and grotesques, also by Sodoma. The scenes follow the account of Benedict's life taken from the *Dialogues* of St Gregory the Great.

The cycle begins on the **east wall** with frescoes **by Sodoma 1**. *Benedict departs from his home at Norcia to study in Rome.* **2**. *Benedict leaves Rome.* **3**. *Benedict miraculously mends a broken tray* (here Sodoma painted his own portrait in the richly clad young man with two tame badgers at his feet). **4**. *The holy monk Romano gives Benedict a hermit's habit* (Subiaco is represented in the background). **5**. *Benedict at prayer in front of his cave, with the devil about to break the bell of his bread basket.* **6**. *A priest is inspired by Christ to take a meal to Benedict on Easter Day.* **7**. *Benedict instructs a group of peasants.* **8**. *Benedict overcomes temptation by throwing himself naked into brambles.* **9**. *Benedict accepts the request of a group of monks to become their abbot.* **10**. *Benedict, with the Sign of the Cross, shatters a glass of poisoned wine prepared by the monks who found his rule too strict.* **11**. *Benedict founds the first twelve communities.* **South wall**: frescoes by **Sodoma**. **12**. *Benedict welcomes Mauro and Placido into the Order.* **13**. *Benedict chastises a monk tempted by the devil.* **14**. *Benedict, in answer to the monks' prayers, makes water spring from Monte Oliveto.* **15**. *Benedict retrieves a scythe which has fallen into a lake.* **16**. *Mauro is sent to save Placido from drowning.* **17**. *The miracle of the flask changed into a snake.* **18**. *Fiorenzo attempts to poison Benedict.* **19**. *Fiorenzo sends a group of loose women to the monastery.*

West wall: **20**, by **Bartolomeo Neroni**, called il Riccio. *Benedict sends Mauro to France and Placido to Sicily.* Nos. **21–29** are by **Luca Signorelli**: **21**. *Fiorenzo's* death. **22**. *Benedict converts the inhabitants of Monte Cassino*. **23**. *Benedict defeats the devil*. **24**. *Benedict rescues a young monk from beneath a collapsed wall*. **25**. *Benedict tells two monks when and where they had dined outside the monastery*. **26**. *Benedict reproaches Valeriano's brother for breaking the fast*. **27**. *Benedict unmasks Riggo disguised as Totila, the Ostrogoth leader*. **28**. *Benedict recognises and welcomes Totila*. The last fresco was destroyed when the door was enlarged. The following frescoes are by **Sodoma**: **30**. *Benedict foretells the destruction of Monte Cassino* (by the Lombards in 581).

North wall: **31**. *Benedict miraculously obtains flour for his monks*. **32**. *Benedict appears to two monks in their sleep and instructs them on how to build a church*. **33**. *Episode of two excommunicated nuns*. **34**. *Miracle of the monk's burial*. **35**. *Benedict forgives the monk who had escaped from the monastery*. **36**. *Benedict releases a bound peasant by merely looking at him*.

In the passage leading to the church are two small frescoes of *Christ carrying the Cross and Christ at the column*, and *St Benedict giving the Rule to the founders of Monte Oliveto*, all by Sodoma. In the vestibule is a statue of the *Madonna and Child* by Fra Giovanni da Verona (1490) and a fresco of *Hermits in the desert* by an anonymous Sienese painter.

The **church**, which has a Latin-cross plan, was renovated by Giovanni Antinori in 1772. The magnificent choir-stalls of inlaid wood are by Fra Giovanni da Verona (1505) and the lectern by Raffaele da Brescia (1520). The *Assumption* in the cupola is by Jacopo Ligozzi, who also painted the *Nativity of the Virgin* behind the high altar. Off the north transept is the Chapel of the Holy Sacrament which has a large polychrome wooden *Crucifix* of the mid-13C. Opposite is the sacristy with cupboards dated 1417.

From the great cloister there is a passageway to the middle cloister, surrounded by a portico, with a *Madonna and Child and angels* over the entrance. A vestibule (with a 17C lavabo), surmounted by a fresco by Riccio) gives access to the **refectory**, a large vaulted hall with frescoes by Paolo Novelli (1670). A staircase from the middle cloister leads up to the early 16C **library** which is preceded by a vestibule hung with portraits of Olivetan monks by Antonio Mueller. The library was built in 1518 to a basilican plan with Corinthian columns by Giovanni da Verona. He also executed the doorway and other carvings, as well as the Paschal candlestick. The library contains some forty thousand volumes, with important manuscripts, choirbooks and incunabula.

A double flight of steps leads to the **pharmacy** which has a fine collection of jars. The **chapter house** (called the Definitorio) dates from 1498. It has a chiaroscuro frieze and a fresco of the *Madonna and Child with Saints* attributed to Matteo Ripanda. In an adjacent room is a small collection of paintings: a *Maestà* by the Master of Monteoliveto, a follower of Duccio, a *Madonna and Child* by Segna di Bonaventura, *St Bernardine* by Neroccio di Bartolomeo, and a *Madonna and Child* by Vincenzo Tamagni. The **Hall of Justice** is also richly decorated and has a fresco of *Christ and the adulteress* by Riccio (1540).

From Monte Oliveto Maggiore a beautiful road leads south to **San Giovanni d'Asso**, on a hill (310m). An enormous **castle** towers over the village. The building is largely intact, with wooden doors, Gothic windows, and a large courtyard with a brick portico, added in the Renaissance period. The back entrance to the castle leads to a rectangular piazza from which there is a beautiful view. To the right, opposite an 18C chapel, is the church of **San Giovanni Battista**, which has a Romanesque brick façade decorated with blocks of travertine and a large oculus over the arched doorway. The interior has been restructured and the Sienese 14C triptych removed to Pienza for safe keeping.

At the far end of the piazza a path leads to the charming little church of **San Pietro in Villore**, surrounded by cypress trees. A very early church (11C–12C), it has an ancient, irregular façade decorated with blind arches and a doorway with carvings and strange anthropomorphic capitals. The structure, of sandstone and travertine, was restored in the upper part in brick at some later date. Beneath the church is a small crypt.

Montisi, nearby to the east is described in Ch. 34.

Buonconvento

Southwest of Monte Oliveto Maggiore, on the Via Cassia (see above), is Buonconvento, a picturesque fortified village at the confluence of the Arbia and Ombrone rivers. Emperor Henry VII, who was planning to lay siege to Siena, died of malaria here in 1313. Later, Buonconvento became one of the primary defences of Siena and its fine brick walls and gates are well preserved. On the charming main street, which crosses the town from north to south, are some medieval houses and Palazzo Pretorio, with a crenellated tower, all in brick. The parish church of Santi Pietro e Paolo dates from the 14C but was entirely rebuilt in the 18C. It preserves a *Madonna and Child* by Matteo di Giovanni and a *Madonna and Child with Saints* by Pietro di Francesco Orioli.

The **Museo d'Arte Sacra della Val d'Arbia** opposite Saint Pietro e Paolo is a museum of religious art from the Arbia Valley (**open** daily, in summer, 10.00–12.00, 16.00–19.00; in winter, 10.00–12.00, 15.00–17.00, closed Mon).

The collection includes several fine works from the parish church, the Compagnia del Corpus Domini, and other churches in the district. The most important include a charming *Madonna and Child* attributed to Duccio, a fine *Crucifix* by the so-called Master of the Buonconvento Cross, a *Madonna and Child with two angels* by Luca di Tommè, an *Annunciation* by Andrea di Bartolo, a large triptych with the *Madonna and Child enthroned and two Saints* by Sano di Pietro, a *Coronation of the Virgin* and other works by Matteo di Giovanni, and an *Annunciation*, by Benvenuto di Giovanni; a particularly luminous work with a charming landscape in the background. There are also some later paintings and liturgical objects including a fine early 14C incense-boat and a 15C copper gilt chalice.

The Val d'Arbia

Lucignano d'Arbia, a pretty village on a hill to the north off the Cassia, has two fortified gates, one at each end of the main street, lined with medieval and Renaissance houses built of brick. At the centre of the village, on a slight rise, is the Romanesque church of San Giovanni Battista beside which is a monumental bell-tower. Inside the church is a *Crucifixion* by Bartolomeo Neroni, called Il Riccio.

A by-road leads southwest to the village of **Vescovado**, which has some charming streets. The parish church is modern but contains a polyptych by Benvenuto di Giovanni of 1475, complete with its painted pinnacles, side-pilasters, and predella, and a small *Madonna and Child* by Andrea di Niccolò.

Murlo

Further south, on a hill, is the tiny village of Murlo (314m), dominating the surrounding countryside. The 12C walls form a complete circle and, although considerably restored, the village preserves its medieval character. The church of **San Fortunato**, medieval in origin and rebuilt in the 16C, has a *Madonna and Child with Saints* by Astolfo Petrazzi and an *Assumption* by Dionisio Montorselli.

In the same piazza is the former bishop's palace, called the *Palazzone*, which houses the **Museo Civico Archeologico** (open summer and Sun 09.30–12.30, 15.30–19.00; winter 09.30–12.30, 15.00–17.00, closed Mon; in July–Aug **open** also 21.00–23.00; ☎ 0577-814213).

The small but choice collection, beautifully displayed and well labelled, includes Etruscan objects, excavated in recent years on the nearby hill of Poggio Civitate. A unique architectural complex with palatial villa has been discovered, dating from the 7C and 6C BC (see below). There are extensive remains of walls and roof tiles and terracotta decorations, including the bust of a bearded man wearing a broad brimmed hat, gorgons and other fantastic animals, besides panels with decoration in relief, some with horsemen. There are numerous refined objects in gold, silver, bronze, and ivory, some of them imported and therefore of interest in establishing the contacts that existed between Poggio Civitate, other districts on the peninsula and other countries. There is also an extensive collection of household objects for daily use, implements, earthenware, and personal ornaments.

The small palace next door, an 18C building called the Palazzina, will eventually house the **Museo d'Arte Sacra del Vescovado**. Its contents will include a *Madonna and Child* by Pietro Lorenzetti, a *Madonna and Child with Angels* by Guidoccio Cozzarelli, a detached fresco of the *Madonna and Child with Saints* by Andrea di Niccolò of 1515, a *Madonna and Child* by Giacomo Pacchiarotti, and two later works, by Alessandro Casolani and Rutilio Manetti.

A short distance southeast of Murlo are the excavations of the site of **Poggio Civitate**, not yet open to the public. These include a building dating from the last thirty years of the 7C BC and another archaic building dating from c 580 BC, which is one of the few known examples of domestic architecture of this period. The building was dismantled by the Etruscans at the end of the 6C BC, and walled in with stones and earth. The terracotta ornaments were buried in trenches and covered over. There is also an interesting large building supported on three rows of piers which was used as a workshop by craftsmen producing objects in gold, ivory and bronze. All the material is now exhibited in the museum of Murlo (see above).

The area around Murlo is rich in castles, some of them romantic ruins in beautiful settings. A map of itineraries is available locally.

North of Lucignano, also on the Via Cassia, is **Monteroni d'Arbia**, the most developed industrial town in the district, specialising in the production of iron, glass and leather. The old *borgo* belonged to the hospital of Siena, Santa Maria della Scala, and preserves a large 14C fortified mill. This area is known for its excellent white wine.

A short distance north, in a conspicuous position above the Cassia, is **Cuna**, a rare example of a fortified medieval granary. Like Monteroni d'Arbia, it also belonged to Santa Maria della Scala, and is entirely built of brick with fortified walls, towers, and an arched gateway. Inside is a small chapel, with a 16C fresco of the *Madonna and Child with Saints*, various houses, beautifully preserved, and a central 13C fortress. An immense ramp leads up to the first floor where grain was stored. There is a fine view of Siena, about 12 km north.

33 · Pienza and the Val d'Orcia

Pienza is famous as an ideal Renaissance town built in the middle of the 15C in five years by Bernardo Rossellino. It¶s 12km west of Montepulciano and 50km south of Siena. **San Quirico d'Orcia** is a well kept interesting little medieval town. The landscape of the **Val d'Orcia** is perhaps one of the best preserved and one of the most beautiful in Tuscany. The river valley, with its characteristic eroded downs or clay hills, is in a majestic setting with the mountain of Cetona on one side, and Amiata on the other. In the wooded foothills are little towns and villages, often with their medieval castles towering above. There are also hot springs in the district known since Roman times.

■ Practical information

Information offices. For **Pienza**: APT Chianciano Terme Valdichiana, Chianciano Terme (☎ 0578-63167), with offices in Pienza, Piazza Pio II (☎ 0578-749071), and (*Pro-loco*) 22 Via Case Nuove (☎ 0578-748072). For **San Quirico d'Orcia** and Bagno Vignoni, APT Siena (☎ 0577-42209); information office in San Quirico, 33 Via Dante Alighieri (☎ 0577-897211). For **Radicofani**, APT dell'Amiata, Abbadia San Salvatore (☎ 0577-778608); information office in Radicofani, 31 Via Renato Magi (☎ 0578-55684).

Getting there
By car. Pienza and the Val d'Orcia are close to the Via Cassia (N2) between Siena and Rome.
Buses. TRA-IN runs buses from Siena and Montepulciano to Pienza and San Quirico d'Orcia.

Hotels
Pienza: ★★★ *Corsignano*, 11 Via della Madonnina (☎ 0578-748501; fax 0578-748166); *Il Chiostro di Pienza Relais*, 26 Corso Rossellino (☎ 0578-748400; fax 0578-748440).
San Quirico d'Orcia: ★★★ *Palazzuolo*, with restaurant, 43 Via Santa Caterina (☎ 0577-897080; fax 0577-898264).
Bagno Vignoni. ★★★ *Posta Marcucci*, with hot thermal swimming pool (☎ 0577-887112; fax 0577-887119), and *Le Terme* (☎ 0577-887150; fax 0577-887497).
Vivo d'Orcia: ★★ *Amiata* (☎ 0577-873790).
Bagni San Filippo: ★★ *Terme San Filippo*.
Radicofani has ★★ hotels.

Restaurants
Pienza. £ *La Buca delle Fate*, 38 Corso Rossellino.
San Quirico d'Orcia. ££ *Vecchio Forno*.

Annual festivals
At **Monticchiello** a remarkable local **open-air theatre** season is held in July (information from the *Compagnia Popolare Teatro Povero*, ☎ 0578-755118).
On the estate of **La Foce** at the Castelluccio Bifolchi an **annual chamber music festival** is held in summer (*Incontri in Terra di Siena*), for information (☎ 0578-69101).

Pienza

Pienza (491m) is a charming compact little Renaissance town (2400 inhab.) created by Aeneas Silvius Piccolomini, afterwards Pius II on his election to the Papacy in 1458. The original fortified village of Corsignano, a Piccolomini feud and Aeneas's birthplace, was renamed Pienza by papal bull in 1462. The architect Bernardo Rossellino was commissioned to design the monumental piazza with its splendid cathedral and palaces, all built between 1459–64. A particularly good sheep's cheese (*pecorino* or *cacio*) is made in the district.

Piazza Pio II, laid out by Bernardo Rossellino, is a remarkable example of Renaissance town planning. It shows the influence of Leon Battista Alberti, Rossellino's master. To one side of the beautifully paved piazza is an elegant well, also designed by Rossellino, flanked by two slender columns with finely carved capitals and an architrave.

Duomo

The Duomo has a superb façade in Istrian stone. The motif of the triumphal arch and the choice of details are evidently inspired by classical Roman architecture. The proportions, the linear clarity and sober decoration conform to the aspirations of dignity, harmony and beauty of the Humanist architect. At the centre of the great pediment are the papal arms of Pius II, on an awe-inspiring scale.

The unusual lofty but compact interior has nave and aisles of equal height, divided by clustered columns with tall dosserets supporting the vault. Five large arched windows, decorated with tracery, one in each of the chapels encircling the east end, fill the church with light. The elegant architecture is clearly influenced by Northern European (French Gothic) models. The painted ribs of the vault, fanning out from the columns, add a beautiful touch of colour and enhance the etherial atmosphere of the church.

The five altarpieces were painted for the cathedral in 1461–63. In the south aisle, *Madonna and Child with Saints Bernardine, Anthony Abbot, Francis and Sabina*, and a *Pietà* in the lunette, by Giovanni di Paolo. **First chapel**: *Madonna and Child with Saints Catherine of Alexandria, Matthew, Bartholomew and Lucy*, and the *Flagellation* in the lunette, by Matteo di Giovanni. **Second chapel** (Chapel of the Holy Sacrament): marble tabernacle attributed to Rossellino, which contains a relic of St Andrew. The central chapel has fine choir-stalls and a bishop's cathedra of 1462. **Fourth chapel**: triptych of the *Assumption with Saints Agatha, Callistus, Pius I and Catherine of Siena*, *Ecce Homo* in the predella, by Vecchietta. **Fifth chapel**: *Madonna and Child with Saints Mary Magdalen, Philip, James, and Anne*, *Ecce Homo* in the gable and *Annunciation* in the predella, by Sano di Pietro. In the north aisle, *Madonna and Child with Saints Jerome, Martin, Nicholas, and Augustine* by Matteo di Giovanni.

The bell-tower to the left of the façade gives access to the crypt of San Giovanni. The Baptismal font in travertine is by Rossellino; the fragments of Romanesque sculpture displayed here come from the former church of Santa Maria.

The whole church has had to be shored up at the east end and the structure is still unstable.

Palazzo Piccolomini

To the right of the Duomo is Palazzo Piccolomini, begun by Pius II and finished by Pius III, his nephew (the main rooms on the first floor are **open** to the public;

guided tours 10.00–12.30, 15.00 or 16.00–18.00 or 19.00, except Mon). It is considered Rossellino's masterpiece, and shows the influence of Alberti's Palazzo Rucellai in Florence. The façade is built of sandstone with two elegant rows of arched mullioned windows alternating with pilasters, separated by horizontal cornices, and simple doorways. The base becomes a projecting bench on three sides of the palace. The elegant courtyard is surrounded by a portico supported on a splendid Corinthian order, above which are two storeys of square mullioned windows with a glazed loggia on two sides of the upper floor. On the right are stairs leading up to the first floor. Opposite, on the left, is the entrance to the hanging garden, onto which faces the magnificent garden front of the palace, composed of three superimposed open loggias. The Italian garden of evergreen box hedges and small trees, has remained unchanged. Seen against the backdrop of the Orcia valley, it is a supreme example of the Renaissance idea of the garden as the intermediary between architecture and nature.

The first floor was inhabited by the Piccolomini family until 1962. The Sala degli Antenati is hung with family portraits. The **dining room** has good furniture and tapestries. In the **music room** is a fine *scagliola* table representing a map of the Sienese State, and Cordova leather hangings. The large **Sala d'Armi** has a display of arms and battle paintings by Borgognone. From the Loggia is a view overlooking the garden and beyond, in the distance, Radicofani with Monte Cetona on the left and Monte Amiata on the right. The **bedroom** has a 17C bed and a fresco over the door with a portrait of *Pius II*. A passage leads to the **library**, interesting for its furniture, carpets, books and documents.

Museo Diocesano

Opposite Palazzo Piccolomini is the **Palazzo Vescovile** (Bishop's Palace), which was modified and enlarged by Roderigo Borgia, later Pope Alexander VI, whose arms it displays on the corner. Here, on the second floor, the new Museo Diocesano has just been installed (**open** 10.00–13.00, 14.30–16.30, except Tues, entrance from the side).

The museum comprises a fine collection of paintings, sculptures, tapestries, textiles, liturgical objects, illuminated choir-books and reliquaries from the cathedral and other churches in the district.

There is an important section of **14C Sienese painting**, beginning with a *Crucifix* of the late 12C from San Pietro in Villore (San Giovanni d'Asso) and another *Crucifix* by Segna di Bonaventura from San Francesco (see below). There are several early *Madonnas* by Niccolo di Segna, Bartolomeo Bulgarini and other unidentified artists. One of the outstanding paintings in the collection is the *Madonna and Child* by Pietro Lorenzetti from Montichiello, a masterpiece by the artist and a work of immense charm. Another charming work is the tabernacle by the Master of the Osservanza, with the *Madonna of Humility between St John the Baptist and St Catherine of Alexandria* and the *Annunciation* in the pinnacles. Sienese painting of the 15C is well represented, the major work being a large altarpiece by Vecchietta, complete with a fine predella and an *Annunciation* which demonstrates the artist's interest in perspective.

There are several fine polychrome wood statues by Domenico di Niccolò dei Cori, and figures of *St Peter* and *St Paul* attributed to Giovanni Andrea Galletti.

Of greatest interest is the collection of objects, many of them of superb quality, which were made for Pius II. His superb crozier of gilded silver, inlaid

PIENZA CENTRE

Palazzo Canonici

Palazzo Vescovile
Museo Diocesano

Palazzo Comunale

PIAZZA DEL MARCATO

CORSO ROSSELLINO

PIAZZA

Duomo

PIO II

Well

Palazzo Ammannati

Palazzo Piccolomini

Palazzo dei Cardinali

San Francesco

0   30 yds
0   30 metres

with enamels, is a very fine example of mid-15C Florentine goldsmiths' work, with an exquisite *Annunciation* scene above a small temple containing six angels holding shields with the papal arms. There are ten enamelled plaquettes from the Pope's original mitre. The treasury commissioned by the Pope includes reliquaries, crosses, an elaborate pax, an incense burner, chalices and plaques. A magnificent cope in *Opus Anglicanum* dating from the first half of the 14C, with scenes from the Life of the Virgin, saints and apostles embroidered in silk and silver gilt thread, is one of the few surviving examples of English medieval ecclesiastical embroidery. There are also other vestments and some fine tapestries from Brussels and Arras, in particular a most beautiful Crucifixion scene woven c1460. The cathedral created by Pius II also had its series of **choirbooks**, many of them illuminated by Sienese and Florentine artists of the mid-15C. A small selection of 16C and 17C paintings and works of art completes the collection.

Opposite the Duomo is **Palazzo Comunale**, with a fine portico supported on travertine columns with Ionic capitals and double windows on the upper floor, also designed by Rossellino. At the further end is a tall clock-tower.

Corso Rossellino leads out of the piazza along the north side of Palazzo Piccolomini, opposite which is **Palazzo Ammannati**, built by Cardinal Ammannati of Pavia, a close friend of Pius II. Its top floor loggia is now bricked in. Next to it is the smaller Palazzo dei Cardinali. A little further on, to the left, is **San Francesco**, an early Gothic church with some late 14C frescoes. The street ends at the 14C **Porta al Prato** (or Porta al Murello), beyond which (on the left) is a public garden. From here there is a charming walk downhill, known as the 'Passeggiata di Santa Caterina', with a fine view.

Via delle Fonti leaves the piazza outside Porta al Prato and continues downhill (600m) to an old fountain. Nearby, beside some picturesque farm buildings, is the beautiful Romanesque **Pieve di Corsignano**, also known as Santi Vito e Modesto. The church is very ancient (10C–11C) and there is an unusual circular tower with eight large arched windows. The doorway at the west end is decorated with reliefs of stylised flowers and palmettes and a strange double-tailed siren; the window has a female caryatid at the centre. On the architrave of the south doorway are carvings depicting the *Journey of the Magi* and the *Nativity*, with animals on the jambs. The **interior** has a basilican plan with piers dividing the nave from the aisles. It still contains the simple baptismal font supported on a Romanesque capital in which Pius II was baptised.

Just inside Porta al Prato, Via Gozzante leads to a delightful raised walkway along the walls on the south side of the town which overlooks the valley. It passes beneath the garden of Palazzo Piccolomini and continues from the Canonica to the **Porta al Ciglio**, at the far end of Corso Rossellino. Outside the gate is a fortified palace with two impressive round towers. The old streets of Corsignano are extemely picturesque.

A road south from Pienza, providing the best view of the garden façade of Palazzo Piccolomini and the great apse of the Duomo, leads to **Monticchiello**, a lovely medieval village. Its 13C castle, walls and towers still exist in a relatively good state. The late 13C church of **Santi Leonardo e Cristoforo** has an elegant doorway and rose window. The interior, rebuilt in the 18C, has 14C and 15C frescoes of the Sienese school. The painting of the *Madonna* by Pietro Lorenzetti is in the new Diocesan Museum in Pienza (see above). The polychrome wood figure of *St Leonard* is by Domenico di Niccolò dei Cori (c 1420). The summer theatre festival is held in the adjacent Piazza San Martino (see above). A by-road leads southeast from Monticchiello to Montepulciano (see Ch. 34).

San Quirico d'Orcia

San Quirico d'Orcia (409m). This little medieval town takes its name from the former church of San Quirico a Osenna, recorded as early as the 8C on the Via Francigena. Little is known of St Quirico (Cyricus) except that he was martyred, allegedly in the 4C. In the 13C the town walls were enlarged and several hospices and hospitals were built to accommodate pilgrims on their way to Rome. Stretches of the walls survive, as well as some of the former watch-towers, partly incorporated into other buildings. The Porta Romana was destroyed in the Second World War.

The Via Francigena

The Via Francigena was the medieval pilgrims' way from France and Northern Europe to Rome, which was especially busy during Jubilee years. Sigeric (also called Siric) travelled along it on his way to Rome from Canterbury to receive the pallium (symbol of investiture) from the hands of the Pope as Archbishop of Canterbury. He described his return journey in 990, with its 80 stopping places, and the manuscript of his chronicle is still preserved in the British Museum in London. The archbishop studied to be a churchman at the Benedictine abbey at Glastonbury in England under St Dunstan.

In the 8C the road was used by the Lombards as a safe route from Pavia to the south, avoiding Byzantine territory, and in the following century it became known as the 'Francigena' because it originated in Frankish territory (it is also sometimes called the 'Via Romea' by medieval chroniclers). The route across France started at Calais and traversed Picardy, Champagne and the Ardennes, then from Switzerland, the Alps were crossed at the Great St Bernard Pass. From Aosta it passed through Northern Italy (Ivrea, Vercelli, Pavia, Piacenza, Fidenza and Parma) and from the Passo della Cisa on the Emilian border it entered Tuscany, where Pontremoli was the first centre of importance. It continued south to Lucca, crossed the Arno at Fucecchio, and then passed through the towns of San Gimignano, Siena, San Quirico d'Orcia, and left Tuscany at Radicofani to cross Lazio (Bolsena, Montefiascone, and Viterbo) before reaching Rome.

This route to Rome was one of three pilgrimage routes in medieval Europe; the other two led to Santiago de Compostela and Jerusalem. The journey from England to Rome took about two and a half months and ordinary pilgrims probably made the entire trip on foot (carrying a characteristic staff), although prelates such as Sigeric may have travelled on horseback. The road was rough and only paved in places, therefore unsuitable for wheeled vehicles. Numerous '*ospedali*' or stopping places grew up along the way which offered help and accommodation to travellers, some of them run by the church (such as the Ospedale di Santa Maria della Scala in Siena which ran many hospices south of the city). The hospice of La Magione (see p. 402) is one of the best preserved to have survived. Castles and villages were also built near the route, and towns such as Lucca and Siena prospered as a result of their proximity to the Via Francigena. Apart from pilgrims, the road was used by merchants and traders and goods as well as works of art were transported along it. Some of the churches in Tuscany built close to the road show the influence of French Romanesque architecture, notably the abbey of Sant'Antimo.

The importance of the Via Francigena diminished after the 13C when other routes were opened over the Alps.

From the medieval **Porta Cappuccini**, an unusual polygonal and well preserved gateway, Via Poliziano passes some interesting houses and ends at Piazza Chigi. The enormous **Palazzo Chigi** was built for Cardinal Flavio Chigi by Carlo Fontana in 1679. After being damaged in the Second World War, it was allowed to fall into a state of neglect, but recently it has been restored inside and the exterior has been consolidated. Many of the rooms are decorated with frescoes by Roman artists. The palace may be visited on request (☎ 0577-898247).

The Collegiata

The Romanesque Collegiata (open all day) was built in the 12C on the site of an earlier church. The **exterior**, built of travertine, has a simple structure, except for the three elaborately decorated **doorways**, parts of which are in contrasting sandstone. The main entrance, beneath a large rose window, dating from the late 12C, is the finest and most elaborate example of a Lombard portal in Sienese territory. It incorporates a frieze of strange animal heads and an arch above four slender clustered columns, tied together with a loop at their centre. These in turn have Lombard lions at their base. A sequence of inner arches, surrounding the lunette with a seated figure, said to be Pope St Damasus at the the centre, are supported on five thin columns with unusual capitals.

The doorway on the south side, with a porch supported on telamons standing on lions, is slightly later in date and is attributed to the school of Giovanni Pisano. It has a fine architrave and is flanked by two elegant Gothic windows; the right window has a kneeling telamon and carved fantastic animals. The smaller doorway, at the end of the south transept, is dated 1298 (both were damaged by shell-fire). The remaining decoration is limited to small blind arches under the roofs. The bell-tower dates from the 18C.

The **interior** has a Latin-cross plan, with three arches supported on piers dividing the nave from the short north aisle. The timber ceiling, parts of which preserve the original paint, was discovered under the Baroque vault. The nave and transept chapels are divided from the crossing by arches. In the north transept is a fine polyptych by Sano di Pietro. The presence of St Quirico and the red-and-white arms of the town in the painting prove that it was painted for this church. The choir was enlarged in the mid-18C to house nine choir-stalls inlaid with trompe l'oeil scenes and half-length figures by Antonio di Neri Barili (possibly on designs by Signorelli) which originally formed a series of 19 in the Baptist's chapel in Siena cathedral. The 17C organ is attributed to Cesare Romani of Cortona; it is used for concerts. In the chapel of the Holy Sacrament is a detached fresco of the *Madonna and Child*, by Girolamo di Benvenuto, known as the *Madonna delle Grazie* or *Madonna del Pomo*. On the side wall is a *Madonna of the Rosary* by Rutilio Manetti. The marble pavement tombstone of Henry of Nassau by Urbano da Cortonais dated 1451.

To the left of the church is the **Oratory of the Misericordia** which has a *Madonna and Child with Saints* by Il Riccio.

The main street, Via Dante Alighieri, crosses the town, past some well-preserved medieval houses and the Renaissance Palazzo Pretorio. In Piazza Libertà is the **Chiesa di Santa Maria di Vitaleta**, also known as San Francesco, which has a (restored) Gothic façade. The interior has a very beautiful white glazed enamel *Virgin Annunciate* by Andrea della Robbiaof 1510 on the high altar and polychrome wood figures of the *Virgin and Angel Gabriel* by Francesco di Valdambrino. The *Preaching of the Baptist* is signed and dated 1597 by Empoli, who also painted the *Immaculate Conception* opposite. The *Miracle of the Loaves and Fishes* is by Vincenzo Rustici.

Across the piazza, next to the Porta Nuova, is the entrance to the **Horti Leonini** (open all day), a beautiful park with an Italian garden created by Diomede Leoni around 1580. At the centre is a marble statue of Cosimo III Medici by Giuseppe Mazzuoli (1688) which was removed from Palazzo Chigi.

The garden, which follows the Renaissance pattern of box hedges in a geometrical design, leading to a *boschetto* or ilex wood on a slope, was intended as a resting place for pilgrims. It is surrounded by remains of the old ramparts, above which stood the tall castle tower.

Farther along Via Dante is a 14C house (No. 38) where St Catherine of Siena is supposed to have stayed. Towards the end of the street is the charming little church of **Santa Maria Assunta** (11C), built of beautiful stone blocks. It has a fine doorway with a porch (which may originally have been intended for Sant'Antimo). The simple interior is dimly lit by small lancet windows. The apse is decorated on the outside with blind arches and zoomorphic heads. Opposite is the **Ospedale della Scala** (which belonged to the eponymous hospital of Siena) dating from the 13C. There are remains of a loggia giving on to the courtyard, which also preserves a 16C well.

The Val d'Orcia

South of San Quirico, approached from by-roads on either side of the Via Cassia, is the Val d'Orcia, the beautiful valley of the Orcia river. West of the Cassia are well-preserved villages, castles and thermal baths in the foothills of Monte Amiata, while to the east the valley widens out on either side of the river with a landscape of eroded clay slopes and small sharp ridges known as *calanchi*, much of it part of the huge estate of La Foce.

Just south of San Quirico, reached through beautiful countryside, is the tiny village of **Vignoni**, from which there is a fine view. It has a truncated medieval tower, and a 15C palace on the main street which leads to the Romanesque church on the edge of the hill.

The road continues to climb towards **Ripa d'Orcia**, a castle surrounded by ramparts in a spectacular, isolated position overlooking the Orcia Valley (it is now a hotel residence ☎ 0577-53023).

Bagno Vignoni is a tiny medieval spa on a small plateau. The warm sulphurous waters, known since Roman times, bubble up into a large *piscina*, constructed by the Medici, in the charming and perfectly preserved piazza. It forms one of the most unusual and evocative sights in Tuscany, especially in winter when the condensation from the hot spring water creates a mist.

Castliglione d'Orcia (540m) is another picturesque little village, built round a ruined castle. The main **piazza**, named after the 15C artist Vecchietta, traditionally believed to have been born here, preserves its old paving of brick and pebbles and there is a well in the centre, dated 1618. The pieve of **Santi Stefano e Degna**, a Romanesque church with a Renaissance façade, has a *Madonna enthroned with four Saints* by Giovanni di Bartolomeo (1531), a large *Crucifixion* by Fabrizio Boschi and two early 16C frescoed lunettes. Three important paintings by Pietro Lorenzetti, Vecchietta, and Simone Martini, have been removed to the new museum in Montalcino (see p. 407). The pretty borgo has narrow streets with some medieval houses and a little Romanesque church, the Chiesa delle Sante Marie. There is a fine view over the Orcia valley.

Nearby **Rocca d'Orcia** is a particularly well-preserved medieval village on a slope, dominated by its spectacular castle, the **Rocca di Tentennano** where exhibitions are held (**open** in summer, 10.00–13.00, 15.30–19.30, in winter at weekends, reduced hours). The piazza has a large octagonal stone well in the centre. The parish church of **San Simeone** preserves a fresco of the *Madonna of Mercy* by a follower of Bartolo di Fredi and a *Madonna of the Rosary* by Francesco Rustici (the *Madonna* by Giovanni di Paolo is also now kept in the museum of Montalcino).

Farther south is **Campiglia d'Orcia** in an elevated position (811m) on the north slope of Monte Amiata, facing Radicofani. It has picturesque medieval streets and a tall bell-tower built on a rocky spur. In the church of San Biagio is a *Madonna and Child with Saints* attributed to Sebastiano Folli.

On the road to Monte Amiata is **Vivo d'Orcia** (870m), surrounded by woods, near the spring of the Vivo torrent. Near the bridge is the **Eremo del Vivo**, an impressive late Renaissance building overlooking the valley. A Camaldolese monastery in the early 12C, it became the property of the Cervini of Montepulciano who built a fortified palace here in 1536. The architect is said to have been Antonio da Sangallo the Younger. The church of San Pietro, opposite, has a Romanesque apse. Nearby are some interesting old farm buildings.

Close to the Cassia is **Bagni San Filippo**. Here the hot sulphurous springs, known since ancient times, are said to be named after St Filippo Benizzi (1238–85), of the Servite Order. There is a thermal station and beautiful cascades. In the village is the church of San Filippo which has an 18C stucco statue of *St Filippo* and busts of *St Filippo Benizzi* and *St Filippo Neri*.

To the east of the Via Cassia (just south of San Quirico) a by-road leads past the fortified farm of **Spedaletto** which belonged to the hospital of Santa Maria della Scala in Siena, and was also used as a hospice for pilgrims on their way to Rome.

A pretty lane diverges for Pienza (see above), while this road runs along the stony shallow river bed where there are gravel works. The interesting landscape has pasturelands and *calanchi* (see above). Its wild aspect was partly altered in the 1980s certain areas were levelled to create arable land. At the end of the valley, where the road begins to climb up to the watershed between the Val d'Orcia and the Val di Chiana, the landscape is better preserved. This was part of the huge estate of **La Foce** (3000 acres) purchased by **Iris** and **Antonio Origo** in 1923 where they spent most of their lives reclaiming the land and cultivating it. They also started a school, nursery school and day clinic on the estate, and Antonio was the founder of the *Consorzio di bonifica* in the Val d'Orcia which ran other schools. During the war, children from Turin and Genoa were taken in by the Origos, and they ran an orphanage here. Iris Origo (1902–88), the historian and biographer, described her life here in her autobiography *Images and Shadows* and her war diary *War in Val d'Orcia*. Her book, *The Merchant of Prato*, about the life of Francesco di Marco Datini, provides a vivid description of life in medieval Italy.

On the skyline the **Castelluccio Bifolchi** can be seen, a small castle where a delightful **annual chamber music festival** (see p. 418) is held in summer (in the courtyard and other localities nearby). From the main road, lined with cypresses and pines, there is also a view of the country road which zigzags up to a farmhouse on the estate, which was planted with widely spaced cypresses by the Origos to provide a picturesque view from the main villa.

At the top of the ridge is the main entrance to the **villa**, still owned by the Origo family and since 1998 the seat of a foundation for the study of the landscape and environment of the Val d'Orcia. The **gardens** may be visited on Wednesdays (15.00–dusk; entrance fee, which is donated to charity). Ask at the farm office in the courtyard to the left of the house. They are usually at their best in May, June and September.

The villa, built in 1498 as a hostel, run by the Ospedale di Santa Maria della Scala of Siena, was restored for the Origos by the Englishman Cecil Pinsent, who designed a number of other gardens in Tuscany, most of them in the environs of Florence (see Ch. 2). Here he added the outside staircase and enlarged the house, as well as designing the lovely gardens and farm outbuildings (water was piped here from a spring seven kilometres away). The numerous cypresses he planted (which also served as wind-breaks) are now suffering from disease and some have had to be felled. Beside the house are two ilexes, one of which is very old, pruned to an unusual shape. The orangery is a handsome building by Pinsent (1924).

From the first garden close to the house (1924/5) which has a low hedge of dwarf pomegranates, a little stone ramp leads up to the gardens outside the larger house, partly built in the 19C (it was given its 16C appearance by Pinsent who added the two upper floors and courtyard), where bay and box hedges feature. The lemon garden, towards the Orcia valley, was designed in 1933. A splendid old wisteria flourishes here. The paths are paved in travertine from Rapolano. A terrace looks down onto a third garden, dating from just before the War. Here the box hedges are planted in an interesting design around four magnolias, and the hedge of cypresses is kept low for the view of the valley, which includes the cypress avenue mentioned above, which zigzags up the hill opposite. Above the second garden is the rose garden, with mixed flowerbeds bordered with lavender, and an herbaceous border. From here steps, lined with cypresses, lead up to the top of the hill. A paved pergola (of vines and wisteria) leads along the side of the hill from the rose garden, past grassy slopes planted with fruit trees and banksia roses. The pergola ends at a large wood crossed by paths, one of which leads to the little cemetery, also designed by Pinsent, where Iris and her husband are buried.

In the middle of the Orcia valley, on a hill is the little well-preserved village of **Contignano**, with a fine castle tower. The church, which was remodelled in the 17C, has a 14C altarpiece of the *Coronation of the Virgin*. There is a splendid panorama embracing Monte Amiata, Radicofani, Monte Cetona and Pienza across the Val d'Orcia.

Radicofani

Due south, in a spectacular position on a basaltic hill (783m) which divides the Orcia and the Paglia valleys, and close to the border with Lazio, is Radicofani. Its pretty medieval streets are mostly built of grey basaltic stone. The remains of the **Rocca** dominate the hill. It is associated with the legendary Ghino di Tacco who imprisoned the Abbot of Cluny here, as related by Boccaccio in the *Decameron*. The Rocca was taken in 1469 and rebuilt by the Sienese but was later forced to surrender, together with other Sienese strongholds, to Cosimo de' Medici in 1559. New fortifications of impressive proportions were constructed by the Medici. The castle was devastated by an explosion in the 18C and partly restored in the 1930s; further consolidation has been carried out in recent years. There are plans to create a local archaeological museum in part of the castle. The position offers a fine view over the Orcia valley to the north and of Monte Amiata to the west.

In the central piazza is the Romanesque church of **San Pietro** above a flight of steps, with a tall campanile rising from the façade. The fine **interior** has cross vaults over the transept and an apse supported on transversal arches. There are several good della Robbia statues and reliefs, a *Madonna and Child* in polychrome wood by Francesco di Valdambrino and over the high altar, a glazed terracotta *Crucifixion with the Magdalen*, by Benedetto and Santi Buglioni. Nearby, in Via Roma, is the Gothic church of **Sant'Agata**, the patron saint of Radicofani. The church was rebuilt in the 18C and has a terracotta altarpiece of the *Madonna and Child with Saints* by Andrea della Robbia.

On a road which descends towards the Via Cassia is a fountain erected by Ferdinando I dei Medici in 1603 with figures of Justice and Abundance flanking the Medici arms. Opposite is **Palazzo La Posta**, a hunting lodge with arched porticoes on two levels, which was built for Grand-duke Ferdinando and is attributed to Simone Genga and Bernardo Buontalenti (1584). It later became an inn at which Montaigne, Chateaubriand, and Dickens all stayed. It is now in a sadly neglected state.

34 · Montepulciano and environs

■ Practical information

Information office. APT Chianciano Terme e Valdichiana (☎ 0578-63167). Information offices in Montepulciano, 9 Via Ricci (☎ 0578-758687); Torrita di Siena, Biblioteca Comunale (☎ 0577-685452); Sinalunga, 5 Piazza Garibaldi (☎ 0577-630364); and Trequanda, Biblioteca Comunale (☎ 0577-685452).

Getting there
By rail. There is a branch line between Siena and Chiusi with stations at Sinalunga, Torrita di Siena and Montepulciano Scalo, 11km north of Montepulciano, but the quickest approach from Florence or Rome is on the main line to Chiusi station where there is a bus service (*LFI*) c every hour for Montepulciano.

By bus. From Siena *TRA-IN* **bus service** (except on Sundays) to Montepulciano. *TRA-IN* buses also run between Montepulciano and Pienza.

Hotels
Montepulciano: ★★★ *Il Marzocco*, 18 Piazza Savonarola (☎ 0578-757262; fax 9578-757530). In the environs, 3km southeast of Montepulciano on the road to Chianciano: ★★★ *Panoramic*, 8 Via di Villa Bianca (☎ 0578-798398; fax 0578-799205).
Torrita di Siena: ★★★ *La Stazione*, 255 Via Mazzini (☎ & fax 0577-685158); ★★ *Belvedere*, 31 Via Traversa Valdichiana Ovest (☎ 0577-686442).
Sinalunga: ★★★★*Locanda dell'Amorosa*, with luxury (**£££**) restaurant, 2km south of Sinalunga (☎ 0577-679497; fax 0577-63200).
Trequanda: ★★ *Casal Mustia*, 3 Piazza della Pieve, ☎ 0577-665310.

Restaurants
Montepulciano: **££** *Il Cantuccio*, 112 Via delle Cantine and *Porta di Bacco*, Via di Gracciano.
Montefollonico: **£££** *La Chiusa*, **££** *Conte Matto*.
Petroio: **£** *Madonnino dei Monti*.
Montisi: **££** *La Grancia*, 3 Via Umberto I.
Sinalunga: **££** *Locanda dell'Amorosa*.

Annual festivals

In Montepulciano the *Bravio delle Botti* is held on the last Sunday of **August**. Two men from each of the eight districts of the town compete in rolling a barrel (*botte*) weighing 80 kilos uphill, from Piazza Marzocco to Piazza Grande. The prize is a painted banner, the *Bravio*, and the privilege of offering the candle to the patron saint of Montepulciano, St Agnese, on her feast day on **1 May**, when an annual fair is held.

Since 1959 a *Convegno Internazionale di Studi Umanistici* has been held here, devoted to the study of Poliziano's work, which ends with a concert of Renaissance music in Palazzo Tarugi.

During the first half of **August**, the *Cantiere Internazionale d'Arte* has a programme of classical and modern music, with performances of plays and dance, and art exhibitions. Throughout August there is a *Mostra Interregionale dell'Artigianato*, an exhibition of local handicrafts.

At **Torrita di Siena** the *Palio dei Somari* is held on the Sunday following 19 March, with a mule race, flag throwing and various festivities.

Montepulciano

Montepulciano is a dignified and interesting hilltop town (14,300 inhab.; 665m) commanding the southeast part of Tuscany near the Umbrian border. It is particularly well preserved, with no ugly buildings on the outskirts towards Pienza. It has many handsome 16C palaces, including some by Antonio da Sangallo il Vecchio who also built the Tempio di San Biagio here, a famous building of the High Renaissance. The area is noted for its red wines, the most famous being the *Vino Nobile di Montepulciano*.

> **History**. After changing hands several times between Siena and Florence, Montepulciano came under permanent Florentine rule in 1511, and its fortifications, including the Porta di Gracciano, were rebuilt by Cosimo I. It was the birthplace of Angelo Ambrogini (1454–94), the great Classical scholar, who adopted the town's late Latin name **Poliziano**. Perhaps the most original genius among writers of his period, he was also famous for his eloquence. Although reputedly extremely ugly, with an enormous nose, Lorenzo il Magnifico employed him as tutor for his sons at Cafaggiolo in the Mugello, see p. 118. He is famous for his poems in the vernacular including *Stanze per la giostra del magnifico Giuliano di Piero dei Medici* (1475–78) and the *Fabula di Orfeo*. Another distinguished native was Cardinal Roberto Bellarmino (1542–1621), a Jesuit, author of the *Catechism of Christian Doctrine*, and hated by British Protestants in James I's days. Another eminent person born here was Riccardo Cervini (1501–55), later Pope Marcellus II.

Outside Porta al Prato stands the 14C church of **Sant'Agnese**, on the site of the convent built by the Dominican abbess, Agnese Segni (1268–1317). She was canonised as St Agnese of Montepulciano in 1726. The modern **façade** incorporates a 14C doorway. The stained-glass rose window, representing St Agnese, is by Bano di Michelangelo da Cortona.

The **interior** has a single nave. In the first chapel to the right is a fresco of the *Madonna* attributed to Simone Martini. A door opens into the Camera di Sant' Agnese, where relics of the saint are preserved. Flanking the main altar on which is a marble urn containing the body of St Agnese, surmounted by a statue by Mazzuoli, are a *Birth of the Virgin* by Raffaello Vanni and the *Martyrdom of San Biagio* by Giovanni da San Giovanni. In the chapel on the left is a 13C

MONTEPULCIANO

SM delle Grazie

✝ S. Agnese

PIAZZA
S. AGNESE

Bus Station

Giardino di
Poggiofanti

V. LE D. SANGALLO

0 _____ 200 yards
0 _____ 200 metres

Porta al Prato ⊠

✝ S. Bernardo

Palazzo
Bucelli

Palazzo
Avignonesi

S. Agostino ✝

GRACCIANO

Palazzo
Tarugi

Palazzo
Cocconi

PIAZZA
MICHELOZZO

S. Lucia ✝

VIA D.

Palazzo
Venturi

Loggia

Porta
Gozzano

V. D. POGGIOLO

S. Francesco ✝

Palazzo
Cervini

Palazzo
Ricci

VIA DI VOLTAIA

Porta d.
Grassi

Museo
Civico

Palazzo
Grugni

VIA RICCI

Palazzo d.
Capitano

Palazzo
Tarugi

✝ Gesù

Palazzo
Comunale

PIAZZA
GRANDE

Palazzo
Contucci

VIA DI ORIOLO

S. Biagio

VIA DI COLLAZZI

✝ Duomo

VIA DELL'OPIO

Teatro
Poliziano

VIA D. FORTEZZA

Politian's
House

Porta d.
Farine

Fortezza

VIA POLIZIANO

✝ S. Maria
d. Servi

N

Crucifix. The **cloister**, which was begun in the early 14C but only completed in the 17C, has frescoed lunettes with stories from the *Life of St Agnes*, by Salvi Castellucci (1652).

Opposite the church is the **Poggiofanti Garden**, dominated by the ramparts built by Antonio da Sangallo il Vecchio, with a fine view over the Val di Chiana. From Porta al Prato, Via di Gracciano del Corso winds up past several 16C palaces including **Palazzo Avignonesi** (No. 91; right), with a rusticated ground floor. Opposite is the Colonna del Marzocco, bearing a copy of the original lion (1511), now in the museum, made in 1856 by Antonio Sarrocchi. On the left is the church of **San Bernardo**, designed by the Baroque architect Padre Andrea Pozzo. The luminous oval interior has a *Madonna in Adoration* over the altar attributed to Andrea della Robbia.

The Corso continues past Palazzo Batignani (No. 85; right), Palazzo Tarugi (No. 84; left), and **Palazzo Cocconi** (No. 70), attributed to Antonio da Sangallo il Vecchio (the top floor was added in the 19C). **Palazzo Bucelli** (No. 73) has Etruscan urns, reliefs, and inscriptions embedded in the lower part of its façade. It housed the Etruscan collection of finds from excavations in the region, created by the 18C scholar and antiquarian Pietro Bucelli, which was donated to Grand-duke Pietro Leopoldo I and is now in the Archaeological Museum in Florence.

Above a flight of steps on the right is the church of *****Sant'Agostino**. The fine **façade** in Istrian stone, and the doorway, with a terracotta high relief of the *Madonna and Child with Saints John the Baptist and Augustine*, are by Michelozzo. The **interior** was redesigned in 1784–91 when the apse and transepts were shortened. On the south side: *Raising of Lazarus* by Alessandro Allori; *St Bernardine* signed and dated 1456 by Giovanni di Paolo; and *Pietà* attributed to Cristoforo Roncalli. On the high altar, polychrome wooden *Crucifix* by Antonio da Sangallo il Vecchio (painted by Antonio di Bastiano). Behind is the **Coro Vecchio** (old choir) of the earlier church, with frescoes and paintings by Bartolomeo Barbiani of Montepulciano, and a *Crucifix* attributed to Pollaiolo. On the third north altar, *Crucifixion* by Lorenzo di Credi, and, on the entrance wall, *Ascension* by Cesare Nebbia (1585), and *Madonna della Cintola* attributed to Federico Barocci.

Facing the church, in Piazza Michelozzo, is an old tower house with a quaint statue of Pulcinella on top which strikes the hours of the clock (the gift of a Neapolitan who settled in the city in the 17C).

The Corso continues past **Palazzo Buratti-Bellarmino** (No. 28; left), with a 17C doorway and frescoes by Federico Zuccari in the vestibule. To the left, Borgo Buio leads to the Gothic **Porta di Gozzano**. Via di Gracciano begins to climb steeply uphill through the Arco della Cavina next to the former hospital of Santa Maria della Cavina, to reach Piazza delle Erbe, the market square. Here is the arched **Logge del Grano** (16C), with the Medici arms. Via di Voltaia continues left past the grandiose **Palazzo Cervini** (No. 21; left), begun for Marcellus II before his pontificate, perhaps by Antonio da Sangallo il Giovane, and **Palazzo Gagnoni-Grugni** (No. 55; left), with a balconied portal by Vignola. Farther on (left), next to the Jesuit College, is the church of the **Gesù**, with a Baroque interior by Andrea Pozzo and illusionistic paintings by his pupil Antonio Colli.

Well in front of Palazzo del Capitano del Popolo

The Corso now becomes Via dell'Opio, lined with more palaces, some of which still reveal their medieval origin. In Piazza dell'Opio, Via del Teatro leads right to Piazza Grande (see below) and Via della Farina leads left to **Porta delle Farine**, a typical example of a Sienese double gate. In Via Poliziano, the continuation of Via dell'Opio, is the 14C house (No. 5; plaque) where Poliziano was born.

Outside the town walls, at the end of Via Poliziano, is the church of **Santa Maria dei Servi**. The simple Gothic façade with an arched doorway and a rose window, dates from the 14C. The elegant Baroque **interior** is by Andrea Pozzo. On the north side (second altar) is a 15C fresco of the *Madonna della Santoreggia*, greatly venerated in the past, and (third altar) a *Madonna and Child* by the school of Duccio, inserted into a larger painting. The road, from which there is a beautiful view, then skirts the rebuilt **Fortezza** and re-enters the walls by Via della Fortezza to reach ***Piazza Grande**, where there is a pretty well.

Duomo

The duomo in Piazza Grande (**open** 09.00–18.00), was designed by Ippolito Scalza in 1592–1630. The façade, unlike the sides, is unfinished. The 14C campanile belonged to the earlier church of Santa Maria.

The **interior** has a Latin-cross plan with three naves and a cupola over the crossing. Fragments of the ***tomb of Bartolomeo Aragazzi**, secretary to Pope Martin V, by Michelozzo (1427–36), include Aragazzi's effigy (right of the west door), two bas-reliefs on the first two nave pilasters, two statues on either side of the high altar, a statue in a niche on the right of the high altar, and the frieze of putti and festoons on the high altar (two kneeling angels from the same tomb are in the British Museum).

South aisle. First chapel, polychrome marble altar by Mazzuoli (1683); **fourth chapel**, two Sienese paintings with gold grounds of the *Redeemer* and the *Assumption*; **fifth chapel**, *Assumption* by Domenico Manetti and *St George* by Angelo Righi (1603). On the **high altar** is a *triptych by Taddeo di Bartolo of 1401, representing the *Assumption of the Virgin with Saints*, predella scenes and pinnacles. In the central nave, on the end piers, are two gilt-wood statues of the *Virgin Annunciate* and the angel *Gabriel* attributed to Francesco di Valdambrino. The marble tabernacle on the right pier of the choir is by Vecchietta.

North aisle. On the pilaster between the fifth and fourth chapels, *Madonna and Child* by Sano di Pietro; in the **baptistery** there is a *font with six bas-reliefs on a base of three caryatid figures by Giovanni di Agostino, c 1340. On the wall, the so-called *Altare dei Gigli* (altar of the lilies), *with Saints Stephen, Bonaventura, Catherine, and Bernardine*, by Andrea della Robbia, enclose a bas-relief of the *Madonna and Child* attributed to Benedetto da Maiano. The statues of *Saints Peter and John the Baptist* in the side niches are attributed to Domenico di Agostino (c 1360).

The crenellated *Palazzo Comunale is surmounted by an impressive clock tower. The building dates from the late 14C. The design of the façade, built in travertine with a rusticated ground floor, has recently been attributed to Michelozzo. There is a fine courtyard with a loggia on two sides and another on the upper floor. The **tower**, which recalls that of Palazzo Vecchio in Florence, is worth climbing to enjoy the view which stretches from Monte Amiata to Siena, and east to Lake Trasimene.

On the corner of Via Ricci is **Palazzo del Capitano del Popolo**, a Gothic palace considerably rebuilt (with fine Gothic arches on Via Ricci), and a bell-cote on the roof. In front is the elegant *Pozzo de' Griffi e de' Leoni attributed to Antonio da Sangallo il Vecchio. The well is framed by an architrave resting on two columns, with the Medici arms, flanked by the lions of Florence and the griffins of Montepulciano. Next to it is the flank of *Palazzo Tarugi, with a triple arched arcade on the ground floor which continues round in the two left bays of the main front, facing the cathedral. The grandiose travertine façade, which is also attributed to Antonio da Sangallo il Vecchio, has Ionic half-columns on high pedestals supporting a balustrade above the pedimented windows of the main floor.

Opposite Palazzo Comunale is **Palazzo Contucci** which was begun for Cardinal Antonio Del Monte (his arms are on the corner) by Antonio da Sangallo il Vecchio. The fine stone façade has five windows on the piano nobile with pediments supported on Ionic columns; the top floor in brick was added later. Inside is an elegant courtyard, and the salone on the first floor is painted with trompe l'oeil frescoes by Andrea Pozzo (1705). The back of the palace rests on the old town walls: the gradient of the site on which the town is built can be appreciated here. To the right of Palazzo Contucci, Via del Teatro leads steeply down and then bends to the right past the **Teatro Poliziano**, built by Giacomo and Sebastiano Barchi and decorated by Giuseppe Castagnoli. It was inaugurated in 1796 by Ferdinando III. The interior is composed of four tiers of boxes.

Museo Civico and Pinacoteca

From Piazza Grande, opposite the Duomo, Via Ricci descends past the 12C–13C **Palazzo Sisti**. Opposite on the left is **Palazzo Ricci**, with a simple 16C façade; the back has a loggia and garden with a fine view overlooking San Biagio. On the right is **Palazzo Neri-Orselli** (No. 15), another Gothic palace, modified in later centuries, which now houses the Museo Civico e Pinacoteca Crociani (closed for restoration and restructuring since 1997). The archaeological collection, with interesting Etruscan finds, is to be rearranged.

The **courtyard** which has a Renaissance loggia and outdoor stairway leading to the upper floors, has sculpture fragments removed from various buildings, the Cocconi and Catenacci arms, the original lion (1511) from the Colonna del Marzocco, and a bust in scagliola of Marcellus II.

On the **first floor** are several della Robbian works including two altarpieces by Andrea della Robbia: one with *God the Father and angels* surrounding a niche with a *Nativity* and *Adoration of the Magi* in the predella; and the other with the *Madonna and Child between Saints Bartholomew and Longinus and two angels holding a crown*. There are also figures of the *Virgin Annunciate* and angel *Gabriel*, and of *St John the Baptist*. The collection of paintings, mostly of the Tuscan and Umbrian schools, is arranged in two large halls. They include: Margaritone d'Arezzo, *St*

Francis; school of Duccio, *Madonna and Child with angels*; Jacopo di Mino del Pellicciaio, *Coronation of the Virgin*; Luca di Tommé, *Crucifixion*; workshop of Filippino Lippi, *Crucifixion*; Raffaellino del Garbo, *Madonna and Child*; Girolamo di Benvenuto, *Nativity*; Giovanni Antonio Lappoli, *Immaculate Conception* (1545).

There are a number of 16C and 17C portraits, including that of *Beata Caterina de' Ricci* by Giovan Battista Naldini, and several by Florentine artists (Sustermans and Santi di Tito). Among the later paintings: Rutilio Manetti, *Holy Family*; Anton Domenico Gabbiani, *Venus and Cupid*; Carlo Cignani, *Venus disarming Cupid and Charity*; Cristoforo Munari, *Still Life with musical instruments* (1712); and Antonio Joli, two views of Arezzo Cathedral. The small 19C collection includes a portrait by Vincenzo Luchini of the tenor *Moriani* in *Lucia di Lammermoor*, and works by Gazzarrini, Morghen, and Ciseri.

Farther down Via Ricci, on the left, is the Baroque façade of the **Oratorio dei Cavalieri di Santo Stefano** and **Palazzo Benincasa**, with a bust of Gian Gastone de' Medici over the doorway. Beyond the Porta San Francesco (from which a street leads through the Porta dei Grassi down to San Biagio, see below) is a piazza with a fine view. Here, in the oldest part of the town, is the church of **San Francesco** which dates from the 13C. Next to the elegant Gothic doorway are the remains of a pulpit from which St Bernardine of Siena is reputed to have preached. The interior has been heavily restored. Via del Poggiolo passes the Piazzetta degli Archi and leads to the church of **Santa Lucia**, built in 1633, which has an elegant façade. On the high altar is a *Crucifix* by Giovanni Battista Alessi di Montepulciano. In the first chapel (right) is a fine, but damaged *Madonna* (c 1495) by Luca Signorelli (locked; light switch behind the grille, operated by a rod).

On the northern outskirts of the town, beyond Sant'Agnese (see above), Viale Calamandrei leads to the sanctuary of **Santa Maria delle Grazie**, designed by Ippolito Scalza, with a porticoed façade (1605). The **interior** was decorated with elegant stuccowork in the mid-18C by Andrea da Cremona. **South side**. *Madonna and Child with Saints* by Niccolò Betti, and (second altar) della Robbian *tabernacle, framing the *Madonna delle Grazie*, and two *Annunciation* figures attributed to Giovanni della Robbia. In the choir is a *Madonna and Child with St Simon Stock* by Giovan Battista Ferretti (1766). **North side**. *St Helena adoring the Cross* by Bartolomeo Barbiani of Montepulciano (1632), a German *Crucifix* (16C), with papier-mâché statues of the *Virgin* and *St John* (1740), and a *Madonna with Carmelite Saints* by Giuseppe Nicola Nasini. The late 16C *organ is the only example of its kind in Italy (there is a comparable one at Innsbruck). Its pipes are of cypress wood and produce a particularly soft and gentle sound, which was recommended by Monteverdi for the accompaniment of his *Orfeo*. Since the organ's restoration in 1983, it has been played by organists from all over the world.

From Piazzale Sant'Agnese Via Bernabei leads to Piazza del Mercato and the 16C Villa La Fantina (unfinished). About three kilometres from the centre of the town is the **Santuario della Madonna della Quercia**, built in the 18C round an earlier chapel. On the façade are two statuettes of the *Annunciation* by Giovanni della Robbia and, inside, an interesting collection of ex-votos.

Tempio di San Biagio

Tempio di San Biagio

Just outside Montepulciano, off the road to Pienza, and approached by a beautiful cypress avenue, is the *Tempio di San Biagio (**open** 09.00–13.00, 15.00–19.00), one of the great church buildings of the High Renaissance. It was built by Antonio da Sangallo il Vecchio (1518–34) for the Ricci family on the site of an earlier church, also dedicated to St Biagio. It has a Greek-cross plan with a central dome. The **exterior** of travertine is of classical sobriety, and the beautifully proportioned design of the façade is repeated on two sides. Only one of the towers was finished, and actually completed in 1545 by Baccio d'Agnolo, who also built the lantern of the dome.

The **interior**, which is also very beautiful, repeats and elaborates the classical features of the exterior, with sculptural decoration carved in high relief in the yellow sandstone. The marble high altar is by Giannozzo and Lisandro di Pietro Albertini (1584). The statues of *Saints John the Baptist, Agnes, Catherine of Siena*, and *George*, are by Ottaviano Lazzari (1617). The venerated 14C fresco in the tabernacle represents the *Madonna and Child with St Francis*. The lunette fresco is by Antonio Righi (1648), and those in the vault are attributed to Bartolomeo Barbiani. The stained-glass window is by Bano di Michelangelo of Cortona (1568). Behind, in the area corresponding to the apse, is the sacristy, from which a staircase leads to the outside balcony. The canons' house, nearby, with open loggias on both floors, was built after Sangallo's death.

The environs of Montepulciano

Torrita di Siena

To the north of Montepulciano is the lovely little red-brick village of Torrita di Siena which was an important stronghold of the Sienese Republic until it became part of the Medici Grand-duchy of Tuscany in 1554. It preserves parts of its walls and is a particularly well-kept village. It is thought to have been the birthplace of the 13C painter and mosaicist Fra Jacopo da Torrita (or Jacopo Torriti), and of Ghino di Tacco.

In the piazza, with a well, is **Palazzo Comunale** (13C; restored), with a bell-tower. Inside is the restored Teatro degli Oscuri (1824). Next to it is the Romanesque church of **Santa Flora e Lucilla**. In the pleasant brick **interior**, on the south side (light on the right) is an exquisite small ***lunette** carved **by Donatello** depicting the *Blood of the Redeemer*. Using the sculptor's typical *schiacciato* technique, in a very small space the figure of Christ is portrayed surrounded by eleven cherubim in the clouds and the busts of the two donors. It is owned by the Spedale Maestri outside Porta Nuova. The church also has some fresco fragments and interesting paintings: on the south altar, triptych with the *Crucifixion and Saints* attributed to Michele di Matteo (1444). In the sanctuary, school of Sodoma, *Madonna in Glory with six Saints*; north side, Francesco Vanni, *Annunciation* (1592); (on the altar), Bartolo di Fredi, triptych with the *Nativity and Saints Anthony Abbot and Augustine*, a charming work; Benvenuto di Giovanni, *Madonna and Saints, with the Trinity* in the lunette above. A painting of the *Madonna and Child* by the school of Ambrogio Lorenzetti was removed for restoration many years ago.

Just beyond the piazza is the church of **Santa Croce** (1642), with a Baroque interior and stucco statuary on the high altar. Outside Porta a Sole (reached along the side of Palazzo Comunale) is the **Madonna delle Nevi** (kept locked) a little brick chapel erected in 1525. It is preceded by a portico with two Ionic columns, and has a cast of Donatello's lunette depicting the *Blood of the Redeemer* (see above) over the portal. The altar wall has fine *frescoes attributed to Girolamo di Benvenuto. Outside Torrita, on the Sinalunga road (see below) is the 16C **Villa La Fratta**, attributed to Baldassare Peruzzi, with a fine garden (admission sometimes on request).

Montefollonico

To the south of Torrita di Siena is Montefollonico, a quiet little fortified village with small houses, Sienese in atmosphere. It stands on a ridge (567m) between the Orcia and Chiana valleys. Probably of Roman origin, the village developed in the Middle Ages. Parts of its medieval walls with three gates remain, including the **Porta Nuova**, a 14C–15C double gate which provides the entrance to the delightful hamlet which has numerous doves and pigeons. The lovely old paving of the main street was destroyed in 1997.

The street leads left past the little 13C **Palazzo del Comune**, with a well-head next to it, to the 13C church of **San Leonardo** (if closed, ring at No. 38, by the east end). The pretty exterior is built of square blocks of local yellow-and-white stone, and is approached by steps on either side of outcrops of rock. The restored interior has a Baroque high altar. In a chapel to the left is a 13C wooden *Crucifix* between two paintings of the *Annunciation* in stone frames. In the nave are very worn frescoes and paintings of the *Birth of the Virgin* and a *Circumcision* (in a good frame). A *Madonna and two Saints* by Guidoccio Cozzarelli which belongs to the church and is now exhibited in the Museo Diocesano in Pienza, has been replaced by a copy.

In the other direction the street leads past the entrance to the little **Chiesa della Compagnia del Corpus Domini** (adm. as for San Leonardo), recently restored. It is preceded by a tiny courtyard with the bell-tower at one corner. Inside is a *Deposition* by the school of Signorelli, and interesting 18C frescoed lunettes with amusing details.

The street leads on past (right) the church of **San Bartolomeo**, privately owned and recently restored (usually open in summer). High up on the façade there is an interesting Romanesque sculpture of a mermaid. **Porta del Triano**, bearing the date 1278, frames a view of Montepulciano on the skyline. Outside the gate is a fine stretch of walls. A footpath continues down to the handsome **Chiesa del Triano** built on rocks in a group of horse-chestnut trees, with a lovely view of Monte Amiata. Its architectural features in brick and stone stand out against the white *intonaco*. It has a pretty domed bell-tower. The date 1609 is above the door. The interior has an attractive crossing with an unusual altar screen. The works of art which belong to the church are now exhibited in the Museo Diocesano in Pienza.

Sinalunga

Sinalunga is now a small industrial town. From the 12C up until 1864 it was known as *Asinalunga*. Here the Sienese defeated the English mercenaries of Niccolò da Montefeltro in 1363; here also Garibaldi was arrested in 1867 by Vittorio Emanuele II, to prevent an ill-timed descent on Rome.

In the ugly, Piazza Garibaldi is the **Collegiata** (San Martino). The **interior** has large white stucco statues of saints. On the south side, the third chapel contains a 16C *Crucifix*. In the south transept is a *Deposition* by Francesco Vanni (1563–1610), with a predella (in a good frame). On the south wall of the sanctuary, *Madonna and Saints* by Benvenuto di Giovanni (1509) with another good predella and frame. On the north wall of the sanctuary a tondo by Pseudo Pier Francesco Fiorentino has been temporarily removed. In the north transept, **Madonna and the standing Child* by Sodoma above *Christ supported by two angels flanked by Saints Bernardine and Catherine.*

To the right of the church is **Santa Croce** with an 18C façade. In the pretty interior is (right altar) a *Marriage of the Virgin* by the school of Luca Signorelli. Also in the piazza is the church of **Santa Maria delle Nevi** with a painting attributed to Benvenuto di Giovanni. On the right of the façade of the Collegiata Via Mazzini winds round to **Palazzo Pretorio**, in an unusual site, between two streets. It is built in brick, decorated with coats of arms and a tower. In front of the palace, a road continues down to **Santa Lucia** (deconsecrated; used by a musical society), which contains a fresco attributed to Benvenuto di Giovanni. Beyond is a view over the Valdichiana. Near Palazzo Pretorio is a **theatre** (1797–1807), with an inconspicuous exterior (No. 17). It is named after Ciro Pinsuti (1824–88), born in Sinalunga.

Outside the town is the Franciscan convent of **San Bernardino** (or the **Madonna del Riposo**; yellow signposts), approached by a short avenue. Off the 18C church (shown by a nun) is an octagonal chapel with some fine paintings: Guidoccio Cozzarelli, *Baptism of Christ* (1470); Benvenuto di Giovanni, *Annunciation* (1470); Guidoccio Cozzarelli, *Madonna and Child with Saints* (1486). A *Madonna and Child* by Sano di Pietro, stolen in 1971, is to be replaced by a copy. Over the high altar is a copy (the original has been removed for safekeeping) of a *Madonna and Child* known as the *Madonna del Rifugio*, attributed to Sano di Pietro.

Trequanda is a medieval village which was once under the dominion of Siena (car park below the fine round tower of the restored Castello dei Cacciaconti). The parish church of **Santi Pietro e Andrea** has a delightful façade chequered in brown-and-white stone. The **interior** contains frescoes by Sodoma and Bartolomeo Miranda and a triptych of the *Madonna and Saints* by Giovanni di Paolo over the high altar. Also here is the fine gilded wood sculptured coffer of

Beata Bonizella (1235–1300). The seated wooden statue of the *Madonna and Child* is attributed to Jacopo Sansovino. The **Palazzo del Comune** has a tower reminiscent of a toy castle.

A lovely road leads south towards Pienza through the beautiful **Valdichiana Senese**, with wooded hills (ilexes and oaks) and cultivated fields past a number of interesting and well preserved small villages.

Montisi is a picturesque village south of Trequanda on a hill (413m). The **castle** preserves some Gothic windows. At the top of the hill, beside a clock tower, is the Romanesque church of the **Annunziata** (key with the caretaker at No. 11). The elegant interior has transversal arches supported on travertine columns. In the sanctuary is a large *polyptych of the Madonna and Child with Saints Peter, Louis, James and Paul*, signed and dated 1496 by Neroccio di Bartolomeo Landi in a fine frame. The predella is in the Museo Diocesano in Pienza. In the north transept chapel is a painted *Crucifix* attributed to Ugolino di Nerio. Among the numerous medieval buildings is a **granary** (at the entrance to the village) which belonged to the hospital of Santa Maria della Scala in Siena. San Giovanni d'Asso, a short way to the west, is described in Ch. 32.

Further south, the village of **Castelmuzio** can be seen from the approach road. There are some lovely old olive trees in the vicinity. Of Etruscan and Roman foundations, and first mentioned in the 9C, it has simple brick and sandstone houses. It is built on a circular plan, so that all the streets are curving. In the piazza is a very unusual *casa-torre*, reconstructed in the 18C as **Palazzo Fratini**, and recently restored. Also here is the **Museo della Confraternità della Santa Trinità e di San Bernardino** (opened on request locally). Next to a hostel for pilgrims on the Via Francigena, the Confraternity of Santa Trinità was founded by 1450. The collection contains a *Madonna and Child* by the school of Duccio; *St Bernardine*, by his friend Giovanni di Paolo; and a *Madonna and Saints*, attributed to Matteo di Giovanni or Pietro di Francesco Orioli. In the sacristy and a room on the upper floor is a charming little collection of Crosses, copes, chalices, musical instruments from the local band founded after the First World War (and disbanded in 1950), Etruscan urns and ceramics.

Outside the village (well signposted) is the **Pieve di Santo Stefano in Cennano**, founded in 1285 on the site of a Roman building. It stands in a group of olive trees beside a farmhouse, and the key is left in the side door. The impressive large church shows the influence of Lombard architecture, with a fine triple apse at the east end. The west door has an arch carved with animals and human heads. In the **interior**, which is awaiting restoration, the columns reach up to the roof. It was poorly restored in the 19C.

A beautiful road, with wide views of Radicofani, Montepulciano, Pienza, and Monte Amiata, leads east past fields and olive groves to **Petroio**. The medieval village is built on an interesting circular plan; a road forms a spiral, leading up to the tower of the impressive 13C brick castle, high above its clustered houses. The parish church of **San Pietro** has a large, but damaged, fresco of the *Crucifixion*, attributed to Andrea di Niccolò, in the choir. A beautiful fragment of a *Madonna and Child* by Taddeo di Bartolo also belongs to the church. **San Giorgio**, an older church, is in need of restoration. Petroio was the birthplace of a famous ascetic, Bartolomeo Carosi, known as Brandano (1483–1554), whose mottoes and prophesies have been handed down to this day.

The locality has been known since the 18C for its production of ceramic vases and pots, using the local ochre-coloured calcareous rock, and there is still a large terracotta works in the woods on the outskirts. To the north of Petroio (on the road to Sinalunga) is the **Abbadia a Sicille**, a 17C fortified farm on the site of a hospice for pilgrims, founded by the Knights Templar in the 11C. The church was built in 1263. The buildings were radically restored in the 19C.

Sant'Anna in Camprena

South of Castelmuzio is the large ex-Olivetan monastery of **Sant'Anna in Camprena** (accommodation available from Easter to September; information from the Curia at Montepulciano). Approached by a long cypress avenue, the monastery is beautifully situated on a peaceful hill which dominates the surrounding countryside (with views of picturesque farms and the little towns of Castelmuzio and Petroio). It was founded by Bernardo Tolomei in 1324, rebuilt in the 15C, and enlarged in the 17C. However, the monastery was abandoned at the end of the 18C. It is now being slowly restored, and can be visited (ring for the caretaker 09.00–12.00, 15.00–18.00).

The **refectory** has very well preserved *frescoes by Sodoma, his earliest works painted in 1503–05, at the age of 25. The splendid colours are extraordinarily vivid, and the landscapes and use of perspective, as well as the expressive figure studies, show remarkable ability. On the **entrance wall**: *Bishop Guido Tarlati approves the Rule of the Olivetan order*; the *Deposition* (a moving scene which includes the figures of St Anna and St Joachim); and *St Anna with the Virgin and Child and two Olivetan monks*. On the **opposite wall**: *Multiplication of the Loaves and Fishes*, divided into three scenes against a background in which the landscape incorporates the Colosseum and the arch of Constantine. The two long walls (the lower parts of which were formerly covered by the refectory benches), bear two frescoed friezes (partially preserved) with roundels of *Saints Gregory, Catherine, and Bernardine*, alternating with monochrome scenes of the lives of St Anna and the Virgin, and grotesques.

Nearby is the splendid old **kitchen** and a charming **walled garden** with a pond. From the 16C **cloister** (which has been partially walled in) is an entrance to the **church** which was built in the 17C and provided with large paintings of the life of Bernardo Tolomei in the 18C.

Near the monastery, an unsurfaced road (signposted *Siena*) leads to the Cassia through superb countryside past little hamlets and *calanchi*, with exceptionally beautiful views.

Pienza, a few kilometres to the south, is described in Ch. 33.

35 · Chiusi and Chianciano Terme

Chiusi, on the south-eastern border of Tuscany close to Umbria, is well-known for its interesting Etruscan museum and painted Etruscan tombs. Nearby is the famous spa town of **Chianciano Terme**. **Sarteano**, with a new archaeological museum, and **Cetona**, a picturesque place, are both villages worth a visit in the district to the south.

■ Practical information

Information offices. APT Chianciano Terme-Valdichiana, 67 Piazza Italia, Chianciano Terme (☎ 0578-63167). The spa centre, Terme di Chianciano S.p.A., is at 12 Via delle Rose (☎ 0578-68111). In Chiusi, tourist office at 67 Via Porsenna (☎ 0578-227667). Sarteano: *Pro-Loco* information office, 1 Corso Garibaldi (☎ 0578-265312). Cetona: *Pro-Loco* information office, Piazza Garibaldi (☎ 0578-239143).

Getting there

By rail. Railway station *Chiusi-Chianciano Terme*, 3km south of Chiusi on the main Florence–Rome line (mostly slow trains only, although a few of the faster trains also stop here).

By bus. Buses every half hour from Chiusi to the railway station. Bus services from Chiusi to Lago di Chiusi, and to Montepulciano via Chianciano Terme.

Car parking in Chiusi off Via Pietriccia and Via dei Longobardi.

Hotels

Near **Chiusi**, at Querce al Pino (4km west): ★★★ *Il Patriarca* (☎ 0578-274407; fax 0578-274594); *Ismaele* (☎ 0578-274077; fax 0578-274069); *Rosati* (☎ 0578-274408; fax 0578-274199).
Numerous (over 200) hotels of all categories in **Chianciano Terme**.
Sarteano: ★★★ *Residenza Santa Chiara*, with restaurant, 30 Piazza Santa Chiara (☎ 0578-265412).
Cetona: ★★★ *Belverde*, just outside the town (☎ 0578-239085; fax 0578-239084).
San Casciano Bagni: ★★★ *Termina* (☎ 0578-58135) and ★★ hotels.

Agriturist accommodation

Near **Sarteano**: *Montemelino*, 106 Via di Chianciano (☎ 0578-265480).
Near **Cetona**: *Podere Verdino*, on the SS 321 Sud road (☎ & fax: 0578-238777); *Caio Alto*, also on the SS 321 road (☎ & fax: 0578-226666); *Fonterucola*, Via Fonterucola (☎ 0578-238345).

Campsites

Sarteano: ★★★★ *Campeggio delle Piscine*, with hot sulphur swimming pool (☎ 0578-265531; fax 0578-265889).
Two ★ sites near **Lago di Chiusi**: *La Fattoria* (☎ 0578-21407; fax 0578-20644) and *Pesce d'Oro* (☎ 0578-21403).

Restaurants

Chiusi: £ *La Solita Zuppa*, 21 Via Porsenna.
Sarteano: £££ *Santa Chiara* in the Hotel Residenza Santa Chiara; ££ *La Giara*, 2 Viale Europa; £ *Trattoria Tripolitania*, Via Garibaldi.
Cetona: £££ *Convento di San Francesco*; £ *Osteria Vecchia*, Sobborgo, and *Da Sacchetta* (just outside the centre). The *Podere Pornelleto*, Traversa Cassia Aurelia 8,an agriturist farm also has a restaurant.

Chiusi

Chiusi is a little hill-top town of 8700 inhabitants. It was an Etruscan town of great importance, as can be seen from the finds in its interesting museum, and the vast Etruscan necropolis which surrounds the town. Under the streets runs a labyrinth of Etruscan galleries.

History. Chiusi was the Etruscan Clevsins. One of the twelve cities of the Etruscan Confederation, it reached its greatest splendour around the 7C or 6C BC. The Latin authors often referred to the fertility of the surrounding countryside, which produced oil, wine, and wheat in abundance. Strabo described how the Lago di Chiusi could be reached by river from Rome up the Tiber and Chiana. Lars Porsena, the Lucumo or king of Chiusi, attacked Rome in 507–06 BC (see Macaulay's Horatius), but after 296 BC the town became subject to Rome and took the Roman name of Clusium. It continued to flourish in the Augustan era, and was then occupied by the Goths from 540 probably up until the 10C, when it became part of the Lombard duchy. The unhealthy marshes of the Valdichiana caused malaria and brought about the decline of Chiusi, but the drainage works begun by Cosimo de' Medici restored some degree of prosperity.

The Duomo

The Duomo and Etruscan Museum (well signposted) are close together. The Duomo (San Secondiano) was founded in the 6C and rebuilt in the 12C, but heavily restored in 1887–94. **Interior**. The splendid *columns and capitals, including one in breccia marble at the west end, come from various local Roman edifices. The nave and apses were painted by Arturo Viligiardi in 1887 in imitation of antique mosaics. In the south aisle is an alabaster font in the style of Andrea Sansovino. Off the left aisle is an *Adoration of the Child* by Bernardino Fungai. At the west end of the north aisle is a monument to San Mustiola (1785). A tall fortified tower was transformed into the campanile in 1585. It covers a huge cistern of the 1C BC (apply for admission to the Museo Nazionale Etrusco, see below).

Under the portico to the right of the façade is the **Museo della Cattedrale**, founded in 1932. It is well-arranged and labelled (**open** daily 1 June–15 Oct, 09.30–12.45, 16.30–19.30; winter 09.30–12.45).

Room I contains tombstones and inscriptions from the local catacombs of Santa Mustiola and Santa Caterina. Also here are Roman fragments from the Duomo, as well as Lombard and late medieval inscriptions, carvings and mosaic fragments. In the Garden, reached by a steep flight of steps cut into the walls in the last century, are remains of Etruscan fortifications which have been in the process of excavation since 1985. These include walls dating from the 3C BC and a square tower on top of an Etruscan building. Nearby is the entrance to a remarkably long Etruscan gallery (open to the public), which may have served as a water channel, or as part of a defence system.

Inside the museum building, at the top of the stairs, **Room II** contains: Girolamo da Benvenuto, *Madonna and Child with Saints* (very ruined; recently restored); church silver and vestments; and 15C ivories by the school of Baldassare degli Embriachi (based in Venice). Stairs continue up to a long passage above the portico with a fine display of **21 antiphonals** from the abbey of Monte Oliveto Maggiore dating from the second half of the 15C, illuminated by Liberale da Verona, Sano di Pietro, Lorenzo Rosselli di Bindo, and others.

The **Catacombs of Santa Caterina**, near the station, can be seen on a guided tour, daily at 11.00, on request at the Museo della Cattedrale (a custodian accompanies visitors in their car). They date from the mid-3C AD and have been illuminated. The **Catacombs of Santa Mustiola**, dedicated to the Roman saint, beneath a farm house, and in use from the 3C to the 5C can also be visited (as for Santa Caterina).

The Etruscan Museum

The *Museo Nazionale Etrusco, opposite the side of the Duomo, was founded in 1871 and opened in this fitting neo-classical building by Partini in 1901 (**open** daily 09.00–14.00; fest. 09.00–13.00; in summer usually 09.00–20.00 on weekdays, and fest. 09.00–13.00).

Chiusi was one of the first Etruscan cities to be explored, as early as the 15C, but unsystematic excavations, especially in the 19C, led to the dispersal of much of the material, and most of the objects in the museum are of unknown provenance; some have been poorly or incorrectly restored. A great number of inscriptions were found in and near Chiusi, but they are now in other museums.

The display is divided into three sections; the first illustrating the history of archaeological research in the area; the second showing the chronological development of local products, and the third section displaying finds arranged topographically. In the centre of the **hall** is prehistoric and Villanovian material, with finds dating from the 9C–8C BC, including canopic vases of the 7C–6C BC. In a small room are displayed Archaic reliefs (late 6C BC), showing Greek influence, and five sculptures of the 6C–5C BC. At the end of the hall are cases of Bucchero ware and 5C Attic black-figure and red-figure vases, terracotta architectural fragments, and 5C–4C bronzes. In the **outer corridor**: Etruscan vases and sarcophaghi and cinerary urns (4C–2C BC) in alabaster and terracotta, including the tomb of Lars Sentinates. The Roman material includes a head of Augustus, architectural and votive terracottas (3C–2C BC) and Hellenistic bronzes, ceramics and sarcophaghi.

The narrow Via della Misericordia leads to the 13C church of **Santa Maria della Morte**, with an unusually-shaped tower. In the pleasant Piazza XX Settembre, with a clock tower and 14C loggia (altered) is the town hall (enlarged in the 19C) and a 19C fountain. At the bottom of Via Lavinia, Porta Lavinia can be seen, with the countryside beyond. Near the clock tower is the church of **San Francesco**, founded in the 13C, with an ancient portal. The interior dates from the 18C; the stained glass windows at the east end were made in 1944 in Florence. Via Paolozzi leads to Piazza Vittorio Veneto, with a panoramic view. In the garden are Etruscan and Roman fragments. Via Arunte descends to a column of 1581 in Piazza Graziani, and then Via Porsenna continues up past several handsome 15C and 16C palaces back to Piazza Duomo.

On the outskirts of the town, in Via della Violella, off the Chianciano Terme road, part of the Etruscan walls of the city can be seen.

Etruscan tombs

The Etruscan tombs in the neighbourhood have all been closed for many years for conservation reasons, except for the Tomba della Pellegrina and Tomba del Leone, which can be visited by appointment at the Museo Nazionale Etrusco (a custodian accompanies you in your car). There are long-term plans to reopen the others. They are approached by pretty country lanes, most of which can be negotiated by car. From Chiusi, on the road to Chianciano Terme, Via delle Tombe Etrusche diverges right for the **Tomba della Pellegrina**, with several urns and sarcophagi. The **Tomba della Scimmia** (of the Ape) has important wall-paintings, and the **Tomba del Leone** has recently been restored. The **Tomba del Granduca**, has eight cinerary urns remaining on their stone benches.

There are more tombs east of the city below the new cemetery: the **Tomba Casuccini** (or *del Colle*), with a fine doorway (now visible through a glass door) and wall-paintings of sports and games and the **Tomba delle Tassinaie**, the only painted tomb from the Hellenistic period.

The **Poggio Gaiella**, a tufa hill to the north, has three storeys of passages and galleries; according to tradition, it is the mausoleum of Lars Porsenna.

To the north of Chiusi are two small picturesque lakes, with reedy shores, the **Lago di Chiusi** (387 hectares) and the **Lago di Montepulciano** (188 hectares), surrounded by cultivated fields and poplars. They are remnants of the huge marsh which once occupied this area. The interesting vegetation includes numerous varieties of aquatic plants, including water lilies. On the shores of Lago di Montepulciano is the Museo Naturalistico del Lago, a small museum illustrating the flora and fauna of the area (the lake can be visited by appointment, ☎ 0578-767518). The lake is frequented by local fisherman.

Città della Pieve, south of Chiusi and Lago Trasimeno to the east of Chiusi, are described in *Blue Guide Umbria*.

Chianciano Terme

Chianciano Terme is one of the most important spa towns in Italy (6800 inhab.). It has warm saline and chalybeate waters. With over 200 hotels of all categories, it is well-equipped to receive its numerous visitors. The **Acqua Santa** (open all year round; high season June–Sept) waters are taken internally for liver complaints. The **Sillene** spring is used for baths.

The place was known to the Romans as *Fontes Clusinae*. In the Middle Ages it was contested between Siena and Orvieto. The spa developed in 1915–29, and most of the thermal buildings were rebuilt in the 1950s.

The pleasant old village of **Chianciano Vecchia** adjoins the spa. The town hall is in the first piazza. A street descends to a second little piazza with Palazzo del Podestà and Palazzo dell'Arcipretura, which contains the **Museo della Collegiata** (ring on the first floor: **open** 10.00–12.00, 16.00–19.00 except fest & Mon; Nov–May only opened on request). The small collection is well labelled. The large *Crucifix* is attributed to the Maestro di San Polo in Rosso (school of Duccio), and the ancona (formerly on the high altar of the church) is attributed to the Maestro di Chianciano (early 14C). The Collegiata, beyond, has a detached fresco of the *Assunta*.

Outside the village, at the crossroads for Montepulciano, the **Museo Etrusco** (**open** 10.00–19.00 exc Mon) was opened in the Granaio Simoneschi, an old granary, in 1997. It contains recent Etruscan and Roman finds from the area. Objects found in the tombs of the necopoli of La Pedata and Tolle include canopic vases, bronzes, and Bucchero ware. There are also finds from the baths at Mezzomiglio, and decorations from a temple pediment discovered at I Fucoli dating from the 2C BC, including a winged female deity.

Sarteano

Sarteano (573m) is a medieval village with its streets laid out in a semicircle at the foot of the castle hill. An Etruscan settlement, it was later contested between Perugia, Orvieto, and Siena, until it passed under the dominion of the latter in 1379. The locality has excellent olive oil. At the entrance to the village is the church of **San Francesco** with a fine Renaissance façade of 1480. In Piazza XXIV Giugno above is a war memorial by Arnaldo Zocchi (1923) and the 14C **Palazzo del Comune** (rebuilt in 1845) which contains the 18C **Teatro degli Arrischianti** (1740; due to reopen soon after restoration).

Via Roma leads up from the piazza past the fine Renaissance **Palazzo Piccolomini**. Opposite is the handsome Palazzo Gabrielli where the **Museo Civico Archeologico** was opened in 1997. On the **ground floor** are displayed finds from the district made during excavations begun in the 19C and continued in this century. The material includes Bronze Age objects but is particularly important for Etruscan ware from 8C–2C BC necopoli (bronzes, vases, and canopic vases). Room 2 displays Bucchero ware with relief decoration (late 7C–early 6C BC). In Room 3 are red-figure vases, and a cippus found in the locality of Sant'Angelo with interesting reliefs (late 6C). Stairs lead down to the **basement** where the small private Bologni collection is displayed, as well as three unusual cinerary statuettes: the one on the left is a Hellenistic original, but the origins of the other two are uncertain. The bas-reliefs once decorated a building of the Augustan period, and two urns displayed here dating from the 1C BC are interesting because they bear the names of the dead in both Latin and Etruscan.

Via Roma continues downhill through an archway to the church of **San Martino**. In the interior, on the north side, is an *Annunciation* by Beccafumi, and a fine painting of the *Madonna with Saints Roch and Sebastian*, complete with its predella, by Andrea di Niccolò. On the south side are two works by Giacomo di Mino del Pellicciaio: *Madonna and Child*, and a triptych with the *Madonna and Saints John and Bartholomew*.

Corso Garibaldi leads from the other side of Piazza XXIV Giugno past several fine palaces including Palazzo Goti-Fanelli (1535), Palazzo Lichini (14C; enlarged in the 16C), and the 17C Palazzo Forneris, and the **Chiesa del Suffragio** with heavy yellow, black and white Baroque altars and some detached 15C frescoes.

The **Collegiata di San Lorenzo** lies beyond. Its foundations are 12C, its structure 16C. In the late 18C **interior**, on the left of the choir, is a chapel with two good paintings of the *Virgin Annunciate* and *Annunciatory angel* by Girolamo del Pacchia. In the chapel to the right of the choir is a marble ciborium by Marrina (1514). Opposite the Collegiata is the 15C Palazzo Cennini (rebuilt in the 18C). Just before Porta Monalda there is another fine palace (at No. 79) with an amusing mock Gothic pink-and-cream wing.

Outside the gate Via della Rocca (right) leads up to the imposing **castle**, first built in the 10C. The present building was fortified by the Sienese in 1467–74. Acquired by the Comune in 1997, there are plans to restore it and reopen it to the public.

Outside Sareano, on the Cetona road, beside a tabernacle, a rough road leads to the **Tomba delle Pianacce**, an Etruscan tomb (5C BC) discovered in 1954, with a dromus some 30 metres long (some of the finds made here are in the Museo Civico Archeologico).

Cetona

Cetona is a beautifully preserved medieval village, which, in the last few decades has become a fashionable place to have a country house. It has fine views of Monte Cetona (see below), and is surrounded by pretty hills planted with cypresses and pine trees.

In the large pleasant **Piazza Garibaldi,** laid out in the 16C, at the bottom of the hill, is the church of **Sant'Angelo.** In the chapel to the right of the high altar (light by the side door) is a highly venerated seated wooden statue of the *Madonna and Child,* and on the second altar on the south side, a 16C painting of the *Madonna and Child with two Saints.*

At the other end of the piazza is a round tower, near which Via Roma goes up past the 16C ex-Palazzo Comunale where the **Museo Civico per la Preistoria del Monte Cetona** was opened in 1990 (**open** 09.30–12.30; Sat also 16.00–18.00; closed Mon. The same ticket allows admission to the archaeological park of Belverde; see below).

A delightful little museum, with childrens' corners and modern facilities, it documents the presence of Man on Monte Cetona from the Paleolithic era to the Bronze Age. Excavations were carried out in 1927–41 by Umberto Calzoni, and most of his finds are now exhibited in the Archaeological Museum of Perugia. Systematic excavations were resumed in 1984 and these finds are exhibited here. The most important material dates from the Bronze Age. The **first room** illustrates the geological formation of the mountain, which was an island in the Pliocene era. **Room 2** has remains of a huge bear found in a cave inhabited by Neanderthal man some 50,000 years ago. In **Room 3** are Bronze Age finds made since 1984 on the Belverde site.

Via Roma continues uphill to the **Collegiata** in a pretty little piazza with attractive paving. It contains a fresco of the *Assumption* attributed to Pinturicchio. From here there is a view of the Rocca above, surrounded by pine trees, and, in the other direction, of Monte Cetona. Farther on (keep left), Via della Fortezza leads up to the **Rocca** (privately owned), and there is a delightful walkway along the walls at the foot of the castle which leads past orchards and little terraces back towards Piazza Garibaldi.

Belverde archaeological park

Belverde (**adm.** with the same ticket and at the same time as the Museo Archeologico in Cetona; guided tours of c 30 minutes; **open** mid-Oct–end of June on request), 6km from Cetona, is the most important Bronze Age site in central Italy, where, for the first time, various phases of Bronze Age habitation were found in one place, untouched by later material. It is reached by

A street in Cetona

taking the Sarteano road, and, just outside the village, Via di San Francesco. This leads up past the ex-**Convent of San Francesco**, founded in 1212. It has been restored by a Roman Catholic community called Mondo X which was founded by Padre Eligio to help young people in need. A member of the community will show visitors the convent including a 14C cloister. The well-known restaurant (*Convento di San Francesco*) is here (see above).

The road continues up to another road for Sarteano: the Monte Cetona road instead proceeds downhill to the left through spectacular countryside, with Monte Cetona conspicuous on the right. An unsurfaced road (yellow signpost) diverges from this road and continues left downhill to **Belverde** on the side of **Monte Cetona** (1148m), a beautiful wooded mountain (with its summit often hidden by clouds), visible, like Monte Amiata, for miles. A Cross was placed on the summit in 1968. Delightful walks may be taken on the mountain side. The road passes the **Parco Archeologico Naturalistico di Belverde**. If you decide on the tour, the guide will point out the interesting vegetation on the calcareous rock with marine deposits (sea-shells, etc). A cavern (lit by solar power), formed by the collapse of travertine outcrops, can be visited. Evidence of Neanderthal habitation was found here. The cave seems to have been used as a store in the Bronze Age. Below the road is an area (no admission) of excavations, begun in 1984, of a Bronze Age settlement.

Just beyond, the road passes the ex-**Convent of Santa Maria a Belverde**, surrounded by lovely old cypresses and ilex trees, with a fine view. A hermitage was founded here in 1367. This is now occupied by a Mondo X community (see above). Visitors are shown the **church**, preceded by a picturesque portico, divided into three oratories and frescoed in 1380–85. The lower church has a barrel vault and is covered with frescoes including a *Crucifixion* and *St Francis receiving the stigmata* attributed, since their restoration in 1973, to Cola Petruccioli. Stairs lead up to the chapel of Santissimo Salvatore with more interesting frescoes of the *Life of Christ* (including the Resurrection) attributed to Petruccioli and Andrea di Giovanni. A few steps lead up to the adjoining chapel of Santa Maria Maddalena, with scenes from the *Life of Mary Magdalene*, also by Petruccioli.

San Casciano dei Bagni

South of Monte Cetona in lovely countryside with vineyards and wooded hills of oak, chestnut and pines is **San Casciano dei Bagni** (582m), a little spa town famous for its hot springs which have existed since Roman times. Mud baths are used here for alleviating rheumatism. The 13C–14C collegiata of **San Leonardo** has a high altarpiece of the *Coronation of the Virgin in a glory of angels, with Saints* (c 1490) by Pietro di Francesco Orioli. In the 16C **Oratorio della Santissima Concezione** is a fresco in a fine tabernacle attributed to Pomarancio. A neo-Gothic castle was built on the site of the Cassero. Just outside the town are the springs, where the Bagno del Portico was built by Ferdinando II. The Chiesa delle Terme is a primitive building founded in the 11C–12C. **Palazzone** to the east is known for its red wine.

36 · Arezzo

Arezzo built on a low hillside (296m) about 5km south of the Arno, is now surrounded to the south by industrial suburbs. It is a lively agricultural provincial town (87,300 inhab.), with several notable churches and interesting museums. In the church of **San Francesco** is the famous **fresco cycle** of the *Legend of the True Cross* painted **by Piero della Francesca**. Its monthly antique market held in the the the streets of the old centre is one of the best known in Italy, and bargains can still sometimes be found here.

■ Practical information

Information offices. APT, 116 Piazza Risorgimento (☎ 0575-23952); Information office (*IAT*), 28 Piazza della Repubblica; outside the railway station (☎ 0575-377678).

Getting there
By rail. Railway station, Piazza della Repubblica, about 500m southwest of San Francesco, on the main Florence–Rome line. Some fast Intercity trains stop here (from Florence in 45mins); otherwise slower trains (frequent service) in c 1hr. Local trains to Sinalunga via Monte San Savino, and (every hour) via Bibbiena and Poppi to Pratovecchio-Stia.

By bus. **Country bus** services run by *SITA* from Arezzo (Piazza Stazione) to Florence (in 1hr 20mins–2hrs); to Sansepolcro (via Anghiari) in c 1hr; to Città di Castello (in 1hr 30mins); to Caprese Michelangelo (in 1hr 30mins–2hrs). A few buses a day to Monterchi (in 45 min). Services run by *LFI* to Siena (in c 1hr 30mins); to Cortona (via Castiglion Fiorentino) in c 1hr; and to Urbino (in c 3hrs).

Car parking near the centre of the town (closed to traffic) is difficult, and most car parks (in Via Niccolò Aretino, Via Alberti, Via Pietro Aretino, etc.) charge an hourly tariff. Free parking in Viale Mecenate, and caravan park outside Porta San Clemente.

Hotels
★★★ *Continentale*, 7 Piazza Guido Monaco (Pl. 1; ☎ 0575-20251, fax 0575-350485); *Europa*, 43 Via Spinello (Pl. 2; ☎ 0575-357701, fax 0575-357703).

Hotels on the outskirts (towards the motorway)
★★★ *Minerva*, 4 Via Fiorentina (☎ 0575-370390, fax 0575-302415).
★★★★ *Etrusco*, 39 Via Fleming (☎ 0575-984066, fax 0575-382131).
★★ *Astoria*, 54 Via Guido Monaco (Pl. 3; ☎ 0575-24361, fax 0575-24362); *Cecco*, 215 Corso Italia (Pl. 4; ☎ 0575-20986, fax 0575-356730).

Hotels in the environs
Montecchio Vesponi: ★★★ *Villa Schiatti*, 131 Via Montecchio (☎ 0575-651481, fax 0575-651482).
Near Castiglion Fiorentino ★★★ *Relais San Pietro*, with restaurant, at Polvano, 5km east (☎ 0575-650100; fax 0575-650255).

Youth Hostel, *Villa Severi*, 13 Via Redi (beyond Borgo Santa Croce; Bus No. 4 from Piazza Guido Monaco (☎ & fax 0575-299047).

Restaurants
£££ *Le Tastevin*, 9 Via dei Cenci (off Corso Italia); *La Lancia d'Oro*, Piazza Grande (with tables outside).
££ *Loggie Vasari*, 19 Via Vasari (Piazza Grande), with tables outside.
£ *L'Agania*, 10 Via Mazzini; *Lucullo*, 10 Borgo Santa Croce (also excellent pizzeria); *La Vigna*, 27 Via Spinello.

Pleasant places to **picnic** include the Parco il Prato and Fortezza Medicea, and the Roman amphitheatre and adjoining public gardens (entrance on Via Francesco Crispi).

Pasticcerie. De' Redi—*Dolcezze Savini*, Piazza Sant'Agostino; *Carraturo*, Corso Italia; *Mignon*, Via Tolletta.

Markets. A popular **antiques fair** is held in Piazza Grande and the surrounding streets on the first Sunday of every month (and the day before). A general market is held every Saturday.

Annual festivals. An important international **choral festival** (*Concorso Polifonico Internazionale Guido d'Arezzo*) is held in the city in late August. The **Giostra del Saracino** is held twice a year: on the penultimate Sunday in June and the first Sunday in September. The contest starts in Piazza Grande at 17.00 and tickets are available in advance (information from the Tourist Office); standing room only on the day.

The Giostra del Saracino

The Giostra del Saracino goes back to the 13C and takes its name from the quintain which is in the form of a Saracen, which probably originated as a representation of the heathen enemy of the Crusader Knights. Two competitors from each of the four districts of the town, mounted and armed with lances, charge in turn across the piazza at a pivoting quintain called *Buratto Re delle Indie* (Puppet King of the Indies) which holds the target in its left hand and in its right a whip, ending in three wooden balls. Points are awarded (from 1–5) for aim, with bonus points for a broken lance, and penalties if the horseman is struck by the wooden balls as the figure turns on its pivot. Each of the four ancient districts of the town enters a team with a captain, standard-bearers, foot-soldiers, bowmen, and a band, which plays the Saracino hymn. The four districts have their own colours: ***Porta Sant'Andrea***, white and green; ***Porta Crucifera***, red and green; ***Porta del Foro***, yellow and crimson; ***Porta Santo Spirito***, yellow and blue. The team (not the individual) scoring the most marks is declared the winner.

History. *Arretium* was one of the more important of the twelve cities of the Etruscan Confederation. The bronze statues of *Minerva* and the famous *Chimera* (c 380 BC) found here in the 16C (now exhibited in the Archaeological Museum in Florence) testify to the quality of the work of local Etruscan artists. From the 3C BC the town became a faithful ally of Rome. It emerged as a free republic in the 10C. Generally supporting the Ghibelline party it was frequently at odds with Florence and was defeated by that city at Campaldino in the Casentino in 1289 when the Aretine leader, Bishop Guglielmino was killed. The town came under the control of Florence in 1384.

As a road junction, the town had tactical importance in the Second World War. Nearly every important building was damaged by bombing.

Ever since the Etruscan period Arezzo has produced notable artists and craftsmen. The famous Arretine pottery, with a bright red glossy finish, was first produced here c 50 BC, and was later mass produced and exported all over the world by some 90 firms working in Arezzo (up to the mid-1C AD). Among the eminent citizens of Arezzo were C. Cilnius Maecenas (d. 8 BC), the

BIBBIENA

AREZZO

N

FLORENCE

0   400 yards
0   400 metres

Porta
S. Clemente

VIA GUIDO TARLATI

Casa del
Vasari

Galleria
e Museo

S. Domenico

Casa del
Vasari

S. Maria in
Gradi

Mus. del
Duomo

Duomo

SS. Annunziata

Palazzo
d. Comune

Casa del
Petrarca

**Parco
il Prato**

Badia

Palazzo
Pretorio

Palazzo
Camaiani

Loggia

**Fortezza
Medicea**

**Teatro
P.O.**

3

Pieve di
S. Maria

PIAZZA
GRANDE

S. Francesco

YOUTH HOSTEL

Prefettura

S. Michele

1

APT

PIAZZA
DANTE

4

S. Croce

**Bus
Station**

S. Agostino

2

Stazione F.S.

SANSEPOLCRO

**Anfiteatro
Romano**

**Museo
Archeologico**

S. Maria delle Grazie

friend of Augustus and the patron of Virgil and Horace; Guido d'Arezzo (c 995–1050), the inventor of the musical scale; Margaritone, the painter (1216–93); Petrarch, the poet (1304–74); Spinello Aretino, the painter (c 1350–1410); Aretino (1492–1566), the most outspoken writer of the late Renaissance; and Giorgio Vasari (1512–74), the architect, painter, and art historian.

The most pleasant approach from the station is by **Corso Italia**, the main street of the medieval town, which leads gently uphill. Via Cavour branches left for **Piazza San Francesco**, a small square created in the 19C. The monument to Vittorio Fossombroni in front of San Francesco is by Pasquale Romanelli, 1863. Fossombroni was a mathematician and hydraulic engineer who drained the marshes of the Val di Chiana.

San Francesco

The church was built by Fra Giovanni da Pistoia in 1322. At the foot of the rough-hewn front is part of the facing which was never finished.

■ **Open** 08.30–12.00, 14.00–18.30. On **Sun** visitors are asked to visit the church 10.00–11.00, 14.30–18.30.
   Admission to the frescoes by Piero della Francesca: it is necessary to book in advance (☎ 0575-355668) for the small guided tours which usually take place on Mon–Fri 09.00–11.00, 15.00–17.30; Sat 09.00–11.00, 15.00–17.00; fest. 15.00–17.00. If tickets are available you can also book a visit on the same day at the office in the lower church (**open** 08.15–12.30, 14.30–17.30; fest. 14.30–17.30). The right wall is still covered while restoration work continues (due to be completed in the year 2000).

The bright Franciscan **interior** contains the world-famous frescoes by Piero della Francesca in the choir, but also numerous other frescoes (mostly fragments) in the nave, many of them showing his influence on the local school. The interior and Piero's frescoes are being restored. **West wall**. The rose window has *stained glass by Guglielmo di Marcillat (William of Marseille, 1520), who also produced windows for the Duomo, showing *St Francis before Honorius III*. The frescoes include: *Supper in the house of the Pharisee* by Giovanni di Balduccio, and the *Mystical Marriage of St Catherine of Alexandria*, an unusual scene with the figure of *St Christopher* attributed to Paolo Schiavo.

   South wall. **First chapel**, frescoes, dated 1463, showing *St Bernardine of Siena leading the Aretines from the church of San Francesco to destroy the Fons Tecta* (connected with a pagan cult), by Lorentino d'Andrea, an assistant of Piero della Francesca. On the wall, Niccolò Soggi, *Sacred Conversation*. **Second chapel**, frescoes with scenes from the *Life of St Bartholomew* by a follower of Piero della Francesca. On the wall, fresco of the *Crucifixion*, and, above an unusual fresco of two figures in monochrome guarding a door closed with chains (from the family name *Catenacci*). Surrounded by a tabernacle in pietra serena, 14C wooden *Crucifix*, and a fresco fragment by Antonio d'Anghiari, master of Piero. Beyond the **third chapel**, with ruined frescoes attributed to Parri Spinelli, in a finely carved tabernacle, is a Roman sarcophagus, the tomb of Beato Benedetto Sinigardi (d. 1282), friend of St Francis. At the end of this wall, *Annunciation* by Spinello Aretino.

   The **chapel** to the right of the sanctuary also has damaged frescoes (restored) by Spinello Aretino: right, *Deeds of St Michael*; left, *Legend of St Giles*. The triptych of the *Madonna of the Holy Girdle* is by Niccolò di Pietro Gerini.

   In the **sanctuary** hangs a huge painted *Crucifix*, with St Francis at the foot of the Cross, attributed from this work to the Master of San Francesco (1250).

   The **Legend of the True Cross by Piero della Francesca**, on the walls of the choir is his masterpiece, and one of the greatest fresco cycles ever produced in Italian painting. A general view of the two upper registers of the restored frescoes on the left wall can now be had from the nave; but you need to book a place on a guided tour (see above) to see them close up from the sanctuary (steps have been installed in front of the lower band with the battle scene showing the victory of Heraclius over Chosroes).

In 1447 the Bacci, a rich Aretine family commissioned Bicci di Lorenzo to paint the sanctuary: he had only painted the *Four Evangelists* on the vault and the *Last Judgement* (restored in 1987) on the triumphal arch before he left Arezzo in 1448 (he died in 1452). Piero della Francesca was called to complete the frescoes, possibly in 1448. He may have interrupted work on them during a stay in Rimini in 1451, and another in Rome in 1459, but the cycle was finished by 1466.

The frescoes illustrate the Legend of the True Cross, taken from the *Leggenda Aurea* by Fra Jacopo Varagine (13C), and the time span runs from the Death of Adam to the Battle of Chosroes in the 7C AD. The frescoes have been undergoing an extremely complicated restoration programme since 1985. They had deteriorated alarmingly for a number of reasons: the wall is particularly thin, the circulation of air in the church was altered when the roof was rebuilt and central heating was installed, and the delicate frescoes were damaged by poor restorations in the past. The left wall was completed in 1998, and restoration on the right wall is expected to be completed by the year 2000.

The chronological order of the scenes, as they illustrate the story is as follows: **right wall (lunette)**, *Death of Adam*. On the right, *Adam seated on the ground, announces his imminent death from old age to his family*; on the left is the dead figure of Adam, and Seth planting a tree on his grave (from which the Cross on which Christ is Crucified will be made). **Right wall (middle band)**, *The Queen of Sheba recognises the sacred wood* (used as a bridge over the Siloam river) and kneels in adoration before it, and (on the right) she is received by Solomon. **Right of the window (middle panel)**, the beam is buried deep in the ground by three men, by order of Solomon. **Right of the window (lower panel)**, *Constantine's Dream in 313 AD*. The Emperor, asleep in his tent the night before battle, dreams that an angel shows him the Cross and announces: 'By this sign, you shall conquer'. **Right wall (lower band)**, *Constantine's bloodless victory over Maxentius* early the next morning. **Left of the window (middle panel)**, *Torture of a Jew named Judas*. He is kept in a dry well until he reveals the secret hiding place of the Cross, stolen after the Crucifixion.

Left wall (middle band), *Discovery and Proof of the Cross*. Judas digs up the Cross before St Helena and her courtiers, and on the right, in a scene in front of a church, its authenticity is demonstrated by the raising of a young man from the dead, while Helena kneels in wonder. **Left wall (lower band)**, *Battle scene showing the victory of Heraclius over Chosroes in the 7C AD*, after Chosroes, king of the Persians, had seized the Cross and placed it near his throne (shown to the right). After his defeat he kneels awaiting execution. **Left wall (lunette)**, *Heraclius restores the Cross to Jerusalem*.

Also by Piero are the two figures of *Prophets* on the window wall, and the *Annunciation* (thought by some scholars to be St Helena receiving the news of her death and thus connected to the main cycle).

In the chapel to the left of the sanctuary is a fine painting of the *Annunciation* by Neri di Bicci, and a damaged fresco of the *Annunciation* attributed to Luca Signorelli or Bartolomeo della Gatta.

North wall. In the last chapel, terracotta funerary monument to Francesco Rosselli, attributed to Michele da Firenze (1439; being restored), and, in a 17C altar, Bernardino Santini, *Ecstasy of St Francis*. On a pilaster, fine fresco of *St Elizabeth of Hungary*, by the school of Spinello Aretino. In the middle of this wall is a chapel with *frescoes (recently restored) of *St Anthony of Padua* and stories from his life, and a lunette of the *Visitation*, by Lorentino d'Andrea, showing the influence of Piero della Francesca (and possibly on a cartoon by him). Beyond are remains of a fresco of *St Francis and Pope Honorius III* by Parri Spinello. The **lower church** (13C–14C) has been restored, but is open only for exhibitions.

The Pieve di Santa Maria

The *Pieve di Santa Maria, at the end of Corso Italia (see above; **open** 08.00–13.00, 15.00–18.30 or 19.00) is a 12C church replacing an earlier building, damaged in 1111. It is one of the most beautiful Romanesque churches in Tuscany. The superbly conceived ***façade** has

a deep central portal flanked by blind arcades which support three tiers of colonnades, the intercolumnations of which diminish towards the top. The 68 diverse pillars include a human figure. The portal bears reliefs of the Madonna, angels and saints (1216) and the months are illustrated in the intrados.

The beautiful tall ***interior** has clustered pillars with good capitals and arches showing the transition to Gothic. The mullioned windows provide a diffused light on the mellow sandstone. The drum was to have supported a dome which was never built. In the raised pres-

The Pieve di Santa Maria, Arezzo

bytery is the ***polyptych by Pietro Lorenzetti** commissioned for the church by Bishop Guido Tarlati in 1320. The crypt below has good capitals, and a reliquary ***bust of St Donato** (1346) by a local goldsmith. In a chapel off the left side of the nave is a polychrome statue of the *Madonna and Child* by the 15C Florentine school.

Piazza Grande

The arcaded apse of the Pieve and its original **campanile** (1330) with its 40 mullioned windows are best seen from the steeply-sloping ***Piazza Grande**, behind the church (reached by Via di Seteria which skirts the interesting flank of the church, opposite medieval shop-fronts). Piazza Grande was laid out c 1200 (some medieval houses and towers survive here). It is still the centre of city life, and the scene of the *Giostra del Saracino* in summer and of the monthly antiques fair.

Beside the apse of the Pieve is the **Palazzo del Tribunale** (17C–18C) with pretty circular steps outside, and the elaborate little **Palazzo della Fraternità dei Laici** in a mixture of Gothic and Renaissance styles. The lower part dates from 1377 (with a detached fresco of *Christ in Pietà* by Spinello Aretino), and in 1434 Bernardo Rossellino added the relief of the *Madonna of the Misericordia* in the lunette above and two statues in niches on either side. The delicate cornice and loggia above were designed in 1460 by Giuliano da Settignano. The bell-cote and clock date from 1552.

One whole side of the square is occupied by Vasari's handsome **Palazzo delle Logge* (1573). The long portico continues northwest back to Corso Italia in which is the 16C **Palazzo Camaiani**, now housing the State Archives. It was restored in 14C style at the beginning of the present century and has painted decorations by Galileo Chini.

Via dei Pileati continues uphill past the 14C **Palazzo Pretorio**, its façade decorated with the armorial bearings of many podestà; it is occupied by the Public Library. The road curves uphill to the left, and at No. 28 Via dell'Orto is the **Casa Petrarca** (open on request here or at the Accademia Petrarca, Via degli Alberghetti, 10.00–12.00, 15.00–17.00; closed Sat afternoon and fest.), the supposed house of Petrarch reconstructed (after its destruction in the Second World War) as an academy and library for Petrarchian studies. Visitors are shown the library with MSS and an autograph letter of the poet (1370).

A huge monument to Petrarch (by Alessandro Lazzerini, 1928) stands in the **Parco il Prato**, an attractive large park with pine trees, lawns and pretty views of the Tuscan countryside. The 14C–16C **Fortezza** (open daily), also in a park, was rebuilt by Antonio da Sangallo the Younger (and partly dismantled in 1800).

Petrarch

Petrarch (Francesco Petrarca), one of the most important Italian poets, was born in Arezzo in 1304. His father had been exiled here from Florence in 1302 because of his Guelf sympathies (Dante Alighieri, who was a friend, had been exiled the same year). The family apparantly soon moved to Ancisa in the Valdarno before following the Pope to Avignon in 1311. It was here in 1327 that Petrarch met a certain Laura and his unrequited love for her inspired some of his greatest sonnets. He travelled in Europe and studied at Bologna university and soon became famous for his learning and his writings in both prose and verse, mostly in Latin (although his masterpiece is considered the *Canzoniere*, a poem in Italian). He studied the writings of Cicero, Virgil, Livy and St Augustine and was particularly important because of the interest he revived in the classics and the culture of Greece and Rome. In many ways he anticipated the Humanist culture of the Renaissance. His beautiful poetry influenced generations of Italian writers and his verse was imitated for centuries, although by the 19C he was held in less esteem.

He became family chaplain and close friend of the Roman Cardinal Giovanni Colonna with whom he travelled widely, and in 1341 was crowned poet laureate on the Campidoglio. From 1353–61 he lived in Milan as a guest of the Visconti. He taught at the university of Padua but left the city in 1362 during an outbreak of the plague and went to Venice where he was offered a house on the Riva degli Schiavoni in return for his promise to leave his books to the city on his death (they formed the nucleus of the Biblioteca Marciana). He spent the last four years of his life in the quiet little village of Arquà in the Colli Euganei near Padua, where he is buried.

Duomo

The *Duomo (**open** 07.00–12.30, 15.00–18.30) was begun in 1278 and continued until 1510, with a campanile added at the east end in 1859 and a façade completed in 1914. Fine travertine steps (1525–29) surround the **exterior**. The handsome southern flank incorporates a good portal (1320–40), with worn reliefs, and terracotta statues of the *Madonna and Child between St Donato and Gregory X*, attributed to Niccolò di Luca Spinelli.

The beautiful Gothic ***interior** has a nave, tribune, and aisles, with clustered columns and pointed arches. The splendid ***stained glass windows** are by Guglielmo di Marcillat (1519–23), a French artist who lived in Arezzo. He also painted the first three vaults of the nave and the first of the north aisle (light at the west end, but extremely difficult to see as they are so high up) in 1521–27. The remaining vaults of the nave were painted in 1661 by Salvi Castellucci.

South aisle. Funerary monument to Cardinal Stefano Bonucci (d. 1589), with a fine bust. The stained glass window by Marcillat illustrates the calling of St Matthew. The sepulchral monument (1320–30) to Pope Gregory X who died at Arezzo in 1276 is a fine Gothic work. The second window by Marcillat shows the *Baptism of Christ*.

To the left of the altar, fragment of a 14C fresco of the *Madonna enthroned with Saints*, and a lunette of the *Risen Christ*, by Buffalmacco. The window by Marcillat shows the *Expulsion of the Merchants from the Temple*. On the third altar are 14C frescoes. The window of the *Woman taken in Adultery* is the last work in the duomo by Marcillat. The medieval **Tarlati Chapel** has a beautiful sculptured canopy by Giovanni d'Agostino. The fresco of the *Crucifix and Saints* is attributed to a local painter known as the Maestro del Vescovado (mid-14C). The fine 4C early Christian sarcophagus rests on a marble tomb with a bas-relief of a bishop saint, and three inscriptions. The window by Marcillat shows the *Raising of Lazarus*. An 18C monument has two busts of members of the Maurizi family.

In the chapel to the right of the apse, marble ciborium of 1783 and a stained glass window of 1477. The Gothic sculptured ***High Altar**, by many 14C artists including Giovanni di Francesco and Betto di Giovanni, encloses the body of St Donato (martyred in 361), the patron saint of the city. The two lateral stained glass lancet windows in the tribune are by Domenico Pecori (16C); the central one dates from 1953.

North aisle. On the left of the sacristy door (and the entrance to the Museo del Duomo, see below) is a beautiful fresco of *St Mary Magdalene*, **by Piero della Francesca** (inconspicuous light on the nave pillar). Next to it is the unusual *tomb of Bishop Guido Tarlati, by Agostino di Giovanni and Agnolo di Ventura, with 16 panels representing the warlike life of this zealous Ghibelline (d. 1327). The small funerary monument to Girolamo Borro (d. 1592) bears his bust. The cantoria is Vasari's first architectural work (1535); the organ dates from 1534 (by Luca Boni da Cortona). Beneath it is a 13C wood statue of the *Madonna and Child*, and 14C fresco fragments. Beyond an altarpiece of the *Martyrdom of St Donato* by Pietro Benvenuti (1794) is a little fresco by Luigi Ademollo of the Aretines receiving the body of St Donato.

The large **Lady Chapel**, preceded by a pretty wrought-iron screen, was added in 1796. On the right, above a funerary monument to Bishop Albergotti (d. 1825), with reliefs by Odoardo Baratta, is an *Assumption* by Andrea della Robbia. On the right wall, large painting of *Judith* (1804) by Pietro Benvenuti, much admired by Canova. In the chapel to the right of the main altar, Andrea della Robbia, *Trinity between Saints Donato and Bernard* (c 1485) (right wall). The main altar was designed by Giuseppe Valadier (1823). In the chapel to the left of the main altar, statue of *Bishop Marcacci* by Stefano Ricci and on the left wall, a polychrome terracotta attributed to Giovanni della Robbia. On the left wall, large painting of *David and Abigail* by Luigi Sabatelli. On the wall near the entrance to the chapel, **Madonna and Child*, by Andrea della Robbia.

In the **north aisle**, funerary monument to Francesco Redi (d. 1697). The **Baptistery** is at the west end of the aisle (closed for restoration). The three beautiful *schiacciato* reliefs on the font are attributed to Donatello or his school.

The Museo del Duomo

The Museo del Duomo or **Museo Diocesano** is entered through the Sacristy off the north aisle (**open** Thurs, Fri, and Sat 10.00–12.00; or by appointment, ☎ 0575-23991).

Room 1 contains three wood **Crucifixes* from the 12C–13C: the oldest one is on the left of the entrance (it was painted in 1264 by Margaritone di Arezzo). The tabernacle with a terracotta bas-relief of the *Annunciation* is attributed to Bernardo Rossellino (1434). The frescoes include an *Annunciation* by Spinello Aretino, a tabernacle, also with an *Annunciation*, by Parri di Spinello, and a *Madonna and Child with Saints James and Anthony Abbot* by Spinello Aretino. The painting of the *Annunciation* is by Andrea di Nerio, master of Spinello. The cases of church silver include the Pax of Siena, in the base of a neo-classical reliquary. It is a 15C Flemish work in enamel surrounded by precious stones, depicting Christ supported by an angel, and the Madonna supported by an angel.

Room 2: Bartolomeo della Gatta, **St Jerome in the desert*, a fresco and its sinopia; detached fresco of the *Madonna and Child* by Lorentino d'Andrea; della Robbian polychrome bust of *St Donato*; Bartolomeo della Gatta and Domenico Pecori, *Madonna and Child with Saints Fabiano and Sebastian*; Domenico Pecori, *Madonna in glory with Saints*; Niccolò Soggi, *Founding of the Basilica Liberiana*; Luca Signorelli, panels from a predella. Cases contain 14C–16C Crosses, reliquaries, and chalices.

Room 3: Vasari, *Preaching of the Baptist*, *Baptism of Christ*, and tondo of the *Madonna della Misericordia* (a processional standard); Santi di Tito, *Christ in the house of Martha*. The last room displays church vestments.

On the cathedral steps stands a statue of Ferdinando I, by Francavilla, after a design by Giambologna. It was erected by the Aretines in 1594 in gratitude for the Grand-duke's agricultural reforms and land reclamation in the Valdichiana. Across Piazza della Libertà is **Palazzo del Comune** of 1333.

San Domenico

The old Via Sassoverde descends right from Via Ricasoli to San Domenico in a square of lime trees. The church, founded in 1275, has a Romanesque portal with a lunette frescoed by Angelo di Lorentino, and a Gothic campanile.

The bright **interior** has a miscellany of fresco fragments of particularly high quality. On the **west wall**, Parri di Spinello, *Crucifixion and Saints* and (in the lunette) two scenes from the life of St Nicholas of Bari. On the **south wall**, in a Gothic canopied altar by Giovanni di Francesco, *Christ with the doctors in the* *temple* by Luca di Tommé. Above, between the windows, *Madonna and Child* by the school of Duccio. In a pretty carved polychrome niche, *St Peter Martyr* by the della Robbian school. The large detached fresco of a triptych with *St Catherine of Alexandria* is by the school of Spinello. Above an 18C wall monument, fragment of a fresco by Parri with angel musicians. Beside the steps, damaged fresco of *Christ blessing the faithful*.

East end. In the chapel to the right of the main altar, a fine stone 14C statue of the *Madonna and Child* and a fresco of the **Annunciation* by Spinello Aretino. The **Crucifix* in the main apse is by Cimabue (light). In the chapel to the left of the apse, Giovanni d'Agnolo, triptych with *St Domenic, Archangel Michael, and St Paul*.

On the **north wall** of the church are frescoes by Giovanni d'Agnolo, Parri di Spinello (*Marriage of St Catherine*), and Jacopo di Landino (stories of St Christopher). Vasari records that the last fresco on this wall of *St Vincent Ferrer* is the only known work by his great-grandfather Lazzaro Taldi Vasari. On the west wall is a large frescoed composition by Spinello Aretino.

Vasari's house

At No. 55 in Via XX Settembre is **Vasari's house** (open 09.00–19.00; fest. 09.00–13.00; ring). He finished building this house after he purchased it in 1540, and then carried out the painted decorations, with the help of assistants (restored in the 19C). It was acquired by the State in 1911 and contains a collection of 16C–17C paintings, many of them by artists in Vasari's circle.

In the **hall** is a late 16C bust of *Vasari*. The **Sala** has ceiling paintings by Vasari of *Virtue, Envy,* and *Fortune,* the *Four Seasons,* the *Four Ages of Man,* and allegorical figures and landscapes. The little **chapel**, with a worn majolica floor, has a *Madonna and Child* by Fra Paolino and small paintings by Michele di Ridolfo del Ghirlandaio, Bernardino Poccetti, and Leonardo Malatesta.

The **Camera d'Abramo**, with a ceiling painted by Vasari in 1548, contains paintings by Vasari (*Deposition*), Aurelio Lomi (*Ecce Homo*), Francesco Vanni (*Flagellation*), Perin del Vaga and Giovanni Stradano.

The **corridor** has a painting of *Ceres* in the vault, and small paintings by Maso di San Friano and Lo Scarsellino. Beyond can be seen the little hanging **garden**. The room which was formerly the **kitchen** was frescoed in 1827 by Raimondo Zaballi date from 1827). Here are hung portraits by Giovanni Maria Butteri and Scipione Pulzone, and two 16C marble bas-reliefs of *Aristotle* and *Plato*. The standard with the *Holy Trinity* by Vasari was restored in 1997.

The **Camera d'Apollo** has the best ceiling by Vasari. The paintings include works by Alessandro Allori, Jacopo Ligozzi, Maso di San Friano, Paolo Farinati and Il Poppi. The painting in a pretty frame of *Prudence* (which may have belonged to Vasari) is attributed to Il Doceno or Alessandro Allori.

The **Camera della Fama** has another good ceiling begun by Vasari and portraits in the lunettes of Lazzaro Vasari, Giorgio Vasari, Luca Signorelli, Spinello Aretino, Bartolomeo della Gatta, Michelangelo, and Andrea del Sarto. The paintings include works by Giovanni Stradano, Girolamo Macchietti, Carlo Portelli, and Giovanni Maria Butteri. The majolica relief of the head of *Galba* is attributed to Andrea Sansovino (purchased by Vasari). The last room has a wooden model by Vasari of the Logge in Piazza Grande, and works by Maso di San Friano. The precious family archives include letters to Vasari from Michelangelo.

Giorgio Vasari

Giorgio Vasari (1511–74) is well known as an art historian, painter and architect. His famous work *Le vite de' più eccellenti pittori, scultori e architettori*, which he first published in 1550, and later revised in 1568, has provided precious information about the lives of artists to generations of art historians and is still considered of fundamental importance to the study of the Renaissance and Mannerist periods. As a boy, Vasari worked in the studio of Giullaume de Marcillat in Arezzo but at 13 he was sent to Florence to study under Michelangelo, Andrea del Sarto and others. He then worked as a painter for the Medici, and in Rome received commissions from Cardinal Farnese and Pope Julius III. But it was under Cosimo I in Florence that he carried out his most important works, which include the Uffizi building and the corridor (known as the Corridorio Vasariano), which links Palazzo Vecchio with Palazzo Pitti across Ponte Vecchio. When Cosimo moved from his private Medici palace into Palazzo Vecchio Vasari was called in to redecorate the building, and he transformed the Salone dei Cinquecento in 1563–65 with frescoes celebrating the duke. He also designed the *Studiolo* for Francesco I in the same palace. In Florence he also founded the first art academy, the Accademia delle Arti del Disegno, and in 1572 he began the fresco of the *Last Judgement* in the dome of the cathedral. In Arezzo he designed the Palazzo delle Logge in Piazza Grande.

The church of **Santa Maria in Gradi**, farther on (left), has a fine **interior** rebuilt in 1592 by Bartolomeo Ammannati. 17C frescoes of the Apostles on the pilasters have been uncovered and restored. On the first altar on the left, *Madonna del Soccorso* by the workshop of Andrea della Robbia. A staircase leads down to the remains of an earlier church or crypt (probably 10C) with a 13C wooden *Crucifix*. The two decorative cantorie (and chapels below) are by Salvi Castellucci (1633) and Bernardino Santini (1629).

The Museum of Arezzo

At the corner of Via Garibaldi is the **Galleria e Museo Medioevale e Moderno**, housed in the fine 15C **Palazzo Bruni** (open 09.00–19.00; fest. 09.00–13.00).

Off the **courtyard**, which has fragments from the Pieve, are two rooms with medieval sculptures and 14C *Madonnas* from gates in the walls, an early 14C statue of *St Michael Archangel*, a late 13C statue of a king (?) and a seated statue of *St Anthony Abbot* by Michele da Firenze.

First floor. Room I: Margaritone, *St Francis*, *Madonna*, and *Crucifix*; school of Guido da Siena, *Madonna*; circle of the Maestro della Maddalena, *Madonna and Child*. **Sculpture**: Agostino di Giovanni, head of a warrior (1330); 13C portrait head; in cases, Romanesque Crosses and Crucifixes. **Room II**: 15C frescoes by Giovanni d'Agnolo di Balduccio (c 1370–1452), pupil of Spinello Aretino. **Room III**: Frescoes of angels and saints by Spinello Aretino and his son Parri di Spinello, and a *Madonna of the Misericordia* by Parri; painting of *St Michael Archangel* by Giovanni d'Agnolo di Balduccio.

Rooms IV and V: Early Renaissance. The chimneypiece is by Simone Mosca, and tournament armour and coins are displayed in cases. Also here: Bartolomeo della Gatta, two paintings of St Roch, the smaller painting including a view of medieval Arezzo. On the opposite wall, Lorentino d'Arezzo, *Madonna and Saints*. **Room V** contains frescoes, some attributed to Signorelli and cases of small bronzes. The next five small rooms contain a magnificent *collection of majolica from Faenza, Gubbio, Deruta, Castel Durante, and Urbino (13–18C), and terracottas by Andrea della Robbia, a bas-relief by Michele da Firenze, and a statuette of *St Luke* by Vincenzo Danti.

The **Mario Salmi Bequest**, arranged in two rooms, includes small works by Il Poppi, Empoli, Agostino Ciampelli, Arcangiolo Salimbeni, Franciabigio, Francesco Granacci, Alessandro Magnasco, Ludovico Carracci, and Adriano Cecioni. In the **gallery** is the *Banquet of Ester and Assuero*, Vasari's largest painting (1548).

Second floor. In the **first room** are 19C works and paintings by the Macchiaioli school. The **second room** has works by Gaspare Dughet, Salvator Rosa, etc. The **third and fourth rooms** contain 16C and 17C works (Jacopo Bassano, Carlo Dolci, Vasari, Alessandro Allori, Cigoli, and Jacopo Vignali), and 16C–19C glass, some of it from the Pharmacy of Camaldoli. The **Salone** has more 16C works (Vasari, Domenico Pecori, and Poccetti).

On the opposite side of Via Garibaldi is the Renaissance church of the **Santissima Annunziata**, with an *Annunciation* by Spinello Aretino on the outside. The beautiful Renaissance grey-and-white *interior is by Bartolomeo della Gatta (1491) and Giuliano and Antonio da Sangallo the Elder (c 1517). The interesting plan includes a columned atrium and a dome over the crossing; the capitals of the columns and pilasters are superbly carved. The stained glass tondo in the atrium is by Guglielmo di Marcillat.

There is a light on the right of the south aisle for the altarpieces. In the chapel to the right of the high altar, *Madonna and St Francis* by Pietro da Cortona, and a 16C terracotta *Madonna and Child with Saints*, and a relief of *God the Father* above. The 17C high altar incorporates Renaissance statues in silver and a venerated statue of the *Madonna* attributed to Michele da Firenze. The chapel on the left of the high altar has an *Annunciation* by Matteo Rosselli and a *Nativity* by Niccolò Soggi (1522). On the third north altar is a 14C *Crucifix*, and on the first altar is a good painting of the *Deposition* painted by Vasari at the age of 18 on a cartoon by Rosso Fiorentino.

On the left, farther on, is the **Badia di Santi Fiora e Lucilla**, built by the Benedictines in 1278, and transformed by Vasari in 1565. The octagonal campanile dates from 1650.

The **interior** is an interesting architectural work by Vasari. On the **west wall** is a delightful *fresco of *St Lawrence*, by Bartolomeo della Gatta (1476). **South side**. Second altar, Baccio da Montelupo, wood *Crucifix*; beyond the third altar, large painted *Crucifix* by Segna di Bonaventura (1320). In the **sacristy** is furniture decorated with intarsia attributed to Giuliano da Maiano.

The **High Altar** has good paintings by Vasari, including the *Calling of the Apostles*, intended for his own tomb. On the right wall of the choir, *Assumption*, also by Vasari. The cantoria of the fine organ dates from 1651 and bears two paintings by Raffaello Vanni. The cupola has a trompe l'oeil fresco by Andrea Pozzo (1702).

On the wall of the **north side**, exquisite marble tabernacle attributed to

Benedetto da Maiano (the bronze door was stolen in 1978). The former monastery preserves a fine 15C cloister.

Via Garibaldi continues southeast, crossing the broad Via Guido Monaco to Piazza Sant'Agostino (where the daily market takes place). The church has a 13C campanile. On Corso Italia is a local Museum of Contemporary Art, containing works mostly dating from the 1960s.

From here Via Margaritone leads to the **Convento di San Bernardo** whose rebuilt double loggie follow the curve of the **Roman amphitheatre** (117–138 AD). The well-kept ruins, adjoining a public park entered from Via Crispi, are open at the same time as the archaeological museum.

The Archaeological Museum

The charming rooms of the convent, overlooking the amphitheatre, now house the Museo Archeologico Mecenate (**open** 09.00–14.00; fest. 09.00–13.00). Other parts of the amphitheatre are visible in the museum rooms. The room numbering is erratic.

Ground floor. Room 1: Archaic finds from Arezzo: architectural fragments and small bronzes. **Room 2**: Hellenistic finds from Arezzo, including terracotta heads. **Room 3** (right): a krater by the potter and vase painter Euphronios (c 510–500 BC). **Rooms 4 & 5** contain material from the Valdichiana, including a fine red-figure amphora (420–410 BC) and kraters and stamnoi from the 5C BC. **Rooms 6 & 7** (right) have an excellent display of the famous Arretine vases mass-produced in Arezzo from 50 BC to 60 AD/70 AD, in a shiny red glaze, usually decorated with exquisite bas-reliefs. Moulds and instruments are displayed as well as the production of individual workshops. **Room 8** continues the display with superb early 1C AD works from the Ateius pottery (which had branch workshops in Pisa and Lyon).

Two small rooms contains a collection of grave-goods from the tomb of a young girl from Apulia (1C BC); a fragment of a circular monument dating from the Claudian era; a marble statue of a man in a toga (1C AD) found in Arezzo in 1994; and a head of Livia, wife of Augustus (35 BC), also found in Arezzo. The last rooms on the ground floor, overlooking the amphitheatre, display Roman mosaics, fragments of *opus sectile* marble pavement, and fragments of poly-chrome stucco wall decorations. There is also a marble head dating from the mid-1C AD, possibly a portrait of Agrippa, which was found in Arezzo, and bronzes, statues, sculpture and urns. A marble altar from the Augustan period is decorated with the legend of Romulus and Remus, and there is a wooden stat-uette of an Oriental divinity (1C–2C AD).

Upper floor. To the left are three rooms of vases: a curious urn with a human head and arms, from Chiusi (7C BC), a good red-figure Greek vases (5C BC) and bucchero ware. Two rooms to the left off a corridor display: Roman glass and a *portrait of a man moulded in gold (Aretine, 1C BC); small bronzes; and the Ceccatelli collection acquired in 1988 with finds from Vulci (7C–6C BC). Off the left side of the long corridor: the Gamurrini collection (small bronzes) and the Vincenzo Funghini (1828–96) collection (mostly 4C–3C BC). Off the opposite side of the corridor are the Palaeolithic and Neolithic collections from the terri-tory of Arezzo. At the end of the long corridor is a display of casts illustrating the finds from the Tumolo del Sodo outside Cortona (see Ch. 37).

Fifteen minutes' walk southeast of the station (reached through an ugly part of the town) is the church of **Santa Maria delle Grazie** in late Gothic style (1449), enclosed in a walled garden. The graceful early Renaissance *loggia is by Benedetto da Maiano. It contains a beautiful marble and terracotta *high altar by Andrea della Robbia and collaborators, which encloses a fresco of the *Madonna of the Misericordia* by Parri di Spinello. On the right wall is a very ruined fresco by Lorentino d'Arezzo. The adjacent oratory of St Bernardine (1450–56) has a pretty vault.

Environs of Arezzo ~ Castiglion Fiorentino

Between Arezzo and Cortona in the Valdichiana, its low hills planted with olives and vines, is **Castiglion Fiorentino**, a walled agricultural market town on a hill dominated by the oddly-shaped Torre del Cassero. From the Porta Fiorentina the Corso leads up past the church of **San Francesco**, in a piazza to the left. It has been undergoing restoration for many years (the entrance is at present through the cloister) and the paintings have nearly all been removed to the museum (see below). In **Piazza Municipio** there is a pretty 16C loggia with some arcades open to provide a view of the valley (the Collegiata is conspicuous on the side of the hill). Palazzo Comunale is opposite.

On the hillside above, built into the rock, is the ancient **Cassero** (castle), with the church of Sant'Angelo, founded in the 11C. It has been restored to house the **Pinacoteca Comunale**, instituted at the beginning of this century and reopened here in 1991 (**open** 10.00–12.30, 16.00–18.30 except Mon).

In this delightful little museum, the works of art are well labelled. Visitors first enter the church of **Sant'Angelo**, with a high altar by Filippo Berrettini. Here is displayed a painted *Cross* by the late 13C Umbrian school (from the church of San Francesco). On the left wall is a painting of the *Madonna and Child with Pope St Silvester and St Anthony* (also from San Francesco), by Vasari. In the **Sacristy** are exhibited two *Crosses* in gilded copper, one dating from the end of the 12C or beginning of the 13C showing northern European influence, and the other an exquisite work of 13C French manufacture. The silver gilt reliquary *bust of *Sant'Orsola* dates from the 14C and is attributed to a French master.

Stairs lead up to the **Pinacoteca** in the **Coro delle Monache**. In the first part of the room: painted *Cross* by an Aretine master of the 13C; bottega of Margarito di Arezzo, *St Francis*; Taddeo Gaddi, *Madonna and Child* (fragment); Pseudo Pier Francesco Fiorentino, *Adoration of the Child*; Bartolomeo della Gatta, *St Michael Archangel*, and *St Francis receiving the stigmata*; Giovanni di Paolo, *St Catherine of Alexandria*, and *Madonna and Child*. Also here is a case of church silver. In the second part of the room: Iacopo del Sellaio, *Pool of Bethesda*; Gian Domenico Ferretti, *St Teresa* (1723); Antonio di Donnino del Mazziere, *Adoration of the Shepherds* (1538); Papacello, *Madonna and Child with St Anne*. Another flight of stairs leads up to the **Saletta della Torre**, decorated with 13C–16C coats of arms, with a fine view.

On the top of the hill is the **Torre del Cassero**. From Piazza Municipio, Via San Michele continues downhill to Piazza Verdi, and by a pretty little Mannerist doorway, Vicolo dei Signori, with good views of the countryside leads steeply down to a piazza with three churches. The neo-classical **Collegiata** contains a della Robbian terracotta of *St Anthony Abbot* (first south altar); Bartolomeo della Gatta,

Madonna enthroned with Saints (recently harshly restored; third south altar); *Annunciation*, another della Robbian relief (altar in the south transept); Lorenzo di Credi, *Adoration of the Child* (chapel to the right of the main altar). In the north transept is a large **Maestà* signed by Segna di Bonaventura. The **Pieve** (deconsecrated), next to the church (half of which was demolished) is entered from the right side of the Collegiata (unlocked on request). Near the 15C font is a *Deposition* by the school of Signorelli and a della Robbian *Baptism of Christ*. Behind the Pieve is the church of the Gesù with a portico.

Via San Giuliano leads downhill to the Porta Romana, outside which is the octagonal **Madonna della Consolazione**. Nearby is the ex-church of **San Lazzaro**, now a small museum of frescoes (including a *Crucifixion* by the school of Giotto).

A short way south of Castiglion Fiorentino, off the road to Cortona, a narrow by-road (signposted) winds through charming countryside up a hill to the castle of ****Montecchio Vesponi**, which was for long contested for its strategic position, and was once owned by Sir John Hawkwood, The splendid 13C walls (the crenellations were added in the 19C) enclosed a village up to the end of the 17C, but now only a tower and 16C house remain (usually shown 11.00–13.00 on Monday; in winter and other times, by appointment, ☎ 0575-651272).

The main road continues south with a splendid view of Cortona and its monumnets strung out along the skyline of the long sloping hillside. A pretty road leads up through beautiful countryside to the Porta Colonia of Cortona (see Ch. 37).

Northwest of Arezzo near Indicatore station is the **Arezzo British Military Cemetery**, with 1267 graves from the Second World War. Across the Arno at **Laterina** long and almost intact stretches of the Via Cassia Vetus were unearthed in 1973.

Sir John Hawkwood

Sir John Hawkwood was born c 1320 at Sible Hedingham in Essex, He came to Italy as captain of a band of mercenaries in 1362. From 1377 onwards he captained the Florentine army, and the castle of Montecchio was given to him (probably around 1375) by the grateful Florentines. Known as *Giovanni Acuto*, he became one of the most famous *condottiere* in Italy. After his death in 1394 he was given a magnificent state funeral by the Florentines, and a procession accompanied his body from Piazza della Signoria to the Baptistery where he lay in state. A splendid stone wall tomb was planned for Hawkwood in the Duomo to be financed by public subscription, even though it had been decreed at the end of the 14C that no tombs should be erected in the church above the level of the pavement. After his remains had, instead, been taken back to England for interment, some years later he was honoured in the Duomo with an equestrian memorial. This famous work, dating from 1436, had to be painted twice by Paolo Uccello, since his first version was not accepted. Its green tones imitate a bronze equestrian monument.

PROVINCIA DI AREZZO

EMILIA
ROMAGNA

FIRENZE

M. FALTERONA

Eremo di
Camaldoli

Passo d.
Consuma
70
Cast. d.
Romena
Stia
Camaldoli
Badia
Prataglia

Borgo
alla Collina
Pratovecchio
Badia

Montemignáio
Porrena
CASENTINO

Castel S. Niccolò
Piano di Campaldino
Poppi

Chiusi
d. Verna

Sestino

Bibbiena
208

3b
258

Badia
Tedalda

PRATOMAGNO
Castel Focognano
Chitignano

Pieve
S. Stéfano

258

Castelfranco
di Sopra
Pieve
Socana
Caprese
Michelangelo

MARCHE

Loro Ciuffenna

Subbiano

Sansepolcro

S. Giovanni
Valdarno
Terranuova
Bracc.
Castiglion
Fibocchi

Anghiari

Cavriglia

Montevarchi
Laterina

AREZZO
Monterchi

Galatrona
Bucine
69

UMBRIA

S. Leolino
Cennina
Pergine
Valdarno

73

540

Civitella in
Val di Chiana
73

SIENA

Ciggiano

327
VAL DI CHIANA
71

Castiglion
Fiorentino

Gargonza
Monte
S. Savino
Montecchio

Marciano
d. Chiana

Lucignano
A1
Camucia
CORTONA

Foiano
d. Chiana
75bis
Terontola

Farneta

Lago
Trasimeno

ARNO

69
A1
VALDARNO

310
71

0   10 miles
0   20 kms

37 · Cortona

Cortona (22,600 inhab.) is a delightful, peaceful little town, particularly well preserved, with olive groves and vineyards reaching up to its walls. It is built on a long hillside with narrow, winding well-kept medieval streets covering the steep slopes. It has numerous interesting churches (including **Santa Maria del Calcinaio**, a famous Renaissance building), and two fine museums. Its works of art include paintings by **Luca Signorelli** who was born here. There are magnificent views over the wide agricultural plain which provides the main source of its economy.

■ Practical information

Tourist information office. (*IAT*), 42 Via Nazionale (☎ 0575-630352).

By rail. There are bus connections from the two nearest stations. *Camucia*, 5km from Cortona, is the nearest station on the Florence–Rome secondary line (a few trains a day from Florence in 1hr 15mins). **Bus** from Camucia station c every 30mins in 10mins to Piazza Garibaldi.

Terontola, 11km from Cortona, is on the main line between Florence and Rome, but only a few fast Intercity trains stop here; local trains in c 1hr 30mins from Florence. **Bus** from Terontola station c every hour in 25mins to Piazza Garibaldi.

By bus. Country buses (*LFI*) from Piazza Garibaldi to Camucia, Terontola, Castiglione Fiorentino, and Arezzo.

Car parking (the centre is closed to traffic). Free car parks in Piazzale del Mercato, Porta Colonia, Porta Santa Maria, or Via Gino Severini.

Hotels

★★★★ *Il Falconiere Relais*, in the countryside at the bottom of the hill, off the road to Castiglion Fiorentino; **località San Martino a Bocena** (☎ 0575-612679; fax 0575-612927); *San Michele*, 15 Via Guelfa (Pl. 1; ☎ 0575-604348, fax 0575-630147).

★★★ *Oasi*, **località Le Contesse** (just outside Cortona), with restaurant (☎ & fax 0575-630354); *San Luca*, 2 Piazza Garibaldi (Pl. 2; ☎ 0575-630460, fax 0575-630105); *Sabrina*, 37 Via Roma (Pl. 3; ☎ 0575-630397, fax 0575-604627); *Italia*, 5 Via Ghibellina (Pl. 4; ☎ 0575-630254, fax 0575-630564).

★★ *Athens*, 12 Via Sant'Antonio (Pl. 5), closed in winter (☎ 0575-630508, fax 0575-604457).

Youth hostel: *Ostello per la Gioventù San Marco*, 57 Via Maffei (closed in winter; ☎ 0575-601392).

Agriturist accommodation

There are numerous agriturist hotels (information supplied by the *APT* office) including the following, both with swimming pools: località Landrucci, near Torontola, *Fattoria Landrucci* (☎ 0575-20446); and località Burcinella, *Agrisalotto*, Santa Caterina di Cortona (☎ 0575-617417).

House to rent near Ossaia (4km south of Cortona), *Il Castagno* (☎ 075-8750083).

Restaurants

£££ *Il Falconiere* (see above); *Il Cacciatore*, 11 Via Roma; *Preludio*, 11 Via Guelfa. ££ *Osteria del Teatro*, 5 Via Maffei.

£ *Dardano*, 19 Via Dardano; *Taccone*, 46 Via Dardano.

Restaurants in the environs
Località Le Contesse. ££ *Oasi.*
Ossaia. £ *La Tufa* (also pizzeria).
At **Castel Gilardi**, on the Città di Castello road, leaving Cortona through the Porta Colonia, there is a trattoria (a cool place to eat in summer).

Café. *Caffè degli Artisti*, Via Nazionale.
A snack bar, *La Casina dei Tigli*, in the public gardens near San Domenico is open in summer.

Picnics. Pleasant places to picnic include Piazza della Pescaia; near Porta Montanina; and in the little garden between San Benedetto and Sant'Agostino. Also on the hillside off Via Santa Margherita.

An **antiques fair** is held in the town in September.

History. The hill on which Cortona stands was occupied by the Villanovan people in the 7C–6C BC. It was in an excellent strategic and commercial position dominating the Valdichiana, on the route between Rome and southern Etruria and northern Etruria and the Po valley, and mid-way between the Tyrrenian and Adriatic coasts. Little is known about the Etruscan town, which was one of the twelve cities of the Etruscan Confederation in the 4C BC. It is thought that the first walls (some 3km in circumference) were built as early as the 4C. By the end of the century the town had come under Roman influence, and large villas were built on the rich agricultural plain in the surrounding territory. However this marshy area was abandoned in the Middle Ages because of malaria. In the 13C and 14C Cortona was a flourishing commune, ruled after 1325 by the Casali family. In the 15C and 16C it was a dominion of the Florentine Republic.

During the 14C and early 15C many Sienese artists were working in the town, including Sassetta. Fra Angelico carried out two altarpieces in the 1430s for the church of San Domenico (now in the Museo Diocesano). The most famous painter born in Cortona was Luca Signorelli (1441–1523), the great precursor of Michelangelo, a number of whose paintings survive here. Another outstanding native painter (and architect) was Pietro Berrettini (1596–1669), called Pietro da Cortona. Gino Severini (1883–1966), the painter was also born here.

Santa Maria del Calcinaio

Half-way up to the town is the church of *Santa Maria del Calcinaio, a masterpiece of Renaissance architecture (**open** 15.00–17.00; summer 16.00–19.00; fest. 10.00–12.30). It is difficult to reach without a car; but there is a request stop outside the church served by buses to Camucia. Otherwise it is a walk of several kilometres (partly on the main road) from Porta Sant'Agostino. It is one of the few works to have survived certainly by Francesco di Giorgio Martini (1485). It is built on a Latin-cross plan with an octagonal cupola. It had been completed only as far as the drum of the cupola at the death of Francesco di Giorgio in 1501. The building was finished under the direction of Pietro di Norbo in 1508–14, almost certainly following the design of Francesco di Giorgio.

Set into the hillside, its beautiful form can be fully appreciated as it is approached from above, along a short road with a few ancient cypresses. It was built on the site of a tannery (called a *calcinaio* from the use of lime), on the wall of which a miraculous image of the Madonna appeared. The Arte dei Calzolai (Guild of Shoe-makers) commissioned the church to house the venerated Madonna from Francesco di Giorgio, on the advice of Signorelli.

Santa Maria del Calcinaio, Cortona

The beautiful light grey-and-white **interior** with clean architectural lines, has a handsome high altar of 1519 by Bernardino Covatti which encloses the devotional image of the *Madonna del Calcinaio* (14C or 15C). The stained glass in the rose window is by Guglielmo di Marcillat, and the two smaller windows are by his pupils.

On the **right side**, the first and third altars have an *Annunciation* and *Assumption* by the local painter, Tommaso Bernabei, called Papacello (1527 and 1526). The *Madonna and Child with Saints* by Alessandro Allori, in the right transept, has been removed for restoration for years. **Left side**: third altar, *Madonna and Saints* (including Thomas Becket), a good Florentine Mannerist painting by Jacopo di Giovanni di Sandro, called Jacone; second and first altars, *Immaculate Conception*, and *Epiphany*, both attributed to Papacello.

Town centre

The road continues up towards the centre (car parks signposted): to the right, near the main entrance to the town is the early 15C church of **San Domenico**. Over the portal is a worn fresco by Fra Angelico. The pleasant **interior** has 17C side altars designed by Ascanio Covatti. The detached fresco on the west wall of *St Roch* is by Bartolomeo della Gatta. On the **south side**, first altar, wood *Crucifix* of uncertain date, and, in the chapel to the right of the high altar, **Madonna and Saints* by Luca Signorelli (1515; removed for restoration). The bright **ancona* on the high altar of the *Coronation of the Virgin* is signed by Lorenzo di Nicolò Gerini (1402). **North side**, third altar, Palma Giovane, *Assumption*; second altar, Passignano, *Circumcision*.

The **Passeggiata** along the hillside behind the church through public gardens has fine views. In Via Santa Margherita is the façade of the lower church of **San Marco**, with a mosaic of St Mark by Gino Severini (1961). The frescoes on the vault of the oratory date from 1665. A staircase leads to the upper church with a 17C high altar sculpted by Andrea Sellari, and an altarpiece (on the right) by Andrea Commodi. Via Santa Margherita continues uphill, away from the centre, to the church of the same name (described below).

At the entrance to the town **Piazza Garibaldi** has a superb view of Santa Maria del Calcinaio and Lago Trasimeno. In **Via Nazionale**, popularly known as *Rugapiana*, because it is the main and only level street of the town, are several

Città di Castello

CORTONA

AREZZO, PERUGIA & STAZIONE

fine 16C palaces, and **Palazzo Ferretti** (No. 45; now the Pretura) built in 1738 by Marco Tuscher.

Via Nazionale ends at **Piazza della Repubblica**, the centre of the town. The 13C **Palazzo Comunale** was enlarged in the 16C and extends to Piazza Signorelli, where the façade has a worn *Marzocco* (the Florentine lion) of 1508.

The Museo dell'Accademia Etrusca

Palazzo Casali (or Palazzo Pretorio), also in Piazza Signorelli is a handsome 13C mansion of the Casali family who became governors of the city. The Renaissance façade was added by Filippo Berrettini in 1613. The 13C flank, on Via Casali, has numerous coats of arms of the governors of the city. The palace houses the *Museo dell'Accademia Etrusca (open 10.00–13.00, 16.00–19.00; winter 09.00–13.00, 15.00–17.00; closed Mon). The museum is entered from the outside staircase in the courtyard. This is also the seat of the Accademia Etrusca, a learned society founded in 1727 for historical and archaeological research. Famous throughout Europe in the 18C, Montesquieu and Voltaire were both early members. The important library has c 30,000 vols, and 620 codices.

On the **first floor** the splendid **main hall (2)** has a fine display of small bronzes. On the platform to the right is an Etruscan *chandelier, a very unusual work probably dating from the late 4C BC. It is decorated on the underside with intricate allegorical carved decorations between the 16 little oil lamps, surrounding a gorgon's head. Also displayed here is an inscription of 2C BC, formerly attached to the chandelier. On the platform to the left are eight fine wooden show cases: in the first, Attic amphora of the mid-6C BC with *Hercules and the Nemean lion* and two lions in an heraldic pose, and an amphora in grey bucchero of the mid-6C BC.

In the **first case on the right**: statuette of *Zeus* (6C BC) and a bronze plaque with Etruscan letters, divinities, and figures of Hercules. **2nd case**: statuettes of athletes, Kourai, votive figures, animals and warriors. **3rd case**: 16C–17C bronzes including a statuette of *Marsyas* (perhaps derived from a work by Antonio Pollaiolo), and early 15C northern Italian ivories. In the **double case at the end**: *Christ crucified* (French or German, 12C–13C), Early Christian glass chalice and a globe of 1710 with the constellations.

In the **cases on the left**: 18C and 19C bronzes in imitation of Antique works, alabaster statuette of *Hecate* (with 3 bodies) of 1C AD; two votive statuettes (with inscriptions on their legs) of 3C–2C BC; and (last case) Italic and Etruscan votive statuettes.

In the **small case opposite the entrance**: the famous *Musa Polimnia* an encaustic painting for long thought to be a Roman work of the 1C–2C AD, but now considered an excellent fake of c 1740. Other paintings displayed around the walls include: a tondo by Francesco Signorelli; Luca Signorelli, *Adoration of the Shepherds*; Pinturicchio, tondo of the *Madonna and Child*; works by Piazzetta, Pietro da Cortona (including a *Madonna and Saints* from the church of Sant'Agostino), Ciro Ferri, Cristofano Allori (self-portrait with Ludovico Cigoli), Empoli, and Santi di Tito, as well as two 18C self-portraits by Zoffany and James Northcote.

In **Room 3**, off the right end of the hall, is an interesting and representative Egyptian collection made by Monsignor Corbelli, Papal delegate in Egypt from 1891–96. It includes a rare wood model of a funerary boat (2060–1785 BC), statuettes, mummies, canopic vases, papyri, etc. In **Room 4**, off the hall, Niccolò Gerini, *Four Saints*; Bicci di Lorenzo, triptych; 12C–13C Tuscan mosaic of the *Madonna in prayer*. The small **Rooms 5–7** to the right contain furniture, material relating to the military architect Francesco Laparelli (1521–70), born in Cortona, who designed La Valletta in Malta, fans, ivories, miniatures, swords, 18C–19C livery, and the portrait of an old lady by Bartolomeo Passarotti. Beyond the **hall (8)** with a good ceiling and two 18C globes, is **Room 9** with an elaborate porcelain *tempietto* presented by Carlo Ginori to the Accademia in 1756, and seals including works by Pisanello and Matteo de' Pasti, and jewellery. **Room 10** (left) contains the numismatic collection, including rare Etruscan coins. The ceramics include Ginori, Delft, Deruta, and Gubbio ware. **Room 11** displays Roman and Etruscan bronzes and terracottas and votive statuettes. **Room 12** contains Etruscan cinerary urns, Bucchero ware, and Attic vases. A door leads out onto a walkway above the courtyard which leads back into the main hall. The last room, next to the ticket office, has a representative display of works by Gino Severini (1883–1966), born in Cortona.

Second floor

At the top of the stairs on the second floor is a room (right) which displays portraits including marble busts of *Luca Signorelli* by Pietro Tenerani (1846) and of *Francesco Benedetti* by Lorenzo Bartolini. Beyond is the 18C **library**, a charming room with c 10,000 volumes in their original bookcases. To the left of the stairs are three rooms which display material from recent excavations in the Eruscan tumulus known as the Secondo Melone del Sodo on the plain below Cortona (described on p. 472). These include fragments of Attic ceramics and a gold fibula dating from 480 BC found in the first tomb in 1990–91; jewellery found in 1991–2 in a second tomb in use from the 6C–2C BC; a cast of the stone griffin which decorates the right side of the altar platform; and models of the tumulus and the second tomb.

Duomo

Via Casali descends to the Duomo on the site of an earlier church (**open** 08.00–12.30 or 13.00, and 15.00 or 15.30–18.30 or 19.00; you are not allowed in if wearing shorts or with bare shoulders).

It was rebuilt in the 16C probably by a local architect, a follower of Giuliano da Sangallo (but was later much modified). Remains of the Romanesque church can be seen in the façade (including a large capital with human heads). The campanile (1566) is by Francesco Laparelli. There is a fine view of the countryside from the terrace here. On the south side beneath a pretty 16C portico is a delightful *doorway by Cristofanello (1550).

The striking **interior**, with a barrel vault, has capitals similar to those in San Lorenzo in Florence. On the west wall is the impressive neo-classical funerary monument to Giovanni Battista Tommasi, by Romualdo Galli (1806). **South aisle**. **Second altar**, Raffaello Vanni, *Transfiguration*; **fourth altar**, Lorenzo Berrettini, *St Joseph*. In the chapel to the right of the sanctuary, 13C terracotta *Pietà* (removed for restoration since 1977). The **high altar**, with four carved angels, is a fine work by the local sculptor Francesco Mazzuoli (1664). In the **choir** (light) are some good paintings (right to left): Cigoli, *Madonna of the Rosary*; Andrea Commodi, *Consecration of the church of San Salvatore*; 16C Florentine school, *Descent of the Holy Spirit*; Luca Signorelli (attributed), *Crucifixion*; Francesco Signorelli, *Incredulity of St Thomas*; Alessandro Allori (attributed), *Madonna of the Holy Girdle*; Giovanni Morandi, *Madonna and Saints*; Andrea del Sarto (or his school), *Assumption*. At the end of the **north aisle**, carved ciborium dated 1491 attributed to Cuccio di Nuccio or Urbano da Cortona, and two mosaics by Gino Severini . **Fifth altar**, Lorenzo Berrettini, *Madonna and Saints*; **fourth altar**, Andrea Sellari, wood *Crucifix*; **third altar**, Pietro da Cortona, *Adoration of the Shepherds*; **second altar**, Lorenzo Baldi, *St Sebastian*; **first altar**, 15C terracotta statue of the *Madonna and Child* (heavily decorated and repainted). On the west wall, fine funerary monument to Giovanni Alberti attributed to Santi di Tito.

The Museo Diocesano

Opposite the façade of the cathedral is the *Museo Diocesano which incorporates the former church of the Gesù, and contains some beautiful paintings (**open** 09.30–13.00, 15.30–19.00; Oct–March: 10.00–13.00, 15.00–17.00; closed Mon).

Room 1, to the right of the entrance, has a Roman sarcophagus (end of the 2C) depicting the battle of the amazons and centaurs, admired by Donatello and Brunelleschi.

Beyond the stairs is the former **Church of the Gesù (3)** which has a fine wooden ceiling by Michelangelo Leggi (1536). Some beautiful paintings are displayed here: Sassetta, *Madonna and Child with four Saints*; Pietro Lorenzetti, large painted *Crucifix*; Fra Angelico, *Madonna enthroned with Saints*, with a fine predella, *Annunciation (1428–30)*, one of his most beautiful works; baptismal font by Ciuccio di Nuccio; Bartolomeo della Gatta, *Assumption of the Virgin*.

In **Room 2**, behind the font, *Madonna and Child* attributed to Nicolò di Segna (formerly thought to be by the Maestro della Madonna di Lucignano; *Madonna enthroned with four angels*, signed and dated 1320 by Pietro Lorenzetti; and *St Margaret* and stories from her life (very damaged) by a 13C Aretine master. The fresco fragments here include the *Way to Calvary* by Pietro Lorenzetti (from the old church of Santa Margherita). A long flight of stairs **(5)**, lined with cartoons (1944) by Gino Severini for his mosaics of the Via Crucis (see p. 472), leads down past a painted *Crucifix* by Pietro Lorenzetti to the **lower church (6)**, the vault of which was painted by Giorgio Vasari, and (lunettes) Cristoforo Gherardi (Il Doceno). The plain stalls are by Vincenzo da Cortona (1517), and the terra-cotta *Deposition* group is a 15C Florentine work.

In **Room 4** (at the end of Room 1): Luca Signorelli, *Deposition*, with a fine predella; *Communion of the Apostles*, signed and dated 1512; and works by his bottega. Off this room **Room 9** has later works: *Ecstasy of St Margaret of Cortona*, by Giuseppe Maria Crespi; *Assumption* by the 16C Roman school; and *Miracle of St Francesco da Paola* by Il Daggiù. Also here are displayed the symbolic bronzes made by Vincenzo Lapi in 1772 for the monument to St Margaret of Cortona in the piazza outside (replaced in situ by copies).

By the entrance another flight of stairs leads down to **Room 8** with the Passerini church vestments of 1515, including a cope made for Leo X's visit to the town, embroidered on designs by Andrea del Sarto and Raffaellino del Garbo. **Room 7** displays the Vagnucci reliquary signed and dated 1458 by Giusto da Firenze, and church silver including a chalice by Michele di Tommaso da Siena (late 14C).

Lower town

From Piazza Signorelli, beyond the **Teatro Signorelli**, built in 1857 by Carlo Gatteschi, the pretty old Via Dardano leads uphill before descending to the simple **Porta Colonia** (which preserves its wooden doors). Here are the most considerable remains of the **Etruscan walls**, the huge blocks conspicuous below Roman and medieval masonry above. The walls stretch away up the hill towards the Fortezza Medicea, above the church of Santa Margherita, the top of which can just be seen in the woods (both described below). Outside the gate (reached by a pretty road), in beautiful countryside on the hillside below the town, the fine centrally-planned church of **Santa Maria Nuova** is well seen. It is known that both Cristofanello (in 1550–54) and Vasari were involved in the construction of the church, which was not finished until 1600 when the cupola was built. It is closed for restoration but contains altarpieces by Alessandro Allori and Empoli, and a 16C organ by Onofrio Zefferini. From the gate Via delle Mura del Duomo, a charming little lane with acacia trees, leads back along the top of the walls to the Duomo.

From **Piazza della Repubblica** three narrow old roads descend to gates in the walls. **Via Roma** passes beneath an archway of Palazzo Comunale and ends at the medieval Porta Santa Maria. On the left is the entrance to the church of **San Filippo** with a cupola, a fine work by Antonio Iannelli (1720). It contains altarpieces by Camillo Sagrestani (high altar) and Giovanni Battista Piazzetta (second altar on the left). Beside the church is the little Porta del Morto of **Palazzo Cinaglia** (No. 25), with a worn carved architrave. Many old houses in Cortona have a second small doorway usually raised above the level of the street (and now often used as a window). This was known as the *Porta del Morto* as it was popularly supposed that it was used only to carry out the coffin when an inhabitant of the house died. Instead it is now thought to have been used as the usual door of the house (which could easily be defended in times of trouble when the larger doorways were barred). On the right (No. 26) is the fine medieval **Palazzo Quintani**. Just before the gate is the pretty Via Jannelli (right) with medieval houses and wooden *sporti*.

Via Janelli, Cortona

Via Guelfa leads south from Piazza della Repubblica steeply down to Porta Sant'Agostino. At the beginning, on the right, is **Palazzo Mancini-Sernini** (No. 4) with an unusually tall *façade incorporating a loggia on the top storey. It was designed by Cristofanello for the Laparelli family in 1533. Lower down is the church and convent of **Sant'Agostino** with a Gothic exterior and a 17C interior (being restored as a conference and exhibition centre). It contains side altars by Filippo Berrettini (1613) and an altarpiece by Empoli. Behind the church (reached by Via del Marzocco) is the unusual exterior of the church of **San Benedetto** (closed) built in 1722 on an elliptical plan. It contains an interesting wooden statue of *Christ at the Column*. Nearby is a medieval house with wooden *sporti* and a 13C public fountain. Outside Porta Sant'Agostino is the church of the **Spirito Santo** (closed) built in 1637 by Filippo Berrettini with a cupola of 1751. It contains an 18C *Madonna and Child with Saints* by Giuseppe Angeli, and a wood statue of the *Dead Christ* by Fabbrucci (1687–1767).

Via Ghibellina leads down from Piazza della Repubblica to the walls where the Etruscan **Porta Ghibellina** has been partially excavated. There is a pleasant walk from here back to Porta Sant'Agostino along the top of the walls.

Upper town

The stepped Via Santucci leads up beneath the **Palazzo del Popolo** in Piazza della Repubblica to the church of **San Francesco**, the first church to be built outside of Assisi by the Franciscans after the death of St Francis. The architect was Brother Elias, friend and disciple of St Francis, who died in the convent of the church in 1253. It preserves a worn Gothic portal.

In the altered **interior** (closed indefinitely for restoration), with 17C side altars, there are attractive pews. On the west wall are interesting remains of fres-coes. **South side**, **first altar**, Niccolò Monti, *St Francis before the Sultan* (1842); **second altar**, Orazio Fidani, *Meeting at Porta Aurea*; **fourth altar**, Cigoli, *Miracle of St Anthony of Padua*. In the chapel to the right of the main altar, Gothic tomb of Ranieri Ubertini by Angelo and Francesco di Pietro (1360). On the left wall of the chapel, *Madonna and Saints* by Ciro Ferri. The 17C marble tabernacle by Bernardino Radi on the **high altar**, encloses a precious Byzantine ivory reli-quary of the Holy Cross. Brother Elias is buried behind the altar. It is thought that Luca Signorelli was buried in the crypt below. **North side**. **Third altar**, **Annunciation*, the last work (left unfinished) by Pietro da Cortona; **second altar**, Camillo Sagrestani, *Martyrdom of St Lucy*; **first altar**, Raffaello Vanni, *Nativity* (in very poor condition). On the wall, 15C fresco fragment.

Beneath the church steps is a 13C public fountain. Opposite the high wall of the church and convent in Via Maffei is the pretty Renaissance portico of the **Ospedale di Santa Maria della Misericordia**. Via Berrettini, a very steep road, leads up from San Francesco through a delightful, quiet residential part of the town, with colourful gardens and plants around the well-kept houses. Beyond a large circular water cistern is the **birthplace of Pietro da Cortona** (No. 33; plaque). The road follows the high convent wall of **Santa Chiara**. The convent and church were built in 1555 by Vasari. The church contains an *Immaculate Conception* by Andrea Commodi, and a *Deposition* attributed as an early work to Pietro da Cortona. In underground rooms are remains of a huge Roman cistern (the most important building of this date to survive in Cortona). The small triangular Piazza della Pescaia is beautifully planted with ilex trees.

Via Berrettini continues to ascend (keep left) towards the charming little Romanesque bellcote of **San Cristoforo** (entered to the left). It contains damaged detached frescoes by the 13C Umbrian school. Beside a large square water cistern a road (right) descends shortly to the 15C church of **San Niccolò**, approached through a peaceful walled garden. The wooden porch, with Ionic capitals, was added in 1930 (opened by the custodian who lives here; ring at the door on the left, 09.00–12.00, 15.00–dusk). Over the altar is a standard painted on both sides by Luca Signorelli with a **Deposition* (in excellent condition) and a *Madonna and Child* (shown by the custodian). On the north wall is a votive fresco of the *Madonna and Saints* by Signorelli or his school.

Via Santo Stefano continues uphill; on the left Via Porta Montanina leads to the edge of the hillside, planted with pine trees, beside the charming **Porta Montanina**, decorated with four arches, with its doors still intact. Remains of the Etruscan walls, and of a second fortified gate can be seen here. A fine stretch of walls leads steeply down the hillside beside orchards, and uphill to the Fortezza Medicea. Outside the gate there is a view of Santa Maria Nuova and the pretty countryside below the town.

Santa Margherita and the Fortezza Medicea

From Via Santo Stefano, Via Santa Croce (signposted for Santa Margherita), a stepped lane with gardens on either side, continues uphill towards the sanctuary (which can also be reached by car off the Città di Castello road at Torreone). Via Santa Croce passes through cypress woods before reaching the sanctuary of **Santa Margherita**, dedicated to St Margaret of Cortona (1247–97).

Born at Laviano, in Umbria, she became a Franciscan tertiary, the third member of the Order after St Francis and St Clare. Her name was associated with numerous miracles after her death in a monastery here; a Gothic church, probably designed by Giovanni Pisano, was built on this site where she was buried. To celebrate her canonization in 1728, Ferdinando Ruggeri built a neo-Gothic cupola over her tomb five years later, but the whole church was rebuilt by Mariano Falcini in 1856–93 in Romanesque-Gothic style. A single rose window was retained from the original church. It contains her *sarcophagus, thought to have been designed by the native artists Angiolo and Francesco di Pietro (1362), but also attributed to Giovanni Pisano). The frescoes (1890–95) are by Giorgio Bandini.

Below the church, Via Santa Margherita descends to the public gardens (see above), past a Via Crucis in mosaic by Gino Severini. A road continues up to the **Fortezza Medicea** or *Girfalco*, in a splendid position dominating the town (651m). There is a magnificent view of Lake Trasimene, and part of the outer circle of walls built by the Etruscans can be seen from here. The castle was built by order of Cosimo I in 1556, and was once thought to be the work of Francesco Laparelli, but is now considered to be by his friend Gabrio Serbelloni. At present the interior is **open** only for exhibitions in summer, 10.00–13.00, 15.00–19.00. Outside is a stone bench carved by Joe Tilson in 1990.

The environs of Cortona ~ Etruscan tombs

On the plain at the foot of the hill are a number of interesting Etruscan tombs. From the road junction, known as the Cinque Vie, near Santa Maria del Calcinaio (see above), a road (signposted for Sodo) leads to the **Tanella di Pitagora** (for **adm.** ☎ 0575-603083), a vaulted circular Etruscan tomb, probably formerly covered by a tumulus. Restored in the 19C, it is now surrounded by cypresses. Despite its name (meaning 'cave-dwelling of Pythagoras'), it has nothing to do with Pythagoras (who lived at Crotone in Southern Italy). It had been discovered by the 16C when Vasari visited it, calling it the tomb of Archimedes. Formerly thought to date from the 4C BC, it may have been built in the 3C or even the 2C BC. Nearby, in Località Piaggette, is the **Tanella Angori**, similar in form, but less well preserved, discovered in 1949.

Near the railway station (entrance on Via Lauretana) is the **Melone di Camucia** ('Melone' or 'melon' refers to its shape), an Etruscan tumulus tomb excavated in 1842 by Alessandro François. It has a perimeter of 200 metres, and was in use from the 7C BC to the 4C BC. Finds from the two burial chambers (the second one discovered in 1964) are in the Archaeological Museum in Florence.

In the locality of Sodo, at the foot of the hill, off the road to Castiglion Fiorentino, are two more tumulus tombs. They are on either side of the road to Foiano. The **Primo Melone del Sodo** (for **adm.** ☎ 0575-612778) was discovered in 1909 and is marked by a pine tree on top of the mound. It has a circumference of 185m, and was in use from the early 6C BC to the 3C BC. Inside is an inscription dating from the 4C BC. On the left of the Foiano road is the **Secondo Melone del Sodo** (usually **open** 08.00–14.00 except Mon; or ☎ 0575-612565) excavated in 1927, and one of the largest tumuli so far found in Etruria. Excavations have been in progress here since 1990 when an altar was discovered on the exterior (east side) of the tumulus, approached by a monumental stairway either side of which are two large sphynxes with warriors carved in the early 6C (this is the only Eturscan tomb known which conserves sculptural elements in situ). Two tombs in use from the 6C–2C BC have been excavated in the tumulus, the finds from which are exhibited in the Museo dell'Accademia Etrusca in Cortona (see above).

Outside Porta Colonia (see above) on the Città di Castello road is the picturesque **Convento delle Celle**, in a beautiful position on the lower slopes of Monte Egidio. The pretty stone buildings, immaculately kept, are grouped beside a river torrent. A hermitage on this site was probably occupied by the Franciscans c 1214–17, who were visited by St Francis in 1226. The convent has been occupied by the Cappuccini since 1537. The hillside has had to be shored up above the convent to prevent landslides. Visitors can see various chapels including St Francis' cell.

Above the convent is **Torreone**, at the watershed between the Valdichiana and Val Tiberina, and **Castel Gilardi**. From here a rough road leads north along the wooded slopes of **Monte Egidio** (1056m) where Villa del Seminario is on the site of the Hermitage of St Egidio. There are particularly beautiful views from this road (of Cortona) and from the Città di Castello road (of Lake Trasimene). From Castel Gilardi a road leads over the Umbrian border to descend into the Tiber valley, joining the road from Umbertide to Città di Castello (see *Blue Guide Umbria*).

Below the Public Gardens of Cortona (see above) Via delle Contesse and Via del Palazzone (left) lead to **Villa Passerini**, known as *Il Palazzone*. It was built for Cardinal Silvio Passerini by Giovanni Battista Caporali (1521), and is now used in the summer by the Scuola Normale di Pisa. The salone has frescoes by Papacello and the chapel is frescoed by Signorelli and his pupils. Nearby, at **Metelliano**, is the 11C church of Sant'Angelo.

A road leads southwest from Cortona towards Mercatale via the **Rocca di Pierle** an impressive, large, square castle dating from before 1098, surrounded by a little hamlet. Mercatale is in Umbria (see *Blue Guide Umbria*).

A road leads across the plain from Camucia to the **Abbazia di Farneta**, probably founded in the 8C. The interesting Romanesque building has a beautiful 10C triple apse and *crypt, restored after 1940. In the priest's house (admission on request) is a local paleontological collection.

38 · The Valdichiana

The **Valdichiana** is a plain southwest of Arezzo, named after the Chiana river which lies between the upper basins of the Arno and the Tiber. In prehistoric times this valley formed the bed of the Arno, which flowed not into the Tyrrhenian Sea but into the Tiber. The Chiana river was once an affluent of the Tiber but was deviated by the Romans into the Arno in an attempt to avoid flooding in Rome. By the late Roman period unhealthy marshes had formed on the plain. In 1388 the Florentines built a drainage ditch (called the Fosso Maestro) for the Chiana and in the 15C Leonardo da Vinci made studies of the area. However, the first serious attempt to drain the marshes was made by Cosimo I when he constructed the Canale Maestro della Chiana in 1551, and draining and irrigation operations continued until 1780 when the situation was more or less resolved by the construction of an artificial watershed between the Tiber and Arno rivers near Chiusi and the building of more canals. The most interesting little towns in this area are **Monte San Savino** and **Lucignano**. The southern part of the Valdichiana with Chiusi is described in Chapter 35.

■ Practical information

Information offices APT **Arezzo** (☎ 0575-377678). In **Monte San Savino**, information office of the Comune (☎ 0575-843098).

Getting there
By car. The A1 motorway from Florence to Rome has exits at Monte San Savino (for Gargonza and Lucignano) and Valdichiana (for Foiano della Chiana).

By rail. A secondary line from Arezzo has stations at Monte San Savino, Lucignano, and Foiano.

Hotels
Monte San Savino. ★★★ *San Gallo*, 16 Piazza Vittorio Veneto (☎ 0575-810049; fax 0575-810220).
Lucignano. ★★★ *Da Totò*, with restaurant, 6 Piazza del Tribunale (☎ 0575-836763; fax 0575-836988).
Houses or flats. These can be rented at **Gargonza**, near Monte San Savino, for short periods (*Residence Castello di Gargonza* (☎ 0575-847021; fax 0575-847054), with swimming pool and restaurant.

An annual **fair** (*Fiera di Santa Caterina*) is held on the last weekend in November in Monte San Savino, when locally-made ceramics are sold including decorative little hand-warmers with whistles on their handles which have been produced in the town for centuries.

Above the northern part of the valley, in a beautiful position on a wooded ridge with fine views, is the delightful little hamlet of **Civitella in Val di Chiana**. Beside the Porta Senese is the **Cassero**, an impressive 13C castle with high ruined walls. It is now a public park (**open** daily 08.00–20.00). The main street, with pretty brick paving (unfortunately unfeelingly renewed on a different design in 1995) and delightful arcades, continues past **Palazzo del Podestà** with coats of arms and a characteristic portico, the lines of which are repeated in the other buildings nearby. The rebuilt parish church in the piazza stands beside an inscription and bronze relief commemorating the inhabitants who lost their lives here in a brutal act of retaliation during the Second World War. An unsurfaced by-road leads downhill to the south through spectacular country-side, via Ciggiano to Gargonza described below).

Monte San Savino

Monte San Savino, a pleasant little town (7300 inhab.) was the birthplace of the sculptor and architect Andrea Contucci, called Sansovino (1460–1529), and preserves a number of works by him.

> **History**. Of Roman foundation, Monte San Savino is named after a church dedicated to the 5C bishop of Chiusi, San Savino. Long hostile to Arezzo, it was destroyed in 1325 by the Aretine, bishop Guido Tarlati. Members of the local Di Monte family (who became Counts of the town in the 16C) included Cardinal Antonio (friend and adviser of Julius II), and Pope Julius III.
> The town has been known since ancient times for its production of ceramics and Andrea Sansovino began his artistic life here as a ceramist.

The town is entered by **Porta Fiorentina** built c 1550 by Nanni di Baccio Bigio Bigio (on a design by Giorgio Vasari). **Corso Sangallo** begins here and crosses the small town past several fine palaces. The paving of the town is being carefully restored. At the far end of Piazza Gamurrini an interesting palace has an unusual ground floor window with two carved herms. The obelisk was set up in honour of Mattias de' Medici who became ruler of the Principality in 1644. The **Cassero** (or castle) is attributed to the Sienese architect Bartolo di Bartolo (1383; restored). The exterior is now hidden by 17C houses. The castle was used as a Monte di Pietà (pawn shop) from 1595 until 1822 and then as a poorhouse (up until 1960). The **Museo del Cassero** (open Easter–Nov on Sat & Sun 09.30–12.30, 16.00–19.00, with longer opening hours in the summer months) contains a collection of local ceramics from the Valdichiana (19C and early 20C), a statue of the *Madonna and Child* (16C–17C) and a wooden 14C *Crucifix* (damaged). It is also used for exhibitions.

The church of **Santa Chiara**, built in 1652, is privately owned and usually kept locked, although there are plans to open it more regularly. Inside there are two paintings (temporarily removed) of saints by Guidoccio Cozzarelli (probably based on a cartoon by Matteo di Giovanni); a splendid *altarpiece of the *Madonna and Child with four Saints* by Andrea Sansovino (c 1490), glazed by Andrea or Giovanni della Robbia; an unglazed terracotta altarpiece of *St Laurence between Saints Roch and Sebastian* (1486), also by Andrea Sansovino; a polychrome terracotta altarpiece of the *Nativity*, attributed to Giovanni della Robbia; and a statue of *St Anthony Abbot*, by Sansovino (and glazed by the della Robbia.

Farther on in Corso Sangallo is the handsome ***Loggia dei Mercanti**, built in 1518–20 by Andrea Sansovino for Cardinal Antonio Di Monte. The high arcade is borne on Corinthian columns and pilasters. Opposite it, in ***Palazzo Di Monte** is the town hall built in 1515 by Antonio da Sangallo the Elder, also for the Cardinal. It has a fine courtyard with two rectangular wells, beyond which is a charming hanging garden designed by Nanni di Baccio Bigio.

The **Pieve** was built c 1100 and the interior remodelled in the mid-18C with stuccoes and marbling. On the left of the west door is the recomposed sarcophagus of Fabiano Di Monte (father of Cardinal Antonio), an early work by Andrea Sansovino (1498). Above the benches towards the east end are two small square reliefs, possibly also early works by Sansovino. On the right of the high altar is a fresco fragment with two angels. The organ dates from the 17C.

On the other side of the Corso is the 14C tower of **Palazzo Pretorio** decorated with coats of arms. Beyond is **Piazza Di Monte**, laid out by Andrea Sansovino in front of his house (plaque). Above the public fountain is a *Marzocco* lion.

The interior of the church of **Sant'Agostino** has a delightful double loggia with Ionic columns at the west end by Andrea Sansovino. The altars date from 1710, and it has an interesting terracotta pavement with numerous tomb slabs. On the west wall are good frescoes of the *Crucifixion*, *Adoration of the Magi*, and *Presentation in the Temple* by Giovanni d'Agnolo di Balduccio (1370–1452). Above is a rose window by Guglielmo di Marcillat. On the right wall, *St Lawrence* with stories from his life. The high altarpiece of the *Assumption* is signed and dated 1539 by Vasari. It is flanked by a *Nativity and Adoration of the Magi* by Orazio Porta. On the left wall is a *Resurrection*, also by Porta (recently restored).

Below the little pulpit is the worn tomb slab of Andrea Sansovino, found in 1969 beneath the pavement of the church. The damaged fresco of the *Pietà*, with five saints below, is by Paolo Schiavo. There is a fine cloister next to the church, probably designed by Sansovino (1528).

The church of **San Giovanni**, which has a door by Sansovino, is usually closed.

In the northwestern district of the town (close to Porta Fiorentina) Via Salomone Fiorentino (named after a native Jewish poet, 1743–1815) recalls the **Ghetto** in this area inhabited from 1627–1799. The 17C synagogue is in a ruined state (there is also a Jewish cemetery outside the walls).

To the east of Monte San Savino (towards the motorway) is the sanctuary of **Santa Maria delle Vertighe**, with a campanile attributed to Andrea Sansovino. In the primitive apse is a copy of an *altarpiece by Margaritone d'Arezzo and Fra Ristoro (which was removed for safety to Arezzo many years ago). When a security system has been installed, it should be returned here, together with the contents of the museum (**adm.** on request at the monastery), which include two saints by Ridolfo del Ghirlandaio, and a painted *Crucifix* by Lorenzo Monaco.

On the other side of the motorway is **Marciano della Chiana** which has scant remains of its walls and towers (being restored). The altarpieces in the church are in very poor condition: the trompe l'oeil frescoes at the east end date from 1750. A road leads south to **Pozzo**, beyond which, by the cemetery, is **Santa Vittoria**, an octagonal chapel with a cupola and lantern thought to have been designed by Ammannati or Vasari in 1572. It was commissioned by Cosimo I to commemorate the battle here of Scannagallo in 1554 in which the Florentines were victorious over the Sienese and French. It is an unusual, but well-proportioned building in brick and *pietra serena* (locked, and in poor repair).

Off the pretty Siena road (No. 73) which runs through woods west of Monte San Savino, is **Gargonza**, a charming little circular medieval hamlet in a peaceful position surrounded by wooded hills, and extremely well preserved. An Ubertini castle in the 13C, it was sold to Siena in 1381, but its possession was subsequently contested by Florence, who ordered the destruction of its walls in 1433. It has been carefully and unpretentiously restored by the Guicciardini family as a hotel-residence where houses or flats can be rented (see above).

Lucignano

Further south is Lucignano, a delightful, cheerful little medieval village laid out on an elliptical form, and well preserved. It has some interesting works of art, and fine views. Above the 14C **Cassero**, with a tall tower, is the large **Collegiata**, approached by a pretty flight of curving steps. The campanile is covered for restoration. The **interior** by Orazio Porta, dates from 1594. The gilded wooden angels were installed in 1706. In the south transept, Giacinto Gemignani, *St Charles Borromeo*. The high altar is by Andrea Pozzo. In the north transept, Matteo Rosselli, *Visitation*. On the north side is a 16C *Crucifix* (third altar) and a *Martyrdom of St Lucy* by Gemignani.

Beyond the Collegiata is the 14C **Palazzo Comunale**, recently restored. It houses the **Museo Comunale** (open 10.00–13.00, 15.30–18.30; closed Mon). In the entrance is a 16C fresco of the *Pietà*. In the entrance corridor is church silver of 1628, and a small painting of the *Madonna enthroned with Saints* attributed to Lippo Vanni. The vaulted **Sala del Tribunale** has delightful frescoes dating from 1438–65 of illustrious people from the Bible and Classical heroes, and a huge gold *reliquary (over 2.5 metres high) known as the 'Tree of Lucignano', made in 1350–1471 and decorated with coral and exquisite miniatures. **Room 3**: lunette by Luca Signorelli of *St Francis receiving the stigmata* (with a lovely landscape), and a *Madonna and Child* attributed to him. **Room 4**: *Madonna and Child enthroned* by the Sienese school (c 1320); *triptych of the *Madonna with Saints John the Baptist and John the Evangelist* by Bartolo di Fredi; *St Bernardine (1448) by Pietro di Giovanni Ambrogio; small *Crucifixion by the 13C Sienese school.

Beside Palazzo Comunale is the church of **San Francesco** (1248), with a Romanesque façade, also recently restored. It has numerous fresco fragments of great interest, attributed to Bartolo di Fredi, Taddeo di Bartolo, and others. On the last altar on the south side is a painted polychrome wood statue of the *Madonna and Child* by Mariano di Angelo Romanelli (1380–90; restored in 1983). Behind the high altar, polyptych of the *Madonna with four Saints* by Luca di Tommè. The organ dates from the 16C.

Other churches of interest (usually closed) include the **Santissimo Crocifisso** and the **Oratorio della Misericordia**, with two della Robbian statues.

The church of the **Madonna della Quercia** is outside the village (indicated by yellow signs). The road passes the ruins of the old Medici fortress on a hill, built by Cosimo I and the cemetery. The church (in poor condition), next to a farm house, is only open for services at weekends. It was built in the late 16C perhaps on a design by Vasari. The fine interior is attributed to Giuliano da Sangallo.

On the other side of the motorway is **Foiano della Chiana**, a small agricultural town, with some industry, near the Chiana plain. From the gate a road leads up to Piazza Cavour where Palazzo Comunale faces the well restored **Palazzo Monte Pio**. It was built by Ferdinando II as a hunting lodge and used as such up to 1670 when it became the pawn shop. It now contains offices belonging to the Comune. A modern flight of steps leads down to the left and across Corso Vittorio Emanuele (which has an 18C loggia) to the church of **San Michele Arcangelo**, with a pretty exterior and campanile. It contains fine carved confessionals and benches dating from the 17C, and 15C choir stalls. On the second south altar is a *Madonna of the Rosary* by Lorenzo Lippi, and on the third north altar, an enamelled terracotta of the *Ascension* by Andrea della Robbia and his son Giovanni (1495–1500) Off the south side is an oratory with elaborate stuccoes in the vault and lunettes.

The Corso continues to **Piazza della Collegiata** where there is a well, imposing brick fortifications (a round tower is being restored) and a row of houses above brick bastions on either side of Porta Castello. The **Collegiata** has a Baroque façade. On the third south altar is a *Madonna della Cintola* (1502) by Andrea della Robbia, and on the second north altar, a *Coronation of the Virgin*, a late work by Luca Signorelli and his school. Steps lead up through Porta Castello, a double brick gate, to the church of **Santa Maria della Fraternità** (not open regularly; ask at the Comune for the key) which contains a 17C ceiling, cantoria, benches, and organ. Four paintings are attributed to Giovanni Camillo Sagrestani, and the beautiful statue of the standing *Madonna and Child* is now thought to be by Andrea della Robbia (c 1460) probably on a model by his uncle, Luca. A 17C gilded wood coffer is being restored.

On the outskirts of the town, by the hospital, is the church of **San Francesco** preceded by a portico (usually open in the afternoon). It contains 16C terracotta statuary, and a large della Robbian altarpiece of *Christ in Glory with Saints*.

From Foiano a road leads over the Chiana, via the Abbazia di Farneta, to Cortona, both described in Ch. 37.

39 · The Valdarno and Pratomagno

The **Valdarno** lies between Florence and Arezzo, overlooked by the Chianti hills and the western slopes of the **Pratomagno**. In the Pliocene era (about 3 million years ago) a huge lake occupied this area and on its shores were tropical forests inhabited by rhinoceros, hippopotamus, and elephants. It later became one of the most fertile areas of Italy, settled by the Etruscans and Romans.

The narrow Arno valley has always been important as the main route between Florence and the South. In the 14C the Florentine Republic founded *Terre nuove* here at San Giovanni Valdarno, Terranuova Bracciolini, and Castelfranco di Sopra. The Humanists Marsilio Ficino, Poggio Bracciolini, and Benedetto Varchi were all born in the Valdarno. The most interesting places to visit in the area include the small town of **San Giovanni Valdarno**, **Montevarchi**, and the monastery of **Vallombrosa**.

Many of the beautiful works of art in churches here by Florentine masters have been carefully restored in recent years: these include a triptych by Masaccio, born at San Giovanni Valdarno (now in the pieve at Cascia), an *Annunciation* by Fra Angelico (exhibited in the museum in San Giovanni Valdarno), and numerous Della Robbian works. A fine red Chianti is produced on the *Colle Aretine*. The hills of the Pratomagno rise to nearly 1000 metres at **Vallombrosa**, famous for its monastery and forests.

■ Practical information

Information offices. APT of **Florence** (☎ 055-290832) for Incisa Valdarno, Figline Valdarno, Reggello, and Vallombrosa. *APT* of Arezzo (☎ 0575-377678) for San Giovanni Valdarno and Montevarchi.

Getting there

By car. The A1 **Motorway** from Florence to Arezzo follows the Valdarno with exits at Incisa (for Figline) and Valdarno (for San Giovanni Valdarno and Montevarchi).

By rail. The main line from Florence–Rome via Pontassieve has stations at Incisa, Figline, San Giovanni, and Montevarchi (slow trains only).

By bus. Services run by *SITA* from Florence via San Donato in Collina to Incisa, Figline, San Giovanni, and Montevarchi. *CAT* services via Pontassieve to the above towns. *SITA* services via Pontassieve, Pelago and Tosi for Vallombrosa and Saltino.

Hotels

Figline: ★★★ *Antica Taverna Casa Grande* (with restaurant), 84 Via Castelguinelli (☎ 055-9544851; fax 055-9544322) and *Torricelli*, 2 Via San Biagio (☎ 055-958139; fax 055-958481).

San Giovanni Valdarno: ★★★ *La Bianca*, 38 Viale Don Minzoni (☎ 055-9123402; fax 055-9121423) and *River*, 10 Via Fratelli Cervi (☎ 055-9122435; fax 055-9120219).

Montevarchi: ★★★ *Delta*, 137 Viale Diaz (☎ 055-901213; fax 055-901727). **Terranova Bracciolini**: ★★★ and ★★ hotels.

Loro Ciuffena: ★★ hotels with restaurants.
Reggello: ★★★★ *Villa Rigacci* in the country at Vaggio (☎ 055-8656718; fax 055-8656537).
Pietrapiana ★★★ *Archimede*, with restaurant (☎ 055-869055; fax 055-868584).
Saltino. ★★★ *Grand Hotel Vallombrosa*, 2 Via Carducci (☎ 055-862012; fax 055-862035) and ★★ *Villino Medici* (☎ 055-862017).

Youth Hostel at Cavriglia, località Cafaggiolo (☎ 055-967418).

Campsites. Figline ★★★★ *Norcenni Girasole Club* (☎ 055-959666), and ★★ sites at **Cavriglia**.

Restaurants
Figline. ££ *Papillon*, 83 Piazza Ficino.
San Giovanni Valdarno. ££ *Adriano VII*, 16 Piazza Masaccio, *Castellucci*, 44 Corso Italia.
Terranova Bracciolini. *Cooperativa Agricola Valdarnese*, open at weekends on a farm at Paterna (booking necessary, ☎ 055-977052).

The Valdarno

At the northern end of the Valdarno is **Incisa Valdarno**, so called from the deep chalky cutting made by the Arno, through which run the road, motorway, and railway. The conspicuous 14C Torre del Castellano was heavily restored in 1952. On the main road is the Municipio beside the church of **Sant'Alessandro** with three fragments of a polyptych by Andrea di Giusto. In the convent of **Santi Cosma e Damiano** (1538; reconstructed in the 17C), preceded by a portico of 1592, are 17C paintings and a polychrome terracotta bas-relief of the *Madonna and Child* attributed to Buggiano (on a design by Luca della Robbia.

A road beyond Sant'Alessandro climbs the hill to the locality known as Castello, where a few pine trees stand on the left of the road. This is the site of the old town of **Ancisa**, and the bellcote of the former church above the high pyramidal wall of the ruined castle provides an odd site. In the hamlet on the left is a house (plaques) where Petrarch spent the first seven years of his life. The road continues up to **Loppiano** in beautiful countryside, before which, on the left, is the **Pieve di Santi Vito e Modesto**. Of ancient foundation, it has a battlemented campanile. The exterior is being restored. Inside (if closed, ring at the house on the right) the painting of the *Madonna of the Holy Girdle* by Francesco d'Antonio (1427) has still not been returned since its restoration in 1987.

To the south, in pretty countryside, near **Brollo**, is the tiny hamlet of **San Pietro al Terreno** (unsignposted), with farm buildings beside the church with a bellcote. In the fine 18C interior (if closed, ring on the right) are frescoes in grisaille, stuccoes, and marble confessionals. On the high altar, *Madonna and Child with four Saints* by an early 16C Florentine master. In the choir, detached 14C fresco of the *Madonna and Saints*. On the left altar, 17C painting of the *Madonna of the Rosary*. The painting of the *Holy Trinity* by Agostino Melissi was removed many years ago for restoration.

Figline Valdarno

Figline Valdarno has been an important market town (13,600 inhab.) since the 12C. The castle of Feghine was first mentioned in 1008, but the town on this site was laid out on a regular plan in 1259 by the Florentines, who also built its walls in 1356.

The lovely large **Piazza Ficino** (market on Tuesdays) is named after the great Humanist scholar Marsilio Ficino (1433–99) who was born here. A friend of Cosimo il Vecchio, he was a leading member of the Medici Platonic Academy in Florence. The square has porticoes and balconies, and a medley of houses. At one end is the 17C **Spedale Serristori** with a loggia. This was founded in 1399 by a certain Ser Ristoro, and the hospital was transferred to Villa di San Cerbone (see below) in 1890. Four very worn frescoes beneath the loggia are by Niccolò Lapi (late 17C).

At the other end of the piazza is the **Collegiata di Santa Maria**, founded in 1257, with a dark **interior** heavily restored in this century. **South wall.** *Madonna and Child with Saints* (including *St Romulus holding a model of Figline*), attributed to Giovanni Andrea de Magistris (1593; restored in 1991). The pretty circular Chapel of the Holy Sacrament, with a colonnade of columns and a lantern above the cupola dates from the 19C. The seated statue of *St Joseph* in polychrome terracotta (temporarily removed for restoration) is attributed to Luca della Robbia 'il giovane' (great-nephew of Luca; c 1505–10. The **Maestà* is ascribed to the Maestro di Figline, named from this work. It was restored in 1975 and is remarkable for its subtle colouring. **North wall**. The 16C font has been placed beside a worn fresco of the *Annunciation*. Beyond a niche with a damaged fresco of the *Crucifixion* is a painting of the *Transition of St Joseph* by the local painter Egisto Sarri (late 19C). A small **museum** (admission on request) has been arranged in two rooms beyond the sacristy. It contains a painting of the *Martyrdom of St Lawrence* by Lodovico Cigoli; two charming angels attributed to Bartolomeo di Giovanni (c 1480) which formerly surrounded the *Maestà* in the church; and church silver, chalices, vestments and illuminated choirbooks.

The narrow Vicolo Libri leads out of the square beside the Collegiata to the 14C **Palazzo Pretorio**, over-restored in 1931, next to a leaning bell tower, at the foot of which is a little open chapel which contains a *Madonna enthroned with Saints* in polychrome terracotta attributed to the workshop of Benedetto Buglioni (the garland, angels, and some details were added in 1930 by the Cantagalli workshop).

In the piazza is the church of **San Francesco**, founded in 1229 and preceded by an attractive portico beneath which, on the left, is a 14C statuette of the *Madonna* in a tabernacle. The **interior** was over restored at the beginning of this century. The **frescoes on the **west wall** (restored in 1984–90) are fine works by Francesco d'Antonio (*Crucifixion and Saints, Annunciation*, and *Coronation of the Virgin*, and *St Francis*). On the **south wall** has been placed a frescoed lunette of the *Madonna and Child with two Saints* attributed to Pier Francesco Fiorentino (detached from the cloister). In the north transept are 14C frescoes of *Christ in Pietà between Saints* and a *Crucifixion* above. On the altar on the **north wall** of the church is a late 15C fresco of the *Madonna of the Holy Girdle between Saints John the Baptist and Julian*, attributed to the school of Botticelli. A door leads into the **cloister** with very worn frescoes of the early 17C, off which is the **Chapter House** (opened on request) which has a 14C fresco of the *Crucifixion* and a painting of the *Madonna and Child* signed and dated 1392 by Giovanni del Biondo.

On the opposite side of Piazza San Francesco is **Santa Croce** (entrance on Via Santa Croce), next to a convent (closed order). In the 18C interior is a 16C painting of the *Crucifixion* and a wooden *Crucifix* by a Tuscan sculptor of the late 15C or early 16C (restored 1991).

A road leads out of Piazza Ficino on the right of the Collegiata to Via Castelguinelli where at No. 86 (marked by two pine trees) is the **Casagrande dei Serristori**, now a hotel and restaurant. The palace was built by the Serristori, the most important family of Figline, and has a Renaissance loggia and Italianate garden (incorporating part of the old walls) which can be seen on request at the restaurant.

Corso Matteotti leads out of the other end of Piazza Ficino beside the Spedale Serristori. It ends in Piazza Serristori with the **Teatro Garibaldi** (being restored), built in 1868–70 by the local architect Andrea Pierallini and decorated by Egisto Sarri. A fine stretch of **town walls** (1356–75) and the Cassero can be seen here.

On the outskirts of the town (reached from Piazza Serristori by Via Vittorio Veneto), beyond the neo-classical cemetery, and next to a palace of 1570, is the sanctuary of **Santa Maria al Ponterosso**, with a fine fresco of the *Madonna and Child* over the high altar by a follower of Perugino.

At the south end of the town (to the right off the main road) is the 17C **Villa di San Cerbone**, seat of the Ospedale Serristori since 1890 (admission on request at the convent). The chapel has an *Annunciation* by Lodovico Cigoli and paintings by Niccolò Lapi. Off the 15C courtyard is the refectory with a *Last Supper* attributed to Giorgio Vasari. The **pharmacy**, founded in 1399, has interesting 16C–19C majolica vases and glass, a painting of the *Madonna enthroned with angels* attributed to the Maestro del 1399, and the head of the *Redeemer* attributed to Matteo Rosselli

This road (signposted Cesto and Gaville) continues past the inconspicuous church of **San Bartolomeo a Scampata**, re-founded in a farm building on the left of the road in 1970, when the old church on the hill above to the right was abandoned. It contains (right wall) a **Madonna and Child* attributed to Segna di Bonaventura or Ugolino di Nerio (restored in 1985). The pretty road continues up to **Gaville** where the Ubertini castle was destroyed by the Florentines in 1252. A road (signposted for the *Museo della Civiltà Contadina*) continues up to the ancient **Pieve di San Romolo**. It stands in a beautiful position, with a fine apse and campanile of 11C–12C. Inside is an *Annunciation* by the Florentine school (c 1500). A painting of *St Christopher* by Bicci di Lorenzo has not yet been returned here since its restoration in 1988. Next door is a local **Ethnographical Museum** illustrating peasant life in the area (**open** Sat 16.00–18.00, Sun 15.00–19.00; or by appointment). The wide view takes in the lignite mines and blast furnaces on the plain (see below).

To the south off the main road for San Giovanni, near the locality of Restone is the church of **Sant'Andrea a Ripalta**, above the road on the right. It is usually locked but has an 18C stuccoed interior and a triptych with a fine predella dated 1436 by Andrea di Giusto.

San Giovanni Valdarno

San Giovanni Valdarno (19,000 inhab.) was founded in 1299 as one of the *Terre nuove* of the Florentine Republic. It is laid out with rectilinear streets on either side of the two central piazze. Some streets have narrow porticoes. San Giovanni was the birthplace of the painters Masaccio (Tommaso Guido or Tommaso di Giovanni Cassai, 1401–c 1428), Mariotto di Cristofano,

Coats of arms on Palazzo Pretorio, San Giovanni Valdarno

1393–1457, and Giovanni di San Giovanni (Giovanni Mannozzi, 1592–1636).

*Palazzo Pretorio (restored in 1991), with a tall central tower (restored in the 19C), stands in the centre of the two main squares, Piazza Cavour and Piazza Masaccio. It is surrounded on four sides by porticoes and covered with coats of arms dating from the 15C to the 18C, some in enamelled terracotta by the della Robbia workshop. The palace was attributed by Vasari to Arnolfo di Cambio. There are long-term plans to open a museum here to display finds from excavations made during restoration work which include medieval ceramics, 15C majolica, 16C–18C local ware, and coins. Outside is a copy of the Florentine *Marzocco* (the original has been placed in the atrium).

In Piazza Cavour, with a monument to Garibaldi by Pietro Guerri (1902) is the 14C **Pieve di San Giovanni Battista** (restored in 1920; often closed), preceded by a portico. It contains a 17C terracotta *Pietà* and a 15C painting of the *Madonna and Child*. In the same square (at No. 12) is the convent of the **Augustinians** (now a school; **adm.** on request). In the oratory (**Santissima Annunziata**) are good works by Antonio Puglieschi (the ceiling fresco, side altarpiece, and high altarpiece of the *Annunciation*, c 1685). On the left altar is a tender **Madonna and Child* on a gold ground by the Maestro della Natività di Castello. In the corridor is a relief of the *Madonna and Child* derived from a prototype by Ghiberti.

The house at 83 Corso Italia is supposed to have belonged to Masaccio (there is a plaque); it is **open** for temporary exhibitions. In Piazza Masaccio, beyond the **Palazzaccio** (or Palazzetto Ricorboli) with three pretty loggias, is **San Lorenzo**, with a plain Gothic façade. The **interior** has been over restored. On the high altar, Giovanni del Biondo, polyptych of the *Coronation of the Virgin*. In the right aisle, remains of frescoes (very ruined) include a fragment of the *Martyrdom of St Sebastian*, the only known signed work by Scheggia (1457; Masaccio's brother, also known as Giovanni di ser Giovanni), and *St Anthony Abbot* with stories from his life (almost illegible) also sometimes attributed to him (or to Mariotto di Cristofano).

The Basilica of Santa Maria delle Grazie

In Piazza Masaccio is the Basilica of Santa Maria delle Grazie, begun in 1484, with a façade of 1856–85, and an unusual portico and double staircase. The east end, with a dome, was rebuilt in the 1950s after severe War damage. At the foot of the staircase is a colourful lunette of the *Assumption of the Virgin with Saints* by Giovanni della Robbia (1515). The church is entered at the top of the right staircase. In the first part, dating from the 18C, with painted vaults, the elaborate high altar has 18C paintings of angels surrounding a venerated image of the *Madonna and Child*. On the altar wall, fresco of the plague which hit the town in 1479. Over a side altar, Domenico di Michelino,

Madonna enthroned with six Saints. The unattractive **rotonda** (in very poor repair) dates from the 1950s. Here is a fresco of the *Marriage of the Virgin* by Giovanni di San Giovanni, detached from the exterior of the church.

The **Museo della Basilica** is entered from a door beside the high altar. (**Open** Tues, Wed, Fri, Sat 10.00–13.30, 16.00–19.00; Thurs 10.00–12.30, 16.00–19.00; fest. 16.00–19.00; closed Mon.) It is arranged in three rooms above the portico overlooking the piazza. In the **first room** Mariotto di Nardo, triptych with the *Trinity and four Saints*; Paolo Schiavo, *St Ansano, St Biagio, Chorus of angel musicians*; works by Lo Scheggia, including a *Chorus of angels*; Giovanni da Piamonte, *Tobias and the archangel Raphael* (also attributed to Bartolomeo della Gatta); Jacopo del Sellaio, *Annunciation*; and works by Mariotto di Cristofano, including *Christ in Pietà between the Virgin and St Lucy.* In the **room to the right**, a beautiful painting of the **Annunciation*, from the convent of Montecarlo. This is generally attributed to the hand of Fra Angelico and dated c 1431 since its restoration in 1984. It is another version of the painting of the same subject by Angelico in the Museo Diocesano in Cortona. In the **room to the left**, Gregorio Pagani, *St John the Baptist, St Lawrence*; Giovanni di San Giovanni, *Beheading of St John the Baptist.*

To the west of San Giovanni Valdarno is **Santa Barbara** laid out in the 1930s next to the open lignite mines and huge blast furnaces (visible from miles around) of an electrical plant. From **Castelnuovo dei Sabbioni** a road continues up through Massa Sabbioni to the **Parco Naturale di Cavriglia** (poorly signposted) on the wooded Chianti hills (800m) overlooking the Valdarno. This is a protected area created in 1978 with a well landscaped zoo (**open** daily 08.00–21.00) with bears, buffalo, wolves, llama, deer and wild fowl. There is a car park outside (if cars are driven into the zoo enclosure a fee is charged), and sports facilities, refreshments, and marked nature trails (wild deer can often be seen in the vicinity).

From Castelnuovo dei Sabbioni a road leads southeast to **Cavriglia**, where a lot of new building has taken place. Above the town is the church of San Giovanni Battista preceded by a garden of lime trees. Its square tower has unusual crenellations. The lunette over the church door of *St John the Baptist in the desert* is attributed to Benedetto Buglioni. The interior has fine Baroque side aisles. A small **Museo di Arte Sacra** has been opened here. It contains a 14C bronze *Crucifix*, and three white enamelled terracotta busts of angels attributed to Benedetto Buglioni.

Southwest of San Giovanni is **Montecarlo**, a Franciscan convent founded in 1429, and now a religious community. An *Annunciation* by Fra Angelico formerly in the church is now in the Museum of San Giovanni Valdarno (see above).

Montevarchi

Montevarchi was also laid out in the early 14C by the Florentine Republic. It has an interesting oval plan with two outer streets, slightly curved, parallel to the two main streets which pass through the central piazza. It is now an important market town (22,700 inhab.) with new suburbs. It is worth exploring for its Art Nouveau and Art Deco buildings.

The Collegiata di San Lorenzo

In the central **Piazza Varchi**, named after the Humanist Benedetto Varchi who was born here (1503–68), is the **Collegiata di San Lorenzo**, with an unusual façade dating partly from the 18C and partly from 1932 (when the bas-relief of the *Martyrdom of St Lawrence* was placed high up on the façade). The campanile (1440) was completed in 1560, and the statue of *St Lawrence* was added by Pietro Guerri in 1894.

The sober **interior** was redesigned in 1706–09 by the local architect and sculptor Massimiliano Soldani Benzi. Pretty stucco frames surround paintings by Giovanni and Camillo Sagrestani and Matteo Bonechi (some have been removed for restoration). The two altarpieces (recently restored) on the right and left side of the *Madonna in glory with Saints* are by Giovanni Balducci (Il Cosci) and Carlo Maratta (1611). In the chapel on the right of the high altar, the dome paintings are attributed to the Sagrestani and Bonechi. At the east end, above the high altar, with the reliquary of the *Madonna del Latte*, by Gherardo Silvani are stuccoes of the *Madonna in Glory* by Giovanni Baratta. The terracotta bust of the *Madonna and Child* dates from the 15C and the bronze statue of the *Madonna* is by Soldani. In the left chapel, Matteo Rosselli, *Adoration of the Magi*.

The Museo della Collegiata

The Museo della Collegiata (**open** Tues, Thurs, Sat 10.00–12.00; or enquire at the door on the right of the façade) is entered off the right side of the church. It is beautifully arranged in two rooms. In the **first room**: large wooden 17C *Crucifix*; three 14C illuminated manuscripts; 16C reliquary bust of one of the Virgins of St Orsola, by Simone di Antonio Pignoni; *Cross* with reliefs by Piero di Martino Spigliati, a pupil of Cellini; a reliquary in the form of a ciborium with 16C paintings by Giovanni del Brina; detached frescoes from the nearby convent of San Ludovico by Roberto (or Luberto) da Montevarchi (an assistant of Perugino).

In the **second room** is the beautiful *****Tempietto Robbiano**. This was formerly the Cappella di Santa Maria del Latte, and it was partly destroyed when it was removed from the church in the 18C. It was reconstructed here in 1973. It was designed to contain a venerated reliquary given to the church in the 13C by Conte Guidoguerra dei Guidi (who had obtained it from Charles of Anjou in gratitude for his valour in a victorious battle in 1266). The enamelled terracottas are by Andrea della Robbia: above the altar are reliefs of *St John the Baptist* and *St Sebastian* in niches on either side of a copy of a terracotta *Madonna and Child*, now on the high altar of the church. Below are four angels protecting the reliquary and a beautiful *Pietà*. The chapel ceiling and friezes of cherubs are also by Andrea. On the wall (formerly on the façade of the church), is a fine della Robbian frieze, also attributed to Andrea, showing the reliquary being presented to the church. Also here are two della Robbian *stemme*, fragments of ceramic oriental draperies, and a stone bas-relief dated 1283.

Via Bracciolini, in front of the church, leads left past **Palazzo del Podestà**, a house with a portico, and **Palazzo Carapelli** with reliefs by Romano Romanelli (early 20C). The church of the **Gesù** has a 19C façade. It contains 18C wooden benches and a large wood statue of *Christ*. At No. 36 is the **Accademia Valdarnese del Poggio**, founded in 1804, in an old monastery with a fine courtyard.

It has a library and an important **Paleontological Museum** (open Tues–Sat 09.00–12.30, 16.00–18.00; fest. 10.00–12.00; closed Mon). In the showcases (1870) are rock, vegetable and animal fossils found in the Valdarno, including the *canis etruscus*, the fossilised head of a dog, studied by the paleontologist Professor F. Major of Glasgow who classified the collection in the 19C. Georges Cuvier, the great French naturalist came here in 1810 to study the collection.

At the north end of the town, near the railway, is the church of the **Madonna del Giglio** with a handsome cupola attributed to Matteo Nigetti (1607–15), a portico, and an early 15C fresco fragment over the altar. In an unattractive part of town to the south (also near the railway), at La Ginestra is the church of **Santa Croce** on a little hill. Thought to have been founded in 614–20, the Benedictine monastery beside it was transformed into a spinning-mill in the 19C (being restored to house a museum illustrating the history of the district). Beyond a door on the right of the church can be seen a fresco of *St Benedict and St Scholastica*. A huge building, once a hat factory, below the hill is being restored and beyond it can be seen the monumental **Palazzo Masini**, an extremely ornate Art Nouveau building with a tower (1924–27).

South of Montevarchi is **Galatrona** with a Romanesque church which contains important works by Giovanni della Robbia (1510–21; key at the priest's house in Mercatale), including a very fine font. Further south, in lovely countryside with farms and woods, is the peaceful little village of **Cennina**, with beautiful views, where a number of houses have recently been restored. The remains of its 12C–13C castle include an isolated gateway. In the attractive little piazza at the top of the hill with a well and houses covered with creepers, is the Sala d'Armi (enquire locally for the key) where concerts are held in August. Near the village is the castle of Lupinari, with a red tower.

Pratomagno

On the east side of the Arno and motorway, almost opposite Montevarchi, is **Terranuova Bracciolini**, now surrounded by ugly new buildings. This was another *Terra nuova* of the Florentine Republic, founded in 1337. The Humanist Poggio Bracciolini (1380–1459) was born here.

Loro Ciuffena, to the east, is also now surrounded by new buildings. The old medieval village is in a fine position on rocks above the Ciuffena river. The church of Santa Maria Assunta has 16C paintings by Carlo Portelli who was born here. The town hall contains a museum (open 09.00–12.00; Sat & fest. 17.00–19.30) dedicated to the works of the local sculptor Venturino Venturi, born here in 1918.

Gropina, in pine woods to the south, is a charming medieval hamlet built around a Romanesque *Pieve (open 08.00–12.00, 15.00–17.00 or 19.00; or ring at the priest's house in front of the side door). The bare interior built in *pietra serena* has delightful carved capitals and a pulpit with interesting carvings. Beneath the right aisle, stairs lead down to remains of earlier buildings on this site (Roman and early Christian finds). On a secondary road to Arezzo is **San Giustino Valdarno**, with another Romanesque pieve.

From Loro Ciuffena a beautiful road (the *Strada dei Sette Ponti*, or the road of the seven bridges), roughly on the line of the Roman Cassia Vetus, leads along the side of the **Pratomagno** hills back towards Florence. It passes the sanctuary of the **Madonna delle Grazie di Montemarciano**, built in 1532 and surrounded by a portico of the early 17C. It contains a fresco attributed to Francesco d'Antonio. The village of **Montemarciano** has remains of its castle destroyed by the Florentines in 1288.

Castelfranco di Sopra was founded by the Florentines in 1299, and laid out on a circular plan perhaps to a design by Arnolfo di Cambio. Outside the village on the left is the Vallombrosan **Badia di San Salvatore a Soffena**, rebuilt in 1394 (and restored in 1966). It contains interesting early 14C frescoes including works by Bicci di Lorenzo, Paolo Schiavo, Lo Scheggia, Mariotto di Cristofano, and Liberato da Rieti.

At **Pian di Scò** the Romanesque pieve of Santa Maria (11C–12C) has interesting capitals, and a fresco attributed to Paolo Schiavo.

Outside **Reggello** (on the Figline Valdarno road) is **Cascia**, birthplace of the 14C musicians Giovanni and Donato da Cascia. Here is the Romanesque pieve of **San Pietro**, marked by its tall bell-tower, and preceded by a 13C portico. It is traditionally thought to have been founded by Countess Matilda, but the present building dates from the late 12C or early 13C (**open** 07.30–12.00, 15.00–19.00; if closed ring at No. 1 in the piazza). At the end of the left aisle (light) is a beautiful small *triptych of the *Madonna and Child with Saints Bartolomeo, Biagio, Giovenale, and Antonio Abate*. Dated 1422, this is the first known work by Masaccio. It was rediscovered in 1961 in the nearby church of San Giovenale, restored in 1984, and installed here in 1988. The church also contains interesting capitals, an ancient *Crucifix* in the apse, an *Annunciation* on the left wall by Mariotto di Cristofano, brother-in-law of Masaccio, and a *Pietà* signed and dated 1601 by Santi di Tito.

Near Montanino, below Cascia, the yellow sandy hills (*calanchi)* have been eroded into strange forms.

Northwest of Reggello is the Romanesque church of **Sant'Agata in Arfoli** beside a Cedar of Lebanon. There is a splendid view of the Valdarno from the terrace. The porch was added in 1928, but the 13C cloister survives. **Interior** (if closed ring at the house on the right). There is a medieval carved pluteus and a fresco of the *Madonna and Saints with the Pietà* surrounded by grottesques, attributed to Raffaellino del Garbo. The fine presbytery was designed in 1928 using old columns and pilasters.

A pretty road leads down between old walls and past vineyards to the hamlet of **Cancelli** and (right) the church of Santa Margherita. It contains a fresco of the *Crucifixion* and, on the left, a fragmentary fresco of good quality by the bottega of Paolo Schiavo. The road continues down past the entrance to the remarkable **Castello di Sammezzano** (a 4-star hotel which was closed in 1999). It is on the site of a castle which was visited by Charlemagne in 781 and was later owned by the Medici. In 1596 the Grand-duke Ferdinando I sold it to Sebastiano Ximenes of Aragon, a Spanish merchant who was trading in Tuscany. In the 19C it was transformed into a fantastic Oriental palace by a wealthy descendant, Ferdinando Panciatichi Ximenes d'Aragona (1813–97). A drive, 2km long, leads up through splendid woods, including numerous sequoia trees, to the huge 'castle', the exterior of which has elements which recall the Taj Mahal. The colourful interior has some splendidly decorated rooms on the piano nobile, some of them modelled on the Alhambra of Granada.

To the north on the main road along the Arno from Incisa (8km) to Pontassieve is the church of **San Clemente a Sociano** (on a curve of the road above to the right), with a portico. In the interior (if closed, ring at the house on the right) there are two lovely marble candle-bearing angels in the sanctuary attributed to Mino da Fiesole, and, in the left transept a marble *bas-relief of the *Madonna and Child* attributed to Antonio Rossellino. The two altarpieces are in poor condition: on the left, *St Michael and Saints* attributed to Giovanni Battista Naldini, and on the right, *Madonna and Saints* by the bottega of Santi di Tito.

Across the Arno is **Rignano**, an unattractive place on the railway on flat ground, surrounded by factories. The 20C church in the centre contains an *Assumption* by Matteo Confortini (1623), and (at the end of the left aisle) a hexagonal font in enamelled terracotta attributed to Benedetto and Santi Buglioni. In a chapel off the left side is a polychrome terracotta relief of the *Birth of the Virgin*, and a 16C *Crucifix* and painting of *St Roch*. The Romanesque pieve of **San Leolino**, north of the town, is being restored.

North of Reggello, beyond Pietrapiana, another road (signposted Donnini) continues along the side of the hill with views of the valley to **San Donato in Fronzano** (if closed ring at the door on the right) with a 17C façade, and an interesting interior. Beyond is the **Pieve a Pitiana** (being restored) with an 11C–12C campanile (if closed ring at the door on the left). Over the high altar is an *Annunciation* attributed to Ridolfo del Ghirlandaio. From Donnini another road, lined with cypresses and olives, leads up towards Tosi (see below) winding round the **Villa Pitiana** with a 19C yellow façade (and 14C and 16C elements).

Vallombrosa

From Pietrapiana the direct road for Vallombrosa winds up through **Saltino** (970m; good views), an old-fashioned resort with large hotels, some of them built at the end of the 19C or early 20C (open only in summer). A rack railway from Sant'Ellero on the Arno up to Saltino, in operation from 1892–1934, may be restored. **Vallombrosa** (997m) is surrounded by a thick forest of pines, firs and beeches, which has been owned by the State since 1867. Cool in summer and conveniently close to Florence, it has a number of restaurants. It is famous for its monastery founded by St John Gualberto in 1040, and the first home of the Vallombrosan order. The monastery was suppressed in 1808, but the Order was reinstated in 1963 and some 20 monks now live here. An avenue leads to the **monastery** with a lawn and fish pond on the left. Beyond a walled garden is the splendid façade with numerous small windows by Gherardo Silvani (1610–40).

The **church** façade dates from 1644. Beneath the portico is a *Madonna and Child* by the bottega of Ghiberti and a statue of *St John Gualberto* by Giovanni Battista Caccini. The **interior** (open 09.00–12.00, 15.30–18.00) contains 18C frescoes and paintings. On the high altar, *Assumption* by Volterrano and 15C carved wooden choir stalls. In the south transept, Cesare Dandini, *Martyrdom of St Sebastian*, and in the north transept, Lorenzo Lippi, *Trinity*. The chapel in the north transept has a fine ceiling with frescoes and stuccoes by Alessandro Gherardini. In the **sacristy**, *Madonna and Saints with donors* by the bottega of Andrea della Robbia and paintings by Raffaellino del Garbo (*St John Gualberto and Saints*), and Luigi Sabatelli.

The **monastery** (for adm. ☎ 055-862029; in summer usually **open** Tues &

Fri 10.30–12.00) has an 18C refectory with paintings by Ignazio Hugford, an enamelled terracotta attributed to Santi Buglioni and a fine kitchen.

Milton is traditionally thought to have stayed in the guest house (known as the *Paradisino*) in 1638 (plaque set up in 1925). Although he mentions both the Valdarno and Vallombrosa in his *Paradise Lost* (Book I) he is not now thought to have come here on his visits to Tuscany in 1638 and 1639.

Fine walks can be taken in the forest, and a road leads up to **Monte Secchieta** (1450m), which has winter sports facilities. A road from Vallombrosa leads to the Passo della Consuma (see Ch. 40), while the direct road to Florence descends steeply through woods past several streams to **Pian di Melosa**. The name of the main road here commemorates the art historian Bernard Berenson (see p. 100) who often stayed nearby at San Miniato in Alpe. **Tosi** is known for its furniture makers. Beyond Pelago (Ch. 2), a lovely hilly road continues down past open fields to Pontassieve and the main road for Florence.

40 · The Casentino

The Casentino is the beautiful wooded upper valley of the Arno in the northeast corner of Tuscany. The scenery is superb and the area has prosperous and well-kept villages. One of the finest forests in Italy can be found at **Camaldoli**, on the border with Romagna.

The valley was dominated from the 10C until the middle of the 15C by the Guidi Counts, whose numerous castles are a feature of the region. Because of its position between Florence and Arezzo, it was long disputed between the two cities, but Florence remained the dominant force after its victory here on the plain of Campaldino in 1289. High up above the valley are the famous monasteries of **La Verna** and **Camaldoli**. Beautiful **walks** can be taken in the Casentino, and in particular in the Parco Nazionale delle Foreste Casentinesi, Monte Falterona e Campigna.

■ Practical information

Information offices. APT of **Arezzo** (☎ 0575-377678). Information office at Bibbiena, 25 Via Berni (☎ & fax 0575-593098). For the Parco Nazionale delle Foreste Casentinesi, Monte Falterona e Campigna, *Comunità Montana Casentino* at Poppi and the *Ente Parco Nazionale Foreste Casentinesi*, 10 Via Roma, Pratovecchio (☎ 0575-504558).

Getting there
By bus. SITA bus services (c 8 times daily) from **Florence** via the Consuma Pass to Poppi and Bibbiena (to Poppi in 2hrs; to Bibbiena in 2hrs 20mins). SITA buses daily also from Florence to Stia in 1hr 45mins. SITA buses from **Arezzo** to Caprese Michelangelo. From **Bibbiena** buses (*LFI*) to Camaldoli and La Verna.

By train. From Arezzo trains and buses run by *LFI* to Bibbiena, Poppi, and Stia.

Hotels
Passo della Consuma. ★★ *Sbaragli*, 3 Via Consuma, Montemignaio (☎ 055-8306500). **Monastery of Camaldoli**. ★★★ *Il Rustichello*, 14 Via del Corniolo (☎ 0575- 556020; fax 0575-556046); ★ *Camaldoli*, with restaurant, 13 Via Camaldoli (☎ & fax 0575-556019).

Poppi. ★★ *Casentino*, 6 Piazza Repubblica, in front of the Castle (☎ 0575-529090; fax 0575-529067). At **Ponte a Poppi**: ★★ *Campaldino*, with restaurant (☎ 0575 529008, fax 0575 529032).
Bibbiena. ★★★ *Brogi*, with restaurant (☎ 0575-536222; fax 0575-536223).
Badia Prataglia. numerous ★★ hotels.
Chiusi della Verna. ★★ and ★ hotels.
Caprese Michelangelo. ★★ hotel, with restaurant, *Buca di Michelangelo*, 51 Via Roma (☎ 0575-793921; fax 0575-793941).

Campsites
Monastery of Camaldoli. ★ sites open in summer, *Fonte del Menchino* (☎ 0575-556157); *Parco Pucini* (☎ 0575-556006).
Badia Prataglia. ★ *Capanno* (☎ 0575-518015).
Chiusi della Verna. ★ *La Verna* at Vezzano, open Apr–Sept (☎ 0575-532121).
Caprese Michelangelo. ★★ *Michelangelo* at Zenzano (☎ 0575-793886).

Restaurants
Passo della Consuma. *Dal Consumi* has good snacks.
Stia. £££ *Caranbar*, 19 Via Adamo Ricci; ££ *Da Filetto*, Piazza Tanucci; £ *La Rana (da Filetto)* in woods on the Arno (by the sports stadium); *Fani Sandro*, Piazza Tanucci (☎ 0575-58824; only by reservation for Sunday lunch).
Pratovecchio. ££ *Gliaccaniti*, 12 Via Fiorentina; £ *La Tana degli Orsi* (open in the evening); *Toscana Twist*, 1 Via della Libertà (good lunches with local specialities).
Monastery of Camaldoli. ££ *Pucini*.
Poppi. ££ *Campaldino*, 95 Via Roma, Ponte a Poppi.
Bibbiena. ££ *Brogi (Da Marino)*; £ *Mon Ami* (also pizzeria). Outside Bibbiena: ££ *Il Bivio di Querceto* at Querceto.
Chiusi della Verna. ££ *La Beccia*.
Caprese Michelangelo. ££ *La Faggeta*, *Il Cerro* and *La Buca di San Francesco*.
Talla. £ *L'Orcello*.

The approach to the Casentino from Florence is via the **Passo della Consuma**, beyond which the road crosses bare hills where some replanting is taking place. There is a fine distant view in the valley below of Poppi Castle with its tall tower. To the north, a pretty by-road traverses woods and then winds downhill to end just before the scanty ruins of **Castel Castagnaio**, an 11C castle.

Further on along the main road a road (well signposted) leads left to the *Castello di Romena**, built in the 11C and perhaps the most important castle in the Casentino, belonged to the Guidi, the Ghibelline family who dominated the area, with whom the exiled Dante sheltered after his expulsion from Florence. Here in 1280 Maestro Adamo, recalled by Dante (*Divina Commedia, Inferno* XXX, 46–90), forged Florentine florins for the Guidi for which he was later burnt by the Florentines. A short cypress avenue leads up to the impressive and well-kept remains which include the three main towers and traces of three circles of walls (**open** by request to the custodian, or by advance booking ☎ 0575-582520). A room contains suits of armour, as well as a model of the castle, and there is a small archaeological collection. Stairs lead up to a loggia and walkway where the views are splendid.

A road (or path from the villa) descends past the **Fonte Branda** (plaque), an overgrown spring, mentioned by Dante (*Divina Commedia, Inferno*, XXX, 78), to the *Pieve di Romena**, the most beautiful Romanesque church in the Casentino. It was built in 1152; remains of the 9C church can be seen beneath the building. It has a splendid east end with blind arcading. The lovely **interior** (only **open** by appointment, ☎ 0575-58725) has a raised presbytery and fine capitals. All the paintings have been removed and restored. They include: parts of a triptych by Giovanni del Biondo and bottega, a *Madonna and Child with two angels* by the Master of Varlungo, a 15C *Madonna and Child with four Saints* by the Florentine school (attributed to the Master of San Miniato), and a 16C *Madonna of the Rosary*.

Stia

Stia is a pretty little town (3100 inhab.) where the Arno meets its first tributary, the Staggia. In the Middle Ages it was the residence of the Guidi family, and it is noted for its small woollen manufactories (some of the abandoned factories along the river are interesting for their architecture). Traditional, very fine handmade textiles are still made here at 49 Via Sanarelli (the firm is called *T.A.C.S.*).

On the right bank of the river is the delightful, sloping **Piazza Tanucci** (with a local tourist office). The 18C public fountain is decorated with lions and snakes.

The Romanesque church of **Santa Maria Assunta** with a plain façade is in the piazza. The **interior** has fine capitals (illuminated by a light switch on the west wall). **South aisle**. First chapel, left wall, 16C *Nativity*, and, on the altar, triptych of the *Annunciation and Saints* with a good predella, by Bicci di Lorenzo. Beneath the altar is a della Robbian stemma. The marble font dates from 1526. On the right wall is another *Annunciation* by the Pistoian school. First altar, Gian Domenico Ferretti, *Preaching of St John the Baptist*. The quaint wooden pulpit dates from 1584.

In the chapel to the right of the high altar, a good 16C Florentine painting of *Supper in the House of the Pharisee* (in very poor condition). On the left is an elaborate (damaged) della Robbian tabernacle. In the pretty **apse** with an ambulatory of four columns is a large 14C wooden *Crucifix*. In the chapel to the left of the high altar, Master of Varlungo, **Madonna and Child*, and (on the right wall), *Madonna and Child* by Andrea della Robbia. **North aisle**. Master of San Miniato, *Madonna enthroned with four Saints*; on the altar, an unusual painting of the *Assumption*, attributed to the Master of Borgo alla Collina. The 14C fresco of the *Madonna and Child* was detached from the Pieve of Stia.

To the right of the church is an archway with a fresco of *St Francis* by Pietro Annigoni (1985). The old streets off the piazza are well worth exploring.

On the other side of the river, an avenue ascends past (left) the church of the **Madonna del Ponte** with a terracotta altarpiece by the della Robbia bottega. Opposite is a 16C painting of the *Holy Family*. The sanctuary is decorated with pretty angels. The avenue continues up to Piazza Mazzini with the modern town hall and a theatre. A road (signposted) leads left for the **Castello di Palagio** reconstructed in 1911 by Giuseppe Castellucci for Carlo Beni, historian of the Casentino. He left it to the Comune and it is open in summer for exhibitions and lectures; the **garden**, with some statuary, is open daily. A huge vault was built here a few years ago, over a spring.

Porciano

Just outside Stia is a by-road (signposted) right for Porciano, approached through pretty meadows. There is a car park below the castle and it is a short

way by foot through the hamlet (reconstructed after an earthquake in 1919)
to the massive tall square tower of
the **castle**, privately owned. It was
restored in 1963–75 (**open**
from 15 May–15 Oct; on
Sun 10.00–12.00,
16.00–19.00; or by
previous appoint-
ment, ☎ 0575-58533
or 055-400517). First
mentioned in 1007, this
may have been the first
Guidi castle in the
Casentino. It remained
in their possession until the
end of the 15C, and Dante
Alighieri is known to have stayed
here as their guest on a number of

Castello di Porciano

occasions when exiled from Florence. It was from here that he wrote to the
Florentines and to Henry VII in 1311.

On the ground floor is a small display of agricultural implements and
domestic tools, as well as a collection of native American material from North
Dakota, made by the father of the present owner George A. Specht (1899–1973)
when a child. The first floor has photographs of the castle before its restoration,
and ceramics (including late 13C and early 14C ware) found during restoration
work. On the second floor is a hall used for lectures etc. The views are splendid.
The upper floors are private.

The church of **Santa Maria delle Grazie** is in an inconspicuous position above
the Londa road, a few kilometres north-west of Stia. Beside the 15C church is
the **Casa del Pellegrino**, built as a hospice for pilgrims with a lovely long loggia
and stairs in the centre of the building. The **church** is only open for services at
weekends. It contains a *Crucifix* attributed to Paolo Schiavo, a 15C *Madonna and
Child*, a pulpit by Mino da Fiesole, and a fresco by Ghirlandaio (1485). A painting
of the *Madonna and four Saints* by Niccolò di Lorenzo Gerini was stolen in 1987.

A fine walk of 4hrs leads north from Stia to the source of the Arno and from
there to the summit of **Monte Falterona** (1654m), now part of a national park
adjoining the Forest of Camaldoli (see p. 492). The adjacent summit of **Monte
Falco**, 4m higher, is more easily reached from the **Passo la Calla** (1296m), on
the road from Stia into Emilia Romagna via the Bidente valley (see *Blue Guide
Northern Italy*). On its slopes, visited by skiers, is a mountain refuge called the
Rifugio La Burraia (1447m).

Pratovecchio

Adjoining Stia to the south is the large village of Pratovecchio surrounded by
some small factories in the valley. From Piazza Paolo Uccello (named after the
painter who was born here), Via Garibaldi with pretty porticoes leads (left)

towards the attractive **Piazza Jacopo Landino** with a group of lime trees. Here is a fine palace (No. 18) with a coat of arms on the corner dated 1621. The parish **church** has a small della Robbian relief above the west door, and paintings by Jacopo Vignali and Francesco Botti inside. To the right of the church, at the end of the piazza, is the entrance (No. 20) to a courtyard in which is the church of **San Giovanni Evangelista** (if closed, ring at the Camaldolese convent). The unusual façade dates from 1909. Over the first left altar is a very well preserved painting of the *Assumption*, attributed to the Master of Pratovecchio, named from this work. It is very difficult to see as it is inserted behind a larger painting. The high altarpiece of the *Coronation of the Virgin* dates from the 16C. In Via XX Settembre, off the upper side of the piazza, is a large della Robbian tabernacle.

On the outskirts of Pratovecchio, just beyond a bridge beside several small factories on the main road to Bibbiena, is the inconspicuous church of **Santa Maria a Poppiena**, partly dating from the 12C, on the left of the road beside a few cypresses. It contains an *Annunciation* attributed to Giovanni del Ponte. From Piazza Paolo Uccello a road leads down across the river with some interesting houses and from the bridge two roads are signposted for the Castello and Pieve di Romena (see p. 489).

From Pratovecchio a beautiful road (signposted *Santo Eremo*), winds up a wooded valley with a view back of the castle of Romena. Before Lonnano it passes close to the little church of **Valiana** (San Romolo), on the right of the road (if closed, ring at No. 1). During restoration work by the local inhabitants in 1984 the original architrave of the door dated 1126 was found beneath the front steps (it is now displayed inside the church). The remarkable painting of *Christ in Pietà with symbols of the Passion* (late 14C or early 15C) is attributed to the Master of the Madonna Straus (it was beautifully restored in 1974). From the church there is a delightful, distant view of the Castello di Romena and the wooded hills of the Casentino.

Camaldoli

The road continues up through Lonnano, entering the splendid **forest of Camaldoli** beyond Prato alle Cogne (1050m). Silver firs and beech trees predominate but other trees include sycamore, manna ash, laburnum, ilex, birch, willow, elm, yew, oak, chestnut, alder, poplar and lime. The forest is crossed by numerous streams and deer run wild here. In 1027 part of the forest was given to the Carthusian monks of Camaldoli, and in 1866 it became the property of the State. The road for the hermitage branches left from the road signposted for Camaldoli.

The forest is part of the **Parco Nazionale delle Foreste Castentinesi, Monte Falterona e Campigna**. The national park was instituted in 1991 to protect the forested area of the Casentino on the Apennine ridge which borders Tuscany and Romagna, and stretches from Monte Falterona (1654m; see above) to the Passo dei Mandrioli (1179m). It is one of the largest areas of forest left in Italy (36,000 hectares) and is administered by the *Ente Parco Nazionale Foreste Casentinesi* in Pratovecchio. Maps are available showing the lovely walks in the park.

The **Hermitage of Camaldoli** (1100m) was founded in 1012 by St Romuald in this *campo amabile*, or 'charming field'; its present name is a corruption of these two words. This is the most important of several hermitages and monasteries founded in Italy and the Pyrenees by this Benedictine saint. The hermits used to live in entire isolation: twelve monks now live here but they no longer choose to live a rigorous hermit's life, and meet for services, meals, and work. The church and cell of St Romuald are **open** 08.30–11.15, 15.00–18.00; fest. 08.30–10.45, 15.00–18.00. The **church** has a grey and white façade of 1713. In the vestibule is a bas relief of the *Madonna and Child* attributed to Tommaso Fiamberti. The chapel of St Anthony Abbot, off the transept which precedes the nave has a tabernacle attributed to Andrea della Robbia and decorations by Adolfo Rollo (1930). The main church has elaborate gilded stucco decoration dating from 1669 and 17C frescoes. The choir stalls date from the 16C and the high altarpiece of the *Crucifixion and Four saints* is attributed to Bronzino. On either side are large marble tabernacles by Gino da Settignano (1531) and in the apse a fresco of the *Transfiguration* by Ezio Giovannozzi (1937). In the **chapter house** is a painting of *St Romuald and his disciples in the forest* by Augusto Mussini (1915). The **refectory**, which dates from 1679, has a fine wood ceiling.

Outside the church is the gateway into the enclosure (no admission) with the 20 **hermits' cells**, really a little village of tiny self-contained houses. Opposite the church is the **cell of St Romuald**, which served as a model for the other cells. Above it the **library** was built in 1622.

A beautiful narrow road descends through the forest to the **Monastery of Camaldoli** (818m), founded in 1046, which now houses about 40 Carthusian monks (**open** daily 06.30–13.00, 15.00–20.00) to the monastery. The huge building on the road, called the *foresteria*, is used for visitors and meetings. Beyond is a piazza with the main entrance . Steps lead down to the **first cloister** (*di Maldolo*) dating from 1100 with primitive capitals, but restored. Off it is the ancient **chapel of Santo Spirito** with a barrel vault and a large column, asymmetrically placed. On the other side of the cloister is the former entrance to the monastery through a tunnel. The **second cloister** has a portico on three sides with pretty Ionic capitals. It was designed by Ambrogio Traversari (1386–1439), the friend and tutor of Cosimo il Vecchio, who was a monk here. From the piazza another door (No. 14) on the left leads into a small courtyard in which is the **church** with an 18C interior. It contains five fine paintings by Vasari, including a *Deposition*, and a *Nativity* and *Madonna with Saints John the Baptist and Jerome*. The **refectory** has a large painting by Pomarancio, a pulpit in *pietra serena*, and paintings attributed to Lorenzo Lippi.

At the other end of the *foresteria* is the entrance to the 16C **pharmacy** (open 09.00–12.30, 14.30–18.30), with lovely carved wood cupboards and panelling dating from 1543. Products made by the monks including honey, liquors and soap, are sold here. Another room is arranged as an apothecary's workshop.

In a separate building across the road is a private **Ornithological Museum** (No. 19; **open** on Sunday, or daily in July and Aug). At the bridge (by a lock) is a road for Bibbiena (another road for Poppi continues beyond the monastic buildings).

At a fork on the main road between Pratovecchio and Poppi a column marks the site of the battle of **Campaldino** on 11 June 1289. Here Dante fought as a young man in the Florentine Guelf army against the Ghibellines of Arezzo, who were defeated, and their leader Bishop Guglielmino Ubertino killed. It is estimated that some 2400 mounted knights and 18,000 foot soldiers took part in the battle which for centuries held almost mythical importance in the imagination of those who lived in the Casentino.

To the northwest is **Borgo alla Collina** (3km), badly damaged in the Second World War. The road runs through a gate beside the tower of the castle. The church of **San Donato**, in a piazza with trees, contains a fine triptych and predella of the *Mystical Marriage of St Catherine*, now attributed to the Master of Borgo alla Collina (1408). The tomb of Cristofano Landini, the Dante scholar and tutor of Lorenzo il Magnifico, was erected in 1848 by Lorenzo Bartolini. Landini, as Secretary of the Florentine Republic was given a palace here, where he died in 1504.

Nearby is **Castel San Niccolò** in a lovely position at the foot of the Pratomagno hills. Beyond Strada, on low ground to the left of the road by an avenue of lime trees, is the **Pieve di San Martino a Vado** (restored in 1968–73). The simple interior, thought to date from the 11C, has charming historiated and foliated capitals. It contains an interesting font, and detached worn frescoes from the church of San Niccolò beside the castle, which is visible from outside the church. The road continues through two piazze and then narrows before reaching **Piazza Matteotti** (or Piazza della Fiera) with an attractive and unusual market building. A medieval paved bridge (reconstructed) leads across the stream and a narrow road (signposted) leads up to the **Castle** (open Sat & Sun afternoon; ☎ 0575-57961). It is surrounded by a tiny hamlet and a Gothic postern gate beneath a tower with a huge clock survives on the side of the hill.

Beyond **Pagliericcio**, with a finely paved street, is **Cetica** in another pretty valley. Outside the village, near a modern school, is the 13C church of **Sant'Angiolo** with a low bell tower and steps at one corner of the building. In the wide interior, at the end of the right aisle, is a *Madonna and Child* by Francesco Pesellino in a beautiful tabernacle. The east end has lancet windows and a handsome altar table. The road ends at **Bagni di Cetica**), an ancient spa rediscovered in 1686, in a beautiful position.

Montemignaio is an attractive village which spreads out along the side of the valley, surrounded by numerous trees. Approaching the village across the valley, the very tall bell tower of its castle, and then the battlemented tower of the church can be seen. The road crosses the bridge: on the right is the **Pieve**, probably dating from the 12C, with three rose windows above its three doors (restored). The **interior** has a deep apse and massive capitals on the two shorter columns at the east end. The two hanging capitals on either side of the presbytery have interesting sculptures representing *Life* and *Death*. On the first north altar, Giovanni Toscani, *Madonna and Child* (fragment of a polyptych). The *Madonna enthroned with four doctors of the church* is by the school of Rodolfo del Ghirlandaio. In the south aisle is a della Robbian terracotta of the *Madonna and Child with two Saints*. On the pilasters are scant remains of frescoes.

A road leads along the side of the hill to another Guidi castle with an oddly-shaped tower. From here there is a distant view of the monastery of La Verna.

In the main valley, just outside Ponte a Poppi is the church of **Certomondo**, approached through an old gate and crumbling courtyard. A convent was founded here in 1262. The church was restored in 1987 when the rose window was exposed. On the right of the presbytery is a fine painting of the *Annunciation* by Neri di Bicci. On pillars in the nave are fresco fragments of saints in very poor condition. On the right of the façade can be seen scant remains of the cloister.

Poppi

From Ponte a Poppi an avenue leads up past a war memorial to the delightful little town (6000 inhab.) of Poppi on a hill. Its splendid castle, which dominates the Casentino valley, can be seen from miles around. The hill is very well preserved, especially on its south side. Its streets have a medley of porticoes, some still built in wood. Poppi is famous as the residence of the Guidi counts who ruled the Casentino until it succumbed to the Florentine Republic in 1440. The sculptor Mino da Fiesole was born here in 1429.

The castle of the Guidi Counts

The approach road passes under a portico into Piazza Amerighi (described below). To the left, Via Conte Guidi continues up to the top of the hill where there is a car park in front of the **Castello* (**open** daily 09.30–12.30, 15.00–18.00) of the Guidi counts. It was begun in 1274 by Count Simone da Battifolle and is the best preserved castle in the Casentino. Built in two stages, the part on the right of the tower is attributed to Lapo, master of Arnolfo di Cambio, and the wing on the left was probably completed by Arnolfo di Cambio himself. Over the door is a relief of a disgruntled Florentine lion, set up by the local sculptor Jacopo di Baldassarre Torriani in 1477.

The **courtyard* has a delightful staircase with old wooden balconies, and numerous coats of arms, and another Florentine *Marzocco*. On the left, a fine vaulted room with one huge column has a display of maps and diagrams illustrating the Battle of Campaldino (see p. 493), and a room below has a delightful scale model of the battle.

First floor. The well-lit Salone has a fine floor and painted walls. The **library* (c 20,000 vols), in two rooms, has a remarkable collection of 519 medieval manuscripts and 780 incunabula (shown in exhibitions every year). Most of the material comes from Fabrizio Rilli-Orsini (1825) and the convent of Camaldoli. At the top of the stairs is a fine stone caryatid representing Count Simone da Battifolle.

Top floor. The chapel has good frescoes by Taddeo Gaddi (1330–40). A room with a pretty little fireplace has a collection of 14C–17C documents from the archives, and the other rooms have painted walls and good views of the Campaldino plain and the castles of Romena and Porciano, and, in the distance, Monte Falterona. Also here is a detached fresco of the *Madonna and Saints*. Outside the castle is a huge underground cistern.

Behind the castle is the church of the **Agostiniani** which has a terracotta *Pietà* attributed to the bottega of Andrea della Robbia above the door. Inside (usually closed) is a *Nativity*, attributed to Benedetto Buglioni. Opposite Palazzo Pretorio is the ancient **Casa dei Guidi** (with a new outside stair) next to a gate into Villa Rita (ex-Giatteschi) in the garden of which can be seen a tower known as the *Torre dei Diavoli* or Devil's Tower.

Below the garden and piazza is Piazza Amerighi with the domed centrally-planned church of the **Madonna del Morbo** begun in 1657 and finished in 1705, dedicated to the Madonna in gratitude for deliverence from the plagues of 1530 and 1631. It is surrounded on three sides by porticoes. Over the high altar is a fine painting of the *Madonna and Child with the young St John* by Pseudo Pier Francesco Fiorentino. Also in the piazza is the church of **San Marco** which contains a *Deposition* and a *Pentecost* by Francesco Morandini, named Il Poppi from this his native town, and a *Raising of Lazarus* by Jacopo Ligozzi.

San Fedele

Via Cavour, the main street, entirely lined with picturesque porticoes, ends at the northern edge of the hill with the abbey church of San Fedele (**open** 10.00–12.00, 15.00–19.00). Built in 1185–95, it is one of the most important churches in the Casentino.

Interior. On the **south side**, Ottavio Vannini, *Madonna and Child with Saints*; first altar, *Crucifixion with the Madonna* and *St John the Baptist and Mary Magdalen* (replica of a painting by Maso di San Friano). **North side**. First altar, 16C *Nativity*; Poppi, *Martyrdom of St John*; Alessandro Davanzati, *Madonna and Child with angels* (a very unusual work by a Vallombrosan monk, 1506); Pietro Sorri, *Martyrdom of St Laurence*, 1596; Carlo Portelli, *Three Saints*. In the south transept is a *Madonna and Child* by the Maestro della Maddalena. On the high altar is a 14C painted Cross.

In the **apse**, *Madonna and Saints*, signed and dated 1527 by Antonio Solosmeo, the only known work by this artist; Passignano, *Two Saints*; Jacopo Ligozzi, *Assumption* and *St Benedict*. Beato Torello (1202–82) is buried in the **crypt**, and his reliquary bust in gilded bronze (15C) is kept here. He was born in Poppi and lived as a Vallombrosan recluse here, walled up in a cell for 60 years.

Below San Fedele is Porta a Porrena, still part of the walls which encircle the town. The other little streets of the town are well worth exploring.

From Ponte a Poppi a road (signposted) leads beneath the railway up the hillside to the **zoo** (open daily 08.00–dusk; picnic places are provided). Pleasantly laid out in 1972, it specialises in European fauna, and includes two bears, buffalo, deer, lynx, llamas, donkeys, and birds.

A by-road leads south from the foot of the hill of Poppi to the pieve of **Santa Maria a Buiano**, one of the oldest churches in the Casentino, built before 1000. It stands beside a farm with round silos (key at the house on the left). It has a charming deep brick apse and crypt. Excavations here in 1977 revealed remains of Roman baths and medieval tombs. This road continues to join another by-road in a pretty, unspoilt valley which passes fields and woods before reaching **Ortignano**. Outside the village, on a curve of the road, is the church of San Matteo. The road ends at the pretty village of **Raggiolo**, clearly visible on one side of the valley, in chestnut woods beneath its ruined castle. The view to the east, back down the valley takes in the headland of La Verna (see below).

Bibbiena

Bibbiena is the chief town (10,300 inhab.) of the Casentino. Built on a low hill, it is now surrounded by numerous small factories, especially on the plain to the south. One of the oldest towns in the Casentino, the name may be derived from *Vibia*, an Etruscan family. It was first mentioned in the 10C and was destroyed by the Guelfs after their victory at Campaldino. The castle was for a long time contested between Arezzo and Florence. Bibbiena was the birthplace of Bernardo Dovizi, called Cardinal Bibbiena (1470–1520), famous statesman and man of letters. He was responsible for the election of Cardinal Giovanni de' Medici to the papal throne as Leo X. He was a friend and patron of Raphael, who painted his portrait (now in the Galleria Palatina in Palazzo Pitti in Florence). He is also well known for his play *La Calandria*, written in Italian, which was first performed in 1513 with a prologue by Baldesar Castiglione. The traditional Shrove Tuesday celebrations here (*Bello Ballo*) date from the mid-14C. A juniper bush is set up in the piazza and everyone dances and sings around it.

The approach road winds up to Via Dovizi, on the left of which is the early 16C **Palazzo Dovizi** (No. 26). Opposite is the 15C church of **San Lorenzo** (restored in 1917) with two fine enamelled terracotta altarpieces of the *Pietà* and *Nativity* (c 1513–20) attributed to Andrea and Girolamo; della Robbia. From Piazza Roma, Via Giuseppe Borghi continues left to **Piazza Tarlati** (car parking). Here is a palace with a portico, a clock tower, and a terrace overlooking the valley.

Behind the clock tower is another tower, once part of the castle of the Tarlati family and on the right is the parish church of **Santi Ippolito e Donato**, usually called *La Pieve*. It was built at the beginning of the 12C as a chapel for the Tarlati castle. The wide **interior**, restored in 1972, has four large arches at the crossing. **South side**. Maestro di San Polo in Rosso (13C), painted *Crucifix*; Jacopo Ligozzi (attributed), *Mystical Marriage of St Catherine* (restored); seated, painted wooden statue of the *Madonna di Giona*, an unusual 12C Tuscan work. **South transept**. Il Poppi, *Annunciation*; Arcangelo di Cola da Camerino, *Madonna and Child enthroned with angels*. Over the high altar, a *Crucifix* replaces a triptych of the *Madonna and Child with Saints* by Bicci di Lorenzo. **North transept**. Jacopo Ligozzi, *Madonna and Child with Saints*, signed and dated 1600; organ of 1552 by Onofrio Zeffirini, brought here in 1700 from the abbey of Vallombrosa; 14C frescoed niche with the *Crucifixion*. **North side**. Good 14C frescoes by the Florentine school of the *Madonna and Child with Saints*, and, above, *Holy Trinity*.

Below the piazza is the **Teatro Dovizi**, a little theatre (200 seats) built in 1842 and reopened after restoration in 1998. It was designed, with a neo-classical façade, by Niccolò Matas. **Concerts** are now held here. Nearby are the Biblioteca Comunale, the 16C Palazzo Comunale, and the restored 14C Palazzo della Pretura.

A short way northeast of Bibbiena is the 15C Dominican convent (closed order) and church of **Santa Maria del Sasso**. It has an attractive portico on the right of the façade with charming frescoed ex-votos in the lunettes (very worn).

In the domed **interior** is a Renaissance tabernacle by Bartolomeo Bozzolini (of Fiesole) with a della Robbian frieze. An elaborate silver frame encloses a fresco of the *Madonna and Child* by Bicci di Lorenzo, and on the back of the tabernacle is an *Annunciation* by Francesco Brina. **South side**. Santi Buglioni, enamelled terracotta of *Christ and St John the Baptist*. **South transept**, Jacopo Ligozzi, *Birth of the Virgin with Saints* (signed and dated 1607). **North transept**. Lodovico Buti, *Madonna with St Giacinto*. On the left wall of the church, Paolino da Pistoia, *Madonna and Saints* (1525). Stairs lead down to the lower church and **Crypt**, with a highly venerated polychrome wooden statue of the *Madonna del Buio*, attributed to Buggiano. The great rock (*sasso*), around which the sanctuary was built can be seen here. Legend relates that the Madonna appeared here miraculously in 1347.

A road from Bibbiena leads northeast to the border with Romagna, passing the hamlet of **Serravalle** with views of Bibbiena and Poppi in the far distance. The impressive church was built in full Romanesque style in 1927. Beyond are remains of a castle around a tower (now privately owned).

The road continues up the deserted valley to **Badia Prataglia** (835m), the most important resort in the Casentino, surrounded by fine woods near the border with Romagna. The 11C **church,** recently well restored, has a Romanesque crypt with interesting worn capitals and primitive reliefs, including one on the left of the altar of a figure in prayer. Fine **walks** may be taken in the wooded hills which surround the village. The main road continues over the Mandrioli Pass (1173m) and descends to Bagno di Romagna in Romagna (see *Blue Guide Northern Italy*).

La Verna

Another pretty road (for Pieve Santo Stefano) leads from Bibbiena up through woods. Ahead there is a view of the oddly shaped, wooded promontory on which the monastery of La Verna was built, and views of the valley behind. Beyond the village of Dama there is another fine view of La Verna, and in the other direction the Pratomagno hills can be seen. From Case Nuove the panorama takes in the whole of the Casentino. The road continues across a plateau, with fewer trees, to the little resort of **Chiusi della Verna** (960m). Just outside (signposted *Castello del Conti Orlando Cattani*), on the right of the road, is a tiny group of houses with the podesteria and the church of **San Michele Arcangelo** (1338) below the ruins of a 10C castle, the highest in the Casentino, built on rocky outcrops.

A road diverges left from the Pieve Santo Stefano and Cesena road to climb up through plantations of fir trees to the famous **Monastery of La Verna**, in a remarkable position on a curiously shaped outcrop of rock (1129m) visible for many miles around. The site was given to St Francis in 1213 by Count Orlando Cattani and here in 1224 he received the stigmata. It is still a Franciscan convent (with about 30 friars) and a retreat. The sanctuary was embellished in 1433 by order of Eugenius IV when a number of altars were commissioned from Andrea della Robbia. His masterpieces of enamelled terracotta sculpture are still here.

The monastery is **open** 06.00–21.30, and there is a procession of the friars every day at 15.00 from the monastery to the Cappella delle Stimmate. A cobbled road leads through woods to the entrance arch, beyond which signs indicate the way (past the side of the Chiesa Maggiore) to the terrace from which there is a spectacular view of the Casentino, with Bibbiena in the distance.

The **Chiesa Maggiore** was begun in 1348, and continued in 1450–70. On the first south altar, *Madonna and Child enthroned between Saints*, attributed to Andrea della Robbia. The two *pietra serena* tabernacles on the right and left of the nave, one with the *Adoration of the Child* and the other with the **Annunciation*, are both by Andrea della Robbia. In the chapel on the left of the presbytery is an **Ascension* surrounded by cherubs and fruit, also by Andrea. At the entrance to the presbytery, the figures of *St Anthony Abbot* and *St Francis* are also by Andrea. The choir stalls date from 1495.

A covered **corridor** with frescoes of the *Life of St Francis* by the 20C Florentine painter Baccio Maria Bacci leads past several sites which recall the life of St Francis here. At the end steps descend to **St Francis' Cell**, with an 18C statue of the saint, beyond which is the tiny **Cappella delle Stimmate**. Above the door is a 13C bas-relief of the saint receiving the stigmata. This was built by order of Count Simone da Battifolle in 1263 on the spot where the Saint received the stigmata, marked by an inscription in the pavement. Over the door, on the inside wall, is a *tondo of the *Madonna and Child* by Luca della Robbia. The intarsia stalls date from 1531 (restored in 1906). The large enamelled terracotta *Crucifixion* (1480–81) by Andrea della Robbia (in a delightful frame), is one of the most monumental della Robbian works ever to have been made.

From the Chapel of San Bonaventura steps lead up and then down again to the Chapel of St Anthony of Padua. From here a door admits to a walkway which leads to the Precipizio (where there is a remarkable view of the sheer rock face), and a cave where St Francis used to pray. Other holy spots are pointed out by the friars.

A ramp leads down from the terrace to the small church of **Santa Maria degli Angeli** (or the *Chiesina*, begun in 1216–18) which contains an altarscreen with two polychrome terracotta altars attributed to Andrea or Giovanni della Robbia, and, beyond, in the earliest church, a blue-and-white altarpiece of the *Assumption of the Virgin*, another fine work by Andrea, and Renaissance stalls. Count Orlando Cattani is buried here. The treasures of the **museum**, including reliquaries and choir books, were stolen in 1978. A path leads up to the summit of the rock (La Penna, 1283m).

Caprese Michelangelo

From Chiusi della Verna (see above) a narrow road winds down through lovely scenery to Caprese Michelangelo, a tiny isolated hamlet (200 inhabitants), with fine views. It is famous because this is where Michelangelo was born in 1475. His father, Leonardo Buonarroti, was appointed *podestà* here the same year.

Cars must be left below the little hill. Beyond the gate is the restored **castle** with the ticket office (**open** daily 09.30–18.30; Nov-mid June 10.00–17.00 exc Mon) in the ground-floor hall. Opposite the **Palazzo Pretorio**, with the room where Michelangelo may have been born, is now a (disappointing) museum with some of Michelangelo's works reproduced in photographs. A garden enclosed by the castle walls has been decorated with sculptures (including works by Emilio Greco and Antonio Berti). A modern building has casts of Michelangelo's most famous works. The great artist was christened in the 13C chapel of San Giovanni Battista below the hill. The district is known for its delicious wild mushrooms (*porcini*).

From Chiusi della Verna the main road continues east to Pieve Santo Stefano (see Ch. 41). A lovely by-road leads southwest from Chiusi della Verna through beautiful countryside to Chitignano and Rassina (see below).

To the south of Bibbiena the Arezzo road follows the Arno, but soon leaves the Casentino valley. At **Rassina**, a busy place with a large gravel works, is **Pieve Socana**. The 11C church has a fine campanile, round below and hexagonal above, beside its lovely apse. The interior (if closed ring at the priest's house on the right) has been heavily restored. A gate on the right of the façade leads to a path which runs beneath a vine trellis and through an orchard to the east end of the church. A large rectangular Etruscan altar (5C BC) and remains of steps which led up to a temple (excavated in 1969) can be seen here.

A by-road leads from Pieve Socana through a pretty valley up to **Castel Focognano**, a compact little village. Beyond the Torre Grande the road leads up to the church beside the Podesteria (early 15C), decorated with coats of arms. Beyond a narrow archway on the left, beneath the campanile, its old loggia with a wooden roof and more coats of arms can be seen, beneath which is an old bread oven. On the right is a palace with two lions. The road continues up through woods with views ahead of the wooded slopes of the Pratomagno. It then descends into a valley with a stream in which is **Carda** a quiet, well-kept little village. In the old district on a hill (keep left) is the church (ring for the key at the priest's house) which contains a precious triptych attributed to Mariotto di Cristofano (restored in 1974).

Another road from Rassina leads southwest to **Talla** birthplace of Guido Monaco (990–c 1050). The beautiful carved 16C organ case in San Niccolò has been restored.

Another by-road leads east from Rassina to **Chitignano**, just before which a signpost (right) indicates the castle of the Counts (now privately owned) above the road on a little hill surrounded by cypresses, with statues high up on its wall. It was from here that Bishop Guglielmino Ubertini, the famous condottiere, set out on 11 June 1289, at the head of the Ghibelline army of Arezzo for the Battle of Campaldino, where he lost his life. The scattered village has mineral water springs.

The main road leads south from Rassina through Giovi, near **Pieve a Sietina**, a lovely little church, to Arezzo (see Ch. 36).

41 · Sansepolcro, Anghiari and Monterchi

Sansepolcro is in the north-east corner Tuscany on the Umbrian border. It can be reached most easily from Arezzo. It is famous as the birthplace of Piero della Francesca and preserves some beautiful works by him. Nearby at Monterchi there is another famous fresco by Piero. The little, well preserved medieval town of Anghiari is of interest for its churches and delightful museum.

■ Practical information

Information offices. APT Arezzo, 22 Piazza della Repubblica (☎ 0575-377678). In **Sansepolcro**, 2 Piazza Garibaldi (☎ 0575-740536). Comunità Montana Valtiberina Toscana, 32 Via San Giuseppe. **Anghiari**: Pro Loco, 103 Corso Matteotti (next to the post office; ☎ 0575-749279).

Getting there
By train. The *Ferrovia Centrale Umbra* links Perugia (see *Blue Guide Umbria*) via Città di Castello with Sansepolcro.

By bus. Buses run by SITA (☎ 0575-742999) from Arezzo and Florence to Anghiari, Monterchi, and Sansepolcro.

Car parking. In **Sansepolcro** there is free parking in Via dei Molini, outside Porta del Castello, and Via Alessandro Volta. Car park with an hourly tariff outside Porta Fiorentina. In **Anghiari** there is a car park off Via Matteotti below Piazza Baldaccio.

Hotels in Sansepolcro

★★★ *Fiorentino*, 60 Via Luca Pacioli (☎ 0575-740350; fax 0575-740370).
★★ *Da Ventura*, 30 Via Niccolò Aggiunti (☎ & fax 0575 742560).

Hotels on the outskirts of Sansepolcro

★★★ *Oroscopo*, 66 Piazza Togliatti, località Pieve Vecchia (☎ 0575-734875, fax 0575-735051).
Anghiari: ★★★ *Oliver*, 16 Via della Battaglia (☎ 0575-789933; fax 0575 789944); *La Meridiana*, 8 Piazza IV Novembre (☎ & fax 0575-788102).
Badia Tedalda has a number of ★★ hotels.

Restaurants

Sansepolcro
£££ *Oroscopo*, 78 Via Togliatti.
££ *Da Ventura*, 30 Via Niccolò Aggiunti; *Fiorentino*, 60 Via Luca Pacioli.
£ *Da Totò*, 140 Via XX Settembre; *Calisti*, 50 Via Pacioli.
There is a student canteen (*mensa*; anyone welcome) open at lunchtime in the convent next to the church of the Cappuccini (outside Porta Fiorentina).
Anghiari. ££ *La Nena*, 12 Via Gramsci; £ *Da Alighiero*, 8 Via Garibaldi.
In the environs: ££ *Castello di Sorci* at **Sorci**, and £ *Antico Posto di Ristoro*, 10km west at **Scheggia** (a cool place in summer); and £ *Vecchia Osteria La Pergola* at **Tavernelle**, with a couple of rooms to let.
Monterchi. £ *La Vecchia Osteria*, 19 Via dell'Ospedale.

Annual festivals

At **Sansepolcro**, the *Palio della Balestra* is held on the second Sunday in September, with a crossbow contest in medieval costume against Gubbio. The town is famous for the skill of its flag-throwers, the *Sbandieratori*. A large fair, the *Mezza Quaresima* is held after the fourth Sunday in Lent, and on 16 August, the *Festa Popolare di San Rocco*, there are various festivities.

At **Anghiari** there is a fair of artisans' work in late April and early May in the streets of the old town.

Sansepolcro

Sansepolcro (properly Borgo San Sepolcro) is an attractive little town (15,500 inhab.) in a plain in the upper Tiber valley, where tobacco is grown. The Buitoni family began their pasta business here in 1827. Most of its buildings date from the 15C. It is famous as the birthplace of Piero della Francesca (1416–92).

History. According to an ancient tradition Sansepolcro is named in honour of relics brought back from the Holy Sepulchre in Jerusalem by two pilgrims named Arcano and Egidio who settled here on their return. In 1012 an abbey was built here which was granted privileges by popes and emperors and held sway over the town. It became seat of a bishopric in 1520. The town was contested between its powerful neighbours Perugia, Città di Castello, Rimini and the Pontifical States, as well as Milan, until it came under Florentine dominion in 1441. It was severely damaged by earthquake in 1351–52, and was again damaged in the Second World War.

Other painters born here besides Piero, were Matteo di Giovanni (c 1430–95), Raffaellino del Colle (1490–1566) and Santi di Tito (1538–1603).

At the centre of the city is **Piazza Torre di Berta**, named after a tower (destroyed in 1944) through which runs the main street of the town, **Via XX Settembre** (usually called the Corso). **Palazzo Pichi-Sermolli** has a fine 16C façade with handsome windows and a central balcony. On the corner of the Corso is another palace with two balconies.

Duomo

The wide Via Matteotti leads out of Piazza Torre di Berta past the **duomo** which has an imposing Romanesque **interior** (13C–14C) with Gothic elements (restored). On the **west wall** are two high reliefs of *St Benedict* and *St Augustine* by Andrea della Robbia and a collaborator. **South wall**. Fine fresco of the *Madonna with Saints Catherine of Alexandria and Thomas Becket* by the Riminese school (1383); first altar: Santi di Tito, *Incredulity of St Thomas* (1575); fresco of the *Crucifixion* by Bartolomeo della Gatta; second altar: Durante Alberti, *Nativity*. At the end of the aisle is a delightful Baroque altar, lit from above by a little oval dome decorated with cherubs. In the **sanctuary**, Niccolò di Segna (attributed), polyptych with the *Resurrection of Christ*, which influenced Piero della Francesca (see below). The organ was built by Tamburini.

In the chapel to the left of the high altar, ***Volto Santo**, a huge wood Crucifix, probably dating from the 10C or earlier (restored in 1989). **North side**. On the right of the sacristy door, polychrome statue of the *Madonna and Child* (14C or 15C), and on the left of the door a della Robbian tabernacle. Second altar, Palma Giovane, *Assumption* (signed and dated 1602); Perugino (attributed, or Gerino da Pistoia on a cartoon by Perugino), *Ascension* (restored in 1998). Beyond the wall monument to Simone Graziani (1509), *Resurrection* by Raffaellino del Colle; first altar: Romano Alberti (16C), *Crucifixion*.

On the right of the façade, at No. 3, is a covered way which leads past part of the cloister with fine capitals towards Via Piero della Francesca. On the wall is a Roman cippus. On the right is the **Cappella del Monacato** or di San Leonardo. It contains a 17C altar and a fresco attributed to Cherubino Alberti around a 15C sculpted *Crucifix*. It is thought that Piero della Francesca is buried here. Opposite the Duomo is Palazzo Gherardi with two 12C towers. Next to the Duomo is **Palazzo delle Laudi** (1592–1609) by Alberto Alberti and Antonio Cantagallina, with a monumental portico. It is now the town hall. Opposite is the 16C Palazzo Aggiunti. In Piazza Garibaldi is **Palazzo Pretorio**, decorated with della Robbian coats of arms. First built in the 14C it was restored in 1843. The Gothic hall on the ground floor with a 16C fresco is used for exhibitions. The fine Gothic windows at the west end are best seen from the museum (see below).

Museo Civico

The Arco della Pesa connects Palazzo Pretorio with the ex-Palazzo Comunale, which has an outside stair. It is now the seat of the Museo Civico (entered around the corner at No. 65 Via Aggiunti), famous for its masterpieces by Piero della Francesca (**open** every day 09.30–13, 14.30–18.00; summer 09.00–13.30, 14.30–19.30). In 1998, the garden courtyard was enclosed for use as a ticket office and bookshop.

Beyond the **Sala del Camino**, the room on the right is at present being used as a restoration laboratory but Piero's polyptych of the *Misericordia* is to be moved here from the Sala della Resurrezione. The **Sala della Resurrezione** contains **masterpieces by Piero della Francesca**. The **Resurrection* was brought to the attention of a new generation of art historians after it had been described by Aldous Huxley in 1925 as the best picture in the world in his *Notes and Essays of a Tourist* (*Along the Road*). Justly one of Piero's most famous works, the remarkable figure of Christ is one of the most haunting images ever produced in Christian art. The soldiers asleep in the peaceful scene below offers a striking contrast. Some scholars formerly believed that it was frescoed in another room of the palace in 1463, and moved here in 1480, but it is now usually agreed that it must have been originally painted for its present position. The ****polyptych of the *Madonna of the Misericordia*** was commissioned from Piero by the local confraternity of the Misericordia (1445–62).

Also here are two frescoes: fragment of the bust of a **Saint* (*St Julian?*), found in the former church of Santa Chiara, and *St Louis of Toulouse* (attributed by some experts to a follower of Piero known as Lorentino, but since its restoration in 1999 now thought to be by the master himself).

The **Sala di Matteo di Giovanni** contains a triptych by Matteo di Giovanni (removed from the Duomo). The central panel, with the *Baptism of Christ*, by Piero della Francesca, is now in the National Gallery, London. Also here are a **standard painted on both sides (*Crucifixion and Saints*) by Luca Signorelli; *Saints Peter and Paul and Assumption* by Gerino da Pistoia; a tabernacle in glazed terracotta of the *Nativity*, recently attributed to Andrea della Robbia (c 1485) and a tondo of the *Madonna and Child* also thought to be by him. From here there is access to a series of small rooms with engravings.

The **Sala di Raffaellino del Colle** contains a fresco and a painting by Raffaellino del Colle and the *Martyrdom of St Quinten* by Pontormo. The **Sala di Giovanni de' Vecchi** has works by the local artist Giovanni de' Vecchi (1537–1615). In the large **Sala di Santi di Tito** are four works by Santi di Tito (including *St Nicholas of Tolentino*, *Pope St Clement among the faithful*, and *Pietà*), and paintings by Agostino Ciampelli (*Destruction of the idols*); and Leandro Bassano (*Adoration of the Magi*).

On the other side of the Sala del Camino (see above), beyond a room with an *Immaculate Conception* by Giovanni Battista Mercati, stairs mount to two rooms with 14C (detached) frescoes, and a view of the two Gothic windows of Palazzo Pretorio (see above). From the courtyard a new flight of stairs leads down to the **Sala delle Pietre** in the **basement** where the **Cathedral treasury** is displayed including church vestments and ecclesiastical objects belonging to Bishop Costaguti (18C). The crown and vestments (mid-14C) used to adorn the Volto Santo in the cathedral (see above), and 13C sculpture. Roman finds from the territory may also be exhibited here.

Piazza San Francesco

In Piazza San Francesco, planted with trees, are two churches. **San Francesco** was founded in 1285, but transformed in 1752. **Interior**. **South side**, second altar, Giovanni de' Vecchi, *St Francis receiving the stigmata* (1614), and, to the right, a profile in marble of Cristoforo Gherardi, the native painter (c 1556). The altar table (1304) in sandstone has reliefs and is surrounded by little Gothic arches. **North side**. Second altar, Francesco Curradi (attributed), *Eternal Father and Saints*; first altar, Passignano, *Christ among the Doctors in the Temple* (in very poor condition). In the adjoining cloister are lunette frescoes (1681–83) of the *Life of St Anthony* (also in very poor condition).

On the other side of the piazza is the church of **Santa Maria delle Grazie**, with a pretty double loggia (1518). The **interior** has fine carved altars. The high altar has a delightful decorated niche around the *Madonna in Prayer* by Raffaellino del Colle, flanked by two marble angels. The carved wood ceiling is by Alberto Alberti. On the south altar is a wooden *Crucifix* and on the north altar a painting of *Saints* by Francesco Gambacciani. The organ dates from the 17C. An interesting (but damaged) detached fresco of *St Lucy with two Saints* also belongs to the church. Beneath the loggia beside the church is a pretty **oratory** (now used for exhibitions) with a vault and 15 frescoed lunettes attributed to Giovanni Alberti and Raffaello Schiaminossi. The *Assumption* in the centre of the ceiling is by Federico Zoi.

In Via Niccolò Aggiunti are a number of interesting palaces: at No. 47 is a very unusual brick building (17C), and at No. 57 a 16C palace with graffiti decoration. On the opposite side is a 15C palace (No. 84). At No. 71 is the **Casa di Piero della Francesca**, a large palace which was probably designed by the famous artist (restored in the mid-16C), and where he may have lived for a time. It has a fine row of windows high up on the façade and has been restored as a study centre. In the garden opposite is a monument to the painter by Arnaldo Zocchi (1892). Just beyond, next to the headquarters of the Misericordia is the church of **San Rocco** (ring for admission). It contains two angels attributed to Alessandro and Giovanni Alberti, and *St Sebastian* attributed to Leonardo Cungi (d. 1569). On the left side is an 18C painting of three saints. Behind the carved and gilded altar is a statue of the *Dead Christ*. The **oratory** beneath the church (also shown on request; ring in Via della Fonte), has frescoed lunettes by the Alberti and a replica of the *Resurrection of Christ* by Raffaellino del Colle in the Duomo. Behind is a copy of the *Holy Sepulchre in Jerusalem*, an imitation of the work by Leon Battista Alberti in the Cappella di San Sepolcro in Florence.

Via XX Settembre (the Corso), which runs across the town from the 16C Porta Fiorentina, beside a fine stretch of walls, to the site of Porta Romana, is well worth exploring, especially at the east end. Outside the gate, a road leads up to the church of the **Cappuccini** (San Michele Arcangelo) which has an interesting high altarpiece of *Paradise* by Paolo Piazza dated 1608. At the west end of the Corso is the church of **Sant'Agostino**, rebuilt in 1771 by Vincenzo Righi with a bright interior decorated with white stuccoes. **South side**, second altar, Annibale Lancisi, *Annunciation* (1762); third altar, 14C *Crucifix*. In front of the high altar, painted wood sarcophagus of 1230, and in the apse, *Madonna della Cintola* by Giovanni Cimica. **North side**, third altar, 17C Florentine school, *Birth of the Virgin*; first altar, Giovanni Cimica, *Madonna in glory with St Nicholas of Tolentino*.

At No. 46 Via XX Settembre is the 18C Palazzo Alberti with a bust of Cosimo II. Beyond Piazza Torre di Berta, Via XX Settembre passes (right) **Palazzo Graziani**, a handsome early 17C palace. Across Via del Buon Umore, with four flying arches, is the 16C **Palazzo Ducci Del Rossi** (No. 131; covered for restoration), seat of the town library. On the left is **Teatro Dante** (now a cinema) built in 1835, and (No. 139) Palazzo Turini with an old tower. The last part of the Corso, with numerous shops, has small side streets, many with arches.

In the southern part of the town (reached from Piazza Torre di Berta by the pretty Via della Fraternità) is the church of **Santa Maria dei Servi**. On the right of the high altar, Matteo di Giovanni (attributed), *Madonna in Glory*, a fine but damaged painting. On either side are two paintings of four *Saints* (with the *Annunciation* in tondoes above), all once part of one work by Matteo di Giovanni. In Via Santa Croce is the deconsecrated church of **San Lorenzo** (open 09.00–13.00, 15.00–19.00), with a Renaissance loggia on one corner. It contains a *Deposition* by Rosso Fiorentino (1528), a dark and crowded composition. Above is a lunette with *God the Father* by Raffaellino del Colle.

The **Fortezza Medicea** (no admission; in urgent need of restoration), at the north-east corner of the old town, was built for Cosimo I in 1561–63 by Alberto Alberti on a design by Giuliano da Sangallo; at the northwest corner is the Cannoniere del Buontalenti, a bastion erected in the 16C in the walls by Bernardo Buontalenti. Other pretty steets in the town include Via San Giuseppe, Via Sant'Antonio, Via Piero della Francesca, and Via Luca Pacioli. To the north of Piazza San Francesco is the old Buitoni factory; a new factory has been erected on the southern outskirts of the town.

Anghiari

From Sansepolcro, beyond the *superstrada* a remarkably long and straight road crosses the plain on the site of the famous battle of Anghiari (see below) and then climbs to Anghiari (6000 inhab.), once called *Castrum Angulare*, in a spectacular position (430m) above the plain. It has a well-preserved old centre, typical of a medieval walled town. In 1440 it was the scene of a Florentine victory, under Francesco Sforza, over the Visconti of Milan (the subject of a fresco commissioned from Leonardo da Vinci for Palazzo Vecchio in Florence, the completed fragment of which has been lost). Later, in 1796, the French defeated the Austrians here.

The local artisans are particularly skilled cabinet makers, and there is an institute for the restoration of antique furniture. On weekends, various artisans' workshops in the old town can be visited.

There is a car park off Via Matteotti below Piazza Baldaccio, with a pretty walk (signposted; keep left) up to an old gate in the walls, which provides an entrance to the medieval town, near Palazzo Pubblico. In **Piazza Baldaccio**, the old market-place, with a statue of Garibaldi, is a monumental arcade, the **Galleria Magi** (1889), an unexpected sight. Beyond it, in Piazza IV Novembre, is the neo-classical **Teatro dei Ricomposti**, with a façade crowned by statues.

On the other side of Piazza Baldaccio is the unspoilt, walled medieval town. From the piazza, the higher road (right) leads to the scenographic Via Trieste, which ascends steeply to **Santa Maria delle Grazie** (the Propositura) at the top. It has an 18C neo-classical interior with a barrel vault. In the north transept are two charming paintings in their original frames by Sogliani: *Last Supper* and *Christ washing the disciples' feet*. The high altar and tabernacle are della Robbian. On the right of the high altar is a *Madonna and Child with four Saints and two angels* by Matteo di Giovanni (from the church of Sant'Agostino, see below), In the right transept is a *Deposition* by Domenico Puligo. Beside the church the town walls and a clock tower can be seen.

The lower road out of Piazza Baldaccio leads shortly to Piazza Mameli which has a number of old houses including the fine Renaissance Palazzo Taglieschi, probably built in 1437 by Matteo Cane (Taglieschi). It now contains the **Museo Statale di Palazzo Taglieschi**, a good local museum, well maintained and carefully labelled (**open** every day 09.00–18.30; fest. 09.00–12.30).

In the **basement** are architectural fragments, and at the foot of the stairs an enamelled terracotta lunette by Benedetto and Santi Buglioni. **Upper floor**. The first room contains a precious 16C organ (still in working order) from Santo Stefano and wooden sculptures including 13C and 14C *Madonnas*, and a seated statue of *St Anthony Abbot* by Giovanni di Turino. In a separate room a *Madonna in polychrome wood is displayed; it is well preserved and one of the best works of Jacopo della Quercia (c 1420). It was made for a church in Anghiari and purchased by the State in 1977. The *Child*, formerly on the Madonna's knee, has been exhibited separately since its restoration. It is not known if it was sculpted at the same time, nor whether it was intended as part of this group. Another room displays an enamelled terracotta *Nativity and Saints* by Andrea della Robbia (from the church of the Badia).

On the **second floor** the 17C paintings include works by Matteo Rosselli, and Giovanni Battista Ghidoni. The collection also includes dolls, terracotta statuettes by Francesco Maria Angiolini, ecclesiastical objects, copes and furniture.

The church of **Sant'Agostino**, also in the piazza, has been closed for many years during excavation work on an earlier church below the foundations. The 12C building was enlarged in 1464. St Thomas Becket is supposed to have stayed here. Beside it a tunnel (signposted) leads down to Porta Sant'Angelo and the walls

A road continues up left from the piazza to the inconspicuous church of the **Badia**, reconstructed in the 14C, with an unusual asymmetrical interior. A carved dossal attributed to Desiderio da Settignano surrounds a painted, wooden high relief of the seated *Madonna, with the standing Child* is by Tino da Camaino. Dating from c 1316 this is the only wooden sculpture known by Tino di Camaino. Around the high altar are four 18C statues.

Opposite the church is the former headquarters (with an interesting old window) of the **Misericordia**, now a delightful little museum (for **adm**. ring at No. 13 Via Nenci, or ☎ 0575-789577) illustrating the history of this charitable institution, still very active all over Tuscany. In the hall, dating from the early 16C, are displayed a carriage (1861) and a litter (1909), surgical instruments, and costumes worn by members of the brotherhood. The archives are kept in a room with traces of 15C frescoes. Uphill to the right (beneath an archway) is **Palazzo Pubblico**, with coats of arms on its façade.

In the other part of the town (see above) Via Matteotti leads straight downhill from the 16C porticoed church of **Santa Croce**, through Piazza Baldaccio, and, near the bottom, past the church of **Santo Stefano** (ring at No. 13), with its little bellcote. This is a remarkable church on a Byzantine Greek-cross plan, thought to date from the 7C–8C, partly enclosed in a later building. It is one of the earliest buildings to have survived in the upper Tiber valley.

Environs of Anghiari

To the east of Anghiari is **San Leo**, near which can be seen **Santa Maria a Corsano**, dating from around 1000, next to an abandoned farm house. It has an unusual campanile attached to the façade, beneath which is the west door of the church.

From Anghiari, a pretty secondary road for Arezzo winds around the hill with wonderful views of the town to the left. It follows an undulating ridge of hills planted with trees and passes a turn left (yellow signpost) for **Pieve a Sovara**, reached in less than 1km along an unsurfaced road. The Pieve stands beside a group of farm buildings. The church, has a prominent campanile and was founded in the 9C but mostly rebuilt in 1480. It contains a 15C font.

The Arezzo road continues to **Tavernelle** where a castellated villa, with a tall central tower, called La Barbolana is conspicuous on a hill to the right. The valley now narrows and the road climbs gently uphill past thick woods (and few houses) to a summit level of 575m at **Scheggia**. It then descends past cypresses, pines, and chestnuts to Arezzo.

A short way north of Anghiari is the church of **Santa Maria a Micciano**, of ancient foundation. It contains a 15C altarpiece of the *Madonna and two Saints*.

Monterchi

Monterchi, south of Anghiari and Sansepolcro, is a quiet little fortified village, damaged by earthquakes in the past, the birthplace of the mother of Piero della Francesca. The famous **Madonna del Parto* by Piero has been kept here, since its restoration in 1993. It is displayed in an old school building in Via della Reglia (**open** 09.00–13.00, 14.00–18.00 or 19.00 except Mon; in July and Aug it is **open** until midnight). The fresco was formerly in the church of Momentana, partially demolished in 1785, and was then included in a chapel in the cemetery at the foot of the hill, just outside the village. It was detached in 1910, and in 1956–69 the chapel was transformed to isolate it from the cemetery. It now seems unlikely that the fresco will be returned to the little chapel: its present display in a stark black glass case with harsh lighting has been justly criticised.

The fresco was painted c 1460 and shows the pregnant Madonna revealed by two angels pulling back the curtains of a tent. It is thought that Piero's mother was buried in the cemetery and this work was intended as a memorial to her. A 14C fresco fragment of the *Madonna and Child*, found beneath the *Madonna del Parto* is displayed in the same room. In other rooms there are instructive displays relating to Piero's fresco technique and recent restorations. There is a fine view from the little garden, where concerts are sometimes held.

At the top of the hill, near a piazza with lime trees, is the **Pieve di San Simeone**, rebuilt in 1966. Its works of art are in poor condition. In the **interior** (only open for services), the first chapel on the south side has a 16C detached fresco of the *Madonna of the Misericordia*. The second south chapel contains a little polychrome terracotta ciborium (its original painted wooden door has recently been stolen). Between the second and third chapels are three interesting 15C bas-reliefs of the *Pietà*. On the third north altar, 15C wooden *Crucifix*. Behind the church is a lovely old medieval passageway. Palazzo Massi-Alberti in Via XX Settembre is used for exhibitions.

At the foot of the hill, the main road to Città di Castello passes the cemetery and the avenue which leads (left) to the chapel which formerly contained the

Madonna del Parto. A by-road continues from the chapel over the hill to the lovely little village of Citerna in Umbria, described in *Blue Guide Umbria*. The interesting town of Città di Castello, to the east, is also described in *Blue Guide Umbria*. West of Monterchi, on the main road to Arezzo in the Cerfone valley is **Pieve a Ranco** (blue signpost). Approached over a very narrow bridge, the church of **Santi Lorentino e Pergentino** (if closed, ring at the priest's house beside the east end of the church) was damaged by an earthquake in 1916. It contains a beautiful 14C polychrome wooden seated statue of the *Madonna and Child* at the east end.

North of Sansepolcro is **Pieve Santo Stefano** (433m), which was systematically mined in the Second World War. The Collegiata was left standing almost alone, amid ruins. The **church**, rebuilt in 1844–81 in neo-classical style, contains a *Martyrdom of St Stephen*, attributed to Spagnoletto, a dossal in enamelled terracotta of the *Assumption* (1514; by Andrea della Robbia), and a 16C polychrome *Madonna*. The church of the **Madonna dei Lumi**, on a domed Greek-cross plan, dates from 1590–1625. In **Palazzo Comunale** is a fine terracotta of the *Good Samaritan* (1511). The Loggia del Grano is an old covered marketplace. The main road continues north to cross the border into Emilia Romagna (see *Blue Guide Northern Italy*).

Another road leads north from Sansepolcro across the Passo di Viamaggio (983m). Here a rough road leads west to the hermitage of **Cerbaiolo**, founded in 722 by the Benedictines and owned by the Franciscans since 1216. The 13C church and cloister survive, in beautiful countryside.

The main road continues to **Badia Tedalda**, a little hill resort (756m). The parish **church** contains enamelled terracotta altarpieces by the Buglioni, including the high altarpiece of the *Madonna and four Saints* commissioned in 1516 from Benedetto Buglioni, a *Madonna of the holy Girdle* (1521), and *Saints Julian, Sebastian, and Anthony* (1522), by Santi Buglioni.

The road continues to **Sestino** an ancient Roman municipium, in the eastern corner of Tuscany, on the border with the Marche. An **antiquarium** (temporarily closed) founded here in 1930–36 displays local Roman finds including statues of the Imperial era. The ancient **Pieve of San Pancrazio** contains a huge painted Cross by the 14C Riminese school. The primitive crypt is also interesting.

To the northeast of Sansepolcro, a by-road leads past the 14C church of Santa Maria near **Montagna**, where local 14C frescoes have recently been restored. The rough road continues up to the convent of **Montecasale**, surrounded by fine woods and cypresses. A hermitage was built here by St Francis (now occupied by Cappuchin fathers). The church contains a 12C wood statue of the *Madonna and Child*.

West of Sansepolcro, on the left bank of the Tiber, is the church of **San Martino di Montedoglio**, restored in 1981. The first church here was probably founded before 1000. It contains a fresco of *St Martin* attributed to the school of Piero della Francesca or to Gerino da Pistoia, and a 15C terracotta statue of *St Sebastian*.

42 · The Islands of Elba and Capraia

The **Parco Nazionale dell'Arcipelago Toscano** which includes the small islands of Gorgona, Pianosa, Montecristo and Giannutri, half of Elba and Giglio, and most of Capraia, was instituted in 1996, a victory for the conservationists after years of debate and considerable local opposition. The Reserve will protect the beautiful landscape of the islands which are covered with low vegetation known as the *macchia mediterranea*, or Mediterranean scrub, which usually includes ilex, broom, strawberry tree, myrtle, cistus rockrose, rosemary, juniper and mastic. Migratory birds visit the islands, and many nest here (shearwaters, shags, Adouin's gulls and herring gulls).

Elba

Elba (29,000 inhab.), is the largest island in the Tuscan archipelago, and is only 10km from Piombino on the mainland. It has an area of 223 sq km, and is 27km long and 18km across at its broadest. The climate is mild and sunny and the sea bathing good, although it is crowded with visitors in summer. It is especially popular as a holiday place with German visitors, many of whom come here in September. It has a particularly interesting geological formation, with numerous varieties of different minerals. The inhabited part of the island has pretty hills covered with the *macchia mediterranea*, while other parts are barren and deserted. The beauty of the island has been threatened in recent years by forest fires, but about half of the island has been protected since 1996 as part of the *Parco Nazionale dell'Arcipelago Toscana*. The excellent red and white wines once produced here are now difficult to find, although the sweet desert wines *Aleatico* and *Moscato* are still sold on the island.

The island became famous in 1814–15 as Napoleon's place of exile, and the two villas where he passed his time can be visited: one is in Portoferraio, but Villa San Martino nearby is more interesting.

Although Portoferraio is the main port, perhaps the most attractive place on the island is Marciana Marina near the scenic Monte Capanne (1019m), covered with chestnut, oak and ilex woods. The resort of Porto Azzurro is in the eastern part of the island.

History. The Greek Aethalia and the Roman Ilva, Elba has been known since ancient times for its iron ore, which has been mined here for centuries. In the 11C the island was in the possession of Pisa and in 1399 it came under the control of Piombino. In 1548 Cosimo I built Portoferraio, and the south-eastern part of the island was taken over by the Spaniards in the 17C as part of the *Stato dei Presidi* (see p. 316). It officially became part of Tuscany in 1809. The English have been coming here since the end of the 18C, and Joseph Conrad based his last unfinished novel, *Suspense* (begun in 1905), on Elba, although he never visited the island. Aldous Huxley probably came here in 1924, and Dylan Thomas in 1947.

■ Practical information
Information offices. *APT dell'Arcipelago Toscano*, 26 Calata Italia, Portoferraio, Elba (☎ 0565-914671; fax 0565-916350). *Comunità Montana dell'Elba e Capraia*, Viale Manzoni, Portoferraio (who publish a map of the numerous footpaths on the island).

Getting there
By sea. The mainland port for Elba is Piombino (see Ch. 19). **Maritime services** are run by *Toremar*, *Mobylines*, and *Elba Ferries*. It is always advisable to book the return trip for cars in advance, especially on holidays and in summer.
Toremar: Piombino office, 13 Piazzale Premuda (☎ 0565-31100); Portoferraio office, 22 Calata Italia (☎ 0565-918080).
Mobylines: Piombino office, 13 Piazzale Premuda (☎ 0565-221212); Portoferraio office, 4 Viale Elba (☎ 0565-914133). Frequent car ferries and hydrofoils (much more expensive) run to Portoferraio on the north coast in c 1hr (hydrofoils in 30mins). Another boat serves Porto Azzurro and Rio Marina on the east coast. Hydrofoil to Cavo.

Rail connections. The slower trains on the main line from Pisa and Livorno to Rome stop at Campiglia Marittima, where there are frequent services to Piombino Marittima for the ferry. In summer there is one return train a day from Florence direct to Piombino Marittima (the *Freccia dell'Elba*) in c 2hrs 15mins connecting with the ferry.

Hotels
There are some 200 hotels and residences of all categories on the island, and only a very small selection is given below.

Near **Portoferraio**. ★★★★ *Villa Ottone*, località Ottone (☎ 0565-933042; fax 0565-933257), and *Le Picchiaie*, località Picchiaie (☎ 0565-933110; fax 0565-933186).

Biodola. ★★★★ *Hermitage* (☎ 0565/936911; fax 0565-969984) and *Biodola* (☎ 0565-936811; fax 0565-969852).

Near **Capoliveri**. ★★★ *Capo Sud*, località Lacona (☎ 0565-964021; fax 0565-964263) and Residence *Costa dei Gabbiani*, località Ripalte (☎ 0565-935122; fax 0565-935233).

Rio Marina. ★★★ *Rio*, 31 Via Palestro (☎ 0565-924225; fax 0565-924162).

There are numerous **campsites** all over the island. These include the ★★★ *Rosselba Le Palme* at località Ottone, east of Portoferraio (☎ 0565-933101; fax 0565-933041). Others on the south coast, particularly near Lacona.

Restaurants
Portoferraio. ££ *Da Vittorio*, 54 Via dell'Amore (near the old port); *La Ferrigna*, Piazza della Repubblica; £ *Da Elbano Benassi*, località Casaccia.
Capoliveri. ££ *Il Chiasso*, Via N. Sauro.
Rio Marina. £ *La Canocchia*, Via Palestro.
Poggio. ££ *Publius*.

Transport on the island
Bus services from near the ferry quay at Portoferraio to Procchio and Marciana; to Cavo via Porto Azzurro and Rio Marina; to Capoliveri via Porto Azzurro; and to Marina di Campo.

Car and bicycle hire available at Portoferraio.

Portoferraio

The chief town and port is Portoferraio (11,500 inhab.), with huge blast furnaces for smelting iron ore. It was founded in 1548 by the Medici Grand-duke Cosimo I when the remarkable fortifications were begun by Giovanni Battista Bellucci and Giovanni Camerini. The modern seafront, where the ferries dock, is unattractive; the old port, now used by private boats, is at the end of the promontory. It was occupied by the British fleet in 1795–97 under Nelson (the Mediterranean fell under British control the following year).

The fortified **Porta a Mare** (1637) leads into the old district, still the centre of the town, with a covered market. The **Museo Archeologico della Linguella**, in the old salt warehouses, was opened here in 1988 (**open** 09.30–12.30, in summer 09.30–12.30, 18.00–24.00; closed Thurs & fest.). It contains late Bronze Age finds from Santa Lucia; a Punic amphora (7C–6C BC); Etruscan material from the fortresses of Monte Castello (above Procchio) and Castiglione di San Martino (5C–2C BC). The exhibits relating to shipwrecked boats found offshore include huge anchors. There are also Etruscan and Roman finds from the necropolis of Profico at Capoliveri, and mosaics from Villa Le Grotte. In the Caserma de Laugier is the **Pinacoteca Foresiana** (open 09.30–12.30, 16.00–19.00; summer 09.30–12.30, 18.00–24.00; closed Mon & fest.), with Tuscan works of the 16C–19C.

A road (or steps) lead up from the main Piazza della Repubblica to the Medici **Forte Stella** (open Apr–Sept 09.30–18.00 or 19.00) which dominates the port and from which there is a good view. Napoleon's principal residence was the **Villetta dei Mulini**, nearby, overlooking the sea. The modest house (**open** April–Oct 09.00–19.00; fest. 09.00–13.00) contains Napoleonic souvenirs.

The main defensive system is to the west around **Forte Falcone**; this can be visited on the descent from the fort to the **Porta a Terra** on the sea front.

Along the coast west of Portoferraio is **Capo d'Enfola** on a rocky promontory with beaches and hotels.

Napoleon Bonaparte

The name of Napoleon Bonaparte is indelibly associated with the island since his enforced residence here. He was born in Corsica in 1769 which up until the year before had belonged to Genoa, and his parents' families were from mainland Italy. As a General at the age of 26 his first Italian campaign was an immediate success. He established the Cisalpine and Cispadane republics in Northern Italy and by the Treaty of Campoformio handed over Venice to Austria. He returned to Italy in 1800 after his Egyptian expedition. The year after he became Emperor (in 1804) he was appointed king of the new 'Kingdom of Italy'. His rule lasted until 1813 when he was defeated at Leipzig. Deposed by the Tallyrand government in Paris in 1814, he was forced to abdicate, but managed to obtain Elba as a principality. He arrived on the island with a guard of honour of some 800 men. In March 1815 he set sail from here for Cannes and re-entered Paris for the 'One Hundred Days' before his final defeat at Waterloo.

On the Marciana road southwest of Portoferraio, beyond the junction with the road for Porto Azzurro (see below) is the by-road left for the **Villa San Martino** (**adm**. as for the Villetta dei Mulini), in a fertile valley, Napoleon's summer residence. The large one-storey neo-classical edifice was built in front of Napoleon's house by Prince Anatolio Demidoff in 1851 as a memorial to him. The Galleria Demidoff, with a collection of engravings was opened here in 1987. Napoleon's simple house above is reached by a path on the left. It is charmingly decorated in the style known as *retour d'Egypte* with frescoes commemorating Napoleon's Egyptian campaign in 1798–1800. They were painted by his official court painter, Vincenzo Antonio Revelli in 1814.

Biodola, a holiday village on a pretty little bay with a sandy beach, has bungalows and a campsite. **Procchio** is a busy resort, with a good beach. Nearby, beyond the little airport for private planes, is **Marina di Campo**, an attractive bathing resort on the coast, with perhaps the best beach on the island, and numerous hotels.

Access to the sea is limited between Procchio and Marciana Marina along the north coast. **Marciana Marina** is a pretty little fishing port with sardine fisheries. The cylindrical tower on the mole was built by the Pisans in the 12C. There are long-term plans to expand the harbour. From here the road runs uphill through chestnut woods to the most beautiful part of the island around **Poggio** (330m) and **Marciana Alta**, both delightful little villages. The Museo Civico Archeologico is closed for restoration. It contains prehistoric material found on the island, including vases of the Rinaldone Copper Age culture; Etruscan and Hellenistic finds; and amphora found offshore. A cable-car (**open** Apr–Sept 10.00–12.00, 14.30–18.00) ascends to the summit of **Monte Capanne** (1018m), which can also be climbed by marked paths in c 2hrs.

The western shore of the island has splendid views and wild scenery. **Sant'Andrea** is an elegant resort, and **Chiessi** is a pretty village amidst vineyards.

The main town in the eastern part of the island is **Porto Azzurro**, a fashionable resort overlooking a beautiful bay. With its great Spanish fort of 1602 (now a prison), it was formerly called *Porto Longone*.

On the road from Portoferraio to Porto Azzurro are the **Terme di San Giovanni**, a small spa, with mud baths rich in sulphur (used to help alleviate rheumatism). Nearby, on the shore, are the remains of **Villa Le Grotte** (open summer daily, 09.00–dusk), a Roman villa of the Imperial era, excavated in 1960. Its swimming pool is one of the largest ever discovered.

In the southern part of the island is **Capoliveri**, a delightful little old miners' town in a charming position. North of Porto Azzurro, reached by an inland road, is **Rio Marina**, of interest as it was once the chief ore-port and centre of the mining area, with tall, grim houses. The local Mineral Museum is **open** Apr–Sept 09.00–12.00, 15.00–18.00; fest. 09.00–12.00. **Cavo**, reached by a coast road from Rio Marina, is at the northernmost point of the island.

Some of the most beautiful scenery on the island can be seen on the unsurfaced road from Bagnaia (east of Portoferraio) to **Rio nell'Elba**, where there is another mineral museum. Another scenic road, the *Volterraio*, leads from Ottone to Rio nell'Elba.

The Tuscan archipelago

Capraia

To the north of Elba, 55km from the mainland at Piombino, is the mountainous volcanic islet of Capraia (20 sq km). The prison here was closed in 1986, and most of the island was protected in 1996, together with the rest of the archipelago, as part of a national park.

■ **Practical information**

Information offices APT dell'Arcipelago Toscano (☎ 0565-914671). *Cooperativa Parco Naturale Isola di Capraia* (☎ 0586-905071), and *Pro-Loco* (☎ 0586-905138).

Getting there

By sea. Ferry (*Toremar*) in 2hr 30mins from Livorno once a day (via Gorgona on Tuesdays). At some periods of the year there is also a service once a week from Portoferraio (in 2hrs). *Toremar* office in Livorno, Porto Mediceo (☎ 0586-896113); in Capraia, Via Assunzione (☎ 9586-905069); in Portoferraio, 22 Calata Italia (☎ 0565-918080).

Hotel

★★★★ *Il Saracino* (☎ 0586-905018; fax 0586-905062) and a number of residences, and rooms to let.

Campsite ★★★ *Le Sughere* (☎ 0586-905066).

The only settlement is **Capraia** (300 inhab.), beneath Forte San Giorgio, reached from the port by the only road on the island. From here paths lead over the wild volcanic countryside, with beautiful vegetation, where cormorants nest. The highest hills reach a level of 400 metres above sea level, and there is a little inland lake. The island was named by navigators from ancient Greece who found numerous goats here (hence Capraia). Skin divers enjoy exploring the rocky shore, with numerous caves.

Gorgona

The tiny island of Gorgona (2.2 sq km), is the northernmost island in the archipelago, 44km north of Capraia, and 37km off the mainland at Livorno. It is still used as a prison. It is also a beautiful wild place, with numerous pine trees and interesting bird life (the island became part of the *Parco Nazionale dell'Arcipelago Toscano* in 1996). **To visit the island it is necessary to book at least one month in advance** at the Comune of Livorno (☎ 0586-884522; fax 0586-895237): a maximum of 40 people are allowed to visit the island on Tuesdays (by the *Toremar* boat from Livorno to Capraia).

Pianosa

14km south of Elba is the low-lying islet of Pianosa, also used as a prison for a hundred years. The prison was closed down in 1998 and there are plans to introduce boat services to the island and open it up to visitors. With an area of 10 sq km, it rises to a maximum of 29 metres above sea level, and has a particularly mild climate. It has interesting flora and fauna. Some 90 amphorae were discovered in 1991 offshore: they have probably remained here exactly as they fell from a Roman shipwreck. The island has been part of the *Parco Nazionale dell'Arcipelago Toscano* since 1996.

Montecristo

Montecristo, the most isolated of the islands in the Tuscan archipelago is 40km south of Elba, and 63km west of the Argentario. It has an area of 10 sq km. This romantic island, now deserted (except for some goats) and declared a European nature reserve in 1988, and part of the *Parco Nazionale dell'Arcipelago Toscano* in 1996, cannot normally be visited. It is formed of a granite mass covered with woods, rising in the centre to Monte Fortezza (645m). Here are the ruins of the Benedictine monastery of San Salvatore and San Mamiliano, devastated by the pirate Dragut in 1553. A legend that the monks had buried their treasure here before abandoning the island inspired Alexandre Dumas (Dumas père) to write his historical novel, *Le Comte de Monte-Cristo* (1844). From the 15C to the 18C expeditions were made from Piombino to search for the treasure.

The island was acquired in 1852 by a wealthy Englishman, George Watson Taylor, who built a villa at Cala Maestra (the only port of the island), later used as a hunting lodge by Vittorio Emanuele III, and surrounded by a luxuriant garden. While in residence here (1853–60) Taylor, who liked to call himself the 'Count of Montecristo', produced an herbarium of the 335 species of flora to be found on the island.

The islands of Giglio and Giannutri, reached by boat from Monte Argentario, are both described in Ch. 23.

Glossary

Aedicule, small opening framed by two columns and a pediment, originally used in classical architecture.
Alberese, white building stone used in Tuscany (especially in the Garfagnana)
Amphora, antique vase, usually of large dimensions, for oil and other liquids.
Ancona, retable or large altarpiece (painted or sculpted) in an architectural frame.
Antefix, ornament placed at the lower corners of the tiled roof of a temple to conceal the space between the tiles and the cornice.
Antiphonal, choir-book containing a collection of antiphonae—verses sung in response by two choirs.
Arca, wooden chest with a lid, for sacred or secular use. Also, monumental sarcophagus in stone, used by Christians and pagans.
Architrave, lowest part of an entablature, horizontal frame above a door.
Archivolt, moulded architrave carried round an arch.
Atlantes (or Telamones), male figures used as supporting columns.
Atrium, forecourt, usually of a Byzantine church or a classical Roman house.
Attic, topmost story of a classical building, hiding the spring of the roof.
Badia, Abbazia, abbey.
Baldacchino, canopy supported by columns, usually over an altar.
Basilica, originally a Roman building used for public administration; in Christian architecture, an aisled church with a clerestory and apse, and no transepts.
Borgo, a suburb; street leading away from the centre of a town.
Bottega, the studio of an artist: the pupils who worked under his direction.
Bozzetto, sketch for a painting or a small model for a piece of sculpture.
Broccatello, a clouded veined marble from Siena.
Bucchero, Etruscan black terracotta ware.
Bucrania, a form of classical decoration—skulls of oxen garlanded with flowers.
Campanile, bell-tower, often detached from the building to which it belongs.
Camposanto, cemetery.
Canephora, figure bearing a basket, often used as a caryatid.
Canopic vase, Egyptian or Etruscan vase enclosing the entrails of the dead.
Cantoria, singing-gallery in a church.
Cappella, chapel.
Cartoon, from cartone, meaning large sheet of paper. A full-size preparatory drawing for a painting or fresco.
Caryatid, female figure used as a supporting column.
Cassone, a decorated chest, usually a dower chest.
Cavea, the part of a theatre or amphitheatre occupied by the rows of seats.
Cella, sanctuary of a temple, usually in the centre of the building.
Cenacolo, scene of the Last Supper (often in the refectory of a convent).
Chalice, wine cup used in the celebration of Mass.
Chiaroscuro, distribution of light and shade, apart from colour in a painting.
Ciborium, casket or tabernacle containing the Host.
Cipollino, onion-marble; a greyish marble with streaks of white or green.
Cippus, sepulchral monument in the form of an altar.
Cista, casket, usually of bronze and cylindrical in shape, to hold jewels, toilet articles, etc., and decorated with mythological subjects.
Cloisonné, type of enamel decoration.

Columbarium, a building (usually subterranean) with niches to hold urns containing the ashes of the dead.

Commune, a town or city which adopted a form of independent self-government in the Middle Ages.

Comune, municipal government (Palazzo del Comune, town hall)

Condottiere, professional military commander.

Confessio, crypt beneath the high altar and raised choir of a church, usually containing the relics of a saint.

Corbel, a projecting block, usually of stone.

Corso, main street of a town.

Crenellations, battlements.

Cupola, dome.

Cyclopean, the term applied to walls of unmortared masonry, older than the Etruscan civilisation, and attributed by the ancients to the giant Cyclopes.

Diptych, painting or ivory panel in two sections.

Dossal, altarpiece.

Dosseret, a second block above the capital of a column.

Duomo, cathedral.

Edicola, *see* aedicule.

Exedra, semicircular recess.

Ex-voto, tablet or small painting expressing gratitude to a saint.

Fresco (in Italian, *affresco*), painting executed on wet plaster. On the wall beneath is sketched the sinopia, and the cartoon (see above) is transferred onto the fresh plaster (*intonaco*) before the fresco is begun either by pricking the outline with small holes over which a powder is dusted, or by means of a stylus which leaves an incised line on the wet plaster. In recent years many frescoes have been detached from the walls on which they were executed.

Giallo Antico, red-veined yellow marble from Numidia.

Gonfalon, banner of a medieval guild or commune.

Graffiti, design on a wall made with an iron tool on a prepared surface, the design showing in white. Also used loosely to describe scratched designs or words on walls.

Greek-cross, cross with the arms of equal length.

Grisaille, painting in various tones of grey.

Grotesque, painted or stucco decoration in the style of the ancient Romans (found during the Renaissance in Nero's Golden House in Rome, then underground, hence the name, from grotto). The delicate ornamental decoration usually includes patterns of flowers, sphynxes, birds, human figures, etc., against a light ground.

Herm (pl. *Hermae*), quadrangular pillar decreasing in girth towards the ground surmounted by a bust.

Hypogeum, subterranean excavation for the burial of the dead (usually Etruscan).

Iconostasis, high balustrade with figures of saints, guarding the sanctuary of a Byzantine church.

Impasto, early Etruscan ware made of inferior clay.

Intarsia (or *Tarsia*), inlay of wood, marble, ivory, or metal.

Intonaco, plaster.

Intrados, underside or soffit of an arch.

Krater, Antique mixing-bowl, conical in shape with rounded base.

Kylix, wide shallow vase with two handles and short stem.

Latin-cross, cross with a long vertical arm.

Lavabo, hand-basin usually outside a refectory or sacristy.

Loggia, covered gallery or balcony, usually preceding a larger building.

Lunette, semicircular space in a vault or ceiling, or above a door or window, often decorated with a painting or relief.

Macchia mediterranea, see p. 288.

Maestà, Madonna and Child enthroned in majesty.

Matroneum, gallery reserved for women in early Christian churches.

Medallion, large medal; loosely, a circular ornament.

Menhir, a long megalithic stone planted vertically in the ground.

Meta, turning-post at either end of a Roman circus.

Monochrome, painting or drawing in one colour only.

Monolith, single stone (usually a column).

Narthex, vestibule of a Christian basilica.

Niello, black substance used in an engraved design.

Nimbus, luminous ring surrounding the heads of saints in paintings; a square nimbus denoted that the person was living at that time.

Oculus, round window.

Opera (Del Duomo), the office in charge of the fabric of a building (i.e. the Cathedral).

Opus Reticulatum, masonry arranged in squares or diamonds so that the mortar joints make a network pattern.

Opus Tessellatum, mosaic formed entirely of square tesserae.

Pala, large altarpiece.

Palazzo, any dignified and important building.

Palombino, fine-grained white marble.

Pavonazzetto, yellow marble blotched with blue.

Pax, a small plaque or tablet used by a priest for the blessing of peace, and offered for the kiss of the faithful. It can be circular or rectangular, and engraved enamelled or painted, usually in a gold or silver frame.

Pendentive, concave spandrel beneath a dome.

Peristyle, court or garden surrounded by a columned portico.

Pietà, group of the Virgin mourning the dead Christ.

Pietre Dure, hard or semi-precious stones, often used in the form of mosaics to decorate cabinets, table-tops, etc., known as *commesso* work in Italian.

Pieve, parish church, often isolated in the countryside (rather than in a town), and the most important in the district.

Piscina, Roman tank; a basin for an officiating priest to wash his hands before Mass.

Plaquette, small metal tablet with relief decoration.

Pluteus (pl. *plutei*), marble panel, usually decorated; a series of them used to form a parapet to precede the altar of a church.

Polyptych, painting or panel in more than three sections.

Porta, gate (or door).

Porta del Morto, in certain old mansions of Umbria and Tuscany, a narrow raised doorway, said to be for the passage of biers of the dead, but more probably for use in troubled times when the main gate would be barred.

Predella, small painting or panel, usually in sections, attached below a large altarpiece, illustrating the story of a saint, the life of the Virgin, etc.

Presepio, literally, crib or manger. A group of statuary of which the central subject is the Infant Jesus in the manger.

Pronaos, porch in front of the cella of a temple.

Putto (pl. *putti*), figure of a small boy sculpted or painted, usually nude.

Quadratura, painted architectural perspectives.

Quatrefoil, four-lobed design.

Reredos, decorated screen rising behind an altar.

Rhyton, drinking-horn usually ending in an animal's head.

Rood-screen, a screen below the Rood or Crucifix dividing the nave from the chancel of a church.

Scagliola, a material made from selenite and used to imitate marble or pietre dure, often used for altar frontals and columns.

Scena, the stage of a Roman theatre.

Schiacciato, term used to describe very low relief in sculpture, where there is an emphasis on the delicate line rather than the depth of the panel.

Schola Cantorum, enclosure for the choristers in the nave of an early Christian church, adjoining the sanctuary.

Sinopia, large sketch for a fresco made on the rough wall in a red earth pigment called sinopia (because it originally came from Sinope on the Black Sea). By detaching a fresco it is now possible to see the sinopia beneath and detach it also.

Situla, water-bucket.

Soffit, underside or intrados of an arch.

Spandrel, surface between two arches in an arcade or the triangular space on either side of an arch.

Stamnos, big-bellied vase with two small handles at the sides, closed by a lid.

Stele, upright stone bearing a monumental inscription.

Stemma, coat of arms or heraldic device.

Stereobate, basement of a temple or other building.

Stoup, vessel for Holy Water, usually near the west door of a church.

Stylobate, basement of a columned temple or other building.

Tablinum, room in a Roman house with one side opening onto the central courtyard.

Telamones, see Atlantes.

Tessera, a small cube of marble, glass, etc., used in mosaic work.

Thermae, Roman baths.

Tholos, a circular building.

Tondo, round painting or bas-relief.

Transenna, open grille or screen, usually of marble, in an early Christian church.

Travertine, tufa quarried near Tivoli.

Triclinium, dining room and reception room of a Roman house.

Triptych, painting or panel in three sections.

Trompe-l'oeil, literally, a deception of the eye. Used to describe illusionist decoration, painted architectural perspectives, etc.

Tufa, porous volcanic rock used as a building stone.

Villa, country house with its garden.

Westwork, west end of a Carolingian or Romanesque church with a massive central tower and, inside, a double story, with the upper room open to the nave.

The terms **Quattrocento**, **Cinquecento** (abbreviated in Italy 400, 500), etc., refer not to the 14C and 15C, but to the fourteen-hundreds and fifteen-hundreds, ie. the 15C and 16C, etc.

Index to Italian artists

Ademollo, Luigi (1764–1849) 107, 221, 222, 261, 277, 378, 454
Adeodato (12C) 181
Agnolo di Ventura (d. 1348) 454
Agostino di Duccio (1418–81) 231
Agostino di Giovanni (fl.1310–d. before 1348) 176, 250, 338, 341, 454, 457
Agostino di Jacopo (14C) 51
Alberti, Alberto (c 1525–98) 502, 504, 505
Alberti, Alessandro (1551–96) 504
Alberti, Cherubino (1553–1618) 502
Alberti, Giovanni (1558–after 1601) 504
Alberti, Leon Battista (1404–72) 74, 78, 81, 86, 154, 419, 420
Albertinelli, Mariotto (1474–1515) 64, 72, 104, 270
Albertini, Lisandro di Pietro (16C) 435
Aldi, Pietro (1852–88) 318, 323, 325, 326, 375
Alessi, Giovanni Battista (16C) 434
Algardi, Alessandro (1598–1654) 82
Allori, Alessandro (1535–1607) 62, 74, 79, 85, 121, 138, 160, 165, 167, 168, 181, 186, 198, 200, 245, 253, 255, 261, 431, 456, 458, 465, 468, 469
Allori, Cristofano (son of Alessandro; 1577–1621) 68, 74, 86, 120, 173, 177, 186, 189, 236, 245, 467
Ambrogio di Baldese (1352–1429) 149, 163
Ammannati, Bartolomeo (1511–92) 60, 62, 67, 68, 71, 73, 77, 82, 83, 87, 90, 104, 105, 108, 146, 198, 201, 214, 222, 236, 272, 276, 456, 476
Andrea d'Ognabene (fl 1287–1316) 178
Andrea da Firenze; see Bonaiuto
Andrea del Sarto (Andrea d'Agnolo; 1486–1530) 64, 68, 70, 73, 74, 76, 95, 146, 167, 168, 198, 236, 456, 468, 469
Andrea di Bartolo (son of Bartolo di Fredi; d. 1428) 381, 416
Andrea di Giusto (Manzini; d. 1455) 143, 159, 165, 171, 479, 481
Andrea di Nerio (fl. 1331–69) 455
Andrea di Niccolò (after 1440–1512) 129, 306, 400, 416, 417, 438, 444
Andreotti, Libero (1875–1933) 187, 188
Andreuccio di Bartolomeo (fl 1389–1404) 270
Angeli, Giuseppe (c 1709–98) 470
Angelico, Fra (or Beato Angelico; c 1395–1455) 75, 96, 100, 122, 251, 287, 464, 465, 469, 483
Angelo di Lorentino (d. 1527) 455
Annigoni, Pietro (1910–88) 107, 123, 184, 187, 490

Antinori, Giovanni (1734–92) 415
Antonio da Colle (fl. 1469–90) 390
Antonio di Ser Cola (early 15C) 158
Aprili, Pietro (fl 1504–58) 225
Arcangelo di Cola da Camerino (fl. 1416–29) 497
Aretino; see Spinello and Parri
Arnoldi, Alberto (d. 1377) 54, 55
Arnolfo di Cambio (c 1245–1302) 52, 55, 61, 82, 84, 119, 351, 395, 482, 486
Arrighi, Giuseppe (fl 1650–80) 269
Aspertini, Amico (1474–1552) 202, 206
Avanzi, Francesco (fl. 1598) 198
Azzolini, Tito (1837–1907) 174

Bacci, Baccio Maria (1888–1974) 498
Baccio d'Agnolo (Bartolommeo Baglioni; 1462–1543) 52, 81, 89, 92, 188, 189, 435
Baccio da Montelupo (1469–1535) 57, 123, 134, 153, 196, 399, 458
Bachiacca (Antonio Ubertini; 1494–1557) 115, 397
Badaloni, Angelo (1849–1920) 281, 284
Balassi, Mario (1604–67) 150, 397
Baldi, Accursio (fl. 1585–90) 353
Baldi, Lazzaro (c 1624–1703) 182
Baldovinetti, Alesso (1425–99) 72, 73, 80, 87, 89, 94, 236
Balducci, Giovanni (Il Cosci; 1560–after 1631) 120, 196, 269, 275, 276, 393, 484
Bandinelli, Baccio (1493–1560) 53, 55, 60, 74, 82, 226
Bandini, Giovanni (Giovanni dell'Opera; 1540–99) 53, 55, 61, 62, 284
Banti, Cristiano (1824–1904) 287
Baratta, Andrea (fl. 1665–90) 221, 222
Baratta, Francesco (c 1590–after 1656) 263
Baratta, Giovanni (1670–1747) 229, 284, 484
Barbiani, Bartolomeo (fl. 1628–42) 431, 434, 435
Barbiere, Alessandro del (Alessandro Fei; 1543–92) 62, 84
Barchi, Sebastiano (18C) 433
Barili, Antonio (1453–1516) 424
Barili, Sallustio (late 15C) 351
Barna da Siena (fl c 1369–81) 389
Barna di Turino (fl. 1378–1410) 342
Barnaba da Modena (fl. 1361–83) 250
Barocci, Federico (Il Baroccio; 1526–1612) 197, 431
Bartolini, Lorenzo (1777–1850) 72, 85, 160, 163, 171, 201, 242, 468, 494
Bartolo di Fredi (c 1330–1410) 304, 358, 373, 389, 392, 397, 401, 402, 407, 426, 436, 477

Bartolomeo della Gatta (Pietro di Antonio Dei; 1448–1502) 271, 451, 455, 456, 458, 460, 465, 469, 483, 502

Bartolomeo, Fra (or Bartolomeo della Porta; 1475–1517) 70, 75, 107, 160, 171, 200, 206, 249, 262, 270

Bassano, Jacopo (da Ponte; 1517/18–92) 64, 198, 458

Bassano, Leandro (da Ponte; 1557–1622) 196, 503

Batoni, Pompeo (1708–87) 194, 198, 207

Battaglia, Francesco (fl. 1668–93) 232

Battistello (Giovanni Battista Caracciolo; c 1570–1637) 160

Bazzani, Giuseppe (c 1690–1769) 361

Bazzicaluva, Ercole (c 1610–61) 188

Beato Angelico; see Angelico

Beccafumi, Domenico (Mecarino; 1485–1551) 88, 196, 237, 338, 342, 348, 350, 352, 354, 365, 366, 367, 370, 374, 375, 444

Bedoli, Girolamo Mazzola (c 1500–69) 362

Bellano, Bartolomeo (1434–96) 77

Bellini, Giovanni (c 1435–1516; son of Jacopo) 64, 87, 163

Bellucci, Giovanni Battista (1506–54) 511

Benci di Cione (1337–1404) 56, 60

Benedetto da Maiano (1442–97) 53, 54, 62, 78, 80, 81, 82, 84, 120, 159, 377, 389, 390, 392, 432, 459, 460

Benedetto da Rovezzano (1474–1552) 53, 60, 80, 83

Benedetto di Bindo (fl. 1411–d. 1417) 350, 365, 378

Benefial, Marco (1684–1764) 251

Benti, Donato (1470–c 1536) 221, 223

Benvenuti, Pietro (degli Ordini; fl. 1458–d. 1484) 145, 454

Benvenuto di Giovanni (1436–d. c 1518) 271, 272, 277, 325, 338, 348, 350, 353, 357, 361, 366, 367, 375, 377, 383, 407, 416, 436, 437

Berardi, Piero (1904–89) 105

Bergamini, Alessandro (1676–1711) 224, 225

Bergamini, Gian Francesco (late 17C) 224, 225

Bergognone (Ambrogio da Fossano; fl 1480–1522) 198

Berlinghieri, Berlinghiero (early 13C) 153, 191, 202, 250

Berlinghieri, Bonaventura (fl. 1235–75) 189

Bernabei, Tommaso (Papacello; c 1500–59) 460, 461, 465, 473

Bernardino di Antonio del Signoraccio (Bernardino Detti; 1460–c 1532) 174, 184, 185, 186

Bernini, Gian Lorenzo (1598–1680) 82, 173, 182, 259, 350

Berrettini, Filippo (1582–1644) 460, 466, 470

Berrettini, Lorenzo (1620–72) 468

Berti, Antonio (1904–90) 499

Berti, Giovanni (fl. 1564) 408

Bertolani, Bastiano (16C) 196

Bertoldo di Giovanni (c 1440–91) 75, 77, 82, 167

Bettarini, Luigi (1790–1850) 281

Betti, Niccolò (fl. 1576–1617) 434

Betto di Francesco (fl. 1369–75) 56

Bezzuoli, Giuseppe (1784–1855) 107, 115, 177, 179, 282

Biagio d'Antonio (fl. 1369–75) 134

Bianchi, Gaetano (1819–92) 119, 229

Bibbiena, Il Antonio Galli; 1700–74) 182, 398

Bicci di Lorenzo (1373–1452) 80, 91, 93, 97, 98, 110, 120, 126, 139, 143, 149, 150, 154, 187, 189, 451, 467, 481, 486, 490, 497

Biduino (late 12C) 203, 205, 243, 249, 259

Bigarelli, Guido (Guido da Como; 13C) 177, 180, 198, 204, 214, 239

Bilivert, Giovanni (1576–1644) 68, 81, 86, 160, 163, 236, 253

Bimbi, Bartolomeo (1648–1730) 170

Bistolfi, Leonardo (1859–1935) 215

Bocciardi, Clemente (1620–58) 251

Boldini, Giovanni (1842–1931) 178, 287

Bonaccorso di Cino (fl. 1347) 174, 176

Bonaiuto, Andrea di (or Andrea da Firenze; fl. 1343–77) 78, 79, 240, 242

Bonanno da Pisa (fl. 1174–86) 236

Bonamico (12C) 401

Bonanni, Vincenzo (16C–17C) 282

Bonastri, Lattanzio (fl. 1550) 375

Bonechi, Matteo (1672–c 1750) 141, 484

Bonistalli, Andrea (fl. 1616–22) 148

Bordone, Paris (1500–70) 64, 362

Bordoni, Francesco (c 1580–1654) 399

Borghetti, Ranieri (fl.1609) 252

Borgognone, Il (Guglielmo Courtois; c 1628–79) 287, 420

Boschi, Fabrizio (c 1570–1642) 135, 425

Boscoli, Andrea (c 1550–1606) 253, 255

Bottani, Giuseppe (1717–84) 230

Botticelli (Sandro Filipepi; 1444–1510) 63, 64, 68, 72, 78, 80, 92, 96, 105, 108, 153, 362, 375, 480

Botticini, Francesco (1446–98) 68, 90, 149, 165

Botticini, Raffaello (son of Francesco; fl. 1474–1520) 148, 150

Bozzolini, Bartolomeo (late 15C) 497

Braccini, Andrea di Pietro (d. before 1391) 178, 179

Bramante, Donato (1444–1514) 253

Brandimarti, Benedetto (fl. 1588–92) 220

Bregno, Andrea (Andrea da Milano; c 1421–1506) 352

Brescianino, Andrea del (Andrea Piccinelli; fl. 1507–25) 338, 356, 361, 366, 371

Brina, Francesco (c 1540–86) 67, 206, 497

Bronzino (Agnolo di Cosimo Tori; 1503–72) 62, 64, 66, 74, 79, 123, 197, 245, 253, 493

Brunelleschi, Filippo di Ser Brunellesco Lapi (1377–1446) 52, 53, 55, 57, 67, 73, 76, 77, 79, 82, 85, 86, 89, 96, 104, 154, 177, 468

Bruni, Giovanni (fl. c 1840) 373

Brusasorci, Felice (Ricci; 1546–1605) 342

Buffalmacco (Bonamico di Cristofano; 1262–1340) 241, 242, 454

Buggiano (Andrea Cavalcanti; Brunelleschi's adopted son; 1416–62) 53, 77, 188, 189, 479, 497

Bugiardini, Giuliano (1476–1555) 86, 272

Buglioni, Benedetto (1461–1521) 80, 119, 135, 146, 148, 150, 181, 186, 214, 216, 225, 251, 428, 480, 483, 487, 495, 506, 508

Buglioni, Santi (1494–1576) 74, 126, 149, 150, 164, 181, 400, 428, 488, 497, 506, 508

Bulgarini, Bartolomeo (formerly known as the 'Maestro della Madonna di San Pietro a Ovile'; fl. 1347–50) 330, 373

Buonfigli, Antonio (18C) 378

Buontalenti, Bernardo (delle Girandole; 1531–1608) 63, 75, 80, 83, 93, 104, 106, 117, 151, 153, 170, 174, 206, 252, 255, 279, 282, 318, 428, 505

Burbarini, Deifebo (1619–80) 397

Buscheto (11C or 12C) 235

Buti, Lodovico (c 1560–1603) 155, 160, 182, 245, 497

Butteri, Giovanni Maria (c 1540–1606) 62, 139, 180, 402, 456

Cabianca, Vincenzo (1827–1902) 287

Caccini, Giovan Battista (1559/92–1613) 89, 138, 272, 399, 487

Cacialli, Giuseppe (1770–1828) 102

Cafaggi, Domenico (1530–1606) 349, 378

Caffà, Melchiorre (1630/35–after 1667) 351

Calamech, Andrea (1514–c 1600) 61

Calcagni, Tiberio (1532–65) 55

Camaino di Crescentino (1285–after 1325) 345, 357

Cambi, Ulisse (1807–95) 157, 194

Cambiaso, Luca (1527–85) 232

Camerini, Giovanni (fl. 1542–70) 318, 511

Camilliani, Giovanni (d. 1566) 159

Canaletto (Antonio Canal; 1697–1768) 66

Candido, Pietro (Pieter de Witte; 1548–1628) 269, 272

Canova, Antonio (1757–1822) 70, 84, 226, 455

Canozzi, Cristoforo (Cristoforo da Lendinara; 1426–after 1488) 205, 244

Cantagallina, Antonio (fl. 1604–09) 282, 502

Canuti, Domenico Maria (1620–84) 349

Capanna, Puccio (fl. 1335–50) 181, 189

Caporali, Giovanni Battista (c 1476–1560) 473

Capra, Alessandro (1608–83) 230

Capriani, Francesco (Francesco da Volterra; late 16C) 269

Caravaggio (Michelangelo Merisi; c 1571–1609/10) 66, 68, 163, 318

Carena, Felice (1879–1966) 218

Caroni, Emanuele (1826–after 1863) 157

Carrà, Carlo (1881–1966) 218

Carracci, Annibale (1560–1609) 66, 70, 236

Carracci, Ludovico (1555–1619) 458

Cartoni, Giovanni Battista (early 17C) 259

Casolani, Alessandro (1552–1606) 298, 335, 342, 350, 365, 372, 374, 375, 377, 385, 400, 417

Cassana, Niccolò (1659–1713) 68

Cassioli, Amos (1832–91) 342, 364, 400, 413

Cassioli, Giuseppe (1865–1942) 107, 123, 413

Castagno, Andrea del (Andrea di Bartolo; 1417/19–1457) 53, 54, 63, 66, 74, 76, 121, 123, 187, 262

Castagnoli, Giuseppe (1754–1832) 433

Castellotti, Lorenzo (born 1718) 196

Castellucci, Giuseppe (1863–1939) 110, 139, 490

Castellucci, Salvi (1608–72) 431, 454, 457

Catena, Vincenzo (c 1470–1531) 198

Cattaneo, Danese (c 1509–73) 82, 159

Ceccarelli, Gaetano (1872–1919) 373

Cecchi, Annibale (fl. 1648) 282

Cecchi, Francesco Antonio (born 1717) 196

Cecco di Pietro (1370–1402) 251

Cecioni, Adriano (1836–86) 458

Cellini, Benvenuto (1500–71) 60, 81, 82, 122, 484

Cellini, Lorenzo (16C) 222

Cellino di Nese (14C) 176, 177, 239

Cenni di Francesco di Ser Cenni (fl. 1369–1415) 135, 136, 143, 144, 149, 262, 272, 275, 393

Cennini, Cennino (c 1370–after 1388) 134, 360, 395, 398, 402

Cercignani, Niccolò see Pomarancio

Cerri, Vincenzo (d. 1903) 284

Chiari, Giuseppe (1654–1727) 397

Chini family 114, 116, 118, 121

Chini, Galileo (1873–1956) 114, 115, 118, 121, 124, 163, 175, 184, 218, 263, 453

Ciampelli, Agostino (before 1577–1642) 188, 458, 503

Cieco da Gambassi (Giovanni Francesco Gonnelli; 1603–64) 277

Cignani, Carlo (1628–1719) 287, 434

Cignaroli, Gianbettino (1706–70) 231

Cigoli (Ludovico Cardi; 1559–1613) 68, 83, 150, 151, 179, 189, 206, 245, 262, 263, 264, 458, 480, 481, 397, 467, 468, 471, 480, 481

Cima da Conegliano (1460–1518) 64

Cimabue (fl. 1272–1302) 51, 63, 78, 85, 87, 146, 154, 237, 456

Cimica, Giovanni (c 1743–88) 04

Cioli, Raffaello (da Settignano; fl. 1522–25) 269

Circignani see Pomarancio

Ciseri, Antonio (1821–91) 67, 435

Ciuffagni, Bernardo (1381–1458) 53, 54, 56

Ciurini, Bernardo (1695–1752) 282

Civitali, Masseo (late 15C) 200, 202, 205, 206

Civitali, Matteo (c 1435–1511) 188, 194, 195, 199, 203, 205, 206, 207, 209, 212, 216, 220, 236, 243

Civitali, Nicolao (1482–1560) 196, 223

Civitali, Vincenzo (1523–97) 196, 202, 204, 207

Colli, Antonio (fl. 1725) 431

Colli, Paolo (d. 1822) 115

Collignon, Giuseppe (c 1776–1863) 230, 365

Colonna, Angelo Michele (1604–87) 71, 191, 202

Commodi, Andrea (1560–1638) 465, 468, 471

Conca, Sebastiano (1680–1764) 204, 236, 251, 318, 353, 364, 370, 376

Confetto, Michele (16C) 138

Confortini, Matteo (c 1565–1616) 487

Consani, Vincenzo (1818–87) 195, 198, 200, 207

Conti, Primo (1900–88) 99

Coppedè, Adolfo (1871–1951) 103

Coppo di Marcovaldo (fl. 1261–75) 51, 81, 91, 134, 176, 177, 371, 391

Cornacchini, Agostino (1685–c 1740) 188

Correggio (Antonio Allegri; 1489–1534) 64

Cosini, Silvio (1502–47) 244, 275

Costanzi, Placido (1688/90–1759) 370

Covatti, Ascanio (d. 1632) 465

Covatti, Bernardino (fl.early 16C) 465

Cozza, Francesco (1605–82) 408

Cozzarelli, Giacomo (1453–1515) 146, 324, 338, 358, 361, 364, 365, 370, 379, 381

Cozzarelli, Guidoccio (1450–1516/17) 306, 322, 348, 350, 367, 386, 407, 417, 436, 437, 475

Crespi, Giuseppe Maria (Il Cerano; 1557–1633) 253, 469

Cristiani, Giovanni di Bartolomeo (fl. 1370–90) 174, 178, 179

Cristofanello (Giovanni Battista di Cristofano Infregliati; early 16C) 468, 470

Cristoforo di Bindoccio (fl. 1361–1406) 306

Cristoforo da Lendinara see Canozzi, Cristoforo

Crogi, Pietro d'Achille (16C) 353

Cronaca (Simone del Pollaiolo; 1454–1508) 61, 81, 87, 90, 94

Cungi, Francesco (fl. 1587) 270

Cungi, Leonardo (d. 1569) 504

Curradi, Francesco (1570–1661) 68, 91, 110, 123, 126, 138, 155, 179, 263, 264, 269, 270, 275, 297, 372, 398, 503

Daddi, Bernardo (c 1312–48) 54, 57, 63, 74, 85, 88, 98, 123, 154, 165, 265, 360

Daddi, Cosimo (d. 1630) 104, 270, 271, 275, 276, 278

Dandini, Cesare (c 1595–1658) 135, 163, 249, 275, 487

Dandini, Ottaviano (c 1707–40) 182

Dandini, Pier (1646–1712) 79, 135, 163, 164, 179, 186, 190, 220, 221, 276, 349, 396, 398

Dandini, Vincenzo (1607–75) 163, 397

Daniele da Volterra (Ricciarelli; 1509–66) 206, 267, 271, 380

Danti, Fra Egnazio (1536–86) 62

Danti, Vincenzo (1530–76) 49, 51, 62, 84, 86, 159, 458

Davanzati, Alessandro (fl. 1596) 496

De Chirico, Giorgio (1880–1978) 218

De Fabris, Emilio (1808–83) 52

De Pisis, Filippo (1896–1956) 218

De' Rossi, Vincenzo (1525–87) 53, 62, 82

Della Robbia, Ambrogio (1470–c 1527) 370

Della Robbia, Andrea (nephew of Luca; 1435–1525) 54, 60, 73, 79, 82, 84, 89, 101, 107, 111, 112, 150, 157, 160, 162, 175, 190, 211, 251, 264, 270, 271, 273, 294, 332, 381, 407, 424, 428, 431, 433, 454, 457, 458, 460, 475, 477, 484, 487, 490, 493, 497, 498, 502, 503, 506, 508

Della Robbia, Giovanni (son of Andrea; 1469–1529) 79, 82, 97, 108, 112, 118, 127, 139, 151, 181, 241, 265, 273, 277, 414, 434, 455, 475, 477, 482, 485

Della Robbia, Luca (1399 or 1400–82) 53, 55, 56, 57, 67, 73, 80, 82, 85, 93, 107, 111, 112, 155, 174, 190, 195, 264, 270, 477, 479, 499

Della Robbia school 81, 85, 104, 106, 108, 109, 114, 117, 119, 123, 135, 124, 137, 145, 146, 148, 150, 155, 162, 188, 192, 202, 206, 214, 215, 261, 270, 333, 372, 402, 428, 433, 434, 477, 480, 482, 490, 497

Desiderio da Settignano (1429/30–64) 77, 80, 82, 85, 101, 117, 506

Diamante, Fra (c 1430–98) 120, 158, 163, 165

Digny, Luigi Cambray (1779–1843) 162

Diotisalvi (12C) 239, 255

Doceno, Il (Cristoforo Gherardi; 1508–56) 456, 469, 503

Dolci, Carlo (1616–86) 68, 159, 163, 196, 458

Domenichino (Domenico Zampieri; 1581–1641) 196, 270

Domenico di Agostino (d. before 1369) 311

Domenico di Bartolo (c 1400–45) 338, 348, 352, 353, 360, 361

Domenico di Cristofano (fl. 1444–56) 353

Domenico di Michelino (15C) 165, 277, 391, 482

Domenico di Niccolò dei Cori (c 1362–before 1453) 299, 338, 342, 348, 349, 356, 373, 407, 408, 420, 422

Donatello (Donato de' Bardi; c 1386–1466) 51, 53, 57, 62, 77, 79, 81, 82, 84, 85, 89, 90, 117, 157, 159, 205, 251, 263, 348, 351, 356, 357, 436, 455, 468

Dosio, Giovanni Antonio (1533–1609) 81, 85

Dossi, Dosso (Giovanni Luteri; 1480–1542) 64

Duccio di Buoninsegna (1260–1319) 63, 66, 297, 309, 312, 338, 344, 350, 358, 366, 367, 371, 395, 400, 407, 415, 416, 432, 434, 438, 443, 456

Dughet, Gaspare (1613–75) 458

Duprè, Amalia (1845–1928) 262

Duprè, Giovanni (1817–82) 241, 242, 339, 342, 354, 364

Duquesnoy, François (1594–1643) 282

Empoli (Jacopo Chimenti; 1551–1640) 68, 86, 96, 112, 137, 141, 148, 149, 162, 166, 173, 179, 245, 249, 282, 311, 424, 458, 467, 469, 470

Enrico di Tedice (13C) 255, 264

Fabbrucci (1687–1767) 470

Falcini, Mariano (1804–85) 155, 472

Falconi, Bernardo (fl. late 14C) 236

Fallani, Bernardo (fl. 1771–78) 141

Fancelli, Chiarissimo (d. 1632) 238, 245

Fancelli, Pandolfo (d. 1526) 236

Fantastici, Agostino (1782–1845) 408

Farinati, Paolo (1524–1606) 456

Fattori, Giovanni (1825/28–1908) 70, 184, 281, 287

Fazzi, Arnaldo (1855–1944) 194

Federighi, Antonio (or Federigo; c 1420–90) 296, 341, 348, 349, 350, 351, 356, 357, 365, 367, 372, 380

Fedi, Pio (1816–92) 60

Fei, Alessandro see Barbiere

Fei, Paolo di Giovanni (fl. 1372–1410) 352, 353, 356, 360, 367

Feliciati, Lorenzo (1732–99) 375

Ferrari, Ettore (1848–1929) 252

Ferrata, Ercole (1610–86) 350

Ferretti, Gian Domenico (1692–c 1750) 112, 141, 143, 160, 230, 244, 268, 276, 460, 461, 490

Ferri, Antonio Maria (1651–1716) 91, 105, 186, 188, 189, 262, 263

Ferri, Ciro (1634–89) 87, 353, 467, 471

Ferri, Simone (fl. 1571) 398

Ferrucci, Andrea (1465–1526) 53, 176, 270

Ferrucci, Francesco (Il Tadda; 1497–1585) 240

Ferrucci, Francesco di Simone (1437–93) 158

Ferrucci, Nicodemo (1574–1650) 110, 192

Fiamberti, Tommaso (d. 1524/5) 398, 493

Ficherelli, Felice (1605–69) 90, 180

Fidani, Orazio (c 1610–56) 141, 264, 265, 471

Filippelli, Filippo d'Antonio (fl. 1483–85) 138

Foggini, Giovanni Battista (1652–1735) 83, 85, 91, 93, 112, 121, 141, 179, 236, 238, 245, 282, 284

Folchi, Ferdinando (1822–93) 148

Folfi, Mariotto di Zanobi (L'Ammogliato; 1521–1600) 61

Folli, Sebastiano (1568–1621) 364, 373, 426

Fontana, Carlo (1634–1714) 226, 385, 423

Fontana, Giovanni (brother of Domenico; 1540–1614) 367

Francavilla, Pietro (Pierre Tranqueville; 1548–1615) 74, 85, 87, 248, 252, 455

Franceschini, Baldassare see Volterrano

Francesco d'Andrea (fl.1466–80) 344

Francesco d'Antonio (fl. 1393–1433) 83, 89, 119, 381, 479, 480, 486

Francesco di Giorgio see Martini

Francesco di Niccolò (late 14C) 177

Francesco di Pietro (fl. 1345–62) 471, 472

Francesco di Valdambrino see Valdambrino

Franchi, Alessandro (1838–1914) 159, 371, 376

Franchi, Antonio (1634–1709) 190, 195, 204, 253

Franchi, Rossello di Jacopo (1377–1456) 137, 149, 179, 262

Franchini, Niccolò (1704–83) 370

Francia, Francesco (Raibolini; 1450–1517) 202, 253

Franciabigio (Francesco di Cristofano Bigi; 1482–1525) 73, 76, 107, 123, 136, 167, 168, 458

Franco, Battista (c 1498–1561) 244

Fungai, Bernardino (1460–1516) 338, 367, 371, 375, 377, 379, 441

Furini, Francesco (1603–46) 68, 134, 150, 163, 196, 362

Gabbiani, Antonio Domenico (1653–1726) 87, 91, 107, 150, 179, 190, 434

Gaddi, Agnolo (or Angelo; son of Taddeo; c 1333–96) 79, 80, 84, 93, 100, 111, 115, 149, 158, 165, 251

Gaddi, Gaddo (di Zanobi; c 1260–1332) 52, 238

Gaddi, Taddeo (fl. 1332–63) 66, 67, 84, 85, 94, 98, 100, 110, 141, 174, 240, 242, 249, 460, 495

Galeotti, Giuseppe (1708–78) 231

Galeotti, Sebastiano (1676–1746) 231

Galilei, Alessandro (1691–1736) 120

Galli, Giovanni Antonio, (Lo Spadarino; fl. 1615–50) 397

Gallori, Emilio (1846–1924) 192

Gambacciani, Francesco (1701–after 1771) 504

Gambarelli, Crescenzio (fl.1702–06) 255, 377

Gambarini, Giuseppe (1680–1725) 179

Gamberini, Italo (1907–1990) 166

Gamberucci, Cosimo (fl. 1598–1619) 111, 262, 397

Garzi, Luigi (1638–1721) 224

Garzoni, Giovanna (1600–70) 68

Gatti, Annibale (c 1827–1909) 230, 287

Gazzarrini, Tommaso (1790–1853) 282, 434

Gemignani, Alessio (d. 1651) 180

Gemignani, Giacinto (1606–81) 476

Genga, Girolamo (1476–c 1563) 361, 397

Genga, Simone (c 1530–95) 428

Gentile da Fabriano (c 1370–1427) 63, 251

Gentileschi, Orazio (Lomi; father of Artemisia; 1565–1647) 196

Gera see Jacopo di Michele

Gerini (Gerino da Pistoia; 1480–after 1529) 179

Gerini, Lorenzo di Nicolò (son of Niccolò di Pietro; fl. 1400–20) 465, 491

Gerini, Niccolò di Pietro (fl. 1368–1415) 67, 84, 109, 143, 162, 163, 164, 189, 249, 360, 450, 467

Gerino da Pistoia (Gerino d'Antonio Gerini; born 1480) 502, 503

Gherardi, Cristoforo see Il Doceno

Gherardi, Filippo (1643–1704) 203

Gherardi, Gaetano (fl. 1835–73) 286

Gherardini, Alessandro (1655–1723) 87, 141, 164, 231, 269, 275, 487

Ghezzi, Biagio di Goro (fl. 1368) 306

Ghiberti, Lorenzo (c 1378–1455) 49, 50, 53, 56, 75, 78, 82, 84, 85, 112, 154, 166, 178, 284, 357, 482, 487

Ghiberti, Vittorio (son of Lorenzo; 1419–96) 49, 85, 292

Ghidoni, Giovanni Battista (early 17C) 141, 506

Ghini, Antonio (fl. 1460–82) 296, 413

Ghini, Giovanni di Cristofori (fl. 1480–88) 344

Ghirlanda, Agostino (d. 1587) 240

Ghirlandaio, Davide (1451–1525; brother of Domenico) 78, 80, 118, 138

Ghirlandaio, Domenico (Domenico di Tommaso Bigordi; 1449–94) 62, 73, 75, 78, 80, 83, 118, 123, 124, 138, 155, 199, 237, 251, 272, 389, 395, 491

Ghirlandaio, Michele di Ridolfo del (Michele Tosini; 1503–77) 127, 135, 138, 215, 456

Ghirlandaio, Ridolfo del (son of Domenico; 1483–1561) 62, 70, 80, 119, 136, 158, 160, 179, 398, 476, 487, 494

Giambologna (Jean Boulogne or Giovanni Bologna; 1529–1608) 56, 60, 62, 73, 74, 78, 79, 81, 82, 104, 106, 186, 200, 226, 236, 271, 397, 455

Giaquinto, Corrado (c 1699–1765) 238

Giarrè, Pietro (fl. 1763–91) 259

Gimignani, Giacinto (1806–76) 173, 179, 180

Gino da Settignano (fl. 1531) 493

Giocchi, Ulisse (fl. c 1600) 273

Giordano, Luca (1632–1705) 74, 76, 91, 196, 342

Giorgione (Giorgio da Castelfranco; c 1478–1510) 64, 70

Giotto del Bondone (1266/67–1337) 54, 55, 63, 79, 82, 84, 88, 92, 115, 122, 201, 273

Giovanni d'Agnolo di Balduccio (c 1370–1452) 134, 250, 450, 456, 457, 475

Giovanni d'Agostino (c 1310–after 1347) 271, 296, 304, 345, 356, 357, 374, 401, 405, 432, 454

Giovanni d'Ambrogio (fl. 1384–1418) 52

Giovanni da Imola (fl. 1502) 202, 356

Giovanni da Milano (fl. 1350–69) 63, 84

Giovanni da Pistoia, Fra (fl. 1322) 450

Giovanni da San Giovanni (Giovanni Mannozzi; 1592–1636) 71, 80, 86, 68, 155, 173, 186, 188, 192, 262, 429, 482, 483

Giovanni da Verona (c 1457–1525) 350

Giovanni dal Ponte (1385–1437) 109, 492

Giovanni del Biondo (fl. 1356–92) 84, 120, 139, 142, 480, 482, 490

Giovanni del Brina (d. 1599) 187, 484

Giovanni delle Bombarde (d. 1478) 380

Giovanni di Cecco (d. 1397) 345, 352

Giovanni di Francesco (c 1428–1459) 86, 454, 455

Giovanni di Nicola (fl. 1358–60) 250, 255

Giovanni di Paolo (c 1403–82) 129, 299, 326, 338, 354, 360, 367, 371, 373, 375, 379, 383, 407, 412, 419, 426, 431, 437, 438, 460, 461

Giovanni di Simone (13C) 238, 240

Giovanni di Stefano (fl. 1246–72) 338, 349, 351, 365, 376, 377, 379, 380

Giovanni di Turino (c 1385–1455) 357, 364, 377, 506

Girolamo da Cremona (fl. 1467–83) 352, 361

Girolamo di Benvenuto (1470–1524) 297, 371, 376, 380, 381, 407, 424, 434, 436, 441

Giroldo da Como (fl 1267–74) 226, 309

Giuliano da Maiano (1432–90) 53, 62, 81, 83, 85, 159, 338, 370, 374, 389, 397, 458

Giuliano da Settignano (fl. 1460) 453

Giuliano di Baccio d'Agnolo (Giuliano Baglioni; 1491–1555) 263, 396

Giuliano di Simone di Lucca (fl. 1389) 205, 216

Giuseppe del Moro (fl. 1740–70) 148, 150

Giusto d'Andrea (1440–96) 145, 271

Giusto da Firenze (fl 1457) 469

Gori, Lorenzo (fl 1842–98) 284

Goro di Gregorio (fl. 1324–43) 309, 338

Gozzoli, Benozzo (Benozzo di Lese; 1420/22–97) 76, 88, 142, 145, 173, 240, 241, 244, 251, 270, 390, 393

Graffione (Giovanni di Michele Scheggini; 1455–c 1527) 87

Granacci, Francesco (1469/70–1541) 72, 102, 126, 141, 262, 458

Grazia, Leonardo (c 1502–48) 200

Greco, Emilio (born 1913) 191, 499
Gregorio di Cecco (fl. 1389–1424) 354
Griselli, Italo (1880–1958) 239, 253
Gruamonte (late 12C) 174, 180, 181
Guardi, Andrea (late 15C) 265, 294
Guardi, Andrea di Francesco (fl mid 15C) 236, 243
Guardi, Francesco (1712–92) 66
Guercino (Giovanni Francesco Barbieri; 1591–1666) 207, 367
Guglielmo, Fra da Pisa (Agnelli; 1256–c 1312) 174, 176, 243
Guidetto da Como (Bigarelli; 13C) 157, 198
Guido da Como see Bigarelli
Guido da Siena (late 13C) 297, 338, 350, 357, 358, 377, 391, 457
Guidocco d'Andrea (fl. 1440–69) 353
Guidotti, Paolo (1560–1629) 196, 202, 241
Guttuso, Renato (1912–87) 218

Hugford, Ignazio (1703–78) 108, 111, 115, 119, 180, 267, 488

Jacopo da Firenze (fl. c 1410) 276
Jacopo del Casentino (Landini; c 1300–49) 57, 120
Jacopo del Sellaio (1446–93) 91, 149, 154, 460, 461, 483
Jacopo di Cione (brother of Orcagna; fl c 1360–98) 109, 120, 267
Jacopo di Michele (Il Gera; fl 1389–90) 250, 262, 272, 288
Joli, Antonio (c 1700–77) 434
Juvarra, Filippo (1676–1736) 201, 209

Lafri, Jacopo (1549–1620) 177
Lamberti, Niccolò di Piero (c 1370–1451) 52, 55, 56, 162
Lanci, Baldassarre (c 1510–71) 377
Landi, Neroccio di Bartolomeo (1447–1500) 205, 327, 338, 348, 350, 351, 360, 376, 415, 438
Landino, Jacopo di (fl 1378–1403) 456
Lando di Pietro (d. 1340) 305, 345, 381
Landucci, Nicolau (1801–68) 204
Lanfranchi, Francesco di Angelo (Lo Spillo; fl. 1525–51) 262
Lanfranco da Como (fl. 1226) 178
Laparelli, Francesco (1521–70) 467, 468, 470, 472
Lapi, Niccolò (d. 1732) 141, 480, 481
Lappoli, Giovanni Antonio (1492–1552) 434
Lasinio, Carlo (1759–1838) 244
Laurana, Francesco (fl. 1458–1502) 82
Lazzari, Ottaviano (fl. 1613–17) 435
Lazzarini, Giovanni (1769–1834) 201, 218
Lazzerini, Alessandro (born 1860) 453
Lazzoni, Giovanni (1617/18–88) 208
Lazzoni, Tommaso (fl. 1672–97) 225
Lega, Silvestro (1826–95) 70, 265, 287
Leggi, Michelangelo (d. 1544) 469

Leonardo da Vinci (1452–1519) 50, 61, 62, 64, 151
Liberale da Verona (1451–1536) 352, 363, 441
Ligozzi, Jacopo (1543–1627) 68, 78, 80, 189, 196, 200, 206, 245, 255, 282, 390, 415, 456, 496, 497
Lippi, Filippino (son of Filippo; 1457–1504) 68, 72, 78, 83, 87, 88, 90, 91, 118, 160, 165, 168, 195, 199, 391, 434
Lippi, Filippo, Fra (1406/7–69) 64, 68, 76, 77, 119, 143, 149, 158, 159, 163, 165, 225, 262
Lippi, Lorenzo (1606–65) 68, 81, 163, 166, 180, 311, 477, 487, 493
Lippo di Benivieni (c 1320) 113, 134, 179
Locatelli, Pietro (c 1634–1710) 353
Lombardi, Giovanni Domenico (1682–1751) 196
Lomi, Aurelio (1556–1622) 90, 206, 238, 241, 244, 245, 248, 252, 255, 259, 262, 456
Lomi, Baccio (late 16C) 248, 255
Longhi, Alessandro (son of Pietro; 1733–1813) 66
Lorentino d'Arezzo (Lorentino d'Andrea; 1430–1506) 450, 452, 455, 458, 460, 503
Lorenzetti, Ambrogio (brother of Pietro; d. c 1348) 63, 134, 310, 329, 334, 338, 342, 344, 354, 360, 363, 367, 374, 375, 383, 404, 407, 412, 436
Lorenzetti, Pietro (brother of Ambrogio; c 1280–1348) 63, 88, 182, 338, 344, 360, 371, 374, 377, 417, 420, 422, 425, 452, 469
Lorenzetti, Ugolino (early 14C) 205
Lorenzetto, Lorenzo di Lotti (1490–1541) 177
Lorenzi, Battista (1528–93) 238
Lorenzi, Stoldo (1534–83) 236
Lorenzo di Bicci (c 1350–1427) 90, 131, 137, 148, 149
Lorenzo di Credi (1439–1537) 64, 72, 90, 96, 177, 179, 214, 431, 461
Lotto, Lorenzo (1480–1556) 66, 362
Luca di Tommè (c1330–after 1389) 251, 260, 330, 335, 358, 367, 370, 378, 386, 407, 408, 416, 434, 456, 477
Lucchesi, Urbano (1844–1906) 218
Luini, Bernardo (c 1475–1532) 64
Luti, Benedetto (1666–1724) 236

Maccari, Cesare (1840–1919) 339, 342, 364
Macchietti, Girolamo (1535–92) 78, 151, 456
Machiavelli, Zanobi (1418–79) 153, 205, 251
Maestro see also Master
Maestro Angelo (late 14C) 407
Maestro degli Ordini (14C) 262
Maestro del 1399 481
Maestro del Chiostro degli Aranci (15C) 83
Maestro del Crocifisso dei Disciplinati (14C) 373

Maestro del Dossale di San Pietro (late 13C) 358

Maestro del Vescovado (14C) 454

Maestro dell'Osservanza (14C–15C) 361, 362, 372, 375, 381, 412, 420

Maestro della Crocifissione di Camposanto di Pisa (fl. 1360–70) 241

Maestro della Maddalena (fl. late 13C) 107, 457, 496

Maestro della Madonna di Lucignano (school of Duccio; 13C–14C) 469

Maestro della Natività di Castello (15C) 159, 251, 287, 482

Maestro delle Clarisse (fl. 1280–85) 391

Maestro di Barberino (fl. c 1360) 110, 111

Maestro di Chianciano (early 14C) 443

Maestro di Città di Castello (fl. early 14C) 358

Maestro di Figline (or Maestro della Fogg Pietà; 1320–60) 85, 480

Maestro di Panzano (15C) 127, 407

Maestro di San Pietro a Ovile see Bulgarini, Bartolomeo

Maestro di Pratovecchio (fl. mid 15C) 165, 492

Maestro di San Lucchese see Cennino Cennini

Maestro di San Martino alla Palma (fl. 1330–50) 108, 156

Maestro di San Polo in Rosso (fl. 13–14C) 443, 497

Maestro di San Torpè (14C) 236, 250, 265

Maestro di Signa (15C) 101, 149

Maestro di Tressa (early 13C) 354, 358, 362

Maestro di Varlungo (13C) 284, 490

Maestro di Vicchio di Rimaggio (early 14C) 101

Maffei, Francesco (c 1625–60) 361

Magi, Luigi (fl. 1846) 297

Magistris, Giovanni Andrea de (fl. 1529–55) 480

Magnasco, Alessandro (Lissandrino; 1681–1747) 253, 458

Mainardi, Sebastiano (c 1460–1513) 84, 78, 155, 389, 393, 396

Maitani, Lorenzo (before 1275–1330) 338

Malatesta, Leonardo, da Pistoia (1483–after 1518) 180, 272, 391, 456

Manetti, Antonio (1423–97) 53, 77, 89, 93, 373

Manetti, Domenico (1609–1663) 330, 374, 376, 378, 432

Manetti, Rutilio (1571–1639) 134, 150, 151, 196, 206, 309, 311, 339, 342, 357, 361, 363, 364, 366, 367, 370, 371, 373, 375, 377, 379, 383, 397, 400, 404, 417, 424, 434

Mannaia, Guccio di (fl. 1292–1318) 375

Mannaioni, Giulio (fl. 1737) 116

Manno di Bandino (early 14C) 390

Mantegna, Andrea (1431–1506) 64

Maratta, Carlo (1625–1713) 179, 189, 224, 225, 350, 364, 484

Marcacci, Leonardo (fl. 1606–27) 182

Marcillat, Guglielmo di (c 1475–1529) 450, 454, 458, 465, 475

Marco Romano (fl. early 14C) 398, 400

Margaritone di Arezzo (13C) 118, 288, 358, 362, 433, 449, 455, 457, 460, 476,

Margheri, Rodolfo (1910–67) 401

Marinelli, Gaetano (1835–1924) 375

Marini, Marino (1901–66) 81, 174

Mariotto di Cristofano (1393–1457) 72, 155, 481, 483, 486, 500

Mariotto di Nardo (c 1373–1424) 80, 81, 99, 101, 109, 127, 149, 179, 362, 483

Marracci, Giovanni (1637–1704) 204

Marrina, Il (Lorenzo di Mariano; 1476–1534) 351, 338, 361, 366, 374, 378, 379, 444

Martelli, Valentino (c 1550–1630) 332

Marti, Leonardo (15C) 200, 205

Martinelli, Giovanni (c 1610–59) 141, 189

Martini, Francesco di Giorgio (1439–1502) 131, 338, 348, 350, 353, 356, 360, 361, 364, 365, 367, 370, 374, 377, 379, 381, 399, 400, 464

Martini, Quinto (1908–90) 171

Martini, Simone (c 1284–1344) 63, 88, 134, 250, 309, 338, 344, 358, 363, 375, 389, 425, 429

Martino di Bartolomeo (d. 1434/5) 200, 250, 260, 344, 389

Marucelli, Giovanni Stafano (1586–1646) 251

Masaccio (Tommaso Guido or Tommaso di Giovanni Cassai; 1401–c 1428) 79, 88, 90, 91, 251, 481, 482, 486

Mascagni, Domenico (1570/74–1637) 272

Mascagni, Donato (1579–1636) 267, 269

Mascagni, Leonardo (fl. 1589–1618) 162

Masi, Tommaso (d. 1806) 241

Maso di Banco (fl. 1341–46) 85, 90

Maso di Bartolomeo (1406–c 1456) 158, 159

Maso di San Friano (Tommaso Manzuoli; 1531–71) 62, 80, 179, 456, 496

Masolino da Panicale (Tommaso Fini; master of Masaccio; c 1383–1440) 91, 149, 150, 174, 263

Master; see also Maestro

Master of 1310 179, 181

Master of 1336   149

Master of 1419 392

Master of Badia a Isola (fl. late 13C) 397, 403

Master of Bagnano (13C; Meliore?) 144

Master of Borgo alla Collina (fl. 1408) 490, 494

Master of Frankfurt (fl. 1470–1538) 179

Master of Marradi (fl. late 15C) 116, 137

Master of Montemerano (15C) 326

Master of Monterotondo (school of Duccio; 14C) 312

Master of Prato (or of Karlsruhe; fl. early 15C) 165

Master of Remole (late 13C) 108

Master of San Francesco (13C) 450
Master of San Martino a Mensola (13C) 100
Master of San Miniato (late 15C) 124, 263, 490
Master of San Remigio (fl. c 1360) 86
Master of Santi Quirico e Giulitta (fl. early 15C) 262
Master of Santo Spirito (15C) 272
Master of Tavarnelle (or dei Cassoni Campana; fl. c 1510–15) 137
Master of the Buonconvento Cross (1300–30) 416
Master of the Horne Triptych (14C) 88, 107, 134
Master of the Madonna Straus (fl 1385–1415) 121, 492
Master of the Triumph of Death (fl. late 14C) 241, 242
Matas, Niccolò (1798–c 1872) 110, 497
Matteo di Giovanni (c 1435–95) 296, 304, 305, 338, 342, 344, 348, 349, 354, 360, 361, 363, 370, 371, 377, 378, 412, 413, 416, 419, 438, 475, 501, 503, 505
Matteucci, Antonio (fl. 1752–83) 379
Mazziere, Antonio di Donnino del (1497–1547) 90, 272, 460, 461
Mazzuoli, Annibale (c 1650–1743) 349, 378
Mazzuoli, Bartolomeo (d. 1749) 351, 367
Mazzuoli, Dionisio (d. after 1661) 367
Mazzuoli, Francesco (d. 1670) 373, 468
Mazzuoli, Giovanni Antonio (born before 1644–d. after 1706) 365, 367, 372, 373
Mazzuoli, Giuseppe (1644–1725) 277, 330, 348, 351, 353, 355, 356, 367, 381, 385, 424, 429
Medici, Don Giovanni de' (1566–1621) 245, 282, 373
Meglio, Jacopo Coppi di (1523–91) 78, 84
Mehus, Livio (1630–91) 162
Mei, Bernardino (1612–76) 163, 339, 362, 363, 373, 375
Melani, Francesco (1675–1742) 244, 251, 265
Melani, Giuseppe (1673–1747) 244, 251
Melchiorri, Giovanni Paolo (1664–1745) 397
Meliore di Jacopo (fl. late 13C) 127, 136
Melissi, Agostino (fl. 1642–75) 479
Memmi, Lippo (fl. 1317–47) 250, 338, 341, 360, 371, 377, 389, 390, 391, 393, 412
Memmo di Filippuccio (fl. 1294–1324) 344, 391, 393, 401
Mengoni, Giuseppe (1829–77) 77
Mengs, Anton Raphael (1728–79) 179
Meo di Piero (1345–70) 376
Meucci, Vincenzo (1699–1766) 148, 150, 230, 276, 370
Michelangelo Buonarroti (1475–1564) 55, 60, 62, 64, 72, 76, 78, 81, 82, 84, 86, 94, 101, 221, 223, 226, 352, 456, 499
Michele da Firenze (Michele di Niccolò Dini; d. after 1443) 151, 451, 457, 458

Michele di Matteo (15C) 253, 436
Micheli, Vincenzo (c 1830–1905) 230
Michelino da Besozzo (fl. 1388–1445) 54, 360
Michelozzo (Michelozzo di Bartolomeo; 1396–1472) 51, 52, 56, 61, 73, 76, 82, 84, 92, 93, 99, 104, 107, 111, 117, 118, 157, 180, 181, 251, 277, 431, 433
Michelucci, Giovanni (1891–1990) 155, 179, 191, 278, 399
Minella, Pietro del (1391–1458) 348, 350, 365
Minerbetti, Francesco (16C) 116
Minga, Andrea del (c 1540–96) 84
Mino da Fiesole (1429–84) 82, 83, 86, 97, 118, 122, 149, 158, 270, 397, 487, 495
Miranda, Bartolomeo (early 15C) 437
Mitelli, Agostino (1609–60) 71
Modigliani, Amedeo (1884–1920) 281
Monaco, Lorenzo (Fra Lorenzo degli Angioli; c 1370–1425) 63, 80, 96, 98, 149, 154, 165, 188, 360, 476
Monaldi, Bernardo (fl. 1588–1614) 144
Montagna, Bartolomeo (1450–c 1523) 362
Monti, Niccolò (born 1780) 471
Montorselli, Dionisio (1653–90) 372, 374, 417
Montorsoli, Giovanni Angelo (1507–63) 74, 270
Morandi, Giovanni Maria (1622–1717) 353, 468
Morandini see Poppi
Morghen, Raffaele (1758–1833) 434
Moroni, Giovanni Battista (c 1525–78) 66, 68, 362
Mosca, Francesco (c 1523–78) 236, 238, 241
Mosca, Simone (Moschini; 1492–1553) 457
Moschino, Simone (1560–1610) 226
Muccio di Rinaldo (14C) 341
Munari, Cristoforo (1667–1720) 434
Muratori, Domenico (c 1661–1744) 236
Mussini, Augusto (1870–1918) 493
Mussini, Luigi (1813–88) 342, 350

Naldini, Giovanni Battista (1537–91) 62, 78, 85, 99, 160, 166, 179, 196, 269, 275, 397, 434, 487
Nanni di Baccio Bigio (Giovanni Lippi; d. c 1568) 90, 474, 475
Nanni di Banco (Giovanni di Antonio di Banco; c 1380–1421) 52, 53, 55, 56
Nanni di Bartolo (fl. 1419–51) 55
Nardo di Cione (brother of Orcagna; 14C) 63, 79, 83
Nasini, Antonio (1643–1715) 297, 311, 331, 378
Nasini, Apollonio (1692–1786) 379
Nasini, Francesco (1621–95) 297, 329, 333, 335, 378
Nasini, Giuseppe Nicola (son of Francesco; 1657–1736) 138, 269, 304, 309, 329, 334, 353, 365, 371, 374, 375, 377, 379, 381, 412, 434

Natali, Francesco (d. 1723) 232
Natali, Giovanni Battista (fl. 1599–1621) 230, 231, 232
Navesi, Giovanni di Raffaello (fl. 1560–77) 353
Nebbia, Cesare (c 1536–1614) 431
Nelli, Pietro (fl. 1375) 111, 112
Neri di Bicci (1418–91) 80, 83, 88, 92, 97, 98, 100, 134, 137, 143, 149, 188, 189, 251, 262, 264, 271, 272, 276, 287, 391, 451, 494
Neri di Fioravante (fl. 1340–84) 56, 66
Neroccio di Bartolomeo see Landi
Neroccio, Goro di Ser (1387–1456) 353, 357
Neroni see Riccio
Nervi, Pier Luigi (1891–1979) 95
Niccolò di Mariano (15C) 181
Niccolò di Segna (son of Segna di Bonaventura; fl. 1331) 358, 371, 405, 502
Niccolò di Ser Sozzo (d. 1363) 390, 392, 401
Niccolò di Tommaso (fl. c 1350–80) 174
Nigetti, Matteo (1560–1649) 77, 81, 96, 253, 485
Nomellini, Plinio (1866–1943) 287
Notari, Francesco (19C) 330
Nottolini, Lorenzo (1787–1851) 203, 204, 218
Novelli, Paolo (fl. 1670) 415

Odazzi, Giovanni (1663–1731) 397
Ognabene, Andrea di Jacopo di (fl. 1287–1316) 177
Orcagna, Andrea (di Cione; fl. 1344–68) 57, 60, 79, 85, 86, 90, 92, 100, 163, 174, 241
Orioli, Pietro di Francesco (1458–96) 311, 338, 351, 357, 361, 381, 416, 438, 446
Orlandi, Deodato (fl. 1288) 204, 205, 250, 257, 263

Paccagnini, Francesco (1780–1832) 408
Pacchia, Girolamo del (1477–after 1533) 361, 365, 370, 374, 376, 400
Pace di Valentino (fl. 1265–90) 177
Paciarelli, Giovanni (19C) 356
Padovanino (Alessandro Varotari; 1580–1648) 362
Pagani, Gregorio (1558–1605) 179, 483
Paggi, Giovanni Battista (1554–1627) 200, 238, 249, 399
Pagni, Benedetto (fl. 1525–70) 188
Pagno di Lapo see Portigiani
Paladini, Filippo di Lorenzo (d. 1608) 181
Palma, Felice (1583–1625) 111, 225, 236, 253, 397
Palma Giovane (Giacomo Negretti; great nephew of Palma Vecchio; c 1544–1628) 255, 362, 465, 502
Palmezzano, Marco (1456–c 1539) 68
Pampaloni, Luigi (1791–1847) 148, 287
Paoletti, Gaspare Maria (1727–1813) 71, 184
Paolini, Pietro (1603–81) 195, 206

Paolino da Pistoia, Fra (1490–1547) 134, 173, 179, 180, 181, 390, 393
Papacello see Bernabei
Pardini, Giuseppe (fl. 1836–79) 212, 227
Parigi, Alfonso (the Elder; father of Giulio; d. 1590) 63
Parigi, Alfonso (the Younger; son of Giulio; d. 1656) 67
Parigi, Giulio (d. 1635) 67, 84
Parmigianino (Francesco Mazola; 1503–40) 64
Parri di Spinello Aretino (1387–c 1444) 342, 450, 452, 455, 457
Partini, Giuseppe (1842–95) 374, 442
Pascucci, Paride (1866–1954) 326
Pasquino di Matteo (c 1425–after 1475) 158
Passaglia, Augusto (1837–1918) 144
Passarotti, Bartolomeo (1529–92) 467
Passignano, Domenico (Cresti; 1560–1638) 90, 93, 111, 138, 139, 150, 177, 182, 189, 199, 204, 206, 238, 249, 255, 282, 390, 465, 496, 503
Pasti, Matteo de' (fl. 1441–64) 467
Pastorini, Pastorino de' (c 1508–92) 349
Pavolini, Jacopo (16C) 269
Pecci, Francesco (18C) 258
Pecori, Domenico (c 1480–1527) 454, 455, 458
Pellegrino di Mariano (Rossini; d. 1492) 353
Pellicciaio, Giacomo di Mino del (c 1315/20–1396) 372, 444
Pelori, Giovanni Battista (1483–1558) 367, 375, 414
Perin del Vaga (Pietro Buonaccorsi; 1500–47) 236, 456
Peroni, Giuseppe (1710–76) 230
Perugino (Pietro Vannucci; 1446–1523) 64, 70, 72, 74, 78, 87, 90, 363, 481, 502
Peruzzi, Baldassarre (1481–1537) 68, 318, 338, 350, 353, 364, 366, 370, 375, 380, 382, 383, 384, 436
Pesellino, Francesco (di Simone; 1422–57) 494
Petrazzi, Astolfo (1579–1665) 357, 363, 366, 371, 374, 395, 397, 417
Petroni, Francesco (1877–1960) 207
Petruccioli, Cola (d. 1408) 446
Piazzetta, Giovanni Battista (1683–1754) 66, 467, 470
Pier Francesco Fiorentino (15C) 149, 391, 393, 396, 398, 480
Pierallini, Andrea (19C) 481
Pieri, Rodomonte (fl. 1680) 189
Pierino da Vinci (nephew of Leonardo; 16C) 61, 104, 190, 252
Piero della Francesca (1416–92) 64, 450, 451, 454, 501, 502, 503, 507
Piero di Cosimo (pupil of Cosimo Rosselli; 1462–1521) 64, 97, 186
Piero di Giovanni Tedesco (fl. 1386–1402) 52
Piero di Puccio (fl. 1370–99) 240, 242

Pieroni, Alessandro (c 1550–1607) 281, 282

Pietro da Cortona (Berrettini; 1596–1669) 67, 68, 70, 182, 206, 374, 458, 464, 467, 468, 471

Pietro di Domenico (1457–c 1506) 297, 361, 401

Pietro di Giovanni Ambrogio (d. 1449) 412, 47

Pietro di Miniato (1366– c 1450) 164, 165

Pignoni, Simone (c 1611–98) 67, 134, 141, 395, 484

Pinturicchio (Bernardo di Betto; c 1454–1513) 225, 348, 351, 352, 361, 391, 445, 467

Pisanello (Antonio Pisano; 1377–1455) 82, 467

Pisano, Andrea (c 1270–1348/49) 49, 54, 56, 91, 177, 205, 250, 309

Pisano, Giovanni (son of Nicola; 1245–1320) 158, 164, 174, 176, 181, 237, 239, 240, 243, 244, 253, 264, 309, 338, 345, 348, 355, 356, 424, 472

Pisano, Giunta (fl. 1202–55) 250

Pisano, Nicola (c 1200–after 1278) 174, 199, 239, 243, 244, 294, 338, 345, 350, 351

Pisano, Nino (son of Andrea; 14C) 78, 177, 249, 250, 253, 261

Pisano, Tommaso (late 14C) 249

Poccetti, Bernardino (Barbatelli; c1542–1612) 74, 75, 92, 103, 110, 131, 259, 456, 458

Poccianti, Pasquale (1774–1858) 102, 167, 170, 281, 285

Poggi, Giuseppe (1811–1901) 94, 265

Poggini, Zanobi (fl. 1549) 159, 164

Pollaiolo, Antonio del (1433–98) 53, 56, 64, 82, 89, 93, 173, 271, 402, 431, 467

Pollaiolo, Piero del (brother of Antonio; 1443–96) 64, 93, 392

Pollastrini, Enrico (1817–76) 179, 286, 288

Pomarancio (Antonio Circignani; 1570/80–1630/40) 375, 446, 493, 342, 354

Pomarancio (Nicolò Circignani; c 1517–96) 270, 271, 275, 277

Pomarancio see also Roncalli, Cristoforo

Ponsi, Domenico (16C) 366

Pontelli, Baccio (c 1450–1492/5) 244

Pontormo (Jacopo Carrucci; 1494–1557) 62, 64, 67, 68, 73, 74, 87, 104, 150, 151, 167, 168, 171, 197, 503

Poppi, Il (Francesco Morandini; 1544–97)) 62, 160, 164, 182, 262, 263, 397, 456, 458, 496, 497

Porrina (Pietro Paolo; fl. 1469–78) 366

Porta, Orazio (late 16C) 475, 476

Portelli, Carlo (d. 1574) 87, 121, 456, 485, 496

Portigiani, Pagno di Lapo (1406–70) 74, 77, 263

Pozzi, Francesco (1779–1844) 281

Pozzo, Andrea (Padre; 1642–1709) 190, 431, 433, 458, 476

Preti, Mattia (Il Cavalier Calabrese; 1613–99) 177, 179, 350, 377

Priamo della Quercia see Quercia

Pseudo Pier Francesco Fiorentino (15C) 120, 437, 460, 461, 496

Pucci, Ambrogio (fl. 1529) 206

Pucci, Nicolao (fl. 1529) 206

Puccinelli, Angelo (14C) 189, 196, 205, 207, 226, 360

Pugliani, Cosimo (d. 1618) 252, 255

Puglieschi, Antonio (1600–1732) 141, 482

Puligo, Domenico (1492–1527) 87, 110, 505

Pulzone, Scipione (c 1550–98) 456

Quercia, Jacopo della (1371/4–1438) 90, 199, 200, 202, 205, 225, 253, 333, 338, 341, 342, 352, 356, 357, 364, 367, 370, 389, 506

Quercia, Priamo della (fl. 1426–67) 205, 353, 272, 273

Radi, Bernardino (1581–1643) 158, 471

Raffaele da Brescia (1479–1539) 415

Raffaellino de' Carli see Raffaellino del Garbo

Raffaellino del Colle (c 1490–1566) 501, 505

Raffaellino del Garbo (Raffaellino de' Carli; c 1466–1524) 72, 90, 97, 126, 146, 155, 165, 204, 401, 434, 469, 486, 487

Raffaello da Montelupo (c 1505–66) 117, 153, 190, 195

Raggi, Antonio (1624–86) 350

Rainaldo (12C) 235, 243

Ramignani, Tommaso (1596–1657) 182

Ranieri del Pace (1681–1737) 141, 275

Raphael (Raffaello Sanzio or Santi; 1483–1520) 64, 68, 70, 87, 253, 351

Redi, Tommaso (1665–1726) 93, 107, 356, 364, 365, 367, 376

Reni, Guido (1575–1642) 68, 70, 206, 253, 367

Ricci, Stefano (1765–1837) 84, 241, 455

Ricciarelli, Leonardo (16C) 269

Riccio Il (Bartolomeo Neroni; c 1500–71/73)) 62, 196, 206, 276, 329, 338, 350, 351, 364, 365, 375, 376, 380, 381, 383, 407, 412, 414, 416, 424

Riccomanni, Leonardo (fl. 1431–72) 221, 223, 224

Ridolfi, Michele (1793–1854) 198, 199

Righi, Angelo (early 17C) 432

Righi, Vincenzo (18C) 504

Riminaldi, Orazio (1586–1630) 236

Ristoro, Fra (d. 1284) 476

Rivalta, Augusto (1827–1925) 284

Robbia see Della Robbia

Romanelli, Giovanni Francesco (1616–62) 251, 364

Romanelli, Mariano d'Agnolo (d. 1390/92) 331, 338, 341, 391, 477

Romanelli, Pasquale (1812–87) 449

Romanelli, Raffaello (1856–1928) 379

Romano, Antoniazzo (fl. 1460–1508) 263

Roncalli, Cristoforo see Pomarancio

Rosa da Tivoli (1655/57–1706) 196, 198

Rosa, Salvator (1615–73) 66, 68, 90, 196, 198, 458

Rosi, Giovanni (1597–c 1673) 397

Rosi, Zanobi (fl. 1626) 236

Rosselli, Bernardo di Stefano (fl. 1474) 127, 138

Rosselli, Cosimo (1439–1507) 72, 87, 90, 97, 101

Rosselli, Domenico (c 1439–1498) 120, 261

Rosselli, Matteo (1578–1650) 74, 80, 81, 86, 87, 102, 107, 112, 115, 120, 154, 163, 164, 173, 179, 180, 186, 203, 221, 223, 224, 248, 262, 269, 270, 390, 458, 476, 481, 484, 506

Rossellino, Antonio (Gambarelli; 1427–79) 82, 84, 93, 149, 158, 173, 177, 487

Rossellino, Bernardo (Gambarelli; 1409–64) 74, 81, 83, 84, 101, 149, 150, 162, 338, 342, 362, 366, 419, 420, 422, 455

Rossetti, Giovan Paolo (d. 1586) 275

Rosso Fiorentino (Giovanni Battista Rosso; 1494–1541) 64, 70, 73, 77, 253, 271, 272, 276, 458, 505

Rosso, Francesco Zanobi del (1724–98) 83, 148

Rubens, Peter Paul (1577–1640) 66, 68, 70

Ruggeri, Ferdinando (c 1691–1741) 67, 148, 151, 472

Rustichino see Rustici

Rustici, Cristoforo (1560–1640) 371

Rustici, Francesco (1474–1554) 50, 145, 146, 365, 373, 378, 400, 411, 426

Sabatelli, Luigi (1772–1850) 115, 177, 179, 455, 487

Sagrestani, Giovanni Camillo (1660–1731) 90, 91, 110, 141, 164, 275, 470, 471, 477, 484

Salimbeni, Arcangelo (1530/40–after 1580) 365, 375, 402, 458

Salimbeni, Simondio (1597–1643) 361

Salimbeni, Ventura (1567/68–1613) 74, 196, 206, 238, 248, 249, 252, 296, 339, 342, 350, 364, 366, 371, 374, 376, 378, 380, 383

Salvei, Rombolus (14C) 178

Salvestrini, Bartolomeo (1599–1633) 141

Salvi d'Andrea (fl. 1457–83) 90

Salviati, Francesco de' (1510–63) 62

Sangallo, Antonio (da) il Vecchio (Giamberti; 1455–1537) 121, 284, 303, 398, 401, 431, 433, 435, 458, 475

Sangallo, Antonio (da) il Giovane (Cordiani; 1483–1546) 426, 431, 453

Sangallo, Francesco da (son of Giuliano; 1494–1576) 52, 57, 74, 103, 104, 162

Sangallo, Giuliano da (1443/45–1516) 79, 80, 83, 84, 87, 90, 155, 161, 166, 255, 322, 396, 401, 468, 477, 505

Sano di Matteo (fl. 1392–1434) 372

Sano di Pietro (1406–81) 297, 309, 310, 326, 330, 338, 344, 352, 354, 361, 362, 367, 371, 375, 378, 381, 395, 406, 407, 416, 419, 424, 432, 437, 441

Sansovino, Andrea (Andrea Contucci; c 1470–1529) 51, 90, 167, 270, 271, 441, 456, 474, 476

Sansovino, Jacopo (Tatti; pupil of Andrea; 1486–1570) 53, 82, 120, 232, 438

Santarelli, Emilio (1801–86) 281

Santi di Tito (1538–1603) 62, 79, 80, 85, 87, 103, 120, 123, 135, 136, 140, 144, 146, 162, 163, 186, 188, 215, 249, 263, 269, 277, 434, 455, 467, 468, 486, 487, 501, 503

Santini, Bernardino (1593–after 1652) 452, 457

Santini, Domenico (19C) 254

Santini, Vincenzo (1807–76) 221

Saraceni, Carlo (1585–1620) 179

Sarri, Egisto (19C) 480, 481

Sarrocchi, Tito (1824–1900) 341, 342, 365

Sarto see Andrea del Sarto

Sassetta (Stefano di Giovanni di Consolo; c 1392–1450) 66, 297, 310, 360, 362, 373, 375, 464, 469

Scaglia, Gerolamo (17C) 196, 206

Scalabrino, Lo (Giovanni Battista Volponi; 1489–after 1553) 379

Scalza, Ippolito (c 1532–1617) 432, 434

Scheggia, Lo (Giovanni di Ser Giovanni, brother of Masaccio; formerly known as the 'Master of the Cassone Adimari'; 1406–86) 53, 72, 482, 483, 486

Schiavo, Paolo (1397–1478) 60, 122, 123, 155, 450, 475, 483, 486, 491

Schiavone, Andrea (Meldolla; 1520–63) 198

Sebastiano del Piombo (Luciani; c 1485–1547) 64

Segna di Bonaventura (fl. 1298–1331) 297, 309, 358, 371, 397, 400, 412, 415, 420, 458, 461, 481

Sellaio see Jacopo del Sellaio

Sellari, Andrea (17C) 465, 468

Serbelloni, Gabrio (1508–80) 472

Severini, Gino (1883–1966) 371, 464, 465, 467, 469, 472

Sgrilli, Bernardo (18C) 190

Signoraccio see Bernardino di Antonio

Signorelli, Francesco (d. after 1553) 467, 468

Signorelli, Luca (c 1441–1523) 64, 68, 87, 165, 272, 364, 414, 424, 434, 436, 437, 451, 455, 456, 461, 463, 465, 467, 469, 471, 473, 477, 503

Signori, Sergio (d. 1990) 227

Signorini, Telemaco (1835–1901) 70, 287

Silvani, Gherardo (1579–c 1685) 81, 86, 111, 158, 484, 487

Silvani, Pier Francesco (1620–85) 81, 90

Sodoma (Giovanni Antonio dei Bazzi; 1477–1549) 103, 198, 237, 338, 342, 344, 354, 361, 363, 365, 370, 371, 373, 374, 376, 378, 383, 391, 414, 415, 436, 437, 439

Soggi, Niccolò (c 1480–1552) 450, 455, 458

Sogliani, Giovanni Antonio (1491–1544) 75, 96, 149, 150, 163, 236, 237, 255, 505

Soldani–Benzi, Massimiliano (1658–1740) 484

Soldini, Domenico (16C) 190

Solosmeo, Antonio (fl. 1525–36) 496

Somazzi, Angelo Maria (d. 1773) 259

Sorbi, Giovanni Battista (18C) 378

Sordo, Giovanni (Mone; 16C)) 255

Sorri, Pietro (c 1556–1621) 352, 374, 375, 496

Sozzini, Giovanni Battista (1525–82) 348

Sozzo, Niccolò di Ser (d. 1363) 344, 371

Spagnoletto, Lo (Giuseppe Ribera; 1590–1652) 179, 508

Spigliati, Piero di Martino (fl. 1552–59) 484

Spinazzi, Innocenzo (d. 1798) 51, 84

Spinelli, Niccolò di Luca (late 14C) 454

Spinello Aretino (fl. 1373–1410) 80, 84, 94, 111, 240, 242, 249, 251, 342, 360, 449, 450, 452, 453, 455, 458

Stagi, Lorenzo (1455–1506) 220, 221, 223

Stagi, Stagio (1496–1563) 220, 222, 225, 236, 238, 242, 243, 275

Starnina, Lo (Gherardo di Jacopo; formerly known as 'Maestro del Bambino Vispo'; c 1354–1413) 149, 205

Stradano, Giovanni (1523–1605) 62, 74, 79, 85, 90, 456

Strozzi, Bernardo ('Prete Genovese'; 1581–1644) 253, 362

Susini, Clemente (1765–1814) 92, 120

Sustermans, Justus (1597–1681) 66, 70, 168, 434

Tacca, Ferdinando (1616/19–86; son of Pietro) 107, 158, 160, 221, 225, 282, 397

Tacca, Pietro (1577–1664) 57, 73, 82, 139, 182, 245, 226, 236, 284, 367, 284, 397

Taddeo di Bartolo (1363–1422) 141, 249, 250, 252, 269, 271, 272, 338, 342, 353, 360, 371, 372, 389, 391, 398, 402, 405, 412, 432, 438, 477

Tais, Giacomo (beginning of 18C) 186, 189

Talenti, Fra Jacopo (d. 1362) 78, 79

Talenti, Francesco (14C) 52, 54, 56

Talenti, Simone (14C) 56, 57, 60

Tallino d'Ognabene (13C) 178

Tamagni, Vincenzo (1492–c 1530) 278, 299, 311, 390, 392, 393, 401, 402, 407, 408, 415

Tarchiani, Filippo (fl. 1619–21) 141, 397

Tarocchi, Mattia (late 18C) 265

Tempesti, Giovanni Battista (1732–1804) 241, 265

Terreni, Giuseppe Maria (1739–1811) 102, 259

Testa, Pietro (c 1611–50) 196

Tiarini, Alessandro (1577–1658) 188, 252

Ticciati, Girolamo (1671–1744) 115, 117

Ticciati, Pompilio (fl. 1731–77) 107

Tiepolo, Giovanni Battista (1696–1770) 66

Tino da Camaino (c 1280–1337) 53, 56, 81, 82, 85, 89, 90, 149, 181, 205, 225, 236, 237, 243, 250, 338, 348, 351, 356, 393, 506

Tintoretto, Jacopo (Robusti; 1519–94) 64, 68, 70, 198, 199

Titian (Tiziano Vecellio; 1480/85–1576) 64, 68, 70, 86

Tofanelli, Stefano (1752–1812) 198, 200, 209, 214

Tommasi, Angiolo (1858–1923) 287

Tommasi, Leone (1903–65) 221

Tonghio, Francesco del (c 1300–88) 350

Tornioli, Niccolò (fl. 1622–40) 357, 397

Torrigiani, Pietro (1472–1528) 352, 390, 391

Torrita, Fra Jacopo da (fl. late 13C) 435

Toscani, Giovanni (c 1370–1430) 151, 159, 494

Traballesi, Giuliano (1727–1812) 375

Traini, Francesco (14C) 205, 241, 242, 249, 250, 253, 362

Traversari, Ambrogio (1386–1439) 493

Treves, Marco (19C) 250

Trevisani, Francesco (1656–1746) 251, 352

Tribolo, Niccolò (Pericoli; 1485–1550) 71, 75, 77, 82, 86, 104, 105, 241, 244

Trombetto, Tommaso di Piero (1464–c 1530) 160

Turapilli, Ventura (d. 1522) 353, 374

Turco, Flaminio del (d. 1634) 309, 349, 350, 364, 366

Turino di Sano (fl. 1382–1427) 357

Tuscher, Marco (1705–51) 466

Uccello, Paolo (Doni; 1397–1475) 53, 54, 64, 79, 144, 159, 165, 263, 491

Ugolino di Nerio (early 14C) 129, 134, 297, 358, 438, 481

Urbano da Cortona (c 1426–1504) 311, 345, 348, 350, 353, 356, 362, 374, 405, 413, 424, 468

Vaccà, Andrea (early 18C) 178, 190, 238, 244

Vaccà, Giovanni Battista (fl. 1711–50) 236

Vagnetti, Italo (1864–1933) 122

Valadier, Giuseppe (1762–1839) 455

Valdambrino, Francesco di (c 1380–1435) 149, 179, 196, 199, 200, 205, 206, 213, 222, 250, 251, 264, 270, 272, 338, 355, 374, 390, 407, 408, 412, 424, 428, 432

Valentini, Giuseppe (1752–1833) 160, 161, 164

Vanni, Andrea (c 1332–1413) 370, 374, 377, 379

Vanni, Francesco (1563–1610) 131, 182, 196, 203, 214, 236, 249, 294, 323, 333, 339, 351, 357, 361, 364, 365, 367, 370, 372, 374, 375, 377, 379, 383, 408, 436, 437, 456

Vanni, Giovanni Battista (1599–1660) 163, 263

Vanni, Lippo (fl. 1341–75) 344, 374, 384, 390, 476

Vanni, Raffaello (1587–after 1657) 249, 310, 349, 357, 364, 365, 367, 370, 373, 378, 429, 458, 468, 471

Vannini, Ottavio (1585–1643) 150, 397, 496

Vanvitelli, Gaspare (Gaspar van Wittel; 1653–1736) 160, 363

Vasari, Giorgio (1512–74) 53, 57, 61, 63, 66, 74, 77, 79, 84, 85, 87, 123, 152, 166, 182, 206, 245, 282, 449, 453, 456, 457, 458, 460, 469, 471, 472, 474, 475, 477, 481, 493

Vasari, Lazzaro (c 1399–after 1452) 456

Vecchietta (Lorenzo di Pietro; 1410–80) 205, 310, 326, 338, 344, 350, 352, 353, 357, 361, 362, 367, 372, 378, 380, 407, 419, 420, 425, 432

Veli, Benedetto (1564–1639) 138

Velli, Cesare (fl. 1591) 115

Veneziano, Antonio (1319–83) 240, 242, 250, 255

Veneziano, Domenico (1404–61) 64, 173

Veracini, Agostino (1689–1762) 110, 141, 269

Veronese, Paolo (Caliari; 1528–88) 64, 70, 196

Verrocchio, Andrea del (1435–88) 52, 56, 61, 62, 64, 77, 82, 85, 87, 90, 173, 177, 215, 262

Viani, Lorenzo (1882–1936) 184, 218

Vignali, Jacopo (1592–1664) 68, 81, 86, 93, 110, 115, 134, 180, 196, 259, 264, 275, 492

Vignola (Jacopo Barocci; 1507–73) 431

Viligiardi, Arturo (1869–1936) 350, 365, 441

Vincenzo da Cortona (fl. 1502–17) 469

Vini, Sebastiano (c 1525/39–1602) 192

Vitale da Bologna (fl. 1320–60) 241

Vite, Antonio (d. 1407) 174

Vitoni, Ventura (1442–1532) 178, 181, 182

Volpi, Stefano (1594–after 1640) 365

Volterrano (Baldassarre Franceschini; 1611–89) 68, 74, 85, 104, 188, 259, 272, 273, 276, 487

Ximenes, Ettore (1855–1926) 287

Zacchi, Zaccaria (1473–1544) 276, 278, 311, 396

Zacchia da Vezzano (fl. 1519–61) 204

Zacchia, Lorenzo (1524–87) 196

Zeti, Giovanni (d. c 1640) 188

Zoboli, Jacopo (1661–1761) 251

Zocchi, Arnaldo (1862–1940) 444, 504

Zocchi, Cesare (1851–1922) 241, 254

Zuccarelli, Francesco (1702–88) 322

Zuccari, Federico (1542–1609) 53, 196, 199, 204, 206, 431

Zucchi, Jacopo (1541–c 1590) 62, 374

Index

Abbadia a Sicille 439
Abbadia Isola 402
Abbadia San Salvatore 330
Abetone 192
Accademia della Crusca 105
Acciaioli, Niccolò 103
Acquacheta waterfall 123
Acton, Sir Harold 95
Agnolo II, Cardinal 103
Agostini, Leonardo 312
Albany, Countess of 87
Alberese 313
Albergotti, Bishop 454
Alberti, Conti 140, 145
Aldobrandeschi family 298, 315, 322, 323, 325, 327, 332, 333
Alexander II 198
Alexander III 337, 342
Alexander VI 420
Alexander VII 362
Alfieri, Vittorio 84
Alfonso of Aragon 299
Algarotti, Francesco 240
Altomena 109
Altopascio 209
Altoviti, Prior Oddo 60
Ammannati, Cardinal 422
Ancaiano 385
Anchiano 151
Ancisa 479
Andrei, Tommaso, Bishop 400
Angeli, Pietro 214
Anghiari 505
Ansedonia 319
Antella 111
Antignano 288
Aragazzi, Bartolomeo 432
Aramo 190
Arcetri 102
Arcidosso 333
Ardenza 288
Aretino, Pietro 449
Arezzo 447
Argegna 216
Argentario 317
Ariosto, Ludovico 215
Arliano 219
Arni 215
Artimino 171

Asciano 412
Atti, Isabella degli 323
Aulla 230
Azzano 223

Baciocchi, Elisa 167, 194, 209, 212
Badia a Conéo 399
Badia a Passignano 137
Badia a Ripoli 110
Badia al Fango 301
Badia del Borgo 116
Badia di Buonsolazzo 121
Badia di Cantignana 209
Badia di Coltibuono 129
Badia di San Salvatore a Settimo 155
Badia di San Salvatore a Soffena 486
Badia Prataglia 498
Badia Tedalda 508
Badiola, La 301
Bagnaia 513
Bagni Caldi 212
Bagni di Cetica 494
Bagni di Lucca 212
Bagni di Petriolo 306
Bagni San Filippo 426
Bagno a Ripoli 109
Bagno alla Villa 212
Bagno Vignoni 425
Balbo, Italo 302, 316
Baratti 292
Barberino di Mugello 118
Barberino Val d'Elsa 139
Barbiana 121
Barbischio 129
Bardini, Stefano 89, 102
Bardini, Ugo 89
Barga 213
Barsanti, Eugenio 220
Battifolle, Count Simone da 495, 499
Bellarmino, Cardinal Roberto 429
Bellosguardo 103
Belverde 446
Beni, Carlo 490
Benincasa, Caterina; see St Catherine of Siena 376
Berenson, Bernard 100
Bertini, Domenico 199

Bibbiani 154
Bibbiena 496
Bilancino 118
Biodola 512
Bivigliano 106
Blagden, Isa 95, 103
Boccaccio, Giovanni 78, 100, 101, 144, 367,427
Boccheggiano 312
Boccherini, Luigi 194, 204
Bolgheri 291
Bonaparte, Paolina 218
Bonizella, Beata 438
Bonucci, Cardinal Stefano 454
Borgia, Roderigo 420
Borgo a Buggiano 186
Borgo a Mozzano 212
Borgo alla Collina 494
Borgo San Lorenzo 114
Borgo San Sepolcro 385
Borro, Girolamo 454
Bosco ai Frati 117
Bosco di Camporena 146
Bottagone 294
Bourbon, Marie Louise de 194, 201, 207
Bracciolini, Poggio 54, 485
Brancacci, Felice 91
Brandi, Cesare 381
Bresci, Gaetano 227
Brolio 129
Brollo 479
Browning, Robert and Elizabeth Barrett 92, 95, 103, 212, 234
Brozzi 155
Brunella 230
Bruni, Leonardo 84
Bucelli, Pietro 431
Buggiano Castello 187
Buitoni family 501
Buonconvento 416
Buriano 303
Burlamacchi, Francesco 194
Byron, Lord (George Gordon) 212, 234, 251, 281, 286

Cafaggiolo 118
Cala Martina 302

Cala Violina 302
Calci 258
Caldana 303
Calomini 214
Calvino, Italo 300
Calzoni, Umberto 445
Camaiore 220
Camaldoli 492
Camigliano 209
Camoggiano 119
Campagnatico 306
Campaldino 493
Campi Bisenzio 155
Campiglia d'Orcia 426
Campiglia Marittima 292
Campo Cecina 229
Campocatino 216
Camporgiano 216
Camucia 472
Cancelli 486
Caniparola 229
Capalbio 320
Capoliveri 513
Cappello, Bianca 92, 121
Cappuccini 334
Capraia (Montelupo
    Fiorentino) 154
Capraia, Island of 513
Caprese Michelangelo 499
Caprona 260
Carda 500
Carducci, Giosuè 222, 291
Carmignano 171
Carosi, Bartolomeo 438
Carrara 225
Casa Rossa 301
Casale Marittimo 290
Casali family 466
Cascia 486
Casciana Alta 265
Casciana Terme 264
Cascina 260
Casentino 488
Casola in Lunigiana 229
Casole d'Elsa 399
Casone 401
Castagneto Carducci 291
Castagneto, Donoratico.
    290
Castagno d'Andrea 123
Castagno, Il 146
Castel Castagnaio 489
Castel del Piano 329
Castel di Pietra 304
Castel Focognano 500
Castel Gilardi 473
Castel Ruggero 127

Castel San Niccolò 494
Castelfalfi 146
Castelfiorentino 141
Castelfranco di Sopra 486
Castelfranco di Sotto 261
Castellina in Chianti 131
Castello del Trebbio
    (Pontassieve) 108
Castello di Trebbio (San
    Piero a Sieve) 118
Castello di Belcaro 383
Castello di Celsa 384
Castello di Porciano 490
Castello di Romena 489
Castello di Volpaia 128
Castelluccio Bifolchi 426
Castelmuzio 438
Castelnuovo Berardenga
    129
Castelnuovo dei Sabbioni
    483
Castelnuovo dell'Abate
    408
Castelnuovo di Garfagnana
    215
Castelnuovo di Val di Cecina
    278
Castelvecchio 190
Castelvecchio Pascoli 215
Castiglion Fiorentino 460
Castiglioncello 290
Castiglione dei Pepoli 172
Castiglione della Pescaia
    299
Castiglione di Garfagnana
    216
Castiglioni 124
Castliglione d'Orcia 425
Castracani, Castruccio 151,
    154, 173, 194, 201,
    203, 213, 220, 221
Catalani, Alfredo 207
Cattani, Count Orlando
    118, 498, 499
Caval
lina 118
Cavo 513
Cavriglia 483
Ceci, Antonio 253
Cecina 290
Celle dei Puccini 212
Celsa, Castello di 384
Cennina 485
Cerbaia 171
Cerbaiolo 508
Cercignani 278
Cercina 104
Cerreto Guidi 151

Certaldo 144
Certomondo 494
Certosa del Galluzzo 103
Certosa di Maggiano 381
Certosa di Pisa 259
Certosa di Pontignano 131
Cetica 494
Cetinale 384
Cetona 445
Cevoli 265
Charlemagne 155, 293,
    337, 409
Charles Edward Stuart (the
    'Young Pretender') 87
Charles IV, Emperor 194, 337
Charles of Anjou 337, 484
Charles V, Emperor 414
Charles VIII of France 234
Chelli, Giovanni 297
Chellini, Giovanni 263
Chianciano Terme 443
Chianciano Vecchia 443
Chianti 124
Chiarone 321
Chiessi 512
Chigi Saracini, Count Guido
    362
Chigi, Agostino 364
Chigi, Cardinal Flavio 385,
    423
Chitignano 500
Chiusdino 405
Chiusi 440
Chiusi della Verna 498
Cino da Pistoia 173, 176
Cintoia 127
Cireglio 191
Civitella in Val di Chiana
    474
Civitella Marittima 306
Clement IX 173, 182
Clement VI 234, 414
Clough, Arthur Hugh 95
Collazzi, I 144
Colle di Casaglia 116
Colle di Val d'Elsa 394
Collodi 190
Colognole 127
Colonnata 228
Comeana 170
Compagno, Gherardo di
    249
Compiobbi 108
Conca di Sotto 220
Conrad, Joseph 510
Consuma 109
Contignano 427

Convento delle Celle 473
Cooper, James Fenimore 285
Corbelli, Monsignor 467
Coreglia Antelminelli 213
Corfino 216
Corsanico 220
Corscia, Baldassarre 51
Cortona 463
Cosa 319
Costaguti, Bishop 503
Cotone 326
Crawford, Francis Marion 212
Crespina 265
Croce Arcana 192
Cuna 417
Cutigliano 192
Cuvier, Georges 485
Cybo, Lorenzo 225

D'Annunzio, Gabriele 164, 218, 222
D'Orso, Antonio 53
Dama 498
Dante Alighieri 49, 83, 84, 123, 148, 176, 229, 248, 304, 387, 395, 402, 489, 493,
Dati, Francesco Leonardo 78
Datini, Francesco di Marco 157, 162, 163, 165
Davidsohn, Robert 95
Davy, Humphry 92
Decio, Filippo 242
Della Ragione, Alberto 61
Della Rovere, Vittoria 212
Demidoff family 106, 512
Dennis, George 324
Di Monte family 474, 475
Diacceto 109
Dickens, Charles 252
Dicomano 123
Diecimo 212
Doccia (Santa Brigida) 105
Doccia (Sesto Fiorentino) 108
Doganaccia 192
Dolci, Carlo 159
Donato da Cascia 486
Donoratico 291
Doria, Andrea 226
Dostoyevsky, Fyodor 92
Dovizi, Bernardo 496
Dudley, Sir Robert 81, 88, 105, 257, 280, 284

Duff Gordon, Lina 230
Dumas, Alexandre 514
Duncan, Isadora 218
Duse, Eleonora 218

Elba 509
Eleonora di Toledo 62, 79
Eliot, George 81
Empoli 147
Equi 229
Eugenius III, Pope 389
Eugenius IV 498
European Universtiy Institute 96

Faggiola, Uguccione della 185
Faltona 121
Fantiscritti 228
Faraday, Michael 92
Farneta 473
Fattori, Giovanni 288
Fattoria di Celle 183
Felici, Cristoforo 374
Ferdinando I; *see* Medici
Ferdinando II; *see* Medici
Ferdinando III (Lorraine grand-duke) 71, 433
Ferrone 127
Ferrucci, Francesco 192, 267
Fibbialla 190
Fibonacci, Leonardo 234
Ficino, Marsilio 480
Fiesole 96
Figline di Prato 171
Figline Valdarno 479
Firenzuola 121
Fivizzano 230
Flaccus, Persius 267
Florence 45
  Badia Fiorentino 83
  Baptistery 49
  Biblioteca Laurenziana 77
  Bibilioteca Nazionale 86
  Biblioteca Riccardiana 76
  Boboli Gardens 71
  Borgo Ognissanti 80
  Borgo degli Albizi 83
  Borgo San Frediano 91
  British Institute 92
  Campanile 54
  Cappella di San Sepolcro 81
  Casa Buonarroti 86
  Cascine 87

Florence cont'd
  Casino Mediceo 75
  Cenacolo di Fuligno 77
  Cenacolo di Santo Spirito 90
  Chiostro dello Scalzo 75
  Church of San Marco 75
  Duomo 51
  English Cemetery 95
  Forte di Belvedere 93
  Fortezza da Basso 94
  Galleria dell'Accademia 72
  Galleria d'Arte Moderna 70
  Galleria del Costume 71
  Galleria Palatina 68
  Galleria di Palazzo Pitti 67
  Galleria degli Uffizi 63
  Giardino dei Semplici 75
  Giardino dell'Orticoltura 95
  Loggia del Bigallo 54
  Market of Sant'Ambrogio 87
  Medici Chapels 77
  Mercato Centrale 77
  Mercato Nuovo 57
  Misericordia 54
  Museo Archeologico 74
  Museo degli Argenti 71
  Museo del Bigallo 54
  Museo di Firenze com'era 83
  Museo Horne 88
  Museo Marino Marini 81
  Museo Nazionale di Antropologia ed Etnologia 83
  Museo Nazionale del Bargello 81
  Museo dell'Opera del Duomo 55
  Museo dell'Opera di Santa Croce 85
  Museo dell' Opificio delle Pietre Dure 73
  Museo di Orsanmichele 57
  Museo di Santa Maria Novella 79
  Museo di San Marco 75
  Museo Stibbert 94
  Museo di Storia della Scienza 88
  Museum of Musical Instruments 72
  Neptune Fountain 60
  Ognissanti 80

Florence cont'd
Oltrarno 67, 89
Orsanmichele 56
Palazzo Antinori 81
Palazzo dell'Arte della
Lana 57
Palazzo dell'Arte dei
Baccai 57
Palazzo dell'Arte della Seta
57
Palazzo Bardi alle Grazie
86
Palazzo del Bargello 81
Palazzo Bartolini Salim-
beni 81
Palazzo Buondelmonti 81
Palazzo dei Congressi 94
Palazzo Corsini 87
Palazzo Davanzati 57
Palazzo Frescobaldi 91
Palazzo Gondi 83
Palazzo Guadagni 90
Palazzo Larderel 81
Palazzo Manetti 91
Palazzo Masetti 87
Palazzo Medici-Riccardi
76
Palazzo Mellini Fossi 86
Palazzo dei Mozzi 89
Palazzo di Parte Guelfa 57
Palazzo Pitti 67
Palazzo Rinuccini 91
Palazzo Rucellai 81
Palazzo Spini-Feroni 80
Palazzo Strozzi 81
Palazzo degli Uffizi 63
Palazzo Vecchio 61
Piazza Beccaria 95
Piazza del Carmine 90
Piazza Donatello 95
Piazza della Libertà 95
Piazza Pitti 92
Piazza della Repubblica 56
Piazza della Signoria 60
Piazza San Felice 92
Piazza San Lorenzo 76
Piazza San Marco 75
Piazza Santa Croce 84
Piazza Santa Maria
Novella 79
Piazza Santo Spirito 90
Piazza Santa Trìnita 81
Piazza Santissima Annun-
ziata 73
Piazza Santo Spirito 90
Piazzale Michelangelo 94
Ponte alla Carraia 87

Florence cont'd
Ponte alle Grazie 88
Ponte Santa Trìnita 87
Ponte Vecchio 66
Porta San Frediano 91
Porta San Giorgio 93
Rotonda di Santa Maria
degli Angeli 73
Russian Church 94
St Mark's Anglican
Church 92
San Felice 92
San Filippo Neri 83
San Firenze 83
San Frediano in Cestello
91
San Gaetano 81
San Giorgio sulla Costa 93
San Jacopo sopr'Arno 92
San Leonardo in Arcetri
93
San Lorenzo 76
San Marco 75
San Martino del Vescovo
83
San Michele Visdomini 73
San Miniato al Monte 93
San Niccolò Sopr'Arno 89
San Pancrazio 81
San Remigio 86
San Salvatore al Monte 94
San Salvi 95
Sant'Ambrogio 86
Sant'Apollonia 76
Sant'Egidio 83
Santa Croce 84
Santa Felicita 67
Santa Margherita
de'Cerchi 83
Santa Maria del Carmine
90
Santa Maria Maddelena
dei Pazzi 87
Santa Maria Maggiore 81
Santa Maria Novella 78
Santa Maria Nuova 83
Santa Reparata 53
Santa Trìnita 80
Santissima Annunziata 73
Santo Spirito 89
Spedale degli Innocenti 73
Synagogue 87
Torre della Castagna 83
Torre Marsili di Borgo 92
Tribunale di Mercanzia 61
Via de'Bardi 89
Via di Belvedere 93

Florence cont'd
Via dei Benci 86
Via de' Calzaioli 56
Via Maggio 92
Via Romana 92
Via di San Leonardo 93
Via di San Niccolò 89
Via Tornabuoni 80
Viale dei Colli 94
Viale Filippo Strozzi 94
Viali 94
Villa La Pietra 95
Zoological Museum 92
Foce di Carpinelli Pass 216
Foce delle Radici Pass 216
Foiano della Chiana 477
Follonica 302
Fonteblanda 314
Fonterutoli 131
Fornovolasco 215
Forte dei Marmi 218
Forte di Bibbona 290
Forteguerri, Cardinal
Niccolò 177, 182
Fosdinovo 229
Franceschini, Canon Pietro
273
Francesco da Barberino
139
Francesco I; see Medici
Franchi, Andrea 173
François, Alessandro 472
Frascole 123
Frassine 312
Frederick II, Emperor 162,
261
Frederick III, Emperor 380
Frosini 405
Fucci, Vanni 176
Fucecchio 151
Fucini, Renato 252, 312
Futa, La 119

Gabbiano castle 127
Gabrielli, Pirro Maria 364
Gaiole in Chianti 129
Galatrona 485
Galilei, Galileo 66, 84, 85,
88, 92, 93, 102, 324,
238, 239, 254
Galliano 118
Gallicano 214
Galluzzo 103
Gambacorti, Pietro 255
Gambassi Terme 145
Garfagnana 210
Gargonza 476

Garibaldi, Giuseppe 186, 252, 302, 314, 437
Gaville 481
Gavinana 191
Gavorrano 304
Geminiani, Francesco 194, 204
Gessi, Romolo 209
Gherardesca family 234, 248, 291
Gherardini, Raffaello Gherarduccio dei 139
Ghiaccioforte 326
Ghini, Luca 245
Ghivizzano 213
Giglio 319
Giannutri 319
Giardino dei Tarocchi 321
Giles, Sylvester 195
Ginori, Leopoldo Carlo 105
Giogo di Scarperia 121
Giovanni da Verrazzano 126
Giovi 500
Giugni, Bernardo 83
Giulia, Beata 145
Giuncugnano 216, 229
Giusti, Giuseppe 186, 252
Golf courses (18-hole) 41
Gombo 257
Gorgona 514
Gori, Giuliano 184
'Gothic Line' 113
Grassina 111
Gregory VII 323, 324
Greve in Chianti 126
Grezzano 116
Gricigliano 108
Gropina 485
Grosseto 296
Grotta del Vento 215
Guarnacci, Monsignor Mario 273, 276
Guidi family 151, 275, 276, 484, 488, 489, 490, 494, 495
Guidiccioni, Giovanni 204
Guido d'Arezzo 449
Guido Monaco 500
Guinigi family 199, 200, 203, 221

Hadrian I, Pope 293
Hawkwood, Sir John 54, 118
Hawthorne, Nathaniel 103
Henderson, George 287

Henry VII, Emperor 236, 243, 416
Hildebrand, Adolf 103
Hildebrand, Bishop 93
Hoefer, Franz 278
Horne, Herbert Percy 88
Hunt, James Leigh 234, 286
Huxley, Aldous 219, 503

Impruneta 111
Incisa Valdarno 479
Indicatore 461
Inghirami, Filippo degli 159
Inghirami, Gimignano 162
Istia d'Ombrone 299

James, Henry 79, 103
John VIII 331
Jones, Inigo 282
Joseph, Patriarch of Constantinople 78
Julius III 474

La Foce 426
La Verna 498
Lago dell'Accesa 312
Lago di Burano 321
Lago di Chiusi 443
Lago di Massaciuccoli 219
Lago di Montepulciano 443
Lago Prile 301
Lagoon of Orbetello 316
Lamartine, Alphonse de 212
Lammari 209
Lamole 128
Landini, Cristofano 494
Landor, Walter Savage 95, 212
Lanfranchi, Abp Ubaldo 240
Larderel family 278, 281
Larderello 278
Lari 265
Lastra a Signa 154
Laterina 461
Lawrence, D.H. 156, 230
Lazzaretti, Davide 334
Lazzari, Filippo 173
Le Grazie 399
Le Quattro Strade 136
Le Sieci 108
Lecceto 383
Leghorn 279
Leo the Great, Pope 267
Leo X 118

Leoni, Diomede 424
Leopardi, Giacomo 234, 244
Leopoldo II (grand-duke) 123, 221, 277, 278, 296, 297, 298, 301, 302, 317, 322, 331
Levigliani 223
Lido di Camaiore 218
Limite 154
Linari 140
Lippi, Lorenzo 154
Liszt, Franz 241
Livorno 279
Londa 124
Longfellow, Henry Wadsworth 285
Longhi, Roberto 218
Lonnano 492
Loppia 214
Loppiano 479
Lorenzini, Carlo ('Collodi') 105, 191
Loro Ciuffena 485
Lubaco 108
Lucardo 135
Lucca 193
Lucignano 476
Lucignano d'Arbia 416
Luco 402
Luco di Mugello 116
Luiano 136
Lunata 209
Lunigiana 230
Lupinari 485
Lutiano Nuovo 121

Macaulay, Thomas Babington 441
Machiavelli, Niccolò 62, 84, 135
Maddalena (convent of) 107
Madonna dei Tre Fiumi 116
Madonna della Quercia 477
Madonna della Tosse 142
Madonna delle Grazie 334
Madonna delle Grazie di Montemarciano 486
Madonna di Pietracupa 139
Madonna di San Pietro 332
Maecenas, C. Cilnius 449
Maffei, Beato Raffaele 275
Maffei, Monsignor Mario 270

Magliano in Toscana 327
Magione, La 402
Maiano 99
Malaspina family 224, 225, 226, 229
Malavalle 302
Malmantile 154
Manciano 325
Mann, Sir Horace 91
Mantegazza, Paolo 83
Marcellus II 429, 431
Marciana Alta 512
Marciana Marina 512
Marciana della Chiana 476
Maresca 191
Maremma 288
Marina di Alberese 313
Marina di Bibbona 290
Marina di Campo 512
Marina di Cecina 290
Marina di Grosseto 299
Marina di Pisa 257
Marina di Vecchiano 257
Marlia 209
Marradi 116
Marsuppini, Carlo 85
Marti, Agostino 195
Martini, Jacopo Magistri 383
Marzi, Bishop Angelo 74
Mascagni, Pietro 281, 286, 288
Massa 224
Massa Marittima 307
Massaciuccoli 219
Massarosa 219
Matilda of Canossa, Countess 226, 241, 261, 265, 486
Mazarin, Cardinal 394
Mazzini, Giuseppe 226, 254
Medici, Alessandro de' 94
Medici, Anna Maria Lodovica de' 63, 71
Medici, Bartolomeo 241
Medici, Carlo dei 159
Medici, Cosimo de' (Cosimo il Vecchio) 49, 61, 75, 76, 77, 96, 99, 104, 117, 118, 280, 441, 493
Medici, Cosimo I de' 61, 62, 63, 64, 71, 75, 105, 107, 222, 230, 245, 248, 254, 258, 294, 318, 337, 377, 406,

427, 429, 472, 477, 505, 510, 511
Medici, Donato de', Archbishop 177
Medici, Ferdinando I de' 73, 93, 104, 118, 170, 252, 259, 280, 297, 299, 334, 380, 428, 455
Medici, Ferdinando II, de' 88, 102, 150, 446, 477
Medici, Francesco I de' 61, 62, 92, 106, 121, 252, 258
Medici, Gian Gastone dei 190
Medici, Giovanni de' ('delle Bande Nere' 118
Medici, Giovanni di Bicci de' 77
Medici, Giuliano de' 77
Medici, Cardinal Leopoldo de' 66, 88
Medici, Lorenzo de' (Lorenzo il Magnifico) 49, 53, 71, 75, 77, 104, 166, 251, 267, 274, 401
Medici, Lorenzo di Pierfrancesco de' 105
Medici, Maria de' 244
Medici, Mattias de' 475
Medici, Pierfrancesco de' 118
Medici, Piero de' 77
Medici, Piero di Cosimo de' (Il Gottoso) 104
Medicina 190
Meleto 129
Meloria 281
Mensano 400
Mercatale 136
Metelliano 473
Metternich, Prince Clemens 209
Milani, Don Lorenzo 121
Milton, John 488
Minias, Deacon 93
Minucciano 216
Mirandola, Pico della 75
Molino delle Pile 405
Mommio 220
Monsummano Alto 186
Monsummano Terme 186
Montagna 508
Montagnola Senese 384
Montaigne, Michel 212
Montaione 146

Montalcino 405
Montanino 486
Montaperti 129
Montarrenti 386
Monte Altissimo 215, 225
Monte Amiata 328
Monte Argentario 317
Monte Capanne 512
Monte Cetona 446
Monte Cimone 192
Monte Egidio 473
Monte Falco 491
Monte Falterona 491
Monte Leoni 307
Monte Morello 105
Monte Oliveto Maggiore 413
Monte Pisanino 216
Monte San Savino 474
Monte Sassoforte 304
Monte Secchieta 488
Monte, Antonio Del 433
Montebonello 124
Montecalvario 131
Montecarlo (Altopascio) 209
Montecarlo (San Giovanni Valdarno) 483
Montecasale 508
Montecastelli 278
Montecatini Alto 185
Montecatini Terme 184
Montecatini Val di Cecina 277
Montecatini Valdinievole 185
Montecchio Vesponi 461
Montecerboli 278
Montecristo 514
Montefeltro, Federico di 64, 267
Montefeltro, Niccolò da 437
Montefioralle 126
Montefollonico 436
Montefortini 170
Montegemoli 277
Montegiovi 329
Montegufoni 143
Montelaterone 329
Monteloro 108
Montelupo Fiorentino 153
Montemarciano 486
Montemassi 305
Montemerano 326
Montemignaio 494
Montemurlo 172
Montenero (Livorno) 288

Montenero (Paganico) 329
Monteoliveto 102
Montepescali 304
Montepiano 171
Montepò 326
Montepulciano 429
Monterappoli 150
Monterchi 507
Montereggi alla Castellina 154
Monteriggioni 402
Monteroni d'Arbia 417
Monterotondo Marittimo 312
Montescalari 127
Montesenario 106
Montespertoli 143
Montesquieu, Charles 466
Montevarchi 483
Monteverdi 434
Montevettolini 186
Monti dell'Uccellina 313
Monticchiello 422
Monticello Amiata 329
Monticiano 404
Montieri 312
Montignoso 225
Montioni 292
Montisi 438
Montopoli in Val d'Arno 263
Montorgiali 326
Montorio 325
Montorsaio 307
Moraduccio 121
Mordini, Antonio 213
Morrocco 137
Mugello 113
Mugnana 127
Mulina 222
Murci 326
Murci, Francesco San-severino 241
Murlo 417

Napoleon I (Bonaparte) 70, 194, 212, 248, 281, 509, 511, 512
Narses 194
Nelson, Lord 281
Nicolò da Tolentino 54, 263
Nightingale, Florence 85, 103
Nipozzano 108
Nocchi 220
Nomadelfia 299

Nozzano 219, 258

Ombrone river 313
Orbetello 316
Orgia 386
Origo, Iris 163, 426
Orsetti, Bernardino 206
Orsini family 322, 323, 325
Orti 294
Ortignano 496
Osservanza 381
Ottieri 325
Ouida (Marie Louise de la Ramée) 212

Pacini, Giovanni 188
Pacinotti, Antonio 254
Paganico 305
Paganini, Niccolò 167, 201, 209
Pagliericcio 494
Palaia 264
Palazzone 446
Palazzuolo sul Senio 116
Palude della Trappola 313
Panna 119
Panzano 127
Papi, Lazzaro 190
Papini, Giovanni 218
Parco dell'Orecchiella 216
Parco dell'Uccellina 313
Parco Faunistico del Monte Amiata 334
Parco Naturale della Maremma 313
Parco Naturale di Cavriglia 483
Parco Naturale Migliarino, San Rossore, Massa-ciuccoli 219, 257
Parco Nazionale delle Foreste Casentinesi, Monte Falterona e Campigna 123, 492
Parco Regionale delle Alpi Apuane 215
Pari 306
Parker, Theodore 95
Pascoli, Giovanni 215
Passerini, Cardinal Silvio 473
Passo dei Pecorai 127
Passo del Muraglione 123
Passo dell'Abetone 192
Passo della Consuma 489
Passo della Futa 119

Passo della Porretta 192
Passo della Raticosa 119
Passo di Viamaggio 508
Passo la Calla 491
Patrizi, Blessed Antonio 404
Pecci, Luigi 166
Pecci-Blunt, Mimì 209
Peccioli 264
Pelago 109
Pereta 326
Peretola 155
Perla, La 278
Pertini, Sandro 283
Pescaglia 212
Pescia 187
Pescia Fiorentina 321
Pescina 330
Petrarch 449, 453, 479
Petrognano 124
Petroio 438
Petroni, Cardinal Riccardo 351
Petrucci, Pandolfo 337, 358
Peyron, Paolo 100
Philibert, Prince of Orange 192
Piaggia, Carlo 209
Pian de' Giullari 102
Pian di Melosa 488
Pian di Scò 486
Piancastagnaio 332
Pianezzoli 150
Pianosa 514
Pianosinatico 192
Piccolomini family 350, 351, 352, 363, 419, 420
Pienza 419
Pierozzo, Antonino 75
Pietrabuona 190
Pietramala 119
Pietrasanta 220
Pietro da Noceto 199
Pietro Leopoldo I (grand-duke) 72, 184, 431
Pieve a Elici 220
Pieve a Pitiana 487
Pieve a Ranco 508
Pieve a Ripoli 110
Pieve a Sietina 500
Pieve a Sovara 507
Pieve di Cellole 393
Pieve di Codiponte 229
Pieve di Coiano 143
Pieve di Compito 209

Pieve di Ponte allo Spino 385
Pieve di Romena 489
Pieve di San Giovanni Battista e Santo Stefano 220
Pieve di San Lazzaro a Lucardo 136
Pieve di San Romolo 481
Pieve di Sant'Appiano 139
Pieve di Santi Giovanni e Felicità 222
Pieve Fosciana 216
Pieve Santo Stefano 508
Pieve Socana 499
Pignotti, Lorenzo 241
Pinsent, Cecil 99, 101, 427
Pinsuti, Ciro 437
Piombino 293
Pirandello, Luigi 218
Pisa 232
Pistoia 172
Pitigliano 322
Pius II 362, 367, 397, 406, 409, 414, 419
Pius III 419
Poggibonsi 401
Poggio 512
Poggio a Caiano 166
Poggio alle Mura 411
Poggio Civitate 417
Poggio Neri 291
Poggio Sterzoni 323
Poggio, Castel di 100
Poggioferro 326
Poggiolo-Salaiole 121
Poliziano 53, 75, 429, 432
Pomarance 277
Pontassieve 108
Ponte a Ema 111
Ponte a Mensola 100
Ponte a Poppi 494
Ponte Buggianese 187
Ponte della Maddalena 212
Ponte Stazzemese 222
Pontedera 266
Ponti di Badia 301
Pontito 190
Pontorme 150
Pontremoli 230
Poppi 495
Poppiano 143
Populonia 292
Porciano 490
Porsena, Lars 441
Portiglione 302
Portinari, Folco 83

Porto Azzurro 513
Porto Ercole 317
Porto Santo Stefano 318
Portoferraio 511
Pozzo 476
Pracchia 192
Prato 156
Prato alle Cogne 492
Prato di Rosello 171
Pratolino 106
Pratomagno 478, 485
Pratovecchio 491
Principina a Mare 299
Procchio 512
Puccini, Giacomo 154, 194, 195, 196, 212, 219, 320, 393
Punta Ala 302
Puntone 325

Quercegrossa 131
Quercianella 290
Quiesa 219
Quinto 105

Radda in Chianti 128
Radicofani 427
Radicondoli 401
Raggiolo 496
Ramsay, Allan 257
Ranieri del Porrina 400
Rapolano Terme 413
Rassina 499
Ravaccione 228
Ravi 304
Redi, Francesco 455
Reggello 486
Restone 481
Retignano 223
Reynolds, Sir Joshua 281
Ricasoli, Bettino 129
Riccobaldi, Alessandro 273
Ridolfi, Cosimo 154
Rifugio di Bolgeri 291
Rignana 128
Rignano 487
Rimaggio 124
Rimigliano 292
Rio Marina 513
Rio nell'Elba 513
Ripa d'Orcia 425
Ripafratta 258
Ripafratta, Beato Lorenzo da 173
Rivoreta 192
Rocca d'Orcia 425
Rocca di Pierle 473

Rocca San Silvestro 291
Roccalbegna 334
Roccamare 302
Roccastrada 304
Roccatederighi 305
Rocchette di Fazio 325
Roncalli 278
Ronchi, I 218
Ronta 116
Rosano 109
Roselle 298
Rosia 386
Rosignano Marittimo 290
Rosignano Solvay 290
Rosini, Giovanni 244
Ross, Janet 100
Rossini, Gioacchino 201
Rovezzano 107
Rucellai, Giovanni di Paolo 78, 81
Ruffo, Titta 234
Rufina 124
Rufus, William 200
Ruskin, John 194, 195

Sagginale 121
St Agnese 429
St Ambrose 76
St Andrew 100
St Antoninus 96
St Appiano 139
St Atho, Bishop 176
St Bernardine 307, 381, 434
St Bartolo 393
St Bonaventura 117
St Catherine de' Ricci 165
St Catherine of Siena 337, 375, 376, 425
St Cerbone 308, 309
St Donato 454
St Egidio 473
St Fausto 131
St Felicity 67
St Filippo Benizzi 426
St Fina 389
St Francis 473, 498, 508
St Galgano 354, 403, 405
St Gimignano 387, 391
St Giovanni Gualberto 80, 137, 138, 487
St Guglielmo 302
St James the Greater 287
St Linus 267
St Lucchese 401
St Margaret of Cortona 471
St Mark, Pope 331

St Minias 261
St Ottaviano 269
St Paul of the Cross 318
St Peter 256
St Quirico 422
St Romanus 201
St Romuald 493
St Savino 474
St Thomas Becket 506
St Ugo 270
St Verdiana 141
St Zeno 176
St Zenobius 56
Saline di Volterra 277
Salmi, Mario 458
Saltarelli, Archbishop
    Simone 249
Saltini, Don Zeno 299
Saltino 487
Salutati, Bishop 97
Salutati, Coluccio 187
Salvani, Provenzano 395
Salviati, Maria 118
Sambuca 216
Sammezzano 486
San Bartolomeo 332
San Bartolomeo a
    Scampata 481
San Bartolomeo in Pomino
    124
San Benedetto 260
San Bruzio 327
San Casciano dei Bagni 446
San Casciano in Val di Pesa
    133
San Cassiano di Controne
    213
San Clemente a Sociano 487
San Cresci (Montefioralle)
    126
San Dalmazio 278
San Domenico di Fiesole 96
San Donato in Collina 110
San Donato in Fronzano
    487
San Donato in Poggio 139
San Galgano 403
San Gavino Adimari 119
San Gennaro 191
San Gimignano 386
San Giorgio a Ruballa 110
San Giorgio di Brancoli 211
San Giovanni al Ponte 402
San Giovanni Battista 306
San Giovanni d'Asso 415
San Giovanni in Sugana
    135

San Giovanni Valdarno 481
San Giuliano Terme 258
San Giustino Valdarno 485
San Giusto in Salcio 129
San Godenzo 123
San Guido 291
San Gusmé 129
San Leo 506
San Leolino 127
San Leonardo al Lago 383
San Lorenzo a Cappiano
    110
San Lorenzo a Merse 405
San Lorenzo al Lanzo 306
San Marcello Pistoiese 192
San Martino a Gangalandi
    154
San Martino a Mensola 100
San Martino a Vado 494
San Martino ad Argiano
    135
San Martino alla Palma
    156
San Martino di Montedoglio
    508
San Miniato (al Tedesco)
    261
San Miniato in Alpe 488
San Pancrazio 135
San Paolo a Mosciano 156
San Pellegrino in Alpe 216
San Piero a Grado 256
San Piero a Sieve 117
San Pietro a Cedda 131
San Pietro a Montepaldi
    135
San Pietro al Terreno 479
San Pietro in Bossolo 136
San Pietro in Mercato 143
San Pietro in Palazzi 290
San Pietro in Villore 416
San Polo in Rosso 129
San Quirico 190
San Quirico a Ruballa 110
San Quirico d'Orcia 422
San Quirico di Vernio 171
San Romano 263
San Romano in Garfagnano
    216
San Savino 474
San Silvestro 291
San Vincenzo 291
San Vivaldo 146
San Viviano 216
Sansepolcro 501
Sant' Alessandro a Giogoli
    144

Sant'Agata 120
Sant'Agata in Arfoli 486
Sant'Agnese a Vignano
    381
Sant'Andrea 512
Sant'Andrea a Ripalta 481
Sant'Andrea in Percussina
    135
Sant'Angelo in Colle 410
Sant'Anna 223
Sant'Anna in Camprena
    439
Sant'Ansano 131
Sant'Ansano in Greti 151
Sant'Antimo 408
Sant'Eustachio 225
Sant'Ippolito 154
Santa Barbara 483
Santa Brigida 108
Santa Cecilia a Decimo 135
Santa Croce sull'Arno 261
Santa Fiora 332
Santa Maria a Bagnano
    140
Santa Maria a Buiano 496
Santa Maria a Casavecchia
    135
Santa Maria a Chianni 145
Santa Maria a Corsano 506
Santa Maria a Micciano
    507
Santa Maria a Monte 261
Santa Maria a Poppiena
    492
Santa Maria a Ripa 150
Santa Maria a Vigesimo
    119
Santa Maria ad Argiano
    135
Santa Maria ad Lamulas
    334
Santa Maria del Sasso 497
Santa Maria delle Grazie
    491
Santa Maria delle Vertighe
    476
Santa Maria in Acone 124
Santa Maria in Camporena
    146
Santa Vittoria 476
Santi Giuliano e Settimo
    155
Santi Lorentino e
    Pergentino 508
Santi Vito e Modesto 479
Santo Stefano a Campoli
    136

Santo Stefano a Rezzano 118
Santo Stefano in Cennano 438
Saracini, Galgano 362
Saracini, Niccolò 383
Sargent, John Singer 209
Sarteano 444
Sassetti, Francesco 80
Sasso d' Ombrone 306
Saturnia 325
Savignano 171
Savonarola, Girolamo 61, 75
Scalvaia 405
Scandicci 156
Scansano 326
Scarlino 302
Scarperia 119
Scheggia 507
Seano 171
Seggiano 330
Segromigno 209
Semifonte 140
Semproniano 325
Senesino 337
Seravezza 222
Sernigi, Niccolò 137
Serra Pistoiese 183
Serravalle 498
Serristori family 481
Sestino 508
Sesto Fiorentino 105
Settefinestre 320
Settignano 101
Sezzate 127
Sforza, Battista 64
Sforza, Francesco 505
Shelley, Percy Bysshe 87, 212, 218, 234, 255, 257, 258, 281, 285, 286
Siena 335
  Accademia dei Fisiocritici 364
  Accademia Musicale Chigiana 362
  Annunziata 353
  Archivio di Stato 366
  Arco delle Due Porte 366
  Baptistery 357
  Biblioteca Comunale 375
  Botanical Gardens 364
  Campo, the 340
  Casa di Santa Caterina 375
  Casato di Sotto 362

Siena cont'd
  Church of the Crocifisso 376
  Conservatorio delle Derelitte 365
  Contrade, the 340
  Contrada dell'Aquila 362
  Contrada del Bruco 378
  Contrada della Chiocciola 366
  Contrada dell Civetta 367
  Contrada Imperiale della Giraffa 373
  Contrada dell'Istrice 380
  Contrada del Leocorno 367
  Contrada della Lupa 378
  Contrada del Nicchio 370
  Contrada dell'Oca 376
  Contrada della Pantera 363
  Contrada della Selva 366
  Contrada della Tartuca 365
  Contrada della Torre 372
  Contrada di Valdimontone 371
  Croce del Travaglio 372
  Duomo 345
  ex-Palazzo dei Bisdomini 363
  Fonte Branda 376
  Fonte Nuova di Ovile 378
  Fonte d'Ovile 378
  Fortezza Medicea 377
  La Lizza 379
  Libreria Piccolomini 351
  Logge del Papa 367
  Loggia della Mercanzia 372
  Maddalena, church of the 364
  Madonna del Rosario 366
  Magione 380
  Misericordia Cemetery 364
  Museo Archeologico 354
  Museo Civico 341
  Museo dell'Opera del Duomo 354
  Oratorio della Cucina 375
  Oratorio della Santissima Trinità 371
  Oratorio della Tintoria 376
  Oratorio dei Tredicini 363
  Oratorio di San Bernardino 374

Siena cont'd
  Oratorio di San Giacomo 372
  Oratorio di Sant'Anna in Sant' Onofrio 379
  Oratorio di Santa Maria delle Nevi 378
  Ospedale di Santa Maria della Scala 352
  Palazzo Bandini Piccolomini 367
  Palazzo Bianchi 370
  Palazzo Buonsignori 358
  Palazzo Chigi 362
  Palazzo Chigi-Saracini 362
  Palazzo dei Diavoli 380
  Palazzo Incontri 365
  Palazzo Marsili 362
  Palazzo Marsilli-Libelli 362
  Palazzo Ottieri (Costantini) 379
  Palazzo Piccolomini 366
  Palazzo Piccolomini Adami 363
  Palazzo Piccolomini delle Papesse 362
  Palazzo Pubblico 341
  Palazzo Salimbeni 374
  Palazzo di San Galgano 370
  Palazzo Spannocchi 374
  Palazzo Tantucci 374
  Palazzo Tolomei 372
  Palazzo Ugurgeri 362
  Palazzo del Vescovo 365
  Palio, the 339
  Pian dei Matellini 365
  Piazza Abbadia 378
  Piazza Postierla 363
  Piazza Salimbeni 374
  Piazza San Francesco 373
  Pinacoteca Nazionale 358
  Porta Camollia 380
  Porta Laterina 366
  Porta Ovile 378
  Porta Pispini 370
  Porta Romana 371
  Porta Tufi 364
  Rocca di Palazzo Salimbeni 378
  San Cristoforo 372
  San Domenico 377
  San Francesco 373
  San Gaetano 370

Siena cont'd
San Giovanni della Staffa 367
San Giuseppe 364
San Martino 367
San Michele al Monte di San Donato 378
San Niccolò al Carmine 365
San Pellegrino a Sapienza 375
San Pietro a Ovile 373
San Pietro alla Magione 380
San Pietro alle Scale 363
San Quirico 363
San Raimondo al Rifugio 370
San Rocco 378
San Sebastiano (in Valle) 366
San Sebastiano (Via Garibaldi) 379
San Vigilio 367
Sant'Agostino 363
Sant'Ansano 365
Sant'Eugenia 370
Santa Maria dei Servi 371
Santa Maria di Provenzano 372, 373
Santa Maria in Portico a Fontegiusta 379
Santa Marta 366
Santi Niccolò e Lucia 364
Santi Pietro e Paolo 366
Santo Spirito 370
Santo Stefano 379
Società Esecutori di Pie Disposizioni 370
Synagogue 372
Torre del Mangia 344
University 367
Via Banchi di Sopra 372
Via di Città 362
Signa 154
Sillano, Rocca di 278
Simoni, Ugolino 184
Sinalunga 437
Sinibaldi, Guittone; *see* Cino da Pistoia
Sinigardi, Beato Benedetto 450
Sismondi, Giovan Carlo de' 188
Sitwell family 143
Sloane, Francis 104

Smollett, Tobias 281, 285, 288
Sobieska, Clementina 212
Sorano 324
Sovana 323
Sovicille 385
Sozzini, Lelio 337
Spano, Pippo 111
Spedaletto 426
Squarcialupi, Antonio 54
Staggia 402
Stagno 257
Stazzema 222
Stephenson, Robert 281
Stia 490
Stiava 220
Stibbert, Frederick 94
Sticciano 304
Stignano 187
Stricchi, Beato Vivaldo 146
Strozzavolpe 402
Strozzi, Filippo 78, 81
Stuart, James 212
Suvereto 292

Tacco, Ghino di 427, 435
Talamonaccio 315
Talamone 314
Talciona 402
Talente 135
Talla 500
Tarlati, Bishop Guido 414, 452, 454, 474
Tavarnelle 136
Tavernelle 507
Taylor, George Watson 514
Temple Leader, John 99, 100, 285
Tennyson, Alfred 212
Tenuta di San Rossore 257
Tenuta di Tombolo 257
Terme di Bagnolo 312
Terme di Firenze 135
Terme di San Giovanni 513
Terme di Saturnia 325
Terranuova Bracciolini 485
Testi, Fulvio 215
Tiburzi, Domenico 321
Tiglio Alto 214
Tignosini, Bonagiunta 204
Tilli, Michelangelo 142
Tirli 302
Tirrenia 257
Tolomei, Bernardo 439
Tolomei, Giovanni 413
Tolomei, Pia de' 304
Tombolo di Feniglia 317

Tombolo di Giannella 318
Tooth, Rev. Charles 92
Torello, Beato 496
Tornabuoni, Giovanni 78
Torniella 305
Torre a Decima 108
Torre del Lago Puccini 219
Torrenieri 408
Torreone 473
Torri 386
Torrita di Siena 435
Toscanelli, Paolo dal Pozzo 53, 92
Tosi 488
Tosina 109
Traballesi, Giuliano 288
Trefusis, Violet 103
Trequanda 437
Triana 334
Trollope, Frances 95
Turini, Baldassare 190

Ubaldini family 114, 116, 118
Uberti, Farinata degli 148
Ubertini family 471, 476, 481, 500
Ubertino, Bishop Guglielmino 493
Uccellina 313
Ugo, Margrave of Tuscany 83, 180
Ugolino 111
Uliveto Terme 260
Umberto I, King 227
Uzzano (castle) 127
Uzzano (Pescia) 190

Vada 290
Vagli 216
Vaiano 171
Val d'Orcia 425
Val di Cornia 291
Val di Nievole 186
Valdarno 478
Valdicastello Carducci 222
Valdichiana 473
Valiana 492
Vallecchia 222
Vallombrosa 487
Valpiana 312
Varchi, Benedetto 484
Vellano 190
Verdi, Giuseppe 184
Verginina, La 183
Verrazzano castle 127

Verrucole 216
Versilia 217
Versiliana, La 222
Vertine 129
Vescovado 416
Vespignano 122
Vespucci family 80, 118, 126, 155
Vetriano 212
Vetulonia 303
Via Cassia 411
Via Francigena 231, 330, 352, 387, 402, 403, 408, 422, 423
Via Volterrana 140
Viareggio 217
Vicchio 122
Vicchio di Rimaggio 101
Vicchiomaggio 127
Vicopelago 209
Vicopisano 260
Vieusseux, Gian Pietro 95
Vignali, Jacopo 458
Vignamaggio 128
Vignoni 425
Villa Basilica 191
Villa Bernardini 209
Villa Calcinaia 127
Villa Capponi 102
Villa Collemandina 216
Villa de le Viterete 121
Villa della Petraia 104
Villa Demidoff (Pratolino) 106
Villa di Artimino 170

Villa di Bellavista 186
Villa di Belvedere 265
Villa di Cafaggiolo 118
Villa di Monastero 383
Villa di Pietrafitta 394
Villa di Poggio Imperiale 102
Villa di Vicobello 382
Villa Frescobaldi a Corte 121
Villa Gamberaia 101
Villa Garzoni 191
Villa Grabau 209
Villa Guiducci a Serravalle 121
Villa I Tatti 100
Villa il Pelagio 121
Villa La Bartolina 121
Villa La Cinquantina 290
Villa La Fratta 436
Villa Le Balze 99
Villa Le Corti 136
Villa Le Grotte 513
Villa Mansi 209
Villa Medicea di Careggi 104
Villa Medicea di Castello 105
Villa Medici, Fiesole 99
Villa Oliva Buonvisi 209
Villa Passerini 473
Villa Pitiana 487
Villa Reale, Marlia 209
Villa Rinuccini di Torre a Cona 110

Villa San Martino 512
Villa Tizzano 127
Villa Torrigiani 209
Villa Vistarenni 128
Villafranca in Lunigiana 230
Villamagna 101
Ville delle Volte 382
Vinchiana 211
Vinci 151
Vincigliata, Castello di 100
Visconti, Gian Galaezzo 234, 337
Viti, Benedetto Giuseppe 272
Vitiano 127
Vittorio Emanuele II 104, 207, 272, 284, 342
Vittorio Emanuele III 104, 514
Vivo d'Orcia 426
Voltaire, François Marie Arouet de 466
Volterra 266

Waterfield, Aubrey 230
Webb, John 213, 286
Whistler, Rex 230
Winizzo, Abbot 331
Wollstonecraft, Mary 212, 234, 286

Zati, Amerigo 100
Zipoli, Domenico 164